The Welfare Economics of
Markets, Voting and Predation

For Samphan, Ann and David

... it is lamentable to think how great a proportion of all the efforts and talents in the world are employed in merely neutralizing one another. It is the proper end of government to reduce this wretched waste to the smallest possible amount, by taking such measures as shall cause the energies now spent by mankind in injuring one another, or in protecting themselves against injury, to be turned to the legitimate employment of the human faculties, that of compelling the powers of nature to be more and more subservient to physical and moral good. [John Stuart Mill, *Principles of Political Economy*, 1848]

One cannot state in any absolute or general way whether the greatest danger at the present time is licence or tyranny, anarchy or despotism. Both are equally to be feared.... [Alexis de Tocqueville, *Democracy in America*, 1835]

The Welfare Economics of Markets, Voting and Predation

Dan Usher

Ann Arbor
The University of Michigan Press

Published in the United States of America by
The University of Michigan Press

1995 1994 1993 1992 4 3 2 1

Library of Congress Cataloging-in-Publication Data applied for

ISBN 0–472–10396–2

—

Typeset in Hong Kong
by Graphicraft Typesetters Ltd.

Printed in Great Britain
by Biddles Ltd., Guildford and King's Lynn

Contents

Contents

List of tables

List of figures

Preface

Two themes differentiate this book from traditional welfare economics: predation as the pattern of what can go wrong in the economy, and the fragile interdependence between markets and voting. Consider predation first. In traditional welfare economics, the quintessential departure from efficiency is the externality, the unpriced by-product of ordinary economic activity, as exemplified by smoke emitted form a coal-fired electricity plant or by the tax-induced diversion of effort from more productive to less productive activities. Alternatively, with the emphasis on predation, the quintessential departure from efficiency is the waste of resources in theft, especially the waste of the labour of the thief in stealing and of the victim in protecting himself. Many activities in the market and in government entail a similar loss of output from the neutralization of the efforts of competing parties, though, for good reasons, such activities may not be illegal. Without denying the importance of externalities, I argue that theft is the more instructive paradigm. A major question, perhaps *the* major question, in welfare economics is how to tell when self-interested economic activity is conducive to the common good. A partial but nonetheless informative answer is that self-interested economic activity is conducive to social welfare when directed toward the making of goods for use or sale, and that it is detrimental when directed toward the taking of goods from others.

One of the advantages of this approach to welfare economics is as an antidote to the world-view of many planners and economists according to which the market generates departures from efficiency and the government corrects them. When taking is emphasized, it becomes immediately evident that neither market nor government has a monopoly on departures from efficiency. Among the varieties of taking in the private sector are theft, rent-seeking, tax evasion, monopolization, over-use of common property, malfeasance and, in some circumstances, advertising, speculation and litigation. Among the varieties of taking in the public sector are corruption by public officials, exploitation by voting, tariffs favouring one industry at the expense of others, subsidies to politically influential firms, overexpansion of departments of government in the interest of bureaucrats and the reservation of jobs for members of privileged groups. Public sector taking may be a pure transfer of income, with no corresponding loss of output or social cost, but it often entails costs varying all the way from expenditure on lobbying to loss of life and property when disputes cannot be resolved without recourse to war. The traditional picture of an economy fine-tuned by a government devoted exclusively to the common good gives way to a new picture in which departures from efficiency in the private sector are, if anything, even larger than was formerly recognized, but departures from efficiency in the public sector are large as well. The design of public policy becomes a trade-off between inefficiencies in the public and private sectors of the economy.

The other major theme of the book is the double entitlement of the citizen as voter and as owner of property. As property-owner, the citizen is entitled to the return from the physical and human capital that society decrees to be his. As voter, he is entitled to influence his expected income through the ballot box, in public decisions about the old age pension, unemployment insurance, welfare, taxation and the rules specifying what one can or cannot do with one's property. The entitlements conflict to some extent.

Though both systems of entitlement are recognized in a great many countries, there seems to be no one word to designate a society with an economy based upon private property and a polity based upon voting by majority rule. Following a long-standing practice among economists of re-defining words in common use as technical terms, I refer to such societies as *liberal*. Specifically, a liberal society is a society with private ownership of a significant part of the means of production and majority rule voting as the principal institution for public decision-making.

Some of the usual connotations of the word "liberal" are preserved in this definition, but others are not. When one hears the phrase "political liberal", one thinks of the struggle for universal franchise in the nineteenth and early twentieth centuries. When one hears the phrase "economic liberal", one thinks of free markets and private property. These resonances of ordinary usage carry over to the usage in this book. On the other hand, the word "liberal" is sometimes used as a synonym for "progressive", where progress is interpreted as an extension of the powers of the state, greater redistribution of income, conformity to the course of history or whatever reform is currently fashionable. These latter connotations are unfortunate, for they tend to rob the word of any precise meaning. They do not extend to the present use of the word as a technical term.

It is sometimes debatable whether the term "liberal" can be appropriately employed, for the liberal society is an "ideal type" that is closely approximated in some circumstances but not in others. Majority rule may be a sham, as, for instance, when there is only one legitimate political party, or when those who refuse to vote for a particular political party can expect to be punished, or when the electorate is so restricted that the great majority of citizens have no say in the choice of a government. One can speak of the liberal society without committing oneself as to just how free an election must be or how wide the franchise must be for the term to be appropriate. Nor is there a clear and precise boundary between societies with economies based on private property and societies with economies based on other principles. Economies lie on a continuum, with private ownership of the entire means of production at one extreme and with complete public administration of the economy at the other. It is sufficient in practice if we can judge when societies are close enough to the ideal type of the liberal society for propositions about the liberal society to become relevant. Men cannot reason without abstractions and must live with the fact that abstractions can never apply exactly to the world at large.

The liberal society is to be contrasted with two other types of society in which predatory behaviour is more prevalent, more overt and more destructive. *Anarchy* is a society with no central authority to enforce property rights. It is a society where one's income is the sum of what he produces and what he takes from others, less what others succeed in taking from him, and where taking and defending entail a major waste of resources and a risk of loss of life. *Despotism* is government by a self-interested ruling class which is unconstrained in the exploitation of its subjects except by rebellion, banditry or the biological link between the income of the subject and his ability to work effectively. Rulers may be modelled as a strict hierarchy or as an oligarchy of equals. Subjects may be modelled as obedient and well protected peasants, or as peasants who are preyed upon by bandits and who may themselves become bandits if their lot as peasants deteriorates. Anarchy and despotism exemplify the pitfalls of the liberal society. They serve at once as paradigms of departure from efficiency in the private and public sectors respectively and as societies in their own right into which the liberal society may disintegrate by mischance or as a consequence of ill-chosen public policy.

As paradigms of departures from efficiency, the models of anarchy and despotism serve to emphasize the predatory aspects of economic activity and the limitations of government as an instrument for setting the market right. The model of anarchy supplies a classification of social costs covering many types of market failure, clarifying the relation between externalities and taking, and dramatizing the role of taking in the private sector of the economy when property rights are, as they must be, ambiguous or imperfectly enforced. The study of despotism is an antidote and corrective to the working assumption in much of traditional welfare economics that self-interest stops at the door of the public sector — that public policy is chosen with no other consideration than to promote the common good as represented by the value of a social welfare function. There is no better way of focusing upon the extremity of that assumption and upon the predatory aspects of government in a predominantly liberal society than to consider the opposite extreme at which government is totally and unreservedly self-interested. The model of despotism can serve as a first step in the modelling of governments that are neither altogether selfish nor altogether altruistic, or which conduct policy for the benefit of one class, interest group, race, religion or language group at the expense of the rest of the population.

As representations of societies in their own right, the models of anarchy and despotism serve to introduce a line of argument that is common enough in ordinary discourse about economic and political questions but which cannot be discussed within the confines of the usual assumptions of welfare economics. It is often said that such-and-such a policy will corrupt the institutions of our society, that it is a step toward anarchy or a step toward despotism. Obviously, statements of this kind may or may not be valid in a particular case; the speaker may be wrong in his assessment. But such statements should not as a class be inadmissible, and one would like to think that welfare economics could be helpful in sorting out the entire range of consequences of economic policy. This line of argument is facilitated by the explicit modelling of the societies into which the liberal society may deteriorate if the consensus holding it together is dissolved. That the liberal society may totter between anarchy on one side and despotism on the other is an idea that was commonplace in the nineteenth century but has, until very recently, been ignored in modern economic analysis. Consideration of the effects of policies on institutions leads naturally to the more general inquiry of how one type of society might evolve into another. Of particular interest is the origin and stability of the liberal society. Much of the modern literature on the social contract can be interpreted as explaining the evolution of the liberal society from anarchy. I shall try to make the case that the more plausible evolution is not the direct path from anarchy to the liberal society but the roundabout path from anarchy through despotism. The difference is not irrelevant for public policy. To imagine a direct path from anarchy to the liberal society is to take an optimistic view of the prospects for constitutional reform. To imagine an indirect path is to perceive the liberal society as the outcome of a slow and painful evolution which societies would be obliged to repeat in any attempt to rebuild institutions from scratch.

The study of the economics of anarchy and despotism virtually compels the introduction of violence into the core of economics. It is a little-noticed but nonetheless remarkable fact about ordinary economic analysis that there is no role for violence at all. Economic man — as portrayed in the textbooks — is never required to defend his possessions, to inflict injury or to experience pain. This caricature can be maintained through the implicit assumption in traditional welfare economics that property is secure; each person's entitlements are protected by a government devoted to the attainment of the common good. With the abandonment of that assumption comes a recognition of the role of actual or threatened violence in the maintenance of the social order, together with the possibility that government entrusted with a near-monopoly of the means of violence may use those means for its own ends as distinct from the good of the ordinary citizen. Violence becomes an essential ingredient in the models of anarchy and despotism, an ingredient without which no equilibrium could be sustained. There is no overt role for violence in the model of the liberal society because the mere threat of violence is assumed sufficient to maintain conformity with the law, to preserve property rights and to induce acquiescence with the outcome of the vote.

This study is both broader and narrower than traditional welfare economics. It is broader in its focus upon the connections among markets, voting and predation. It is narrower in that many important aspects of welfare economics are not covered at all. There is little discussion of the precise conditions for the existence of the social welfare functions, or of rules for optimal taxation, cost–benefit analysis, tariffs and the pricing of public services. The extensive discussion of departures from efficiency in the public and private sectors of the economy is not followed by detailed prescriptions for improving matters once departures from efficiency have been identified. The reasons for this choice of topics are that the recognition of the circumstances of the liberal society constitutes the necessary first step toward the development of public policy and that the topics covered are those about which I may have something useful to say.

The book begins with a brief critical analysis of the virtues and defects of traditional welfare economics, covering the fundamental theorems on the existence and optimality of the competitive economy, market failure when actual economies differ from the competitive ideal and the social welfare function as a criterion for public policy. The second chapter covers much of the same ground from an historical point of view, showing how traditional welfare economics developed and how it has come to be modified, largely as a consequence of the study of self-interest within the public sector. There follow chapters on anarchy, despotism, the liberal society and transitions from one society to another. The next two chapters are more within the domain of traditional welfare economics. A chapter on departures from efficiency in the private sector of the economy is followed by a chapter on the tasks of government in a society where government itself is reasonably benign and where the social cost of public policy is often magnified as citizens reorganize their affairs to evade taxes and to become eligible for public largess. The final chapter is about predatory government: how public officials, agents in the private sector or coalitions of voters may employ the power of the government to take, one way or another, from the rest of the population, and how predatory government may be contained within acceptable bounds by the institutions of the liberal society.

Acknowledgments

Thanks to Gordon Tullock for comments on an earlier draft, to E.G. West of Carleton University and Bob Rutherford of the University of Tasmania for commanding me to read John Stuart Mill and to colleagues and students at Queen's, whose suggestions or influences are acknowledged at appropriate places in the book. A grant from the Social Science and Humanities Research Council of Canada freed me from a term of teaching responsibilities to complete the final draft. I must also acknowledge the great influence upon my thinking of the Virginia school — the public choice approach to economics of James Buchanan and Gordon Tullock — though I suspect Buchanan and Tullock are not altogether content with the use I have made of their ideas.[1]

As is usual with longish books in economics, the writing of this book spun off a series of discussion papers and articles. My first thoughts were put out as "Production and Predation, I: The Sources of Inefficiency" and "Production and Predation, II: The Welfare Economics of Theft", Queen's University, Institute for Economic Research, Discussion Papers 534 and 535, 1983. Chapter II appeared independently as "The Rise and Fall of the Public Sector in the Estimation of the Economists", in A. Asimakopulos, R. Cairns and C. Green (eds.), *Economic Theory, Welfare and the State: Essays in Memory of Jack Weldon*, Macmillan, 1990. Part of Chapter III was published as "Theft as a Paradigm for Departures from Efficiency", *Oxford Economic Papers*, June 1987. Parts of Chapters IV and VI are taken from "The Distribution of Income in a Despotic Society" (with Merwan Engineer), *Public Choice*, 1987, 261–76, from "The Dynastic Cycle and the Stationary State", *American Economic Review*, December 1989, 1031–44, and from "The Birth of the Liberal Society", Queen's Discussion Paper 770, 1990. The material on advertising in Chapter VII is a development of "Six Models of Advertising and Welfare", Queen's Discussion Paper 756, 1989. Some of the material in Chapter VIII is from "The Hidden Cost of Public Expenditure" in R. Bird (ed.), *More Taxing than Taxes:*

Implicit Taxes in Developing Countries, I.C.S. Press, 1991, "Police, Punishment and Public Goods", *Public Finance*, 1, 1986, 96–115, and "Tax Evasion and the Marginal Cost of Public Funds", *Economic Inquiry*, October 1986, 563–86. Parts of Chapter IX have appeared as "Intensity of Preference under Representative Government", Queen's University, Institute for Economic Research, Discussion Paper 686, 1987, and as "The Significance of the Probabilistic Voting Theorem", Queen's Discussion Paper 785, 1991.

I have been particularly fortunate in the secretarial assistance at the Economics Department at Queen's. A sequence of pleasant and helpful people grappled with my handwriting and my propensity not to leave well enough alone, typing and retyping, correcting and recorrecting the manuscript as it took shape. Thank you Sharon Sullivan, Angie Dunphy, Lisa Graham, Sandy Lee and especially Elaine Constant, who did the final draft, for your speed, accuracy, concern and good humour.

Note

1   The working hypothesis that there are three fundamental types of society — anarchy, despotism and the liberal society — bears the unmistakable stamp of the Virginia school, specifically, the Center for Study of Public Choice, now at George Mason University. The Virginia school emphasizes both the evils of anarchy and the propensity of government to turn nasty if given half a chance. The very title of one of James Buchanan's books, *The Limits of Liberty: Between Anarchy and the Leviathan*, University of Chicago Press, 1975, conveys the threefold classification, and sharply differentiates that book from the milieu of ordinary economic analysis. On the mechanism of the despotic society, see Gordon Tullock, *The Social Dilemma: the Economics of the War and Revolution*, University Publications, 1974 and *Autocracy*, Kluwer Academic Publishers, 1987.

The Virginia school has the additional virtue that it avoids the tendency, fostered unintentionally by the organization of universities into departments, for students of the market (economists) not to think much about voting and for students of voting (political scientists) not to think much about the market. The journal of the Virginia school, *Public Choice*, publishes many articles that could be classified as economic analysis of voting behaviour. See also Buchanan and Tullock's *The Calculus of Consent*, University of Michigan Press, 1962. A victim of its own success, the Virginia school is less unique today than it has been in the past. Increasingly, models of voting and of self-interested behaviour by government are employed within economics as explanations of public policy, and articles in political science journals make use of economic constructs and assumptions. Long ago, economics and politics would often be taught together within the same university department. The departments split because the two subjects came to differ too greatly in style and in content. The Virginia school has helped to forge a new accommodation.

My analysis of anarchy, despotism and the liberal society draws so heavily upon the Virginia school that it seems worthwhile to state how I differ from the Virginia school, if only to reassure myself that I have something new to say. Among the differences are (i) the explicit incorporation of violence and mortality rates into economic models, (ii) the explanation of the distribution of income between rulers and subjects and within the ruling class of a despotic society, (iii) the study of the dynastic cycle, (iv) the emphasis in the study of the liberal society on voting by majority rule rather than on constitutional restraints, (v) the rejection of the social contract as an explanation of the origin of the liberal society or as a basis for reorganizing society, (vi) a greater explicit reliance on the social welfare function to represent one's sense of the common good in the analysis of public policy and departures from efficiency, and — as a consequence of (iv) and (v) — (vi) the mistrust of constitutional solutions to political and economic problems.

Chapter I

A change of emphasis

Economics is an advice-giving profession. Economists are called upon to advise on tax reform, anti-trust, budgeting, industrial policy, free trade, the allocation of resources to alternative uses in medical care, assistance to the poor, education and so on. To deal with such matters, the economics profession has evolved a particular view of the world, not a true or realistic view — for much of the colour and substance of the world has been abstracted away — but a view encompassing just those aspects that need to be considered for the purpose at hand. I shall refer to this view as *traditional welfare economics*. At the risk of oversimplification, traditional welfare economics can be said to consist of three components: a doctrine of the virtues of the market, a list of market failures, and a concept of the common good expressed as a social welfare function that serves as a criterion for public policy to set the market right.[1]

It is most definitely not the purpose of this book to overthrow traditional welfare economics altogether. This view of the world has been and continues to be a powerful "engine for the discovery of concrete truth" in many aspects of society and government. I shall nevertheless argue that this world-view tends to suppress analysis of some important aspects of society. It takes too little account of what might be called predatory activity in the economy and in government. Nor does it allow for the inevitable tension between property and voting in public choice and in the allocation of the national income among citizens. Like most economists today, I am ambivalent about traditional welfare economics. I am prepared to use it as a framework of analysis, and do so readily at several points in this book. At the same time, I am acutely aware of its limitations and of its propensity to mislead if not carefully and critically applied. The doctrine as described here is to some extent a caricature of welfare economics as taught and practised today, an extreme statement of general tendencies. Its limitations are typically embodied not in propositions to the effect that such-and-such is irrelevant to economic policy, but in silence — in what is ignored in books and in teaching rather than in what is actually said.

The evaluation of traditional welfare economics in this chapter and in the chapter to follow sets the stage for the remainder of the book. The division of labour between these chapters is that this chapter is analytical while the next chapter tells the story of the emergence of welfare economics from Adam Smith to A.C. Pigou and of its partial disintegration under the influence of recent developments in the analysis of, among other topics, the role of self-interest within the public sector. In this chapter, a brief description of the doctrine of traditional welfare economics is followed by more extensive discussions of the fundamental theorems about the virtues of the market, of the assumption in those theorems that property is secure, and of the status of the social welfare function in the design of economic policy.

Traditional welfare economics

The three components of traditional welfare economics — the theorems about the virtues of the market, the list of market failures and the social welfare function as a criterion for public policy to set the market — are described briefly in turn:

The virtues of the market
The economist's doctrine about the virtues of the market is encapsulated in two great fundamental theorems: that a competitive equilibrium exists, and that it is Pareto optimal. The first establishes that there is a set of prices at which all markets clear simultaneously when all actors in the economy are price-takers. The second establishes that the outcome when all markets clear is optimal in the sense that nothing is wasted; no re-arrangement of production or reallocation of goods could make everybody better off simultaneously. The significance of these theorems will be discussed in some detail in the next section.

Market failure
The second component of traditional welfare economics is a list of the ways in which actual markets fail to conform to the assumptions of the competitive equilibrium model. Four sources of failure are usually identified: monopoly, externalities, public goods and distributional inadequacies.

When production of a good is monopolized, the monopolist firm or cartel is no longer a price-taker and is instead confronted by a set of price–quantity combinations along a demand curve. The monopolist chooses his profit-maximizing output where the marginal gain from selling an extra unit at the going prices and costs is just balanced off by the marginal loss from the fall in price and rise in unit cost on all intramarginal units. As described in detail in any introductory textbook in economics, monopolization leads to a reduction of quantity supplied, a rise in price to the consumer and a departure from efficiency in the sense that the composition and allocation of output in the economy could be altered to make everybody, including the monopolist, better off.

Externalities occur when unpriced goods or bads are generated along with ordinary production for use or sale. A railroad emits sparks that ignite wheatfields along the track. Cows wander into fields of crops. Industrial processes emit pollutants. It is characteristic of most of the formal analysis of externalities that the harm is not generated maliciously or as the main objective of the perpetrator. The harm is the incidental by-product of otherwise normal production. The key questions in the study of externalities are why they are unpriced in the market and how a corrective to ordinary pricing can be established.

Public goods are like externalities carried to an extreme. They are goods that benefit everybody at once, with no trade-off between your benefit and mine. Typically such goods are supplied by the public sector because a private supplier could not recover his cost of production from the beneficiaries and because, once produced, public goods are no longer a scarce commodity in the economist's sense of the term.

Distributional inadequacies represent a market failure because the absence of waste is not the only desirable characteristic of an economy. Any initial allocation of property among citizens gives rise to a competitive equilibrium, with some waste-free allocation of income among citizens, but there is no guarantee that the actual distribution will not yield great wealth for the few and stark poverty for the many. If equality is recognized as a second desirable characteristic of an economy, then the competitive equilibrium may be faulted in that equality is not automatically promoted, and public action to promote equality may be advantageous on balance. This final market failure is unlike the preceding three in that it represents a defect in the competitive ideal rather than a discrepancy between actual markets and the competitive ideal.

The social welfare function
The social welfare function, in this simplistic interpretation of traditional welfare economics, is at once the proper criterion for evaluating developments in the economy as a whole and the rule that is employed by the public sector in correcting for market failures and in redistributing income where warranted. The only constraint upon the public sector in the performance of these tasks is the perverse response of the private sector to taxation and to public provision of services.

The critique of traditional welfare economics to follow will deal differently with each of the three parts of the doctrine. On the first, it will be argued that the importance of the competitive ideal is, if anything, underemphasized and that the fundamental theorems of welfare economics are more powerful, more surprising and of greater significance for society than is generally realized. On the second, it is claimed that the greatest market failure is overlooked. While not denying the existence or importance of the market failures listed above, I would argue that the absence of full and complete security of property is the major source of departures from efficiency in the private sector. Full and uncontested security of property is an essential assumption in the proof of the optimality of the competitive economy. In actual economies, property is inevitably less than fully secure, and resources are inevitably employed in the resolution of disputes about ownership. On the third, I emphasize the double error in assuming the social welfare function to be an objective property of society as a whole and in assuming that an actual government might be expected to adopt the social welfare function as the sole criterion in policy formation and execution. Necessary as it may be as a component in certain types of argument, the social welfare function is a slippery concept that is frequently misinterpreted and misused, especially when it substitutes for a close study of self-interest in the public sector.

The task of prices in the economy: the first theorem of welfare economics

The first of the two fundamental theorems of welfare economics[2] is that there exists a competitive equilibrium in an economy where all agents, suppliers and demanders alike, are price-takers. To be a price-taker, in this sense of the term, is to believe or to act as though you believe that you, personally, can have no influence upon market prices. Prices are what they are, regardless of what you choose to do. "Existence" in the context of the theorem means that there is a set of prices, one for each good or service, at which all markets clear at once. Everybody knows that prices respond to developments in the economy, but each seller and each buyer believes that he is too small a part of the market to affect prices to any significant extent.

The nature of the theorem and logic of the proof are inherent in the ordinary demand and supply diagram, as shown in Figure 1, with the quantity of a good on the horizontal axis and its price on the vertical axis. The demand curve reflects the tastes of the buyers of a good; it is drawn downward sloping because buyers are assumed to want more of the good when the price declines. The supply curve reflects the technology of production of the good; it is drawn upward sloping because sellers are assumed to offer more of the good when the price rises. The demand and supply diagram carries some fairly strong assumptions about the nature of markets. In particular, it carries the implicit assumption that technology and taste are linked only by prices. Suppliers know nothing about demanders,

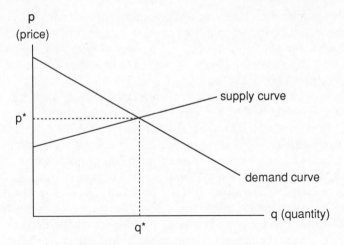

Figure 1 The competitive equilibrium

and demanders know nothing about suppliers, except the price at which they are prepared to trade. The market-clearing, or equilibrium, price equates supply and demand. Nobody need fear that he cannot buy or sell what he pleases at that price. There can be no excess supply or excess demand. That is the essence of the first fundamental theorem of welfare economics. The combination of downward sloping demand curve and an upward sloping supply curve virtually guarantees the existence of a market-clearing price, the price p* in Figure 1. The corresponding quantity is q*.

The theorem is obvious and trivial for a single, isolated market, though, even in a single market, there are a few odd exceptions.[3] The theorem becomes subtle and difficult when extended to all the markets in the entire economy. Then the theorem asserts, not that one price clears one market, but that there "exists" a set of prices that clear all markets simultaneously. The difficulty in extending the theorem from one market to all markets is that the location of each and every curve in each and every market is affected by prices and quantities in all other markets. The theorem rules out a situation where the establishment of an equilibrium, market-clearing price in market A shifts the demand and supply curves in market B, the re-establishment of the equilibrium price in market B shifts the demand and supply curves in market C, the re-establishment of equilibrium in market C shifts demand curves in markets A, B and D, and so on *ad infinitum*, with no stopping place at which all markets are in equilibrium at once. That there is such a stopping place is the first fundamental theorem of welfare economics. The theorem rules out a situation comparable to what would occur in a game of matching pennies if the losing party could always take back his move after he had seen the move of his opponent. The theorem was known in its practical implications since the time of Adam Smith, but the formal proof — together with an exact specification of the assumptions required for the proof to hold — was developed gradually over a period of a hundred years.[4]

The power of the theorem derives to a large extent, not from what it says, but from what it need not say. The theorem establishes that there is a set of prices at which all markets clear, at which each item put up for sale has a buyer, and at which no demands are unfulfilled. To get that result, it is necessary to assume the existence of uncontested property rights to factors of production, a matter to be discussed later on in this chapter and then extensively in the course of this book. But, given property rights, it is not necessary to invoke additional activity by the public sector to make markets work. The theorem is a demonstration that the market can be autonomous, that the market supplies order without orders, that it converts selfishness into a kind of cooperation, that the world's business can be done without the direct intervention of a planning commission or any agent presumed to understand the entire economy and to direct people accordingly. As we proceed, the theorem will have to be qualified in many important respects, but the central core of the theorem — the autonomy of the market, without which the liberal society would be impossible — will be preserved.

This remarkable theorem is made commonplace by familiarity. Every student of economics knows that price signals create a degree of coherence in the economy, but, to quote Arrow and Hahn, it "is important to understand how surprising this claim must be to anyone not exposed to this tradition. The immediate 'common sense' answer to the question 'What will an economy motivated by individual greed and controlled by a very large number of different agents look like?' is probably: 'There will be chaos.' . . . quite a different answer has long been claimed true and has indeed permeated the economic thinking of a large number of people who are in no way economists."[5]

A second and closely connected implication of the theorem concerns the role of prices as transmitters of essential information about the economy, a matter already mentioned in connection with price formation in a single market. Prices encapsulate just the information that each person requires to play his part in the economy, to cooperate in producing the infinite variety of goods and services in the economy and do so without actually intending to cooperate.[6] Cooperation in a modern economy is so vast, so pervasive, so automatic, and so silent in its operation that we sometimes forget it is there at all. Nobody understands the world economy as a whole, yet everybody is guided by prices — by, in Adam Smith's words, an invisible hand — to direct his skills and resources in a vast and intricate division of labour that is the foundation of all prosperity. The market economy behaves as though it were guided by an omniscient central planner, but it is not.

Who knows, Milton Friedman is fond of asking, how to make a pencil? The manufacturer must know how to combine the wood, graphite, tin, rubber and paint into a serviceable pencil. The manufacturer does not know how to convert trees into wood — how best to cut down a tree, how to transport logs to the mill, how to operate a mill, how to dry wood so it will not warp, or, going further back, how to convert sheet metal and wood into a saw to cut the tree, what minerals to combine into the metal for a blade, how to extract metal from ore, how to build the smelting equipment, and on and on through a list that could by one route or another include any and every industrial process, agricultural technique and system of organization of production that is or has ever been employed. Somehow the entire economy of the world is organized so that just the right amounts of several metals are provided, to make just the right number of saws, to cut just the right number of trees, to produce just the right amount of wood, to make just the number of pencils we wish to buy. No explicit cooperation — not among men, as in the organization of the army, or in nature, as in the organization of a beehive — can match the intricacy and detail of the silent, implicit cooperation in the economy.

Cooperation to make a pencil has several dimensions. It is geographical cooperation in which, to name only a small fraction of the ingredients and only one of each of the many sources of supply, wood from Canada, tin from the Congo, rubber from Indonesia, pumice (an ingredient of the eraser) from Iceland, graphite from Sri Lanka, clay from England, zinc compounds (for yellow pigment) from Australia and oils (for the paint binder) from the Congo are combined into a pencil that is stamped as made in Germany for export to the United States. It is also cooperation in the division of labour. Machine operators, engineers, paint mixers, accountants, lawyers, foremen, janitors, secretaries and many other trades participate in the final production and distribution of pencils; every conceivable occupation is involved at some stage in the intermediate products. It is cooperation among the possessors of different kinds of information. One man knows how to mix paints, another how to print, another how to operate a lathe, another how best to sell the pencils, another where to find credit, another how to deal with suppliers of materials. Geography, division of labour, and the acquisition and use of many bits of information possessed by many different people are all part of the cooperation that the production and sale of any good requires, and which the market automatically supplies.

It is remarkable how remote from each man's consumption is his contribution to the world's productive capacity. We all eat similar food, wear similar clothes, live in houses that differ more in size than in function, and enjoy similar forms of entertainment, drawing in one way or another on a large proportion of the world's skills and techniques of production. But one man builds furniture (that and nothing else), another cuts down trees, another drives a taxi, another writes advertising copy, another types letters, another repairs television sets, another cures the sick, and another writes books on welfare economics.

Notice the precise wording of Friedman's question. Not "Who makes a pencil?" to which the answer is "Almost everybody" if the chain of production is followed back far enough, but "Who knows how to make a pencil?" to which the answer is "Nobody." Each man knows a tiny part of the process, and all men's efforts to advance their own interest constitute a vast system of cooperation in which prices guide pencils to appear in the right place, time and quantity.

The phrase "perfect competition" as descriptive of what happens when everybody is a price-taker is too well entrenched within the science of economics to be abandoned now but is, in one respect, extremely misleading. The ordinary word "competition" conveys a sense of struggle and rivalry. One thinks of runners in a race, of losing and winning, of businessmen haggling over the terms of a deal, each trying to get the best of his competitors. Perfect competition as the economist employs the term is not like that at all. It refers to an economy without direct rivalry among people, without bargaining, without competition as the term is commonly understood. It refers to an economy where people respond to prices rather than to other people and where the world's work gets done in a conflict-free, infinitely complex interaction that has the appearance but not the substance of a high degree of organization.

The market's receptiveness to particular items of information in the possession of particular people is nowhere more important or more conducive to the general welfare than in the creation of new ideas, products or processes. To a very great extent, the market is the womb of invention. By contrast, there is a lamentable tendency for hierarchies to ossify, to become geriatric, to squelch innovation as a threat to established privilege and authority or to passively deny the innovator an opportunity to try out his ideas because, as a "mute inglorious Milton" at the periphery of society, he has no channel of communication with the people who matter. Markets give the innovator a chance to back his ideas with his own resources, if he has any, or to persuade the guardians of one of the many thousands of competing pools of capital that his ideas are potentially profitable. Wide-ranging competition among firms virtually guarantees that any firm's market will, sooner or later, be invented away by rival firms if the firm itself fails to innovate. It is more than an historical accident that countries with free markets grow prosperous, while centrally controlled economies decay.

The link between market and innovation is more complex than the preceding paragraph would suggest. As discussed in some detail in Chapter VII, there are reasons why a liberal society may not provide the optimal amount of resources for the development of new ideas and products and why the resources that are provided may not be allocated optimally among competing uses. But the exceptions do not destroy the rule altogether. As long as the state is prepared to create property rights in newly invented products and processes (and even in some circumstances where it is not), the encouragement of innovation is a major virtue of a price-driven, property-respecting economy.

The efficiency of the competitive economy: the second theorem of welfare economics

The second fundamental theorem of welfare economics is that "a competitive equilibrium is Pareto optimal". Once again, the meaning of the theorem can be exhibited with the aid of an ordinary demand and supply diagram, but now it becomes necessary to rely on the interpretation of the heights of the curves. So far, the demand curve has been seen as an indicator of the amounts of a good that people are willing to buy at each and every price. Equivalently, it may be seen as an indicator of the buyers' marginal valuation of the good at each and every quantity that might be offered for sale, where marginal valuation is the cost of the minimum amount of other goods that would make the demander just as well off as he would be with the "last" unit purchased. A person buys q units of a good when the price is $p per unit. To do so, he must prefer the qth unit to whatever else $p might be used to buy, and he must prefer something else costing $p to an additional, (q + 1)th, unit. Thus the negative slope of the demand curve becomes a reflection of the buyer's diminishing marginal valuation of the good in question. Similarly with the supply curve. Its height reflects the marginal cost of production, where marginal cost is the value of goods that could have been produced instead if the resources required to produce the last unit of the good in question were diverted efficiently to other goods. Within the context of a single market, the second theorem of welfare economics is that the equilibrium is efficient in the sense that — referring to Figure 1 — if less (or more) than the equilibrium, q*, of the good were produced, the marginal valuation of an extra unit of the good would exceed (or fall short of) its marginal cost, so that, with appropriate rearrangements, everybody in the economy could be made better off by increasing (or decreasing) the quantity of the good produced.

There is a simple and well known "proof" of the second fundamental theorem of welfare economics for a two-good economy. The proof makes use of the demand and supply curve diagram as illustrated in Figure 2, which is like Figure 1 with additional information. It is worth reviewing this proof briefly as a basis for the discussion of other matters later on in the book. The demand and supply curves are assumed to pertain to the

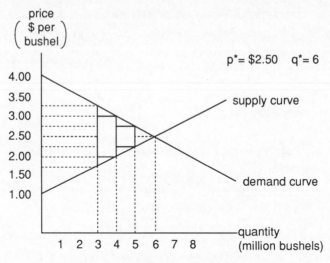

Figure 2   Equilibrium and optimality

market for wheat, and the axes are graduated. The equilibrium quantity and price are 6 million bushels and $2.50 per bushel. Suppose, however, that production is for some reason restricted to 3 million bushels. One can read off the diagram that people "demand" 3 million bushels when the price is $3.25 a bushel. Why do they demand 3 million bushels, no more no less? They do so because the 3 millionth bushel is worth exactly $3.25, in the sense that people are indifferent between the last bushel and any other good or bundle of goods costing $3.25. If the bushel were worth less, people would buy less. If it were worth more, people would buy more. Similarly, as shown by the supply curve, the producers of wheat are un-willing to restrict output to as little as 3 million bushels unless the price they receive has been reduced to $1.75, which is the cost to the firm of the labour required for the production of the 3 millionth bushel. (Ignore other factors of production and intermediate products, as their presence does not change the story to any significant extent). But if workers are prepared to supply a given amount of labour in return for $1.75 and if these same workers could earn the value of their marginal products in other indus-tries, then these workers must be able to produce $1.75 worth of other goods instead. When total production of wheat is 3 million bushels, the value of the "last" bushel produced is $3.25, while the value of other goods that might have been produced instead is only $1.75, leaving a gap of $1.50 which is the gain to society as a whole, from the production of one extra bushel.

One can immediately read off the diagram that, ignoring the little triangles at the tops and the bottoms of the bars, the gain from increasing total production from 3 million to 4 million bushels is $1 million, the gain from an additional increase from 4 million to 5 million bushels is $500,000, and so on, until production reaches 6 million bushels, at which point the marginal valuation of the last bushel is just equal to the marginal cost and no additional production is socially advantageous.

Generalizing slightly, it can be said (i) that the value of being able to buy wheat at the market-clearing price as against not being able to buy wheat at all is the total triangular area between the demand curve and supply curve up to the equilibrium quantity (this area is called the total surplus), (ii) that, if production is restricted (for example, by the imposition of a tax), the social cost of the restriction is the area of the remaining triangle to the right of the restricted quantity (this area is called the loss of surplus), and (iii) that the market equilibrium output (q* in Figure 1, on 6 million bushels in Figure 2) is the "best" output in the sense that there is no loss of surplus; people as a whole are better off at that output than they would be if the output were either more or less. The third proposition is the core of the theorem that a competitive equilibrium is optimal — best, in some sense, for everybody.[7]

Any proposition to the effect that the output in a competitive economy is, in some sense, best must take account of the interactions among markets for the different goods and of the inevitable conflict of interest among people over the allocation of the total national income. The second of these considerations is especially problematic and was quite deliberately ignored in the discussion of surplus in the preceding paragraph. An economy may be organized to provide a high income for Scrooge and a low income for Cratchit or, alternatively, to provide a low income for Scrooge and a high income for Cratchit. Obviously Scrooge prefers the former and Cratchit prefers the latter. How then can a competitive equilibrium outcome — or any other outcome — be said to be best for all?

The problem of defining a social best is compounded by the fact that the competitive equilibrium is not unique. The first theorem of welfare economics is that, for a given allocation among people of labour power and property, there exists a set of prices at which all markets clear. The theorem holds regardless of the allocation of labour power and property, but each allocation gives rise to its own set of equilibrium prices, and the allocation of goods among people is a reflection of the initial allocation of resources. A social best in this context might be defined with regard to either of two criteria, efficiency and full social welfare. What is being called the second theorem of welfare economics is a theorem about efficiency. Social welfare will be discussed presently.

Efficiency, as the term is understood within the discipline of economics, is the absence of waste. At a minimum, efficiency means that a given output is produced with the fewest inputs possible, that ten hours of labour are not expended when five would do. The term is extended to cover the mix of goods produced and the allocation of goods among people. The mix of goods is said to be efficient if there is no way to reorganize the economy — producing more of some goods and less of others — to make everybody better off. The economy is inefficient in this sense if all cars are painted black though some buyers would prefer other colours instead and there is no significant cost-saving in painting all cars the same colour. The economy does not cease to be inefficient in this sense if these black cars are produced with the minimum possible input of labour and other resources. The allocation of goods among people is said to be efficient when all potential gains from trade have been exhausted so that no additional exchange of goods could make everybody better off.

To speak of efficiency as the absence of waste is to say that an economy is efficient when no change in the technology of production, the mix of goods produced or the allocation of goods among people can make everybody better off. The waste in this context is of utility rather than of things. In the standard terminology of economics, a situation without waste is said to be Pareto optimal, defined formally as a condition such that no rearrangement of production or reallocation of goods among people can make anybody better off without making somebody else worse off. The second great theorem of welfare economics is that a competitive equilibrium is efficient, free of waste, Pareto optimal. An "economy motivated by individual greed and controlled by a very large number of agents" is more than coherent in the sense that demands and supplies are matched at the equilibrium prices. Such an economy is efficient as well in the sense that an omniscient and omnipotent planner could not rearrange production and distribution to everybody's advantage. The planner could make some people better off at the expense of others, but not everybody at once.

Observe that the planner could make everybody better off, in the circumstances described by the demand and supply curves in Figure 2, if the actual output of wheat were less than (or more than) the competitive equilibrium output. The equilibrium output is 6 million bushels. If the actual output were 3 million rather than 6 million, an extra bushel would be worth $3.25 to each and every consumer, and would have an alternative cost of only $1.75. Thus, by arranging for the production of an extra million bushels, the planner could generate a surplus of $1 million that might be allocated among consumers to make everybody better off. Only when output reaches 6 million is this type of manoeuvre no longer possible. The generalization from a single market to a complete competitive economy presents complications — that surpluses for different goods are not additive, that the locations of the curves depend on the initial distribution of resources, and that the curves in one market are affected by transactions in other markets — but the basic idea in the demonstration does carry over to the full-fledged proof.

An additional, admittedly very strong, assumption converts the second theorem of welfare economics into an unambiguous statement about the common good. It is useful for some purposes to suppose that everybody in society is alike in his tastes and in his command over resources so that, by symmetry, everybody's consumption is the same too, as long as public policy is not discriminatory. The advantage of this supposition is that it permits an unambiguous evaluation of alternative policies or institutions.

To reason about what is in effect a society of identical twins is to analyse policies or institutions in two stages, with distributive considerations put aside until the second stage. Indeed, there may be no second stage if one is prepared to make a rough judgment that distributive considerations are relatively unimportant for the matter at hand. Within a "twins" model of the economy, the second theorem of welfare economics establishes that the representative person is better off in a competitive market than he would be with any deviation from or modification of the competitive market. The "twins" model sidesteps interpersonal comparison of utility because, within the terms of reference of the model, everybody gains or loses together. It is only with reference to this model that monopoly is unambiguously inferior to competition, for the case where monopoly can be justified on distributive grounds — because the monopolist is poor while the consumer is rich — is assumed away. The "twins" model is employed extensively in the analysis of departures from efficiency in Chapter VII below, especially in the discussion of the social costs and benefits of advertising. It is also employed in the design of tax systems and of rules in commercial law where, or in so far as, the parties affected by taxes or rules are more or less alike in the relevant respects.

Together, the two fundamental theorems of welfare economics tell a highly counter-intuitive story about how selfishness mimics cooperation within the domain of the economy. Plato *knew* that the ideal republic would require the detailed guidance of a superior class of philosopher-kings. The "economist" *knows* that philosopher-kings are unnecessary — worse than unnecessary because their "folly and presumption" would destroy the economy they attempt to guide. Admittedly, the actors in the market do not intend to cooperate. Each is entirely selfish. Each is uninterested in the welfare of his fellow citizens. Yet the combined effect of selfishness on everybody's part is precisely what would have transpired if people did cooperate and if people knew what the right cooperative actions would be. Certainly, the assumptions of the fundamental theorems of welfare economics are very strong, and the conclusions of the theorems are modified as the assumptions are relaxed in important respects. The theorems are significant nevertheless. That there is a broad domain of economic activity within which self-interested behaviour is at least Pareto optimal and possibly desirable for everybody is the great lesson of economic science.

Competition over the allocation of property

Widespread mistrust among non-economists in the efficacy of competition may be traced to a discrepancy in paradigms about the relation between selfishness and waste. Within the bounds of the assumptions of the fundamental theorems of welfare economics, it is quite true that selfishness mimics cooperation. Outside these bounds, the proposition is usually if not invariably false. There is no analogue to the fundamental theorems of welfare economics in marriage, international relations, crime or war, where unrestricted selfishness is indeed a recipe for chaos and where central control or voluntary self-restraint is required to promote the welfare of the community as a whole.

In sharp contrast to competition as the economist understands the term is the wasteful competition for property, income, rights or privileges in circumstances where the prize for which people compete is what it is regardless of whether people compete for it, and where everybody, including the competitors, could be made better off *ex ante* by an agreement to allocate the prize by lot or to share the prize without competing. Wasteful competition is exemplified by the contest between the thief and his victim. Both would be better off if they could figure out how much would be stolen and quietly agree to pass the value of the stolen goods from victim to thief without the wasted effort of the thief in evading the law, the risk of injury to the victim and to the thief in the process of stealing, and the expense of locks on the victim's doors, police, judges and prisons. It is, of course, the essence of the "market" for theft that there is no mechanism in society to effect such an agreement. If there were, the thief's loot would for all practical purposes be the thief's property, and theft as we now understand the term would be absent altogether. This example will be discussed in detail in Chapter III.

Theft is just the most flagrant example of a kind of behaviour that is abstracted away in the assumptions of the fundamental theorems of welfare economics. The proof that a competitive equilibrium exists and is optimal rests on the assumption that property is costlessly secure, an assumption which restricts analysis for the most part to domains of life where competition is not wasteful. To the extent that property is insecure, there is scope in the economy for actions that are competitive in the derogatory sense of the term as employed in common speech; there is scope for actions that are privately advantageous and socially wasteful at the same time.

Wasteful competition can take many forms, all of which can (perhaps with a grain of salt) be interpreted as competition over property. Plaintiff and defendant pour resources into a legal conflict which may in the first instance be over the interpretation of the terms of a contract but is ultimately a dispute over a sum of money that is what it is regardless of who

wins. Advertisers compete for shares of a market of a given size. Speculators devote resources to discovering whether the city is destined to develop to the east or to the west in order to buy property advantageously,
though the ownership of property has no effect on development itself.
Would-be importers compete for quotas in the gift of the government. All
these cases will be discussed at some length at various places in the book.
All are abstracted out of sight by the assumptions of the fundamental
theorems of welfare economics. All are examples of activities in which
selfishness cannot be said to mimic cooperation and for which the non-
economist's scepticism about the relation between selfishness and cooperation is entirely justified. As will be discussed in Chapter VII, the most
interesting cases are those in which productive competition and wasteful
competition interact in complex and unexpected ways.

The world of perfect competition is a safe place, with no thieves, no
muggers, no dishonesty, no direct conflicts of any sort between one man
and another, no policemen, no judges, no prisons, not even lawyers. The
assumed security of property eliminates all these features of any real society.
It is this assumption, above all, that accounts for the nice attributes of
perfect competition. As already mentioned in the preface, a central theme
of this book is the contrast between making and taking, one the domain
of all of the attractive implications of the fundamental theorems of welfare
economics, the other the domain, in the words of the quotation at the
outset of this book, of "actions neutralizing one another". The contrast is
between use of one's resources, including labour, to make goods for use
or sale and the use of one's resources to take property away from others.
To assume full and complete security of property is to assume the latter
away.

In parallel with the assumption that property rights are secure is the
assumption that all promises are kept to the letter. Until quite recently,
this assumption was rarely, if ever, questioned or abandoned within economic analysis because nobody knew what to put in its place. The assumption is, for example, that the cost of supervision of labour may be
ignored because workers automatically supply a mutually agreed upon
effort for a mutually agreed upon wage. Malfeasance by workers in their
relation to managers, by managers in relation to their stockholders, by one
firm under contract to another, and, most important, by public officials in
their collective and individual dealings with the public and with one another would all be assumed away. Progress in analysis has made it possible
to model these phenomena. Monitoring, moral hazard, principal–agent
relations and a variety of other terms having to do with actual or potential
promise-breaking have become part of the stock-in-trade of the practising
economist.

Equally important, once property rights are no longer automatically
secure, is the role of actual or potential violence as the rock-bottom sanction

upon people to respect property rights and other rules of society. Even punishment by fine has to be extracted by force or by the threat of force. To postulate secure property rights or to suppose that a given expenditure by the state is sufficient to ensure that property rights become secure is to abstract from the role of violence in society, in particular to ignore the fact that violence can be misused. One of the purposes of this book is to give violence its due. Violence plays a central and overt role in the models of anarchy and despotism in Chapters III and IV. In the liberal society, it is only implicit, an ever-present threat that need not necessarily be exercised.

The postulated security of property is an abstraction, not only from theft and theft-like activities, but from voting, for a legislature can take actions that are the equivalent for all practical purposes of the reassignment of property from one person to another. To raise the old age pension is to transfer property from the young to the old. To increase agricultural price support is to transfer property from city folk to country folk. Taking by voting has some of the economic attributes of theft, but the analogy between them is with reference to certain of their consequences rather than to their moral or political status. One can draw this analogy without at the same time subscribing to the view that all property is sacrosanct or that legislative decisions to circumscribe, abridge or change the rights of property are necessarily immoral.

Actual liberal societies — by which I mean societies that are more or less democratic in their politics and more or less capitalist in their economic organization — have two partly contradictory systems of entitlement. As a citizen of such a society, I may possess property and I have the right to vote, where voting might easily be on matters involving a restriction of property rights. A major theme of this book is the mediation between these entitlements. In principle, a majority of voters could overthrow property rights entirely, but, as will be argued in detail later on, there are strong reasons for believing that no majority of voters would have an interest to do so. In any actual liberal society, there is an uncomfortable but unavoidable tension between the two sources of entitlement. As discussed in Chapters VIII and IX, a community of rational voters may take actions that are wasteful in the sense that everybody could be made better off by a reallocation of property rights together with a ban on "predatory voting", though such a ban could not, in practice, be put into effect without destroying the liberal society.

Traditional welfare economics abstracts completely from the problems that arise in the double entitlement of people as voters and as holders of property. It abstracts, in particular, from the political consequences of economic policy. To postulate that economic policy is conducted to maximize the value of a social welfare function is, for all practical purposes, to postulate the existence of an omniscient, omnipotent (within limits) and benevolent despot who can effortlessly enforce compliance with the law and who need look no further in assessing the effects of economic policy than the private sector response of labour supply, saving rates, and the allocation of income among goods consumed. Welfare economics becomes the provision of advice to a Monarch who has no fear of political opposition among his subjects.

Introduce the right to vote and the consequences of economic policy begin to extend beyond the usual economic considerations. It is an undeniable fact of political life that democracies crumble from time to time, sometimes to re-emerge after a period of dictatorship, sometimes not. It is an equally undeniable fact that democratic governments are invariably associated with the private ownership of at least part of the means of production. By postulating what is in effect an omniscient, omnipotent and benevolent despot, traditional welfare economics diverts attention from the possibility that particular economic policies can make government by majority rule more, or less as the case may be, difficult to maintain.

The ownership of the social welfare function

The social welfare function is intended as a precise representation of one's sense of the common good. It may be claimed, for example, that free trade is good for the country as a whole, that no-fault insurance is preferable to strict liability upon the perpetrator of an accident, that deficits are desirable in certain circumstances, that optimal taxes can be computed or that competition is better than monopoly. Never mind whether the statements are true or false. The relevant consideration here is that, as each statement is about what is best for society, such statements cannot be either true or false except with reference to a criterion for deciding whether society as a whole is better off. Since every conceivable policy is detrimental to somebody, each statement requires a criterion for weighting gains to some people against losses to others. A precise representation of such a criterion is a social welfare function. The social welfare function is intended to translate vague intuitions about the common good into precise criteria by which the actions of government may be judged.

The social welfare function is like an ordinary utility function in that both depict welfare as dependent upon other entities and both can be thought of as summaries of answers to a long series of questions directed to the person to whom the function belongs. In an ordinary utility function, the welfare of the individual depends upon the amounts of the different goods consumed. In a social welfare function, the welfare of the community depends upon the incomes or utilities of the different people in the community. In principle, an ordinary utility function is a summary of the information derived from answers to questions of the form "Do you prefer this to that?" For instance, "Would you rather have four apples and three pears than three apples and nine pears?" Extending the questions from apples and pears to bundles of various amounts of all goods consumed, one can represent a person's answers as a set of indifference curves such that the bundles of goods q^1 and q^2 lie on the same indifference curve whenever the person says he is indifferent between q^1 and q^2, and the bundle q^1 lies on a higher indifference curve than the bundle q^2 whenever the person says he prefers q^1 to q^2. A function $u(q)$ is then constructed by attaching numbers to indifference curves. Any numbering will do as long as the utility assigned to q^1 is higher than the utility assigned to q^2 (i.e. $u(q^1) > u(q^2)$) when the person prefers q^1 to q^2.

So too with the social welfare function, except that (in the simplest version of the social welfare function) the comparison is among bundles of incomes of different people rather than among bundles of goods consumed by one particular person. The data from which one's social welfare function is derived are a set of answers to questions of the form "Is the common good promoted if the incomes of Charlie and Joe are changed from \$10 and \$50 respectively to \$20 and \$30?" The questionnaire is broadened to cover the incomes of every person in society. The answers are represented as a set of indifference curves such that the bundles of incomes y^1 and y^2 (where, for instance, y^1 is a set of incomes, y^1_1, y^1_2, ... y^1_m, for each of the m persons in society) lie on the same indifference curve whenever the person whose sense of the common good is being investigated says that he is indifferent between y^1 and y^2, and the bundle y^1 lies on a higher indifference curve than the bundle y^2 whenever the person says that the common good is enhanced by a move from y^2 to y^1. A social welfare function $W(y)$ is then constructed by attaching numbers to indifference curves.[8] Any numbering will do as long as $W(y^1) > W(y^2)$ whenever a person prefers the income distribution y^1 to the income distribution y^2.

The use of income as a surrogate for utility or welfare is a harmless simplification as long as prices are invariant, but is unsatisfactory when prices are not invariant, as they are unlikely to be in comparisons among alternative forms of economic organization or major policy options. When prices are not invariant, it is no longer appropriate to employ *money income* as the representation of individual welfare within the social welfare function. The social welfare function must be reconstructed as $W(u)$ rather than as $W(y)$, where y is a vector of incomes for each and every person in society, u is the corresponding vector of utilities and each person's utility is dependent on the bundle of goods consumed. However, individual welfare can still be represented within the social welfare function by *real income*, interpreted as a money-metric measure of utility; in this measure, a person's real income is defined as the amount of money he requires to be as well off at some fixed set of prices as he is in his present circumstances.[9]

From the construction of the social welfare function, it follows automatically that the function itself represents some person's judgment of the common good. The function should really be written as $W^i(u)$ rather than as $W(u)$, where i refers to one of the n people in the community; the function $W^i(u)$ differs from the function $W^j(u)$, where j denotes another person, unless their conceptions of the common good are exactly alike. This might, but certainly need not, be so. One person may place a high weighting on the size of the national income, but be relatively uncon- cerned about the degree of equality in the distribution of income. Another person may be more concerned about equality and less about the size of the national income. A third person may see inequality as a public virtue. For one person, a country's common good encompasses the standard of living of everybody in the world; for another, it encompasses nothing outside the immediate welfare of the citizens of his country. Of course, the social welfare function is meaningless to one for whom there is no concept of the common good, and the function is not particularly interesting unless it can be supposed that people's conceptions of the common good are similar.

The significance of the social welfare function derives from the context in which it is employed. Within economic analysis, the function is used in arguments of the following form: "If *your* (the reader's) sense of the common good can be represented by such-and-such a social welfare function, and if these are the social, technical, behavioural and political features of the society in which you live, then it must be your opinion that (depending on the context of the argument) (i) such-and-such actions in the private sector are (or are not as the case may be) socially advantage- ous, or (ii) such-and-such rules are appropriate, or (iii) the government should do such-and-such."[10]

At the outset of this chapter, I spoke of economics as an advice-giving profession. The basis of the economist's advice is, in part, his acquired skill at digging out and organizing data that are relevant to the problem at hand, but it is also in part his skill at working out the implications of preferences regarding the organization of the economy and society. Man's ability to calculate, to draw inferences from a set of preferences and cir- cumstances, is limited. The economist is trained to engage in certain routines of calculation about economic matters, just as the physicist is trained to engage in certain routines of calculation about the world of nature. In employing a social welfare function or some logically equivalent construc- tion, the economist is not imposing his preferences upon society. He is postulating that somebody else's sense of the common good can be represented by such-and-such a function, and he is drawing out the im- plications of that person's preferences. One who rejects the postulated representation of the common good would, to a greater or lesser extent, reject the implications of the analysis.

Though, ideally, the social welfare function is discovered by questioning the citizen in accordance with the hypothetical experiment as described above, it is customary, and I think unavoidable, in welfare economics to postulate a form for the function as a basis for the analysis of public policy. The rationale for this procedure is that strong inferences about public policy can sometimes be derived from simple specifications of the social welfare function in circumstances where not too much depends upon the exact form of the function or upon aspects of moral judgment that are being ignored. In practice, it is rarely possible to induce citizens to supply accurate and honest information about their choices among hypothetical alternatives. General features of social welfare functions and specific functional forms have both to be imposed.

Assumptions about the specification of the social welfare function are not strictly or invariably imposed. They are working assumptions designed to focus on the essence of the problem at hand and to facilitate the establishment of clear rules for public policy and for ranking alternative forms of economic organization. They are relaxed or modified from time to time as the occasion warrants. They are for the most part adhered to in this book, but not rigidly or without exception. In the course of this chapter I express reservations about how the social welfare function is employed in traditional welfare economics, but these reservations do not extend to the postulates about the form of the function itself.

Among the general features imposed upon welfare functions — individual and social — are that they are limited in scope, non-paternalistic and exogenous. A person's utility function is "limited in scope" when it depends exclusively on quantities of ordinary purchasable goods and services. Longevity, leisure, friendship, public esteem, freedom of movement, the state of one's health and many other aspects of life that influence one's personal welfare and one's judgment about the common good are usually ignored. Longevity will be incorporated as a good in the models of anarchy and despotism in Chapters III and IV. Otherwise the ordinary assumptions about the scope of the welfare function will be maintained.

By "non-paternalism", I mean that, when your well-being enters as an argument into my social welfare function, the measure of your well-being is a reflection of your tastes and preferences exclusively. When altruism is non-paternalistic, an increase in your consumption of frogs' legs enhances my assessment of the social welfare if and only if you like frogs' legs and regardless of whether I like them or not. If your welfare affects my assessment of the common good, if you prefer good A to good B, and as long as your having good A rather than good B is not injurious to a third party whom I care about as well, then social welfare as I see it is enhanced when you have good A rather than good B. The non-paternalistic assumption is maintained throughout this book.

"Exogeneity" is a more fundamental assumption. Welfare functions are exogenous when one's tastes and one's sense of the common good are fixed and immutable characteristics of a person, regardless of the society in which one lives or one's place in that society. Tastes influence events.

Events do not influence tastes. There is no analogue in traditional welfare economics to the propositions that socialism will create a new and better man or that people will behave more decently to one another in a society that is free than in a society that is not free. There is no false consciousness, no obedience induced by propaganda, no structure influencing super-structure, and certainly no "spirit of the times". I do not dismiss such considerations as *a priori* nonsense, unscientific or unworthy of notice by the social scientist. Following the usual practice in welfare economics, I ignore them all the same.

When stated in this bald and uncompromising way, it is at once evident that the exogeneity assumption is far from innocuous, for it is undeniable that material and moral preferences are conditioned to some extent by one's circumstances. One's ideals and aspirations are undoubtedly influenced by one's upbringing and one's place in society, as well as by the mores, technology and organization of the community in which one lives. Enculturation, to use the sociologists' term, is a fact of life. The exogeneity assumption in traditional welfare economics is that the phenomenon of enculturation may be ignored in the contexts where economic analysis is typically employed.

These assumptions need no apology. All analysis in the social sciences — formal and informal — is based on concepts which are by their very nature simplifications of and abstractions from the virtually infinite complexity of the world. It is always possible that a richer set of assumptions *might* give rise to a model with very different implications. No analysis whatsoever is defensible against that assertion, but, equally, the assertion is of no practical importance unless it can be shown that more realistic assumptions *do* alter the implications of the analysis in significant respects. The burden of proof in this matter lies with the critic, who must show, not just that enculturation, for instance, exists, but how tastes and values are affected by changes in economic organization and how important propositions in a model without enculturation are not merely muted but obliterated when enculturation is taken into account.

Nor, of course, is it unreasonable to suppose that enculturation is worth considering for some purposes but not for others. It has been claimed that the treatment of enculturation marks the main boundary between the assumptions of economics and sociology.[11] Economics almost always abstracts from enculturation; a major task of sociology is to explain how people's aspirations are affected by the mores and circumstances of their society. In so far as the claim is valid and with two minor exceptions — the discussion of the ideology of despotism in Chapter IV and one of the models of advertising in Chapter VII — this book is true to type as a work of economics.

Though enculturation may be of fundamental importance in the study of culture, narrowly defined as art, literature, music, relations within the family and so on, it is probably of less importance for the study of the grosser aspects of life, the getting and spending, which are the typical subject-matter of economics. To use a homey analogy: as a consequence of climate, geography and technology, the Chinese tend to like rice and the Europeans tend to like potatoes — preferences that persist for generations after the economic determinants of differences in taste cease to be relevant, as among people in North America today. But at a more basic level the dietary needs of Chinese and Europeans are the same; they have the same needs and "tastes", as economists understand the term, for nutrients — protein, fats, carbohydrates, vitamins and so on. Chinese and Europeans may differ about the definition of a good meal, but not about the meaning of hunger, malnutrition or starvation. Economics is mostly about hunger, not gastronomy. Economics is focused upon human traits that persist regardless of the form of economic organization.

There is another consideration. To serve its purpose within economics as the criterion for choosing among alternative policies, the social welfare function has to be invariant with respect to the policies themselves. The social welfare function must not be allowed to wobble. Otherwise, there may be no basis for choice among alternative policies, as each policy could be best in the light of the social welfare function that it enculturates. In a world where the good guys do not always win, where public choice is not always in the interest of the citizens, and where the verdict of history is no certification of the merits of a cause, the exogenous social welfare function, as the representative of one's sense of the common good, is a vantage point for an independent assessment of the actions of the society in which one lives.

In considering the form of the social welfare function, it is convenient to begin with the simplest representation and to add complexity bit by bit. For some purposes, the social welfare function can be adequately represented by national income.[12] When rules or policies do not affect market prices to any significant extent and when one cannot tell in advance who gains and who loses from the application of a given rule or policy, it may be satisfactory in practice to say that the best rule or policy is that which generates the largest national income, for everybody could be better off with a large national income than with a small one. This simplest of criteria is often satisfactory for commercial law where no businessman can say when the law is passed whether he will be affected as plaintiff or as defendant. An application of this interpretation of the social welfare function is the "Hand rule" for identifying negligence: that a party is guilty of negligence when injury to a second party might have been prevented by precautions undertaken by the first party, if and only if the expected cost of the injury exceeds the cost of the precaution. A more complicated specification of the common good might serve only to muddy the waters, opening the courts to complex judicial interpretations that would in practice impart a vagueness to the law with no compensating advantage.[13]

Similarly with cost–benefit analysis. The Ministry of Transport must set policy for the location, width, construction and repair of roads. If I had my way, I would of course arrange for the Ministry to spend lavishly on roads I am likely to use frequently and to skimp on expenditure on other roads. If I cannot influence the Ministry to favour me over my fellow citizens, and if, besides, I am uncertain where I and my descendants will wish to travel, I can do no better than to have the Ministry undertake projects where benefits exceed costs, "to whomsoever they may accrue", a policy more or less equivalent to maximizing total national income.

National income is a poor surrogate for one's sense of the common good in evaluating changes in society that affect relative prices or the distribution of income. For changes that affect relative prices without at the same time having any significant differential impacts upon the rich and the poor (or any other identifiable groups of people), the national income can be replaced as a criterion for public policy by a postulated utility function for the representative person within a "twins" model of the economy, that is, within a model in which everyone is assumed to be just like everyone else in his tastes, his skills, his ownership of the means of production, his political rights and, consequently, his pattern of consumption. Alternative rules, laws or policies would be assessed with regard to their effects upon the *real* income of the representative consumer rather than aggregate *money* income. One knows perfectly well that people's tastes differ, but one cannot always incorporate this knowledge into the analysis in any useful way. Instead, one reasons that such-and-such would occur within a twins model and hopes the discrepancy between the model and the world does not matter too much. One reasons *as if* the twins model were an accurate representation of the economy, for the only alternative may be silence on important questions of the day.

A different tack is adopted when alternative rules, policies or laws have differential effects upon identifiable groups or between the rich and the poor. A rule prohibiting people from sleeping on park benches might be efficient in the sense of augmenting the national income (with appropriate quantification of the non-monetary benefits), but most people's sense of the common good would require that some account be taken of the special circumstances of those who are harmed by the rule. Most people's sense of the common good would require that dollar values of benefits and costs to the poor be more heavily weighted than dollar values of benefits and costs to the rich.

In this context, one may appeal to the "veil of ignorance" hypothesis about the meaning of the common good.[14] The hypothesis links the common good to personal utility, by means of a restricted version of the conceptual experiment discussed above: a choice has to be made between, for instance, the passage or the rejection of a law. The veil of ignorance hypothesis is that the common good, as I see it, is reflected in the course of action that I, in my own interest, would recommend if I forgot my own circumstances in society and believed myself to be confronted with an equal chance of occupying the circumstances of each and every person who would be affected by the proposed law. In this conceptual experiment, I am presumed to remember a good deal about society and about the effects of the proposed law, but to remember nothing about myself. Imagine a three-person society in which the proposed law would increase the income of the first person from 100 to 101, decrease the income of the second from 200 to 185, and decrease the income of the third person from 300 to 205. If I am the first person, I favour the law because it leads to an increase in my income. On the veil of ignorance test, I would claim that the law serves the common good only if I would prefer equal chances (1/3) of enjoying incomes of 101, 185 and 205 to equal chances of enjoying incomes of 100, 200 and 300. This interpretation of the common good allows people's assessments to vary with their taste and their understanding of society, but not with their own circumstances, except in so far as one's beliefs affect one's understanding of how society works.

A few additional assumptions translate the veil of ignorance test into a precise utilitarian social welfare function which can be particularly useful for the analysis of public policy. If everyone is alike in his tastes, if each person's choice behind the veil of ignorance is a reflection of risk aversion rather than altruism, and if personal utility is a function of nothing more than one's bundle of goods consumed, the social welfare function becomes

$$W = v(q^1) + v(q^2) + \ldots + v(q^3)$$

where q^i is the bundle of goods consumed by person i, and v is the assumed common utility function cardinalized to represent one's choices among risky prospects.[15] As discussed above, the utility function can sometimes be simplified so that it depends only on one's income rather than on the entire bundle of goods consumed; $v(q^i)$, becomes $v(y^i)$ where q^i is the bundle of goods consumed by the person i and y^i is his income. The simplification is possible when each person can be assumed to allocate his income among goods to maximize his utility and when all prices of goods are invariant over all the situations that are being compared.

In practice, the trade-off between the maximization of national income and the promotion of equality can be reflected in the postulated curvature of the individual utility function v. On the extreme assumption that $v(y) = y$, the social welfare, W, and national income are one and the same; the disparity between rich and poor has no bearing on social welfare at all. On the more general assumption that $v(y) = y^\alpha$ for some value of α between 0 and 1, the trade off between national income and equality is reflected in the value of the parameter α. The smaller α, the greater the weight on equality and the smaller the weight on national income until, in the limit where α approaches 0, the social welfare W depends upon nothing other than the income of the worst off person in society.[16] Within the literature of economics, the implicit or explicit use of this version of the social welfare function is an ingredient in the analysis of redistributional policy, especially in theorizing about the optimal degree of progressivity of the income tax and about optimal taxation in general.

The main link in the chain of inferences from the veil of ignorance test to the utilitarian social welfare function is the fusing of altruism and risk aversion. When, from my vantage point behind the veil of ignorance, I express a willingness to sacrifice a certain amount of national income in exchange for a greater degree of equality among citizens, I may do so because I am risk averse or because I am altruistic. I may fear that I will be included among the poor when the veil of ignorance is lifted, or I may be uncomfortable in a society with a large gap between rich and poor, regardless of who I personally turn out to be. The motives are quite distinct. There is nothing illogical or inconsistent in a person being willing to take big chances in the conduct of his own affairs — to choose to be a speculator or a rock star rather than a university professor — while at the same time believing that the common good is promoted by measures which reduce the gap between rich and poor or by the imposition of constraints on the transmission of wealth or privilege from one generation to another. Nevertheless, these motives are juxtaposed when a social welfare function is derived with reference to a person's choices behind the veil of ignorance among alternative distributions of income. Risk aversion and altruism are both conducive to reducing the gap between the incomes of the rich and the poor, but the motives are not translatable into one another, and only the former leads directly to the utilitarian social welfare function.

My unease with the social welfare function as an ingredient of traditional welfare economics is not about its construction as discussed so far or about its use as a criterion for public policy, but about the manner in which it is used. The typical pattern of analysis in traditional welfare economics is that the government chooses certain parameters, such as the progressivity of the tax system, to maximize the value of a postulated social welfare function subject to constraints reflecting the response of the private sector to these parameters in the choice of, for instance, the supply of labour, the rate of saving and the mix of goods purchased. Useful as such models may be in the context where they are typically employed, they do abstract from important domains of life. They abstract, in particular, from the influence of self-interest within the public sector and from the risk of subversion of the liberal society through the choice of economic policy.

Assume for the sake of argument that people agree completely in their assessments of the common good, so that a unique social welfare function may be defined. Can one then be confident the social welfare function will be reflected in public decision-making? There are several reasons why it might, at least to some extent. Fear of the consequences of breaking the law must serve as a restraint upon fraud, malfeasance and corruption. Fear of loss of office in an election has some impact on the behaviour of politicians. Perhaps people are spontaneously more public-spirited in their participation in the public sector than in their participation in the economy, where, after all, self-interest is expected to reign. Even despotic rulers may find, as Hobbes claimed in the quotation at the beginning of Chapter IV, that their own interests are bound up with the prosperity of the ruled. Some degree of public-spiritedness is almost implied by the notions of the social welfare function and the common good. Barring total hypocrisy, there must be a disinterested corner in one's psyche if political discourse about what is best for the country is to proceed at all. Talk of the common good presumes a community of people who are prepared to listen.

That cannot be the whole story. Men who are predominantly self-interested in their behaviour within the private sector are unlikely to abandon self-interest altogether at the door of the public sector. Public officials have interests of their own that sometimes conflict with the interests of those whom they are expected to serve. Pressure can be applied by individuals and by organized groups to turn the government's favour in their direction. Votes are cast for politicians expected to adopt policies in the voters' immediate interest regardless of whether their immediate interest is in conformity with the common good. Predatory behaviour within the public sector can be restrained to some extent by the application of the law, but the law is never so well constructed or so well enforced as to block every possibility for employing the instruments at the disposal of the public sector to procure a small, relatively risk-free benefit for oneself while imposing a larger cost on the general public. The common good may be an important consideration in governmental decision-making, but not the only consideration.

Careless application of traditional welfare economics may give rise to two connected fallacies in the interpretation of the social welfare function. The first, which might be called the "displacement fallacy", is to take the social welfare function away from the individual to whom it rightfully belongs and either to objectify it as a single, universal ideal or to place it within the government where it serves as the sole and exclusive driving force of public policy. Once one begins to talk about a social welfare function, there is a tendency to lapse into the implicit assumption that the social welfare function can exist apart from particular people's sense of the common good. One forgets the social welfare function is the individual's assessment of the welfare of society, and not society's assessment of the welfare of individuals. What exists is my sense or your sense of what is best for society. What does not and cannot exist is the great social welfare function in the sky, the one overarching principle that resolves all disputes, the Platonic ideal of the good society, the economic counterpart of Rousseau's general will that supersedes all particular wills and prescribes what is right, fitting and good regardless of anybody's preferences or sense of the common good.

From the objectification of the social welfare function it is a small step to the supposition that the social welfare function is the embodiment of the motivation of the government of the day. This is a useful and necessary assumption for some purposes, and it is employed from time to time in this book. Following standard practice in the study of public finance, it is drawn upon in the analysis of public goods and the redistribution of income in Chapter VIII, where, for simplicity, other motivations of government are abstracted away, and where the problem is to determine what an ideal government would do, regardless of whether any actual government can ever be expected to behave in accordance with the ideal. It is a dangerous assumption, nonetheless, for it diverts attention from the less honourable and more self-interested motives of government. The implied dichotomy in much of traditional welfare economics between public sector altruism and private sector greed is at best an exaggeration and at worst a threat to the liberal society. A salutary lesson in the models of despotism in Chapter IV is that there need be no such dichotomy. Members of the ruling class in these models are every bit as greedy and self-interested as ordinary citizens are normally supposed to be. In practice, the antidote to the displacement of the social welfare function is the close study of the role of self-interest in the behaviour of the personnel of the government.

The displacement fallacy inculcates a systematic blindness to the political consequences of economic policy. Among the baggage of traditional welfare economics is a theory of government as the maximizer of the social welfare function. To suppose that governments have no other objective is to abstract from politics altogether and to ignore the possibility that economic policy can be corrosive to democratic institutions or to the liberal society. The chain from economic policy to political consequences is not as well forged in this book as I would have liked, but the juxtaposition of the study of anarchy and despotism with the study of the liberal society calls attention to the intrinsic fragility of the liberal society, and the analysis of predatory government, especially the section on voting in Chapter IX, deals with this matter more directly. The study of predatory government, especially its extreme in the despotic society, serves to emphasize the risk of the disintegration of the liberal society and suggests types of economic policy that might contribute to its preservation.

The second fallacy — which is the practical counterpart of the displacement fallacy and which might be called the Pigovian fallacy in recognition of a particularly clear instance to be discussed in the next chapter — is the proposition that any deficiency in the private sector of the economy should be remedied by public action. Public action is alleged to be warranted whenever there emerges a discrepancy between the outcome in the private sector of the economy and the outcome dictated by the maximization of a social welfare function subject to the existing technical and behavioural constraints. Though unobjectionable in certain contexts, the proposition is open to dangerous and harmful interpretations. Consider a proposal to expropriate the wealth of a very rich and very obnoxious old man, for the benefit of the poor. Most readers would, I suspect, have "a little list" of people for whom it could be said that the common good, as the reader understands the term, would be served if their fortunes were substantially less and if a good number of poor people were a little better off instead. We can perhaps agree that the world would be a better place if Scrooge were less wealthy and Cratchit were more so. Does this consideration provide sanction for the state to expropriate the wealth of some suitably rich and obnoxious person? A crude reading of the utilitarian criterion would suggest that expropriation would be warranted.

There are three reasons why a more circumspect interpretation of the utilitarian criterion would suggest otherwise. The first pertains to the re-action of the private sector to a policy of expropriation of the rich and obnoxious. Knowing that wealth will be expropriated, one loses the incentive for enterprise and for saving. Discouragement of enterprise and saving lowers the national output, with the possibility that everybody, even the poor, becomes worse off than if wealth were not expropriated. This argument should not be pushed too far. It is a valid argument against massive and discriminatory expropriation of the wealthy. It is not, as discussed in detail in Chapter VIII, a valid argument against partial, systematic and universal redistribution of income as a balance between the loss of national output and the gain from the attainment of a greater degree of equality in society.

A second reason for circumspection pertains to the behaviour of government in the administration of a policy of selective expropriation. A department of government would be required to choose the suitably rich and obnoxious. I am not speaking here about punishment for well specified crimes, such as any society can and must impose. I am speaking about selective redistribution where no crime has been committed. The common good might possibly be served by a programme of selective redistribution if God himself were prepared to select the expropriates or if officials could be found whose probity was universally recognized as beyond question and beyond dispute. Otherwise, officials of the Department of Expropriation would have to be appointed through the normal channels of government. Some officials might be entirely honest, disinterested and dedicated to their work. Other officials would be careless or would allow themselves to be influenced by characteristics of candidates for expropriation that most citizens would not consider to be relevant for the purpose at hand. Still other officials might be influenced by the threats or inducements of the candidates for expropriation. A Department of Expropriation could become a means for the influential to harm their enemies. In practice, a policy of selective expropriation might create uncertainty for everybody, because nobody, no matter how innocent and modest his life, can be entirely sure that he will not in the end be designated for expropriation. Selective expropriation is an extreme example of a policy that is undesirable because it is almost certain to be misused.

A third reason for circumspection is closely related to the second. Recognizing the authority that is lodged in the Department of Expropriation, the political party in office will be sorely tempted to employ that authority for partisan ends, and voters will choose among political parties according to who the parties are expected to victimize. In the Canadian context, English voters would favour political parties with "little lists" composed primarily of French Canadians, while French voters would favour political parties with "little lists" composed primarily of English Canadians. The effect of such developments is to erode the willingness of citizens to abide peacefully by the outcome of majority rule voting. The rules of equity and the common understandings at the foundation of the liberal society could not be preserved if the powers of government extended to the extreme of discrimination that the expropriation of the rich and obnoxious would entail. In this imperfect world, governments will inevitably exercise discriminatory powers to some extent, but some rules of entitlement have to be respected nevertheless. The Pigovian fallacy in this context is to disregard entitlements and to suppose that governmental action is warranted whenever it can be said that the common good would be served if entitlements were different from what they actually are.

Beyond this consideration, the Pigovian fallacy is a failure to draw the implications of self-interested behaviour within the public sector. A government that embodied and internalized the social welfare function need look no further in its choice of policies, laws and programmes than the response of the private sector to the instruments at the disposal of the government. In particular, regulation, taxation or subsidization of markets would be warranted whenever markets work imperfectly as assessed in the light of the ideal of perfect competition. There are few markets that cannot be rendered more efficient by such regulation as an omniscient, omnipotent and benevolent government might impose, and even fewer markets that would not on balance be rendered less efficient by such regulation, subsidization or taxation as might be expected from the partly disinterested, partly predatory government in societies of ordinary, fallible men. The proper scope of the public sector in a liberal society depends on the nature of government as it is and not as it might be if the maximization of the social welfare function were the single and unmixed objective. It is the common failure to recognize this consideration which accounts, in my opinion, for the considerable distaste for the notion of the social welfare function among those who are most fearful of the predatory propensities of government. The logic of their position is questionable because neither they nor anyone else can assess public policy — not excluding the policy of leaving the market alone — without the guidance of some criterion of the common good, and once that concept is introduced, it might as well be made precise. The politics of their position is understandable because the misuse of the social welfare function can provide a spurious but persuasive argument for the unwarranted expansion of the public sector.

A change of emphasis

As I said at the beginning of the chapter, there is no attempt to overthrow traditional welfare economics altogether. Quite the contrary, I shall make extensive use of the assumptions and methods of traditional welfare economics and I appeal, where I think it appropriate, to the reader's conception of the common good as represented and made precise in a social welfare function or in an ordinary utility function for a postulated representative consumer. There is nonetheless a major difference in tone between this book and, for instance, Pigou's *The Economics of Welfare* (discussed in the next chapter) or many modern treatments of welfare economics. The big question of welfare economics — of when and under what circumstances self-interested behaviour serves the common good — is posed with regard to actions in the public sector as well as to actions in the private sector, and not just with regard to the private sector, as is the practice in much of traditional welfare economics. Consideration is given to the interdependence of property and voting as the two principal, defining institutions of the liberal society. There is a special emphasis on the taking of property as the paradigmatic departure from efficiency. Violence is incorporated into economic analysis as an essential ingredient of the equilibria in anarchy and despotism and as the silent but fundamental last resort in the enforcement of the rules of the liberal society. Anarchy and despotism play a dual role as paradigms of opposing tendencies within a liberal society and as states of society into which the liberal society may in certain circumstances deteriorate. This last consideration represents an automatic withdrawal of the implicit assumption in the practice of traditional welfare economics that the institutions of the government and of the market are eternal, and that effects of economic policy extend no farther than to the bundle of goods consumed.

As used in this chapter, the term "traditional welfare economics" refers to a style of analysis that was most current some years ago before the expansion of the discipline of economics into the territory of voting, rent-seeking, moral hazard, incentives and the role of self-interest within the public sector. The story of the emergence and subsequent modification of traditional welfare economics is told in the next chapter.

Appendix I.1 Self-interested actions and the common good

Selfishness mimics cooperation in some domains of life but not in others, and it is a large part of the task of the economist to determine which is which. The general problem is illustrated in a partial equilibrium context in Figure 3. Every action that one may or may not take involves a certain gain or loss for oneself and a certain gain or loss to others, where "others" may be another person or an aggregate of the rest of one's community. Presumably one gains from one's actions, for it would be irrational to undertake them otherwise. Others may gain, lose or be unaffected, and, if one is selfish, one does not really care which. Good actions, such as those within the bounds of perfect competition, are such that the sum of one's own gain and the gain or loss to others is positive; if everybody undertakes such actions, then the national income must be maximized. Bad actions are those for which this is not so.

Figure 3 illustrates the relation between one's own gain from one's action and the gain to others in each of three types of activity: production by a price-taker in Figure 3(a), production by a monopolist in Figure 3(b), and theft in Figure 3(c). In each case, the agent chooses a certain level of activity (not shown on the diagram), yielding gain G^s to himself and a gain G^o to others. In each case, the directed curve from the origin to the point α shows corresponding values of G^s and G^o for various levels of activity, where G^s and G^o are measured on the horizontal and vertical axes of the figure. Think of G^s and G^o as additions to real income over and above what it would be with none of the activity in question; the appropriate interpretation of real income in this context is the money measure of utility evaluated at current prices. The advantage of this measure of gain is that the values of G^o and G^s are usually, though unfortunately not always, commensurate in the sense that an increase in the sum of G^o and G^s, coupled with the appropriate transfer of income between them, would make both parties better off. In the following paragraphs, this will be assumed to be so.

For the price-taker in Figure 3(a), the directed curve hugs the horizontal axis. Think of the agent as a supplier of labour in a large labour market. The value of G^s at the point α is his gain when he supplies his preferred number of hours of labour; points on the directed curve to the left of α indicate his gain from supplying a sub-optimal number of hours of labour at the going wage. Clearly selfish action is socially advantageous in this case because others are unaffected at the margin by one's behaviour.

For the monopolist in Figure 3(b), the directed curve connecting G^s and G^o begins along the horizontal axis because the consumer gets no surplus from the first bit of production of the monopolized good when price reflects the consumer's marginal valuation. Then the directed curve rises to reflect the consumer's surplus associated with the consumption of intramarginal units of the monopolized good once output begins to increase. For a time, both the monopolist and the consumer benefit from an increase in the output of the monopolized good. This state of affairs continues to the point α, which is, once again, the agent's optimal level of activity; monopoly profit is maximized at α. Beyond α the directed curve turns back on itself, signifying that the monopolist becomes worse-off as output increases, but the sum $G^s + G^o$ continues to grow until the point β on the vertical axis, which is the competitive equilibrium at which the monopoly profit is wiped out altogether.[17]

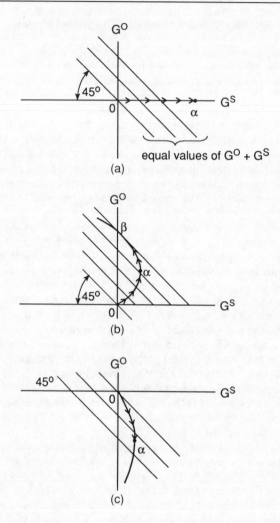

Figure 3 Beneficial and harmful activities. (a) The price-taker. (b) The monopolist. (c) The thief

Theft, on the other hand, is socially disadvantageous right from the beginning. The directed curve connecting gains to the thief and losses to his victim must lie to the right of the vertical axis as long as theft is advantageous to the thief, and it must be below the horizontal axis as long as theft is disadvantageous to others. As the curve is drawn it is steeper than the 45° line, signifying that the gain to the thief is less than the loss to his victim, a proposition to be spelled out in detail in Chapter III, though it should, on the face of it, seem reasonable to the reader. The sum $G^s + G^o$ diminishes steadily as the amount of theft increases. The thief's optimal amount of theft is indicated by the point α at which G^s is maximized. By contrast, the sum $G^s + G$ is maximal at the origin of the figure (signifying that the potential thief desists from theft altogether), where it is equal to zero by definition. If everybody steals, then everybody may be worse off than if nobody did so. Protection of property rights and the provision of the entire paraphernalia of the criminal justice system — laws, police, courts and prisons — becomes the first, indispensable duty of the state, as discussed in Chapter VIII.

In principle, the effects on people of any type of behaviour, socially advantageous or otherwise, can be illustrated on a diagram like those in Figure 3. There are, however, two important limitations to the figure. The first is the implicit assumption that the overriding social objective is the maximization of the real national income, an assumption which is valid in some circumstances, but not universally so. The other is that the analysis is strictly partial equilibrium. In general, the effects of any person's actions on his own gain and that of others depends on what others are doing. The consequences of my holding a piece of red-hot metal over an anvil are not independent of whether you are wielding a mallet. The logic of the relation between my gain and the gain to others is developed against an implied background of other actions in the rest of one's community. Though the partial equilibrium assumption is more blatant in this case than, for instance, in an ordinary demand and supply diagram, there is no real difference in kind. The moral of the story — that some self-interested actions are, and others are not, conducive to the common good — survives the restricted assumptions.

Notes

1 For an up-to-date treatment of welfare economics, see Robin W. Boadway and Neil Bruce, *Welfare Economics*, Blackwell, 1984. A major component of contemporary welfare economics is the study of how to tell from observed prices and quantities — which is all the market ever reveals — whether a person is moving up the scale of indifference curves or whether a community is in some sense becoming better off. This is the central problem in cost-benefit analysis of public projects or policies. It is also at the core of the measurement of real national income and economic growth. This aspect of welfare economics is ignored altogether here, not because it is deemed unimportant, but because the book is about a different aspect of the subject.

2 The first and second theorems of welfare economics are stated and proved with the utmost rigour in Kenneth J. Arrow and Frank H. Hahn, *General Competitive Analysis*, Holden Day, 1971. For a more accessible presentation, see David M. Kreps, *A Course in Microeconomic Theory*, Princeton University Press, 1990, Chapter 6.

3 For instance, there need be no equilibrium when one of the curves is discontinuous, as illustrated in Figure 4. To say that an equilibrium, market-clearing set of prices "exists" is not necessarily to say that the set of prices will be "discovered" by the market. In principle, a situation could arise in which all markets would clear if a certain set of prices obtained, but markets do not clear in fact because actual prices differ from equilibrium prices; traders may have no way of discovering the market-clearing prices, or something within the market may generate a different set of prices instead. Theorizing about the process by which traders discover

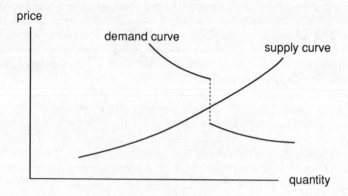

Figure 4   An absence of equilibrium

market-clearing prices has given rise to a number of theorems about the "stability" of the competitive economy. In this chapter, it is assumed that the equilibrium, if it exists at all, is unique and is discovered, one way or another, by the traders in the market. This assumption will be modified to some extent in the latter half of Chapter VII. Theorems about stability are discussed in the references cited in note 2.

4   The story is told in Kenneth J. Arrow, "Economic Equilibrium", *International Encyclopedia of the Social Sciences*, Macmillan, 1968, Vol. 4, 376–86.

5   See p. vii of the reference to Arrow and Hahn in note 2.

6   The *locus classicus* of this way of thinking about prices is F. Hayek, "The Use of Knowledge in Society," *American Economic Review*, 1945, 519–30. Hayek draws the fundamental distinction between "scientific knowledge" and "knowledge of the particular circumstances of time and place", the latter being so dispersed among the actors in the economy that no one person or organization can command more than a tiny fraction of what is necessary in the running of a modern economy. The price mechanism is the device society employs to utilize that infinitely dispersed information in the common enterprise of producing the world's goods and services. Consider a rise in price of a raw material generated by a new source of demand.

The marvel is that in a case like that of a scarcity of one raw material, without an order being issued, without more than perhaps a handful of people knowing the cause, tens of thousands of people whose identity could not be ascertained by months of investigation, are made to use the material or its products more sparingly, i.e., they move in the right direction.

I am convinced that if it were the result of deliberate human design, and if the people guided by the price changes understood that their decisions have significance far beyond their immediate aim, this mechanism would have been acclaimed as one of the greatest triumphs of the human mind. Its misfortune is the double one that it is not the product of human design and that the people guided by it usually do not know why they are made to do what they do. But those who clamor for "conscious direction" — and who cannot believe that anything which has evolved without design (and even without our understanding it) should solve problems which we should not be able to solve

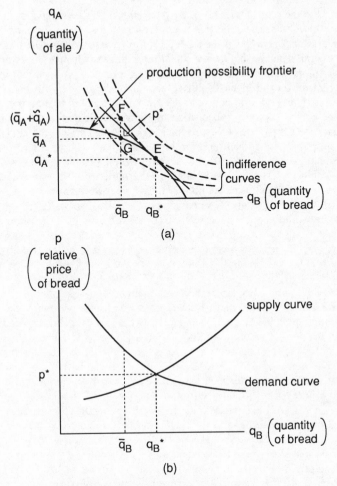

q_A
$\begin{pmatrix} \text{quantity} \\ \text{of ale} \end{pmatrix}$

production possibility frontier

$(\bar{q}_A + \hat{q}_A)$
$\bar{q}_A$
q_A^*

F
p^*
G   E

$\Bigr\}$ indifference
curves

q_B $\begin{pmatrix} \text{quantity} \\ \text{of bread} \end{pmatrix}$

$\bar{q}_B$ q_B^*

(a)

p
$\begin{pmatrix} \text{relative} \\ \text{price} \\ \text{of bread} \end{pmatrix}$

supply curve

p^*

demand curve

q_B $\begin{pmatrix} \text{quantity} \\ \text{of bread} \end{pmatrix}$

$\bar{q}_B$ q_B^*

(b)

Figure 5   The measurement of surplus

consciously — should remember this: The problem is precisely how to extend the span of our utilization of resources beyond the span of the control of any one mind; and, therefore, how to dispense with the need of conscious control and how to provide inducements which will make the individuals do the desirable things without anyone having to tell them what to do. (p. 527)

7   The meaning of surplus and its connection with the second fundamental theorem of welfare economics are best illustrated in a context without conflict of interest among people and with only two goods. Robinson Crusoe consumes only ale (A) and bread (B), and his production possibility frontier — the locus of all possible combinations of ale and bread he is able to produce — is as indicated on Figure 5(a). The figure also contains a set of indifference curves summarizing Robinson Crusoe's preferences for alternative combinations of ale and bread; he prefers any combination of ale and bread represented by a point on a "higher" (above and to the right) indifference curve to any combination on a lower one. The shapes of the curves reflect the assumed increasing rate of transformation between goods in production (which is the essence of the upward slope of the supply curve) and the assumed decreasing rate of substitution in use (which is the essence of the downward slope of the demand curve). Robinson Crusoe produces at the point E, placing himself on the highest indifference curve consistent with his production possibilities. The output of ale is q_A^*, the output of bread is q_B^*, and the "price" of bread, the common rate of substitution between the ale and bread in production and in use, is p^*, the slope of the production possibility curve at the equilibrium E.

Now suppose that production of bread is restricted to $\overline{q}_B$ on the understanding that production of ale rises to $\overline{q}_A$ consistent with the production possibility curve. Clearly Robinson Crusoe is worse off with the bundle $(\overline{q}_A, \overline{q}_B)$ than he would be with his unrestricted choice, the bundle (q_A^*, q_B^*). How much worse off? One way to quantify the loss is to ask — starting from the mix of goods $(\overline{q}_A, \overline{q}_B)$ how much extra *ale* he would need to be as well-off as he would be with the original bundle (q_A^*, q_B^*). The answer is the amount $\tilde{q}_A$ which leaves Robinson Crusoe with a bundle $(\overline{q}_A + \tilde{q}_A, \overline{q}_B)$ that is on the same indifference curve as the equilibrium bundle (q_A^*, q_B^*). One can define the amount $\tilde{q}_A$ as the loss of surplus in choosing the wrong bundle, $(\overline{q}_A, \overline{q}_B)$, instead of the right bundle, (q_A^*, q_B^*).

Precisely the same story can be told with demand and supply curves. Figure 5(b) is a conversion of Figure 5(a), with the identical horizontal axis, showing the quantity of bread, but a different vertical axis. Now the vertical axis is the relative price of bread, the derivative of q_A with respect to q_B, i.e. dq_A/dq_B. The supply curve on Figure 5(b) is the relation between q_B and the slope of the production possibility frontier. The corresponding demand curve is the relation between q_B and the slope of the indifference curve *through the point E*. By construction, the curves cross at the equilibrium price p^* and the equilibrium quantity of bread q_B^*. Clearly, in this case, the crossing of the demand and supply curves signifies that Robinson Crusoe is as well-off as he can be with the technology of production at his disposal.

Furthermore, the measure of Robinson Crusoe's loss in the event that he must produce $\overline{q}_B$ loaves of bread rather than q_B^* — the amount $\tilde{q}_A$ on Figure 4(a) — is exactly the area between the demand and supply curves of Figure 5(b) over the range from $\overline{q}_B$ to q_B^*. The usual measure of surplus in Figure 2 turns out in this case to be a vertical difference between indifference curves. This follows immediately from the usual relation between derivatives and integrals. By construction, the increase in the height of the indifference curve through the point E between E and F is the area under the demand curve, and the increase in the height of the production possibility curve between E and G is the area under the supply curve, so the vertical distance between F and G has to be the appropriate triangular area between the demand and supply curves.

There is a complication. If the output of bread were really restricted to $\overline{q}_B$ (for instance, by an excise tax), the observed demand price would be the slope of the indifference curve at G rather than at F, and the equality between the observed triangular area and the true measure of surplus $\overline{q}_B$ would fail to hold exactly. The degree of correspondence has been the subject of considerable debate among economists. See Robin Boadway and Neil Bruce, *Welfare Economics*, Blackwell, 1984, Part II, for an exhaustive discussion of this topic.

8   The *locus classicus* on the social welfare function is A. Bergson, "A Reformulation of Certain Aspects of Welfare Economics", *Quarterly Journal of Economics*, 1938, 310–34. For an up-to-date discussion of the construct, see Boadway and Bruce, *Welfare Economics*.

Much unnecessary confusion has been introduced into the analysis of the social welfare function by Arrow's impossibility theorem. The theorem establishes that there is no way to aggregate individual *orderings* of different states of society into one unique social ordering with certain "reasonable" properties. The theorem does not get in the way of a person's social welfare function because a social welfare function is a utility of utilities rather than an ordering of orderings. The theorem does signify that a well defined social welfare function does not reflect a fixed relation between individual orderings and a social ordering, regardless of the circumstances in which these orderings arise. The distinction between a social welfare function (which A.K. Sen calls an s.w.f.) and a social ordering based on individual orderings (which Sen calls an S.W.F.) is discussed in A.K. Sen, *Collective Choice and Social Welfare*, Holden Day, 1970. For further discussion of these matters, see Boadway and Bruce, chapter 5. What Arrow's impossibility theorem really shows, in my opinion, is that there is no escape from the paradox of voting (discussed in Chapter V) by replacing ordinary majority rule voting procedures with some more sophisticated procedure.

9   Real income is a "money-metric" measure of a person's utility. Let u(q) be any arbitrarily chosen utility function where q is a vector representing a person's bundle of goods consumed. The vector q is $(q_1, q_2, \ldots q_n)$ for each of the n goods in the economy. Real income is a monotonic transformation of the function u constructed with reference to an arbitrarily chosen vector of prices p which may, but need not be, the current prices for the goods. The vector p is $(p_1, p_2, \ldots p_n)$. Real income associated with the bundle of goods q and defined with regard to the set of reference prices p is

$$R(q \mid p) \equiv \min_{x} \{p_1 x_1 + p_2 x_2 + \ldots + p_n x_n, \text{ subject to } u(x) \geq u(q)\}$$

where x is any other bundle of goods. It is easily shown that real income depends on the person's indifference curves and on the arbitrarily chosen reference prices but not at all on the cardinalization, u, by which indifference curves are numbered.

This measure is useful because it allows current income to serve as a reference point for evaluating any and every bundle of goods. When the reference prices are the actual market prices that obtain today, a person's real income and his money income are one and the same as long as he is purchasing rationally. At these reference prices, the real income associated with any bundle of goods whatsoever is the amount of money I would need today to make myself as well-off as I would be with that bundle of goods.

This measure of real income is discussed in detail in D.Usher, *The Measurement of Economic Growth*, Blackwell, 1980, chapter 2.

10   The form of a typical statement in welfare economics is, "If you would attain such-and-such an end, and if these are the means at your disposal, then you ought to do thus-and-so," in other words, if U(q) is your utility function, and if $T(q,c) = 0$ is your constraint, where q is a vector of arguments in the utility function and c is a vector of parameters at your disposal, then choose ĉ.

This description of the practice of welfare economics raises the question of whether welfare economics, so described, is "normative" or "positive" as these terms are commonly interpreted. In *An Introduction to Positive Economics* (Weidenfeld and Nicolson, 1963, p. 4), Richard Lipsey identifies normative and positive with the old philosophical distinction between "is" and "ought", and he asserts that all statements have to be one or the other:

It is possible to classify statements into POSITIVE statements and NORMATIVE statements. Positive statements concern what is and normative statements concern what ought to be. Positive statements, assertions or theories may be simple or they may be very complex but they are basically about what is the case. *Thus disagreements over positive statements are appropriately settled by an appeal to the facts.* Normative statements concern what ought to be. They are thus inextricably bound up with whole philosophical and religious position, they are bound up, that is, with our VALUE JUDGMENTS.

Disagreements may arise over normative statements because different individuals have different ideas of what constitutes the good life. Such disagreements cannot be settled merely by an appeal to facts.

To which category does welfare economics belong? My answer to this question is "neither". It is not positive because it does not communicate facts. It is not normative because it does not advocate anything. It does not advocate because the utility function is conditional. It is rather the explication of the logic of choice: *if* these are your objective and constraints, then this is *your* best policy. The speaker does not say what he thinks is best, as when one talks about "what ought to be". The speaker does no more than draw out the implications of a possible view of a good society.

Of course, the logic of choice could be subsumed under the heading of normative economics. On that interpretation, the convenient identification of "positive" with "is" and of "normative" with "ought" would have to be abandoned, and a new distinction would have to be drawn within normative economics between advocacy *per se* and the logic of choice. This procedure would formally save the positive–normative distinction but at the cost of draining the distinction of its principal function in economic discourse. The challenge and the threat and the fun of the methodology of positive economics lay in the implicit or explicit assumptions that the positive and normative headings were all-encompassing, that real scientists did only positive economics and that normative economics was just moralizing. Recognize that man's calculative faculty is weak and limited, that we need complex patterns of reasoning to assess the social consequences of our actions, and that the provision of such patterns is a serious and worthy enterprise — recognize these considerations, and the practice of welfare economics becomes a socially useful occupation. Welfare economics is not rendered less valuable by the fact that we would have no need of it if we had better brains.

The distinction I am drawing between "ought" statements and the logic of choice was recognized by John Neville Keynes in *The Scope and Method of Political Economy*, Macmillan, 1891, pp. 34–5. Restating what I suspect was a commonplace at the time the book was written, Keynes proposed a *threefold* classification: "a *positive science* . . . a body of systematized knowledge concerning what is; a *normative* or *regulative science* . . . a body of systematized knowledge discussing criteria of what ought to be . . . ; an *art* . . . a system of rules for the attainment of a given end". What Keynes meant by "art" is certainly close and possibly identical to what we now call applied welfare economics. In *The Principles of Political*

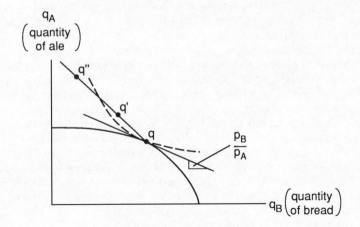

Figure 6   Income and utility

Economy (1883, to be discussed in Chapter II), Sidgwick included under the heading of the art of political economy much of the same material that was later contained in Pigou's *The Economics of Welfare*, and defined the art of political economy as follows (Sidgwick p. 397, cited in Keynes, p. 78):

we may take the subject of political economy considered as an art to include, besides the theory of provision for governmental expenditure, (1) the art of making the proportion of produce to population a maximum ... and (2) the art of rightly distributing produce among members of the community, whether on any principle of equity or justice, or on the economic principle of making the whole produce as useful as possible.

My own view is that this statement comes as close to the definition of welfare economics as we know it as was possible at that time.

Oddly enough, though the passage from J.N. Keynes in the preceding paragraph was quoted verbatim in the opening paragraph of Milton Friedman's essay "The Methodology of Positive Economics", *Essays in Positive Economics*, University of Chicago Press, 1953, which initiated the modern discussion of the positive-normative distinction, Friedman proceeded directly to "The Relation between Positive and Normative Economics", ignoring "art" altogether in the rest of the essay, as though the term referred to painting and dance. Nor was the three-way classification discussed by Richard Lipsey in his *Introduction to Positive Economics*.

11 For a development of this argument, see Scott Gordon, *The History and Philosophy of the Social Sciences*, Routledge, 1991.

12 Consider an economy of twins, and assume that ale and bread are the only goods consumed. In Figure 6, the quantity per head of ale, q_A is shown on the vertical axis and the quantity per head of bread, q_B, is shown on the horizontal axis. The solid curve is a production possibility frontier per head. The broken curve is an indifference curve of the representative consumer; it is the indifference curve containing the equilibrium point, q, at which utility is maximized over the production constraint. The point q is a vector (q_A, q_B) of amounts of bread and ale consumed.

The slope of the common tangent of the two curves at q is the relative price of bread in terms of ale, p_B/p_A. Any point above this line corresponds to a higher national income than that at q, i.e. $p_A q'_A + p_B q'_B > p_A q_A + p_B q_B$ whenever the point q' is above the common tangent.

Now consider any line, such as qq'q" in the figure, that begins at q and that extends above the tangent at q so that all points on the line (other than q itself) yield a higher value of the national income (at prices p_A and p_B) than q. From the general shape of the indifference curve, it follows that the representative person must be better off at points like q' that are close to q, but that he need not be better off at points such as q" that are further away. Since relative prices reflect the slope of the indifference curve at the bundle of goods consumed, one can be sure that a change in rules, laws or policies that increases the national income must also increase the utility of the representative person as long as relative prices do not change "too much". That justifies the use of the national income as a surrogate for the social welfare function in those circumstances where relative prices do not change significantly.

13 The "Hand rule" is discussed in detail in R. Cooter and T. Ulen, *Law and Economics*, Scott Foresman, 1988, 361–2.

14 The probabilistic interpretation of utilitarianism was originally proposed by John Harsanyi in "Cardinal welfare, individualistic ethics, and interpersonal comparisons of utility", *Journal of Political Economy*, 1955. The term "veil of ignorance" is from John Rawls, *A Theory of Justice*, Harvard University Press, 1971. Rawls argues that what one means when one uses the word "justice" is what one would choose behind the veil of ignorance. Economists have employed Rawls's conceptual experiment as an indicator of "welfare" rather than "justice".

15 The function v is not any old cardinalization of indifference curves. For W to be the sum of $v(q^1)$, $v(q^2)$, $v(q^3)$ and so on, a particular cardinalization is required. The required function v is called a Neumann–Morganstern utility function, named after John von Neumann and Oskar Morganstern, who introduced the function in *Theory of Games and Economic Behaviour*, Princeton University Press, 1944. To construct the function, begin by assigning a utility of 0 to some very "undesirable" bundle of goods, q^u, and assigning a utility of 1 to a very "desirable" bundle q^d. The utility of any bundle q that is better than q^u but worse than q^d is then assigned a value of v, where v is determined in the following conceptual experiment: The subject of the experiment is required to choose between a bundle q with certainty and a gamble in which he wins q^d with probability v and q^u with probability $(1 - v)$. The subject's (Neumann–Morganstern) utility of q is defined as the value of v at which he is indifferent between the certainty and the gamble. A value of v can by this means be determined for every bundle q, so that there is a function $v(q)$. From the laws of probability, it follows immediately that one gamble is preferred to another if and only if the expected value of $v(q)$ in the former is greater than the expected value of $v(q)$ in the latter. The subject of the conceptual experiment chooses among risky prospects to maximize expected utility when utility is cardinalized in this manner. The expected utility of a person behind the veil of ignorance is

$$\left(\frac{1}{n}\right) v(q^1) + \left(\frac{1}{n}\right) v(q^2) + \ldots + \left(\frac{1}{n}\right) v(q^n)$$

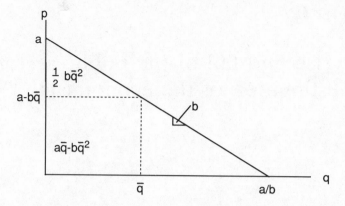

Figure 7   Benefits to the consumer and to the monopolist

because the probability of that person emerging from behind the veil in the circumstances of any given person is exactly (1/n). To maximize the above expression is equivalent to maximizing the value of W in the text.

For a given set of prices, a Neumann–Morganstern utility function can be constructed with regard to incomes rather than bundles of goods — $v(y)$ rather than $v(q)$, where y is a person's income. It is easily shown that a person's risk aversion is reflected in the concavity of the function $v(y)$. To say that the function v is concave is to say that $v' > 0$ and $v'' < 0$. The degree of risk aversion can be measured by an expression such as $- v''/v'$ or $- v''y/v'$. For a careful exposition of these matters, see H. Raiffa, *Decision Analysis: Introductory Lectures on Choices under Uncertainty*, Random House, 1968.

16   For a proof of this assertion, see H. Varian, *Microeconomic Analysis*, Norton, second edition, 1984, section 1.7. Formally, the proof refers to production functions, but it carries over with nothing more than a reinterpretation of symbols to the social welfare function.

17   Suppose, for simplicity, that the monopolized good is costless to produce and that the demand curve for the good is

$$p = a - b\,q$$

where p is price and q is quantity supplied. If the good were provided free, the quantity demanded would be a/b. When an amount $\bar{q}$ is provided at the price the market will bear, the benefit to consumers, G^o, is the surplus $(1/2)b\bar{q}^2$ and the benefit to the monopolist, G^s, is $a\bar{q} - b\bar{q}^2$. Clearly G^s and G^o are both positive when q is small, G^s maximized when q = a/b, and the sum $G^s + G^o$ is maximized when q = a/b, at which $G^o = a^2/(2b)$ and $G^s = 0$.

Chapter II

The rise and fall of the public sector in the estimation of the economists

Several themes of this book have deep roots in the history of economic doctrine. Enumeration of sources of inefficiency in the public and private sectors of the economy has been a major preoccupation of economists since the very beginning of the subject. The distinction between making and taking was well recognized by John Stuart Mill, as is evident from the quotation at the outset of this book. Even the spectre of despotism as an extreme of what might go wrong with the public sector was commonplace in the writings of the classical economists. In fact, what I have been calling traditional welfare economics is traditional only in the sense of being, until quite recently, widely accepted, and not in the sense of being very old. The tradition has solidified in the middle years of the twentieth century and does not, as we shall see, represent the views of an earlier age.

This chapter is a brief and selective history of economists' views about departures from efficiency in the public and private sectors of the economy. The texts to be discussed — Smith's *Wealth of Nations*, Mill's *Principles of Political Economy*, Sidgwick's *Principles of Political Economy*, Pigou's *Economics of Welfare* and several modern works — are chosen to exemplify dominant views of their day. Undoubtedly there were always cross-currents of opinion, but I make no attempt in this chapter to produce an extensive assessment of the state of opinion at any time. The story I want to tell is of the gradual emergence and the disintegration in recent years of what I have been calling traditional welfare economics. It is a story of a sharpening of the tools of economic analysis together with a gradual forgetting and subsequent relearning of much that was once central to the discipline.

Over the last two centuries, there has been a great cycle of opinion among economists about the sources of inefficiency, from Adam Smith's sharp and unqualified contrast between private sector enterprise and public sector sloth, to Mill's qualified and reluctant allowance of large domains within the economy where the public sector must act because the private sector would not or could not do so, to Sidgwick's concern in the latter part of the nineteenth century with what we would now call market failure and his willingness to trust the public sector to put things right, to Pigou's detailed analysis in the early years of the twentieth century of the defects of the competitive economy coupled with an almost complete disregard of the possibility of public sector inefficiency, to a recent revival of interest in public sector economics and a reassessment of public sector efficiency reminiscent of the views of Adam Smith.

Our story begins as theology. Before he embarked upon the serious study of economics, Adam Smith, the speculative philosopher, knew that there was a divinely ordained harmony in society. Not benevolence, but the pursuit by each man of his own self-interest, leads in the end to the best possible state of affairs for society as a whole.

The idea of that divine Being, whose benevolence and wisdom have, from all eternity, contrived and conducted the immense machine of the universe, so as at all times to produce the greatest quantity of happiness, is certainly of all the objects of human contemplation by far the most sublime . . . The administration of the great system of the universe . . . the care of the universal happiness of all rational and sensible beings, is the business of God and not of man. Man is allotted a much humbler department, but one much more suitable to the weakness of his powers, and to the narrowness of his comprehension; the care of his own happiness, his friends, his country.

Thus self-preservation, and the propagation of the species, are the great ends which nature seems to have proposed for the formation of all animals . . . But though we are . . . endowed with a very strong desire of those ends, it has not been entrusted to the slow and uncertain determination of our reason to find out the proper means of bringing them about. Nature has directed us to the greater part of these by original and immediate instincts. Hunger, thirst, the passion which unites the two sexes, the love of pleasure, and the dread of pain, prompt us to apply those means for our own sakes, and without any consideration of their tendency to those beneficient ends which the great Director of nature intended to produce by them.[1]

What we have here, as seen from today's perspective, is the second fundamental theorem of welfare economies deduced, not from a detailed analysis of the interaction of self-interested agents, but as a manifestation of God's purpose on earth.

Smith preserved something of this theological optimism when he turned to the study of the economy in *The Wealth of Nations*, but he had to contract the range of compatibility between private interest and the common good. In principle, a theory that self-interested actions promote the common good may or may not extend to the actions of the government. If public as well as private actions are conducive to the fulfilment of God's plan, then the theory has no economic implications and becomes quite useless as a basis for the reforms Smith wished to advocate. On the other hand, if only private actions are acceptable, there can be no role for government whatsoever, not even the protection of persons and property or the administration of justice. Smith could not subscribe to the latter view, for he believed that a market requires a framework of laws and substantial public expenditure on defence, justice and public works.

Theological optimism could not support the proposition that there is a "higher" agenda for government, an agenda which may differ substantially from the actual agenda of the government of the day. To advocate free trade and the abolition of restrictions on the economy while at the same time justifying the role of government in other spheres, one must be prepared to examine in detail how, and to what extent, self-interested actions are conducive to the common good, and one must study the consequences of public sector acts and decisions. That is exactly what Smith did. Smith specified the roles of the public and private sectors as follows:

All systems either of preference or of restraint, therefore, being thus completely taken away, the obvious and simple system of natural liberty establishes itself of its own accord. Every man, as long as he does not violate the laws of justice, is left perfectly free to pursue his own interest his own way, and to bring both his industry and capital into competition with those of any other man, or order of men. The sovereign is completely discharged from a duty, in the attempting to perform which he must always be exposed to innumerable delusions, and for the proper performance of which no human wisdom or knowledge could ever be sufficient; the duty of superintending the industry of private people, and of directing it towards the employments most suitable to the interest of the society. According to the system of natural liberty, the sovereign has only three duties to attend to; three duties of great importance, indeed, but plain and intelligible to common understandings: first the duty of protecting the society from the violence and invasion of other independent societies; secondly, the duty of protecting, as far as possible, every member of the society from the injustice or oppression of every other member of it, or the duty of establishing an exact administration of justice; and, thirdly, the duty of erecting and maintaining certain public works and certain public institutions, which it can never be for the interest of any individual, or small number of individuals, to erect and maintain; because the profit could never repay the expense to any individual or small number of individuals, though it may frequently do much more than repay it to a great society. [651][2]

Notice particularly Smith's uses of the phrase "system of natural liberty", once to prescribe the proper role of the private sector and again to prescribe the proper role of the public sector. The phrase itself is wonderfully ambiguous, standing halfway between the medieval concept of natural law and the modern concept of economic welfare, with strong overtones of civil rights. It would not be completely wrong to say that Smith advocates what he does because it is right, moral and in accordance with God's purpose for mankind. Nor would it be completely wrong to say that Smith advocates what he does because it is conducive to economic welfare in the modern sense of the term. Jacob Viner described Adam Smith as the great eclectic. "Traces of every conceivable sort of doctrine are to be found in that most catholic book, and an economist must have peculiar theories indeed who cannot quote *The Wealth of Nations* to support his special purposes."[3] I adopt the latter interpretation, not because it is necessarily right, but because it conforms to my special purpose.

By assigning defence, justice and public works to the public sector, Smith, in effect, claims that these activities would not be undertaken by an unfettered private sector or that they would be undertaken inadequately. Smith does not explain why he believes this to be so, why these activities cannot be consigned to the private sector along with the allocation of labour and capital to the production of ordinary goods and services. A defender of Smith's position might say that some things are too obvious to warrant full-blown explanation, but that is no help in our search for a list of actual or potential sources of inefficiency. The matter was only to be sorted out many years after the publication of *The Wealth of Nations*. It will have to do for our purposes to say that there are essential undertakings — justice, defence, and public works — that the private sector will not provide.

Smith wrote extensively and vigorously about departures from efficiency in the public sector, but his argument was developed by precepts and examples rather than by formal theorems, and one can only speculate as to how Smith might have categorized such departures. I suggest a classification under the headings of incentives, corruption, information, presumption and monopoly.

Under the heading of incentives, I would include a class of problems that have been the object of a great deal of attention in recent economic literature. When two parties engage in a common undertaking and establish an implicit or explicit contract specifying each party's privileges and obligations, it is in the personal interest of each party to shirk his obligations and to slant the enterprise to his own benefit, though both parties would be better off if neither behaved in that way. The worker is less diligent than he might be. The employer skimps on expenditure for the safety and convenience of his worker. The civil servant does not bother to put in the time and effort to perform his duties well. Of course, the incentive problem is not unique to the public sector. It arises whenever performance can be enforced only imperfectly. But it is hardly surprising that Adam Smith paid particular attention to incentives in the public sector. Hierarchy was more extensive in the public sector, and the control over the civil service by Parliament or the King was likely to be looser than the control over the employee by his employer in the private sector, where incentives were automatically provided by the options not to buy goods offered for sale, not to employ an unenthusiastic worker, and not to work for an unsatisfactory employer.

In modern times, the diligence of public teachers is more or less corrupted by the circumstances which render them more or less independent of their successes and reputation in their particular professions ... A man of real abilities can scarcely find out a more humiliating or more unprofitable employment to turn them to. The endowments of schools and colleges have, in this manner, not only corrupted the diligence of public teachers, but have rendered it almost impossible to have any good private ones. [733]

As a departure from efficiency, corruption is an extreme manifestation of the absence of an incentive to perform work conscientiously. However, the word "corruption" usually refers to an active, frequently illegal, abuse of authority, while the incentive problem is the passive unwillingness to exert oneself in the interest of one's partners in an enterprise. Smith was particularly indignant about the selling of favours to the private sector and the direct exploitation by the ruler of his subjects. "The violence and injustice of the rulers of mankind is an ancient evil, for which I am afraid, the nature of human affairs can scarce admit a remedy." Speaking of bounties from the public sector to particular firms or industries, Smith says,

though it can very seldom be reasonable to tax the industry of the great body of the people, in order to support that of some particular class of manufacturer: yet in the wantonness of great prosperity, when the public enjoys a greater revenue than it knows what to do with, to give such bounties to favourable manufactures may be natural. [489]

A third source of public sector inefficiency concerns the production and use of information. Only the private sector has the information required to direct the economy effectively. To be sure, no individual in the private sector is as well informed about the economy as a whole as are the servants of the great Ministries. But each manufacturer knows what he needs to know to conduct his business, and prices can be relied upon to coordinate decisions. In the summary of the roles of the public and private sector cited above, Smith speaks of public direction of industry and capital as a duty for which "no human wisdom or knowledge could ever be sufficient".

A fourth departure from inefficiency is presumption on the part of the civil servant who comes to believe that he alone knows what is best for the economy and that the businessman who does not willingly accept good advice should be compelled to do so. Smith's views in this matter appear in his discussion of Colbert's system of mercantilism in France:

The industry and commerce of a great country he endeavoured to regulate upon the same model as the departments of a public office; and instead of allowing every man to pursue his own interest his own way, upon the liberal plan of equality, liberty and justice, he bestowed upon certain branches of industry extraordinary privileges, while he laid others under as extraordinary restraints ... and kept down agriculture of that country very much below the state to which it would naturally have risen in so very fertile a soil and so happy a climate. [627–8]

Colbert, as Smith describes him, was not corrupt, not dishonest, and not disinclined to serve the King of France with all the ability and energy at his command, but was led by presumption to policies that were in the end harmful to his country. The

statesman, who would attempt to direct private people in what manner they ought employ their capital, would not only load himself with a most unnecessary attention, but assume an authority which could safely be trusted, not only to no single person but to no council or senate whatever, and which would nowhere be so dangerous as in the hands of a man who had folly or presumption enough to fancy himself fit to exercise it. [628]

A final source of public sector inefficiency is its tendency to support and maintain monopoly, that "great enemy of good government". The evil of monopoly is that

all other subjects are taxed very absurdly in two different ways; first by the high price of goods, which, in the case of free trade, they could buy much cheaper; and second, by their total exclusion from a branch of business, which it might be both convenient and profitable for many of them to carry on. It is for the most worthless of all purposes too that they are taxed in this manner. It is merely to enable the company to support negligence, profusion, and malversation of their own servants, whose disorderly conduct seldom allows the dividend of the company to exceed the ordinary rate of profit .... [712]

Elsewhere Smith notes that:

People of the same trade seldom meet together, even for merriment and diversion, but the conversation ends in conspiracy against the public, or in some contrivance to raise prices. It is impossible indeed to prevent such meetings, by any law which either could be executed or would be consistent with liberty and justice. But though the law cannot hinder people of the same trade from sometimes assembling together, it ought to do nothing to facilitate such assemblies, much less to render them necessary. [125]

The passage on the system of natural liberty, as quoted above, could be interpreted as including a recognition of the existence of natural monopolies which have to be administered or regulated by the state. Smith's famous invective against monopoly is for the most part directed toward state-created monopoly that could not be preserved without the direct prohibition of potential competitors.

Though Adam Smith had much to say about the effects of public policy on the economy, *The Wealth of Nations* is not a study of government itself. Quite the reverse. One of the great innovations in the book is the study of the economy in isolation from the rest of society. The sub-sections of the book are labour, capital, money, economic growth, international trade and public finance — topics that still constitute the sub-divisions of a textbook of economics — combined for the first time as a separate and distinct field of inquiry. What the book lacked, and what Ricardo was later to supply, was a formal model of the economy in which the central concepts were clearly and forcefully abstracted from the detail of economic life. The formalization of economic science proceeded throughout the nineteenth century, revealing with ever greater precision the exact sense in which it might be said that one may promote the public interest indirectly by attending to one's own private interest. Intensive study of the competitive economy could not help but focus attention on to a growing list of exceptions, while at the same time diverting attention from the strengths and weaknesses of the public sector.

In *The Principles of Political Economy*,[4] published in 1848, John Stuart Mill differed from Smith more in his preoccupations than in his analysis. He was preoccupied, first and foremost, with liberty. His advocacy of *laissez-faire* was no less enthusiastic than that of Smith, but it was as a requirement for personal liberty and not just as a means of generating wealth. Also, as a disciple of Bentham, Mill could hardly avoid being preoccupied with the content of law. Smith was most emphatic about the need for the state to protect the citizen from force and fraud, but he disposed of the matter in a couple of sentences. Mill dealt with the matter at length, adding the definition of property rights, the resolution of disputes, and the specification of the range of permissible contracts to the list of activities that had to be undertaken by the public sector.

It is at least arguable that, to Mill, the great departure from efficiency was predation, the violence and the waste of labour when one man attempts to take property from another and the other is compelled to divert effort from production to defence. The quotation at the front of this book is the expression of an idea that must have been of great significance in Mill's scheme of thought, for it occupies the closing paragraph of *The Principles*. Recall Mill's lament for "efforts and talents . . . neutralizing one another" and his assertion that "the proper end of government [is] to reduce this wretched waste to the smallest possible amount" (979).

Though the great departure from efficiency is insecurity and though the ultimate defence against insecurity lies in the public sector, it does not follow that a large and ubiquitous public sector is conducive to liberty or to prosperity. At several critical points in *The Principles*, Mill raises the spectre of despotism, which is associated for the most part with the governments of Asia, but is not rigidly or permanently confined there. One gets the impression that Mill, unlike his successors to be discussed below, was not absolutely certain that England would be free of despotism forever. Security

consists of protection *by* the government, and protection *against* the government. The latter is the more important. Where a person known to possess anything worth taking away, can expect nothing but to have it torn from him, with every circumstance of tyrannical violence, by the agents of a rapacious government, it is not likely that many will exert themselves to produce much more than necessaries.

This is the acknowledged explanation of the poverty of many fertile tracts of Asia, which were once prosperous and populous. From this to the degree of security enjoyed in the best governed parts of Europe, there are numerous gradations. In many provinces of France before the Revolution, a vicious system of taxation on the land, and still more the absence of redress against the arbitrary exactions which were made under colour of the taxes, rendered it the interest of every cultivator to appear poor, and therefore to cultivate badly. The only insecurity which is altogether paralyzing to the active energies of producers, is that arising from the government, or from persons invested with its authority. Against all other depredators there is a hope of defending oneself. [113–14]

Mill begins the *Principles* with some "preliminary remarks" in which, after a brief discussion of the meaning of wealth, he launches into a thumbnail sketch of economic history, looked upon primarily as a history of the growth of security. He speaks first of Asia, where a nomadic society gives way to agriculture, yielding a "surplus" which,

whether small or great, is usually torn from the producers, either by the government to which they are subject, or by individuals, who by superior force, or by availing themselves of religious or traditional feelings of subordination, have established themselves as lords of the soil. . . . Under the regime in question, though the bulk of the population are ill provided for, the government, by collecting small contributions from great numbers, is enabled, with any tolerable management, to make a show of riches quite out of proportion to the general condition of the society. [12]

Mill is explicit about the effect of despotism on industry.

The ruler of a society of this description, after providing largely for his own support, and that of all persons in whom he feels an interest, and after maintaining as many soldiers as he thinks needful for his security or his state, has a disposable residue, which he is glad to exchange for articles of luxury suitable to his disposition: as have also the class of persons who have been enriched by his favour, or by handling the public revenues. A demand thus arises for elaborate and costly manufactured articles, adapted to a narrow but a wealthy market. . . . The insecurity, however, of all possessions in this state of society, induces even the richest purchasers to give a preference to such articles as, being of an imperishable nature, and containing great value in small bulk, are adapted for being concealed or carried off. Gold and jewels, therefore, constitute a large proportion of the wealth of these nations, and many a rich Asiatic carries nearly his whole fortune on his person, or on those of the women of his harem. No one, except the monarch, thinks of investing his wealth in a manner not susceptible of removal. [13]

Europe is alleged to have avoided a similar fate. Speaking of the early Middle Ages, Mill states that the

productive classes, therefore, when the insecurity surpasses a certain point, being unequal to their own protection against the predatory population, are obliged to place themselves individually in a state of dependence on some member of the predatory class, that it may be his interest to shield them from all depredation except his own. [881]

In the new frame in which European society was now cast, the population of each country may be considered as composed, in unequal proportions, of two distinct nations or races, the conquerors and the conquered: the first the proprietors of the land, the latter the tillers of it. [17]

This gave rise to a sort of European counterpart of the economical condition of Asiatic countries; except that, in lieu of a single monarch and a fluctuating body of favourites and employees, there was a numerous and in a considerable degree fixed class of great landholders; exhibiting far less splendour, because individually disposing of a much smaller surplus produce, and for a long time expending the chief part of it in maintaining the body of retainers whom the warlike habits of society, and the little protection afforded by government, rendered indispensable to their safety. [17–18]

Security of person and property grew slowly, but steadily; the arts of life made constant progress; plunder ceased to be the principal source of accumulation; and feudal Europe ripened into commercial and manufacturing Europe. In the latter part of the Middle Ages, the towns of Italy and Flanders, the free cities of Germany, and some towns of France and England, contained a large and energetic population of artisans, and many rich burghers, whose wealth had been acquired by manufacturing industry, or by trading in the produce of such industry. The Commons of England, the Tiers-Etat of France, the bourgeoisie of the Continent generally, are the descendants of this class. As these were a saving class, while the posterity of the feudal aristocracy were a squandering class, the former by degrees substituted themselves for the latter as the owners of a great proportion of the land. This natural tendency was in some cases retarded by laws contrived for the purpose of detaining the land in the families of its existing possessors, in other cases accelerated by political revolutions. Gradually, though more slowly, the immediate cultivators of the soil, in all the more civilised countries, ceased to be in a servile or semi-servile state: though the legal position, as well as the economical condition attained by them, vary extremely in the different nations of Europe, and in the great communities which have been founded beyond the Atlantic by the descendants of Europeans. [18]

Like *The Wealth of Nations*, Mill's *Principles* contains no formal list of departures from efficiency, just as it contains no formal proof of a theorem about the efficiency of a competitive economy, but one can easily derive a list of departures from efficiency in the public and private sectors of the economy from the discussion of "the limits of the province of government".

The general presumption is

in favour of restricting to the narrowest compass the intervention of a public authority in the business of the community: and few will dispute the more than sufficiency of these reasons, to throw, in every instance, the burden of making out a strong case, not on those who resist, but on those who recommend, government interference. *Laissez-faire*, in short, should be the general practice: every departure from it, unless required by some great good, is a certain evil. [950]

But if *laissez-faire* has the residual authority and each departure from *laissez-faire* has to be justified by some great good, there is nonetheless a formidable list of justifiable public sector activities. Foremost among these, as might be expected in view of Mill's concern with security, is "protection against force and fraud" [796]. Mill is quick to emphasize that protection against force and fraud is a more extensive responsibility than some proponents of strict *laissez-faire* are inclined to recognize. It entails the establishment of the rules of inheritance, especially when the deceased is of unsound mind or fails to specify the disposition of his property. It entails the establishment of laws specifying what types of contracts "are fit to be enforced" . . . for "there are promises by which it is not for the public good that persons should have the power of binding themselves" (798). It entails the drawing up of rules concerning the consequences of non-fulfilment of a contract owing to fraud, negligence or occurrences which make the contract impossible to fulfil, as well as the resolution of disputes that "arise between persons, without *mala fides* on either side, through misconception of their legal rights, or from not being agreed about the facts, on the proof of which those rights are legally dependent" (799). The admissible forms of contracts may be chosen, not so much because one form is intrinsically superior to another, but to minimize the frequency of disputes.

Over and above protection against force and fraud which is a requirement for the existence of a market, the government, according to Mill, should undertake certain activities which the private sector would attend to inefficiently or not at all:

(i) The provision of education:

any well-intentioned and tolerably civilized government may think, without presumption, that it does or ought to possess a degree of cultivation above the average of the community which it rules, and that it should therefore be capable of offering better education and better instruction to the people, than the greater number of them would spontaneously demand. [953]

Every child should be provided with instruction, but the state ought not to appropriate a monopoly of elementary education.

It is not endurable that a government should, either *de jure* or *de facto*, have a complete control over the education of the people. To possess such a control and actually exert it, is to be despotic . . . . It would be justified in requiring from all people that they possess instruction in certain things, but not in prescribing to them how or from whom they shall obtain it. [956]

(ii) The protection of lunatics (957).
(iii) The protection of children from cruel or uncaring parents:

Whatever it can be clearly seen that parents ought to do or forbear for the interests of children, the law is warranted, if it is able, in compelling to be done or forborne, and is generally bound to do so . . . . Labouring for too many hours in the day, or on work beyond their strength, should not be permitted to them . . . . Freedom of contract, in the case of children, is but another word for freedom of coercion. [958]

Mill would impose no similar restriction on the employment of women. He classifies the common subjugation of women to their husbands together with slavery, but goes on to argue that women freed of that burden need no legal restraints and are "as capable as men of appreciating and managing their own concerns" (959).

(iv) Natural monopoly:

There are many cases in which the agency, of whatever nature, by which a service is performed is certain, by the nature of the case, to be virtually single; in which a practical monopoly, with all the power it confers of taxing the community, cannot be prevented from existing. [962]

Among these practical monopolies, Mill includes gas and water companies (though these may be local in scope), roads, canals and railways. He adds that "the state may be the proprietor of canals and railways without itself working them . . . they will almost always be better worked by means of a company renting the railway or canal for a limited period from the state" (963).

(v) Avoiding prisoners' dilemmas:

The principle that each is the best judge of his own interest, understood as these objectors understand it, would prove that governments ought not to fulfil any of their acknowledged duties — ought not, in fact, to exist at all. It is greatly the interest of the community, collectively and individually, not to rob or defraud one another: but there is not the less necessity for laws to punish robbery and fraud; because, though it is the interest of each that nobody should rob or cheat, it is not anyone's interest to refrain from robbing and cheating others when all others are permitted to rob and cheat him. Penal laws exist at all, chiefly for this reason — because even an unanimous opinion that a certain line of conduct is for the general interest does not always make it people's individual interest to adhere to that line of conduct. [966]

(vi) Provision for the poor:

The claim to help, therefore, created by destitution, is one of the strongest which can exist; and there is *prima facie* the amplest reason for making the relief of so extreme an exigency as certain to those who require it as by any arrangements of society it can be made. [967]

Mill recognized the force of the standard objection to assistance for the poor, that assistance destroys industry, but he believed that the case for assistance was so strong as to outweigh the cost of the attendant inefficiency, and that programmes of assistance could be designed to reduce costs to an acceptable level.

. . . in all cases of helping, there are two sets of consequences to be considered; the consequences of the assistance itself, and the consequences of relying on the assistance. The former are generally beneficial, but the latter, for the most part, injurious; so much so, in many cases, as greatly to outweigh the value of the benefit. [967]

(vii) Public goods. Mill speaks of cases where "important public services are to be performed, while yet there is no individual specially interested in performing them, nor would any adequate remuneration naturally or spontaneously attend their performance" (975). His examples are "a voyage of geographical or scientific discovery", maintenance of lighthouses and buoys and "the cultivation of speculative knowledge" which "gives no claim on any individual for a pecuniary remuneration" (976).

(viii) Externalities. It is arguable, though not beyond dispute, that Mill had a concept of externalities. Part of the difficulty in interpreting the text is that he was concerned primarily with the question of what the state ought to do rather than of why the state ought to do it. He comes close to the concept of externalities in a discussion of colonies.

If it is desirable, as no one will deny it to be, that the planting of colonies should be conducted, not with an exclusive view to the private interests of the first founders, but with a deliberate regard to the permanent welfare of the nations afterwards to arise from these small beginnings; such regard can only be secured by placing the enterprise, from its commencement, under regulations constructed with the foresight and enlarged views of philosophical legislators; and the government alone has power either to frame such regulations, or to enforce their observance.... the removal of population from the overcrowded to the unoccupied parts of the earth's surface is one of those works of eminent social usefulness, which must require, and which at the same time best repay, the intervention of government. [970]

The passage (and subsequent discussion) can be interpreted as meaning that the provision of the infrastructure of colonization is an ordinary public good. The passage can also be interpreted as meaning that each colonist by helping to create a community that others may enter conveys an externality to future colonists and to the mother country, where labour becomes less plentiful and real wages rise.

Though Mill does have a considerable list of activities and actions that the public sector does sometimes undertake inappropriately and to the detriment of society as a whole, his discussion of government places particular emphasis on general problems within the public sector and on reasons why the size of the public sector *per se* may become a matter of concern.

(i) The risk of despotism. To Mill, the great and most costly departure from efficiency associated with the public sector occurs when government ceases to be the servant of society and becomes despotic.

... oppression by the government, whose power is generally irresistible by any efforts that can be made by individuals, has so much more baneful an effect on the springs of national prosperity, than almost any degree of lawlessness and turbulence under free institutions. Nations have acquired some wealth, and made some progress in improvement, in states of social union so imperfect as to border on anarchy: but no countries in which the people were exposed without limit to arbitrary exactions from the officers of government ever yet continued to have industry or wealth. [882]

Fear of despotism should constitute a check on the activity of government.

... every increase in the functions devolving on the government is an increase of its power, both in the form of authority, and still more in the indirect form of influence. The importance of this consideration in respect to political freedom, has in general been quite sufficiently recognized, at least in England; but many, in latter times, have been prone to think that the limitation of the powers of government is badly constituted when it does not represent the people, but is an organ of a class, or coalition of classes: and that government of sufficiently popular constitution might be trusted with any amount of power over the nation, since its power would only be that of the nation over itself. That might be true, if the nation, in such cases, did not practically mean a mere majority of the nation, and if minorities were only capable of oppressing, but not of being oppressed. Experience, however, proves that the depositaries of power who are mere delegates of the people, that is of a majority, are quite as ready (when they think they can count on popular support) as any organs of oligarchy to assume arbitrary power, and encroach unduly on the liberty of private life. [944–5]

(ii) Administrative overload:

Every additional function undertaken by the government is a fresh occupation imposed upon a body already overcharged with duties. A natural consequence is that most things are ill done; much not done at all, because the government is not able to do it without delays which are fatal to its purpose; that the more troublesome, and less showy, of the functions undertaken, are postponed or neglected, and an excuse is always ready for the neglect; while the heads of the administration have their minds so fully taken up with official details, in however perfunctory a manner superintended, that they have no time or thought to spare for the great interests of the state, and the preparation of enlarged measures of social improvement. [945]

(iii) Technical inefficiency:

in all the more advanced communities the great majority of things are worse done by the intervention of government, than the individuals most interested in the matter would do them, or cause them to be done, if left to themselves. The grounds of this truth are expressed with tolerable exactness in the popular dictum, that people understand their own business and their own interests better, and care for them more, than the government does, or can be expected to do. [947]

(iv) Loss of initiative in the private sector:

Even if the government could comprehend within itself, in each department, all the most eminent intellectual capacity and active talent of the nation, it would not be the less desirable that the conduct of a large portion of the affairs of the society should be left in the hands of the persons immediately interested in them. The business of life is an essential part of the practical education of a people; without which, book and school instruction, though most necessary and salutary, does not suffice to qualify them for conduct, and for the adaptation of means to ends. [948] ...

The only security against political slavery is the check maintained over governors by the diffusion of intelligence, activity, and public spirit among the governed. Experience proves the extreme difficulty of permanently keeping up a sufficiently high standard of those qualities; a difficulty which increases, as the advance of civilization and security removes one after another of the hardships, embarrassments, and dangers against which individuals had formerly no resource but in their own strength, skill, and courage. [949]

Finally, Mill lists a number of activities that governments of his time did undertake, but ought to have avoided because on balance their effects were to discourage industry rather than to promote it: protection of domestic goods against foreign competition, fixing of prices and wages, prohibition of usury, and regulation of forms of partnership. Mill was particularly adamant about the ill-effects of restrictions on the formation of joint-stock companies with limited liability, for, barring outright fraud, persons dealing with such companies would be quite capable of assessing the risks associated with limited liability and of taking whatever steps might be necessary to protect themselves.

The world of Henry Sidgwick's *The Principles of Political Economy* is quite different from that of either Smith or Mill. The book first appeared in 1883.[5] By that time, England had passed from what Dicey (1905)[6] has called a period of Benthamism or Individualism into a period of Collectivism and, though Sidgwick opposed socialism, he did not share Smith's views about the intrinsic incompetence of government or Mill's brooding concern about despotism. The hundred years since the appearance of *The Wealth of Nations* had seen considerable progress in the British economy and in the science of economics. There had also been considerable progress in the art of government, so that, by Sidgwick's time, Great Britain was much further along the road from absolute monarchy to pure democracy than had been the case in Smith's day, and there had been a radical reform of the civil service. Sidgwick could justifiably assume that some functions of government would be performed well. He may well have supposed the liberal society in England to be absolutely and unshakably secure.

Much of what Sidgwick had to say about the art of political economy — his distinction between the science and art of political economy corresponded more or less to what we would now call economic theory and applied welfare economics — was conditioned by his response to socialism. As a contrast and alternative to the ideal organization of the economy, socialism played somewhat the same role in *The Principles of Political Economy* that mercantilism played in *The Wealth of Nations*, though Sidgwick was too ambivalent and too gentle to deal with his intruder upon the true doctrine as vigorously or as scornfully as Smith had done. Sidgwick's view of the system of natural liberty — he employed Smith's term — was of a trade-off between inequality and efficiency. On the one hand, he could see no moral justification for great disparities of inherited wealth. The *"prima facie* ground . . . on which the interference of government with the distribution of produce that results from the individualistic organization of industry appears economically desirable, lies in the very great inequalities of income to which this organization leads" (519). On the other hand, the system of natural liberty is in most circumstances more productive than any other system men knew how to devise. "I object to socialism not because it would divide the produce of industry badly but because there would be so much less to divide" (517).

Sidgwick's criterion was utilitarian, the maximization of the sum of the utilities of each person in society on the assumptions that everyone's utility function is, for all practical purposes, the same and that there is a diminishing marginal utility of income. Thus in assessing the system of natural liberty he is on the lookout for inefficiencies that might justify the intervention of government, which, once involved in a branch of industry, might use its influence to equalize income somewhat. Sidgwick has a long list of instances in which "the system of natural liberty would have, in certain respects and under certain conditions, no tendency to realize the beneficent results claimed for it":

(i) The use of wealth to gratify a lust for power. Not all utilities are socially desirable:

among these utilities . . . we must include the gratification of the love of power, the love of ease, and all whims and fancies that are wont to take possession of the minds of persons whose income is far more than sufficient to satisfy ordinary human desires. [404]

(ii) Misuse of income by the old. Total utility may not be maximized because the old "spend larger and larger sums on smaller and smaller enjoyments" or impose "posthumous restraint on bequeathed wealth [which] will make it less useful to the living" (405).

(iii) Slavery.

If all contracts freely made are to be enforced, it is conceivable that a man may contract himself into slavery; it is even conceivable that a large mass of the population of a country might do this, in the poverty and distress caused by some widespreading calamity. [406]

The state ought not to permit such contracts. Similarly, the state ought not to uphold contracts agreed to under pressure, as when merchant seamen alienate part of their claims to wages at sea under "undue influence which the needful discipline of a ship gives to its master" (429).

(iv) Externalities. There are "some utilities which, from their nature, are practically incapable of being appropriated by those who produce them or who would otherwise be willing to purchase them" (407). Examples include (a) "a well-placed lighthouse", (b) "forests on account of their beneficial effects in moderating and equalizing rainfall", (c) inventions where the cost of discovery is greater than the prospective income from a patent but less than the value of the invention to society, (d) education, when the returns are

more than sufficient to repay the outlay necessary to provide them — while at the same time it would not be profitable for any capitalist to provide the money, with a view to being repaid out of the salary of the laborer educated, owing to the trouble and risk involved in the deferred payments. [408]

(v) Monopoly, among workers or among firms (411).

(vi) Advertising (412).

(vii) Balancing the interests of present and future generations. The "purely individualistic or competitive organization of society . . . does not necessarily provide to an adequate extent for utilities distant in time" [412].

(viii) Ignorance on the part of the consumer. "As the appliances of life became more elaborate and complicated through the progress of invention . . . an average man's ability to judge the adaptation of means to ends . . . is likely to become continually less" (417). "Our own government does not trust its subjects to find out for themselves and avoid unhealthy food or improperly qualified physicians, surgeons, and apothecaries" (425).

(ix) Public goods "which if left to private enterprise . . . would not be provided at all" (439), or would be provided under conditions of monopoly. Among these are roads, canals, railways, the post office and above all the currency.

Sidgwick does not proceed direct from the identification of what we would now call market failure to the prescription of public policy to set things right. It "does not of course follow that whenever *laissez faire* falls short government interference is expedient; since the inevitable drawbacks and disadvantages of the latter may, in any particular case, be worse than the shortcomings of private industry" (414). Thus parallel to the list of the shortcomings of the market is a list of the shortcomings of the public sector:

(i) Corruption: "the danger of increasing the power and influence capable of being used by government for corrupt purposes" (415).

(ii) Special interest politics: "the danger . . . that the exercise of [the government's] economic functions will be hampered and prevented by the desire to gratify influential sections of the community — certain manufacturers, certain landlords, certain classes of manual laborers, or the inhabitants of certain localities" (415).

(iii) Public extravagance: "the danger . . . of wasteful expenditure under the influence of popular sentiment — since people, however impatient of taxation, are liable to be insufficiently conscious of the importance of thrift in all details of national expenditure" (415).

(iv) The social cost of taxation and regulation:

when action of the government requires funds raised by taxation, we have to reckon — besides the financial cost of collection and any loss of production caused by particular taxes — the political danger of adding to a burden already impatiently borne ... where again it requires prohibition of private industry, we must regard ... the repression of energy and self-help that tends to follow from it; where, on the other hand the interference takes the form of regulations ... we may often have to calculate on a certain amount of economic and political evils due to successful or unsuccessful attempt to evade them. [415]

Speaking particularly of protection, Sidgwick said that the gain

in particular cases is always likely to be more than counterbalanced by the general bad effects of encouraging producers and traders to look to government for aid in industrial crises and dangers; instead of relying on their own foresight, ingenuity and energy. [489]

(v) Incentives:

the work of the government has to be done by persons who — even with the best of arrangements for effective supervision and promotion by merit — can have only a part of the stimulus to energetic industry that the independent worker feels, who may reasonably hope to gain by any well directed extra exertion, intellectual or muscular, and must fear to lose by indolence or neglect. [416]

Similarly, if workers were remunerated by need rather than according to effort, as would be the case under some definitions of socialism,

we can hardly doubt that the labour thus purchased by the state could not, even by good organization, be made to pay the cost of its support ... he would have much less motive than at present either for working energetically or for seeking and qualifying himself for the employment in which he would be most useful. [533]

Moving ahead another forty years, we come to A.C. Pigou's *The Economics of Welfare*, which first appeared in 1920 and remained influential until after the Second World War. Pigou's world — the world of the upper classes of late nineteenth and early twentieth-century England — was a world free of tyranny and secure for democracy, a world in which, as Yeats expressed it, "rogues and rascals had died out" or, in so far as they remained here on earth, were confined to the somewhat nasty realm of commerce and were not to be found among the Cambridge-educated gentlemen of His Majesty's civil service. Pigou, quoting Alfred Marshall, stated that

during the past century in England, there has been a vast increase in the probity, the strength, the unselfishness, and the resources of government ... And the people are now able to rule their rulers, and to check class abuse of power and privilege, in a way that was impossible before the days of general education and a general surplus of energy over that required for earning a living. [333[7]]

In fact, Marshall had gone so far as to speak of the civil servants of his time as motivated by an "economic chivalry" in their concern for the welfare of ordinary people.

Pigou recognized, in principle, that public "authorities are liable alike to ignorance, to sectional pressure and to personal corruption by private interest" and that "companies, particularly when there is continuing regulation, may employ corruption, not only in the getting of their franchise, but also in the execution of it"; but the message of the book was that such considerations could well be ignored in practice. The entire subject of misbehaviour in the public sector occupied two pages in an 800 page book. The only example was where special interests in the private sector exert undue influence on the public sector. There was no mention of the possibility that civil servants might be less diligent than their counterparts in the private sector, and no hint that they might fall victim to "folly and presumption".

By implication, if not in so many words, the reader is told that potential defects of government can be safely ignored. "When there is a divergence between" marginal private net product and marginal social net product "self-interest will not therefore, tend to make the national dividend a maximum; and, consequently, certain specific acts of interference with normal economic processes may be expected, not to diminish, but to increase the dividend" (172; "dividend" refers to real national income).

In any industry, where there is reason to believe that the free play of self-interest will cause an amount of resources to be invested different from the amount that is required in the best interest in the national dividend, there is a *prima facie* case for public intervention. The case, however, cannot become more than a *prima facie* one until we have considered the qualifications which government agencies may be expected to possess for intervening advantageously. [332]

But the "broad result is that modern developments in the structure and methods of government agencies have fitted these agencies for beneficial intervention in industry under conditions which would not have justified intervention in earlier times" (335). The reader, who is told very little about conditions when intervention is still unjustified, cannot help receiving the impression that the entire question is irrelevant in practice. Hence the reference to the Pigovian fallacy in Chapter I above.

Silence in this context is tantamount to bias. One version of the second fundamental theorem of welfare economics is that a competitive economy is as efficient as an "ideal" planned economy — as efficient, but not more so. Hayek has spoken of the ideal as a "communist fiction", a convenient way of organizing one's thoughts about the optimality of a competitive economy. The fiction is harmless as long as it is recognized that an actual planned economy is no more likely to realize the ideal than an actual market economy. Pigou does recognize, in a passage cited above, that no planned economy can measure up to the ideal. But, with no systematic attempt to identify the conditions where the actual and ideal diverge, there can be no basis for judging when departures from efficiency in the private sector should not be corrected by the public sector because the cure would be worse than the disease. By specifying in detail the inefficiencies of the private sector, and saying virtually nothing about the inefficiencies of the public sector, Pigou inevitably creates a presumption in favour of the latter.

In fact, the public sector is always preferable when the choice is presented in this manner, for a competitive economy can at best yield one among many possible Pareto optima, while the planner can pick the superior Pareto optimum from a utilitarian point of view. The outcome of a competitive economy depends on the initial distribution of property rights, which may be very unequal, while the "ideal" planner knows no such constraint and can pick the Pareto-optimal outcome corresponding to what a competitive economy would yield with a different and presumably more equal distribution of property.

Pigou's list of departures from efficiency in the private sector includes many of the items that have already been identified by Sidgwick. There are now four main categories: tenancy, externalities, monopoly and scale.

(i) The separation of tenancy and ownership. The tenant may not have a sufficient incentive to maintain the quality of the farm, or to make warranted improvements in drainage, buildings, etc. The landlord may be unwilling to undertake long-term investments when the contract between owner and tenant specifies a fixed rent for a given term of years.

(ii) Externalities. Though Pigou does not employ the term "externalities", he speaks of a class of divergences between social and private net product such that

one person, A, in the course of rendering some service for which payment is made to a second person, B, incidentally also renders services to other persons . . . of such a sort that payment cannot be extracted from the benefited parties. [183]

Here Pigou provides examples that are still the stock-in-trade of welfare economics: (a) the lighthouse; (b) roads, parks and "resources invested in lamps erected at the doors of private houses, for these necessarily throw light on the street" (184); (c) research,

resources, devoted alike to the fundamental problems of scientific research . . . perfecting inventions and improvements in industrial processes . . . of such a nature that . . . the whole of the extra reward, which they at first bring to the inventor, is very quickly transformed from him to the general public in the form of reduced prices. [185]

(d) neighbourhood effects, as when a new factory destroys amenities in a residential area; (e) foreign investment when it

consists in a loan to a foreign government and makes it possible for that government to engage in a war which otherwise would not have taken place, the indirect loss which Englishmen in general suffer, in consequence of the world impoverishment caused by war, should be debited against the interest which British financiers receive. [187]

(f) the injury to the foetus when a pregnant mother works in a factory. Pigou calls this the "crowning illustration of this order of excess of private over social net product" (187).

(iii) Monopoly. Pigou identifies several departures from efficiency that arise when an industry is monopolized or limited to a few firms, each with a large enough share of the market to exert an influence upon the market price. Among the departures from efficiency due to monopoly or oligopoly are: (a) reduction of output to raise the market price; (b) competitive advertising "directed to the sole purpose of transferring the demand for a given commodity from one source of supply to another" (196). Pigou distinguishes between competitive advertising, which is socially wasteful, and informative advertising, which is not; (c) bargaining costs, which arise from the theoretical indeterminateness of bilateral monopoly and "open up the way for the employment of activities and resources in efforts to modify the ratio of exchange in favour of one or another of the monopolists" (200). The obvious example is the strike, but negotiation among businessmen over prices and terms of contracts also falls under this heading; (d) deception, as when false weights and measures are employed; (e) destruction of the "educative ladder" through the trustification of industry, "the lessening of the opportunities for training in the entrepreneurial function" when a market consisting of many small firms is cartelized (207).

(iv) Increasing returns to scale:

in a many-firm industry the value of the marginal net product of any quantity of investment is greater than, equal to or less than the value of social net product according as the industry conforms to conditions of increasing, constant or decreasing supply price from the stand point of the industry. [222]

There is "a presumption in favour of State bounties to industries in conditions of decreasing supply price" (224).

The *reductio ad absurdum* of Pigou's reasoning was the economics of socialism as understood by economists in the 1930s and 1940s. If every departure from efficiency in the private sector of the economy warrants public activity to set it right, and if the Pareto-optimal outcome in an ideal competitive economy is still distributionally inferior to what the public sector can provide, then why tolerate private ownership of the means of production at all? Why not incorporate the entire means of production into the public sector? A central planner would announce prices, managers of publicly owned firms would maximize accounting profits at these prices, temporary shortages and gluts would signify which prices are too low and which prices are too high, and the planner would adjust prices next period, more or less as a competitive economy is supposed to do. Much of the debate about socialism centred around the question of whether a planning commission could solve the "millions of equations" that a competitive economy solves automatically in the determination of prices of all goods and rents of all factors of production. The debate on this point was inconclusive, though the socialists seemed to have the best of the argument, since large firms appeared to engage in such planning already and the planning mechanism in the Soviet Union, while hardly ideal in its operation, had not yet led to a complete breakdown of the economy and appeared to be amenable to improvement with the advance of statistical and mathematical techniques.

Socialism, defined as the complete ownership of the means of production by the state, was seen to have two distinct advantages over the private ownership of the means of production. The first was that the national income could be divided equally among citizens except for variations among incomes to compensate for disamenities of certain kinds of jobs. The second was that any departure from efficiency which would arise in a market economy could be eliminated in a socialist economy by means of a compensating divergence between the producer price and the consumer price. Oskar Lange has stated that an

economic system based on private enterprise can take but very imperfect account of the alternatives sacrificed and realized in production. A socialist economy would be able to put *all* the alternatives into its economic accounting. Thus it would evaluate *all* the services rendered by production and take into account of the cost of *all* the alternatives sacrificed; as a result it would also be able to convert its social overhead cost into price cost. By doing so it would avoid much of the social waste connected with private enterprise. As Professor Pigou has shown, much of the waste can be removed by proper legislation, taxation and bounties within the framework of the present economic system, but a socialist economy can do it with much greater thoroughness.[8]

Obviously, socialism is preferable to capitalism if you ignore the innards of the public sector and suppose, implicitly or explicitly, that there is a well defined common good, and that the public sector can direct the economy accordingly, deploying resources to the production of commodities and distributing commodities to people to maximize social welfare subject only to technical and physical constraints.

It was precisely these assumptions that were about to be abandoned. A disenchantment with the public sector developed gradually but with ever-growing intensity since about the end of the Second World War. The change was no doubt a response to historical events, the growth of the public sector in most countries in the Western world, the absence of severe depressions, the superior economic performance of capitalist countries as compared with socialist countries, and the abundant evidence that extreme socialism was not conducive to justice, prosperity or personal liberty. But it was also a response to two major developments within the science of economics itself: the disintegration of the concept of social welfare as criterion for public sector intervention in the economy, and the close study of the economics of the public sector, which raised serious doubts as to whether a public sector would in practice act to maximize economic welfare, even if such a thing could be shown to exist.

The failure of the new welfare economics was by no means complete. "During the nineteenth century," wrote John Hicks in the year 1939,

it was generally considered to be the business of an economist, not only to explain the economic world as it is and as it has been, not only to make prognostications (so far as he was able) about the future course of events, but also to lay down principles of economic policy, to say what policies are likely to be conducive to social welfare, and what policies are likely to lead to waste and impoverishment.[9]

Though the capacity of the economists to "lay down the principles of economic policy" had been challenged off and on for some time, the decisive challenge in the English-speaking world was the publication in 1936 of Lionel Robbins's *The Nature and Significance of Economic Science*. From our point of view, the essence of Robbins's critique is that principles of economic policy which economists had supposed to be well grounded in the science of economics were at bottom dependent on ethical premises without which costs and benefits to different people could not be compared. In practice, there can be no economic policy, however beneficial to the greater part of the population, that does not make somebody worse off. If one man's good cannot be balanced against another's bad, then nothing definitive can be said about economic policy and much of the *raison d'être* of the economist would seem to be lost.

The immediate object of Robbins's attack was the law of diminishing marginal utility, which had been interpreted to imply that "anything conducive to greater equality, which does not adversely affect production, is said to be justified by the law: anything conducive to inequality condemned" (156). The brunt of the attack was not that the law was necessarily wrong, but that it was not economics, and could not be justified by economic reasoning. The law of diminishing marginal utility is part of the doctrine of utilitarianism, which can be summarized in four propositions: that the satisfaction of different people may be compared on a common scale; that the relation between utility and income is approximately the same for most people; that for any person, and at any given set of prices, utility increases with income at a steadily decreasing rate; and that the object of public policy is to maximize total utility. On these propositions, the case for the mitigation of inequality can indeed be established, and Robbins, whose own political philosophy was what he called "provisional utilitarianism", was prepared to act *as if* they were true in many instances. His argument was that these propositions were ethical rather than scientific. Policy based on the utilitarian calculus is compelling only to someone who accepts the principles of utilitarianism or who can justify such policy by some other ethical principles. Robbins tells the story of a brahmin whose response on hearing about utilitarianism was "But that cannot possibly be right. I am ten times as capable of happiness as that untouchable over there."[10] One may well argue, in defence of utilitarianism, that people should be treated as though they were equally capable of happiness, and one may believe it immoral to treat people otherwise, but there is no test, no experiment, no evidence from sample surveys that will demonstrate the brahmin's error, if he persists in his point of view. Nor, for that matter, is there any scientific basis for the view that the object of economic policy is the maximization of the sum of each person's utility. One either accepts this as a first principle or one does not.

Robbins's critique was to provoke an extensive reformulation of the criteria for the evaluation of economic policy. One response was to reduce the objective from social welfare to Pareto optimality. On the old utilitarian criterion, a policy was said to be desirable if it led to an increase in the sum of everybody's utility (where equality as a component of social welfare could be assigned a greater or lesser weight by increasing or decreasing the curvature of the postulated utility of income function). To replace social welfare with Pareto optimality is to say that a policy is on balance beneficial if it eliminates waste, that is, if it represents a move toward a state of the economy from which no further change can simultaneously make everybody better-off. As a criterion for the choice of public policy, Pareto optimality is satisfactory as long as everybody gains or loses together, or the effect of public policy on the distribution of income is irrelevant to the problem at hand. Otherwise Pareto optimality is an inadequate criterion because the efficient outcome is not unique. As discussed in Chapter I, Pareto optimality provides no basis for choosing between outcome A, in which Scrooge is prosperous and Cratchit is unprosperous, and outcome B, in which the reverse is the case. Nor can it be said that an efficient outcome (in the sense that nothing is wasted) is necessarily better than an inefficient outcome, except in the special case where literally everybody becomes better off. For a time, it looked as though the old certainty could be preserved by what came to be known as "compensation criteria", according to which there is an unambiguous improvement in the economy as a whole if the gainers can compensate the losers. It turned out after much discussion that the test was internally inconsistent and could not be reformulated to provide an acceptable criterion for deciding when the population as a whole is materially better off.[11]

A second and complementary response was to reinterpret the role of the objective function in economic argument. If it is no longer possible to identify an economically given criterion for public policy, it is at least possible to model the logic of public choice. One cannot say that a particular policy is beneficial in some absolute sense, but one can say to the reader that if such-and-such is *your* criterion and these are *your* society's constraints, then *your* best policy under the circumstances is whatever the maximization procedure determines that policy to be. This interpretation of welfare economics was discussed in detail in Chapter I. On this interpretation, the skill of the economist is to represent the essence of a complex situation in a model, to discover the consequences of the interactions among agents, each doing the best he can for himself with the means at his disposal, and to explicate the logic of choice. This interpretation of welfare economics was facilitated by the development of the probabilistic interpretation of the utilitarian calculus in which the social welfare function becomes an indicator of what I, in my own interest, would choose from a vantage point behind the veil of ignorance.

Useful as this construction may be in eliciting the meaning and content of the social welfare function representing my assessment of the common good, it does not circumvent the ethical problem of why I should act, or favour government actions, to maximize the value of a social welfare function when it is not in my own personal interest to do so. It is still open to me to say that, though I would prefer policy A if I had an equal chance of being anybody in society, I actually prefer policy B because I know perfectly well who I am and I know that I would be best off if policy B were adopted. Furthermore, since I and other like-minded people have the power to effect policy B, we will do so regardless of the interests of the rest of the community. The utilitarian has no response. Either I am persuaded by the ethical argument that I should work for the installation of policy A, or I am not. Policy implications of economic models are valid only to someone who accepts the ethical premises from which the policies are derived and who agrees that the constraints in the model are a proper representation of the circumstances in which a decision has to be made.

The effect of the new welfare economics was probably to swing the climate of opinion away from the more extreme version of interventionism. To be sure, the absence of a clear-cut criterion for economic policy is not an argument for *laissez-faire*. No economic policy can be justified on the grounds that we have no firm basis for the evaluation of economic policy. Nevertheless, the effect of the new welfare economics was probably to inculcate circumspection and modesty on the part of economists, a willingness to let the economy run according to its own laws except where the consequences of intervention seem obviously and overwhelmingly beneficial.

The other major source of the change in the perspective of the economists toward the role of government was the serious study of the mechanism of government itself. If the reformulation of welfare economics showed that economic policy could not be rendered independent of ethical prescriptions, the study of public choice made it clear that governments could not be relied upon to serve the public in a totally disinterested manner. The one knocked away the scientific basis of economic policy while the other cast doubt upon the capacity of government to adopt sound policy, even if such policy could be identified. It is as though Smith's dictum about the folly and presumption of government, after falling out of view for a hundred years, were suddenly thrust back into the center of economic analysis.

The earliest and perhaps most devastating component of the new study of the economics of government was the analysis of voting. Government can be presumed to serve the common good only if it is motivated by altruism or if there is a mechanism in society to resolve conflicts of interest among citizens and to induce government to act appropriately. Altruism might take the form of a benevolent dictatorship or of an electorate each member of which is prepared to subordinate his personal interest to the common good. While few would deny the presence of a degree of altruism in society, it is hard to imagine that altruism alone is sufficient to hold modern government in check. Something more than altruism is required. Most people would point in this context to our democratic institutions, an essential component of which is the principle of majority rule in the election of legislators and in voting on bills within the legislature. Yet the closer one looks at the mechanism of voting by majority rule the more evident it becomes that the outcome in a community of self-interested voters need not correspond to any reasonable conception of the common good. Depending on the constellation of interests among the voters and upon the rules of parliamentary procedure, there may be no equilibrium outcome such that a majority of voters can be found to favour that outcome over all other outcomes, or the equilibrium outcome, if there is one, may be inefficient.[12] The voting mechanism may be used by a majority stratified along the lines of wealth, race, language or religion to expropriate the property or rights of the minority.[13] The order of presentation of issues may be manipulated by officers of the legislature to yield an outcome more favourable than otherwise to the officers themselves. A group of legislators may devise voting strategies to procure an outcome more favourable to the members of the group and less favourable to others than the outcome that would arise if all votes reflected the true preferences of the voters on every issue.[14]

The upshot of such theorizing was the realization that voting by majority rule is a less than ideal conduit from the interests of citizens to public policy. Voting may yield an outcome that is more or less satisfactory to most people most of the time. It may be the only mechanism we possess to subordinate the rulers to the ruled, for the alternative may be government by a small, self-interested ruling class. It may be a satisfactory basis for political action to correct for departures from efficiency in the private sector when those departures are large, glaring and likely to be detrimental to a significant proportion of the population. It is not guaranteed to produce the appropriate corrective action in every case. It is no foundation for the Pigovian principle that "specific acts of interference" by government are warranted for any and every market failure. Recognition of difficulties with voting by majority rule tended to destroy the old confidence that an observed spread between private and social cost is itself sufficient to justify public intervention in the market.

This moral was reinforced by developments in the theory of public finance leading to the realization that there is typically a very large gap between the dollar value of public expenditure on a project or programme and its full social cost when the response of the private sector is taken into account. There are several components to the gap. On the tax side, the excess cost of public expenditure — over and above its cost as recorded in the public accounts — includes the deadweight loss as taxpayers switch from highly beneficial but highly taxed activities to somewhat less beneficial activities that happen to be less heavily taxed, for example, from taxed purchases of goods and services to untaxed leisure and do-it-yourself activities. Also on the tax side is the social waste of effort and resources on the part of the taxpayer to minimize his tax bill in schemes of legal tax avoidance or outright tax evasion, and the corresponding social waste of effort and resources on the part of the public sector to foil these schemes. To say that these activities are wasteful is not to say that taxpayer and government are acting irrationally under the circumstances; it is merely to assert that the activities neutralize one another and that everyone would be better off if tax avoidance and tax evasion could somehow be costlessly eliminated.[15] There is a similar problem on the expenditure side of the public accounts. Whenever the government provides a good, service or transfer to any category of firms or people, there is automatically created an incentive for people or firms to devote resources to persuading the government to include them among the beneficiaries; or, if the provision of the good, service or transfer is conditional on misfortune, the perverse incentive is to take less care to avoid the misfortune in the first place. Provision of tariffs or investment subsidies generates "rent-seeking" activity on the part of would-be beneficiaries.[16] Provision of support for the unemployed, for single mothers or for the destitute has some effect upon the incidence of these conditions; the argument here is not that support should be denied to those in great need but that the full cost of support should be recognized.

A third development is the theory of predatory government. Regardless of whether a social welfare function exists or can be identified, the government may have objectives of its own that conflict with the good of the greater part of the citizens. Predatory government may be in the interest of one or more dominant groups in the private sector or it may be in the interest of the personnel of the government. The archetype of government as the servant of one class in society is Marx's view of the public sector in a capitalist economy as "a committee for managing the common affairs of the whole bourgeoisie". On a more modest scale, the view of government as the servant of special interests is reflected in the "capture" theory of regulation, according to which the regulators of an industry may come to serve the interests of the regulated industry rather than the interests of the public at large. Regulators may allow themselves to be influenced by the prospect of remunerative employment in the regulated industries, or they may, quite innocently, assimilate the attitudes of the industries' representatives. When regulators can be "captured", it may be best to leave the market alone in many circumstances where the outcome could be improved under an ideal regulatory regime.[17]

That the government's monopoly of the means of violence may be employed in the interest of the king, bureaucrats, mandarins or soldiers rather than to maximize the value of a social welfare function is a possibility that was recognized by Smith and Mill, was subsequently ignored to a great extent, and is now taken seriously once again by the economics profession. Marx himself allowed that the ruling class may be characterized by a monopoly of the means of violence rather than by a monopoly of the means of production. In an analysis that might have come straight from John Stuart Mill and can almost certainly be traced to a common source, Marx allowed for the existence of an "Asiatic mode of production" in which the servants of the emperor constitute a class that rules society in its own interest, without at the same time acquiring a significant amount of property.[18] Though Mill's *Principles* contains discussions of Asiatic society and communism, and though Mill speculates on "how far the preservation of 'liberty' would be found compatible with the communistic organization of society" (210), he nowhere associates communism with Asiatic despotism and he does not appear to believe that communism and the preservation of liberty are necessarily and permanently incompatible.

It has been a perennial criticism of Marx that a communist society instituted by the party as the vanguard of the proletariat and with public ownership of the means of production would be indistinguishable in practice from the Asiatic mode of production. As early as 1872 the anarchist Bakunin stated that:

This government will not content itself with administering and governing the masses politically, as all governments do today. It will also administer the masses economically, concentrating in the hands of the State the production and division of wealth, the cultivation of land, the establishment and development of factories, the organization and direction of commerce, and finally the application of capital to production by the only banker — the State. All that will demand an immense knowledge and many heads "overflowing with brains" in this government. It will be the reign of *scientific intelligence*, the most aristocratic, despotic, arrogant, and elitist of all regimes. There will be a new class, a new hierarchy of real and counterfeit scientists and scholars, and the world will be divided into a minority ruling in the name of knowledge, and an immense ignorant majority. . . . for the proletariat this will, in reality, be nothing but a barracks: a regime, where regimented working men and women will sleep, wake, work, and live to the beat of a drum . . . .[19]

This idea was taken up by Karl Wittfogel,[20] who argued that the great despotic empires of China and the Middle East were made possible by the development of large-scale waterworks requiring an army of administrators who by their numbers and capacity to coordinate actions came to dominate the state. At about the same time, the Yugoslavian theorist Milovan Djilas[21] claimed that the communist party itself constituted a ruling class with no less capacity or willingness to exploit the rest of society than the property-based ruling classes in the traditional Marxian framework.

Contemporary study of the economics of predatory government is a major preoccupation of the "public choice" school of economics associated particularly with James Buchanan and Gordon Tullock, whose book *The Calculus of Consent: Logical Foundations of Constitutional Democracy*[22] played a large role in the inculcation of the new, more modest assessment of the capacity of the public sector to promote economic welfare. Their favourite metaphor for the all-encroaching government is the Leviathan, a biblical beast originally incorporated into the study of government by Thomas Hobbes. What the public choice theorists add, both to the deviant Marxists' analysis of the new class and to Hobbes's theory of government, is the close study of the mechanism of predatory government and of means keeping the Leviathan in check. The aetiology of the Leviathan is investigated by James Buchanan in *The Limits of Liberty* and by Gordon Tullock in *The Social Dilemma* and *Autocracy*.[23] Applications to constitutional limits on taxation are discussed in Geoffrey Brennan and James Buchanan, *The Power to Tax*.[24] These lines of analysis suggest that severe limitations be placed upon the use of government as a corrective for the defects of the market, the argument being that, if you empower the beast to manipulate the private sector and to redistribute income at will, he will use those powers for purposes of his own and may well leave the ordinary citizen worse off than before.

The study of information and incentives over the forty years since the Second World War has altered the perception of economists about efficiency in the private sector and the public sector of the economy. Traditionally, it had been assumed that buyer and seller in any transaction are both completely informed of the quality of the product or service. Equilibrium changes radically if, for example, the worker knows his level of competence but the employer does not, the insured knows more about his state of health than the insurer can hope to learn until it is too late, or the seller knows more than the buyer about the characteristics of the product.

Differential knowledge on the two sides of the market may result in an "adverse selection" of goods for sale that is always inefficient and sometimes destroys the market altogether.

Though economists have always been aware that one may work more or less diligently according to the probability and severity of punishment for malfeasance, this consideration has usually been ignored in formal economic analysis because it could not be incorporated into well specified models from which clear propositions might be derived. Only recently have models been developed in which one party acts as the agent of another and the outcome is necessarily less than Pareto optimal, at least by comparison with a world in which effort can be costlessly observed, because resources are used up in monitoring or because too little diligence is applied. Relations between stockholder and manager, manager and worker, landowner and sharecropper, insurer and insured, client and contractor all conform to this general pattern. Agency problems present special difficulties for the study of departures from efficiency because the obvious ideal with which actual behaviour is to be compared — a world in which effort can be costlessly observed and agency problems do not arise — is, almost by definition, unattainable. Hence evaluation of forms of organization must be comparative. Output under one set of institutions must be compared, not with reference to the ideal, but with reference to other feasible sets of institutions.[25]

The economics of information and incentives has a natural application to the study of the public sector. There would be no malfeasance if the performance of the agent could be observed costlessly by the principal and if the agent could be appropriately punished for failing to comply with the full terms of his contract. Consequently, one would expect malfeasance to be more extensive in responsible managerial jobs, where the agent must exercise discretion and where effort is not easily observed, than in routine work where performance is easier to monitor. The work of the civil servant is usually such that his performance is more difficult to scrutinize than the performance of a manager in a firm in the private sector. Parliament has probably less control over, and less power to discipline, the bureaucracy than a board of directors has over the executives of a firm. In a sense, the theory of bureaucracy as a ruling class is the outer edge of the theory of incentives, the extreme where the principal (in this case the citizen as voter) has the least control over his agents.

Surveying the history of the rise and fall of the public sector as a remedy for the undeniable departures from efficiency in the private sector, one can identify two great concepts that have moulded our views about the role of the public sector in the economy. The first of these is the system of natural liberty, a classic juxtaposition between *is* and *ought*, for an economy where people are free to follow their own interests is best for the community and ought to be unfettered by public policy. The development of economics after *The Wealth of Nations* might, with some exaggeration, be looked upon as the evolution of the *is* into propositions about the existence and Pareto optimality of the competitive equilibrium together with an ever-growing list of exceptions, and the merging of the *ought* into utilitarianism as a guide for public policy. In the course of this transformation, the concentration of economists' attention upon the private sector tended to emphasize its faults and failures, while the faults and failures of the public sector were quietly forgotten. Economists came to look upon government as the self-effacing devotee of the welfare of the governed, anxious to maximize the sum of the utilities of all citizens when informed by the economists how best this is to be done. More recently, the critical examination of the social welfare function and the study of the economics of political behaviour have modified these views to some extent.

The second great concept is despotism. Government may be seen, not just as relatively inefficient, but as having a propensity to turn nasty, to become predator, Leviathan or instrument for the exploitation of subjects by a ruling class. Fear of despotism is more evident in the writing of Mill than in that of Smith, though Mill's preoccupation with security as a requirement for liberty and his rudimentary analysis of society without government led him to see a larger role for government than Smith was inclined to allow. Fear of despotism waned throughout the latter part of the nineteenth century and the early part of the twentieth, primarily, I suspect, because governments in Europe appeared increasingly responsive to the needs and desires of citizens and because of a growing confidence that economic and political progress had become permanent and irreversible. Despotism was mentally relegated to Asia and destined to disappear as European enlightenment spread throughout the earth. That the role of government in society might be chosen with a view to minimizing the risk of a slide into despotism ceased for a time to be a serious consideration in economic and political analysis. Absence of any real fear of government becoming despotic or even moderately self-serving, tacit acceptance of utilitarian principles for the formation of public policy and the detailed study of market failure characterized the high point of the public sector in the estimation of the economists, just as renewed fear of despotism, the disintegration of utilitarianism as a criterion for public policy and the detailed analysis of self-interest within government, an analysis reminiscent of the strictures of Adam Smith, all contributed to the public sector's decline.

Notes

1   Adam Smith, *The Theory of Moral Sentiments*, cited by Jacob Viner in "Adam Smith and Laissez-faire", an essay in J.M. Clark *et al.*, eds., *Adam Smith, 1776–1926*, University of Chicago Press, 1928.

2   Except where otherwise specified, all quotations of Adam Smith are from *The Wealth of Nations*, Modern Library edition, 1937.

3   Viner, *op. cit.*, 126.

4 All references are to the 1909 edition, W.J. Ashley, Longman.

5 All quotations following are from the second edition, which appeared in 1887.

6 A.V. Dicey, *Lectures on the Relation between Law and Public Opinion in England during the Nineteenth Century*, Macmillan, 1905.

7 All quotations are from the fourth edition, published in 1932 by Macmillan.

8 Oskar Lange, "On the Economic Theory of Socialism", originally published in the *Review of Economic Studies*, October 1936 and February 1937, and reprinted with modifications together with an article by Fred M. Taylor in a book of the same title edited by Benjamin E. Lippincott in 1952; the quotation is from p. 104. For a contemporary collection of studies generally hostile to socialism, see F.A. Hayek, ed., *Collectivist Economic Planning*, 1935.

9 J.R. Hicks, "The Foundations of Welfare Economics", *Economic Journal* 1939, 696–712.

10 Lionel Robbins, "Interpersonal Comparisons of Utility: a Comment", *Economic Journal*, 1938, 635–41, p. 636.

11 The original idea is credited to Nicholas Kaldor, "Welfare Propositions of Economics and Interpersonal Comparisons of Utility", *Economic Journal*, 1939, 549–52; its tortuous history is reviewed in E.J. Mishan, "*A Survey of Welfare Economics, 1939–59*", *Economic Journal* 1960, 197–256, and S.K. Nath, *A Reappraisal of Welfare Economics*, Kelley, 1969.

12 Duncan Black, "On the Rationale of Group Decision Making", *Journal of Political Economy*, 1948, 23–34.

13 Gordon Tullock, "Problems of Majority Voting", *Journal of Political Economy*, 1959, 571–9.

14 Robin Farquharson, *Theory of Voting*, Yale University Press, 1969.

15 See A.B. Atkinson and N. Stern, "Pigou, Taxation and Public Goods", *Review of Economic Studies*, 1974, 119–28.

16 James Buchanan, Robert Tollison and Gordon Tullock, eds., *Toward a Theory of the Rent-seeking Society*, Texas A & M University Press, 1980, which contains the seminal articles on the subject.

17 On the capture theory, see George Stigler, *The Citizen and the State*, University of Chicago Press, 1980.

18 The story of the Asiatic mode of production is told in an appendix to Perry Anderson's *The Lineages of the Absolute State*, Verso, 1974.

19 Quoted in David Miller, *Anarchism*, Dent, 1984, 11–12.

20 Karl Wittfogel, *Oriental Despotism: a Comparative Study of Total Power*, Yale University Press, 1958.

21 Milovan Djilas, *The New Class: an Analysis of the Communist System*, Thames & Hudson, 1957.

22 University of Michigan Press, 1962.

23 James Buchanan, *The Limits of Liberty*, University of Chicago Press, 1975; Gordon Tullock, *The Social Dilemma: the Economics of War and Revolution*, University Publications, 1974, and *Autocracy*, Kluwer, 1987.

24 Cambridge University Press, 1980.

25 A good selection of articles on these matters is contained in P. Diamond and M. Rothschild, eds., *Uncertainty in Economics*, Academic Press, 1978.

Chapter III

Anarchy

Anarchy has two parts to play in this book.[1] It is a type of society in its own right, and it is a paradigm of what can go wrong with the economy. As a society in its own right, anarchy is characterized by the absence of government. It is a society — in the words of John Stuart Mill quoted at the front of the book — where a great "proportion of all the efforts and talents in the world are employed in merely neutralizing one another", a society distinct both from despotism, which is dreadful in a different way, and from the liberal society where government protects property and other entitlements and where the actions of government are determined, at least in part, by voting. As a paradigm of what can go wrong with the economy, anarchy is a substitute, generalization and improvement upon the economist's old workhorse, the externality. In the study of departures from efficiency, a model of anarchy tends to emphasize the waste of effort and resources in taking what others have produced and in defence against taking as distinct from the unintended by-products of ordinary economic activity. The purposes of the model of anarchy are complementary. Anarchy as a society in its own right is the end point of a continuum on which lie a great variety of departures from efficiency in the private sector of a liberal society.

The model of anarchy is to be built up in three distinct stages. The first, based on a legal example, is a demonstration of the waste of resources when "talents are employed in neutralizing one another". The second, based upon an example of an act of theft, introduces externalities and destruction of product. The third, encompassing the risk of losing one's life in conflict over the allocation of goods, contains the full model of anarchy which will serve as the foundation of and foil for the main model of despotism in the next chapter.

Attack and defence: litigation

The reader might think it strange to begin a study of anarchy with a legal example, for law and anarchy are as far apart as social phenomena can be. The example serves nonetheless, for it highlights a central feature of anarchy — the waste of resources in competition over a fixed reward — and carries the lesson that this feature of anarchy cannot be entirely extricated from societies that have advanced well beyond anarchy in most respects.

Two parties, 1 and 2, are engaged in a dispute over a sum of money, R. They might agree between themselves as to how the money is to be divided or they might have to resort to litigation. They both know that, if they go to court, the entire sum will be awarded to one party or the other and that each party's chance of winning is improved by his effort to win the case. For the purpose of this example, it is sufficient to suppose that probabilities and efforts are connected by the following simple functions. The probability of the award going to the first party is

$$p_1 = \alpha + (1 - \alpha - \beta) \frac{E_1^\delta}{E_1^\delta + E_2^\delta} \tag{1}$$

and the probability of the award going to the second party is

$$p_2 = \beta + (1 - \alpha - \beta) \frac{E_2^\delta}{E_1^\delta + E_2^\delta} \tag{2}$$

where E_1 is dollars, worth of effort by the first party to win the case; E_2 is dollars, worth of effort by the second party to win the case; α is the probability of the award going to the first party, even if he makes no effort to win the case, i.e. $p_1 = \alpha$ if $E_1 = 0$; β is the probability of the award going to the second party even if he makes no effort to win the case, i.e. $p_2 = \beta$ if $E_2 = 0$, and δ is a parameter between zero and 1. The significance of δ will be explained presently. Note that $p_1 + p_2 = 1$ regardless of the values of E_1 and E_2, for somebody has to win the case. The expenditures E_1 and E_2 cover legal fees, the value of the contestants' time spent on the case, and so on.

In these circumstances, each party chooses his expenditure to maximize his expected net benefit from the lawsuit. The first party chooses E_1 to maximize

$$p_1 R - E_1 = \left[\alpha + (1 - \alpha - \beta) \left(\frac{E_1^\delta}{E_1^\delta + E_2^\delta} \right) \right] R - E_1 \tag{3}$$

while the second party chooses E_2 to maximize

$$p_2 R - E_2 = \left[\beta + (1 - \alpha - \beta) \left(\frac{E_2^\delta}{E_1^\delta + E_2^\delta} \right) \right] R - E_2 \tag{4}$$

Think of each party as choosing his effort in the belief that the other party's effort is determined independently of his own. By symmetry, it follows immediately that both parties choose the same effort[2]

$$E_1 = E_2 = E \tag{5}$$

and that the common value of effort is

$$E = \frac{\delta(1 - \alpha - \beta)R}{4} \tag{6}$$

Thus, for instance, if R is a million dollars, if $\alpha = \beta = 0$ signifying that neither party stands any chance of winning the law case without some effort and if $\delta = 1$ signifying that each party's chance of winning is just equal to his share of total effort, then $E_1 = E_2 = R/4 = \$250,000$. Each party devotes a quarter of a million dollars to the case, so that half the potential gain of a million dollars is lost in the effort to grasp the prize from the hands of one's opponent. If δ were as large as 2, the entire potential benefit would be wasted in legal effort to win the suit.

As modelled here, the law case is a prototype of wasteful competition. The prize, R, is what it is regardless of the expenditures of the contending parties in the attempt to win it. The net gain to both parties together is the difference between the value of the prize and the combined value of the efforts of both parties. Knowing the equilibrium values of p_1 and p_2, the two contending parties would both be better off — and nobody else would be worse off — if they resolved the matter between them, all at once, by the flip of an appropriately weighted coin.

This model of wasteful competition can be generalized in many directions, with no more than a change in the meanings of the symbols. Within the courts, it becomes a model of competition over the size of an award — as in a divorce settlement — by interpreting p_1 and p_2 as shares of R accruing to the first and second parties. As discussed in some detail in Chapter VII, it is a model of common property where the parties are competing fishermen each of whose catch is reduced by the presence of the other; it is a model of advertising for shares of a market of a given size; it is a model of rent-seeking where E_1 and E_2 are efforts to persuade the government that one is a fitting recipient of a licence to import a product protected by a quota on total imports; it is a model of wasteful speculation. It is also a model of political competition among pressure groups where transfers to some groups must be at the expense of transfers from others, and resources are wasted as each group strives to be among the beneficiaries of public largess.[3]

The model is easily generalized to any number of contestants. Consider the special case where there are n contestants, where E_i is the effort of contestant i and where the probability that the prize goes to contestant i is

$$p_i = \frac{E_i}{E_1 + \ldots + E_n} \tag{7}$$

so that the expected profit of contestant i becomes $p_i M - E_i$. Again by symmetry, it follows that the effort of each contestant is the same

$$E_1 = E_2 = \ldots = E_n \equiv E \tag{8}$$

The common value of effort turns out to be[4]

$$E = R(n - 1)/n^2 \tag{9}$$

Furthermore, the total effort by all n contestants to win the prize is nE, which is equal $R(n - 1)/n$. A fraction $(n - 1)/n$ of the prize is wasted in the efforts of all n contestants to obtain it. The waste approaches 100 per cent when the number of contestants is unlimited.

Note before we proceed (i) that not all prize-seeking behaviour is wasteful, as has been implicitly assumed so far, and (ii) that some "wasteful" behaviour should be tolerated because it cannot be prevented except at a cost that exceeds the cost of the wasteful behaviour. As so far described, the efforts to win the lawsuit were of no social value in themselves. The effort of the first party is nothing more than his attempt to use the legal system to gain advantages at the expense of the second. The effort of the second party is to gain advantages at the expense of the first. Both efforts are wasted in the sense that everybody would be better off if both parties' efforts were reduced in whatever proportion is necessary to keep the probabilities of winning the same. This strong assumption will be relaxed in Chapter VII, where the efforts themselves will have a direct effect on output, generating a useful by-product, or affecting the magnitude of the prize. An example of the former is the spin-off of public information from speculative activity. An example of the latter is the patent race.

The other qualification is essentially a reminder of the Pigovian fallacy discussed in Chapter II. Efforts to win the law case are wasteful in the sense that the omnipotent, omniscient and benevolent dictator of traditional welfare economics would never allow a lawsuit to proceed. He would calculate each party's probability of winning, and would award the disputed sum on the flip of a suitably weighted coin. There are no judges, policemen, lawyers or law courts in traditional welfare economics. Our society employs these "wasteful" institutions because we have no omnipotent, omniscient and benevolent dictator and because the waste in these institutions must be borne if society is to function at all. One could argue, of course, that what is necessary cannot at the same time be wasteful, but that is mere playing with words. Waste can be defined as the use of resources for purposes that would have no place in the ideal world of traditional welfare economics. One may say, for example, that resources employed in taking and defending are wasteful, while at the same time recognizing that part of what we call waste is unavoidable. One need not constrain the word "inefficiency" to cases where the economist's advice is ignored.

Externality and destruction: a model of production and banditry

A thief approaches me on the street, sticks a gun in my ribs and — politely, so as not to cause me undue distress — says, "Your money or your life." As a proper economic man, I make a lightning calculation of the consequences of the alternatives, decide that I prefer the latter, and hand the thief my wallet. He takes my money, returns my wallet and goes on his way, he richer and I poorer by the amount of money he took.

The unwary economist might be inclined to evaluate this transaction according to its effect upon the social welfare function, where, in practice, social welfare is said to increase if the national increase becomes larger — the efficiency criterion — or if the distribution of income among people becomes narrower — the equality criterion. Efficiency and equality are the criteria by which public policy is typically evaluated in, for example, the realms of public finance and international trade. One might suppose that the criteria are relevant here as well. In a sense they are, but they must be applied carefully. Consider equality first. The transfer of money from me to the thief is equalizing as long as the thief is less well off than I. We can assume this to be so, especially if we take account of the non-monetary rewards of the academic life and the risk of misfortune in the life of a thief. With equality as the criterion, and on the assumption that the thief is worse off than his victim, we can say that theft is desirable and ought to be encouraged by the state. What about efficiency? There is really nothing wrong with theft if one considers the act all by itself. The thief is better off by the amount of money he takes, I am correspondingly worse off, but the national income is not reduced; the thief can be thought of using the money he steals to buy what I would have bought instead. Crudely applied, the usual criteria for the evaluation of public policy would seem to suggest that theft is desirable, for it improves matters on one criterion and has no effect on the other.

Yet a society that is free of theft is obviously preferable for everybody, even the would-be thief, to a society where theft is prevalent. Theft appears costless in our example because the comparison is between situations before and after a particular act of theft, rather than between societies with and without theft. A society where people steal if it is in their interest to do so bears four distinct costs that would be avoided in a society where property rights are secure. The first is the alternative cost of the labour of the thief.

The man who devotes himself to a life of crime deprives society of the services of the garbage man, professor, taxi driver or doctor he might have become instead. The second is the alternative cost of resources devoted to the prevention of crime. Such cost may be private or public. The potential victim protects himself by building a fence around his house, by installing locks on his doors and bars on his windows, by training himself to overpower a thief and so on. He also protects himself through the intermediary of the state, which employs a police force, operates prisons, and so on. A third cost is the diversion of resources from the production of goods that can be stolen to the production of goods that cannot be stolen. If television sets can be stolen but houses cannot, the potential victim of theft spends less of his income on the former and more on the latter than he would in an economy where all possessions are secure. When all goods can be stolen, he devotes more of his time to leisure and less to work. This third cost may be called a deadweight loss, for it is similar to the "excess burden" of taxation. To a risk-averse consumer, it makes no difference whether he must pay a tax of 10 per cent on an item of consumption or must bear a 10 per cent risk of having the item stolen; his response is the same. The fourth and final cost is the injury to people and property in the scuffle that occurs when the thief tries to take property by force. In taking my money, the thief may also take my wallet, which contains pictures of great value to me but not to him. Or my watch may be broken. Or the thief may consider it necessary to hit me over the head to reduce my capacity to defend my property. Or one of us may be accidentally or intentionally killed. This fourth cost is like the first two in that it constitutes pure waste; neither party gains from injury and both could be made better off if a more amicable way could be found to effect the transfer from victim to thief. It differs from the first and second costs in that the loss of welfare may be the disappearance of goods and services already produced rather than the diversion of resources from the making of goods and services. For the present, think of this cost as destruction of product exclusively. Later on in this chapter it will encompass the loss of life as well.

Of these four costs of theft, the first two are entirely analogous to the efforts of the two parties to the lawsuit. The plaintiff seeks to take and the defendant seeks to preserve what he has. The third and fourth costs are different.

There is a terminological difficulty. Though the study of anarchy follows naturally from the story of the thief, the word "theft" is inappropriate in the context of the formal analysis of an anarchic society because to steal is to violate well established property rights which cannot exist without a government to call these rights into being and to invest them with greater security than a mere squatter can command through his own strength. Theft is a legal concept that can have no meaning without the existence of publicly enforced law. We can, however, distinguish between making and taking. Among activities that are advantageous to the actor, some must be devoted to producing things if people are to subsist at all, but others are predatory and intrinsically wasteful. At the margin, both types of activity must be equally profitable. To avoid the legal implications of the word "theft", I shall from here on refer to predatory activity as "banditry".

The story of the thief will be developed into a formal model of the allocation of the resources of society among production, banditry and defence against banditry. To incorporate deadweight loss, a distinction is drawn between types of goods that have to be defended against bandits and types of goods that are intrinsically secure. People are assumed to choose among three occupations, farming, clothing manufacture and banditry, where farmers have to divide their time between producing food and defending their crops, but clothiers can devote all their time to production because, by assumption, clothing cannot be appropriated by bandits. Though agents in a real anarchic society would in all probability be generalists, dividing their time optimally among the available occupations, it is convenient to assume instead that people specialize but that incomes are equalized by free mobility of labour among occupations. The model in this section makes no allowance for loss of life in the conflict between farmer and bandit. Loss of life will be incorporated into a more realistic model of anarchy in a later section (p. 89). An essential feature of both models is the absence of coordination among people in production, predation or defence.

These are the assumptions:

(i) Society consists of n people who choose among the three occupations so that

$$n = n^F + n^C + n^B \tag{1.1}$$

where n^F is the number of farmers, n^C is the number of clothiers and n^B is the number of bandits. (Equations in this section are numbered according to their place in Table 1; (1.1) means the first equation in Table 1, etc.)

(ii) Bandits take food but not clothing. Bandits pillage farms before the food can be consumed or sold. Clothing manufacture and markets where farmers and bandits exchange food for clothing are both safe from banditry.

(iii) Each person has an endowment of one hour of time, which should be thought of as available time in excess of necessary leisure. Bandits and clothiers work full-time at their occupations. Farmers divide their endowment of time between L^F hours producing food and L^G hours of "guard labour" defending their produce:

$$L^F + L^G = 1 \tag{1.2}$$

(iv) The output of clothing per producer is a constant, r, so that society's total output of clothing is rn^C.

Table 1   *An economy with farmers, clothiers and bandits*

(1) $n = n^F + n^C + n^B$	allocation of people among occupations
(2) $L^F + L^G = 1$	allocation of farmer's time between production and defence
(3) $f = f(L^F)$	production function for food
(4) $g = g(L^G, n^B/n^F)$	production function for guard labour
(5) $T = f(L^F)g$	amount taken per farmer
(6) $f'/f = -(\partial g/\partial L_G)/(1 - g)$	optimal allocation of farmer's time
(7) $Y^F = f(L^F) - T$	income per farmer
(8) $Y^C = r\,p$	income per clothier
(9) $Y^B = X(1 - D)$	income per bandit
(10) $p = p(f(L^F)n^F - DXn^T, rn^C)$	goods market equilibrium
(11) $n^B X = n^F\,T$	Say's law of crime
(12) $Y^F = Y^C$	labour market equilibrium for farmers and clothiers
(13) $Y^B = Y^F$	labour market equilibrium for farmers and bandits

The three exogenous variables are

n	number of people in the economy
r	output of clothing per worker
D	proportion of loot destroyed

The thirteen endogenous variables are

n^F	number of farmers
n^C	number of clothiers
n^B	number of bandits
Y^F	*per capita* income of farmers
Y^C	*per capita* income of clothiers
Y^B	*per capita* income of bandits
L^F	hours of farm labour
L^G	hours of guard labour
f	output of food per farmer
g	proportion of farmer's output stolen
T	amount taken per farmer
X	amount stolen per bandit
p	price of clothing
F	consumption of food per head
C	consumption of clothing per head

(v) The output of food per farmer, f, is a function of the number of hours of work devoted to farming, that is

$$f = f(L^F) \tag{1.3}$$

The function f is best thought of as a concave production function with $f' > 0$ and $f'' < 0$, as would be the case if each farmer occupied a fixed amount of land. Alternatively, land may be so abundant that its marginal product falls to zero, but the technology may be so primitive and the productivity of land so low that distance alone accounts for the diminishing marginal product of labour in farming.[5]

(vi) A good many analytical complications are avoided by ignoring the inevitable randomness in the interaction among bandits and their victims. When a group of uncoordinated bandits appropriates food from a group of uncoordinated farmers, the amount taken must differ from one farmer to the next because — just by chance — some farmers will be victimized more frequently than others. Suppose instead that when all farmers supply the same amount of guard labour (as they do because they are alike in tastes and circumstances) the amount of food, T, taken from each farmer is the same, and the amount of food acquired by each bandit over the year, X, is the same as well. The actual values of T and X are endogenous to the model. Think of each bandit as taking a small amount of food from each of many farmers over the course of the year.

(vii) A fraction D of all food taken from farmers is destroyed in the act of banditry. Bandits who take X can only preserve $X(1 - D)$ for themselves.

(viii) The proportion of the farmer's output that is stolen, g, depends on the amount of guard labour, L^G, he supplies and on the incidence of crime in society as a whole, n^B/n^F

$$g = g(L^G, n^B/n^F) \tag{1.4}$$

where $g_1 < 0$, $g_{11} > 0$ and $g_2 > 0$. The total amount stolen, T, from any given farmer is the proportion stolen, g, multiplied by the amount produced, $f(L^F)$.

$$T = f(L^F)g \tag{1.5}$$

It is important to think of L^G as determined before the bandit arrives at the farmer's door, and of the bandit as unable to observe L^G until he has irrevocably committed himself to a predatory act. Otherwise there would develop a competition among farmers, each devoting an especially large amount of his time to guard labour in the hope of provoking bandits to take from other farmers instead.

Say's law of crime requires that

$$n^B X = n^F T \tag{1.11}$$

in market equilibrium where all farmers are alike and all bandits are alike.

(ix) The market for food and clothing works as follows. Once a certain amount of food has been stolen from the farms, everybody — farmers, clothiers and thieves — goes to the market place, where farmers and thieves peacefully trade food for clothing at market-clearing prices. The price of food is set arbitrarily at 1. The price of clothing, as determined by the market, is p.

By definition, the incomes per head of the three classes of people, farmers, clothiers and bandits, are

$$Y^F \equiv f(L^F) - T \tag{1.7}$$

$$Y^C = r \, p \tag{1.8}$$

$$Y^B = X(1 - D) \tag{1.9}$$

Free mobility among occupations guarantees that these incomes are all the same,

$$Y^F = Y^C = Y^B \tag{1.12 \quad 1.13}$$

but Y^B might differ from Y^F and Y^C if the number of bandits were somehow fixed.

(x) Everyone has identical preferences for food and clothing as represented by a common utility function

$$U = U(F,C)$$

where F and C are amounts of food and clothing that a person consumes. When the market equilibrium is such that everyone consumes the same amount of both goods, then

$$F = [f(L^F)n^F - DXn^B]/n$$

and

$$C = rn^C/n$$

where $f(L^F)n^F - DXn^B$ is the difference between the total output of food and the amount destroyed in the act of theft. The inverse demand function for clothing becomes

$$p = p(f(L^F)n^F - DXn^B, rn^C) \tag{1.10}$$

where p, the market equilibrium price of cloth, is equal to U_C/U_F and where the partial derivatives, p_1 and p_2, are positive and negative respectively.

Also assume that the common utility function is homothetic; the relative price of clothing depends only on the ratio of C to F and remains unchanged when F and C increase or decrease proportionally. As long as everyone is confronted with the same relative price of food and clothing, the marginal valuation of clothing with respect to food, U_C/U_F, is also the same regardless of whether the incomes Y^F, Y^C and Y^B are the same or different.

That completes the assumptions.

There are two decisions in this economy; everyone must choose his profession, and farmers have to allocate their time between production and defence against bandits. Since everyone is essentially alike, each person chooses the profession yielding the highest income, a process ensuring that Y^F, Y^C and Y^B have to be the same in equilibrium. Then treating n^F, n^C, n^T and p (the price of clothing) as market characteristics over which he has no control, the farmer chooses L^F and L^P to maximize Y^F where

$$Y^F = f(L^F) - T = f(L^F)[1 - g(L^G, n^T/n^F)]$$

subject to his time constraint

$$L^F + L^G = 1$$

Thus the rule for dividing his labour-time between production and defence becomes[6]

$$\frac{f'}{f} = -\frac{\partial g}{\partial L^G}/(1 - g) \qquad (1.6)$$

which may be interpreted as equating "the percentage increase in output resulting from an extra minute in productive labour" to "the percentage of the crop saved by an extra minute of guard labour".

Now we can pull the story together. As summarized in Table 1, the model consists of thirteen equations and thirteen unknowns with three exogenous variables. One can normally expect there to be a solution to the system, though there is no assurance that anyone chooses to be a bandit. The equilibrium number of bandits, n^B, is positive or zero depending on whether or not $Y^B > Y^F$ when $n^B = 0$.

Some interesting properties of the model are displayed in Figure 8. The figure contains two curves illustrating the income of workers and the income of bandits as functions of the number of bandits. The figure is constructed by dropping equation (13) of Table 1, setting Y^W, where W is mnemonic for worker, to be the common value of Y^F and Y^C, and expressing every variable in the model, including Y^B and Y^W, as a function of n^B.

The existence of such curves is a direct consequence of the model, but their shapes have to be justified. As drawn, the curves are downward sloping, signifying that both groups are made worse off by an increase in the number of bandits.[7] The income-of-the-bandit curve starts higher than the income-of-the-worker curve ($\overline{Y}^B > \overline{Y}^W$) but is steeper, and there is an equilibrium number of bandits at which $Y^W = Y^B$ and all thirteen equations are satisfied. The reason for requiring $\overline{Y}^B > \overline{Y}^W$ is that, if it were not so, there would be no incentive for anybody to divert labour from farming to banditry, and there would be no banditry at all. The reason for requiring the income of the bandit curve to be relatively steep is that, if it were

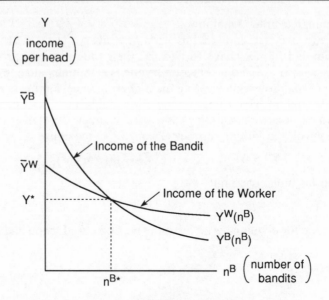

Figure 8   Equilibrium in anarchy

not so, there would be no production of food or clothing. Both situations are possible. The parameters of the model might be such that no banditry occurs or that no production occurs. We are examining an economy where the parameters are such that there is some production and some banditry. The solution need not be unique. With multiple solutions, the first from the left would be stable, the next unstable, and so on.

Two simple propositions follow immediately from the comparative statics of Figure 8. The first is that crime always pays. The market equalizes the profitability of farming and banditry, just as it equalizes profitability in any two legitimate occupations, except for compensating differences — assumed away in our model — due to training or the innate ability of the practitioners. In general, the criminal can be expected to work as diligently at his trade as the law-abiding citizen, but the crime of theft is not rendered socially beneficial on that account.

The second and more interesting proposition is that whatever harms the bandit is beneficial both to the worker and to the bandit. The proposition is strictly true if interpreted to mean that any set of changes in the market such that the income-of-the-worker curve is unmoved, and the income-of-the-bandit curve is lowered, makes both parties better off. This is illustrated in Figure 9. The income-of-the-worker curve is fixed, the income-of-the-bandit curve shifts downward as indicated by the arrows, and the equilibrium shifts from E^0 to E^1, leading to an increase in the common value of Y^W and Y^B as long as the income-of-the-worker curve is downward sloping. The bandit is worse off for any given value of n^B, but

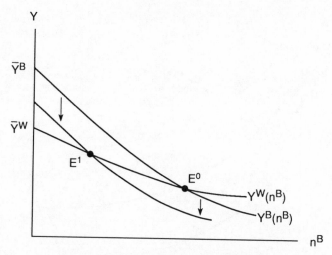

Figure 9 Alternative anarchic equilibria

he is better off in the final equilibrium because the number of bandits is reduced, and the equilibrium moves up the income-of-the-worker curve. The proposition is usually, but not necessarily, true if interpreted to refer to the effects of changes in the parameters of the model, for changes in parameters could affect both curves at once. A spontaneous change in equation (9) such that D increases for any given value of X would lower $Y^B(n^B)$ without shifting $Y^W(n^B)$ at all.

The four costs of theft

In a society with farmers, bandits and clothiers, with free mobility among occupations and with no cooperation or organization, the social cost of banditry may be classified under the headings of the four costs of theft in the example at the outset of the last section.

(i) The loss to society of the alternative cost of the labour of the bandit.
(ii) The loss to society of the alternative cost of the guard labour of the farmer.
(iii) The destruction of product in the act of banditry.
(iv) The deadweight loss incurred because people produce and consume too much of the good (clothing) that is safe from theft and too little of the stealable good (food).

The social cost of predation is the difference between *per capita* real income in a world without banditry and *per capita* real income in a world with banditry. To measure this cost, we cannot simply observe the difference between $\overline{Y}^W$ and Y^W in Figure 8 because banditry influences the

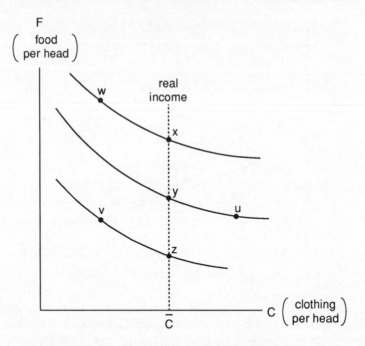

Figure 10 The measurement of real income

ratio of the outputs of food and clothing, which in turn influences the relative price of clothing. The cost of banditry has to be measured as a change in *real* income defined as a cardinal indicator of the indifference curve attained. A set of indifference curves for food and clothing is illustrated in Figure 10.

A particularly useful indicator of real income for our purposes may be defined as follows. Real income corresponding to any bundle of goods, F and C, is indicated by the amount of food, $\overline{F}$, such that — for some arbitrarily chosen amount of clothing $\overline{C}$ — the bundles (F,C) and $(\overline{F},\overline{C})$ lie on the same indifference curve. Thus real incomes are shown on Figure 10 as distances above the horizontal axis of on the line xyz$\overline{C}$. Real income associated with the point w is the distance x$\overline{C}$; real income associated with the point u is the distance y$\overline{C}$; real income associated with the point v is the distance z$\overline{C}$.

Formally, for any arbitrarily chosen quantity of clothing $\overline{C}$ and for any arbitrarily assigned utility function $\phi(F,C)$ which conforms to the given set of indifference curves — in other words, where $\phi(F^1,C^1) = \phi(F^2,C^2)$ whenever the bundles (F^1,C^1) and (F^2,C^2) lie on the same indifference curve and where ϕ_F and ϕ_C are always positive — we define a new utility function U(F,C) so that, for all possible combinations of F and C,

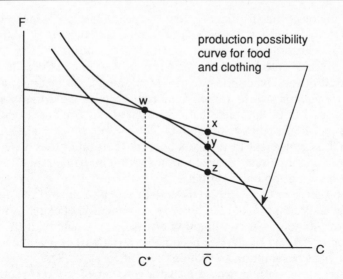

Figure 11 Sources of waste in anarchy

$$U(F,C) \equiv [\overline{F} \text{ such that } \{\phi(F,C) = \phi(\overline{F},\overline{C})\}] \qquad (1.14)$$

The numbered equations in this section should be thought of as additions to the system of thirteen equations in Table 1. Obviously, the function U is a monotonic transformation of the function ϕ. The function U serves as a measure of real income, for, by definition, it is calibrated in units of F and it has the property that $U(F,\overline{C}) = F$ for all values of F.

The welfare loss from banditry can now be illustrated as a quantity of food corresponding to a distance between indifference curves, where $\overline{C}$ in equation (1.14) is not just any arbitrary quantity of clothing, but is the quantity of clothing consumed per head in the equilibrium of the model in Table 1. Figure 11 is an extension of Figure 10 with the addition of a *per capita* production possibility curve for food and clothing. The new curve represents combinations of food and clothing that would be available if there were no banditry. It is the locus of attainable F and C as they would be if n^B and L^G were set at zero. The competitive equilibrium would be optimal, and the economy would settle down at a combination of F and C represented by the point w corresponding to a real income of x. When there is banditry, the economy settles down at a point z which is necessarily below the production possibility curve (because banditry wastes resources) and which is probably, but not necessarily, to the right of w (because banditry is like a tax on the stealable good, raising its price relative to the unstealable good and inducing consumers to change from the one to the other).

It is obvious from the diagram that the *per capita* loss from banditry is the vertical distance x–z which is at once an amount of F and a well specified reduction in real income as an indicator of utility. This is immediately divisible into two parts, y–z and x–y. The first is the reduction in the output of food when the quantity of clothing is set at $\overline{C}$. As we shall show, it encompasses the three of the four costs of theft: the loss of the potential output of the thief, the loss of the alternative cost of defensive labour, and the destruction of product. The second, which can legitimately be called a deadweight loss, occurs because theft interposes a wedge between the marginal rate of substitution and the marginal rate of transformation between food and clothing.

The subdivision of y–z proceeds as follows. The height of the point z is the actual consumption of food, F, when consumption of clothing is $\overline{C}$. The height of the point y is consumption of food as it would be if there were no banditry (so that the farmer need not divert a part of his time to guard labour) but consumption of clothing remained at $\overline{C}$. The value of y is therefore $f(1)(n - \overline{n}^C)/n$, where $\overline{n}^C$ is the number of workers required to produce $\overline{C}$ *per capita*, and $f(1)$ is output of food per farmer as it would be if there were no banditry. To measure y–z, the loss of food due to banditry when output of clothing is $\overline{C}$, observe the equalities between the value of consumption and the incomes of suppliers of food and of clothing.

$$nF = n^F Y^F + n^B Y^B \qquad (1.15)$$

and

$$nC = n^C r \qquad (1.16)$$

From equation (1.8), it immediately follows that $n(F + pC) = n^F Y^F + n^B Y^B + n^C Y^C$, which signifies that national expenditure equals national income. From equation (1.12), it follows that $z = F = Y^F - pC = Y^F(1 - \overline{n}^C/n)$. Consequently,

$$
\begin{aligned}
y-z &= [f(1) - Y^F]\frac{(n - \overline{n}^C)}{n} \\
&= \left[f(L^F + L^G) - \frac{n^F}{n^F + n^B} f(L^F + L^G) \right] \frac{(n - \overline{n}^C)}{n} \\
&\quad + \frac{n^F}{n^F + n^B} [f(L^F + L^G) - f(L^F)] \frac{(n - \overline{n}^C)}{n} \\
&\quad + \left[\frac{n^F}{n^F + n^B} f(L^F) - Y^F \right] \frac{(n - \overline{n}^C)}{n} \\
&= \left\{ \frac{n^B}{n} f(L^F + L^G) \right\} + \left\{ \frac{n^F}{n} [f(L^F + L^G) - f(L^F)] \right\} + \left\{ \frac{DTn^F}{n} \right\}
\end{aligned}
\qquad (1.17)
$$

= {alternative cost of the labour of the bandit}

+ {alternative cost of the guard labour of the farmer}

+ {destruction of product}

where Tn^F is the amount of food stolen and D is the proportion destroyed in the act of banditry.

The expression $y-z$ is decomposed into three expressions by successive subtraction and addition of components: the second term in the first expression is the same as the first term in the second, and so on. These three expressions are then simplified so that their interpretation as elements of the costs of theft is straightforward. The only difficult step is to show the equivalence between[8]

$$\left[\frac{n^F f(L^F)}{n^B + n^F} - Y^F \right] \frac{(n - \bar{n}^C)}{n}$$

and $DT(n^F/n)$.

That $x-y$ is a deadweight loss is obvious from inspection of Figure 11. It is the loss of utility from choosing a sub-optimal point on the production possibility curve depicting all combinations of food and clothing that would be available for consumption if there were no banditry. Along this curve, both quantities can be expressed as functions of n^C. Consumption of food is $f(1)(n - n^C)/n$, consumption of clothing is rn^C/n, and utility is $U(F, C) = U(f(1)(n - n^F)/n, rn^C/n)$. The point x is the maximum of utility over all possible values of n^C, and the point y is the utility corresponding to the value, $\bar{n}^C$, chosen in the equilibrium when there is banditry. Consequently,[9]

$$x-y = \int_{\bar{C}}^{C*} \frac{U_C}{U_F} dC - T \int_{\bar{C}}^{C*} \frac{f(1)}{r} dC \tag{1.18}$$

where $\bar{C}$ is the actual output of clothing per head, $C*$ is the optimal output of clothing when there is no banditry or guard labour, the first integral is the area under the compensated demand curve for clothing (as read off the indifference curve through w and x) between $C*$ and $\bar{C}$, and the second integral is the area under the supply curve for clothing (as read off the production possibility curve as it would be if $n^B = 0$) between $C*$ and $\bar{C}$. Thus the meaning of equation (1.18) is that the deadweight loss can be measured in the usual way as the triangular area between the demand curve and the supply curve over the range from the actual output to the optimal output.

Utility and survival

The model of the preceding section has been silent about the nature of the encounter between farmer and bandit. Equations (1.4) and (1.5) say that the amount stolen per farmer depends on the number of bandits per farmer in the economy and on the number of hours of guard labour per farmer, but they do not say how bandits appropriate food or how the guard labour is deployed. I might plead in defence of the model that production functions never really explain production. They specify how much output is generated by given inputs of labour and capital, not what happens to the factors of production as output is created. On the other hand, it is fairly evident what happens when farmers encounter bandits. They fight. They are injured or perhaps killed. By contrast, following well trodden paths of economic analysis, the model of farmers, clothiers and bandits has so far allowed for nothing worse than a partial destruction of property.

Normally, economics is the most peaceful of sciences. Economic man may work, consume, trade and adopt strategies, but he does not fight. He is acquisitive (or its opposite, altruistic) but never aggressive. He experiences pleasure from goods, but not physical pain. There is no overt denial of fear, violence, combat, pain or death, but these are not woven into the fabric of economic analysis. Abstraction from these aspects of life is not just an oversight on the part of the economist. These aspects of life tend to be ignored because they are not central to the phenomena with which economists are primarily concerned: taxation, international trade, project assessment, etc. These aspects of life are effectively excluded by the implicit assumption in the usual model of a competitive economy that property is completely secure. But to drop that assumption is to force oneself to deal with the fact that society must rely upon some physical sanction, imprisonment, pain or death, to ensure respect for property rights or for any other rule for dividing society's goods and services among its citizens.[10]

The model of anarchy does not contain a full description of the encounter between farmers and bandits, but it does break with the pacifist tradition in economics by allowing the encounter to be lethal. The encounter could be modelled as a game of hide-and-seek in which the bandit creeps up to the farmer's stock of grain, carries off a ton if he is undetected, and waves goodbye empty-handed if he is detected. That is not the procedure here. Instead the encounter between bandit and farmer is dangerous as well as costly; the life of man in the state of nature is "solitary, nasty, brutish and [especially] short". The danger in the encounter might consist of the risk of pain, broken limbs, and so on. We shall concentrate here on only one possible consequence. It will be supposed that there is a fight which entails a certain risk of death to both parties. This extreme consequence is chosen because mortality is more easily modelled than, for instance, the risk of breaking a limb, because it fits particularly well into the study of despotism to come, and because it establishes a connection between the circumstances of the economy and the rate of population growth.

Utility must now be defined as a function of one's survival rate as well as of one's consumption of ordinary goods and services. Ideally, survival rates should be introduced in the context of an intertemporal model in which people live for an uncertain number of years. That will not be the procedure here. We shall remain within the static model, but will assume that each person's utility, W, is

$$W = Su(Y)$$

where S is his overall survival rate, Y is his annual income, and u is his atemporal, static utility of consumption function. This specification of utility might be thought of as pertaining to people whose risk of death each year depends upon the choice of occupation but not upon age. The function u is assumed to be the same for everyone in the model, but values of S and Y may differ. In choosing whether to be a farmer or to be a bandit, each person observes the going values of W^F and W^B, and he becomes a farmer if $W^F > W^B$, or he becomes a thief if $W^F < W^B$. Consequently, $W^F = W^B$ in equilibrium.

To simplify matters, we drop the clothing industry and change the terminology somewhat. As there is now only one good and no investment in the model, we can denote total output by Q, which is at once the total production of food and the national income with food as the numeraire.

The total population, n, consists of n^F farmers and n^B bandits. As before, the farmers' time is divided between guard labour, L^G, and productive labour, L^F. Total output of food, Q, depends on the total input of farm labour $L^F n^F$, and on consumption per farmer, Y^F,

$$Q = F(L^F n^F, Y^F) \qquad (2.3)$$

where F is the production function, $F_1 > 0$, $F_2 > 0$ wherever Y^F falls short of some adequate level $\overline{Y}^F$ and $F_2 = 0$ otherwise. Output is dependent upon consumption per farmer, on the assumption that farmers cannot work hard unless they are adequately fed. (The compound numbering of equations in this section is in accordance with their place in Table 2. Some of the equations in the table need not be discussed in the text because they are self-explanatory.) By definition

$$Y^F = Q/n^F - T \qquad (2.4)$$

where T is once again the amount of food taken per farmer.

The income, Y^B, of a bandit is the product of the number, E, of encounters with farmers during the year and the amount stolen, H (heist), per encounter, i.e. $Y^B = EH$. The number of encounters with bandits per farmer is therefore equal to En^B/n^F. It follows immediately from Say's law of crime that $Tn^F = Y^B n^B$. In setting out these equations we are deliberately ignoring the fact that some farmers may be robbed more than others, merely by chance. As in the second section above, we are assuming that every farmer is robbed the same number of times during the year and that all farmers choose the same allocation of time between L^F and L^G.

The key assumption about the danger in banditry is that farmers and bandits are equally adept at fighting, so that each bears the same risk of losing his life in an encounter. The bandit approaches the farm, takes an amount H, and then either gets away undetected or is compelled to fight the farmer, where the risk, to farmer and bandit alike, of getting killed in such a fight is ψ. This risk, ψ, depends on three considerations. It increases with the amount of guard labour of the farmer, L^G, because, the more guard labour supplied, the greater the probability that any given act of banditry will be detected. It also increases with the amount stolen, H, because a big heist is, by assumption, easier to detect than a small one. And it increases with the number of encounters, E, because, the more appropriations attempted, the less care one can take in each to avoid detection. Thus $\psi = (L^G,H,E)$ where all first derivatives are positive. The farmer's probability of surviving all his encounters with bandits, V^F, is therefore,

$$V^F = [1 - \psi(L^G,H,E)]^{En^B/n^F} \tag{2.7}$$

and the corresponding survival probability of the bandit is

$$V^B = [1 - \psi(L^G,H,E)]^E \tag{2.8}$$

These are not the only risks that people must bear. In addition, both groups bear the ordinary risks of mortality by natural causes; let the corresponding survival rates be

$$M^F = M(Y^F) \quad \text{and} \quad M^B = M(Y^B) \tag{2.9 \quad 2.10}$$

where the function M has the properties that $M(Y) = 0$ whenever $Y \leq \underline{Y}$, $M' > 0$ and $M'' < 0$ whenever $\underline{Y} < Y < \overline{Y}$ and $M = \overline{M}$ whenever $Y > \overline{Y}$, as illustrated in Figure 12. You need to consume at least $\underline{Y}$ to survive at all and your chance of survival increases with Y up to $\overline{Y}$, beyond which additional income has no effect upon your survival rate. The significance of $\overline{M}$ being less than one is that no amount of consumption eliminates all risk of death by natural causes.

Equilibrium in anarchy requires that the population divides itself between farmers and bandits so as to equalize the utilities in the two occupations,

$$V^FM^Fu(Y^F) = V^BM^Bu(Y^B)$$

Finally, the farmer chooses L^G to maximize his utility, given the behaviour of the bandit, and the bandit chooses H and E to maximize his utility, given the behaviour of the farmer. This maximizing behaviour adds three extra equations to the system:[11]

$$L^G = L^G(H,E,n^B) \tag{2.11}$$

$$H = H(L^G,n^F) \tag{2.12}$$

$$E = E(L^G,n^F) \tag{2.13}$$

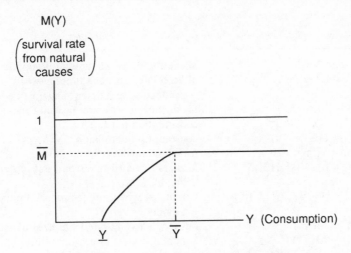

Figure 12 Consumption and survival

Once again, the equilibrium in anarchy can be represented as a number of equations — set out in Table 2 — determining an equal number of unknowns, and the equilibrium can be illustrated on a diagram like that in Figure 8, except that incomes, Y^F and Y^B, would have to be replaced by utilities W^F and W^B. The construction of the new diagram is exactly the same: drop the final equation, in this case equation (2.16), and express all endogenous variables as functions of n^B, the number of bandits. The utility of the farmer curve is $W^F(n^B)$, and the utility of the thief curve is $W^B(n^B)$. For there to be an equilibrium in which n^F, n^B, L^F and L^G are all positive, the utility-of-the-bandit curve must start high when $n^B = 0$ and decrease faster than the utility-of-the-farmer curve until the two meet in the interior of the diagram. The equilibrium is now characterized by higher mortality rates from natural causes and from violence than would occur if banditry could be costlessly prohibited.

The introduction of violence and mortality into our model of anarchy gives rise to a dynamics of population growth. By definition, the rate of growth of population is the difference between birth rate and death rate, that is:

$$\frac{\dot{n}}{n} = b + \frac{n^F}{n}S^F + \frac{n^B}{n}S^B - 1 \qquad (10)$$

where b is the birth rate, which, for convenience, we suppose to be constant and less than 1, and S^F and S^B are survival rates of farmers and bandits: $S^F \equiv V^F M^F$ and $S^B \equiv V^B M^B$.

A rudimentary Malthusian dynamics emerges through the production function in equation (2.3). To assume, as we have, that $F_1 > 0$ and $F_{11} < 0$

93

Table 2 *A model of anarchy with endogenous survival rates*

(1) $n = n^F + n^B$	allocation of people among occupations
(2) $L^F + L^G = 1$	allocation of farmer's time between production and defence against banditry
(3) $Q = F(L^F n^F, Y^F)$	production function in agriculture
(4) $Y^F = (Q/n^F) - T$	consumption per farmer
(5) $Y^B = HE$	consumption per bandit
(6) $Tn^F = Y^B n^B$	total amount taken
(7) $V^F = [1 - \psi(L^G, H, E)]^{En^B/n^F}$	farmers' survival rate from encounters with bandits
(8) $V^B = [1 - \psi(L^G, H, E)]^E$	bandits' survival rate from encounters with farmers
(9) $M^F = M(Y^F)$	farmers' survival rate from natural causes
(10) $M^B = M(Y^B)$	bandits' survival rate from natural
(11) $L^G = L^G(H, E, n^B)$	optimal amount of guard labour
(12) $H = H(L^G, n^F)$	optimal heist
(13) $E = E(L^G, n^F)$	optimal number of encounters per bandit
(14) $W^F = V^F M^F u(Y^F)$	welfare of farmers
(15) $W^B = V^B M^B u(Y^B)$	welfare of bandits
(16) $W^F = W^B$	labour market equilibrium

The endogenous variables:

n^F	number of farmers
n^B	number of bandits
L^F	hours of farm labour
L^G	hours of guard labour
Y^F	consumption per farmer
Y^B	consumption per bandit
T	amount taken per farmer
H	amount taken per encounter
E	number of encounters per bandit
M^F	farmers' survival rate from natural causes
M^B	bandits' survival rate from natural causes
V^F	farmers' survival rate from banditry
V^B	bandits' survival rate from banditry
Q	total production of food
W^F	welfare of farmers
W^B	welfare of bandits

Note that total population, n, is exogenous.

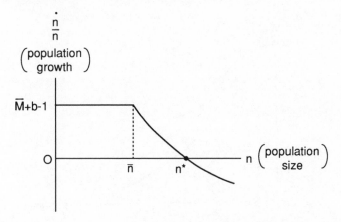

Figure 13 The effect of population size on population growth

is to impose diminishing returns to labour in agriculture and to ensure that output per hour of labour $(Q/n^F L^F)$ falls as labour input increases. To see how population grows, and when it stops growing, it is useful to begin by imagining an economy without banditry so that $n^B = L^G = 0$ and $V^F = 1$. In such an economy, population growth depresses output per person, while the fall in output per person lowers the rate of population growth, until the economy evolves into a stationary state with no further change in output or population. Output per farmer, Y^F, is $F(n,Y^F)/n$, which declines steadily as n increases. As illustrated in Figure 12, the mortality rate from natural causes, $1 - M(Y^F)$, is constant as long as $Y^F > \overline{Y}$, but it begins to rise as Y falls below $\overline{Y}$. Equation (10) reduces to $\dot{n}/n = M(Y^F) + b - 1$, where $M(Y^F) = \overline{M}$ whenever $Y^F > \overline{Y}$, and $M(Y^F) < \overline{M}$, otherwise. The expression $\overline{M} + b - 1$ is assumed to be positive, for otherwise population would decline indefinitely.

The relation between population size, n, and population growth, $\dot{n}/n$, in a world without banditry is illustrated in Figure 13. The pattern of population growth is marked by two critical values of the size of population, $\overline{n}$, below which the income per farmer is high enough that the mortality rate from natural causes is minimal and therefore unaffected by small changes in income, and n*, beyond which income per farmer is so low, and the corresponding mortality rate from natural causes so high, that population declines. Clearly, $n^* > \overline{n}$. As long as $n < \overline{n}$, populational growth is constant and as large as it can ever be. When population is between $\overline{n}$ and n* population continues to grow but at a decreasing rate. All growth stops when the population reaches n*. Specifically, the value of $\overline{n}$ is the solution to the equation $Y = F(\overline{n},Y)/\overline{n}$ when $Y = \overline{Y}$, the lowest value of Y for which the mortality rate is minimal. The values of n* and Y* (consumption per head when the population is n*) are determined simultaneously

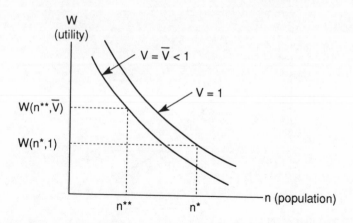

Figure 14 Violence and welfare in the long run. W(n*,1) is utility in the stationary state without violence, W(n**,$\overline{V}$) is utility in the stationary state with violence

from the equations $Y^* = F(n^*,Y^*)/n$ and $M(Y^*) + b - 1 = 0$, where the latter equation signifies that the birth rate just equals the death rate and the population remains constant for ever.

Though population *growth* remains constant until n reaches $\overline{n}$, output per head is declining steadily and utility is declining as well. This is illustrated by the downward sloping curves in Figure 14. For this economy without banditry, the outer curve shows how the typical person's utility (on the vertical axis) declines as total population (on the horizontal axis) increases. The inner curve is drawn on the assumption that mortality is somehow reduced by spontaneous violence; the survival rate is reduced from $M(Y^F)$ to $VM(Y^F)$, where $V < 1$. Equation (10) becomes $\dot{n}/n = VM(Y^F) + b - 1$, where $V = 1$ in the absence of spontaneous violence, and $V < 1$ otherwise. With or without violence, the response of population growth to real income leads the economy to a stationary state. When $V = 1$ (the outer curve), the equilibrium population in the stationary state is n*, as in Figure 13, and the welfare of the typical person is W(n*,1). When $V = \overline{V}$ < 1 (the inner curve), the equilibrium population is n** (where n** < n*) and the welfare of the typical person is W(n**,$\overline{V}$).

A curious feature of this model of anarchy can be summed up in the proposition that a little violence is good for you in the long run. Necessarily, the birth rate must equal the death rate when population is stationary. For an economy without violence, this implies that $b = 1 - M(Y_1)$ for some value Y_1 of Y^F. Add a certain risk of death by violence and the identity between birth rate and death rate becomes $b = 1 - \overline{V}M(Y_2)$ for some other value Y_2 of Y^F. Comparing these equations, it follows immediately that $1 - b = M(Y_1) = M(Y_2)\overline{V}$ which can only be so if $Y_2 > Y_1$. Welfare in the stationary state without violence is $W(n^*,1)$, which is equal to $(1-b)u(Y_1)$. Welfare in the stationary state with violence is $W(n^{**},\overline{V})$, which is equal to $(1-b)u(Y_2)$, and is necessarily larger than $W(n^*,1)$. The effect of the introduction of violence is to decrease the size of the equilibrium population but, at the same time, to increase the welfare per head.

This seemingly perverse relation among stationary states is illustrated in Figure 14. For any given population, people are, of course, worse off if there is a risk of violent death; among stationary states, people become better off if there is a risk of violent death. To maximize the welfare of the representative person, it is better to curb population growth by violence than not at all, for the stationary-state survival rate is $1-b$ regardless, and stationary-state income is higher in a violent society than in a peaceful one. The argument requires that welfare depends on the annual survival rate regardless of whether death is by violence or by natural causes. In the first section of this chapter it was shown that everyone becomes better-off when banditry is (costlessly) eliminated, when people keep what they produce and never steal. That proposition must now be qualified. It is true of societies with fixed populations, but not necessarily among stationary states.

The inclusion of the survival rate in the welfare function introduces an additional complication. Mobility among occupations guarantees that farmers and bandits are always equally well-off, that $W^F = W^B$. It does not guarantee that they have the same incomes or mortality rates, the typical situation being that $V^B < V^F$ and $Y^B > Y^F$. Consequently the stationary state is characterized by an excess of births over deaths among farmers, an excess of deaths over births among bandits, and a slightly greater propensity for children of farmers to become bandits than for children of bandits to become farmers.

Theory and content

Anarchy as described here is the nastiest society imaginable, a society so unpleasant that Hobbes could employ the spectre of anarchy to frighten his readers into embracing the Leviathan, which, so he argued, is the only real alternative. Yet primitive societies without formal government are often quite different from the picture we have drawn. Our model abstracts completely from the possibility of informal cooperation. Tribal societies, with populations small enough that people get to know one another and with military technology simple enough that domination of the many by the few can be prevented, do evolve informal rules of behaviour that people feel obliged to respect and to enforce. There is voluntary cooperation. Members of such societies recognize one another's rights as specified by the traditions of the group. It seems doubtful whether the efficacy of voluntary cooperation in small primitive societies extends to large industrial societies. The model of anarchy may be a better description of relations among societies than of relations among people within them. Tribal warfare, the chaos in Europe in the early feudal period before the establishment of national states, or the uglier aspects of modern international relations do conform to some extent to our model of anarchy.

But our model of anarchy is not intended as a description of societies as they are or as they have been. It is an ideal type — comparable in this respect to perfect competition or to the despotic society in the next chapter — put forward to exemplify tendencies rather then to describe societies as a whole. We wish to be able to say of certain rules, events or institutions that they represent a move toward anarchy or that they entail social costs similar to the social cost of anarchy. That is the context in which a full-blown, uncompromising model of anarchy is useful.

The model is also useful as a foil for other models of society. The model of anarchy tells us something about the model of perfect competition, for example, by emphasizing the implications of alternative assumptions. From our point of view, the main assumption of the model of perfect competition is security of property, attained effortlessly and at no cost to the participants in the economy. There is no better way of pointing out the implications of that assumption than by designing a society where the only security is one's ability to defend what one has from predators and where the process of taking and defending is costly and dangerous.

Having described anarchy, with its total absence of cooperation or collective security, we now proceeed to examine the two other types of society, despotism, where cooperation is to be found only within a ruling class that exploits the rest of society for its own purposes, and the liberal society, where some degree of collective security is attained in the interests of the entire population.

Notes

1 The classic study of the economics of anarchy is Winston Bush, "Individual Welfare in Anarchy", in Gordon Tullock, ed., *Explorations in the Theory of Anarchy*, Center for the Study of Public Choice, 1972. Some of the ideas in that paper are developed in W. Bush and L.S. Mayer, "Some Implications of Anarchy for the Distribution of Property", *Journal of Economic Theory*, 1974, 401–12. Though I draw heavily on the analysis in these articles, I argue in Chapter VI that there are *no* implications of anarchy for the distribution of property. See also Gordon Tullock, ed., *Further Explorations in the Theory of Anarchy*, University Publications, 1974.

There would seem to be two opposite pictures of anarchy in the literature on the subject, the nasty picture and the nice picture. To Winston Bush, as to Hobbes, a state of nature without government is unreservedly nasty, with no redeeming features. There is, however, a school of anarchist thought according to which people without government do somehow cooperate, while government is nothing more than the exploitation of one lot of people by another. John R. Umbeck (*A Theory of Property Rights with Applications to the California Gold Rush*, Iowa State

University Press, 1981) argues that property rights can be respected in the absence of a magistrate. Michael Taylor (*Community, Anarchy and Liberty*, Cambridge University Press, 1982) examines the social organization of tribes that manage to live peacefully without governments or formal mechanisms for enforcing rules, and he speculates on whether and to what extent a modern industrial society could do the same. For a history of anarchist thought, see David Miller, *Anarchism*, Dent, 1984.

So far as I can tell, the essence of the "anarchist" position, as exemplified by Umbeck, is that anarchy is not inefficient because potential inefficiencies are always eliminated through mutually advantageous trades. Referring to Figure 8, the anarchist argument is that if ever a situation arises where the presence of banditry, or some other source of inefficiency, reduces the income per head to Y^* from a higher potential value of $\overline{Y}^w$, the participants in society will strike a bargain that raises the income per head to $\overline{Y}^w$ and shares the surplus ($\overline{Y}^w - Y^*$), so as to make everybody better off.

Such a bargain can only be struck if three conditions are met. The parties must be able to communicate with one another. They must be able to agree on a rule for sharing the surplus. Their promises to one another must be credible; each party must be confident that, if he keeps his part of the bargain, the other parties will keep theirs. The model of anarchy in this chapter is of a world where none of these conditions holds. Umbeck, on the other hand, constructs a model where they do. He imagines a group of gold miners who occupy a territory suitable for mining and who must allocate the territory among themselves before mining can begin. There is no government and nothing stops one person from taking land from another, except the latter's willingness to resist. By assumption, land is taken — never output. Taking and defending are labour-using processes. The potential inefficiency in the model is the reduction in the total output of gold as labour is diverted from mining to fighting. Umbeck proposes a mechanism through which this potential inefficiency is avoided.

The essence of the mechanism is this. If I want an acre of your land, I present myself to you and demand it. Recognizing the alternative use of labour in gold mining, each of us calculates the number of man-hours he would be willing to devote to taking or defending. It is assumed that each of us knows what the land is worth to the other and who would win the fight over the land if we each devoted as much labour to fighting as the land is worth. The would-be winner takes the land, and the other party — the original occupant or the predator as the case may be — withdraws. The fight, if it occurred, would be resource-using, but the confrontation is not, by assumption, as long as one party backs down. Umbeck argues — correctly, in my opinion — that there is an allocation of land for which no marginal predation is advantageous to the predator. That allocation is the anarchic equilibrium.

The key assumption in the model, without which nothing is established, is that each person "offers" to devote as many man-hours to the fight over the land as the land is worth to him — no more, no less — despite the fact that (on the assumptions of the model) each person knows that he could have the land for nothing if he offered more than the land is worth and more than is offered by his opponent. On this assumption, Umbeck's conclusion is valid; without it, the model seems to break down completely. There is, of course, no provision in the model for one man to shoot another and take all his land, or for two people to gang up on a third, or for the possibility that labour in taking and defending must be irrevocably committed before it is determined who gets what.

There is some question in my mind whether Umbeck has a theory of anarchy or a theory of government. The model at the beginning of the book is of a balance of terror which is almost efficient; there is no waste of resources in fighting, but the influence of fighting capacity upon the allocation of land among people does not lead to the maximization of the total output of gold. Later on in the book, Umbeck describes how small groups of miners heading for the wilderness do form contracts which are enforced by the willingness of the entire group to discipline any of members who break the rules. I have no difficulty with the latter claim or with Umbeck's assertion that the contracts are often efficient. Primitive tribes and small isolated groups of people do establish implicit government, just as large, complex societies establish large, complex governments. What the anarchist must show, and what Umbeck fails to show convincingly, is that a balance of terror, or what in practice amounts to the same thing, a sense of goodness, justice and decency in all uncorrupted men, is sufficient, in itself, to generate an efficient economy with no government at all.

The model of anarchy in this chapter is about what happens when a government is not established and when rules are not collectively enforced. The model of despotism in the next chapter is about what happens when the enforcer has interests of his own. The virtues and limits of bargaining will be discussed in Chapter VII.

2 It is being assumed that E_1 and E_2 are determined in a Nash equilibrium where the first party chooses E_1 to maximize $p_1 R - E_1$ in the belief that E_2 is invariant and where the second party chooses E_2 accordingly. It is also assumed that there is no risk aversion; contestants are indifferent between a probability p of an award R and a certainty of pR. Party 1 chooses E_1 to maximize

$$\left[\alpha + (1 - \alpha - \beta) \left(\frac{E_1^\delta}{E_1^\delta + E_2^\delta} \right) \right] R - E_1$$

The first-order condition is

$$(1 - \alpha - \beta) R \frac{E_2^\delta}{(E_1^\delta + E_2^\delta)^2} \delta E_1^{\delta-1} - 1 = 0$$

By symmetry, E_1 and E_2 have to be the same in equilibrium; their common value is E. Therefore

$$(1 - \alpha - \beta) R \frac{E^\delta}{(E^\delta + E^\delta)^2} \delta E^{\delta-1} = 1$$

or

$$(1 - \alpha - \beta) R \frac{(E^\delta)^2}{(2E^\delta)^2} \frac{1}{E} = 1$$

which implies that

$$E = \frac{\delta(1 - \alpha - \beta) R}{4}$$

3 Such a model is presented in Gary S. Becker, "A Theory of Competition among Pressure Groups for Political Influence", *Quarterly Journal of Economics*, 1983, 371–400. Each group's net transfer from the government is an increasing function of the pressure that the group exerts. The model contains no explanation of the innards of government or of what the government is supposed to be maximizing in responding as it does. The model is discussed in Chapter IX.

4 The expected net revenue of contestant i is

$$p_i R - E_i = M\left(\frac{E_i}{E_i + \ldots + E_n}\right) - E_i$$

Maximizing this with respect to E_i yields the first-order condition

$$\frac{R}{(E_1 + \ldots + E_n)^2}[(E_1 + \ldots + E_n) - E_i] - 1 = 0$$

Since all E_i are the same in equilibrium, it follows at once that

$$R(n - 1)/n^2 = E$$

which is equation (9) in the next.

5 Absence of land from the production function is not as unrealistic as the reader might at first suppose. Pure anarchy, where each person is literally solitary and the enemy of every other person, has never to the best of my knowledge been observed. Relations approaching anarchy may occur among tribes. Disease or mortality from intertribal warfare could reduce population to the point where the marginal product of land falls to zero. On the absence of property rights in pre-colonial Burma, see J.S. Furnival, "Land as a Free Gift of Nature", *Economic Journal*, 1909, 552–62.

6 The Lagrangian of the problem is

$$\pounds = f(L^F) [1 - g(L^G, n^T/n^F)] - \lambda[L^F + L^G - 1]$$

The first-order conditions are

$$\partial\pounds/\partial L^F = f'[1 - g] - \lambda = 0$$

and

$$\partial\pounds/\partial L^G = -fg_1 - \lambda = 0$$

Eliminating λ, we see that

$$f'[1 - g] = -fg_1$$

7 The income-of-the-worker curve is necessarily downward sloping. Substituting equations (1.2) and (1.5) into equation (1.7) and differentiating equation (1.7) totally, we see that

$$dY^F = -[(1 - g) f' + fg_1] dL^G - fg_2 \frac{d}{dn^B}\left(\frac{n^B}{n^F}\right) dn^B$$

Eliminating the expression in square brackets by means of equation (1.6), we see that

$$\frac{dY^F}{dn^B} = -fg_2 \frac{d}{dn^B}\left(\frac{n^B}{n^F}\right) < 0$$

because f, g_2 and $d/dn^T(n^B/n^F)$ are all positive.

8 The equivalence follows from equations (1.7), (1.9), (1.11) and (1.13) of the original model, namely $Y^F = f - T$, $Y^B = \pi (1 - D)$, $n^B\pi = n^FT$, and $Y^F = Y^B$. Substituting these equations into the expression $DT(n^F/n)$, we see that

$$DT(n^F/n) = \left(1 - \frac{n^B(f - T)}{Tn^F}\right)\frac{Tn^F}{n} = \frac{Tn^F - n^BfT}{n}$$

$$= \left[\frac{(f - Y^F)(n^F + n^B) - n^Bf}{n^F + n^B}\right]\frac{n - \overline{n}^C}{n}$$

$$= \left[\frac{n^Ff}{n^F + n^B} - Y^F\right]\frac{n - \overline{n}^C}{n}$$

9 By definition,

$$x-y = \max_{n^C} U\left(\frac{n - n^C}{n} f(1), \frac{n^Cr}{n}\right) - U\left(\frac{n - \overline{n}^C}{n} f(1), \frac{\overline{n}^Cr}{n}\right)$$

$$= \int_{\overline{n}^C}^{n^{*C}} \left(\frac{dU}{dn^C}\right) dn^C$$

where n^{*C} is the utility-maximizing value of n^C

$$= \int_{\overline{n}^C}^{n^{*C}} \left(-U_F\left(\frac{f(1)}{n}\right) + U_C\left(\frac{r}{n}\right)\right) dn^C$$

$$= \int_{\overline{n}^C}^{n^{*C}} \left(\left(\frac{U_C}{U_F} - \frac{f(1)}{r}\right) U_F \frac{r}{n}\right) dn^C$$

$$\cong \int_{\overline{C}}^{C^*} \frac{U_C}{U_F} dC - \int_{\overline{C}}^{C^*} \frac{f(1)}{r} dC$$

where $dC = (r/n)dn^C$ because $NC = n^Cr$, where $\overline{C}$ and C^* are the values of C corresponding to $\overline{n}^C$ and n^{*C}, and where U_F can be dropped from the equation because it is approximately equal to one — exactly so at the point x. Note that U_C/U_F is the demand price of clothing, $f(1)/r$ is the supply price of clothing, the two integrals on the last line of equation (1.17) are the areas under the demand and supply curves for clothing between C and C^*, and the difference between these integrals is the ordinary measure of deadweight loss.

10 Real-life anarchy is dangerous too. The anthropologist Napoleon A. Chagnon found that normal intertribal warfare accounted for 24 per cent of male deaths among the Yanomamos of Brazil and Venezuela. See *Yanomamo: the Fierce People*, Holt Rinehart & Winston, 1968, 20.

11 The variables E, H and L^G are determined in a Nash equilibrium; bandits choose H and E, anticipating farmers' choice of L^G, while farmers choose L^G, anticipating bandits' choice of E and H.

Chapter IV

Despotism[1]

Webster's dictionary defines despotism as "rule or government by a despot; autocracy". That is not quite the usage in this chapter. The term is used to denote government in the interest of a ruling class that may be organized as a strict hierarchy with a semi-divine figure at the apex or as an oligarchy with little differentiation in wealth or status among its members. The ruling class, or upper stratum of society, is unconstrained by elections, though, as we shall see, there must be constraints of a different kind.

To say that rulers serve their own interest rather than that of their subjects is not to say that the subjects are necessarily worse off under despotism than they would be in a state of anarchy. Hobbes's argument to the contrary is probably right, though it does not touch upon the question of whether some other form of government altogether — neither anarchy nor despotism — might be decidedly better than either. Hobbes justified obedience to an absolute sovereign by pointing to the dreadful state of mankind under anarchy and to the self-interest of the sovereign in promoting the welfare of his subjects. Of anarchy Hobbes observed

that the estate of man can never be without some incommodity or other; and that the greatest, that in any form of Government can possibly happen to the people in generale, is scarce sensible, in respect of the miseries and horrible calamities, that accompany a Civill Warre; or that dissolute condition of masterlesse men without subjection to Laws, and a coërcive power to tye their hands from rapine and revenge.

Of despotism, he observed that

the greatest pressure of Soveraign Governours, proceedeth not from any delight, or profit, they can expect in the dammage, or weakening of their own Subjects, in whose vigor, consisteth their own strength and glory.[2]

The main task of this chapter is to deal with Hobbes's second assertion precisely — to explain the distribution of income between rulers and subjects and, in some cases, among the grades in the ruling hierarchy.

Economists are accustomed to explain incomes of people in different occupations by their marginal products of labour or, more generally, by the marginal products of the factors of production they possess. This type of explanation is clearly inappropriate for a ruling class which, almost by definition, need not respect the outcome of the market. Yet the ruling class must decide how much of the national income to take for itself and how much to leave in the hands of the ordinary subjects. Something must be constraining rulers from appropriating the entire national income. The bulk of the chapter is a sequence of simple models, each incorporating a different constraint. At a minimum, rulers are constrained by the need to leave their subjects with a subsistence income, where subsistence may be interpreted as the physiological minimum to keep alive and working or as the demographic minimum to enable the working class to reproduce itself. A more stringent constraint emerges from the connection between the worker's income and his efficiency; people may be unable to work hard when they are poorly paid. If so, rulers have an incentive to pay what has come to be called an efficiency wage. Beyond that, rulers may be constrained by the prospect of banditry. In a development of the model of anarchy in Chapter III it will be shown that there is an equilibrium division of the population of subjects between tax-paying farmers and bandits who must be hunted down by the ruling class, and that the number of bandits is low when the return to farming is high. The prospect of rebellion by their subjects is an additional constraint upon the rulers. Where rebellion is dangerous for rulers and rebels alike, and where everyone's utility depends on his mortality rate as well as upon his income, there is an incentive on the part of the ruler to provide his subjects with incomes high enough that it is not in their interest to rebel. Finally, the distribution of income within the ruling hierarchy can be modelled as depending on the risk of a *coup d'état* at each level of the ruling hierarchy. These five models of the exploitative income distribution — subsistence, efficiency, banditry, rebellion, and *coup d'état* — are logically distinct, but they exert a cumulative influence upon the rulers' choice of incomes for their subjects and for themselves.

Models of despotism can be useful in several ways. The first and most obvious is to explain income distributions in societies that really are despotic. The incomes of the mandarins of imperial China, the bureaucracy of ancient Rome, the kings and nobility in the Middle Ages and the Nomenklatura in contemporary communist countries were determined in a manner that cannot be represented by the models of non-violent, property-respecting, benevolently governed societies which are the stock-in-trade of ordinary economic analysis. Our models of depotism are intended to fill the gap. Second, a model of the ruling class in a purely despotic society may serve, together with the model of government-as-maximizer-of-social-welfare in traditional welfare economics, as polar cases between which the actual real-life governments lie. No government is exactly like either model. All governments share some of the features of both. The substantial growth of the public sector over the last fifty years in virtually every country in the world has been accompanied by an increasing dissatisfaction with the political assumption of traditional welfare economics, but, as discussed in Chapter IX, it has proved rather difficult to construct a model that reflects what actual governments do and how they are motivated. A model of despotic government may be of some help in this context, if only as an antidote to the extreme assumptions in traditional welfare economics. Third, and most important in the context of this book, the models of anarchy and despotism may serve as representations of opposing tendencies within a liberal society. Markets that work badly share some of the characteristics of anarchy. Governments that work badly share some of the characteristics of despotism, though the beneficiaries of public sector predation are not confined to the personnel of the public sector and may include groups in the private sector as well.

How to model despotism

The distribution of income in a despotic society is a complex phenomenon which I attempt to analyse by isolating each of five constraints upon the ruling class in a separate model of the despotic economy. The models themselves share common features and common assumptions about such matters as cooperation within the ruling class, the objectives of the ruling class, the functions of rulers in society, the organization of rulers, the sources of rebellion and population growth. These and other features of despotism are discussed in this section, before I proceed to the detailed presentation of the models.

Cooperation and expectations
It is hardly surprising that there is no role for cooperation in our model of anarchy, for anarchy is almost synonymous with the absence of cooperation. By contrast, rulers must cooperate in the deployment of violence to punish disobedient subjects and to suppress rebellion. The first law of fighting is that, other things being equal, the larger force can defeat the smaller one. The ruling class must therefore ensure that the disobedient subject or rebel will in the end be outnumbered in battle. This does not imply that there need be more rulers than subjects, only that rulers can always pull together a larger force than disobedient subjects or rebels can command. A small class of rulers can dominate a large class of subjects if cooperation among subjects can be thwarted, so that each subject is powerless against the combined weight of all members of the ruling class. Ten rulers dominate 100 subjects as long as conspiracy among the subjects can be detected before the number of conspirators exceeds five and as

long as the technology of battle is such that the ten always emerge victorious.

The role of expectations may be critical in cementing the required co-operation among rulers.[3] Imagine a society with five people called A, B, C, D and E where the technology of fighting is such that any three can defeat (and impose severe punishment upon) the remaining two. It would be an 'expectational equilibrium' for A to be the leader, and the others to obey A regardless of whether his commands serve their interests, as long as each of B, C, D and E has come to believe (i) that the other three will come to the aid of A in fighting him if he ceases to obey A and (ii) that if, for instance, B ceases to obey A and C refuses to help A fight B, then A, D and E will fight and defeat B and C together. With these expectations, each party believes that the others would punish him for disobedience, just as he himself would participate in punishing others. The leader could demand whatever he pleased of his followers as long as compliance remained less painful than defeat and punishment.

The example requires at least five people for the structure of expectations to be credible. With only three people — A, B and C, of whom A is the leader — B might say to himself that he need not obey because, if he disobeys and is fought by A, it will become immediately evident to C that he can equally well fight on the side of B as on the side of A. Putting themselves in the place of C and imagining what they would do in his shoes, both A and B realize that C will not fight on the side of A unless A's rule is mild enough that C would rather accept A's rule than trust his luck to the outcome of a three-way battle. Once B has shown his disobedience to A, there can be no more uncertainty for C because C can always place himself in some two-to-one majority. The addition of a fourth person, D, is not yet sufficient to make expectations credible, because once B disobeys, C can still combine with B to form a coalition that will not be outnumbered no matter what D chooses to do. The addition of the fifth person is, strictly speaking, sufficient to ensure that B's announcement of disobedience gives no other person the assurance that he can join B and not be on the weaker side in a battle.

With five people, the expectations that generate the example are consistent though hardly plausible. They are consistent in the sense that nobody expects disobedience and it does not occur. They are implausible in the sense that, if there really were only five people in a community and if the leader were appropriating a great deal more income for himself than was allocated to his followers, the followers would soon begin to complain to one another and communication among the followers would lead to a change in expectations about who would support whom in battle.

These expectations become more plausible when ten rulers confront forty subjects in circumstances where the spoils of office are shared more or less equally among the ten and where distance or surveillance by rulers places limits upon the number of subjects who can coordinate their actions in a conspiracy to rebel. No such conspiracy can succeed if rulers can always detect the conspiracy when the number of conspirators grows to — say — fifteen and if rulers can intimidate the remaining subjects to assist in defeating the conspirators. When the total population is increased from five to fifty, it becomes more difficult for potentially rebellious subjects to coordinate their activities and more likely that subjects not directly involved in the rebellion will be afraid not to support rulers against rebels, for concerted action among thirty is very much more difficult than among three.

What rulers maximize

However much they may differ in their opportunities and their constraints, rulers and subjects are always assumed to be alike in their tastes. When the consequences of one's actions include a risk of death, as was the case in the complete model of anarchy, then the rulers, like the farmers and the bandits, arrange their affairs to provide themselves with high incomes and low mortality rates. Specifically, in a stationary state where one year is like the next, they are assumed to maximize welfare, W, defined as

$$W = Su(Y) \tag{1}$$

where S is the survival rate per decade, Y is income and u is a concave "utility of income" function. The mortality rate, $1 - S$, is a compound of mortality from natural causes and from violence. The source of violence may be an encounter with bandits or rivalry within the ruling class.

What rulers do

Rulers collect taxes, hunt bandits and suppress rebellion. The income of the rulers is acquired by taxing peasant proprietors or by dividing the land among the rulers and collecting rents. Tax rates or rents are set to maximize the rulers' welfare regardless of the consequences for their subjects. This need not imply that wages are forced down to bare subsistence, or that subjects are literally on the brink of starvation. Rulers may have an interest in keeping wages high for a variety of reasons to be discussed in this chapter. The chapter will conclude with a brief discussion of whether and in what circumstances the subjects are enslaved.

As tax collectors, landowners or slave owners, rulers are in opposition to their subjects, for any increase in the income of one class is necessarily at the expense of the other. As hunters of bandits, rulers convey benefits to their subjects by reducing the share of the farmer's crop that is appropriated by bandits and by diminishing the risk to the farmer's life in defending his crop. It cannot be said *a priori* whether farmers are on balance better off under despotism than in anarchy. Farmers are better off to the extent that the incidence of banditry has been reduced. They are worse off in having to pay taxes to predatory rulers.

The organization of the ruling class

The ruling class may be organized as a Spartan oligarchy or as a strict hierarchy. A Spartan oligarchy is a group of rulers who are strictly equal among themselves and who collectively exploit their subjects as best they can. It is analytically convenient to assume a strict equality among members of the ruling class because the assumption confines the analysis to three supposedly homogeneous groups — farmers, rulers and bandits. The size of the ruling class may be historically determined or it might have been chosen to maximize the welfare of the typical member of the class. It is easy enough to imagine a ruling class increasing its size by elevating some subjects to the status of rulers, if the ruling class is initially too small. It is not so easy to imagine how the ruling class might go about reducing its numbers, though a reduction might be arranged gradually by strict primogeniture or by some other rule of social organization. On the other hand, members of a ruling class would normally be unable to act cooperatively in suppressing rebellion and hunting bandits unless they were organized in a hierarchy. A complete model of hierarchy would require an explanation of the number of ranks, the size of each rank, the distribution of income among ranks, and the pros and cons of rebellion at each rank.

No attempt will be made to construct a complete model of a hierarchical ruling class. Instead, it will be assumed in one of the models in this chapter that there is a strict hierarchy, with fixed, technically given numbers at each rank. One king can supervise ten dukes, each duke can supervise ten counts, and so on, through as many ranks as are necessary to supervise the serfs who ultimately do the work and who, in the limit and in a society with rulers and farmers but no bandits, constitute eight-ninths of the population.

Sources of rebellion

Rulers are never entirely secure. They may be displaced by the armies of other states, by rebellion within the ruling hierarchy, by a peasant revolt or by a gang of bandits who become gradually stronger and stronger until they are in a position to challenge the state. We shall be primarily concerned here with peasant revolts and rebellion within the ruling hierarchy. We ignore external threats to concentrate on the innards of a despotic society.

The distribution of income

A major point of contrast between an ordinary competitive economy and a despotic society, as modelled here, is that the distribution of income in a competitive economy is based on the marginal productivity of owned factors of production, while the distribution of income in a despotic society is based on fear. In our models of despotic society, total output must, of course, depend on the productivity of factors of production, but the income of rulers depends on what they can effectively take rather than upon their contribution to production. Rulers and bandits are alike in this respect.

Income must be allocated among social classes, within the ruling class and among successful rebels displacing a defeated ruling class. The distribution among rulers, farmers and bandits is most conveniently analysed by assuming that rulers share the spoils of office equally and that bandits act individually and alone rather than in gangs. When the hierarchy among rulers is taken into account, the distribution of income within the ruling class is determined by the ability of the occupants of the lower ranks of the hierarchy to rebel. Rebellion is always dangerous, for rulers and for rebels. The potential rebel desists from rebellion as long as the risk to his life (for there is only one punishment in the model) outweighs his expected gain as a successful rebel. The ruler sets wages high enough at each rank of the hierarchy for this to be so. Wages increase with rank because occupants of high ranks are particularly well situated as potential rebels and require larger incomes as obedient functionaries if rebellion is to remain unattractive.

The allocation of roles
Where there is a choice, each actor in the economy chooses his role to maximize his welfare, inclusive of income and the mortality rate. The choice between becoming a farmer or a bandit is the same under despotism as in anarchy, except that the bandit's mortality rate is increased when he is opposed by organized rulers as well as by the unorganized farmers on whom he preys. Presumably, rulers will not choose to become bandits or farmers as long as the income of rulers exceeds that of bandits and farmers. Rulers occupying junior posts in a strict hierarchy might choose to rebel, but the man at the top has an incentive to provide his subordinates with incomes high enough that rebellion is not on balance advantageous.

The initial allocation of places in a ruling hierarchy will not be explained. Though one can imagine a process by which anarchy gives way to despotism as a ruling class gradually eliminates its rivals and solidifies its authority, we shall think of the allocation of places in the hierarchy as an historical fact, exogenous to the model of despotism, just as the distribution of property and talent is exogenous to a model of perfect competition. Our theory of despotism is primarily a theory about its stability, though the origin and possible evolution of despotism will be discussed in Chapter VI.

Population growth
It is a small step from mortality rates to population growth. As in the model of anarchy, the economy may evolve into a stationary state when the birth rate remains constant and mortality increases with the size of the population. But there is another possibility. As will be explained in Chapter

VI, a society may alternate over time between anarchy and despotism in a manner reminiscent of the dynastic cycle in Chinese history.

Five principles of income distribution in a despotic society

Features of a despotic society are incorporated into a sequence of five models, each with a different constraint upon predation by the ruling class: the subsistence wage, the efficiency wage, control of banditry, fear of rebellion, and fear of a *coup d'état*.

The subsistence wage

Imagine a society with n^R rulers and a subject population of n^F farmers who are so intimidated by the ruling class that they accept whatever income the rulers choose to allow and nobody turns to banditry. Rulers set the farmers' income, Y^F, and determine the number of farmers, L, who are permitted to work at that income. Excess farmers must emigrate or starve. There is a fixed supply of land. Total output, Q, depends on inputs of land and labour, but, as the input of land is invariant, the production function, F, can be represented as dependent on labour alone as long as there is a diminishing marginal product of labour.

$$Q = F(L), F(0) = 0, F' > 0 \text{ and } F'' < 0 \tag{2}$$

where $L \leq n^F$, and $L = n^F$ means that all farmers are employed. For convenience, it is assumed that the number of hours of work per farmer per year is invariant, so that input of labour is represented completely by the number of farmers employed.

A subsistence wage may be defined with reference to physiology or to demography. With reference to physiology, the subsistence wage, $\overline{Y}$, is an income below which one cannot afford to buy food and other necessities to keep oneself alive and working. To postulate a subsistence wage in this extreme sense of the term is to say that a farmer's marginal product drops precipitously to zero whenever the wage falls below $\overline{Y}$. Define $\overline{L}$ to be the number of workers such that their marginal product is just equal to $\overline{Y}$; that is, $F'(\overline{L}) = \overline{Y}$. With reference to demography, the subsistence wage is an income at which the birth and death rates are the same, so that the population neither increases nor decreases over time. When the birth rate, b, is assumed constant, and the survival rate, S(Y), is an increasing function of income, the subsistence wage, $\tilde{Y}$, is that for which

$$S(\tilde{Y}) + b = 1 \tag{3}$$

Define $\tilde{L}$ to be the number of workers such that their marginal product is just equal to $\tilde{Y}$; that is, $F'(\tilde{L}) = \tilde{Y}$. Assume, for convenience, that the demographic subsistence wage exceeds the physiological subsistence wage; that is, $\tilde{Y} > \overline{Y}$.

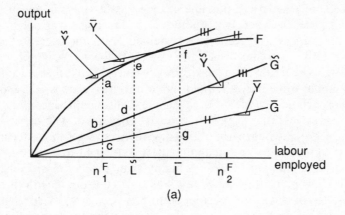

(a)

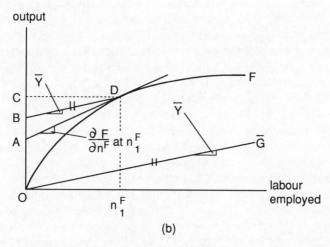

(b)

Figure 15 Incomes of rulers and farmers. When there are n_1^F farmers the return to land is OA with free labour, OB with slave labour

The rulers' options are illustrated in Figure 15(a), with total output represented on the vertical axis and input of labour represented on the horizontal axis. Three curves are shown: a production function, F, specifying how total output depends on the input of labour; a return-to-labour curve, $\overline{G}$, specifying how total income of labour varies with the number of farmers employed when the wage is fixed at $\overline{Y}$; and a second return-to-labour curve, $\tilde{G}$, specifying how total income of labour varies with the number of farmers employed when the wage is fixed at $\tilde{Y}$. Rulers' total income is the difference between the heights of the production function and the return-to-labour curve at the going wage and at the actual input of labour. Since the wage must be at least equal to $\overline{Y}$ if workers are to produce at all, the largest possible income for the rulers in any given year is the distance (fg) when $\overline{L}$ workers are employed at a wage of $\overline{Y}$. But an income as large as (fg) cannot be sustained over time because the population of farmers declines when the wage is as low as $\overline{Y}$. To preserve the work force, the ruling class must offer a wage of $\tilde{Y}$. At that wage the best size of labour force from the point of view of the rulers is $\hat{L}$, yielding the rulers an income of (ed) — their maximal sustainable income — which is necessarily less than (fg). The ruler is a fisherman who can choose to maximize his catch each year, allowing the stock of fish to decline over time, or to maintain the maximum sustainable yield from his resource.

If the actual number of farmers at any given time were n_1^F which is less than either $\overline{L}$ or $\hat{L}$, the ruling class would be confronted with three main options. It could act myopically, setting the wage at $\overline{Y}$ for which the rulers' income, (ac), is maximal in the current year but destined to decline as the population of farmers declines. It could set the wage at $\tilde{Y}$, for which the rulers' income, (ab), is less than ac but sustainable over time. Or it could choose a wage in excess of $\tilde{Y}$ so as to allow the population of farmers to rise gradually toward $\hat{L}$, at which the rulers' sustainable income is maximized. On the other hand, if the actual number of farmers were n_2^F, which is greater than either $\hat{L}$ or $\overline{L}$, and if the ruling class were myopic, the ruling class would immediately banish $n_2^F - \overline{L}$ workers and set the farmers' wage at $\overline{Y}$. Otherwise, depending on the rulers' rate of discount, some farmers might be banished and the wage would be set at or close to $\overline{Y}$. Over time, the wage would gradually rise to $\tilde{Y}$ and the number of farmers would gradually fall to something less than $\hat{L}$.

Note particularly that the ruling class in this model of despotism is more than the collectivity of landowners, and need not own land at all. The ruling class chooses the number of farmers and exacts tribute, which may be called tax or rent. In a competitive economy with constant returns to scale for land and labour together, and where the financial role of the public sector may be ignored, the income of the landless farmer is the full marginal product of labour. In a despotic society the income of the farmer, as set by the ruling class, is less — perhaps very much less — than the marginal product of labour. Suppose the population of farmers is n_1^F, where $n_1^F < \overline{L}$. Figure 15(b) reproduces the production function from Figure 15(a). With a labour force of n_1^F, the marginal product of labour is represented by the slope of the tangent, AD, to the production function at n_1^F. Thus the total income of the farmers when they are paid the value of their marginal products is the distance AC, and the corresponding rulers' income is the distance OA. But rulers are not as a class compelled to offer farmers a total income of AC. They can offer as little as CB, which is the physiological subsistence income as indicated in Figure 15(a). Myopic rulers would offer a wage of as little as $\overline{Y}$, raising their total income from OA (which is the return to land in a competitive economy) to OB. Rulers with some concern for the future would offer workers more than CB but not necessarily as much as AC.

The economic organization of agriculture depends critically on the technology of tax collection and the organization of the ruling class. Rulers may be content to allow farmers to "own" the land if ample public revenue can be obtained from a head tax on farmers, if rulers are confident that their privileges will be maintained indefinitely once they have divorced themselves from production, and if rulers are not deterred by the prospect of life in the strict hierarchy that an administrative ruling class must be. Otherwise, if rulers insist on owning land themselves, and if it is very much easier for rulers to extract income by rent than by taxation, the wage that is best for the ruling class as a whole can be sustained only by tying the worker to the land, so that a worker who is dissatisfied with his wage on one farm cannot seek a higher wage in another. Whether this condition is tantamount to slavery will be discussed at the end of the chapter.

The efficiency wage[4]

The concept of the efficiency wage is a generalization of the concept of the subsistence wage. Instead of supposing that there is a fixed wage, $\overline{Y}$, above which the farmer works at 100 per cent efficiency and below which he cannot work at all, it might be supposed that there is a continuous relation between wage and productivity. Specifically the production function becomes

$$Q = F(L, Y^F) \tag{4}$$

where Q is total output, L is input of labour and Y^F is the farmers' wage, which is assumed to affect output continuously. By assumption,

$$F_L > 0, \ F_{LL} < 0, \ F_Y \geq 0 \ \text{and} \ F_{YY} \leq 0 \tag{5}$$

where F_Y and F_n mean $\partial F / \partial Y^F$ and $\partial F / \partial n^F$ respectively. The inequalities are not strict, signifying, for instance, that Q may increase with Y^F up to some limiting value of Y^F, beyond which $F_Y = 0$. To focus upon the peculiarities of the efficiency wage, it is assumed initially that the population of farmers, n^F, is invariant over time.

Now the ruling class has two decisions: whether to employ the entire work force, and how high a wage to allow. If all farmers are employed (i.e. if $L = n^F$), then the wage, Y^F, is chosen to maximize the rulers' income, $F(n^F, Y^F) - n^F Y^F$, and the optimal wage from the point of view of the rulers is identified by the first-order condition

$$F_Y(n^F, Y^F) = n^F \tag{6}$$

The optimal wage is that for which the cost saving, n^F, from a \$1 reduction in the wage is just equal to resulting fall in output, F_Y, because farmers work less well at the lower wage. In general, the optimal wage from the point of view of the ruling class is less than the marginal product of labour, the only exception being when the number of subjects is so large that it becomes advantageous to employ less than the entire work force. If rulers could choose n^F as well Y^F, the surplus would be maximized when both $F_Y = n^F$ and $F_n = Y^F$. If n^F were smaller than is necessary to satisfy the latter equation, then F_n would exceed Y^F, signifying that the subject's income falls short of his marginal product of labour.

The situation may be clarified by a simple example. Suppose the production function is

$$Q = F(L, Y^F) = 100 \, L^{1/2}(1 - 1/Y^F) \tag{7}$$

as long as $Y^F > 1$. This is an ordinary Cobb–Douglas production function connecting total output, Q, to the number of farmers employed, L, except for the term $(1 - 1/Y^F)$ which signifies that no output is produced unless farmers have an income, Y^F, of at least 1, and that output increases steadily with Y^F (for any given L) but at a progressively decreasing rate.

By maximizing the rulers' surplus, $Q - LY^F$, with respect to L and Y^F, it is easily shown[5] that the rulers' surplus is as large as it can ever be when 123 farmers are employed and that each employed farmer is paid a wage of 3.[4] In that case, total output is 741, of which 371 accrues to the rulers. Rulers can never do better than that, and would not willingly employ more than 123 farmers. Whenever n^F is less than the rulers' optimal number of farmers (123), the rulers' income is less than 371 and the efficiency wage is less than the marginal product of labour. Whenever n^F is greater than the rulers' optimal number of farmers, the excess farmers, $n^F - L$, are (if possible) removed from the economy.

Table 3 shows the effects of the number of farmers *employed*, L, upon the efficiency wage of farmers, the marginal product of labour, total output, Q, and the surplus to the ruling class, $Q - LY^F$. These effects are measured at four alternative values of L, the rulers' optimal values (123), two smaller values and one larger value. From the table one can see at a glance that the farmer's income falls from 5 to 3 as L increases from 16 to 123, that the farmer's income is below his marginal product within that range, that the marginal product of labour would be larger still if farmers had been paid the value of their marginal product, and that the surplus appropriated by the rulers is maximal (among the four values of L) when L = 123. If the number of farmers exceeds the optimal from the point of view of the rulers, the rulers would prefer to exile the surplus people. Should that be impossible, the income of the farmer is actually set above his marginal product of labour. When L rises to 256, the income of farmer is set at 2.5 though his marginal product is only 1.9. The surplus accruing to the rulers is reduced from 371 to 320.

Optimal policy toward farmers — the choice of Y^F and, if possible, L — is so far independent of the number of rulers, for rulers do not work and

Table 3   *The efficiency wage of farmers and the income of the ruling class*

Number of farmers employed (L)	Efficiency wage of farmers (Y^F)	Marginal product of labour when farmers are paid the efficiency wage	Marginal product of labour when farmers are paid their marginal product	Total output (Q)	Surplus to rulers ($Q - LY^F$)
16	5	10	11.4	320	240
81	$3^{1/3}$	3.9	4.2	630	360
123	3	3	3	741	371
256	2.5	1.9	–	960	320

The construction of the table is explained in note 5.

Of the values of L in the first column, three are fourth powers of 2, 3 and 4 respectively (so that the reader can easily check the arithmetic) and the fourth (123) is the value of L yielding the largest surplus to the rulers.

In the second column Y^F is the wage to the farmers that maximizes the income of the rulers.

The last row is calculated on the assumption that rulers must hire 256 farmers, even though they would prefer to hire no more than 123.

have no function in the model other than to collect tribute. It is not even necessary for *per capita* income of rulers to exceed the *per capita* income of subjects, though this would always be so if members of the ruling class could choose to become farmers instead. Nothing in our assumptions excluded the case where there is only one ruler, who takes the entire surplus for himself. However, this becomes unlikely if the ruling class is thought of as a monopolist-bandit who is, individually or collectively, strong enough that no one else dares become a bandit, and farmers surrender whatever portion of the crop the ruler demands.

The evolution of a despotic society can be modelled once birth rates and mortality rates are introduced. This is done by assuming that the birth rate is constant, that there is no violence and that mortality from natural causes is inversely related to income because people can expect to live longer when they are prosperous. Suppose the birth rate, b, is constant at 3 per cent per year and the mortality rate is (i) 100 per cent whenever Y is less than 2 (signifying that the physiological subsistence income, $\overline{Y}$, is equal to 2), (ii) 2 per cent whenever Y is greater than 5 (signifying no income beyond 5 has a marginal beneficial effect on one's health) and (iii) $0.01(7 - Y)$ for all Y within the range from 2 to 5. These rates are illustrated in Figure 16.

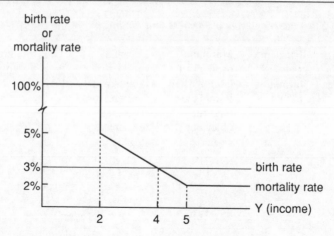

Figure 16 Income, birth rates and mortality rates in a despotic stationary state. $\overline{Y} = 2$, $\tilde{Y} = 4$

It is immediately evident from the figure that the demographic subsistence income, $\tilde{Y}$, is equal to 4; the mortality rate exceeds the birth rate whenever Y is less than 4 and the birth rate exceeds the mortality rate whenever Y is greater than 4. Suppose the rulers adopt a wage policy to guide the economy toward the stationary state in which the surplus to the ruling class as a whole is maximized. In that stationary state the farmer's wage must, of course, be 4. The population of farmers for which the surplus is maximized is 88 [the L at which Q − 4L is maximized when $Y^F = 4$]. The rulers' surplus would be 352. Initially rulers would set Y^F above or below 4, depending on whether the number of farmers was greater or less than 88. If the relation between birth rates, mortality rates and income were the same for rulers as for farmers, the number of rulers would increase over time until their income per head fell to 4. In the long run, population growth wipes out the advantage of being a ruler.

If the birth rate were 4 per cent rather than 3 per cent, the stationary state income would fall to 3 and the optimal population of farmers (from the point of view of the rulers) would rise to 123. If the birth rate rose $4\frac{1}{2}$ per cent, the stationary state population of farmers would rise to 256, which would be larger than is in the interest of the ruling class. The rulers would then have to choose between constantly restricting the population of farmers and accepting a smaller surplus than they might otherwise enjoy.

Control of banditry[6]

Rulers have so far played a sinister but shadowy role in the models of the despotic distribution of income. They set wages to maximize their own revenue, and they are so intimidating that their subjects passively accept whatever income the rulers allow. The means by which rulers dominate society have not been examined at all. The present model introduces a different constraint upon the ruling class and requires a closer look at the rulers' behaviour. Now the rulers' incentive for not appropriating the entire national income is to restrict the number of bandits in the subject population; the provision of high incomes to farmers reduces the incidence of banditry because the equilibrium proportion of bandits to farmers depends on the income of the farmers.

Rulers have two roles to play. They are tax collectors and they are policemen. As tax collectors, they take what they please from the farmers. As policemen, they engage bandits in combat, reducing the attractiveness of banditry relative to farming by lowering the survival rate of bandits. It is best to think of rulers as organized and of bandits as unorganized, so that a small number of policemen might constitute a serious threat to a large number of bandits. Banditry is not eliminated altogether because, as the number of bandits is reduced, farmers devote progressively less of their time to guard labour, and the reward to successful banditry grows accordingly. The new model of despotism is a modification of the final model of anarchy in the last chapter. In that model, there is an ordinary production function according to which output depends on input of labour but not upon the wage of labour, one's utility depends upon one's mortality rate as well as upon one's income and the encounter between farmers and bandits is dangerous to both parties.

The model of despotism builds upon the sixteen-equation model of anarchy set out in Table 2, changing equations and adding new equations to account for the introduction of the ruling class. All equations but (2.1), (2.4) and (2.5) are carried over unchanged from the model of anarchy in Table 2. Modifications to equations are indicated by primes and new equations in the model of despotism are presented in Table 4. Equations in this section are numbered according to their place in Table 4.

Equation (1) from Table 2 becomes

$$n = n^F + n^B + n^R \tag{2.1}$$

where n^B is the number of bandits. Equation (4) has to be adjusted because farmers are now confronted with two deductions from total output, one by bandits as in the original model of anarchy and a second by the tax collector. Thus equation (4) becomes

$$Y^F = [(Q/n^F) - T] (1 - t) \tag{2.4'}$$

where t is the tax rate chosen by rulers. It is assumed that tax is collected as a fixed percentage of farmers' net income left over after part of the crop has been appropriated by bandits.

Equation (2.15) is adjusted to take account of the risk to the bandit when he is hunted by rulers. The survival rate of the bandit becomes

Table 4   *Conversion of the model of anarchy in Table 2 into a model of despotism*

New variables:

t	tax rate
W^R	welfare of rulers
V^{RB}	rulers' survival rate in encounters with bandits
V^{BR}	bandits' survival rate in encounters with rulers
Y^R	rulers' income
n^R	number of rulers

New equations:

$(1')$ $n = n^F + n^B + n^R$

$(4')$ $Y^F = (1 - t) (Q/n^F - T)$

$(15')$ $W^B = V^{BR} V^{BF} M(Y^B) u(Y^B)$

(17) $Y^R = t(Q - Tn^F)/n^R$

(18) $W^R = V^R M(Y^R) u(Y^R)$

(19) $V^{RB} = v(n^R/n^B)$

(20) $V^{BR} = s(n^R/n^B)$

$(21A)$ $t = q(n, \bar{n}^R)$

$(21B)$ $t = q(n)$

$(21C)$ $n^R = p(n)$

The functions s and v determine the bandits' survival rate in encounters with rulers and the rulers' survival rate in encounters with bandits.

Depending on whether or not n_R is invariant at some value $\bar{n}_R$, rulers maximize welfare by choosing t in accordance with equation (21A) *or* by choosing t and n_R in accordance with equations (21B) and (21C).

$M^B V^{BF} V^{BR}$ where, as in anarchy, M^B is the survival rate associated with natural causes, V^{BF} is the bandit's survival probability in encounters with farmers and V^{BR} is the bandit's survival probability in encounters with rulers. Equation (2.15) becomes

$$W^B = M^B(Y) V^{BF}V^{BR}u(Y^B) \tag{2.15'}$$

The bandit's survival rate associated with encounters with rulers is assumed to be decreasing function of the ratio of the number of rulers to the number of bandits.

$$V^{BR} = s(n^R/n^B) \qquad s' < 0 \tag{2.20}$$

Some new equations are required to represent the behaviour of the rulers. Rulers do not protect farmers directly. They hunt bandits, catch some of them and execute the bandits who are caught. Let Y^R be the rulers' income per head. As an accounting identity, the total income of rulers equals the total tax collected from farmers.

$$n^R Y^R = [Q - n^F T]t \qquad (2.17)$$

Rulers' survival rate becomes $M^R V^{RB}$ where M^R is the survival rate associated with natural causes and V^{RB} is the survival rate associated with encounters with bandits, which is assumed to be function of the ratio of the number of rulers and the number of bandits.

$$V^{RB} = v(n^R/n^B) \qquad v' > 0 \qquad (2.19)$$

The welfare of a ruler becomes

$$W^R = M(Y^R)\, v(n^R/n^B)\, u(Y^R) \qquad (2.18)$$

To the original sixteen equations and sixteen unknowns in the model of anarchy in Table 2 this model of despotism adds four more equations, (2.17), (2.18), (2.19) and (2.20), and six more unknowns, Y^R, t, V^{BR}, V^{RB}, n^R and W^R, leaving two free parameters. The model can now be closed with either of two assumptions about the ruling class. It might be supposed that the number of rulers is fixed, an unchangeable fact of history. In that case, rulers choose the tax rate, t, to maximize their welfare, W^R in equation with all the other equations in the model as constraints. The optimal t would then be a function of the total population, n, and the number of rulers, $\bar{n}^R$.

$$t = q(n, \bar{n}^R) \qquad (2.21A)$$

The other possibility is that rulers can choose the size of the ruling class, n^R, in addition to the tax rate, t. They choose n^R and t to maximize the welfare, W^R, of those who remain in the ruling class. The optimal t and n^R would then be functions of population.

$$t = q(n) \qquad (2.21B)$$

$$n^R = p(n) \qquad (2.21C)$$

Alternatively, and equivalently, the set of equations consisting of the original sixteen (appropriately modified) plus (2.17), (2.18) and (2.19) can be looked upon as generating alternative combinations of V^{RB} and Y^R, among which rulers choose the combination that maximizes welfare as defined in equation (2.18).

In principle, one could derive the optimal rate of tax, t, from the functions and parameters in the model. All that will be attempted here is to identify the main effects of a change in the tax rate upon the behaviour of farmers and bandits. Suppose t is increased. The first-order effect through equation (2.4′) must be to increase the rulers' revenue, for, if this were not so, the economy would be on the wrong side of the Laffer curve and the original value of t would be too large. There are secondary effects, all tending to reduce the welfare of the ruler. The reduction in Y^F lowers the welfare of the farmer relative to the welfare of the bandit, causing some

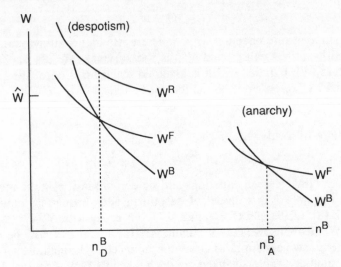

Figure 17 A comparison of welfare in anarchy and despotism

farmers to become bandits instead. This lowers the rulers' revenue, in part because total output declines and in part because farmers divert labour from growing food to protecting the crop. Furthermore, the increase in the number of bandits reduces the bandits' mortality rate and increases the mortality rate of the rulers accordingly, through the functions V^{BR} and V^{RB}.

One cannot say *a priori* whether subjects are better off in a despotic society than in anarchy, but it seems reasonable to assume that it would usually be so. Other things equal, the farmer is made worse off because he is taxed, but there is a corresponding gain from the reduction in the incidence of banditry, which permits him to devote less of his time to guard labour, increasing his gross output and reducing the mortality rate associated with defence against banditry. It is reasonable, though not strictly necessary, to suppose that welfare in anarchy and in despotism are as illustrated in Figure 17. The figure is drawn on the assumptions that total population is the same in both regimes, that subjects always allocate themselves between farming and banditry to equalize welfare in the two occupations, and that the size of the ruling class in a despotic regime is historically fixed. In both regimes, welfare of all social classes is illustrated as a decreasing function of the number of bandits. Let n_A^B be the equilibrium number of bandits in anarchy, and n_D^B be the equilibrium number of bandits in the despotic society. As the figure is drawn, n_A^B is larger than n_D^B, and the equilibrium level of welfare of farmers and bandits is less in anarchy than in a despotic society. The welfare of rulers is also a downward sloping function of the number of bandits but it is greater than the welfare of either farmers or bandits. Despotism improves the lot of the subjects but it improves the lot of rulers even more. The point $\hat{W}$ on the vertical axis represents the welfare of farmers as it would be if there were no rulers or bandits, and if the available land were divided equally among the farmers. Obviously $\hat{W}$ is greater than the equilibrium values of W^F under anarchy or despotism, but it is not necessarily greater than W^R, for the rulers may be better off under despotism than they would be as ordinary citizens in a society with neither rulers nor bandits.

Fear of rebellion by subjects

Rebellion against a despotic regime may be to replace the despotic regime with another from of government, or it may be nothing more than the attempt by a group of dissatisfied subjects to displace the original ruling class and to become the rulers instead. Though these two types of rebellion are conceptually distinct, it is difficult to differentiate between them in practice because rebels seeking the support of non-committed subjects always claim to be the harbingers of a regime of sweetness and light — a claim most persuasive if it is sincere — and rulers always claim that the rebels in power will be no kinder to their subjects than was the old, displaced ruling class. Transformation of one type of regime into another will be the subject of Chapter VI. The model in this section is of rebellion to displace the ruling class rather than to change the regime itself. The core of the model is a specification of the costs and benefits of rebellion. The potential rebel's welfare is compared if the rebellion succeeds, if it fails and if it does not take place at all because it has been successfully deterred by the ruling class. To make the analysis precise and to keep the model reasonably simple, we adopt the extreme assumption that the rebellion takes the form of a battle between rulers and rebels, in which all the losers are killed and all the winners survive to become the new ruling class.

It has been assumed in the model of rulers, bandits and farmers that only rulers act collectively, while farmers and bandits act alone or in groups small enough to pose no threat to the ruling class. Bandits are like rabbits that can sometimes evade their predators but can never challenge them. To incorporate the possibility of rebellion, it is necessary to enable the would-be rebels among the farmers, bandits or dissident rulers to cooperate in overthrowing the ruling class. This adds considerably to the complexity of the model, making it imperative to simplify somewhere, so as to keep the entire model within manageable bounds. The main simplification is the removal of bandits, leaving only farmers and rulers. Two types of rebellion will be examined. The first, discussed in this section, is a peasant revolt in which an undifferentiated and cohesive ruling class is confronted by a group of rebellious farmers. The second, discussed in the next section, is a *coup d'état* in which a hierarchically organized ruling class is challenged from within.

One general law governs the behaviour of all parties at all times. In choosing among courses of action to promote alternative outcomes in society, a rational person does not necessarily act in support of the outcome he prefers. In this, as in all else, he maximizes utility, and, in doing so, may embark upon an entirely different course of action. To formalize the law, imagine that a social decision has to be made between two possible outcomes, A and B, and that each person in society has to choose between two possible actions, a and b. Action a promotes A, action b promotes B, and a person's action to promote an outcome increases the probability of its occurrence. The critical assumption is that a person's utility does not just depend on the outcome in society — upon which party wins the election or upon whether the revolution succeeds in toppling the old regime. A person's utility depends upon his own action as well as upon the outcome in society; that is the essence of the free rider problem. Suppose, for instance, that outcome A is that the revolution succeeds, outcome B is that it fails, action a is to support the revolution, and action b is to oppose it. For person i, the utilities associated with actions and outcomes are $U_i(A,a)$, $U_i(A,b)$, $U_i(B,a)$ and $U_i(B,b)$, where $U_i(A,a)$ is his utility if the revolution succeeds and he supports it, etc. The corresponding probabilities are $p_i(A|a)$, $p_i(A|b)$, $p_i(B|a)$ and $p_i(B|b)$, where $p_i(A|a)$ is the probability as seen by person i of outcome A if he takes action a, etc. For actions to be effective, it is necessary that $p_i(A|a) > p_i(A|b)$ and $p_i(B|b) > p_i(B|a)$.

The law, first put forward in this context by Tullock,[7] is that an individual chooses between a and b, not according to whether he prefers A or B, but to maximize his expected utility. If he chooses a, his expected utility (dropping the subscript i) is

$$Exp(U|a) = p(A|a) \ U(A,a) + p(B|a)) \ U(B,a) \qquad (8)$$

and, if he chooses b, his expected utility is

$$Exp(U|b) = p(A|b) \ U(A,b) + p(B|b)) \ U(B,b) \qquad (9)$$

It could easily happen that a person chooses action b because $Exp(U|b) > Exp(U|a)$ despite the fact that he would really prefer outcome A. A person can be said to "really prefer outcome A" when $U(A,a) > U(B,a)$ and $U(A,b) > U(B,b)$, that is, when he is better off with outcome a regardless of whether his action is a or b.

From a purely analytical point of view, this perverse behaviour — a person rationally choosing an action to bring about an outcome that he does not prefer — can occur for someone who prefers outcome A, when $U(B,b) > U(B,a)$ and when $p(B|a)$ and $p(B|b)$ are both large. Though the person prefers outcome A to outcome B, he is very badly off if he takes action a rather than action b and if outcome B occurs regardless.

The law becomes interesting in a contest between rulers and would-be rulers, both vying for the support of subjects and both prepared to reward their friends and punish their enemies if they are victorious. A rebellion need not occur just because a great many people expect to be better off if the rebellion succeeds. To have a rebellion, there must be a large group of rebels who believe that their gain if the rebellion succeeds will outweigh the risk of punishment by the ruling class if it fails. The same analysis implies that one might assist the revolution, though one would really prefer it to fail, if the rebels were vengeful whilst the original rulers were not.

Now imagine a society without banditry, but where dissatisfied subjects may rebel to displace the ruling class. The society consists of n^R rulers and n^F farmers. The ruling class is homogeneous and without hierarchy. Total output, Q, is a function of the number of farmers

$$Q = F(n^F) \tag{10}$$

Rulers allocate the national income, allowing Y^R to each ruler and Y^F to each farmer.

$$Q = Y^R n^R + Y^F n^F \tag{11}$$

To rebel, in this model, is to join an alternative ruling class which grows until it is "discovered". Discovery is immediately followed by a battle between the old rulers and the would-be rulers in which one party is destroyed and the other party becomes the new ruling class. The technology of rebellion and suppression of rebellion can be represented by two probability functions, ϕ and θ, the first signifying the size of the rebel army at the moment when it is discovered and fought, and the second signifying the rebels' chance of winning the battle as a function of the numbers of rulers and rebels.

Let $\phi(m, n^R)$ be the probability that the conspiracy to rebel is discovered at the moment when the rebel army has grown to a size m. As the task of the ruling class is to sniff out and eliminate conspiracy to rebel, it is reasonable to assume that, for any given m, an increase in the size of the ruling class must raise the probability that the conspiracy is detected before it becomes as large as m. Specifically,[8]

$$\frac{\partial}{\partial n^R} \int_0^m \phi(s, n^R) \, ds > 0 \tag{12}$$

for all values of m. The effect of n^R on the probability of detection is illustrated in Figure 18.

The technology of combat can be summarized in the proposition that numbers matter. Let $\theta(X, Y)$ be the probability that an army of X people defeats an army of Y people. When neither side has the edge in arms or organization, it is reasonable to suppose that $\theta(X, Y)$ is symmetrical in X and Y, so that $\theta(k, k) = 1/2$ for any value of k, and $\theta(X, Y) + \theta(Y, X) = 1$ for all X and Y. It is also reasonable to suppose that there is some minimal

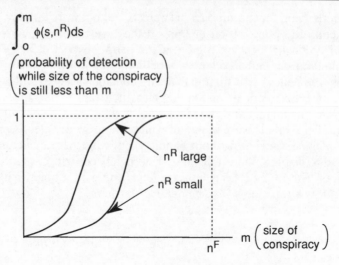

Figure 18 The detection of conspiracy

ratio of X to Y below which $\theta(X,Y) = 0$ and that $\theta_X > 0$ and $\theta_Y < 0$ as long as neither army is too small relative to the other. Hence, if a rebellion has grown to a size m when it is finally detected by the ruling class, there is a probability $\theta(m,n^R)$ of the rebels defeating the rulers and becoming rulers in their place, and a probability $1 - \theta(m,n^R)$ that the rebels are destroyed and the old ruling class remains in power.

Define π as the probability that a rebellion succeeds. Once begun, a rebellion has a probability, π, of displacing the old ruling class. This probability depends on the technology of discovering rebellion, ϕ, the technology of combat, θ, and the number of rulers, n^R. Specifically,

$$\pi(n^R) = \int_0^{n^F} \phi(m,n^R)\, \theta(m,n^R)\, dm \tag{13}$$

At this point, the utility function must be reconstructed to take account of the fact that an act of rebellion involves a large risk of losing one's life today, balanced against a high future income and low future mortality rate in the event that the rebellion succeeds. A person's welfare, W, has so far been defined as the product of his annual survival probability, S, and his annual utility, u. This formulation has been satisfactory because the analysis has been restricted to alternative stationary states where nothing changes from one year to the next. Now welfare must be defined over a person's lifetime because mortality rates may change over time.

Let lifetime welfare be the discounted sum of expected utility every year, where a person's expected utility in any given year is his utility if he survives through the year weighted by the probability that he does so.

When a person's income is the same in every year of his life, his lifetime welfare, L, becomes

$$L \equiv \int_0^\infty S(t)\, u(Y)\, e^{-rt}\, dt \tag{14}$$

where $S(t)$ is his probability of survival to the year t, $u(Y)$ is his annual utility of income, Y is his annual income, and r is his rate of discount. Though this function is far from realistic as a description of a person's objective in decisions affecting income and mortality rates over his entire life, it is adequate in the context of a model of rebellion and it has some very convenient properties.[9] In particular, lifetime welfare in accordance with equation (14) reduces to

$$L = \frac{\pi u(Y)}{r + \delta} \tag{15}$$

when the individual is confronted with a risk $(1 - \pi)$ of losing his life immediately, a constant annual mortality rate of δ in the event that he survives the large risk of death at time zero, and an annual income of Y for as long as he is alive.[10]

Now consider the decision to rebel. The decision is based on a comparison by the potential rebel of his welfare as an obedient subject with his expected welfare as a rebel. His welfare as an obedient subject is $u(Y^F)/(r + \delta^F)$, where δ^F is the farmer's annual mortality rate associated with natural causes of death and is approximately equal to $1 - M(Y^F)$. The farmer need not look beyond his survival rate associated with natural causes because, by assumption, he is not endangered by a rebellion as long as he does not himself rebel. A man's expected welfare as a rebel depends upon three considerations: anticipated income, Y^{R^*}, as a ruler if the rebellion succeeds, survival rate from natural causes, $M(Y^{R^*})$, as a ruler if the rebellion succeeds, and the probability of success of the rebellion, $\pi(n^R)$. The rebel's welfare becomes

$$\frac{\pi(n^R)\, u(Y^{R^*})}{r + \delta^*} \tag{16}$$

where δ^* is approximately equal to $(1 - M(Y^{R^*}))$.

Finally, suppose the potential rebel believes that his circumstances as a ruler would be the same as those of the current rulers against whom he rebels. The rebel believes that $Y^{R^*} = Y^R$, so that $\delta^* = \delta^R$ where δ^R is approximately equal to $(1 - M(Y^R))$. On these assumptions, a rebellion occurs if and only if

$$\frac{\pi(n^R)\, u(Y^R)}{r + \delta^R} > \frac{u(Y^F)}{r + \delta^F} \tag{17}$$

Rebellion is now the welfare-maximizing course of action for all subjects or for none. In the former case, the ruler is certain to be overthrown, for

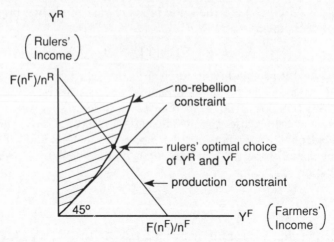

Figure 19 Incomes of rulers and farmers when farmers might rebel. Rebellion is averted as long as Y^R and Y^F are outside the shaded area

all subjects are alike, all conspire to rebel, and one of the rebellions must eventually succeed. In the latter case, the ruler is quite safe. Consequently, the ruler must choose Y^F to reverse the inequality above. When the number of rulers is n^R and the number of farmers is n^F, the rulers' problem is to choose the largest possible Y^R consistent with the national accounting identity equating production and consumption

$$F(n^F) = n^F Y^F + n^R Y^R \tag{18}$$

and the no-rebellion constraint

$$\frac{\pi(n^R)\,u(Y^{R)}}{r + \delta^R} \le \frac{u(Y^F)}{r + \delta^F} \tag{19}$$

The ruler's choice is illustrated in Figure 19, with the ruler's income on the vertical axis and the farmer's income on the horizontal axis. For fixed n^F and n^R, the national accounting identity between total product and total national income is represented by a downward sloping straight line, and the no-rebellion constraint is an upward sloping curve. To be safe from rebellion, the ruler must choose a combination of Y^R and Y^F outside the shaded area. Since no point to the right of the production constraint is feasible, his best choice is the point where the two constraints meet.

The size of the ruling class is optimal when the rulers' loss from having to share the surplus with extra members of the ruling class is just balanced by the gain from the reduction in the farmers' income, Y^F, made possible by the improvement in the rulers' ability to detect and fight rebels. Increases in n^R are easily arranged, because subjects are delighted to join the ruling class. Reducing n^R would be more difficult, but it might be effected gradually over time. Rebels also have a size problem. As their number increases, the rebels may eventually find themselves in a position where their gain from the increase in the probability of the rebellion succeeding is outweighed by the loss in income per head to the members of the new ruling class. In that event, the conspirators would proclaim the existence of the rebellion and begin to fight the old rulers immediately, rather than wait to be discovered.

Among the unrealistic features of the model is the implication that the probability of the occurrence of rebellion — as distinct from the probability of success once the conspiracy has begun — is either 0 (if Y^F is above some critical limit) or 1. This follows from the assumption that the behaviour of the potential rebel is deterministic. A more plausible alternative is that the probability, p, of a rebellion within any period of time is a function, h, of the disparity between the welfare of an obedient subject and the welfare of a rebel, taking into account the risks and rewards of both options. Specifically, the annual risk of rebellion would be

$$p = h\left[\frac{\pi(n^R)\,u(Y^R)}{r + \delta^R} - \frac{u(Y^F)}{r + \delta^F}\right] \qquad (20)$$

Necessarily, $0 \leq p \leq 1$, because p is a probability. There might be a certain high value to the argument above which p is always equal to 1 and a certain low value below which p is always 0, or there may always be some risk of rebellion, however small, regardless of the values of n^R, Y^R and Y^F.

To the ruler, the annual risk of death in combat, $1 - V^R$, becomes $p(1 - \pi)$, where p is the probability of the occurrence of rebellion and π is the probability that the rebellion, once begun, will be successful in displacing the old ruling class. For any n^R and n^F, the ruler's problem is now to choose Y^R to maximize his lifetime welfare, L, where

$$L^R = u(Y^R)/(r + \delta^R), \qquad (21)$$

$$\delta^R = -\ln\left[(1 - V^R)\,(1 - M(Y^R))\right] \qquad (22)$$

and V^R depends as explained above on Y^R, Y^F, n^R, n^F, the subject's propensity to rebel and the conditions of production.

This story of rebellion introduces a fourth constraint upon the treatment of subjects by rulers. The first constraint was a generalization of the simple notion that subjects require a subsistence wage if they are to produce at all. The second was that rulers need to take account of the efficiency of the farmers. The third was that impoverished subjects would turn to banditry. A \$1 reduction in the subject's income diverts a number of subjects from farming to banditry, decreasing the number of farmers, increasing the amount stolen per farmer, increasing the magnitude of the ruler's task in hunting thieves and, possibly, making rulers worse off than they were before. The optimal wage in these circumstances may be well above the subjects' subsistence wage. The fourth was fear of rebellion. Rulers trade income for security, in the belief that well remunerated subjects are less likely to rebel. The constraints were examined in separate models to save the reader (and the writer) from having to consider too many phenomena at once. An unfortunate consequence of our procedure is that we have overlooked the continuum between banditry and rebellion. In times of trouble, gangs of bandits expand, acquire internal organization not unlike that of governments, and, in some instances, usurp the power and authority of the state. Part of the reason this possibility has not been modelled is that we have as yet no internal organization of rulers, rebels or bandits. It is to this aspect of despotism that we now turn.

Fear of a coup d'état

A *coup d'état* is defined for our purpose as a rebellion from within the ruling class, as distinct from a rebellion by dissatisfied subjects against the ruling class as a whole. A *coup d'état* is an attempt by junior members of the ruling class to displace their superiors and to rule in their place. Once again the stakes are high. The rebels must either succeed in displacing their superiors or die in the attempt, and the old rulers can expect to lose their lives if the rebellion succeeds. The study of the *coup d'état* introduces complications that we have so far been able to avoid. First, we can no longer rely on a two-party (rulers and subjects) or three-party (rulers, farmers and bandits) economy, but must consider the entire set of ranks in the ruling hierarchy. Income at each rank must be explained as the consequence of utility-maximizing behaviour. Second, the decision to rebel becomes complex. The potential rebel must draw a balance among his utility as an obedient member of the old hierarchy, if the rebellion succeeds and if it does not, the probability of success of the rebellion, and his anticipated status and utility in the new ruling class that would emerge if the rebellion is successful. Clearly, the model of a *coup d'état* will require gross simplification and deep abstraction (in the sense of deep surgery, not deep philosophy) if it is to yield implications at all.

Simple and unrealistic as it is, the model of fear of a *coup d'état* as the basis of the distribution of income in a despotic society has the virtue that it provides a distinct despotic alternative to the theory of marginal productivity that dominates economic analysis now. The model yields a distribution of income in the entire society and not just among the rulers. This virtue is obtained at the cost of relying on crude assumptions about the rebels' expectations and other matters. The model is simple enough that there can be constructed a numerical example in which income at each rank in the hierarchy is determined as a function of total population.[11] The assumptions are these:

Hierarchy. Society is organized as a strict hierarchy with a fixed span of control of X — one king, X counts, X^2 dukes and so on. At the bottom of the hierarchy, at rank m, are at most X^m serfs. With all ranks full, the total population, N, must be

$$N = 1 + X + X^2 + \ldots + X^m = (X^{m+1} - 1)/(X - 1) \qquad (23)$$

In our example, we set $X = 9$ so that, with six ranks in society, we have one king, nine counts, eighty-one dukes, 729 lords, 6,591 knights, 59,049 bailiffs and 531,441 serfs, for a total population of 597,871. If the population were somewhat less than 597,871, there would not be nine serfs for each bailiff to supervise. For simplicity, we restrict our example to populations with all ranks complete.[12]

Production. Food — the only consumption good — is produced on farms worked by serfs. Total output, which constitutes the income of the entire population, is determined in accordance with an ordinary production function $F(n^F)$ where n^F is the number of serfs, and $n^F = X^m$ when there are m full ranks in society. The identity between national income and national expenditure becomes

$$Y_0 + XY_1 + X^2Y_2 + \ldots + X^mY_m = F(X^m) \qquad (24)$$

where Y_i is the income of a person at rank i ($i = 0, 1 \ldots m$). Assume, for the purposes of the example, that $F(n^F) = (n^F)^\beta$, where $\beta = 2/3$.

Supervision. The role of the upper classes in this model — everybody but the serfs — is to supervise the serfs and to punish them if they do not produce grain as required. The production function, $F(n^F)$, signifies total output when the serfs are well supervised. Nothing is produced, otherwise. The span of control X is a technical parameter; an extra serf supervised by a bailiff who already has X serfs to supervise produces no extra output.

Rebellion. A *coup d'état* is undertaken by an association of junior members of the ruling hierarchy who can expect to occupy the top posts if the *coup d'état* succeeds. A person participates in the *coup d'état* if and only if his expected welfare as a participant exceeds his expected welfare when he desists from participating. An essential ingredient in this calculation is his expectation about his rank in the new ruling class. To represent this calculation by the would-be rebel, the model focuses upon the leader of the rebellion, who sees himself at the top of the new hierarchy if the rebellion succeeds. No *coup d'état* takes place unless the leader's expected utility — the average of his utility as king and of his utility associated with losing his life in the event that the rebellion fails, weighted by the probabilities of success and failure — exceeds his utility in his station of life prior to the rebellion.

The probability of success of a rebellion depends largely on the proportion of the population that can be persuaded to support it, and this in turn depends on each person's expected income in the event of success, the perceived probability of success, and the facility of communication among potential rebels. We make no attempt to model these considerations explicitly, but rely instead on the simple and convenient assumption that the probability of success of a rebellion — whatever its ultimate cause —

depends upon the rank of the leader. One might suppose, for example, that a leader of a rebellion can maintain the loyalty of all of his original subordinates in the hierarchy, so that a baron has a far greater chance of leading a successful rebellion than does a serf. Specifically, we assume that the probability of success of a rebellion is

$$\pi_i = X^{-i\alpha} \tag{25}$$

where i refers to the rank of the leader and $\alpha = 1/2$ in our example.

Welfare. As in the model of rebellion, each person's welfare depends on his expected time-streams of income and mortality rates, from the present into the indefinite future. Specifically a person who bears a risk, $1 - \pi$, of losing his life today, followed by an annual survival rate of S per year forever, who will enjoy an income of Y per year as long as he survives and who discounts future utility at r per cent per annum, has a lifetime welfare, L, of

$$L = \pi u(Y)/(r - \ln (S)) \tag{26}$$

(Remember that ln (S) is a small negative number because S is slightly less than 1.) A person choosing among several options picks the option for which the corresponding value of L is the largest. The example is constructed on the assumptions that the annual utility function is

$$u(Y) = Y \tag{27}$$

and that S is independent of Y.

The decision to rebel. A person chooses to lead a rebellion if and only if his expected utility as a rebel exceeds his expected utility as an obedient subject. If he is initially at rank i, his welfare as an obedient subject is $u(Y_i)/(r - \ln (S))$, where S is everybody's normal survival rate in peaceful times, and his utility as a rebel is $\pi_i u(Y_0)/(r - \ln (S))$. Thus he desists from rebellion as long as

$$u(Y_i) \geq \pi_i u(Y_0) \tag{28}$$

The king's optimum. The king chooses everybody's income. He chooses the entire set Y_0 (his own income), $Y_1, Y_2 \ldots Y_m$ (the income of the serfs) to maximize his own utility. In doing so he is bound by two constraints, the production constraint and the set of no-rebellion constraints, one for each rank in the hierarchy. The source of the no-rebellion constraints is that, if it were in the interest of anyone at rank i to rebel, it would be equally in the interest of everybody at that rank, and one of the rebellions would eventually succeed.

The absence of banditry. The ruling class is the only predator in this economy.

These assumptions together imply a unique distribution of income among the ranks of society as a function of the span of control X, the exponent

Table 5   *The distribution of income among ranks in a hierarchy*

No. of ranks	Popu-lation	Y^0	Y^1	Y^2	Y^3	Y^4	Y^5	Y^6	Total income	Income *per capita*
0	1	1.00	–	–	–	–	–	–	1.00	1.000
1	10	1.08	0.36	–	–	–	–	–	4.33	0.433
2	91	1.44	0.48	0.16	–	–	–	–	18.72	0.206
3	820	2.03	0.68	0.23	0.075	–	–	–	81.00	0.099
4	7381	2.88	0.96	0.32	0.107	0.036	–	–	350.47	0.047
5	66430	4.17	1.39	0.46	0.154	0.051	0.071	–	1516.38	0.023
6	597871	6.00	2.00	0.67	0.222	0.074	0.025	0.008	6561.00	0.011

of the production function β, the exponent of the success of rebellion function α, the form of the utility function, and the number of ranks in society. In the example we assume $X = 9$, $\beta = 2/3$, $\alpha = 1/2$ and $u(Y) = Y$. Plugging the no-rebellion constraints into the production constraint, we see at once that

$$Y_0(1 + X^{1/2} + X + X^{3/2} + \ldots + X^{m/2}) = X^{(2/3)} \qquad (29)$$

from which Y_0, and consequently the entire set, Y_i, can be determined. A distribution of incomes for societies with up to six complete ranks is presented in Table 5.

Though the model is simple and arbitrary, the table is not uninteresting. It establishes that a distribution of income can be derived from the balance between repression and rebellion rather than from marginal products of factors of production. Nobody owns anything in this society, yet a unique distribution does emerge. In addition, the table illustrates a conflict of interest between the rulers and the ruled over population growth. The ruler sees his income rise sixfold as population grows from 1 to 597,871, and income also rises at each level of the hierarchy. Nevertheless, the income of the serfs at the bottom falls by more than nine-tenths of its original value, from 1 to 0.008. Malthusian considerations are not inconsistent with a significant gain to the ruling class from population growth.

Liberty, property and slavery

The word "despotism" has ugly connotations that are not immediately evident in our models of despotism as set out above. One thinks of despotism as cruel, oppressive and without scope for personal liberty or enterprise. But if the sole object of the ruling class were to maximize the revenue of the state — if, for example, the efficiency wage story in the second model were the entire truth of the matter — then a despotic government would have every reason to establish and protect property rights, to encourage science and the arts, to give entrepreneurs the maximal opportunity to establish new firms, and to foster the mobility of labour among locations and occupations; for the wealth of rulers increases automatically with the wealth of nations.

Some of the ugly connotations of the word "despotism" are implicit in the fourth and fifth models, where the ruling class has to take account of the prospect that it may be overthrown. This is most evident in the fourth model, where the major function of rulers is to hunt down conspiracies before they grow large enough to be really dangerous. Rulers in that model would be prepared to sacrifice a good deal of national income and economic growth to make rebellion less likely. Freedom of religion becomes a danger to the state, because an organization originally designed to facilitate common worship may be diverted to secular purposes, as is frequently alleged to have occurred in Tudor England, where Puritan congregations became the nuclei of opposition to the ruling monarch.[13] A state religion (or anti-religion) with publicly appointed priests and a doctrine to which everyone must subscribe would provide the ruling class with greater security than if everyone were free to believe what he pleased and to combine with like-minded people in common observance of religious rites. Freedom of speech on political matters would of course be out of the question. The incorporation of survival rates in violent encounters as arguments in the welfare functions of rulers and subjects conveys something of the flavour of actual despotic societies.

Other aspects of despotism should be mentioned, though they play a minor role in our story. The privilege of the ruling class goes well beyond income. The law itself may take account of rank or status. In Anglo-Saxon times, when recognition by the courts was restricted to the kindred group, the punishment for murder was the payment of compensation, called *wergild*, from the kinsmen of the murderer to the kinsmen of his victim. The amount of compensation depended on the status of the victim, 1,200 shillings for the death of an immediate dependant of the king, though 200 shillings would do for an ordinary landowner.[14] During the third century A.D. there evolved in the Roman Empire a broad distinction between the *humiliores* and the *honestiores*, names which should speak for themselves. The *humiliores* could be flogged, tortured or put to death for certain crimes, but the *honestiores* could at most be exiled or deprived of property.[15] In Imperial China, scholars who passed the Confucian examinations and thereby established themselves as members of the ruling class were exempt from corporal punishment, no small privilege when torture with wooden presses was routinely employed to exact confessions from persons accused of crimes. The legal privileges of the upper classes were enhanced by the rule that punishment, not excluding strangulation or beheading for many crimes, was commutable to cash at rates that the upper classes could afford but the lower classes could not.[16] Though discrimination by rank may not be built into the law, it is present in all societies to a greater or lesser extent, the more so, one would imagine, the more insulated is the ruling class from the rest of society. There is no doubt that the Nomenklatura in most communist societies had material advantages over and above mere salaries. It has been claimed that, in practice, the Nomenklatura was so favoured in the application of the law that there might as well have been two distinct codes of law.[17]

Legal and economic privilege cannot help but inculcate a belief, among the oppressed as well as among the oppressors, in the intrinsic superiority of the upper classes. The emperor is not merely privileged; he is divine. I once saw a Thai Buddhist illustration of reincarnation from (I have forgotten the exact details) ant to frog, to dog, to buffalo, to peasant, to official, to king, to angel, to the Buddha himself, with no intimation that any gap in the chain, except possibly the very last, was larger than any other. The sentiment seems strange now, but it would not have seemed so to Western Europeans a few hundred years ago. This quotation from Sir Walter Raleigh reflects a view common in his time.

For that infinite wisdom of God, which hath distinguished his angels by degrees, which hath given greater and less light and beauty to heavenly bodies, which hath made differences between beasts and birds, created the eagle and the fly, the cedar and the shrub, and among stone given the fairest tincture to the ruby and the quickest light to the diamond, hath also ordained kings, dukes and leaders of people, magistrates, judges and other degrees among men.[18]

A "great chain of being" at once unifies all nature and separates mankind into into what amounts to sub-species with no more in common and no greater respect for one another than the eagle and the fly. A residue of this view of the world is evident in in-house magazines of departments of government, large corporations and universities. On arising each day the King of Dahomey, a great pre-colonial state on the west coast of Africa, would show his gratitude to the Gods for providing him with a good night's rest by sacrificing a couple of slaves.[19]

At several points in this book I contrast the equality of people as voters with their inequality as owners of human and non-human capital. There is an even greater inequality among people as holders of ranks in the governmental hierarchy, an inequality that may extend to the very core of one's humanity. By contrast, money becomes the equalizer. The market supplies a certain equality, if only among dollars, that may be worlds away from the deep and pervasive inequalities endemic in thoroughly non-market economies. It is perhaps more than an accident that the first realistic, sympathetic and respectful paintings of ordinary people in the ordinary business of life appeared in sixteenth-century Holland, a society dominated by commerce to a degree that few societies had ever been before. Thus, as we turn our attention to the liberal society in the next chapter, it should be borne in mind that we are focusing upon a different tone and quality of life as well as on a different means of production and allocation of goods.

This line of inquiry raises a question that was touched upon in the discussion of the subsistence wage but might be examined in more detail. The question is, are farmers slaves? Is the study of despotism really the study of slavery under a different name, or can one institution exist independently of the other?

The question itself is somewhat ambiguous because there are degrees of subservience. The status of subjects in a despotic society may lie on a continuum, with taxpaying property-holders at one extreme, outright slavery at the other and serfdom as one of many forms of subservience in between. A serf is bound to the land, the terms of his implicit or explicit contract with the landowners may depress his income to bare subsistence, but he lives in a family unit, has kin, brings up his own children and has customary rights in his use of the land. A slave is in every respect subservient to his master. He has no kin. He may be sold away from the land. He may be kept in barracks, worked in gangs under an overseer and confronted with the threat of punishment rather than the lure of gain as an inducement to exert himself. Though the distinction between serf and slave is, of course, of the utmost significance to the serf or slave, it may be of less significance to the master who seeks to maximize the return to his "property". What is important — as shown in the model of subsistence income as a constraint on the rulers' capacity to exploit their subjects — is that the serf or slave be tied to the land as a means of keeping the wage well below the marginal product of labour.[20]

Much depends on the internal organization of the ruling class. A ruling class may be strictly military and bureaucratic. Its role may be no more than to intimidate farmers and to extract the maximal tax revenue, subject to the various constraints discussed in this chapter. Alternatively, the ruling class may hold land as well as office. Within the frame of reference of our models of despotism, there is no particular reason for rulers to prefer one form of dominance to another, but good reasons can be found, based on other considerations.

Land-owning may be advantageous for fiscal reasons. A ruling class need not own land, and may restrict itself to administrative and military duties, as long as the instruments of tax collection and public administration are effective enough to allow the government to collect a great deal of revenue from the taxation of output. Otherwise, it may be preferable for rulers to allocate land among themselves, to provide for their own subsistence from their property, and to impose upon themselves the obligations of furnishing soldiers in times of war and supplying the king with revenue to maintain the peacetime operation of the state.

There is another, more important reason why rulers may want to own land. An administrative and military ruling class must, necessarily, be organized in a hierarchy, like that in the model of the *coup d'état* as a basis of the income distribution, with inequality among the ranks, not only in income but in social status, rights and dignity. Members of the ruling class may not want that for themselves. They may prefer to live in a society where each member of the ruling class is more or less the equal of every other. It is hard to see how such equality, or some approximation to it, can be established and maintained unless each member of the ruling class has his own economic base, so that his income does not depend entirely on his standing with the rest of the ruling class. Of course, equality *within* the ruling class does not require equality between the ruling class and its subjects.

On the contrary, it is at least arguable — and has been so argued by a number of historians and economists[21] — that liberty within the ruling class is a direct cause of the enslavement of subjects. As long as the ruling class is purely administrative and military, and as long as the tax system works reasonably well, there is no reason why farmers should not be landowners as well as workers, for taxation can generate as much income for the ruling class as the models in this chapter suggest is in the rulers' interest to acquire. But if rulers are landowners, if wages cannot be taxed directly, and if rulers as a class seek to drive the incomes of their subjects below the marginal product of labour, then subject workers cannot be set free to seek employment where they please. They must be tied to the land or to their masters. They must be serfs or slaves. Though slavery was not un-known in the great despotic empires of the past — in Egypt, Mesopotamia, the Islamic world, India and imperial China — the institution of slavery did not dominate agriculture or handicrafts.[22] Slavery in production was far more important in the city states of ancient Greece.

Property fares better than liberty. Despotic rulers would seem to have several reasons for respecting property rights, though their record in this regard has been far from perfect. The first, alluded to above, concerns the efficiency of the economy. Particularly in primitive conditions such as have characterized most of the great empires of the past, an economy with private property is very much more efficient than a command economy at producing ordinary goods and services. Rulers are better off taxing a private sector for what it will bear than trying to exploit the entire economy as one giant firm. A second reason is that conditional grants of property may be the most efficient means of compensating the ruling class, especially when the ruling class consists of soldiers who are desperately needed from time to time to deal with insurrection or foreign wars but who have little to do in times of peace. It makes sense for the king to allocate income to his men in the form of "stipendiary tenement" rather than as salary that has to be financed out of tax revenue. A senior man in the hierarchy acquires a tract of land yielding an income out of which he must finance a number of soldiers in time of war. There is a saving in administrative cost when the army can be made to finance itself. Feudal organization of the ruling class is not quite private property as we know it today, but it is closer to private property than to the ownership of the means of production by the state. A third reason has to do with the security of the occupants of the top ranks of the ruling class. The hierarchy itself may constitute the springboard of rebellion, as when the officers' mess becomes the nucleus of conspiracy. It may be said that people in the same hierarchy seldom meet together, even for merriment and diversion, but the conversation ends in conspiracy to overthrow the established ranks. The ruling class might be safer with an unorganized competitive market than with a well structured hierarchy encompassing the entire range of the economy; the ruling class may ultimately be safer with businessmen who only conspire to monopolize. This consideration is not always decisive, for rebellion among subjects may be more easily observed within a hierarchy than in a market where people in different firms are linked only by prices. The most effective way of controlling the behaviour of ordinary people is to confine them to organizations within which they can be penalized for failing to display the required degree of enthusiasm for the regime. Perhaps one can say that hierarchy protects rulers from rebellion by subjects while a well developed market, by reducing the need for hierarchy, protects rulers from *coups d'état*.

The willingness of a despotic ruling class to tolerate subjects' rights and to rely for its income upon the tax system depends to a large extent on the security of the ruling class from rebellion or *coups d'état*. A secure ruling class would probably allow subjects a good deal of liberty in the conduct of their private lives and would willingly protect property rights. An insecure ruling class might act differently, fearing all independence of subjects as potentially rebellious. One might therefore expect to see an evolution in a despotic society from regimentation of subjects and public ownership of the means of production, when a regime is new and the successful rebels are gradually finding their way into the leading and most remunerative positions in society, to the re-establishment of property rights once the new ruling class is securely in place.

Notes

1 Though there is a great deal of literature on despotism by historians and political scientists, Gordon Tullock appears to have a near-monopoly on the economic analysis of the subject: see "The Edge of the Jungle" in Gordon Tullock, ed., *Explorations in the Theory of Anarchy*, Center for the Study of Public Choice, 1972, *The Social Dilemma: the Economics of War and Revolution*, University

Publications, 1974, and *Autocracy*, Kluwer Academic Publishers, 1987. See also J.E. Roemer, "Rationalizing Revolutionary Ideology", *Econometrica*, 1985, 85–108; a model of revolution can be isomorphic to a model of despotism.

2　Thomas Hobbes of Malmesbury, *Leviathan or, the Matter, Form and Power of a Common-Wealth Ecclesiastical and Civil*, 1651, p. 238.

3　On actions and expectations, see George Akerlof, "The Economics of Caste and the Rat Race and other Woeful Tales", *Quarterly Journal of Economics*, 1976, 599–617.

4　A good collection of readings on efficiency wages is George Akerlof and Janet Yellen, ed., *Efficiency Wage Models and the Labour Market*, Cambridge University Press, 1986.

5　For any L and Y^F, the rulers' surplus is

$$Q - LY^F = 100L^{1/2}(1 - 1/Y^F) - LY^F$$

This is maximized when

(i)
$$\frac{\partial}{\partial L}(Q - LY^F) = 0$$

(ii)
$$\frac{\partial}{\partial Y^F}(Q - LY^F) = 0$$

Specifically, these equations are

(i) $50(1 - 1/Y^F)/L^{1/2} = Y^F$ and (ii) $100/(Y^F)^2 = L^{1/2}$

which together require that $Y^F = 3$ and $L = (100/9)^2 = 123$. Only the second of these equations holds when L is fixed and rulers optimize over Y^F alone. Alternatively, if farmers were paid the value of their marginal product, their wage would be the solution, x, to the equation

$$x = (50L^{-1/2})(1 - 1/x)$$

for various values of L. There is no solution when $L = 256$.

6　Based on D. Usher, "The Dynastic Cycle and the Stationary State", *American Economic Review*, December 1989.

7　See Gordon Tullock, *The Social Dilemma*, p. 61.

8　Since ϕ is a probability density, it must be the case that

$$\int_0^\infty \phi(m, r^R) = 1$$

for all values of n^R. The role of n^R in the function is to increase ϕ for low values of m and to decrease ϕ for high values of m. Hence equation (12).

9　The additive functional form of the lifetime utility function is discussed in Henry Y. Wan, Jr, *Economic Growth*, Harcourt Brace Jovanovich, 1971, p. 274.

10　With a steady probability of death of δ per year, one's probability, S(t), of being alive after t years is $e^{-\delta t}$. Equation (15) follows immediately. If one's annual survival rate is M, then M and δ are related by the equation $e^{-\delta} = M$, which implies that δ is approximately equal to $1 - M$.

11　Based on D. Usher and Merwan Engineer, "The Distribution of Income in a Despotic Society", *Public Choice*, 1987, 261–76.

12　In treating the span of control as fixed and exogenous I follow Oliver E.

Williamson, "Hierarchical Control and Optimal Firm Size", *Journal of Political Economy*, 1967, 123–38. A more realistic model might explain the span of control as the outcome of utility maximizing behaviour on the part of the king.

13 M. Walzer, *The Revolution of the Saints: a Study of the Origins of Radical Politics*, Harvard University Press, 1965.

14 G.O. Sayles, *The Medieval Foundations of England*, Perpetua Edition 1961, 122–5.

15 A.H.M. Jones, *The Later Roman Empire, 284–602: a Social, Economic and Administrative Survey*, Blackwell, 1964, 17, 751.

16 J.D. Spence, *The Search of Modern China*, Norton, 1990, 125.

17 M. Voslensky, *Nomenklatura: Anatomy of the Soviet Ruling Class*, Bodley Head, 1980, 179.

18 Sir Walter Raleigh, quoted in E.M.W. Tillyard, *The Elizabethan World Order*, Chatto & Windus, 1960, 9.

19 M. Herskovits, *Dahomey*, 1938, cited in Eli Sagan, *At the Dawn of Tyranny: the Origins of Individualism, Political Oppression and the State*, Knopf, 1985, 124.

20 In an essay on the decline of the Roman Empire, Max Weber argued that slavery evolved into serfdom in the later Roman Empire because serf families bore enough children to preserve the supply of labour over time while slaves on farming estates could not, by the very definition of slavery, form the families within which children might be raised. Slavery was an efficient method of farming. Serfdom was less profitable day by day to the landowner but renewed itself over time. Slavery was the preferred method of large-scale agriculture as long as conquest generated a regular supply of new slaves. Serfdom was preferable once conquest ceased. See Max Weber, "The Social Causes of the Decay of Ancient Civilization" in Eugene D. Genovese, ed., *The Slave Economies* I, *Historical and Theoretical Perspectives*, Wiley, 1973.

21 More bluntly put, the cities in which individual freedom reached its highest expression — most obviously Athens — were cities in which chattel slavery flourished. The Greeks, it is well known, discovered both the idea of individual freedom and the institutional framework in which it could be realized. The pre-Greek world — the world of the Sumerians, Babylonians, Egyptians, and Assyrians; and I cannot refrain from adding the Mycenaeans — was, in a very profound sense, a world without free men, in the sense in which the west has come to understand that concept. It was equally a world in which chattel slavery played no role of any consequence. That, too, was a Greek discovery. One aspect of Greek history, in short, is the advance, hand in hand, of freedom and slavery. [M.I. Finlay, "Was Greek Civilization Based on Slave Labour?" in Eugene D. Genovese, ed., *The Slave Economics* I, *Historical and Theoretical Perspectives*, Wiley, 1973, 44–5.]

A compatible argument was put forward by Evsey Domar to explain the emergence of serfdom in sixteenth-century Russia. At the core of Domar's argument is the proposition, already discussed in connection with the subsistence wage, that (ignoring military considerations) there is nothing to be gained by rulers in tying farmers to the land unless the marginal product of labour exceeds the subsistence wage. Domar argues that the establishment of the Russian state in the sixteenth century, after a Time of Troubles in which the man–land ratio was considerably reduced, raised the marginal product of labour well above the subsistence wage, generating precisely the conditions in which serfdom was profitable to the land-owning ruling class. See Evsey D. Domar, "The Causes of Slaves or Serfdom: a Hypothesis", *Journal of Economic History*, 1970, 18–32. I am indebted for this reference and for useful discussions about slavery to my colleague Professor Marvin McInnis.

22 On slavery in despotic empires, see Karl A. Wittfogel, *Oriental Despotism: a Comparative Study of Total Power*, Yale University Press, 1957, section 802 on slavery.

Chapter V

The liberal society

Anarchy and despotism are alike in this respect: that in neither society are all men bound by rules in the pursuit of their aims. Bandits take what they can. Farmers hold what they can. Rulers exploit their subjects as completely as technology and demography allow. The distribution of income among social classes is an equilibrium of violence. Under despotism, the law is imposed by and in the interest of rulers exclusively. In anarchy, there is no law at all.

By contrast, societies we are inclined to call democratic, liberal or just are rule-bound to a very great extent. Everybody in such societies is constrained by rules that everybody (or the great majority of people) is prepared to respect and to defend. A policeman arrests me. If he does so in accordance with the rules — that is, because he has reason to believe that I have committed a crime — then he can rely upon the entire apparatus of government — other members of the police force, the judiciary, the prison guards and so on — to support him against me, should I choose to resist. If he arrests me in violation of the rules, because, for instance, he dislikes me or wants something I possess, if he knows that I have committed no crime and if others understand what he is doing, then the system of justice, which would otherwise support him against me, turns in the opposite direction and supports me against him instead. The system of justice supports my use of a piece of property when the rules determine the property to be mine and when my use of that property is in accordance with zoning laws and other rules prescribing limits on what one may do with one's property. The Prime Minister can rely upon the army and the police as long as his actions are in accordance with his constitutionally established authority, but the very people who enforce his commands when they are appropriately given must turn away from him and, on occasion, block him when he exceeds his authority. That, at any rate, is how the rules are supposed to work and, to some extent, how they do work in practice.[1]

To say that a society is rule-bound is not to say that violence has been banished altogether. No society can avoid the ultimate appeal to violence to enforce its determination of who gets what. A rule-bound society differs from anarchy and from despotism in the way that violence is employed and in the subordination of violence to custom or to law. Violence is employed when citizens combine, directly or through agents appointed for that purpose, to punish those who break the rules. There must be an expectational equilibrium, similar in some respects to the five-person society in the last chapter, in which each person believes (i) that he will be attacked if he breaks the rules and (ii) that he will be treated as a rule-breaker if he does not play his prescribed part in attacking other rule-breakers. Everyone participates in the attack on the person who takes what the rules of society determine to be mine, just as everyone would attack me if I took what the rules assigned to another. Why do people behave in this way? Possibly because they believe such behaviour to be right, but also because refusal to take part in collective action — for instance, by not contributing one's share of public expenditure — would itself be punished.

A distinction can be drawn between rules of public decision-making and rules of entitlement. That you may speak to the assembly if and only if you hold the talking-stick (a rule among some tribes of North American Indians), that there must be at least one federal election every five years, that the winner in an election is the person with the plurality of votes or, alternatively, that candidates with the fewest votes are dropped in each of a sequence of elections until a clear majority emerges — these are rules of public decision-making. That I may forbid you to trespass upon my land, that I may not build a factory on land designated as my property if that property is zoned as residential, that the state may not prevent me from writing a letter to a newspaper or prevent the newspaper from publishing the letter, that I may not be arrested for no better reason than that the policeman dislikes me, that I, like any other citizen, am to receive a certain sum of money from the government when I grow old, that my children can attend public schools — these are rules of entitlement. There are, of course, some rules (such as the rule that every adult has the right to vote) which partake of both categories. Other rules (such as the rule that one must drive on the right side of the road) do not fit neatly into either. Most of society's rules fall naturally into one category or the other.

What I am calling a liberal society is an abstraction in which the vast and complex web of rules that people are prepared to respect is reduced to two: voting by majority rule as *the* rule for public decision-making, and private property as *the* rule of entitlement. The place of the liberal society in this book is as a crude and provisional distillation of essential features of any society that has succeeded in subordinating violence to rules. The reader will, I suppose, readily agree that public decision-making by voting is a necessary condition for such a society whenever technology and social organization are at all complex. The reader may balk at my insistence on private property. I hope to show in this chapter that property and voting are highly interdependent institutions and that an economy based on private property is a requirement for majority rule voting as well as a source of efficiency in production and distribution. It is not just an accident or a coincidence that a considerable scope for markets and for private property is maintained in every society where majority rule voting is effectively employed in the choice of leaders, legislation and policies. The purpose of this chapter is to show how property and voting reinforce one another, how together they give rise to an allocation among people of tasks and rewards, and how a society with property and voting can be stable, avoiding the slide into anarchy on the one hand, while defending itself from despotism on the other.

The chapter begins by examining the virtues and defects of voting, with special emphasis on the anti-democratic argument that voting is generally unacceptable as an instrument for public sector decision-making because it empowers the majority to expropriate the minority completely. There follows a discussion of property, with special emphasis on the efficiency of markets with private property and on the essential injustice of a distribution of income and property in which some people are very rich and others are very poor. Finally, there is an attempt to show how property and voting fit together, each compensating to some extent — though not completely — for the defects and weaknesses of the other. A liberal society with voting and property together can be prosperous and stable, though neither voting nor property is sufficient on its own.[2]

This chapter is doubly elementary. It reviews some straightforward material, and it develops an argument in a simple-minded way, overlooking qualifications and reservations that may be important in practice. Many of the themes in this chapter will be revisited later on in the book, where the virtues and vices of the market and the place of government in a liberal society will be discussed in greater detail.

Voting

Public decisions can be made by custom, by the despot or by voting. To decide by custom is to recognize the authority of the *status quo*. Custom may be codified in a written constitution or it may consist of rules that are respected and obeyed but not prescribed in any hallowed document.[3] Custom is an essential ingredient of a liberal society, but it is never sufficient for all public decisions. It is essential, not just in the allocation of property rights, but in the procedural rules of government, in laws and in rights of citizens against the state. It is never sufficient because society must often choose among alternatives, none of which has the authority of the *status quo*. Monarchy provides a *status quo* for the choice of the head of state, but there is no equivalent in any other form of government. Rarely can a *status quo* be identified for the choice of economic policy in a changing environment. Nor is it safe for a country to rely upon custom in the choice of alliances with other countries. As an alternative to blind custom, despotism is usually inefficient, frequently dangerous even for the despot, and particularly unattractive for those not privileged to belong to the ruling class.

Voting, on the other hand, may be looked upon as a peaceful substitute for a test of strength. The minority gives way to the majority because voting is respected as a method of public decision-making and because, if voting were replaced by warfare, the majority would be the more likely to win. Voting by majority rule has two principal virtues. Unlike custom, it can, in principle, be employed for any matter whatsoever. There is no technical limit to the range of questions that might be put to a vote. Unlike despotism, it comes as close as is humanly possible to providing everybody with some input into public sector decision-making, restricting the prerogatives of the more influential members of society and generating outcomes most favourable to a hypothetical person (behind a veil of ignorance) who has an equal chance of occupying the income and status of every person in the society. As will be amply demonstrated in Chapter IX, this statement has to be qualified in some important respects, yet I stand by it because the alternative to government by voting, in an advanced industrial society, is despotism.

The emphasis here is, nevertheless, on the defects of voting, studied in the same spirit that a doctor studies disease with a view to keeping the patient well. As a method of public sector decision-making, voting by majority rule is potentially inconsistent and it empowers a majority of voters — any majority — to exploit and expropriate the remaining minority. Following a brief examination of these defects, there is some discussion of single-peaked issues for which these defects do not arise.

The paradox of voting[4]

The potential inconsistency in voting by majority rule may be illustrated in a simple, much-used example. Imagine three alternatives A, B and C. If I prefer A to B and B to C, one would expect me to prefer A to C and one might well consider me irrational, or even insane, if I did not. Similarly, one would expect a legislature composed of rational people to choose rationally among alternative bills. One would expect the legislature to vote for bill A as against bill C, if it is prepared to vote for bill A as against bill B and for bill B as against bill C. It may do so, but need not.

Suppose there are three voting members in the legislature, 1, 2 and 3, and that decisions are reached by majority rule voting. It is certainly possible that one of the three bills wins unambiguously because two of the three voters prefer that bill to any other. This is not the only possibility. An inconsistency would emerge if Mr 1 prefers A to B to C, Mr 2 prefers B to C to A and Mr 3 prefers C to A to B. In that case, the decisions of the legislature in a sequence of pairwise votes are to choose A when the vote is between A and B, to choose B when the vote is between B and C, and to choose C rather than A when the vote is between A and C. No outcome — not A, not B, and not C — wins unambiguously over the other two. A legislature composed of rational people may behave irrationally; that is the "paradox of voting".

There are two important implications. The first is the susceptibility of the legislature's decision to manipulation by the person or committee empowered to set the agenda of the legislature. When no option commands a clear majority of votes over all other options, the order in which the different options are presented to the legislature is critical in determining the ultimate winner. Suppose the established procedure for voting among three options is that the agenda-setter chooses a pair of options, the legislature votes to reject one of the two, and then the legislature votes again between the two remaining unrejected options. With that procedure, and if no option wins over each of the other two, the agenda-setter can manipulate the legislature to choose whatever option he prefers. If he wants option A to win, he arranges for the first pairwise vote to be between B and C; the winner is B, which then loses to A. If he wants option C to win, he arranges for the first pairwise vote to be between A and B; the winner is A, which then loses to C.

The scope for manipulation of the legislature by the agenda-setter extends well beyond the simple example. In particular, the process by which matters are combined into bills can have a significant effect upon what the legislature decides. Suppose each of the three voters in the legislature lives in a separate district, that there is a firm rule in this society according to which all public revenue is raised by a proportional income tax on all voters, and that the question at hand is road-building. For each voter, the road in his own district is worth considerably more to him than his share of the cost of construction, the roads in the other two districts are worth less *to him* than his share of the cost of construction, but all three roads together, as a package, are worth more to him than his share of the total cost of construction. If each road is voted separately, then no road gets built, for only one voter is in favour of each road and two are opposed. If all three roads are voted together, then all roads get built. If two roads are combined in a package bill and the third is considered separately, then only the two get built; voters in districts where these roads are built are better off than they would be if all three roads were built because their taxes are reduced by their share of the cost of a road in the third district. The agenda-setter who chooses which bills to present to the legislature may be empowered to decide whether there are to be three roads, two or none. To be sure, his influence in this example is so blatant that voters would be unlikely to allow themselves to be manipulated as the example suggests. The example takes no account of the voters' right to propose amendments. There are, however, many subtler ways for the agenda-setter to manipulate the legislature, in the wording of bills, organization of committees, rules of debate, timing and so on.

A second implication of the potential inconsistency in voting by majority rule is that it may be advantageous for members of the legislature (or citizens voting in elections) to vote strategically rather than sincerely. Return to the original example and suppose that the agenda-setter has arranged for a first vote between A and B, where the winner will be matched in a pairwise vote with the remaining option, C. If everyone votes sincerely, as we have so far assumed, then C wins. Mr 1 particularly dislikes this outcome because he prefers A to B to C. Nothing he can do will induce the legislature to adopt A, but he can induce the legislature to adopt B instead of C by switching his initial vote from A to B. Now the legislature votes for B rather than A in the first round, and again for B over C in the second. One cannot predict the outcome when all voters behave strategically.

Exploitation of minorities[5]

The other, greater defect of majority rule voting is that it may become a means whereby a majority can exploit or expropriate the remaining minority. The west, where the line between east and west is drawn sufficiently eastward that the west constitutes a majority, may impose tariffs on imports that compete with goods produced in the west, subsidize western production and western infrastructure, provide westerners with the best jobs in the civil service, make life difficult for firms that fail to employ the appropriate proportion of westerners in leading positions, exempt westerners from certain types of taxation and, in the extreme, disenfranchise and enslave easterners. In principle, any majority coalition may play the role of exploiter, regardless of the badge by which members of the coalition recognize one another. Language, religion, location and race have all at one time or another served as axes of division — not, it should be stressed, because these are intrinsically divisive, but because any badge can serve as a catalyst or trigger for this particular mode of behaviour. Division into majority and minority is primary; the source of the division is secondary and relatively unimportant.

The temptation for the majority to exploit the minority is especially great when the legislature votes about the allocation of income. If, for example, the legislature bore responsibility for the setting of all wages, there would arise an almost irresistible pressure upon each trade or category of workers to form alliances with other trades or categories of workers so as to create a majority coalition designed to channel a large share of the national income to its members. Even workers who would desist from political activity to raise wages if they could be confident that others would do so too find themselves driven in that direction as they become suspicious of others who might be tempted to form coalitions behind their backs, coalitions from which they are excluded.

Any public decision has some bearing upon the allocation of income, but that consideration may be central, as in the determination of relative wages, or it may be peripheral, as in a vote about the severity of punishment for crimes or about foreign affairs. A decision to go to war has an impact on relative wages in military and civilian occupations, but that impact is typically less important to the average voter than the direct consequences of war upon the lives of soldiers and the prosperity of the community as a whole. When the effect of a public decision upon the allocation of income among people is small and peripheral to the main purpose of the decision, there is reason to expect that all or almost all voters will be prepared to live with the outcome of the vote because the preservation of the system of public decision-making is considered more important than the content of the decision in any particular case. When the effect of a public decision on the allocation of income among people is large and central, that may no longer be so, for the voter's loss of income may outweigh his concern for the maintenance of the decision-making procedure.

Exploitation by voting has led on many occasions to the disintegration of democracy. A potential majority is disenfranchised and must be held down by force. A minority group is increasingly deprived of wealth and access to the more remunerative occupations, until a moment comes when rebellion seems preferable to continued submission. A party in power, having used its majority in the legislature to acquire wealth and privilege, refuses to give up its advantages at the ballot box and chooses to rely on the army instead. Better to establish a one-party state than risk losing an election to a group of rascals who would probably establish a one-party state themselves if they got the chance. Reasoning along these lines is always seductive and sometimes compelling. Much depends upon the economic significance of the vote. The more there is at stake, the less willing is a group in power to be replaced by another group that happens to win an election.

The median voter theorem[6]
At this point in the argument, there would seem to be little chance that a democratic government could be maintained for any length of time. A reader without knowledge or experience of democratic government could be forgiven for supposing that democracy simply would not work. The main line of argument of this chapter is that the prospects for democratic government are not as bleak as they seem because the defects of voting

are to a degree overcome in the presence of an economy with private property. There is, however, a subsidiary argument about the technology of voting; inconsistency in voting and the exploitation of minorities are circumvented when issues before the legislature are single-peaked. Single-peakedness is a characteristic of, or restriction upon, the preferences of voters with regard to an issue to be resolved by majority rule voting. An issue is single-peaked when (i) each option can be represented by a number on a scale, (ii) each voter has a preferred option, and, (iii) as between two options with numbers both above or both below the number corresponding to his preferred option, the voter always chooses the option that is closer to his preferred option. I want the school board to spend $2 million. I vote for $2.5 million when the alternative is $3 million, and I vote for $1.5 million when the alternative is $1 million. If all voters behave as I do (though with respect to a first preference on spending by the school board that may be greater or less than $2 million), then spending by the school board is a single-peaked issue.

Why does this matter? It matters because, for any single-peaked issue, there can be identified a median voter whose first preference wins in a pairwise vote with any other option. Suppose, in a five-person legislature, Mr A wants the school board to spend $1 million, Mr B wants $2 million, Mr C wants $2.5 million, Mr D wants $3.5 million and Mr E wants $5 million. The median voter is Mr C, who can combine with Mr A and Mr B in a majority coalition to oppose any expenditure in excess of his first preference of $2.5 million, and who can combine with Mr D and Mr E to oppose spending less. Once Mr C's first preference gets on to the voting agenda, it wins over any other alternative and becomes the decision of the legislature. On a single-peaked issue the agenda-setter is relatively power-less, and there is little scope for strategic voting or exploitation of one group by another. The proposition that voting over single-peaked issues is free of the inconsistencies of the paradox of voting is known as the median voter theorem.

Voting about single-peaked issues has two "nice" properties. There is an electoral equilibrium — an outcome preferred by some majority of voters to all other outcomes — and the outcome is reasonably satisfactory for most voters. Mr A, who is at one extreme of the spectrum of preferences, may be disappointed with the outcome of the vote, but he is at least assured that the voting procedure does not lead to the opposite extreme. If the legislature does not adopt the first preference of Mr A, who wants the least educational expenditure, neither will it adopt the first preference of Mr E, who wants the most. People in the middle of the spectrum get more or less what they want.[7]

In view of these nice properties of single-peaked issues, it becomes important to know when issues are single-peaked and when they are not. As a general rule, any public decision that can be represented as the choice of *one* parameter, such as a sum of money, is single-peaked. Examples are educational expenditure (already discussed in this context), military expenditure, total public expenditure on medical care, and so on. An additional requirement is that people's preferences be regular over the scale of options as specified above. This requirement is usually, but not invariably, met.[8]

Three important issues are not single-peaked. The first is the choice among candidates for office. Candidates cannot as a rule be lined up so that the preferences of voters conform to the requirements of the median voter theorem. If A, B and C are candidates for office, there is no guarantee that A will defeat C in a pairwise race when A defeats B and B defeats C. That might happen, but need not. It is because choice among candidates is not single-peaked that elections in the British tradition are based on plurality voting, a procedure that would never be tolerated in the choice among bills in Parliament. The candidate with the most votes wins the election, even if, as often happens when there are more than two candidates, the winner gets less than 50 per cent of the votes and he would have been defeated in a pairwise vote with one (or even all) of the losing candidates. Within Parliament, a vote is always to accept or reject a motion. Members of Parliament are not asked to vote for bill A *or* bill B *or* bill C, on the understanding that the bill with the most votes is passed into law.

Second, voting among platforms of political parties need not be single-peaked, even if the issues covered in the different platforms are each in themselves single-peaked.[9] This is best shown in a simple example. Imagine society with two issues and three voters as illustrated in Figure 20(a). The issues are aggressiveness toward one's enemies, measured on the vertical axis of the figure, and the extent of redistribution of income, measured on the horizontal axis. Every pair of public decisions can then be represented as a point. A move to the north-east represents an increase in aggressiveness abroad and an increase in the redistribution of income at home. Let the voters be A, B and C, and label the first preference of each voter accordingly. Each voter's indifference curves are loops around his preferred point. One sees immediately that if the two issues were resolved in separate and independent votes, the degree of aggressiveness would be the distance G_A on the vertical axis, corresponding to the first preference of A, who is the median voter on that issue, and the amount of redistribution would be R_B, corresponding to the first preference of B, who is the median voter on that issue. Resolved one at a time, the two issues are single-peaked and there is a well specified "plebiscites equilibrium" represented by the point (G_A, R_B).

This is no longer true when voting is between platforms, even though each issue within a platform is single-peaked. A platform in this context is just a pair of outcomes for each of the issues that have to be resolved. A

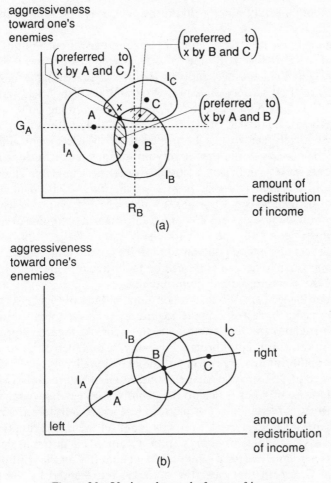

Figure 20 Voting about platforms of issues

political party seeking office would usually present such a platform to the electorate. Consider the platform represented by the point x, which may or may not be the same as the plebiscites equilibrium (G_A, R_B), and let I_A, I_B and I_C be the indifference curves of A, B and C passing through the point x. It is immediately obvious that x is not preferred by a majority of voters to every other platform. Platforms preferred to x (the "win set" of x) are represented by the shaded trillium-shaped area, each leaf of which is preferred to x by a different pair of voters. For instance, points in the bottom leaf are preferred to x by a majority consisting of A and B; these points are "closer" to the first bests of both A and B than is the point x. With the constellation of preferences represented by Figure 20(a), there is no voting equilibrium among platforms. There is no point in the figure without its win set.

To this general rule there is an interesting exception. Politics is often discussed in terms of "left" and "right". It is said that one politician is more left-wing than another, implying that the former adopts a more leftist stance on a great variety of issues. Programmes of political parties are thought of as left, right or centre. Voters choose among political parties accordingly. Such language makes sense only if the multiplicity of issues in a modern society can in fact be projected onto a left–right continuum. How this is done is to me profoundly mysterious, but it is done to some extent. Talk of left and right is not altogether meaningless. The political language of left and right may have a bearing on the virtues and defects of the voting mechanism. Contrary to what one might suppose when positions on individual issues are combined in platforms of political parties, it may be possible to look upon the totality of public sector decision-making as one vast single-peaked issue on a left–right continuum. Politics becomes one-dimensional, a median voter can be identified and his first preference becomes the electoral equilibrium outcome.

Consider, once again, the two-dimensional politics of Figure 20(a) where public decisions have to be made regarding aggressiveness toward one's country's enemies and redistribution to the poor. As Figure 20(a) is drawn there is no electoral equilibrium, for every point, such as x, has its win set. An equilibrium emerges when the dimensionality of public decision-making is reduced from two to one, as indicated in Figure 20(b), where the first preference of voter B lies on the "contract curve" between A and C. This contract curve is the set of platforms at which indifference curves of A and C are tangent; starting from any point on the contract curve, it can never be advantageous for *both* A and C to move to a different point. The point B is a unique electoral equilibrium when it lies on the contract curve of A and C, for, in that case, the outcome represented by the point B defeats any and every other outcome in a pairwise vote. With more than three voters, choice among platforms remains single-peaked if the first preferences of all voters lie along the contract curve for some given pair of voters (who may be thought of as the extremists) and subject to certain other conditions regarding the tangencies of indifference curves. The electoral equilibrium becomes the first preference of the median voter along the contract curve of the extremists on the left–right continuum.[10]

The third and most significant of the matters that are not single-peaked is the allocation, or reallocation, of income among voters. This matter has already been discussed as the exploitation problem. It remains only to formalize that discussion in the context of the median voter theorem. Again a simple example will show what is at stake. Imagine a society in which the entire national income has to be allocated by a legislature with majority rule voting. The legislature consists of three voters, A, B and C. The total

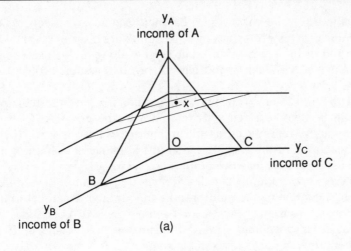

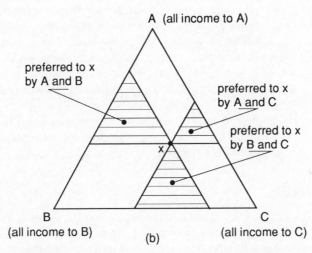

Figure 21 Allocations of income among three voters

national income is fixed at Y per head. The legislature's task is to choose y_A, y_B and y_C, the incomes of Mr A, Mr B and Mr C, subject to the constraint that

$$y_A + y_B + y_C = 3Y$$

The situation is illustrated in Figure 21(a), a three-dimensional diagram with axes representing the magnitudes of y_A, y_B and y_C. On the diagram, the set of all efficient distributions of income is represented by a plane that cuts each axis at a distance 3Y from the origin; the points of intersection, A, B and C, are such that $0A = 0B = 0C = 3Y$. Each voter is assumed to be totally selfish; he cares about his own income exclusively. Thus the indifference curves of, for instance, person A are a set of planes, stacked one on top of the other at different heights along the y_A axis. One such indifference curve is shown in Figure 21(a). It is assumed to contain the point x.

That the allocation of income among voters is never a single-peaked issue can be demonstrated with reference to the plane ABC in Figure 21(a), which is reproduced as the triangle ABC in Figure 21(b). Each point, such as x, in the triangle represents a unique allocation of income among the three people. Now indifference curves are parallel straight lines opposite the appropriately labelled vertices. For instance, the indifference curve of A containing the point x is the line through x parallel to the BC axis. Starting from any point x, a movement toward A increases the income of A, a movement toward B increases the income of B and a movement toward C increases the income of C. It is immediately evident from the figure that there is no electoral equilibrium allocation of the national income among the three voters. For instance, the point x is not an electoral equilibrium because any point in the shaded area is preferred to the point x by two out of three voters. The shaded area is the win set of x. There is a similar win set for every point in the triangle. Starting from any triplet of income $\{y_A, y_B, y_C\}$, it is always possible to construct another triplet $\{y_A + \varepsilon, y_B + \varepsilon, y_C - 2\varepsilon\}$ such that all incomes sum to 3Y and the latter triplet is preferred to the former by a majority of two out of three votes. The exploitation problem, as discussed above, is an especially unfortunate implication of this fact.

Private property

Private ownership of the means of production entitles one to earn income from one's property by selling it, using it, renting it, or combining it with other factors of production to make goods and services that may be sold. Property may be owned directly, as when one owns a factory outright, or indirectly, as when one owns stocks or bonds. Since the liberal society is an ideal type — an abstraction to which actual societies may conform to a greater or lesser extent — it would be possible to require of a liberal society that *all* the means of production are privately owned. That is not the definition here. Instead a liberal society is one where a large part, but not necessarily all, of the means of production is privately owned. There is no clear-cut answer to the difficult question of how large the public's share of property can be before a society stops being liberal. My not very satisfactory answer must be that the share cannot be so large that the society begins to look like despotism.

The virtues and defects of markets with private property as a basis of economic organization are implicit in the two principal theorems of welfare economics which are discussed briefly in Chapter I: that there exists a competitive equilibrium and that the equilibrium is Pareto-optimal. The first theorem establishes that there exists a set of prices at which all markets clear, all resources are employed in the production of goods, and all goods are purchased by consumers as long as all resources are privately owned and subject to certain other conditions. The second establishes that the outcome of a competitive economy is not wasteful; no rearrangement of production and no reallocation of goods among people could make everybody better off. The second theorem shows how the pecuniary motive may induce people to direct their actions in a socially optimal way, and it provides some basis for the presumption that an economy with private property is likely to be more prosperous than an economy where all the means of production are owned and administered by the state. Public administration of the entire economy does not provide a comparable pecuniary motive, and the whip has proved to be an unsatisfactory substitute.

The autonomy of the private sector

The first of the principal theorems of welfare economics — on the existence of a competitive equilibrium — is especially significant for its silence about the role of the government in the economy. Given the distribution among people and firms of the means of production and the distribution among people of the ownership of firms (and subject to other qualifications discussed in Chapters I and VII), the competitive economy is entirely autonomous. It attends to the production and distribution of goods without the intervention of the government. Government may choose to intervene for a variety of reasons, good and bad, but it has the option not to do so.

The competitive economy is altogether independent of the government in one respect, but altogether dependent in another. To prove the existence and efficiency of the competitive economy, there had to be postulated an initial allocation among people of the means of production, including labour. The assumption is not just that property is owned. It is that property is secure, that banditry is deterred absolutely and that the costs of banditry, as discussed in Chapter III, do not reappear in some other form. Hence the absolute dependence of property upon the state as the protector and guarantor of property rights.

No uncoordinated activity by property-holders can protect property adequately or avoid a condition of anarchy where one's "property" is nothing other than what one can defend. Protection of property — defined broadly to include civil rights and entitlement to one's own labour power as well as ownership of the means of production — requires an army and a police force which must necessarily be collectively organized and financed. Protection of property requires the government to maintain a preponderance of the means of violence and coercion. Inevitably, this arrangement entails a risk that the government's monopoly of violence will be employed to take from property-holders rather than to defend them. There is always a danger of the army and the police transforming themselves into a self-serving, despotic ruling class. Some societies succeed in subordinating the army and the police; others do not. This particular danger to the liberal society compounds with and magnifies the danger, discussed above in connection with voting, of expropriation by some majority of the corresponding minority. Majority rule implies majority control over the state's monopoly of the instruments of coercion. Regardless, protection of people and property is the rock-bottom minimal task of government in a liberal society.

Protection of property rights necessarily extends to the resolution of disputes about the content of rights. Rights of people to the use of property, or rights over other people by virtue of one's ownership of property, are never unlimited. My right to the enjoyment of my house and garden does not extend to the point where I can install a swimming pool that is not properly fenced, or build an extension to my house that significantly alters the appearance of the neighbourhood. Rights associated with residential property are always constrained by national laws or local by-laws. Similarly, rights associated with ownership of industrial property or machinery are never unconditional. Such property cannot be used in a way that would excessively endanger the health or life of an employee, even if he fully understands the risk. Nor can it be used to produce and sell substances considered dangerous to the user. The content of ownership is also in dispute when, for instance, title to a piece of land is unclear or when questionable means have been employed in a take-over bid for a corporation. In such cases the government must ultimately determine who owns what, through legislation and by adjudication. Intellectual property is especially problematic. Rarely does an important and valuable patent go unchallenged in the courts.

Similar ambiguities arise in the interpretation of contracts. The intrinsic unpredictability of the future makes it virtually impossible to write a contract covering every eventuality relevant to the obligations of the parties to the contract, or to specify enforceable penalties for every instance of non-fulfilment. Implicitly or explicitly, every contract contains a provision that it will be interpreted in a reasonable manner, according to the mores of the community to which parties to the contract belong. To some extent, the pressure of the community can be relied upon to enforce compliance. Each party to the contract knows that others will not enter into contracts with him tomorrow if he breaks his contract today; such considerations are often alleged to explain the commercial success of many small, close-knit minority groups within large and poorly administered societies. Nonetheless, the ultimate determination of what is reasonable when a dispute arises among parties to a contract rests with the court's decision as to how and to what extent a contract is to be enforced.

Vagueness and imprecision at the edges of property rights have a two-fold effect upon the role of the institution of private property in the economy. On the one hand, the required public administration of the institution of private property entails a considerable cost which must be balanced against the benefits of the institution as an efficient way of organizing an economy. More important, the need for public administration of private property reduces the effectiveness of the institution as a means of allocating the national income among people, for the resolution of disputes over property rights is not strictly mechanical and is influenced to some extent by political considerations. The autonomy of the institution of private property must be less than complete when the public sector has to resolve disputes over the interpretation of contracts and the limits of private rights.

Should property rights be respected?

A case can be made that they should not. Bear in mind that a competitive economy is at best efficient in the limited sense that there is no waste. Efficiency in this sense places no constraints on the allocation of income among people. In the technical language already employed in Chapter I, the outcome of a competitive economy is efficient but need not lead to the maximization of social welfare. Each and every initial distribution of human and physical resources yields an efficient allocation of goods among people, but there are millions and millions of efficient allocations corresponding to the millions and millions of possible allocations of property. Depending on the initial distribution of ownership of resources, the resulting efficient allocation may provide vast incomes for the prosperous few and bare subsistence or outright starvation for the impoverished many. Mere efficiency is a dubious virtue.

The fundamental theorems of welfare economics provide not a hint of justification for the existing allocation of property. The form of the theorems is: given the allocation of property and certain other conditions, there is an equilibrium allocation of goods among people and there is no waste. Nothing in the theorems explains why the distribution of property is what it is or suggests that the given distribution of property, which favours some people at the expense of others, should be tolerated when citizens have the means to change it. On this matter the theorems are mute.

Nor can one take much comfort in Locke's famous derivation of property rights from one's entitlement to one's own labour. The key passage from *The Second Treatise of Civil Government*[11] is this:

27. Though the earth and all inferior creatures be common to all men, yet every man has a property in his own person; this nobody has any right to but himself. The labour of his body and the work of his hands, we may say, are properly his. Whatsoever then he removes out of the state that nature hath provided and left it

in, he hath mixed his labour with, and joined to it something that is his own, and thereby makes it his property. It being by him removed from the common state nature hath placed it in, it hath by this labour something annexed to it that excludes the common right of other men. For this labour being the unquestionable property of the labourer, no man but he can have a right to what that is once joined to, at least where there is enough and as good left in common for others.

The argument is, in my opinion, open to three objections, any one of which would be sufficient to invalidate the argument as a justification for existing property rights. First, the mixing of labour conveys no title unless people have already agreed that it should do so.[12] Second, present ownership of things is a complex outcome of a process in which force, violence and fraud have all played major roles. The roots of present ownership extend back to a time when tribes took what they could from neighbouring tribes and no rights were respected that could not be defended by force of arms. Third, even the product of my own labour, if such can be identified at all, is mine only by virtue of a prior social convention. "My" skills are a result of my training, which was purchased for me by my parents with the income from property to which they were not in any cosmic sense entitled. The product of "my" labour is the consequence of the entire organization of society — the protection I am afforded against my neighbours, the tax system and the accumulated knowledge of science and technique. At no time did labour power stand pristine and apart from other people, land and capital.

A majority of voters can overturn the existing allocation of property among people, and we have at this stage of the argument produced no good reason why a majority should desist from doing so. A linguistic, social, regional or economic majority cannot be prevented from voting away the prior distribution of property, to socialize the means of production or to appropriate the means of production for itself. What is mine is mine by virtue of a social convention which could be overturned at any time. Nor are there moral grounds for the present disparity between rich and poor or for the existing allocation of property. Property cannot be justified because property-holders are worthy or meritorious folk. The institution of private property must somehow be justified on prudential grounds if it is to be justified at all. To justify private property is to show that a society where private property is protected is a very much better place, even for the relatively poor, than a society without well specified and well protected property rights.

The interdependence of property and voting

Voters in a liberal society may respect and preserve property rights for three reasons: because an economy based on private property is efficient, because the institution of public decision-making by majority rule voting cannot be sustained in the absence of private ownership of the means of production, and because the potential inequalities in a system of private property can be mitigated by redistribution of income without overturning property rights altogether. Of the first reason — that an economy with private property is efficient — nothing need be added to the discussion in Chapter I, except perhaps to say that some important qualifications will be discussed in Chapter VII.

The second reason needs to be examined in detail. The role of property as a defence of majority-rule voting is a consequence of the exploitation problem. Majority-rule voting is the only means in an organizationally and technically complex society of subordinating the government to the will of the great majority of citizens. It is, all the same, entirely defective as a means of allocating the national income among citizens. Allocation by voting leads inevitably to the exploitation by some majority of voters of the corresponding minority. The prospect of exploitation leads in turn to the abandonment of the institution of majority-rule voting as some faction seizes power to exploit others permanently or to defend itself from exploitation. Recognition of this prospect is the basis of the classic anti-democratic argument: if government must allocate, and if government by majority rule cannot do so, then some other form of government — perhaps monarchy — is required instead.

By providing an allocation of the national income among people, the institution of private property exempts the institution of voting from the task which it can never perform without destroying itself, and, thereby, frees voting for the tasks which it can perform well, among which are the choice of leaders, the conduct of foreign affairs and the overall administration of the economy. The first theorem of welfare economics is especially important in this context. The theorem is that, if property rights are defended, the economy will of itself generate a set of market-clearing prices and a distribution of income among people with no additional input or influence from the government. One rule resolves a great many disputes. Under private ownership, the distribution of income among people is in accordance with the returns to the factors of production they possess, including, of course, their own labour. Given the distribution of resources among people, there is no need for explicit public decisions about the allocation of goods and services, no conflict, no wastage of resources or loss of life in taking or defending as is characteristic of anarchy, and no balance of terror as is characteristic of despotism. Private ownership of property ensures that the allocation among people of goods and services is effected quietly, costlessly and efficiently. The first theorem of welfare economics — that a competitive equilibrium exists — carries precisely that message.

The political role of private property is to direct production and to allocate income among people independently of decisions by the legislature. The legislature need not vote about the allocation of labour between farming and fishing, the relative incomes of farmers and fishermen, the choice of executives in large corporations or who is to keep his job and who is to become unemployed. These matters are arranged in the market, more or less as depicted in the general equilibrium model. To be sure, the separation of market from voting is incomplete. Legislatures cannot avoid influencing the detail of the economy as an indirect consequence of their responsibility for the provision of public goods, tax collection and general economic policy. But it is one thing to influence allocation, quite another to determine it altogether. A legislature could choose to ignore property rights and allocate incomes as it sees fit, but it need not do so. It has the option of not discussing the allocation of the national income among people and of relying on the market for the organization of the economy.

In short, voting requires property for self-preservation. Voting works as a method of social decision-making when the minority accepts the verdict of the majority and desists from going to war with the majority to get its own way. Such restraint will not be forthcoming unless members of the minority group believe themselves to be better off in the long run under a system of voting than they would be if voting were abolished. This expectation is justifiable only when the degree to which the majority can use the vote to dispossess the minority is limited. A general respect for property rights provides that limitation. We respect the institution of private property and, within limits, must accept the distribution of property as we find it, for the alternative is despotism.

It may be objected at this point that (i) a legislature which can accept the market's verdict on the allocation among people of the national income could, equally well, establish that allocation by decree without the intermediary of the market at all, and (ii) some other, extra-parliamentary method of allocation would do equally well. With regard to the first objection, it is sufficient to observe a major difference between economic and political allocation. When incomes are determined in the market, the legislature's only decision is to let the market be; the legislature could intervene but has the option of silence, of not discussing the allocation of income at all. When incomes are determined in the legislature, the option of silence is removed. Directly or indirectly, the legislature would have to choose incomes for each and every person in society. The exploitation problem would descend with a vengeance, and democratic government would in all probability self-destruct. Concerning the second objection, all that need be said is that in practice there is no other extra-parliamentary method of allocation. The only conceivable alternative, full equality of income, would destroy incentives to work and save and would in any case be incongruent with the considerable degree of hierarchy that an advanced society requires.

To deny that the legislature can allocate the national income among people is not to proscribe redistribution of income from rich to poor. The distinction is between choosing an entire set of incomes from scratch and the adoption of a rule that transfers some income from rich to poor without at the same time altering the ordering of people on the scale of rich and poor or eliminating altogether the advantages of being rich. The progressive income tax, the provision of welfare for the very poor and socialized medicine are redistributions in this sense of the term.

The essence of the distinction is that, with certain qualifications and within certain limits, the redistribution of income is a single-peaked issue for which there is a unique electoral equilibrium. Suppose, for example, redistribution is the only object of public expenditure and that it is conducted as follows: all incomes are taxed at a flat rate, t, and the revenue from the tax is redistributed equally to every person. The tax rate, t, is the measure of redistribution because, the larger t, the more equal does the post-tax distribution of income become. Redistribution of income is a single-peaked issue in this case because there is only one variable, t, to be chosen. Each person has a preferred value of t and would presumably vote for the rate that is closest to his preferred value in a contest between two other rates. By the median voter theorem, there must then be a certain tax rate t* which beats every other tax rate in a pairwise vote.

One might suppose that if the pre-tax distribution of income is skewed in the usual way — with a substantial majority of people whose incomes are somewhat below the average income in the country as a whole, and a minority of peoples whose incomes are well above average — a majority of the poor would be inclined to vote for a tax rate of 100 per cent. That would be true if redistribution had no effect on pre-tax incomes. As discussed in detail in Chapter VIII, that is no longer true when redistribution reduces the size of the pie because resources are used up in tax collection, because taxation creates a disincentive to work and save, and because resources are wasted in tax evasion. When the pie shrinks as you redistribute it, the post-tax income of the median voter is maximized while the tax rate is well short of 100 per cent.

The redistribution of income is not quite a single-peaked issue when the marginal tax rate is allowed to increase, to a greater or lesser extent, with the pre-tax income of the taxpayer, or when redistribution is undertaken on the expenditure side of the budget — through the old age pension, unemployment insurance, welfare to the poor or public provision of medical care. With some freedom to allow tax rates to vary according to pre-tax income, the poor and the rich can combine to exploit the middle to some extent without violating the redistributional requirement that the orderings of pre-tax and post-tax incomes be the same. But the original exploitation problem is not reproduced in voting about the degree of redistribution. The risk of exploitation is nothing like as serious when transfer programmes are bound by the constraints of progressive taxation, as when the legislature is unconstrained in its choice of a distribution of income. Redistribution is almost single-peaked, which is good enough in practice.

Conflict between rich and poor is not confined to the allocation of income. It spreads to the demarcation of the line between the domain of voting and the domain of property. Those who have more property naturally wish to expand the range of what money will buy, and those who have less property naturally wish to expand the range of goods, services and privileges associated with being a citizen, just as occupants of hierarchies in the public and private sectors wish to enlarge the organizations to which they belong. Generally speaking, the poor are more inclined to favour the redistribution of income and the public provision of services, like medical care and education, which are supplied equally to all but financed in most countries by taxes levied more or less in proportion to income.

Rights of people as equal voters and as unequal holders of property may conflict in less obvious ways. The rich might wish to interpret the right of assembly as the right to hire a hall for political meetings, while the poor might wish to expand that right to include the right to congregate in parks or on streets. The rich would prefer fixed fines for given offences, while the poor would prefer fines levied in proportion to income. The rich would prefer that a person convicted of a crime be given the option of paying a fine or going to prison, while the poor would rather that a prison term be mandatory. Each group wants a set of punishments with major deterrence on other groups and minor deterrence on itself. Notwithstanding the interdependence between property and voting, there is, inevitably, a conflict over the border between their domains. People differ according to their interests and circumstances in their views about where the fence posts belong.

One need not deny the place of violence and fraud in the original establishment of property rights or the absence of a compelling moral justification for the existing allocation of property or the insultingly wide gap between rich and poor in most capitalist countries to recognize the essential role of the allocation of property among people, and of the widespread acceptance of the entitlements, as the great indispensable bulwark in the defence of the liberal society. Property rights, quite apart from the property itself, are a significant part of the overhead capital of the nation. It is when property rights are in dispute — as, for instance, when opinion is split over the desirability of land reform, or when squatters on the outskirts of cities have ambiguous title to land (some rights but less than the full rights of ownership), or when title to natural resources is precarious, or when zoning laws are subject to change day by day, or, in the extreme, when there is a good deal of support in the general population for the outright expropriation of all private property — that the liberal society is in danger of dissolution. It is when property rights are accepted that civil liberties, freedom of speech and general prosperity are most likely to be found. In saying this, I am not advocating any particular rule of entitlement. I am maintaining that a country with widespread acceptance of some rule is fortunate. The process of forging a set of property rights is long, unpleasant and often bloody. A country without property rights is not a liberal society.[13]

The liberal society is a coherent form of organization, and not just a juxtaposition of voting and property, for the two institutions are indispensable to one another. Government by voting is the only real alternative to despotism, but it is altogether unsuitable for the allocation among people of the national income. An economy based on private property is efficient, but it needs the protection of the state and may give rise to an intolerably unequal distribution of income. Property frees voting from the allocation of income, while voting attends to the redistribution of income so that, on balance, the entire system becomes acceptable to the great majority of people who might otherwise employ the power of the vote to abolish property rights. That, at any rate, is the simple schema of the liberal society.[14]

As we proceed, the simple schema of the liberal society, in which property compensates for the principal defects of voting and voting compensates for the principal defects of property, will be confronted with a range of other considerations. Actual economics are less than completely efficient and less than completely autonomous. Monopoly, pollution, waste of resources in bargaining, predatory speculation, advertising, involuntary unemployment and other vestiges of anarchy drive the national income well below what it would be if the assumptions of the theorems of welfare economics were strictly true. The need for the state to clarify and redefine property rights in a thousand instances where rights become ambiguous — because new technology requires new rights or because of the intrinsic imprecision at the edges of all contracts — compels the government to choose between competing claims and eats away at the autonomy of the competitive economy. A large government comprising, as most governments in the democracies do, a third to a half of the national income cannot avoid influencing the allocation of income among people, though governmental influence may be greater or smaller depending on how economic policy is conducted. On the other hand, the conduct of government is infinitely more complex than is accounted for in our simple model of voting. Representative government, political parties' lobbying in the private sector, the intricate rules of parliamentary procedure and the complex motivations of politicians, soldiers and officials (each with private interests that are reflected to some extent in their actions), all serve to modify the simple pattern that is developed in this chapter.

These phenomena and others are discussed in the final three chapters of the book. They are discussed for their own sake, as vestiges of anarchy and despotism in the contemporary embodiment of the liberal society, with a view to the design of economic policy to keep the liberal society going, and in the belief that enough of the simple interdependence between property and voting survives the complexities of actual societies to make the whole enterprise worth while.

Notes

1 On rules, see G. Brennan and J. Buchanan, *The Reason of Rules: Constitutional Political Economy*, Cambridge University Press, 1985.

2 The argument that voting requires property is developed at greater length in D. Usher, *The Economic Prerequisite to Democracy*, Blackwell and Columbia University Press, 1981.

3 James Buchanan has for many years been advocating a constitutional safeguard for property rights and a constitutionally sanctioned limit on tradition to block the encroachment of the government on the private sector. See J. Buchanan, *The Limits of Liberty*, University of Chicago Press, 1975 and J. Brennan and J. Buchanan, *The Power to Tax*, Cambridge University Press, 1980.

4 For a good introduction to the paradox of voting and its implications, see W. Riker, *Liberalism vs. Populism: a Confrontation between the theory of Democracy and the Theory of Social Choice*, Freeman, 1982. On the generalization of the paradox of voting to public decision-making in a broader context, see Kenneth J. Arrow, *Social Choice and Individual Values*, Wiley, 1951.

5 The spectre of government by majority rule leading to the expropriation of property has been evoked for centuries as an argument against the establishment of democratic government. This anti-democratic argument was recognized by Aristotle, used by Oliver Cromwell against the Levellers (A.S.P.W. Woodhouse, *Puritanism and Liberty*, University of Chicago Press, 1938, 75), used by Macaulay against James Mill (J. Lively and J. Rees, *Utilitarian Logic and Politics*, Oxford University Press, 1978) and recognized, though, of course, opposed, by James Madison in the tenth Federalist letter (B.F. Wright, ed., *The Federalist*, Harvard University Press, 1961). The argument was introduced into the study of public finance by G. Tullock ("Problems of Majority Voting", *Journal of Political Economy*, 1959, 571–79).

6 The classic on this subject is Duncan Black, *The Theory of Committees and Elections*, Cambridge University Press, 1958.

7 The first preference of the median voter is not usually Pareto optimal. When a public good is financed by a proportional income tax, the first preference of the median voter is identified by the condition

$$MB_m = MC \left[Y_m / \sum Y_i \right]$$

while the necessary condition for Pareto optimality is

$$\sum MB_i = MC$$

where the subscript i refers to any voter i, the subscript m refers to the median voter, MC is marginal cost, MB_i is the marginal benefit to voter i, Y_i is the income of voter i and Σ refers to the sum over all voters. An amount of expenditure that satisfies one of these equations will not normally satisfy the other.

8 The choice of public expenditure for education could fail to be a single-peaked issue when some parents send their children to private schools. A paradox of voting could emerge if some people preferred high public spending to low public spending but at the same time preferred low public spending to medium public spending, a preference which would be rational for someone who would send his children to the state school when there is high public spending and a correspondingly high quality of public education, but who would send his children to private school when there is medium or low public spending on education. A person sending his children to a private school prefers low to medium public spending to minimize his tax bill.

9 See C. Plott, "A Notion of Equilibrium and its Possibility under Majority Rule, *American Economic Review*, 1967, 143–70, where it is shown that the median voter theorem fails in more than one dimension except in the special circumstances described in Figure 21(b).

10 On left and right as political language, see D. Usher, *The Economic Prerequisite to Democracy*, Blackwell, 1981, 32.

11 John Locke, *The Second Treatise of Civil Government*, 1690, chapter 5, para. 26, in Thomas I. Cook, ed., *Two Treatises of Government*, Hafner Press, 1947, 134.

12 As Robert Nozick argued in *Anarchy State and Utopia* (Blackwell, 1974, 175), one might as well say that I own the sea because I owned a can of tomato juice and poured it into the sea.

13 Redistributive programmes are sometimes looked upon as "new property", new forms of entitlement, comparable to ownership of the ordinary means of production. This is true in some senses but not in others. My entitlement to medical care at public expense if I am sick and to a publicly provided old age pension when I am old provide me with benefits that are comparable to what I would obtain from private medical insurance or from a privately purchased annuity; thus far, the new property and the old property are alike. New and old property differ in that the new property is not directly associated with factors of production and is more dependent on ongoing decisions in the public sector. The divorce between ownership and entitlement is exemplified by the old age pension, which has to be financed by current taxes or by a fund of assets that must necessarily be owned and administered in the public sector. Dependence on ongoing decisions in the public sector arises from the fact that, though the programmes themselves may persist over long periods of time, their benefit to recipients changes frequently. Parliament does not have to choose the wages of different kinds of labour or the returns to different kinds of capital, for factor prices are set in the market and owners of factors are compensated accordingly. Parliament does have to choose the size of the old age pension, the level of payment to the unemployed, the rules determining eligibility for welfare and the payments to people on the welfare roll. On the legal implications of new property see Charles Reich, "The New Property", *Yale Law Journal*, 1961, 733–87.

14 Though this consideration is peripheral to our main concern, it is worth mentioning that property can be a corrective to political overload or congestion. In a planned economy, there are too many items to vote about, too many complex issues for voters and legislators to master and resolve. The legislator, no matter how hard he tries, cannot become well informed on all the subjects about which he must vote. The voter, knowing that he can have no effect upon the outcome of the election except in the extremely unlikely event that his vote is pivotal, has no incentive to take the trouble to become well informed. The larger the scope of government, the more important these considerations become. The voters' lack of incentive to become well informed may be overcome to some extent by the role of politics as a spectator sport. One watches the activity of politicians with the same fascination that one watches a good hockey game, and one's enjoyment is enhanced by knowing something about how the game ought to be played.

Chapter VI

Transitions

Having described the three ideal types of society and the conditions in which they are stable, it seems natural to ask how one type of society may evolve into another. With three types of society, there can be at most six transitions: anarchy to despotism, anarchy to the liberal society, despotism to the liberal society, and their opposites. This chapter is a speculation about when, and under what circumstances, a society may be stable, about the process of transition when a society is not stable and about which transitions are likely to occur from time to time.

Our real interest is in the origin of the liberal society. The starting point is anarchy, which is really the absence of social organization. One way or another, the liberal society must evolve out of anarchy, but it may do so directly or indirectly, with despotism as an intermediate step. Whether the passage from anarchy to the liberal society is direct or indirect is, in a sense, a peculiar question. To learn how Canada evolved, one reads the history of the country, going back, of course, to the origins of its institutions in Europe and the Middle East — a history too complex to be pigeonholed as either direct or indirect evolution out of anarchy. Our question about the origin of the liberal society cannot be a straightforward historical question. It is, rather, a question posed about an imaginary past, but intended to identify the consequences of alternative courses of action today. The logic of the question is similar to the logic of Adam Smith's famous history of the progress of opulence, or of Marx's description of the transition from feudalism to capitalism to socialism, or of the accounts in Hobbes and Locke of the social contract — all highly stylized summaries of the great sweep of history, telling us, not what really happened, but what we can or ought to do now. Locke's account of the social contract reinforced the Whigs' devotion to individualism and liberty, just as the story of Abraham's willingness to sacrifice Isaac reinforced the Israelites' aversion to the sacrifice of human life.

To ask whether the liberal society evolved directly or indirectly is to contrast two presumptions about the prospects of reform. To say that the liberal society evolved directly out of anarchy is, on most versions of the story, to say that reform is quick and painless. If we do not like the way society is organized, we can reconstitute the state of nature, hold a constitutional convention, and rebuild society from scratch. To say that the liberal society evolved indirectly from anarchy, with despotism as an intermediate step, is to say that the evolution of the liberal society has been a slow, painful process that nobody would want to repeat. Reform of society so radical as to be tantamount to a return to anarchy would not create the better society that the reformers genuinely desire. People would be condemned to relive the passage through despotism, with the attendant risk that there might be no exit from despotism next time. One story is optimistic and the other is pessimistic about the prospects for large-scale social transformation.

Broadly speaking, the argument in this chapter is as follows. The transition from anarchy to despotism is straightforward because anarchy becomes unstable as soon as people learn to coordinate their activities. Once established, a despotic society may persist indefinitely, revert to anarchy or evolve into a liberal society. A model is developed in which population growth *might* destabilize a despotic society, causing a sudden reversion to anarchy, accompanied by a rapid and painful decrease in population and a restoration of the initial conditions from which despotism first emerged. There may be a recurrent cycle of anarchy and despotism, reminiscent of the dynastic cycle in the historiography of imperial China. The direct transition from anarchy to the liberal society is often portrayed as the outcome of a social contract establishing a government to preserve order. I argue that this much-told story is implausible because government emerging out of anarchy is almost certain to be despotic. Another theory of the direct emergence of the liberal society relies upon spontaneous self-interested behaviour to generate rules of cooperation that everyone has an incentive to respect. This too, I shall argue, is implausible as an explanation of the birth of the liberal society. A more convincing story can be told about the evolution of the liberal society out of despotism. Reversion of the liberal society to despotism is perhaps avoidable but by no means impossible.

To explain the transition from despotism to the liberal society is to postulate a process by which private ownership of the means of production and majority rule voting might gradually evolve in a society that is initially despotic. Private ownership is easy, for a ruling class soon discovers that it is more profitable and less troublesome to tax a market economy than to appropriate the surplus from a planned economy. An income-maximizing ruling class has reason to respect private property. Majority rule voting is more difficult to explain. I attempt to model the development of majority rule voting with a universal, or almost universal, franchise as the final stage of a gradual evolution out of the king's council. The first step is for the leading men of the kingdom to demand rights from the king, rights that cannot be exercised collectively except by voting. Then the franchise is gradually extended as rebellion by the unenfranchised is again and again averted through the enfranchisement of the wealthiest of the potential rebels. The model is developed with an eye to the history of England rather than France or the United States, where revolution had a more important part to play in the final establishment of democratic government (though conditions prior to the revolution cannot be fairly described as full-fledged despotism). In so far as this story is correct, the liberal society must be seen as the outcome of a long, frequently unpleasant evolution rather than as something men can create all at once.

From anarchy to despotism

The anarchic equilibrium in Chapter III was stable because there was no cooperation to take advantage of economies of scale in banditry and in defence against banditry. Allow for cooperation and immediately the bandits begin to organize. Gangs of bandits compete over territory — fighting, destroying and absorbing one another in the attempt to monopolize the exploitation of as large a population as possible. The gangs coalesce, until eventually there is only one large gang, and its leader becomes a king. Think of gangs as organized in a hierarchy, not just in ranks but as a complete pecking order from top to bottom. The gradual consolidation of society into a single hierarchy can be modelled as a random process in which pairs of gangs are combined, with or without a battle. The process begins in extreme anarchy where each gang consists of just one member. By chance, gangs meet and confront one another. The larger gang challenges the smaller to battle, and the smaller must accept the challenge or submit. The outcome in either case is that one of the gangs is tacked on to the end of the pecking order of the other. If the smaller gang submits, its members must occupy the lower ranks of the hierarchy of the new consolidated gang, but there is no loss of life. If the smaller gang chooses to fight, there is some chance of its winning a place at the top of the hierarchy of the consolidated gang, but this chance is purchased at the risk of some loss of life in the battle for priority. Assume that equal-sized gangs must fight.[1]

To formalize the process by which gangs coalesce, suppose (i) that each gang's probability of winning is a function of its size and of the size of its enemy, and (ii) that the probability of losing one's life in fighting is lower for the winner than for the loser in any battle. Specifically, define $\phi(n_1,n_2)$ as the probability that a gang of size n_1 defeats a gang of size n_2. The function ϕ is endowed with the properties that $\phi(n_1,n_2) + \phi(n_2,n_1) = 1$ (because winning and losing are mutually exclusive events), that $\phi(n_1,n_2) > 1/2$ whenever $n_1 > n_2$ (signifying that the larger gang has a better than even chance of winning), and that $\phi(n_1+x,n_2) > \phi(n_1,n_2)$ and $\phi(n_1,n_2+x) < \phi(n_1,n_2)$ for any positive x (signifying that an increase in the size of a gang must increase its chances of winning). Let V_W be the survival probability of someone on the winning side, let V_1 be the survival probability of someone on the losing side, and suppose that $V_W > V_1$.

In this context, a person's utility is assumed to depend on the size of the gang of which he is a member and on his rank within the gang. A person's utility is

$$U = U(i,j) \tag{1}$$

where j is the size of his gang and i is his rank within it. If he is the leader, then i = 1; if he is second-in-command, then i = 2, and so on. The dependence of utility on rank has the properties

$$U(i,j) > U(i+1,j) \tag{2}$$

and

$$U(i,j+1) > U(i,j) \tag{3}$$

For a gang of any given size, j, a person's utility increases with his rank in the hierarchy, and it is preferable to hold a given rank, i, in a large gang rather than in a small one. The function $U(i,j)$ is intended to represent all the advantages and all the risks of the person who occupies the i rank of a gang of size j. A more realistic utility function would take account of the number and size distribution of rival bands, but I have made no attempt to allow for this consideration. The utility function in equation (1) should be thought of as consistent with our earlier assumptions about utility — specifically, that a person whose utility would otherwise be U experiences a reduction in utility to VU when confronted with a once-and-for-all risk to his life of $1 - V$.

When a gang of two members submits to a group of five members, everybody in the original five-member gang becomes better off, for it is preferable to be the i member of a seven-member gang than to be the i member of a five-member gang. The utility of the leader of the five-member gang is $U(1,5)$. His utility increases to $U(1,7)$ when his gang acquires two more members. At the same time, the utility of the former leader of the two-member gang decreases from $U(1,2)$ to $U(6,7)$. If the leader of the smaller gang chooses to fight rather than to submit, and if fighting entails no loss of life, the expected utility of the leader of the five-member gang would be $\phi(5,2) U(1,7) + \phi(2,5) U(3,7)$ and the expected utility of the leader of the two-member gang would be $\phi(2,5) U(1,7) + \phi(5,2) U(6,7)$. If fighting entails the loss of one randomly chosen person on each side (so that the risk to each person in the smaller gang is much higher than the risk to each person in the larger gang), the expected utility of the leader of the five-member gang becomes

$$(4/5)[\phi(5,2) \, U(1,5) + \phi(2,5) \, U(2,5)]$$

and the expected utility of the leader of the two-member gang becomes

$$(1/2)[\phi(2,5) \, U(1,5) + \phi(5,2) \, U(5,5)]$$

where the numbers 4/5 and 1/2 are survival probabilities, and where $\phi(5,2)$ is considerably larger than $\phi(2,5)$. The leader of the two-member gang chooses to submit rather than to fight if

$$U(6,7) > 1/2[\phi(2,5) \, U(1,5) + \phi(5,2) \, U(5,5)]$$

He submits unless the small chance of becoming the leader of a five-member gang outweighs the risk of combat.

More generally, imagine a confrontation between a gang of n_1 members and a gang of n_2 members where $n_1 < n_2$, where V_W and V_L are survival probabilities of winner and loser in the event of a fight, and where the leader of the smaller gang (n_1 members) has no option other than to fight or submit. If the leader of the smaller gang chooses to submit, his utility becomes $U(n_2+1,n_1+n_2)$. If he chooses to fight, his utility becomes

$$\phi(n_1,n_2) \, V_W U(1,n_1 V_W + n_2 V_L) + \phi(n_2,n_1) \, V_L U(n_2 V_W + 1, n_2 V_W + n_1 V_L)$$

The expression requires some explanation. The total number of survivors of a fight is $n_1 V_W + n_2 V_L$ if the smaller gang wins, and $n_2 V_W + n_1 V_L$ if the larger gang wins. Thus the expected utility of the leader of the smaller gang is the sum of (i) his expected utility if his gang wins, $V_W U (1,n_1 V_W + n_2 V_L)$, weighted by the probability of the event, $\phi(n_1,n_2)$, and (ii) his expected utility if his gang loses, $V_L U(n_2 V_W + 1, n_2 V_W + n_1 V_L)$, weighted by the probability of that event, $\phi(n_2,n_1)$, where, of course, the probabilities sum to 1 because winning and losing are mutually exclusive events. The leader of the smaller gang chooses his utility-maximizing course of action, and the two gangs are combined, either by the submission of the smaller gang or as the outcome of a battle. In either case, the number of independent gangs in society is reduced by one at each encounter until, eventually, only one large hierarchy remains.

The reader need hardly be reminded how much of the reality of warring states is being ignored. There is no territory in the model. To win a battle is to acquire one's opponent's soldiers so as to be in a better position to confront the next opponent who comes along. The assumption that a person's utility increases with the size of the gang to which he belongs is consistent with the supposition that large gangs control large territories or can command disproportionate shares of the national product, but these considerations are not part of the formal model. There is no distinction in the model between a battle and a war. A side cannot lose some of its territory or some of its men and keep going. The only possibilities are total victory or total defeat. Nor are there alliances between gangs. Gang A and gang B, fearing the greater strength of gang C, cannot combine to defeat C and divide up its men and resources.

More important, the model contains within it no limit to the size of nations. Wars cannot end in a stand-off between rival gangs, each in possession of its own territory. There is no natural stopping place within the model between extreme anarchy and world government. It is not difficult to imagine how a stand-off between nations may arise. Seas, mountains or rivers may separate nations that are strong enough to protect their borders but not to expand their territory. Transport and communication may limit a country's capacity to engage an enemy located at a distance from the centre of gravity of the country's population and resources.[2] Organization alone may be a barrier to the development of very large states. Distant provinces may be ultimately uncontrollable, for a king who keeps a tight rein upon his provincial governors may deny them the freedom of action required for the suppression of organized banditry, while a king who keeps a loose rein upon his provincial governors may run the risk of rebellion as subordinates become accustomed to the exercise of independent authority. A leader of extraordinary organizational talent — an Alexander — may establish a great empire which disintegrates upon his death. In view of these limitations, the reader should look upon this model as part of a larger but unspecified model characterizing the limits as well as the sources of the growth of nations. My purpose in constructing the model is merely to emphasize the instability of anarchy and the natural tendency toward despotism once people learn to act in concert.

Strictly speaking, this model of the evolution of despotism leaves no residue of bandits once the evolution is complete, but a permanent place could have been found for banditry by supposing that the probability of an encounter between any two gangs increases with the size of both gangs. The probability of an encounter between the ruling hierarchy and a bandit could then be made small enough not to deter banditry altogether. The hierarchy would encompass the entire population except for a fringe of outlaws whose survival probabilities are reduced by the activity of the rulers, but not sufficiently to convert outlaws into obedient subjects.

One aspect of the reality of warring states is accounted for reasonably well. The evolution of anarchy into despotism is a "time of troubles" for the warring bandits themselves and for the innocent bystanders whose means of subsistence is appropriated by one side or another in the conflict, or is destroyed by one side so as to weaken the other. A part of this process is captured within the model by the assumptions about the loss of life in combat.[3]

From despotism back to anarchy

Despotism may be stable. Having once evolved out of anarchy, a despotic society might persist for ever, with only the occasional mishap, as when an incompetent ruler is displaced or the succession is contested. In the absence of technical change, the standard of living in a despotic society is highest at the time when the despotic society first emerges out of anarchy. All social classes — farmers, bandits and rulers — are better off at that time than they will ever be again because the population is small and can be expected to grow rapidly thereafter. The population is small because the sustainable population in an anarchic society is considerably less than the sustainable population in a despotic society and because of the loss of life during the time of troubles when the new dynasty was establishing itself. Income per head is high because the land–man ratio is high and because resources formerly devoted to warfare can for the first time be devoted to the production of useful goods and services. In these conditions, birth rates can be expected to exceed death rates and the population increases. Population growth leads to a fall in output per farmer for the usual Malthusian reasons, and this in turn causes birth rates to fall or death rates to rise. Eventually the despotic society may settle down into a stationary state with net population growth among the wealthy, net population decline among the poor, some movement from one class to the other, and constant total population.

There is another possibility. Population growth may eventually render despotism unstable by wiping out the advantages of the ruling class. In our examination of the despotic society, we identified five principles of income distribution, of which the first four — maintenance of a subsistence wage, maintenance of an efficiency wage, control of banditry and discouragement of rebellion — all place limits on the rulers' capacity to exploit their subjects. When the population is small, the rulers can, within these limits, provide themselves with incomes that are well above the incomes of their subjects. These limits become increasingly restrictive as population growth reduces potential output per head. The subject, as always, is paid whatever income serves to maximize the welfare of the rulers. Though the subjects' income per head falls as population grows, it may not fall fast enough to keep the rulers' residual from falling even faster until a point is reached where the gap between rulers' income and subjects' income is eliminated altogether. At this point the largest income per head that the rulers can extract from the economy is no greater than the income of their subjects. Beyond that critical point the rulers who are now worse off than farmers or bandits begin to desert their posts and to become bandits instead. A chain reaction ensues; the number of bandits increases, the incomes of the rulers decline, and more rulers abandon their class, until the ruling class disappears altogether.

This second possibility has a strong resemblance to the dynastic cycle in Chinese history. The rise and fall of dynasties was connected anthropomorphically with the health of society at large: prosperity when the dynasty is young and flourishing, misery and poverty in its decline . . .

politics, like men, have their periods of birth, growth, maturity, senescence and death . . . In its genesis a dynasty received the mandate to rule from Heaven, which recognized the justice and promise of the new regime. And at its end a dynasty lost the mandate when its performance . . . destroyed the moral basis of a good society.[4]

There seem to be two main versions of the theory, one "moral" and the other "economic". The moral version attributes the breakdown of a dynasty to the corruption of the rulers themselves: luxury, impiety, excessive influence of eunuchs or women, astrological portents of Heaven's displeasure and so on. The economic version attributes the breakdown to more mundane causes associated primarily with population growth, peasant rebellion and the difficulty of squeezing tax revenue from an increasingly impoverished peasantry to finance the civil service and the army. Obviously, it is the latter version that connects with our models of anarchy and despotism. The cycle itself begins with the emergence of a despotic society out of anarchy as described above. Prosperity under despotism gives rise to population growth. Population growth undermines the basis of despotism. The dissolution of despotism is accompanied by population decline, recreating the anarchic society, and the cycle begins again.

The place to start in examining the dissolution of despotism under the impact of population growth is the model in Table 4. A ruling class of equals maximizes its own welfare, W^R, in circumstances where the rulers' capacity to exploit farmers is limited by the farmer's option of becoming a bandit. The proportions of farmers and bandits in the population depend upon the tax rate that the rulers impose. The higher the tax rate, the more bandits there will be. The model was constructed for a fixed population, n. Since survival rates of members of each social class are already endogenous to the model, the model itself becomes dynamic as soon as the birth rate is determined. Suppose the birth rate is constant at b and is the same for all social classes. Population growth becomes

$$\frac{\dot{n}}{n} = \frac{n^F S^F + n^B S^B + n^R S^R}{n} + b - 1 \qquad (2.22)$$

where S^F, S^B and S^R are the survival rates of the three social classes; $S^F = V^{FB} M(Y^F)$, $S^B = V^{BF} V^{BR} M(Y^B)$ and $S^R = V^{RB} M(Y^R)$. The equation for population growth under anarchy is the same except that the term $n^R S^R$ drops out because there are no rulers in an anarchic society. (The numbering of this equation refers to the models of anarchy and despotism in Tables 2 and 4.)

Let $W^A(n)$ be the welfare of a person in anarchy, $W^F(n)$ the welfare of farmers in a despotic society and $W^R(n)$ the welfare of rulers in a despotic society when the total population is n; $W^R(n)$ is the most rulers can extract for themselves and $W^F(n)$ is whatever farmers' incomes turn out to be when rulers act that way. Following Thomas Hobbes, we are adopting the working assumption that anarchy is so dangerous and so nasty that everybody, subjects as well as rulers, becomes better off with the establishment of a despotic society. The burden of the taxes that the rulers impose on farmers does not outweigh the benefit to farmers of the reduction in the incidence of banditry. Thus $W^F(n) > W^A(n)$ for all values of n. The welfare of the subject is greater under despotism than under anarchy for any given population. However, the assumption does not imply that farmers in *any* despotic society are better off than people in *any* anarchic society. A person's welfare may be greater in an anarchic society with a small population than in a despotic society with a large population. Population growth reduces the standard of living of farmers and bandits as long as there are diminishing returns to labour in agriculture, as specified by the production function in the model of the despotic society in Table 4.

The welfare of farmers in an anarchic society, of farmers in a despotic society and of rulers in a despotic society is illustrated as functions of total population in the three downward sloping curves in Figure 22. The welfare of bandits is always the same as the welfare of farmers because people cannot be prevented from switching from one occupation to another. In both anarchy and despotism the welfare of farmers decreases with total population, as a consequence of diminishing returns to labour in agriculture and because, beyond some point, any reduction in the income of the farmer reduces his efficiency at work. The curve depicting the welfare of farmers in anarchy is always below the curve depicting the welfare of farmers in a despotic society, reflecting our assumption that the farmer is worse off in anarchy than under despotism for any given population. The welfare of rulers usually exceeds the welfare of farmers, but it can be expected to decline more rapidly as population grows. Any reduction in the farmers' incomes leads eventually to a reduction in their survival rate associated with natural causes. This neutralizes the farmers' advantage over the bandits in having no risk of death in conflict with rulers and leads to an increase in the proportion of bandits in the population if the welfare of farmers and bandits is to remain the same.

Population cannot grow indefinitely. A moment must come when population growth stops because the birth rate no longer exceeds the average of the death rates among all social classes. Since everyone is better off in despotism than in anarchy, the maximal population must be correspondingly larger. In Figure 22 the maximal populations in anarchy and under despotism are indicated by n_A and n_D. (Note that populations

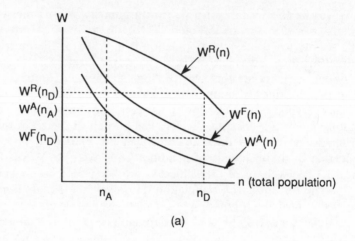

(a)

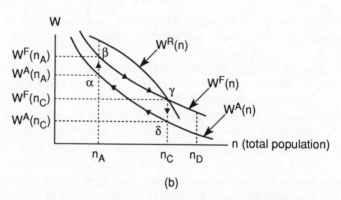

(b)

Figure 22 Alternative paths of the welfare of rulers and farmers as population grows

of social classes are indicated by superscripts, while alternative values of total population are indicated by subscripts.)

Two possible paths of W^R as a function of total population are shown in Figure 22. Figure (22a) is drawn on the assumption that the welfare of rulers, while declining faster than the welfare of farmers for the reasons set out above, remains larger when population growth finally stops at n_D. This is the situation which gives rise to a despotic stationary state with no tendency to revert to anarchy. The other possibility is illustrated in Figure 22(b). There may come a time, while the population is still growing, when the best the rulers can do for themselves — the maximal value of W^R over all possible values of n^R and t — is no greater than the associated value of W^F. In this case, the W^R curve crosses the W^F curve at a population of n_C(C is mnemonic for catastrophe) which is still less than n_D, at which population growth stops. Once population growth reaches n_C there is no longer an advantage in belonging to the ruling class. The slightest increase in population above n_C creates an incentive on the part of each member of the ruling class to become a bandit again. Desertion from the ruling class reduces W^R still further. The ruling class collapses. Despotism reverts to anarchy.

The disintegration of the despotic society and its collapse into anarchy are accompanied by a precipitous fall in the welfare of subjects from $W^F(n_C)$ to $W^A(n_C)$. Population then declines because n_C is considerably greater than n_A, which is the stationary state population of an anarchic society. This is a time of troubles, and of rapidly declining population, between the destruction of one dynasty and the formation of another. Perhaps a new gang of bandits can assert itself and assume the mandate of Heaven before population has fallen all the way down to n_A, or perhaps a long period of anarchy intervenes between the end of one dynasty and its replacement by another.

When the disintegration of despotism entails a reduction in population to the anarchic equilibrium, the welfare of subjects over the cycle is as indicated by the path in Figure 22(b). Start with an anarchic equilibrium at α. The establishment of a despotic society creates an era of prosperity when the welfare of subjects (the height of the point β) is as great as it will ever be. Population growth gradually reduces W^F to $W^F(n_C)$ at the point γ. Then W^F falls sharply to $W^A(n_C)$ at the point δ, followed by a gradual rise to its original level in the anarchic equilibrium as population declines from n_C to n_A, and the cycle begins again.

A despotic society disintegrates periodically into anarchy or evolves into a permanent stationary state, depending on whether the population at which mortality rates finally catch up with birth rates is greater or less than the population at which the welfare of the rulers can no longer be made to exceed the welfare of subjects and the advantage of being a ruler is lost.

A numerical example may help at this point. The equations describing a despotic society are difficult to solve, but the flavour of the model and the conditions determining the paths of evolution — the dynastic cycle or the stationary state — can be conveyed with the aid of simplifying assumptions about the technology of banditry and policework. Suppose:

(i) Everyone works the same number of hours per day.
(ii) The aggregate production function is

$$Q = 100\sqrt{n^F} \tag{4}$$

where Q is total national income in billions of dollars and n^F is the number of farmers in millions.

(iii) Each person's utility function is

$$W^i = M(Y^i)\, V^i \ln (Y^i) \tag{5}$$

where M is survival probability associated with natural causes, V is survival probability associated with violence, and the superscript is either F, B or R.

(iv) Neither farmers nor rulers bear any risk of losing their lives at the hands of bandits ($V^F = V^R = 1$), but the life of a bandit is dangerous.

(v) Rulers are able to control bandits to some extent but not altogether. For the rulers to have an effect on banditry, the number of rulers must be at least as large as the number of bandits. If there are fewer rulers than bandits, the entire crop is stolen and bandits are not endangered by rulers ($V^B = 1$). If there are more rulers than bandits, the amount stolen is limited to half the crop and bandits bear a 40 per cent chance per decade of losing their lives at the hands of rulers ($V^B = 0.6$). Once the number of rulers equals the number of bandits, the presence of additional rulers has no effect upon the amount stolen or upon the risk borne by bandits. Thus when the ruling class is no larger than is necessary to limit the extent of banditry

$$n^R = n^B \quad \text{and} \quad n^B Y^B = Q/2 \tag{6}$$

(vi) Survival probability associated with natural causes depends on income. Specifically,

$$M(Y) = 0.9 \min(1, \ln (Y)/\ln (5)) \text{ when } Y > 1 \tag{7}$$

and

$$M(Y) = 0 \text{ when } Y \text{ is 1 or less,}$$

where Y is measured in thousands of dollars. The best survival probability one can hope for is 90 per cent, which occurs when one's income is in excess of \$5,000. Survival probability declines steadily with income until it reaches a floor of zero at an income of \$1,000, as illustrated in Figure 23.

(vii) There is free mobility of labour between farming and banditry, ensuring that welfare is the same in both occupations ($W^F = W^B$), that is

$$(0.9) M(Y^F) \ln (Y^F) = (0.9) (0.6) M(Y^B) \ln (Y^B) \tag{8}$$

(viii) Rulers choose Y^F and n^R to maximize their own income per head. For any given total population, n, rulers choose Y^F and n^R to maximize Y^R subject to the above equations as constraints and to the additional constraint that

$$n^F + n^B + n^R = n \tag{9}$$

On these simplifying assumptions one can deduce all the characteristics of a despotic society, including its aggregate survival rate, for any given total population. This information is presented in Table 6 for alternative values of total population as indicated in the first column. Numbers in all the remaining columns are inferred.

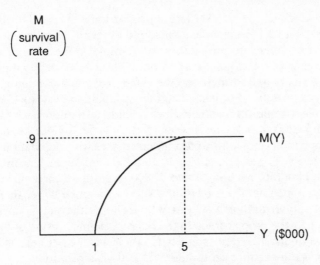

Figure 23　Survival rate per decade associated with natural causes of death

Table 6　*The distribution of income by social class in a despotic society*

Population (millions)			National income ($ billions)	Income per head ($ thousands)			Aggregate survival rate per decade
Total n	Farmers n^F	Bandits n^B	Q	Farmers Y^F	Bandits Y^B	Rulers Y^R	
25	12.3	6.3	351	7.3	27.7	13.4	0.809
50	21.8	14.1	466	5.4	16.5	8.2	0.798
75	34.7	20.1	589	5.0	14.6	6.0	0.803
100	40.0	30.0	633	4.5	10.6	4.5	0.752
125	43.8	40.6	661	4.2	8.1	3.7	0.690
150	47.4	51.3	668	3.9	6.7	3.1	0.643

When the population is as low as 25 million, about half the people are farmers and everyone is quite well off, though rulers are very much better off than farmers. Bandits have higher consumption than rulers, but not sufficiently higher to compensate for the difference in survival rates. Rulers' survival rate is 0.9, the maximal value of M; bandits' survival rate is 0.54, the product of their survival rate associated with natural causes, 0.9, and their survival rate associated with encounters with rulers, 0.6. Thus the welfare of rulers, W^R, is 2.3 ($W^R = (0.9) \ln (13.4)$) while the welfare of bandits, W^B, is only 1.8 ($W^B = 0.54 \ln (27.7)$).

As population grows, an ever larger proportion is diverted to ruling and to banditry, output per person declines, and everyone's income declines as well. However, rulers' incomes decline more rapidly than farmers' incomes, and a moment comes when, as total population reaches 100 million, the incomes of rulers and farmers are the same. Beyond 100 million, despotism becomes unstable. For instance, if the population grew to 125 million, the best rulers could do for themselves would be to allow each farmer an income of $4,200, which leaves rulers with only $3,700 per head.

The proportion of bandits to farmers increases with population because all *per capita* incomes and survival rates decline. When the incomes of farmers and bandits are both above $5,000 the ratio of their survival rates is 0.6 and the income of the bandit must be very much larger than that of the farmer if their utilities (W^F and W^B) are to be the same. Since, by assumption, half the crop accrues to the bandit, the proportion of bandits in the population must be quite small when their income per head is high. As the income of the farmer drops below $5,000 his mortality rate associated with natural causes drops below 0.9, the ratio of the survival rate of the bandit to the survival rate of the farmer rises above 0.6, the disparity in their incomes falls accordingly and the number of bandits required to "use up" half the crop increases as well.

The last column of the table shows aggregate survival rates, the population-weighted sum of the survival rates of all social classes. Except for a blip where $Y^F = 0.5$, the rate declines steadily with output per head, slowly at first owing to the gradual increase in the proportion of bandits, and then rapidly once consumption per head of farmers falls below $5,000. The aggregate survival rate when population reaches the critical level of 100 million (at which rulers are no longer better off than their subjects) is 0.752. Thus the despotic society described in this example evolves into a stationary state if the birth rate is less than 0.248 per decade, and it is unstable if the birth rate exceeds 0.248 per period.

If despotism cannot be maintained, society reverts, at least temporarily, to anarchy. Suppose the birth rate is 25 per cent so that population continues to grow beyond 100 million and the despotic society disintegrates because rulers became worse off than bandits. Suppose also that anarchy may be characterized as follows. (i) Banditry and guard labour together occupy nine-tenths of the available labour time, leaving only one-tenth for farming. This assumption is consistent with the assumptions that bandits steal half the crop while farmers devote four-fifths of their time to guard labour. (ii) Banditry and the protection of one's crop from bandits entail mortality rates, for bandits and farmers alike, of 20 per cent, i.e. $V^F = V^B = 0.8$. (iii) There is unrestricted mobility of labour between farming and banditry.

At a population of 100 million an anarchic society provides an output per head of only $3,160 ($(1/n) \, 100 \, (n/10)^{1/2}$ where n = 100), and the survival rate per decade is only 0.57 (0.8 ln $(10^{1/2})$/ln 5). Thus population declines at an initial rate of 18 per cent [43–25] per decade. The decline is arrested only when the population becomes small enough — and the marginal product of labour large enough — that birth and death rates equalize once again. This occurs once the population has fallen from 100 million to 48.9 million. The steady-state population in anarchy is the solution, n, to the equation {0.8 ln [(1/n) 100 $(n/10)^{1/2}$]/ln 5 = 0.75}. *Per capita* income in the anarchic stationary state with a population of only 48.9 million is \$4,520 ((1/48.9) 100 $(4.89)^{1/2}$), which is not significantly different from the income of farmers in a despotic society with 100 million people.

Thus, with the parameters we have chosen, there is a perpetual dynastic cycle. It begins in anarchy with an equilibrium population of just under 50 million. The anarchic equilibrium is disturbed when rival gangs compete to form the new dynasty. The eventual establishment of the dynasty ushers in a period of prosperity and tranquillity in which the income per head of farmers is initially in excess of \$5,000, incomes of rulers and bandits are higher still and farmers experience minimal mortality rates. The birth rate exceeds the death rate, population grows and *per capita* income gradually falls. Eventually population exceeds the critical point at which rulers become worse off than bandits. Despotism dissolves, population declines, and the cycle begins again.

The birth rate is critical in this process. If the birth rate were 24 per cent rather than 25 per cent, population growth would stop at a population just short of 100 million, and the despotic society would evolve into a stationary state.

The birth of the liberal society

So far, it has been shown in this chapter how anarchy may evolve into despotism and how despotism may either evolve into a stationary state or revert, under the impact of population growth, to anarchy. That must not be the end of the story, for there is as yet no mechanism by which the liberal society might evolve. I will consider three simple models of the birth of the liberal society: the spontaneous emergence of cooperation, the social contract, and the disintegration of despotism. The first two models are of the direct evolution of the liberal society from anarchy. The third entails a circuitous route from anarchy to despotism and from despotism to the liberal society. I will argue that the stories of the direct evolution from anarchy to the liberal society are inherently implausible and, more seriously, since we are dealing here in political myths, fundamentally misleading as guides to action. The story of the indirect evolution through despotism is better on both counts.

The spontaneous emergence of cooperation

Can spontaneous, self-interested and uncoordinated actions by a large number of people lead to the gradual abandonment of anarchy and the emergence of a liberal society with voting and property rights? Note that we already have a model of the abandonment of anarchy, but that it leads to the wrong place; it leads merely to a society where one big gang of bandits has suppressed many, though not necessarily all, little gangs of bandits. The question at hand is whether anarchy can be made to evolve spontaneously into something less nasty.

This has been claimed to be possible. The basis of the claim, as I understand it, is the demonstration of how certain simple institutions might have evolved through the uncoordinated activity of many self-interested agents. The demonstration that these institutions could evolve spontaneously becomes by analogy the justification for the proposition that more complex institutions may have evolved that way as well. Two examples of the spontaneous evolution of institutions are the choice of a market day, a variant of a problem examined by Schotter,[5] and the repeated prisoners' dilemma game as examined by Axelrod.[6] I discuss these examples briefly, primarily to show that they do not provide a basis for the presumption that the liberal society may have evolved spontaneously out of anarchy. *Some* institutions may evolve spontaneously; *many* institutions have not, unless the word "spontaneously" is given so extended a meaning as to cover all possible events.

Spontaneous evolution of institutions is exemplified by the choice of a market day, when a group of farmers, whose only interest in one another is to have a large choice among trading partners and who cannot communicate with one another at all, do ultimately establish a universally recognized market day by a process of choosing days at random and updating probability weights in the light of past experience. Farmers go to market once a week. Each farmer knows the location of the market and the number of other farmers at the market on the days when he himself is present. He does not know the total number of farmers or the number of other farmers at the market on those days when he is absent. Someone who goes to market on Tuesday, for example, knows how many other farmers are there on Tuesday, but not on any other day. Farmers home in on one particular day by rational use of their observation of the numbers of farmers on various days over a long series of weeks. In the first week of the process, when nobody has any idea which day is likely to be more crowded than any other, each farmer picks a day at random in a lottery where every day has the same weight. Then gradually, as the farmer acquires experience, he places more weight on days that are observed to be more crowded. Eventually, and purely by accident, one day acquires an edge over the rest. As the weeks go by, more and more farmers are present at the market on that day, until, finally, all farmers appear at the market on that day alone.

Let N be the total number of farmers, and let n(d,t) be the number who go to market on day d of week t. A farmer who goes to market on that day observes n(d,t). He does not observe n(d*,t) where d* refers to any other day of the week. The farmer dare not go to market on the same day every week until he is confident that he has found the best day, but he does learn from experience. His choice each week is biased toward the day which he has observed to have been most crowded. He balances uncertainty and experience by choosing a day each week on the throw of a weighted seven-sided die where the weights change from week to week according to what the farmer observes. Define $p^i(d,t)$ to be choice of farmer i of the probability (or weighting of the die) of going to market on day d of week t. By definition,

$$p^i(1,t) + p^i(2,t) + \ldots + p^i(7,t) = 1 \qquad (10)$$

for all i and t. The process begins at week 0. Having no information about how many people to expect at the market each day, farmers set $p^i(d,0) = 1/7$ for all d. Thereafter, each farmer gets one piece of information per week. He observes the number of other farmers who appear at the market on the same day as himself. Farmers get different information because they go to the market on different days of the week.

In updating probabilities, the farmers' problem is to avoid a situation where, for instance, one group of farmers goes to the market regularly on Tuesday, another goes regularly on Wednesday, and the advantages of all going on the same day are lost because neither group knows of the existence of the other. Farmers must adopt an updating procedure in which the sampling of the days of the week does not stop altogether until farmers are absolutely sure they have discovered the day when the market is most crowded.

Considerable sophistication could be employed in constructing a set of estimates, $n^i(d,t)$, of the number of people at the market on each of the seven days of that week and in transforming these estimates into probabilities $p^i(d,t)$, but a simple rule of thumb, such as the following, might be sufficient.

In estimating the number of people at the market on any day this week, the farmer might look no further than his most recent observation of the number of people who did appear on that day. The estimate $n^i(d,t)$ would be the most recent observation by farmer i at the start of the week t of the number of people who appeared at the market on day d. If t is the fiftieth week, if the last time farmer i went to the market on a Tuesday was in the fortieth week and if he observed sixty-five people there, then n^i (Tuesday, 50) = 65. In the event that farmer i has never gone to the market on day d̂, the value of $n^i(\hat{d},t)$ would have to be set equal to the average of $n^i(d,t)$ for those days d when he has gone to the market. The terms $n^i(d,t)$ are defined for all t except t = 0. If farmer i observed 100 people at the market on Wednesday of week 0, 110 people on Tuesday of week 1 and ninety people on Friday of week 2, then n^i (Tuesday,3) = 110, n^i (Wednesday,3) = 100, n^i (Friday,3) = 90 and $n^i(d,3)$ = 100 for all d different from Tuesday, Wednesday and Friday.

The important consideration in converting the seven estimates, $n^i(d,t)$, into probability weights, $p^i(d,t)$, is to keep all of the $p^i(d,t)$ from falling to zero prematurely, because a day for which $p^i(d,t)$ is equal to zero will never be sampled again. This pitfall can be avoided by weighting all days equally, except for the one day for which $n^i(d,t)$ is largest. Define $d^i(t)$ to be that day for farmer i in week t; by construction $n^i(d^i(t),t) > n^i(d,t)$ for any other day d. The farmer might choose his probability weights as follows. For the day estimated to be the most crowded,

$$p^i(d^i(t),t) \equiv \frac{n^i(d^i(t),t)}{\sum_{d=1}^{7} n^i(d,t)} \tag{11}$$

and for all other days d,

$$p^i(d,t) \equiv 1/6[1 - p^i(d^i(t),t)] \tag{12}$$

By construction, $p^i(d^i(t), t)$ is larger than $p^i(d,t)$ for any day d, other than $d^i(t)$. Also $p^i(d^i(t),t)$ approaches 1 and $p^i(d,t)$, for all d other than $d^i(t)$, approaches 0 whenever six out of the seven values of $n^i(d,t)$ approach 0.

In week 0, at the beginning of the process, no farmer has any reason to choose one day over another, all farmers' weights for all seven days are 1/7, and more or less the same number of farmers go to market on each of the seven days. At the beginning of the following week 1, each farmer has one observation, but that still provides no basis for differentiating among the days of the week in setting probability weights. Again all farmers set all weights at 1/7. In week 1, however, each farmer gets a second observation and a unique $d^i(2)$ can be identified. The probability that farmer i attaches to the days in week 2, though similar, are no longer quite the same. Eventually, entirely by chance, one day acquires an edge over the rest. From then on, farmers gradually increase their probabilities of going to market on that day and the probability of going to market on any other day becomes closer and closer to zero.

The essence of the example is that this eminently satisfactory result does not emerge through central planning or because farmers act in accordance with their conception of the common good. The rules for choosing probabilities each week may be thought of as representing prudent self-interested behaviour on the part of farmers who are always searching for

Player B

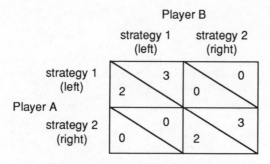

Figure 24 The coordination game

the day with the largest n. A clear example of the spontaneous evaluation of a social institution!

What are we to make of this story? Do we have here a paradigm of the evolution of the liberal society out of anarchy, or do we have an instance of spontaneous evaluation embedded in a larger and very different mechanism? I would argue that the latter is almost certainly the case.

The story is not particularly convincing, even as an explanation of the choice of a market day. The Sunday market could have evolved spontaneously, but it could, equally well, be the consequence of an explicit public decision. The king might have decreed that henceforth the market will be held on Sunday. Some prehistoric Paul Revere may have ridden among the farmers shouting, "It's Sunday!" Other institutions that might have emerged spontaneously in the process described above — driving on the right-hand side of the road or the use of standardized weights and measures — could also have been established by decree.

A more important criticism of the story of the Sunday market as a basis for an explanation of the emergence of the liberal society is that the story lacks essential ingredients of social interaction in anarchy and abstracts from the real impediments to spontaneous cooperation. The Sunday market example is a particular case of what Ullman-Margalit[7] has called coordination norms, defined as social conventions emerging from situations representable as games of the form in Figure 24. Each of two players (the essence of the game is unaffected by the addition of more players) chooses between two (easily generalized to any number, for instance, seven) available strategies. The essence of the game is that neither player cares which strategy is played as long as everybody plays the same strategy — the same day to bring one's goods to market, the same side of the road, the same weights and measures. The players would immediately agree upon a coordinated strategy — either left or right, it makes no difference — if they could communicate. The choosing of a strategy at random and

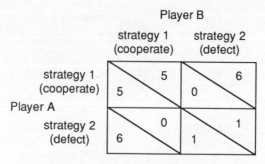

Figure 25 The prisoner's dilemma

updating one's probability on the basis of the observed behaviour of other players is a substitute for communication in this game.

Ullman-Margalit includes the coordination game as one of three fundamental games representing basic types of social interactions. The other games are less amenable to an ideal, unanimously agreed-upon solution. The second game is the standard prisoner's dilemma in Figure 25, where the outcome when each player does what is best for himself is different from, and worse for everybody than, the outcome when players cooperate. To cooperate in this example is to choose strategy 1. When both players cooperate, they both get an income of 5. When neither cooperates, they both get an income of 1. Yet the only equilibrium of the game is for neither of them to cooperate. Defection from cooperation is the individually rational strategy, despite the fact that cooperation is best for everybody. Consider the options of player A. If player B chooses to cooperate, the best strategy for player A is to defect, so that his pay-off is 6 rather than 5. If player B chooses to defect, the best strategy for player A is still to defect, so that his pay-off is 1 rather than 0. Defection is the best strategy for player A regardless of what player B chooses to do. Player A defects, and so too does player B, because their situations are entirely symmetrical. By following individually rational strategies the parties make themselves worse off than they would be if they could arrange to cooperate. As in the coordination game, communication among the players might lead to an agreement to cooperate, but now each player has an incentive to double-cross the other. The games differ in that the agreement in the prisoners' dilemma game needs to be enforced, while the agreement in the coordination game is self-enforcing. The prisoner's dilemma game looks like a model of anarchy with no escape, no route to any analogue of the liberal society.

The third fundamental game in Ullman-Margalit's classification is like the coordination game in that both players must choose the same strategy to avoid the "worst" outcome, but it differs from the coordination game

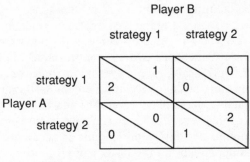

Figure 26 The partiality game

in that there is a direct conflict of interest between the players as to which strategy is chosen. Each player has a preferred strategy and is better off when he and the other player both adopt that strategy than he would be if they were to adopt the other strategy. Somehow, society must evolve what Ullman-Margalit calls "norms of partiality" to determine who the favoured party will be; a norm of partiality may be thought of as a rule for picking a point on a utility-possibility curve. An example of this game is presented in Figure 26. Player A prefers strategy 1. Player B prefers strategy 2. Something outside the game, some appeal to tradition or to violence, is required to settle the matter. The game captures an aspect of despotism. Everyone, subject and ruler alike, is better off, let it be assumed, in a despotic society than in anarchy, but nobody willingly becomes the subject rather than the ruler. The game also captures the essential inequality in the allocation among people of property rights within a liberal society.

The basic hypothesis in the studies of the emergence of cooperation is nicely expressed by Schotter:[8] "Just as Adam Smith's invisible hand can, in a decentralized fashion, lead economic agents to reach a Pareto optimal competitive equilibrium, it can also lead them to create social institutions when competitive outcomes are not optimal." Against this view I would assert (i) that the implied distinction between centralized and decentralized activity takes no account of limited cooperation exemplified by a predatory government or a gang of bandits, (ii) that there is no justification for the presumption that institutions created by invisible hands are necessarily optimal. They may, like the Sunday market, turn out to be optimal, or they may turn out to be nasty. There is, to my knowledge, no general theorem comparable to the fundamental theorems of welfare economics specifying a broad class of conditions under which the interaction of many self-interested agents creates institutions superior to some prior set of institutions. The Sunday market example goes one way; organized banditry goes the other.

The institution-creating invisible hand is sometimes benevolent in circumstances where one might not at first expect benevolence. An interesting instance is Axelrod's repeated prisoner's dilemma tournament. The basic unit in the tournament is a two-person prisoners' dilemma game like that in Figure 25. Once again, each player has a choice between two strategies, cooperation and defection. The tournament itself is among a number of participants, each of whom plays a round of approximately 200 prisoners' dilemma games against every other participant in turn. Each participant chooses a "compound strategy" signifying his choice of a primary strategy in every game as dependent on the history of all preceding games in that round. Once all compound strategies are announced, the games themselves are played by computer.

Recall that in the original, one-shot prisoner's dilemma game in Figure 25, it was advantageous for each player to defect (strategy 2) regardless of the strategy chosen by the other player. This fundamental property of the prisoners' dilemma game — that the combined outcome of individually rational actions may be universally disadvantageous, or, to use the economist's terminology, that certain equilibria may not be Pareto-optimal — does not necessarily carry over to a sequence of games. By analogy with the ordinary prisoner's dilemma game, one might suppose that the winning compound strategy in Axelrod's tournament would be to defect in every game. That turns out not to be so. Instead, the champion compound strategy was tit-for-tat — begin with a cooperative move and thereafter imitate the move of one's opponent. Tit-for-tat won the tournament because a player who chose that compound strategy did quite well against another player who also adopted tit-for-tat, and because players who adopted nasty compound strategies got very low scores in contests against one another.

The moral of the story is that, in social interactions that take the form of repeated prisoners' dilemma games, as opposed to simple once-and-for-all prisoners' dilemma games, one would expect to see strictly self-seeking behaviour in the choice of compound strategies leading to a situation where most people behaved *as though* they were acting cooperatively most of the time. The example which served for years as the paradigm contrast between private and social interest has been turned round. Where once there was a discrepancy between private and social interest, there appears now to be an identity, or a reasonable approximation thereto. Among the examples of behaviour that appears to conform to the repeated prisoners' dilemma are the commercial morality of members of minority groups in close and repeated contact, norms of behaviour in tribes or small groups, such as the occupants of wagon trains in the western migration in America in the nineteenth century, norms of behaviour of soldiers in respecting a truce and, perhaps, cooperative behaviour in certain species of animals.[9]

The story of the search for a market day and the story of the repeated prisoner's dilemma game can be thought of as encapsulating different aspects of what we normally call cooperation. In the former, everybody wants to cooperate — to appear at the market on the same day — but does not initially know how to do so. In the latter, everybody knows how to cooperate — to play strategy 1 — but may not want to do so. In general, society is confronted with both problems at once. Normally cooperation implies an organized allocation of tasks and greater productivity for the group as a whole than could be attained if each person worked alone. It is Adam Smith's pin factory. It is "I'll drive the bus, and you collect the fares." It implies communication among agents so that each knows what to do and what to expect of others. Cooperation, in the sense of coordination, normally requires a hierarchy in production and collectively imposed sanctions on those who break the rules upon which such coordination depends.

I am not convinced that the story of the repeated prisoners' dilemma is the essence of the missing theorem about the optimality of self-interested institution-forming behaviour. Like the story of the search for a market day, it seems to account for no more than a narrow range of social interaction under the umbrella of a larger system that operates on very different principles. There are too many fundamental differences between the repeated prisoners' dilemma and the conditions of anarchy for the one to serve as a model of the other.

(i) The repeated play *between two given players* has no counterpart in anarchy. It is essential to the repeated prisoner's dilemma game that A and B meet over and over again, 200 times, before A is allowed to confront C, D or E. If, instead, we suppose there to be a large population with a new choice of participants for each play of the game and little prospect of any two participants meeting again for a long time, then each game represents a separate and distinct prisoner's dilemma from which the usual moral can be drawn.

(ii) The near Pareto optimality of the outcome of the repeated prisoners' dilemma is due in large measure to the essential orderliness of the game. The prizes are set. The partners are chosen at random. The number of encounters is established in advance of the play. Nobody runs off with the prize after he has lost a game.

(iii) The emergence of cooperation depends on the assumed rewards of the game. Different and no less realistic sets of rewards could yield very different results. For instance, if winning or losing *per se* were what mattered, rather than the total score, and if types of people (as distinguished by their strategies) reproduced or failed to reproduce according to whether they won or lost, then the evolutionary stable strategy would be to defect rather than to cooperate. Cooperation would not emerge in that case. Mutual cooperation as the outcome of the universal adoption of the tit-for-tat strategy might also be forestalled if society consisted initially of some people who always cooperate, some who play tit-for-tat and some who always defect, and if the groups gradually expanded or contracted in accordance with their success at each round of play. Such a society could evolve into a state where only defectors remain, because cooperators do better than tit-for-tatters in these conditions and defectors do better than cooperators.[10]

(iv) An equilibrium with some tit-for-tatters and some defectors could easily evolve if the return to each strategy depended on the number of people who play it, as was the case in the bandit and farmer model of anarchy. Suppose, for instance, that the tit-for-tatter's return in confrontations with defectors depended on his preparation, and that preparation is costly. The smaller the proportion of defectors, the less likely is a tit-for-tatter to encounter one, the smaller his optimal preparation will be, and the larger is the return to the strategy of defection. What emerges from this process is not universal cooperation, but an equilibrium of cooperation and defection with some of the characteristics of anarchy.

(v) The repeated prisoner's dilemma can be thought of as a story about crime deterred by punishment. Normally, when we think of crime and punishment, we imagine crimes as committed by individuals and punishment as meted out by the state. In this context, the essence of the repeated prisoners' dilemma game is that the threat of private punishment, as part of the tit-for-tat compound strategy, is sufficient to induce cooperative behaviour, that is, to deter crime. Thus one way of deciding whether the story is general enough to account for the emergence of the institutions of a liberal society is to ask oneself whether the threat of privately administered retribution is likely to be sufficient without the paraphernalia of the repeated prisoner's dilemma game. If the answer to this question is "yes", then the usual function of the state as law-giver and law-enforcer would seem to be superfluous. If the answer is "no", then the story reduces to the valid, but uninteresting, proposition that it is in each man's interest to obey the law if he will be punished for disobedience. My own answer is unambiguously no. The essence of anarchy is that the privately optimal response of the victim of non-cooperative behaviour is insufficient to deter such behaviour altogether. It is of some interest that *any* model can be designed in which the private response is sufficient. The repeated prisoner's dilemma model must be set against other, no less realistic models of social interaction in which laws have to be enforced by the state.

(vi) The players in a repeated prisoner's dilemma game are forbidden to choose for themselves with whom and against whom to cooperate. This in my opinion is the most serious objection to the repeated prisoners' dilemma game as an explanation of the birth of the liberal society. Starting from a condition of anarchy, cooperation is far more likely to emerge in small sub-groups of the population than in the population as a whole, and the purpose of such cooperation may be to exploit outsiders. Cooperation may be honour among thieves. It may consist of ganging up on helpless victims and of surveillance to ensure that the victims remain unorganized and helpless. The rulers in a despotic society are the first cooperators, who succeed in establishing their organization before anybody else can do so, who fight off competitors, and who, once established, allow no rival organization to develop. In the repeated prisoner's dilemma game, all conflict is one-against-one. The design of the game eliminates the incentive — which is essential in the evolution of despotism — for A and B to cooperate in subjugating C.

Whatever else it may represent, the model of the emergence of cooperation in the repeated prisoner's dilemma game does not represent the emergence of the liberal society from anarchy. One seeks in vain for an isomorphism between the repeated prisoner's dilemma and some plausible story of the development of property rights and of voting by majority rule. There is, so far, little to support the hypothesis that a liberal society can emerge spontaneously out of anarchy as the unintended consequence of uncoordinated, self-regarding actions by a large number of people.

The social contract[11]
The social contract is in a sense the opposite of spontaneous evolution. A social contract establishes society by design. Expressed baldly and crudely, the social contract is this: imagine a condition of anarchy, with some lethal violence and much wasted effort as people regularly take what others have produced and try to defend what they have produced from predatory neighbours. One day it occurs to somebody that there is a better way for people to live together, that everyone would be happier if property were divided up and a police force hired to punish those who refuse to respect property rights. The entire population is called to a meeting. Everyone, or almost everyone, agrees that property and government are desirable, and these institutions are established on the spot. Hobbes argued that people who understood their true interest and appreciated the difficulties in governing by an assembly would opt for absolute monarchy. Others have argued that people would opt for a liberal society.

Whether the story is convincing depends critically on what aspect one chooses to emphasize. Emphasis may be placed on (i) the implied obligation to be loyal to one's society, (ii) choice within the constitutional convention as a model of one's sense of the common good, (iii) the constitutional convention as the central event in an encapsulated or stylized history of the development of modern political institutions, or (iv) the process by which the contract was assumed to have emerged as a model for political action today.

Of these four aspects of the social contract, it is, I believe, the first two that account for most people's sense that "there is something to the story", but it is the last two that are relevant to the inquiry in this chapter. One can appreciate the story as a myth, parable or cautionary tale about loyalty or about the identification of the common good while dismissing it altogether as potted history, as a guide to action or as a serious competitor for spontaneous evolution out of anarchy and for the disintegration of despotism in explaining the birth of the liberal society. To place the social contract in a proper context for comparison with other explanations of the birth of the liberal society, these four aspects of the story will be discussed in turn.

One cannot fail to be moved by Plato's use of the story of the social contract as a parable about loyalty in his description of the death of Socrates. Socrates[12] appeals to this view of the social contract to explain his obedience to the law, even to the point of acquiescing in a sentence of death. Socrates says that

he who has experienced the manner in which we order justice and administer the State, and still remains, has entered into an implied contract that he will do as we command him. And he who disobeys us is, as we maintain, thrice wrong; first, because in disobeying us he is disobeying his parents; secondly, because we are the authors of his education; thirdly, because he has made an agreement with us that he will duly obey our commands . . .

The story dramatizes one's sense of duty. I am obliged to obey the laws of my country because they are my laws, and because I, in some sense, established them.

Notwithstanding its emotional appeal, the social contract as a story about loyalty is open to the objections (i) that the terms of the supposed contract are ill specified and (ii) that the contract itself is redundant. The first objection is that the social contract may be employed to justify both sides of almost any political argument. A conservative might attach the contract to society as it was at a time in the past, before the terms of the contract were violated in some objectionable reform. Obedience to the king, subservience to the law, however cruel and unjust, and acceptance of the allocation of income and privilege are all mandated by my implied promise at the moment when society was established. Someone else might attach the contract to society as it is today. Never mind that society has been changing from the beginning of time; today it is complete, and one must accept it as is. But as society changes, the terms of the contract change too, so that, in practice, the story of the social contract does not serve to justify any particular laws or policies. The story can at most be employed to inculcate among citizens a sense that it is one's duty to obey the law and to engage oneself in one's community.

It can be helpful in this context to distinguish between two types of social contract: the contract of society and the contract of government.[13] The first is an arrangement among people regarding law, property and possibly other matters. The second is an arrangement between citizens and government in which the rights and obligations of each are specified; government protects property, punishes criminals, but must not itself violate the law, etc. The significance of the distinction is that some authors reason as though the two contracts were made sequentially, so that the contract of society takes precedence over the contract of government and thereby places a ban on what the government may do. Locke and, to a greater extent, Nozick look upon the contract of society as inviolate, and thereby deduce that nothing more than a minimal state can be justified. A book (Nozick's *Anarchy, State and Utopia*) beginning with the assertion, "Individuals have rights, and there are things no person or group may do to them (without violating their rights)," can hardly be expected to arrive at any other conclusion.[14] Hobbes easily avoided that conclusion by refusing to differentiate between the two contracts; when people meet in a state of nature to draw up a social contract, they must design society and government together, for no private rights can exist without a magistrate to enforce them. Hobbes's contract was an agreement among subjects to obey the sovereign, who, not being himself a party to the agreement, was not bound by it and therefore free to violate the law if reasons of state compelled him to do so. A major premise of the argument was, in my opinion, technical. Hobbes's sovereign had to be absolute because the absolute sovereign was the only viable alternative to the horrors of the state of nature, a proposition which is hardly self-evident today but may have seemed so to many Englishmen in the year 1651 when *Leviathan* was published.

The other objection — that the contract is redundant — has been well put by David Hume:[15]

What necessity, therefore, is there to found the duty of allegiance or obedience to magistrates on that of fidelity or a regard to promises, and to suppose, that it is the consent of each individual which subjects him to government, when it appears that both allegiance and fidelity stand precisely on the same foundation, and are both submitted to by mankind, on account of the apparent interests and necessities of human society? *We are bound to obey our sovereign, it is said, because we have given a tacit promise to that purpose. But why are we bound to observe our promise?* It must here be asserted, that the commerce and intercourse of mankind, which are of such mighty advantage, can have no security where men pay no regard to their engagements. In like manner, may it be said that men could not live at all in society, at least in a civilized society, without laws, and magistrates, and judges, to prevent the encroachments of the strong upon the weak, of the violent upon the just and equitable. The obligation to *allegiance* being of like force and authority with the obligation to *fidelity*, we gain nothing by resolving the one into the other. The general interests or necessities of society are sufficient to establish both.

As a tale or parable about the identification of the common good, the story of the social contract is closely related to standard assumptions in welfare economics. Good laws, sound public policy and appropriate constraints upon government action are not what *was* chosen in an ancient constitutional convention, but what *would be* chosen if the convention were held today. There are reverberations of this aspect of the social contract when, for instance, the optimal tax structure is defined as that which maximizes a — typically, utilitarian — social welfare function subject to behavioural and technical constraints or when alternative public policies are evaluated with reference to welfare triangles. There is an especially close connection between the social contract story and traditional welfare economics when social welfare is seen as a person's choice for his community "behind the veil of ignorance", that is, when social welfare reflects the criterion that I would apply in a choice among alternative public policies if I had an equal chance of occupying the circumstances of each and every person who was affected by that choice. It is arguable, of course, that the paraphernalia of conventions and contracts is redundant in this context, as exemplified by the fact the "veil of ignorance" approach to social welfare could be discussed in Chapter I above with no reference to contracts at all. Against this, it may be claimed that the contract is implicit or that the story of the contract heightens and dramatizes important aspects of one's sense of the common good.

A particular virtue of the story of the social contract as a test of the meaning of the common good is that the common good is automatically dependent on the technical, social and behavioural constraints of one's society. A person with an equal chance of occupying the social and economic status of each and every member of society would choose a very different set of laws, rules and customs if confronted with the technology of the Middle Ages from what he would choose if confronted with the technology today. Absolute monarchy serves the common good in a society where democracy is a recipe for chaos. The abandonment of aged and infirm parents serves the common good in a nomadic society, such as that of the Eskimos, where no other course of action is consistent with the preservation of the lives of the rest of the people in the community. Whipping may serve the common good in a society that cannot establish prisons. One's sense of the common good may also depend to a great extent on one's knowledge of and presumptions about social science. The optimist favours a loose rein of government for a citizenry that is expected to behave decently most of the time. The pessimist favours a tight rein on people who can be expected to behave miserably unless terrorized into order by rack and the dungeon.

As already mentioned above, the social contract was never intended as literal history. There may, nevertheless, be an historical aspect to the story. The social contract may be seen as an extraction from the infinite detail of the historical record of the one central, quintessential happening that makes sense of the record as a whole. From this point of view, the crucial event in the development of the liberal society is the agreement among people that a degree of social organization is advantageous for all. The moral of the story of the social contract as encapsulated history is that explicit agreement as distinct from spontaneous evolution is what drives history along.

So broad an interpretation of the great sweep of history is not subject to definitive verification or rejection, but it is open to criticism on its internal consistency and its conformity to what we believe the laws of society to be. Three objections are discussed here: that it obscures the role of predation, violence and exploitation, that it fails to differentiate between explicit agreement and tacit consent, and that it blurs the distinction between past agreement and present agreement.

That the story of the social contract tends to obscure the role of violence and exploitation in the development of political and economic institutions is at once evident from a consideration of the plausibility of the story itself. A minimal requirement for the coming together of people in a constitutional convention is the absence of any group in society with the incentive and the means to stop it. This requirement is most unlikely to be satisfied in the primitive state of society where the contract is assumed to be established. By the time people learn to cooperate on a large enough scale for a constitutional convention, they have probably known for some time how to cooperate on a smaller scale, as in a gang of bandits or army of *condottieri*. There must already have formed embryonic despotisms with ruling classes that do better by organized plunder then they would expect to do as obedient and law-abiding citizens once the social contract has been established. A well organized coterie of bandit-rulers would not stand idly by and allow the contract to be arranged. The natural successor to anarchy is despotism, not the liberal society.

In the words of David Hume:[16]

Almost all the governments which exist at present, or of which there remains any record in story, have been founded originally, either on usurpation or conquest, or both, without any pretense of a fair consent or voluntary subjection of the people. When an artful and bold man is placed at the head of an army or faction, it is often easy for him, by employing, sometimes violence, sometimes false pretenses, to establish his dominion over a people a hundred times more numerous than his partisans. He allows no such open communication, that his enemies can know, with certainty, their number or force. He gives them no leisure to assemble together in a body to oppose him. Even all those who are the instruments of his usurpation may wish his fall; but their ignorance of each other's intention keeps them in awe, and is the sole cause of his security. By such arts as these, many governments have been established; and this is all the original contract which they have to boast of.

The face of the earth is continually changing, by the increase of small kingdoms into great empires, by the dissolution of great empires into smaller kingdoms, by the planting of colonies, by the migration of tribes. Is there any thing discoverable in all these events but force and violence? Where is the mutual agreement or voluntary association so much talked of?

Second, delegates to a constitutional convention would normally be confronted with two types of decisions at once: the design of a good society (about which everyone might agree) and the choice of the occupants of privileged positions. The postulated veil of ignorance in some versions of the contract story is intended to focus attention on the first type of decision. It does so at the cost of de-emphasizing the second, of ignoring the essentially irresolvable bargaining problem that arises whenever privilege cannot as a matter of practice be eliminated and a norm of partiality, as defined in the discussion surrounding Figure 26 above, must somehow be established. The Israelites decide that they need a king to lead them against their enemies. In some circumstances the king might be chosen by lot or by God through the intermediary of the prophet Isaiah. More commonly, people cannot or will not allow major allocative decisions to be made by chance and they disagree in their interpretations of God's word. The constitutional convention is ill equipped to set norms of partiality by agreement.

The best one can hope for is the establishment of norms of partiality by tacit consent. After much negotiation, and no small loss of blood, there may develop an acceptance of a *status quo* with a well defined structure of privilege. The description, in the next section, of the emergence of the liberal society through the disintegration of despotism can be thought of as a crude and simple example of the development of tacit consent. But only by a quite unreasonable stretching of the meaning of words can the development of tacit consent be described as an agreement within the terms of the story of the social contract.

The difficulty in reaching agreement over the assignment of privilege is most immediately manifest in the allocation of property among citizens. The social contract may be imagined to have been drawn up so long ago that property could have been equally divided among citizens, in which case present inequalities would be the consequence of post-contractual transactions. This interpretation of the contract will be discussed presently. A more common interpretation of the contract as it pertains to property rights is that people enter the constitutional convention in unequal circumstances and on the understanding that the increase in the national income generated by the establishment of order will be allocated so as to make everybody better off.

Imagine a society in a condition of semi-anarchy where people's incomes differ according to their strength or according to the property they have amassed, but where the national income could be increased substantially by the establishment of public order. Prior to the social contract, the incomes of the n people in the society are, from lowest to highest, $y_1^0, y_2^0 \ldots y_n^0$, for a total of Y^0. Total income in the new society established by the social contract is Y^1, where Y^1 must be greater than Y^0 if the contract is to be useful at all. A candidate for a norm of partiality is to divide the surplus in proportion to the original incomes;[17] the new incomes, $y_1^1, y_2^1 \ldots y_n^1$ are chosen so that, for each person i, $y_i^1 = y_i^0 Y^1/Y^0$.

To postulate such a rule is to assume away real conflicts of interest in the allocation of income among people. The rule has no natural superiority over many other rules that might have been chosen instead and that might have been preferred by large numbers of the delegates to the constitutional convention. The poorer half of the population would prefer an equal sharing of the surplus, so that $y_i^1 = y_i^0 + (Y^1 - Y^0)/n$. Better still, from the point of view of the poor, would be a rule that allocates the total surplus to the poorest in society, so that the first m incomes (where m < n) are equal and the incomes of the rest of the population remain as they were before. How are delegates to a constitutional convention to agree on one among the multitude of possible rules when each delegate knows how he personally would be affected by each rule? More important, it has been assumed so far that delegates to the constitutional convention would respect the prior distribution of income, at least to the extent of not making anybody worse off than he was before. Delegates may refuse to do so when they know that the prior distribution of income is the outcome of power relations that are automatically dissolved as the constitutional convention begins. To say that the delegates are compelled to do so by the original ruling class would be to degrade the social contract into an incident in the history of exploitation. A contract under duress is unlikely to be respected when the power of the ruling class is removed.

With no veil of ignorance to transform post-contract inequality into *ex ante* equality among the delegates to the constitutional convention, with no natural rule for the allocation of the surplus, and without even a higher authority to command respect for the distribution of income that precedes the calling of the constitutional convention, there is no basis for agreement among the delegates concerning the distribution of income, wealth, office or status in the newly founded society. One can imagine how the existing distribution of property may have evolved in a gradual process in which entitlement, enterprise, force, politics, theft and fraud all may have played some part. One can imagine how the existing distribution of property may come to be respected as people realize that the redistribution of income would, beyond some limit, be so detrimental to enterprise as to harm the great majority of people, and that failure to respect the *status quo*, at least to some extent, might lead to the disintegration of the liberal society. It is difficult to imagine how people would reach a specific agreement as to who is to be rich and who is to be poor in a society where the gap between rich and poor cannot be eliminated altogether.

The third inadequacy in the contract story is its failure to differentiate between present and past agreement. The story makes no allowance for the fact that some agreements are simply not enforceable. There is an unwarranted extension in the story from private contract to social contract. The state's monopoly of the means of coercion will suffice for the enforcement of private contracts. There is no comparable instrument to compel compliance with a social contract by a majority of voters who, through their elected representatives, are themselves in command of government. Behind the veil of ignorance, there may be unanimous agreement that law A is preferable to law B if law A can be enforced, but the delegates to the constitutional convention may choose law B regardless because law B can be enforced while law A cannot.

An example may clarify the distinction between enforceable and unenforceable social contracts. Imagine a society with 1,000 people and a potential national income of $50 million in the event that property rights are protected. A constitutional convention is established to design a government for the protection of property and to choose a rule for the allocation of the national income among citizens. The veil of ignorance descends and delegates are confronted with the choice between two designs for the economy. Design A provides every person with an income of $50,000. Design B establishes two classes of people with membership to be determined by chance, a large lower class of 900 people, each with an income of $10,000 per year, and a small upper class of 100 people, each with an income of $410,000 per year. A risk-averse person would prefer design A; a risk-loving person might prefer design B. I suspect that most people in this world are risk-averse, but there is nothing illogical in supposing that the delegates to the constitutional convention are risk-loving, and would, in fact, be quite happy to accept design B as long as places in the upper class were allocated by lot. Design A is adopted nonetheless because each delegate knows that, if he were among the unlucky 900, he would immediately employ the power of the vote to redistribute the national income in his favour. Some disparities of income may be tolerated because, as discussed in Chapter VIII, the cost of redistribution, in the resulting decline of the total national income, outweighs the potential advantage to the ordinary voter. Other disparities of income may be too large for this consideration to serve as a barrier to redistribution.

Careless interpretation of the story of the social contract as encapsulated history places too much emphasis on the objectives in the design of society and government and too little emphasis on the constraints. The impression may be conveyed that, if people want government to do thus-and-such, they can recreate the state of nature, hold a new constitutional convention and establish a government in conformity to their desires. If you want everyone to have equal incomes or, alternatively, if you want a society with strong barriers to the redistribution of income by the state, and if others agree, it is entirely within your power to institute a government to achieve your aims. That is often true, but subject to the major qualification that reforms sometimes come in packages. Substantially greater equality of income might be attainable only at the expense of enlarging the powers of the bureaucracy, thereby creating a new inequality based on position in the hierarchy rather than wealth. Or too much respect for property rights might convert those without property into enemies of the state. Citizens might want A without B, but their wants might be denied, not by wilful opponents, but by the technology of social interaction. The story of the social contract tends to hide the very basic proposition in social science that actions often have consequences quite apart from the genuine intentions of the actors. That is why there is no mileage in supposing that property was divided equally among citizens in a social contract established long ago. A contract established long ago supplies no protection for property-holders today if the majority of voters are bent on expropriation. Reasons why a majority of the poor might not be bent on expropriation of the rich were discussed in Chapter V and will be discussed in greater detail in Chapter IX. Those reasons are valid, if they are valid at all, regardless of whether or not the distribution of wealth can be traced back to an original contract.

Interpretation of the terms of a social contract is invariably problematic. The enforcement of contracts — private contracts and social contracts alike — requires the establishment of some public body, such as the Supreme Court, with the ultimate authority to supply the definitive interpretation in the event of disputes. However, the interpretation of social contracts is far more contentious than the interpretation of ordinary private contracts because there is a major difference in the degree of independence of the judiciary from the parties to a dispute. The judiciary is necessarily appointed by the government, which, ideally, stands outside and above disputes over private contracts but which may, as the instrument of a majority of voters, be a party to a dispute over the interpretation of the social contract as manifest in a written or unwritten constitution.

There is no denying that constitutions do bind government to some extent. Elected governments often back down when the judges decree that a law or an administrative procedure is in violation of the constitution. Majorities do allow themselves to be thwarted by pronouncements of the judiciary, especially with reference to such matters as "basic civil rights", "cruel and unusual punishments" and parliamentary procedure. Deference to the courts is especially forthcoming in situations, such as the law regarding abortion, where people want their government to adopt the "right" law or the "right" course of action but are genuinely puzzled or ambivalent as to what the right may be. Deference is also extended in "coordination problems" where any number of procedures of government would do but one particular procedure must be chosen.

Constitutional safeguards are particularly efficacious and particularly respected when they pertain to the "assurance" problem. There are some actions in the political realm that nobody would ever want to take against his opponents as long as he is assured that his opponents will desist from such actions as well. The leaders of a political party with a majority in Parliament could perhaps employ their authority over the army and the police to imprison the leaders of the opposition party, who might otherwise displace them in the next election. Politicians in office today may desist from such actions as long as they are confident that their successors in office will desist in their turn. They do so because they understand the consequences of their actions for the preservation of the liberal society and because they prefer the liberal society to any likely alternative. Only mistrust can destroy the consensus placing bounds upon the politicians' use of the powers of government to remain in office. In this context, a written constitution can be especially helpful in providing the assurance required to keep the electoral process going.[18]

But deference is a fragile emotion, judges of the Supreme Court are, after all, men appointed by politicians, and the interpretation of the constitution could degenerate into partisan politics if the courts were seen as employing their authority in the interest of a minority that could not prevail at the ballot box. It is one thing to observe that the dictates of the Supreme Court are respected and the judges are chosen in a reasonably non-partisan manner within the present scope of their authority. It is quite another to believe that respect for the Court can be preserved no matter what its task may be.

Of course, the constitution is never an absolute barrier to the majority of the day, for constitutions can be amended. Typically, amendment requires a super-majority of, perhaps, two-thirds or three-quarters of the population or legislature, or it requires a complex procedure that is more or less the equivalent of a super-majority. What this means in practice is that a minority can block a majority on certain matters. Emphasis on mere agreement in the social contract story can create the impression that an agreement expressed in suitably dignified language must enforce itself. Shrewd delegates to a constitutional convention would be aware that this is not so and would exercise restraint in the imposition of constitutional checks and limits to majority rule.

These considerations extend with a vengeance to the story of the social contract as a model for reform. Somehow, contractarian ideas have appealed to those who believe that the government has got out of hand. The growth of governments over the last fifty years and the growth of the U.S. deficit over the last decade are seen as failures of government by majority rule, failures than can be rectified only by extraordinary means. There is pressure in the United States for tax limitation by constitutional amendment,[19] and there is talk in Canada of extending the Charter of Rights to the protection of property. There is at the same time a considerable nostalgia for the pristine constitutional convention in which anarchy was deemed to be replaced by government subservient to the will of the people.[20]

As a parable about reform, the story of the social contract may be no more than a rebuttal of the argument that the existing government must not be altered because it was established by decree from on high that takes precedence over the mere desires of the citizens at any given time. You must not alter the government, so it is said, because the monarch rules by divine right, or, to cite the modern equivalent, because the present government is the vanguard of the proletariat, whose will is historically destined to prevail. No, say the contractarians. God does not arbitrarily specify a right form of government independently of the interests of the governed. Nor does the proletariat communicate its will to a select few who happen at the moment to hold the reins of government. The Will of the People is the will of the people, or it is nothing at all.

As an elaboration of the virtues of the constitutional amendment, the contract story is open particularly to the third objection to the story as history, namely that not all agreements — even those embodied in formal constitutions — can be enforced. An amendment to limit taxation would be especially susceptible to political manipulation. With such an amendment as part of the constitution, prospective judges of the Supreme Court would be required to swear that certain tax-like instruments were not true taxes under the terms of the constitution. The Supreme Court might be packed. Political trickery might displace majority rule as the basis of public decision-making. On economic questions, there may in practice be no appeal from the will of the majority of voters. Either they are persuaded to vote for politicians prepared to cut public expenditure, or expenditure will not, and should not, be cut. The constitutional detour may have very detrimental side effects.

As a basis for the restoration of the constitutional convention today, the contract story is opened to all the objections that were raised in connection with its interpretation as encapsulated history. A constitutional convention would by its very nature entail a root-and-branch reconstruction of the rules of society. It would automatically involve the destruction of the complex overhead capital in established institutions and the painfully constructed web of common understandings on which the liberal society depends. Norms of partiality that have evolved over hundreds of years would be wiped out at a stroke. Tacit agreements would necessarily be abrogated. Even property rights, which the contractarians wish so fervently to defend, might be disregarded, leaving the allocation of the national income in an economic limbo with no guiding principle at all.

As a story about the birth of the liberal society the social contract is worse than wrong. It is misleading. It misleads by conveying the impression that the ascent out of anarchy has been painless, and that we could, if we chose, reconstruct anarchy for the purpose of establishing a new and better contract. The story of the contract conveys the impression that anarchy is transformed into the liberal society in one colossal act of consent

— a passage from darkness to light with no necessary unpleasantness in between. That is false. The liberal society is the end product of a long and brutal process that nobody would care to live through again. The process began in anarchy which was dreadful, and there is reason to believe that the first "civilizations" to evolve out of anarchy were dreadful too.[21] Somehow, over the years, people established rules within which they can sometimes live peacefully together. The social contract is no model for political action because it would place all rules in jeopardy at once, because the required descent into anarchy might not be brief or painless, and because the new society to emerge from this process would in all probability be despotic, notwithstanding the good intentions of the contractarians. Reform, to be effected at all, must be forged from the materials at hand today. Reform of political and economic institutions is "like replacing the rotten boards on a leaky ship while staying afloat". Society is a going concern that cannot be dismantled and reconstructed as we please.

To speak, as some authors do, of returning temporarily to a state of nature is to imagine an impossible or unacceptably costly voyage. Our description of the formation of the social contract was of a reasonably friendly process in which people who have hitherto been murdering one another quietly sit down together to design a state. If the picture is more or less accurate, we might suppose that the temporary return to the state of nature would be tolerable, perhaps even exhilarating. But if the picture is inaccurate as encapsulated history — as, I have argued, it is — if the evolution of society as we know it was slow, brutal and terrifying — not something anybody would consent to relive — then return to the state of nature is out of the question as an aspect of reform.[22]

From despotism to the liberal society

We have reached a point in our analysis where we must either construct a plausible account of the emergence of the liberal society from despotism or give up trying to explain the emergence of the liberal society within the framework of analysis we have so far employed. What needs to be explained is how a society governed by a narrow, self-interested ruling class may evolve into a society with private ownership of the means of production and majority-rule voting for collective decision-making. To "explain" the transformation of despotism into the liberal society is to present a plausible, commonsense account of how the event might have occurred as the consequence of interactions among self-interested people or groups, regardless of whether it actually occurred that way. An explanation is an account of why a despotic society might choose to protect private property, why voting by majority rule might be adopted as the method of decision-making within the ruling class, and why the franchise might be gradually expanded to take in the entire adult population.

Property is easier to explain than majority-rule voting because private

ownership of the means of production is not inconsistent with the existence of a cohesive ruling class. Consider how the rulers in a despotic
society might go about extracting revenue from their subjects. As discussed briefly at the end of Chapter IV, there would seem to be three
main possibilities. The entire country could be administered by the rulers
as one great collective farm. Office-holders with civil or military responsibilities might be compensated with entitlements to exploit particular pieces
of property, entitlements that might or might not include rights over groups
of people attached to the land. Or rulers might be paid from the proceeds
of taxation upon subjects who own property which they are free to use as
they please. In short, communism, feudalism or military dictatorship.

The first of these methods is particularly advantageous when the ruling
class is insecure, for it combines revenue collection with surveillance. A
ruling class that administers the economy as well as the army and the
police can be quite large and, therefore, relatively defensible against rebellion by subjects. Disrespectful behaviour by subjects is easily identified
and expeditiously punished when subjects owe their livelihoods directly to
the state. The disadvantage of this method is that the rulers' income per
head may be quite low by comparison with what it could be if the economy
were organized differently. There is little prospect of productivity growth
or the development of new products when fear of punishment is the subject's
only inducement to produce. Rulers themselves lack the incentive to innovate or to administer their bits of the economy well, for the surplus from
an enterprise is shared among the entire ruling class. This method of
generating income for the ruling class also requires a better system of
communication among the parts of the economy than has been feasible
except in modern times.

The second method is a cross between collective administration of the
economy by the ruling class and full private ownership of the means of
production. Property is divided up among members of the ruling class, but
ownership is conditional upon the discharge of well defined duties to the
state — administration of the law within one's domain, recruitment and
financing of soldiers in time of war, etc. This method may have worked
reasonably well in predominantly agricultural economies that did not require much communication and coordination among different enterprises.
It is not an efficient way to run a modern economy. Even in feudal times,
some branches of the economy, notably foreign trade and commerce in
cities, were left to the market.

The advantages of the third method are that it mobilizes the immediate
pecuniary interest of the subject in maximizing the national income and
that it enhances the privilege of membership of the ruling class by restricting the number of rulers among whom the surplus must be shared. In a
society where predation by the ruling class is the only activity of the public
sector, the revenue per head of the ruling class, Y^R, is the product of the

national income, Q, and the rulers' share, t (where t can be thought of as the tax rate), divided by the number of rulers, n^R; $Y^R = tQ/n^R$. Rulers in these circumstances have as much interest in augmenting Q as in augmenting t, and they prefer to keep n^R small if they can do so without placing their authority over their subjects in jeopardy. Thus rulers have a double incentive to foster and protect private ownership of the means of production by their subjects: by comparison with a centrally administered economy, an economy with private property and with markets that are unrestricted except by taxation requires a smaller ruling class and generates a larger national income for rulers to tax. Of course, taxation itself is a disincentive to enterprise. For reasons discussed in Chapter VIII, the size of the national income is a decreasing function of the tax rate ($Q = Q(t)$ and $Q' < 0$) and there is, from the point of view of the rulers, an optimal, revenue-maximizing rate. The case for relying upon taxation rather than upon some other means of exploiting one's subjects is particularly strong in poor countries where subjects must absorb much of the national income merely to maintain their strength as workers and small percentage increases in the national income translate into large percentage increases in the take of the ruling class.

Initially, rulers may not care who is rich and who is poor among their subjects because tax revenue is the same regardless. But one would expect that, over time, there would be a fusing of rulership with wealth. The same set of people would serve as rulers and as holders of large tracts of land or other forms of property. Membership of the ruling class would convey financial privileges, such as contracts with the public sector or inside information that makes speculation profitable. Those who become wealthy in dealings within the private sector might be permitted to buy membership of the ruling class.

The danger to the rulers in a system of private property is that the same independence and flexibility which enable subjects to generate a large national income may also generate centres of opposition to the ruling class. Thus one would expect to see subjects participating in a free market with private property in societies where, for one reason or another, the ruling class is secure, where there is intermingling between the rulers and the rich, and where a tradition of civility has evolved in which deposed rulers are dealt with gently — by exile, for example, rather than by execution at the hands of their successors. Of the two defining characteristics of the liberal society — private property and voting by majority rule — it is not difficult to imagine how the first may be nurtured in a despotic regime, for the maintenance of a system of private property is in the rulers' own interest as long as their position as rulers is reasonably secure.

Government by voting is much more difficult to explain, for the rulers of a despotic society have strong reasons *not* to submit their privileges, lives and fortunes to the whims of a legislature. In this democratic age we tend to forget how totally privileged the rulers can be. The story is told in Clarendon's *History of the Rebellion* that in the reign of King Charles I, at a time when the average working man could expect an annual income of about £6, it was possible for the King to bestow upon one of his favourites, the Earl of Carlisle, a fortune of at least £400,000, which the earl succeeded in spending "in a very jovial life" on his own pleasure and amusement.[23] The great museum of St Petersburg was named the Hermitage because the empress Catherine the Great felt like a hermit there; it was her personal museum for her exclusive enjoyment. The indulgences that so incensed Martin Luther and allegedly played a role in the splitting of Christianity were very largely to finance the personal pleasures and aggrandizement of the Medici Popes. A legislature with majority rule voting and unlimited scope for decision-making could transform a king into a serf or a serf into a king. What has to be explained is why — and especially in what circumstances — a group of despotic rulers would be prepared to run such risks. A ruling hierarchy forged in combat and enjoying vast privileges must somehow be induced to risk those privileges at the ballot box. How might this come about?

To this question I cannot produce an entirely satisfactory answer. Ideally, the answer would be contained in a fully articulated intertemporal general equilibrium model within which the interaction among rational and self-seeking agents leads from anarchy at one moment of time to despotism later on. I have no such model. The best I can do is to supply a few hints — analogous to a partial equilibrium explanation — about how the process may have occurred. The sketch to follow is of the gradual increase in the extent of the franchise reaching down into successively lower orders of society. Two considerations will be especially important: changes over time in the risk to those already enfranchised of the granting of political rights to some people who were formerly excluded, and changes over time in the extent to which the disfranchised can be troublesome to the privileged portion of society.

In principle, voting by majority rule with universal suffrage could be instituted all at once in a great outburst of democratic enthusiasm. That possibility cannot be ruled out, but is unlikely for several reasons. Rulers would probably not permit the required freedom of movement and communication among their subjects. Successful rebellion against a determined ruling class would require a disciplined army of rebels who, if the rebellion succeeded, might be more inclined to set themselves up as a new ruling class than to permit the establishment of a liberal society. Partisans of a successful democratic revolution, being mostly poor, might be unwilling to respect existing property rights or unable to construct a more widespread distribution of property. Thus, even if a system of majority-rule voting with universal franchise were initially established, it would be in danger of destroying itself in conflict over the allocation of the national income and positions of authority. Revolution may be a crucial event *within* the slow evolution toward a liberal society; a despotic society is unlikely to transform itself all at once.

Our account of the origin of majority rule voting is of an evolution from the top down. Voting is first adopted for decision-making within the ruling class. The franchise is then gradually expanded to the entire adult population. I think of this story of the origin of voting as a stylized and encapsulated history of England. In the years immediately following the Conquest, England was as despotic as any state in Europe. Thereafter political rights evolved slowly. Barons acquired rights against the King. The King's Council evolved into a Parliament with limited membership and limited powers. The franchise was extended gradually, first to the wealthier members of the community, then to successively lower strata of society, and finally, in the present century, to the entire adult population.[24] The model of the birth of the liberal society is an abstraction from these events.

In considering this model, it should be borne in mind that there are really two quite distinct aspects to the development of the independence of Parliament from the King: the growth of the privileges of Parliament and the growth of the franchise. Originally Parliament was called at the King's pleasure, its purpose was largely to facilitate tax collection, its rights were few, and the advantages of being able to assist in the choice of a member of Parliament were questionable. As late as the reign of Queen Elizabeth I, the right of free speech within Parliament was the right to say more or less what one pleased on matters submitted to Parliament by the Queen; certainly not the right to choose topics for debate or to say virtually anything at all, as is the case today. The franchise for such a Parliament was not the sought-after privilege that it subsequently became. Medieval Parliaments were a feature of a society with little in the way of a civil service, and a good deal of local autonomy. In the words of one historian, it was a matter of "self-government at the King's command".[25] With the development of the King's civil service the medieval parliaments died in most European countries. The acquisition of new powers in the Parliament of England during the seventeenth century gave the extent of the franchise an importance that it had never had before.

The King is the King because the barons are prepared to obey his commands. If the barons could be kept apart from one another (except when necessary to discipline a rebel against the King), then a strict chain of command could probably be maintained intact. If, on the other hand, the barons must meet as advisers to the King, or if the King simply cannot stop them from meeting, then the barons might assert what would henceforth become their rights: the right to transmit property to their children, a clear specification of their obligations as taxpayers, and so on. Furthermore, the barons cannot exercise collective rights without a mechanism for resolving disputes among themselves and for determining when a collective decision has in fact been made. A voting rule is required.

Whether barons seek to establish rights against the King depends on several considerations. They would certainly desire security against arbitrary behaviour by the King, against dismissal from the ruling class or confiscation of their estates. They would also wish to keep a large share of the total revenue that is extracted by the ruling class from its subjects. On the other hand, they would have to recognize that defence against their country's enemies or against rebellion at home requires a unified command. The King must not be deprived of the authority and the funds to attend to these matters. Too much liberty for the barons, who may not always acquiesce peacefully to the will of the majority, may be a recipe for civil war that everyone, King and barons alike, would wish to avoid. Even when the franchise is restricted to the barons, voting requires a consensus among the barons as to the extent of their property rights and a prior agreement not to vote about property; voting has to be constrained to prevent a majority of the barons from utilizing the vote to expropriate the rest. The barons might agree to transform the King's Council into an embryonic legislature with a very limited franchise and very limited powers.

The expansion of the franchise can be seen as a gradual process generated by fear of rebellion. The process begins with the establishment of the House of Lords. (Our theoretical England has only one House of Parliament.) Members of the House of Lords would of course prefer not to expand the franchise, but, like the King, they may eventually be confronted with the choice between sharing power and succumbing to rebellion. Their best course may be to forestall rebellion by buying off some of the potential rebels, granting the franchise to classes of people who would be especially dangerous as rebels or would present the least threat within the legislature. The franchise might be granted to occupants of the next rank down the hierarchy or to the wealthiest among the unenfranchised portion of the population.

Return to the assumption already employed in modelling the transition from anarchy to despotism, that societies are organized as complete orderings of their members from top to bottom rather than in ranks with equality among the holders of any given rank, and suppose, for convenience, that wealth and rank are perfectly correlated. In this formulation, the distinction between ruler and subject turns on the right to vote. The enfranchised are the rulers. The disfranchised are the subjects. To model the extension of the franchise, imagine a society part way along its evolution out of despotism, with the franchise already granted to the top n_v people out of a total population of N, where people are ordered according to their wealth — Mr 1 is the richest, Mr 2 is next, and so on. The electorate consists of Mr 1, Mr 2, up to Mr n_v; the disenfranchised are Mr $n_v + 1$, Mr

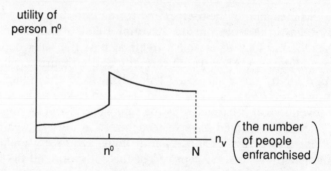

Figure 27 The utility of a person of rank n^0 as a function of the size of the electorate

$n_V + 2$, up to Mr N. Think of membership of the electorate as desirable, because Parliament passes laws that augment the incomes and privileges of the classes included in the electorate at the expense of the rest of the population. To take the classic example, when the time comes to dismantle feudal arrangements, a Parliament of nobles would naturally decide that property rights reside with the nobles, while a Parliament of serfs would naturally decide that property rights reside with the serfs. Consequently, a person's utility is a function of his wealth (which can be represented by n, since people are ordered according to their wealth) and the composition of the electorate, n_V; that is,

$$U = U \text{ (rank, size of the electorate)} = U(n, n_V) \qquad (13)$$

Figure 27 illustrates the utility of the $n^0 + h$ wealthiest person (shown on the vertical axis) as a function of the size of the electorate (shown on the horizontal axis). His utility increases gradually with the size of the electorate as long as the electorate remains small enough that he himself is not entitled to vote, that is, if $n_V < n^0$. His utility increases abruptly when he becomes enfranchised because his interests are taken into account in public decisions; $U(n^0, n_V)$ increases abruptly at $n_V = n^0$. However, his utility declines as the electorate increases still further because there are fewer and poorer people left to exploit.

Utilities of different people are compared in Figure 28. Now points on the horizontal axis represent different people as indexed by their order, n, on the scale of rich and poor, and the vertical axis represents utility. Each curve in Figure 28 is drawn for a given franchise, n_V, and it shows how utility declines with n. The decline is steady and continuous except for a sharp drop in utility at $n = n_V$. The two extremes of the franchise are represented by the unbroken curves. The lower curve, labelled $U(n,0)$, shows utility as a function of wealth (more precisely, of one's order on the scale of wealth) when nobody is entitled to vote. The higher curve, labelled

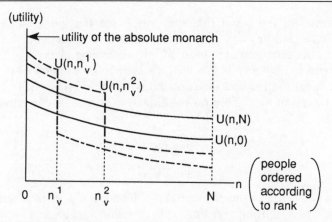

Figure 28 Utility by rank for four values of the size of the electorate, 0, n_V^1, n_V^2 and N

U(n,N), shows utility as a function of wealth when everybody is entitled to vote. Otherwise all curves are broken. They are drawn on the assumption that any increase in the franchise, n_V, (that is, any reduction in the amount of property one must possess in order to be entitled to vote), increases the utility of the newly enfranchised people but reduces the utility of people who were already entitled to vote.

The curve $U(n,n_V^1)$ shows the utility of wealth as a function of n when only the first n_V^1 people are entitled to vote and the rest are disfranchised. This curve starts quite high because voting is a valuable privilege when the electorate is small, but it falls below the curve $U(n,0)$ for people $(n > n_V^1)$ not included in the electorate. Now suppose that the electorate is increased from n_V^1 to n_V^2. The shape of the curve $U(n,n_V^2)$ is similar to the shape of the curve $U(n,n_V^1)$, but $U(n,n_V^2)$ is substantially greater than $U(n,n_V^1)$ in the range between n_V^1 and n_V^2 because this range covers those people who are entitled to vote when the franchise is extended to the first n_V^2 people but who were not entitled to vote when the franchise was restricted to the first n_V^1 people. In a society where property is respected and where the franchise depends on wealth, it is in each person's interest to expand the electorate up to, but no further than, the point where he is included in the electorate.

The franchise expands when a majority of those already entitled to vote can expect to gain from the enlargement of the electorate. The model of utility and the franchise as illustrated in Figures 27–8 does not so far provide the electorate with the appropriate motive because the utility of each original voter decreases, rather than increases, as the franchise expands. Something extra is required. The postulated motive is fear.[26] The electorate extends the franchise as a defence against rebellion by the disfranchised. The franchise is extended to the wealthiest among the disfranchised in the belief that they would be the the least disruptive within the legislature and the most dangerous if excluded. The natural leaders of the rebellion are co-opted into the ruling class.

The main ingredients of this analysis are the probability of the occurrence of rebellion (p) and the probability of the success of the rebellion (π). At any given time, both probabilities are decreasing functions of the size of the electorate, that is,

$$p = p(n_V) \tag{14}$$

$$\pi = \pi(n_V) \tag{15}$$

where n_V is the size of the electorate, $p' < 0$ and $\pi' < 0$. Both functions can be thought of as shifting over time or in response to changes in society and in technology so that the equilibrium size of the electorate today is not the same as it was yesterday or will be tomorrow. Now make the following assumptions.

(i) Decisions regarding the size of the electorate are made in accordance with the interests of the median voter on the scale of rich and poor. Voters wealthier than the median voter would probably want a smaller electorate. Voters less well off than the median voter would probably want a larger electorate. In this context, the median voter is to be understood as the median among the electorate, not among the population as a whole.

(ii) In the event that a rebellion is successful, the expected utility of the members of the deposed ruling class (the former electorate) falls to U_S, which reflects their new low status as subjects of the new ruling class. Even if the rebellion is unsuccessful, the utility of the members of the ruling class is reduced somewhat, for there is a cost, in income and risk of injury, to suppressing a rebellion. Define the utility of the nth member of the ruling class in the event of an unsuccessful rebellion to be $U(n,n_V;\#)$. Necessarily,

$$U(n,n_V) > U(n,n_V;\#) > U_S \tag{16}$$

as long as the ruling class would rather suppress the rebellion than be suppressed by it.

The equilibrium number of voters, n_V^*, at any given time is that which maximizes the utility of the median voter, $n_V^*/2$. If there is such an equilibrium, it is determined by the maximization with respect to n_V of the expression

$$(1 - p) [U(n_V^*/2,n_V) + p(1 - \pi) [U(n_V^*/2,n_V;\#] + p\pi U_S$$

where $n_V^*/2$ in the first argument of the utility function is treated as a constant in the maximization procedure. The expression is the expected utility of a voter of rank $n_V^*/2$ as a function of the size of the electorate, n_V. The weights $(1 - p)$, $p(1 - \pi)$, and $p\pi$ are, respectively, the probabilities that there is no rebellion, that there is a rebellion which is defeated by the ruling class and that there is a successful rebellion. An equilibrium franchise is one for which the value of n_V which maximizes this expression is just equal to n_V^*.

Maximization of this expression with respect to n_V yields a first-order condition

$$p' [U - (1 - \pi)U_\# - \pi U_S] + \pi'p[U_\# - U_S] = U'(1 - p) + U_\#' p(1 - \pi) \tag{17}$$

that must hold whenever the franchise is in accordance with the wishes of the median voter. In equation (17) the term U is shorthand for $U(n_V^*/2,n_V)$, the term $U_\#$ is shorthand for $U(n_V^*/2,n_V;\#)$ and the terms U' and $U_\#'$ respectively are their derivatives with respect to n_V. The equation may be interpreted as follows. The size of the electorate is optimal for the median voter when the expected increase in safety resulting from a small expansion of the electorate is just worth the corresponding expected loss of income and privilege. The value of the expected increase in safety, represented on the left-hand side of the equation, is the combined effect of the reduction, p', in the probability of rebellion and of the reduction, π', in the probability that a rebellion succeeds. The first of these gains is $p'[U - (1 - \pi) U_\# - \pi U_S]$, where the term in square brackets is the expected loss of utility in the event of a rebellion. The other gain is $\pi'p[U_\# - U_S]$, where the term in square brackets is the reduction in utility when a rebellion succeeds. The value of the expected loss of income, represented on the right-hand side of the equation, is the sum of the expected losses of utility, $U'(1 - p)$ and $U_\#' p(1 - \pi)$, if the rebellion does not occur and if the rebellion occurs but is unsuccessful. The electorate is too small if the risks of the occurrence and of the success of rebellion are both rather high and the gain from reducing these risks by expanding the franchise more than outweighs the loss of privilege to those originally entitled to vote. The electorate is too large if the opposite is the case.

Thus our model of the growth of the electorate becomes a model of the forces causing the components of equation (17) to change over time. First, and perhaps most important, improvements in communication coupled with ever-increasing urbanization lead to increases in p and π for any given n_V and presumably in p' and π' as well. The disenfranchised constitute a greater danger to the state when they are concentrated in a place where they can hear the call to rebel than when they are scattered about the country, unable to communicate with one another or to rise simultaneously. As $p(n_V)$ and $\pi(n_V)$ increase for any given n_V, the optimal n_V must increase as well. Second, changes in the technology of redistribution may have given the rich less cause to fear the enfranchisement of the poor, thereby reducing U' and increasing the median voter's preferred value of n_V. It is one thing for the rich to acquiesce in the enfranchisement of the poor when the poor are expected to use their votes to increase the progressivity of the income tax or to raise welfare payments; it is another when the poor, having no other means of redistribution, are expected to use their votes to expropriate the property of the rich. Third, economic growth converts the poor into supporters of the system of private property. The higher the general standard of living the larger is the fraction of the population that can be admitted into the electorate without fear that property will be expropriated. Of course, the dispersion of the income distribution is also relevant, but for any given distribution, as represented, for instance, by the Gini coefficient, one would expect support for the institution of private property to increase together with the general standard of living. Thus economic growth lowers U' in our equation and increases the equilibrium value of n_V.

That completes the account of the transformation of despotism into the liberal society. The account is not put forward as an inevitable development of despotism, but as a possibility, even a remote possibility. Despotism does not often evolve into a liberal society. It may persist indefinitely, with the occasional reversion to anarchy and periodic changes in the personnel of the ruling class. Nor is the account put forward as in any way original. I hope the reader's reaction to the account will be that it is more or less what he was taught in school and that I am formalizing what is already well known.

I would emphasize, however, that this story is quite different from the story of the spontaneous emergence of institutions or from the story of the social contract. My main objection to those stories as explanations of the birth of the liberal society is that they require the introduction of implicit or explicit cooperation in the entire population. It is far more likely that cooperation would begin on a small scale and that the first cooperators would cooperate in exploiting the rest of society and not just in passively protecting themselves. The institutions of property and voting are not the natural successors of anarchy, for they are both dependent on a degree of order and security that they cannot themselves supply. Despotism supplies the order within which these institutions may evolve.

To be sure, the institutions of the market may evolve spontaneously under the umbrella of the magistrate or the prince. The courts may well come to respect traditional business practice or social customs. But commercial institutions cannot evolve, spontaneously or otherwise, unless a degree of order is first established. The picture I want to convey is of a liberal society as the end product of a complex, long and often brutal evolution. Reform is often possible and desirable, but not, as is sometimes supposed, by returning to the state of nature and building a new structure from the ground up.

From the liberal society back to despotism

About this transition there is little to explain. The liberal society is neces-sarily fragile, depending as it does on the determination of citizens to accept the outcome of the vote, regardless of whether that outcome is favourable or unfavourable to their particular interests and concerns. The vote itself must be more important than the subject of the vote. It is a common theme of democratic theory[27] that voting requires a degree of consensus among citizens. The liberal society cannot withstand a division of citizens into two camps with opposing platforms so strongly held that partisans of each would rather fight than compromise or accept defeat at the polls. The liberal society may be terminated by *coup d'état*, by civil war leading to a despotism imposed by the victor, by rebellion on the part of a well organized minority of citizens, or as the consequence of general understanding among citizens, reflected in one final election, that decision-making by majority rule is unworkable and that the true will of the people is reflected in the great leader or the great party.

The termination of a liberal society may be the termination of the in-stitution of private property, or the institution of voting by majority rule, or both; but the liberal society cannot limp along with only part of its institutional support. A central argument in Chapter V was that the insti-tutions of property and voting are highly interdependent and that, in par-ticular, the preservation of decision-making by majority rule requires private property. The crux of the argument was that voting cannot be employed as a means of allocating the entire national income among citizens without at the same time destroying the minimal consensus upon which the institu-tion of voting depends. If so, there is no possibility of preserving demo-cracy in a society without private property. The reverse is not true. Pri-vate property can be preserved to some extent within a despotic society.

The overthrow of a liberal society may give rise to despotism with or without private property. The latter is usually more burdensome to the subjects and more difficult to displace. First, despotism without private property goes deeper into the economy and exercises a more pervasive influence upon the lives of the subjects. When the institution of private property is preserved, the ruling class may have no greater concern for the rest of society than to preserve order, fight off challenges to its author-ity and, of course, collect tax revenue. Otherwise, the ruling class is obliged to concern itself with every aspect of life — production, news, education, health and so on — leaving no corner where a person can live independently. Second, private property carries within it the embryo of a new liberal society. A market economy requires a good deal of private communication and private organization which can be turned from commerce to politics, just as, in an earlier time, independent religious organizations served as the nucleus of rebellion. Third, the ruling class in a despotism with private property is smaller than it would otherwise be and correspondingly easier to overthrow. There are fewer rulers to be deposed in rebellion and fewer people prepared to support the established regime, for the personnel of the army and of businesses can expect to be maintained in their posts regardless. Despotism without property rights is not so easily displaced.

Regular and persistent alternation between a liberal society (admittedly with a certain despotic colouring) and despotism with property rights is a pattern common enough that it is almost a system of organization in itself. Something in the liberal society is amiss in certain countries and seems to call for the suspension of political rights from time to time; something in the resulting despotism is unstable and leads to the re-establishment of the liberal society.

Notes

1 On possible specifications for a conflict function and for a brief bibliography of literature on the subject, see J. Hirshleifer, "Conflict and Rent-seeking Success Functions: Ratio vs. Difference Models of Relative Success", *Public Choice*, 1989, 101–12.

2 A model of the size of nations might be constructed by analogy with standard models of catchment areas of towns. Suppose the army is "centred" on the capital city and its probability of defeating an opponent decreases with the distance from the capital city to the border where the battle takes place. The army's probability of winning a battle becomes $F(n_1, n_2, d_1, d_2)$, where the subscripts 1 and 2 refer to the army and its opponent, the variable n refers to the size of the forces, and the variable d refers to distances from the capital city to the border. There may be an optimal size of countries at which there is no incentive to engage in combat for additional territory. For a very different explanation of the size of nations, see D. Friedman, "A Theory of the Size and Shape of Nations", *Journal of Political Economy*, 1977, 59–77.

3 Everyone would be better off if all fights were replaced by lotteries in which each group's probability of winning is precisely the probability that it would have won the fight. Expected incomes and ranks would remain unchanged, but survival probabilities associated with violence would immediately rise to 1. It is interesting to speculate why this never happens.

4 Arthur F. Wright, "Generalizations in Chinese History", in L. Gottschalk, ed., *Generalizations in the Writing of History, A Report*, University of Chicago Press, 1963, 41.

5 Andrew Schotter, *The Economic Theory of Social Institutions*, Cambridge University Press, 1981.

6 Robert Axelrod, *The Evolution of Cooperation*, Basic Books, 1984.

7 Edna Ullman-Margalit, *The Emergence of Norms*, Clarendon Press, 1977.

8 Schotter, *op. cit.*, 4.

9 Axelrod's results require that the players' discount rates are not too high and that there is some randomness in the length of the sequence of games, so that the entire strategy of cooperation does not unravel from the last game backwards.

10 Models with these implications are presented in Jack Hirshleifer and Juan Carlos Martinez Coll, "What Strategies Can Support the Evolutionary Emergence of Cooperation?", *Journal of Conflict Resolution*, 1988, 367–98.

11 For an informative history of the doctrine of the social contract, see J.W. Gough, *The Social Contract: a Critical Study of its Development*, Clarendon Press, 1936.

12 *Crito*, in Irwin Edman, ed., *The Works of Plato*, Modern Library, 1928, p. 102.

13 The distinction between the contract of government and the contract of society is discussed extensively by Gough. See note 11.

14 Robert Nozick, *Anarchy, State and Utopia*, Blackwell, 1974, ix.

15 David Hume, "On the Original Contract", in E. Barker, ed., *Social Contract*, 1947, 228.

16 *Ibid.*, 215. I doubt whether Hobbes would have disagreed with this passage. Hobbes allowed that a commonwealth could originate by institution (discussed in chapter XIX of *The Leviathan*) or by conquest (discussed in chapter XX), but one has the impression that the former is seen as rare or non-existent. In "A Review and Conclusion" at the end of the book, Hobbes had this to say:

In the 29. Chapter I have set down for one of the causes of the Dissolutions of Common-wealths, their Imperfect Generation, consisting in the want of an Absolute and Arbitrary Legislative Power; for want whereof, the Civill Soveraign is fain to handle the Sword of Justice unconstantly, and as if it were too hot for him to hold: One reason whereof (which I have not there mentioned) is this, That they will all of them justifie the War, by which their Power was at first gotten, and whereon (as they think) their Right dependeth, and not on the Possession. As if, for example, the Right of the Kings of England did depend on the goodnesse of the cause of William the Conquerour, and upon their lineall, and directest Descent from him; by which means, there would perhaps be no tie of the Subjects obedience to their Soveraign at this day in all the world: wherein whilest they needlessely think to justifie themselves, they justifie all the successefull Rebellions that Ambition shall at any time after raise against them, and their Successors. Therefore I put down for one of the most effectuall seeds of the Death of any State, that the Conquerors require not onely a Submission of mens actions to them for the future, but also an Approbation of all their actions past; when there is scarce a Common-wealth in the world, whose beginnings can in conscience be justified.

17 Such a rule has been proposed in R. Epstein, *Takings: Private Property and the Power of Eminent Domain*, Harvard University Press, 1985.

18 See A.K. Sen, "Isolation, Assurance and the Social Rate of Discount", *Quarterly Journal of Economics*, 1967. The assurance problem may be illustrated in a simple two-person game, as in Figure 29. Nobody in this case has an incentive to break the rules, but either party may do so out of mistrust. The situation is especially treacherous in an intertemporal context if the first party to break the rules automatically acquires the means to stop the other party from doing so.

19 See, for instance, Lewis K. Uhler, *Setting Limits: Constitutional Control of Government* (with a foreword by Milton Friedman), Regnery Gateway, 1989.

20 California's proposition 13 was not a constitutional detour in this sense. My critique of the social contract does not extend to the use of a referendum for the passage of what is, in effect, an ordinary law. There is nothing to stop those

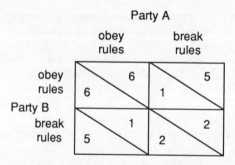

Figure 29 The assurance problem

opposed to proposition 13 from putting it on to the ballot once again in the hope that the majority of voters will reject it next time.

21 On what happens when anarchy, among tribes if not among people, first gives rise to "civilization" with a well developed hierarchy of rulers, see Eli Sagan, *At the Dawn of Tyranny*, Knopf, 1985.

22 For a different view of the prospects for the establishment of a new social contract, shoring up the rights of property and restricting the encroachment of government on the individual, see James M. Buchanan, *The Limits of Liberty: Between Anarchy and Leviathan*, University of Chicago Press, 1975. Buchanan believes passionately that a new contract is feasible and desirable. Though I have drawn heavily on Buchanan in the development of my own ideas, I cannot follow him on this matter.

23 G. Huehns, ed., *Clarendon: Selections from "The History of the Rebellion" and "The Life by Himself"*, Oxford University Press, 1978, 85.

24 From 1831 to 1979 the British electorate increased from about 2 per cent to 73 per cent of the total population. The increase came about through a gradual reform of Parliament: the relaxation and eventual removal of property qualifications, the elimination of elements of unfairness in electoral procedure (like the famous constituency of Old Sarum with only seven voters and the open ballot that allowed landowners to intimidate their tenants) and the enfranchisement of women. The main events were the Catholic Emancipation Act of 1829, the First (1832), Second (1867) and Third (1884) Reform Acts, that greatly reduced property qualifications, the introduction of the secret ballot in 1872, the abolition of property qualifications and the enfranchisement of women over thirty in 1918, and the lowering of the voting age from twenty-one to eighteen in 1969. The ratio of the electorate to the total population at various dates was as follows:

Date	Electorate as % of population
1831	2.0
1832	4.6
1868	8.0
1885	15.8
1918	49.6
1929	63.2
1979	73.1

These data are from F.W.S. Craig, ed., *British Electoral Facts, 1832–1980*, Parliamentary Research Service, 1981, supplemented by J. Cannon, *Parliamentary Reform, 1640–1832*, Cambridge University Press, 1973.

25 A.B. White, *Self-government at the King's Command: a Study of the Beginnings of English Democracy*, Oxford University Press, 1933.

26 This is not a novel idea. Fear of rebellion is given the principal role in John Cannon's account of the history of the agitation that led to the passage of the Great Reform Act of 1832. See note 24.

27 See, for instance, Elias Borg, *Democracy and the Majority Principle*, Studies in Politics 3, Political Science Institute, University of Göteborg, 1965.

Chapter VII

Departures from efficiency in the private sector of the liberal society

Anarchy, despotism and the liberal society have so far been looked upon as three complete and entirely distinct forms of organization. Anarchy and despotism were, each in its own way, malevolent, while the liberal society represented what is best for the ordinary citizen, not in the absolute sense that nothing better can be imagined, but in the prosaic sense that nothing better can be attained. Transitions from one society to another were discussed, but the possibility that actual societies might have attributes of all three pure types was hardly considered at all.

From here on, the threefold classification of societies is employed as a device for the analysis of institutions and behaviour within societies that are more or less liberal because they are based on property and voting but that differ in important ways from the pure type described in Chapter V. The focus is now upon actual liberal societies, that is, upon the capitalist and democratic societies that we know today.

Anarchy and despotism are assigned new roles in the analysis. Total collapse of the liberal society into anarchy or despotism remains a possibility, but these alternative societies will also serve as models or paradigms of defects, weaknesses and inefficiencies within a primarily liberal society that need not be on the verge of collapse. From anarchy we draw the fundamental distinction between making and taking, as well as the four-fold classification of the social cost of predatory behaviour. From despotism we draw the picture of government as predator, a picture which must somehow be juxtaposed and fused with the apparently opposite picture of government as the upholder of property rights and defender of the law-abiding citizen from the predation of his neighbours.

Departures from efficiency in a primarily liberal society are to be looked upon as vestiges of anarchy and despotism. Departures from efficiency in the private sector are like anarchy in that resources are diverted from the making of goods to the taking of goods made by others and to the defence of income and property. Departures from efficiency in the public sector are like despotism in that resources are diverted from production to the dispensation of privileges through the intermediary of the government and to the acquisition of influence over public sector largess. Actual liberal societies tread a narrow path between anarchy on one side and despotism on the other.

So broad a picture of possible malfunctionings in the economy and the government can never be completely and strictly accurate. The world is too diverse and contrary a place to be pinned down by such a simple scheme. Yet the representation of departures from efficiency as vestiges of anarchy and despotism within the liberal society may be helpful in several ways. It identifies common features in what might otherwise appear as separate and disconnected phenomena. It may serve as an antidote to the point of view — still implicit in some studies of welfare economics though rarely expressed in so many words — that departures from efficiency are a monopoly of the private sector and that government is a disinterested agency for putting matters right. It calls attention to possible trade-offs between departures from efficiency in the economy and in the government. It provides an alternative to the model of the isolated and self-sufficient economy that has been the stock-in-trade of the economics profession since *The Wealth of Nations*, that has over the years constituted an immensely powerful "engine for the discovery of concrete truth", but that does constitute a one-sided and frequently misleading picture of society.

Departures from efficiency in the public sector will be dealt with in the following two chapters: Chapter VIII is about the role of government, on the working assumptions that the government is reasonably disinterested in its administration of the economy and that departures from efficiency arise from manoeuvres by citizens to avoid tax or to make themselves eligible for public largess. Chapter IX is about the acquisition of privileges through the intermediary of the government. This chapter is about departures from efficiency within the private sector.

Anarchy and market failure are alike in their social cost. Recall the demonstration in Chapter III of how the social cost of banditry can be divided into four mutually exclusive components: (i) the waste of the labour power of the bandit, (ii) the waste of the labour of the farmer when he defends himself, (iii) the deadweight loss from excessive production of non-stealable goods or leisure, and (iv) the destruction of product in the act of banditry. Two morals can be drawn from that story. The first and more comprehensive moral is that costs associated with departures from efficiency can be placed in one or more of these four categories. Banditry is the paradigmatic departure from efficiency in which all four costs are liberally represented. Other departures from efficiency, to be discussed in this chapter, entail some but not necessarily all of these costs. The story of the farmer and the bandit provides a classificatory device. The other narrower but more interesting moral is that many departures from efficiency are theft-like. They arise from efforts of agents to appropriate goods that others have made, as distinct from production of goods for use or sale — taking as distinct from making. Many departures from efficiency in the private sector can be thought of as tendencies toward anarchy, where anarchy is the extreme limit of a society without publicly imposed impediments to private appropriation. The analogy between market failure and anarchy is most enlightening when the predator can be identified, as he can in the analysis of advertising and speculation below. Pure, unmixed predation would normally be made illegal, but there are activities in which making and taking are so intertwined that it would on balance be disadvantageous to criminalize the activity altogether, though some regulation may do more good than harm. In this chapter I propose to push the distinction between taking and making as far as it can be made to go, and to cover as much as possible of what can go wrong with the private sector of the economy.

Two main assumptions of the economist's model of perfect competition as set out in Chapter I are that property is privately owned and that all agents are price-takers. The first assumption is that society's means of production are divided up among people who may use, rent or sell their share without fear that it will be taken away. The second assumption is that each person believes the observed market prices to be beyond the control of any one agent in the economy, so that no action on his part — no sale or purchase — can cause any price to rise or fall perceptibly. On these assumptions (among others), it is established that there exists a set of market-clearing prices and that the outcome when everybody trades as he pleases at these prices is Pareto optimal. The right mix of goods and services is produced and the right bundle of goods is allocated to each person, in the special and limited sense that no change in the mix of goods produced and no additional exchanges of goods are advantageous to everyone. Nobody can be made better off without someone else being made worse off. There is, in short, no waste. The outcome need not be distributionally ideal. There may be some very rich and some very poor. A social welfare function that puts some weight upon the distribution of income may rank the particular Pareto optimal outcome lower than some other Pareto optimal outcome arising from a different initial set of endowments of property. Nevertheless, if there are secure property rights and if everyone is a price-taker, then all the resources of society are devoted to making as distinct from taking and nothing of the waste of resources in the model of anarchy is observed. Departures from efficiency in the private sector arise because property is not completely secure and because prices are not wholly market-determined or wholly unaffected by the actions of any single person or firm.

This is almost tautological. With secure property rights, inclusive of one's property rights in goods purchased and in goods produced but not yet sold, and with market prices seen by all agents as invariant, there can be no predatory behaviour; there can be no use for one's resources other than to produce goods for sale or personal consumption. Departures from efficiency in actual competitive economies may be seen as tendencies toward anarchy arising for the most part because stubborn reality will not conform to the assumptions of the model.

Our examination in this chapter of departures from efficiency in the private sector of a liberal society is organized under the headings of the two main assumptions of the model of perfect competition. Departures from efficiency may be associated with misplaced, non-existent or insecure property rights, or they may be associated with limitations upon price-taking behaviour. These matters will be discussed in turn.

Property rights

Among the assumptions required to prove that a competitive economy is efficient, in the sense of Pareto optimality, are that property is privately owned, that it consists of entitlement to objects — land, factories, one's own labour power, and so on — rather than to the exclusive use of knowledge or the exclusive right to serve certain markets, that taste is impervious to manipulation by self-interested firms, and that everyone has the same information, want of information or probability distribution about future events. Reasonable as these assumptions are in many of the contexts where economic analysis is employed, and useful as they undoubtedly are for concentrating one's attention on significant features of many practical problems, they are all descriptively false. A recalcitrant world will not always conform to the assumptions in our models, and departures from efficiency frequently arise when it stubbornly refuses to do so.

Disconformity of the world to the assumptions about property rights is a possible source of inefficiency in several important respects. Property may be held in common, as exemplified by unrestricted access to fishing grounds. Property rights may be assigned to markets rather than to things or to labour power (monopoly). Property in knowledge about technology and in natural resources may be created by the state as an inducement to firms to invest in the acquisition of knowledge. Property is contested in litigation and rent-seeking. Property in markets is enhanced by advertising. Property in knowledge of future events is created by speculation. Monopoly is placed here under the general heading of "property rights" rather than under the heading of "limits upon the domain of prices" in the latter half of this chapter because the emphasis there is on the absence of equilibrium prices rather than upon discrepancies between equilibrium prices and true rates of trade-off in production or use.

Table 7 *Marginal and average product with common property*

Number of fishermen	Total catch ($)	Catch per fisherman ($)	Contribution of the "mrginal fisherman" ($)
1	3,000	3,000	3,000
2	5,500	2,750	2,500
3	7,500	2,500	2,000
4	9,000	2,250	1,500
5	10,000	2,000	1,000
6	10,500	1,750	500
7	10,500	1,500	0
8	10,000	1,250	−500
9	9,000	1,000	−1,000
10	7,500	750	−1,500

Property in common

The absence of property rights is a state of anarchy. A condition resembling anarchy, but far less nasty in its effects, can arise when some property is unappropriated and made available to whoever wishes to use it. Such property is called "common property", where the word "common" in this context refers to common access rather than common ownership. The city hall is not common property in the economist's sense of the term, though it is owned collectively by all the inhabitants of the city. The medieval commons on which everyone might set his cows to graze, the road with free access to all vehicles because it is infeasible or prohibitively expensive to impose tolls, the lake available to anyone who wishes to fish there and the air we breathe are common property because they are open to everyone to be used privately for his own personal benefit.[1]

The departure from efficiency when property is used in common is best introduced by the well known example of unlimited access by fishermen to a lake. To keep matters simple, suppose that the going wage of fishermen elsewhere is $1,000 for the fishing season, that anyone who wishes to fish on this lake may do so, and that the lake is remote enough from other fishing grounds that one must fish there exclusively for the entire season — forgoing the alternative wage of $1,000 — if one is to fish there at all. Suppose also that every fisherman on the lake gets an equal share of the catch; no fisherman has better luck over the season than any other. The catch as a function of the number of fishermen on the lake is assumed to be as in Table 7. As the number of fishermen increases from one to ten, the total catch first increases, reaching a maximum when there are six fishermen, and then declines. The assumed decline in the catch once there are more than six fishermen on the lake does not make much sense in the context of a static model of fishing, though one may suppose that fish are destroyed as fishermen compete too closely. The real justification for the assumption is as a static counterpart of certain dynamic effects to be discussed below. The contribution of the marginal fisherman, as shown in the right-hand column, is the amount by which the total value of the catch would be reduced if there were one less fisherman on the lake.

The crux of this example is the discrepancy between the socially optimal number of fishermen on the lake and the actual number of fishermen when each fisherman chooses a course of action to maximize his earnings. The optimal number of fishermen on the lake is that which maximizes the total value of the catch, *on the lake and elsewhere*, for any given contingent of fishermen. The optimal number is identified by the condition that the marginal product of a fisherman is the same on the lake as elsewhere — $1,000 in each case. Thus the optimal number is five, despite the fact that the value of the catch per fisherman when there are five fishermen on the lake is $2,000, which is twice what fishermen can earn elsewhere — a discrepancy that cannot be maintained when fishermen are free to choose where to fish. The equilibrium number of fishermen is that for which the value of their average product on the lake is just equal to the earnings of fishermen elsewhere. The equilibrium number of fishermen is nine, despite the fact that the total value of output is actually less with nine fishermen than with five. The total output of the nine fishermen could be increased from $9,000 to $14,000 if four fishermen were to go elsewhere instead; the five remaining on the lake would produce $10,000 worth of fish and the four surplus fishermen would together produce $4,000 worth elsewhere.

Note that it is not sufficient for four particular fishermen to agree to depart, because they would be replaced immediately by new fishermen drawn to the lake by the new higher average product of labour. To prevent this from happening, the right to fish on the lake would have to be restricted. For example, the right to fish on the lake might belong to nine particular fishermen who would have every incentive to assign five of their number to the lake and the remaining four elsewhere, on the understanding that total earnings, on the lake and elsewhere, would be shared equally. Alternatively, the lake might be privately owned. The owner would have an incentive to hire fishermen up to the point where their marginal product on the lake equalled the going wage. Or access to the lake might be taxed at a rate of $1,000 per fisherman.

The departure from efficiency in this example is sometimes described as an externality. Each fisherman is said to impose a negative externality upon every other fisherman. While there is nothing wrong, in my opinion, with this terminology, I find it unhelpful because the word "externality" conveys little information or insight once it is recognized that there is a departure from efficiency. By contrast, the analogy with anarchy is less than complete but perhaps still helpful in comparing this departure from efficiency with others. The analogy with anarchy emphasizes the waste of resources in taking and defending (though, as in the legal example in Chapter III, all agents are simultaneously predator and prey), as well as the destruction of product in the contest over possession. Deadweight loss, on the other hand, is absent in this example because the price of fish is assumed to be invariant.

Utilization of common property is especially inefficient in an inter-temporal context, as may be illustrated in a simple extension of the fishing example. For analytical convenience, we make the following assumptions. All fishing takes place in the summer. The size of the catch each summer depends on the number of fishermen and the stock of fish. Fish live for no more than one year. They are born in the winter, live through the summer if they escape the fishermen, spawn in the autumn and die the following winter. On these assumptions, the spring and autumn stocks would be the same if there were no fishing. The relation between the autumn stock in one year and the spring stock in the next is Malthusian. With a limited supply of nutrients in the lake, the rate of growth of the stock over the winter (which may in some circumstances be negative) diminishes with the size of the autumn stock.

The technology of fishing may be represented by three equations. The first is the production function relating the size of the catch in any year, C, to the number of fishermen, N, and the stock of fish in the spring, S.

$$C = C(N,S) \tag{1}$$

where $\partial C/\partial N > 0$, $\partial C/\partial S > 0$ and $\partial C^2/\partial N^2 < 0$, signifying that there are diminishing returns to labour in fishing. The production function is illus-trated in Figure 30, with the catch, C, on the vertical axis and the number of fishermen, N, on the horizontal axis. The information in Table 7 can be thought of as representing a production function for some given stock, S. The values of the variables C, S and N would normally change from one year to the next, so that these variables should really be written as C(t), S(t) and N(t) respectively. The second equation is an accounting identity connecting stocks and flows of fish.

$$A(t) = S(t) - C(t) \tag{2}$$

The autumn stock each year, A(t), is equal to the spring stock, S(t), less the catch, C(t). The third equation depicts our admittedly unrealistic as-sumption about the life cycle of fish. It shows the dependence of the stock, S(t + 1), in the spring of the year t + 1 upon the stock, A(t), in the autumn of the preceding year t.

$$S(t + 1) = f(A(t)) \tag{3}$$

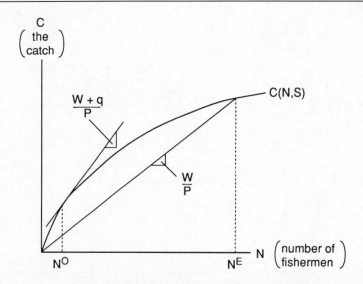

Figure 30 The production function for fishing. N^E is the equilibrium number of fishermen when the wage is W and the price of fish is P, N^O is the optimal number of fishermen when q is the shadow price of uncaught fish, and S is the stock of fish; an increase in S rotates the curve C(N,S) anticlockwise

where the function f is concave (f' > 0 and f" < 0), reflecting our Malthusian assumption about population growth in the presence of a limited supply of nutrients. The natural growth function, f, is illustrated in Figure 31, with S(t + 1) on the vertical axis and with both stocks in the year t, S(t) and A(t), on the horizontal axis. The 45° line signifies points of equality between stocks this year and stocks next year.

The effect of fishing this year on the stock of fish next year can be read off Figure 31. Let the stock in the spring of this year, t, be S(t). With no fishing in the year t, the spring and autumn stocks would be the same (by assumption) and the stock the following spring would grow to f(S(t)), which, as the curve is drawn, is larger than S(t). Alternatively, with a catch, C(t), equal to the distance cd in the figure, the stock in the following spring would be f(A₁(t)), where A₁(t) = S(t) – cd; the stock f(A₁(t)) is less than f(S(t)) but still greater than S(t) itself. The sustainable yield from a stock of S(t) is indicated by the distance db. When the catch is db, the autumn stock becomes A₂(t). This grows over the winter to f(A₂(t)), which is, by construction, just equal to S(t). The catch in any year could exceed the sustainable yield, but only at the cost of a reduction of the stock of fish the following year. For instance, if the catch were as large as ad, the autumn stock would be only A₃(t) and the stock in the spring of the following year would be f(A₃(t)), which is less than S(t).

Much depends on the assumed shape of the natural growth function, f.

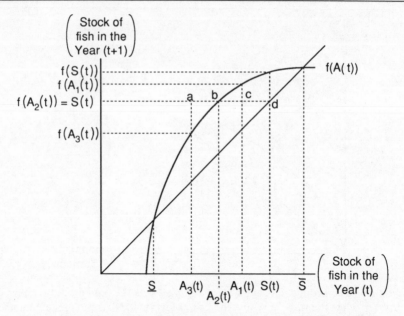

Figure 31　The growth of a stock of fish from one year to the next

Referring to Figure 31, it must lie above the 45° line at some values of
$A(t)$, for otherwise the fish population would become extinct, even in the
absence of fishing. It must cross the 45° line at some high value, $\bar{S}$, of the
stock, for otherwise there would be no natural limit to the stock of fish.
The function cannot intersect the vertical axis, for the obvious biological
reason. It might be assumed to begin at the origin, signifying that the fish
population can never become extinct as long as some fish, no matter how
few, survive the summer's fishing. Instead, it is assumed to cross the 45°
line from below at a minimal biologically sustainable stock of $\underline{S}$. If, perhaps by over-fishing, the autumn stock is once allowed to fall below $\underline{S}$, it
can never recover, for the stock then declines year after year until there
are no fish left. The maximal sustainable yield accrues where the slope of
f is parallel to the 45° line.

Once again, as in the simple numerical example, free access of fishermen
to the lake leads to over-fishing, but now there are two aspects to the
departure from efficiency. There is a disregard on the part of each
fisherman for the effect of his actions on the productivity of other
fishermen today and there is a similar disregard for the effect of today's
actions upon the size of the stock of fish tomorrow. Let P be the price of
fish and W the going wage of labour; suppose these remain constant over
time.

When the lake is treated as common property, the number of fishermen each year, N^E, is such that the value of the catch per fisherman is just equal to the externally given wage, W.

$$PC(N^E,S) = WN^E \tag{4}$$

where, for convenience, the dependence of P, S, w and N^E upon time is ignored. In these conditions the market may evolve over time into a steady state or the stock of fish may be wiped out.

By contrast, the socially optimal rate of fishing on the lake is that which maximizes the present value of the net social benefit from fishing until the end of time. In any given year the net benefit from fishing would be maximized when the number of fishermen was such that the value of the marginal product was just equal to the wage; $P\partial C(N,S)/\partial N = W$. This is not the optimal number of fishermen, for, at this number of fishermen, the removal of one fisherman has no effect upon the national income in the current year but *does* have an effect upon the stock of fish in the following year. The removal of one fisherman in these conditions is advantageous because it leads to an increase in national income next year without reducing national income this year at all. Thus the optimal number of fishermen, N^0, is identified by the equation

$$P\partial C(N,S)/\partial N - W = q > 0 \tag{5}$$

where q is the present value of the net benefit next year made possible by a reduction in N this year.[2]

That the equilibrium number of fishermen, N^E, exceeds the optimal number, N^0, may be seen by comparing equations (4) and (5), and is illustrated in Figure 30 above. The equilibrium catch is indicated by the intersection of the production function with a line through the origin at a slope of W/P, as signified by equation (4). The catch is optimal when the slope of the tangent to the production function is just equal to $(W + q)/P$, as signified by equation (5). The value of N^E exceeds the value of N^0 because the assumed diminishing marginal product of labour in fishing guarantees (i) that the value of N for which $C/N = W/P$ is greater than the value of N for which $\partial C/\partial N = W/P$ and (ii) that the value of N for which $\partial C/\partial N = (W + q)/P$ is smaller still. Note that equations (4) and (5) are based on the assumption that it is profitable to fish on this lake. Nothing in the analysis itself guarantees this to be so. In certain circumstances it might be best to let the lake lie undisturbed for a few years until the stock of fish has increased.

Harm from the over-use of common property is not confined to the reduction of the marginal product of labour in any given year. The lesson to be learned from the intertemporal extension of the common property example is that the greatest harm in practice may be the gradual destruction of the stock from which each year's yield is derived. Failure to take account of the effect of one's actions on the welfare of other people may be especially harmful in this context because tomorrow's losers may not be in a position to plead their cause or to bargain for better treatment today.

Over-use of common property becomes a classic externality when the benefit and the harm of an activity (both associated with fish in our example above) accrue in different products or contexts. A refrigerator keeps food cold *and* emits freon gas that harms the ozone layer of the atmosphere. Gasoline is fuel for cars *and* a source of air pollution. DDT protects crops from non-human predators *and* endangers species of plants and animals. These types of harm to common property are called externalities, in part by historical accident as discussed in Chapter II and in part because they are external to the purpose of the transaction, though they are no less harmful on that account. The owner of a refrigerator does not want to harm the ozone layer but, as the ozone layer is common property without restrictions upon its use, he has no real incentive to refrain from harming it.

I know that my refrigerator emits freon gas which damages the ozone layer. In principle, my benefit from using the refrigerator and the full worldwide damage to the ozone layer from the freon gas that my refrigerator emits can both be valued in dollar terms. It is entirely possible that the social cost exceeds my private benefit. I use the refrigerator nonetheless because the full benefit accrues to me while the resulting harm is shared more or less equally among three billion people. I use the refrigerator because I get all the benefit and bear one three-billionth of the cost, and because I know that giving up the use of my refrigerator would not provoke others to give up using theirs.

Refrigeration is one of many instances where making and taking are so bound together that they cannot be separated and where one cannot always tell in practice which predominates. Refrigeration is making in so far as it keeps food cold. It is taking in so far as it endangers people through the effect of freon gas on the ozone layer. Perhaps the sum of the benefits when everybody uses refrigeration exceeds the sum of the costs. Making dominates taking in that case, and refrigeration is socially advantageous on balance, though regulation might still be appropriate to reduce the amount of freon gas that escapes from the cooling system. Alternatively, the total social cost might exceed total social benefit, so that taking dominates making and it would be advantageous to ban refrigeration altogether unless a way could be found to change the impact upon the atmosphere. The social cost of refrigeration is best placed in the category of destruction of product, where the product in this case is an aspect of the environment in which we live.[3]

International common property is especially troublesome. Warming of the atmosphere from the emission of carbon dioxide and destruction of the ozone layer from the emission of chlorofluorocarbons are analogous to the depletion of the stock of fish in the lake. Each person's use of his car or refrigerator is of benefit to himself alone; the cost of each person's action is borne by everybody collectively; the harm, though potentially massive, is slow to appear. These standard problems are compounded by the want of any single jurisdiction to bear the responsibility for restraint. Each country would like to be an international free rider, reaping the benefit of others' restraint but restraining its own citizens as little as possible. If each country contributed to global warming in the same way, then perhaps a common programme of restraint could be established. It is especially difficult for countries to agree upon a common programme when one country cuts down forests, another is a heavy user of automobiles and a third is dependent on coal for its industry.

Several distinctions are important for the assessment of the nature and magnitude of the departure from efficiency from the holding of property in common. Common property may be land or capital, part of the world as it appeared to Adam and Eve or something that people have made. The distinction between land and capital is significant in this context because a secondary departure from efficiency arises from the absence of an incentive within the competitive market for the production of common property, even in circumstances where the social return on the investment is high. No individual is prepared to bear the expense of building a road or an artificial lake if the road or the lake are designated as common property so that the builder is not entitled to levy a toll on its use.

Common property may be distinguished from "public property" and from "public goods". The three concepts are alike in that property is possessed by the community collectively. They differ according to how the property can or may be used. Common property, as exemplified by a lake full of fish, is subject to congestion but unrestricted in use. Public property, as exemplified by the city hall or nationalized firms, yields benefits that accrue in the first instance to the government but ultimately to citizens, equally or according to some well specified rule such as in accordance with tax payments.[4] Public goods, as exemplified by a television signal, do not need to be allocated among users because they are uncongested; the quality of the signal to any given viewer is independent of the number of other viewers. Subject to qualifications to be discussed in the next chapter, the army is another public good. The atmosphere was like a public good in primitive conditions where the use of carbon for fuel was minimal. It has recently acquired the attributes of common property.

Common property may be atemporal or intertemporal as exemplified by the two versions of our fishing example. When common property is atemporal, each user is at once the bandit and the victim, and it is relatively easy to remove the departure from efficiency by taxation or by the establishment of property rights. When common property is a stock that deteriorates over time, the present generation becomes the bandit, the next generation becomes his victim, and people's willingness to remove the departure from efficiency depends on the strength of the identification between one generation and the next.

Common property is a social institution rather than an intrinsic quality of the property itself. The lake is common property, in our sense of the term, because nobody is prevented from fishing there. It ceases to be common property if ownership is assigned or, equivalently, if access is appropriately taxed. Nonetheless, the fact that some property is held in common while other property is strictly private suggests that there might be common characteristics of each type. It may be best to hold certain kinds of property in common despite the well known departure from efficiency that common property entails.

One characteristic of a great deal of common property is that it flows. Unlike a steel plant, which is fixed in one place, or a truck, which is in only one place at a time, the air is everywhere at once. It is physically impossible to fence off your share of the atmosphere from mine. The air would not be common property if it could be divided into three billion compartments and if the air pollution from a factory could be contained within the compartments of the stockholders of the firm to which the factory belonged. Similarly, the lake cannot be usefully divided up into areas for each fisherman unless the fish can be taught to respect property rights. Of course, the lake as a whole can be owned; many lakes and streams are private property. The ocean, on the other hand, cannot be privately owned without at the same time creating a monopoly of a substantial part of the world's food supply, a property right that few would be inclined to respect.

A second, and partly overlapping, characteristic of property held in common is that it would be costly, sometimes prohibitively so, to charge for access. If tax collection were costless, automobiles could be taxed according to their impact upon the cost of maintenance and congestion on each yard of road they travel. No such tax is imposed because the cost of collection, including the extra congestion at the toll booths, would exceed the cost of using roads in common; this statement is probably true with the technology of tax collection today, though it may not continue to be true tomorrow. The designation of a lake as private property or the taxation of access might be inappropriate if the owner's rights could be ignored by poachers or if the tax could easily be evaded. There is no way to determine *a priori* where the balance of advantage lies, though a calculation may be feasible in many cases. It is often said of public goods that they are "nonexclusive", which is usually interpreted to mean that there is simply no way to block access. This is equivalent to saying that the cost of collecting taxes or enforcing property rights would be infinite.

Examination of the characteristics of property that tends to be held in common, and recognition of the reasons society may choose to put up with the departure from efficiency that common property entails, raise the question of whether there is really a departure from efficiency at all. How can common property be a departure from efficiency in circumstances where it is best for society to maintain property in common? The problem is more semantic than real. To say that there are departures from efficiency which ought not to be rectified by public action is implicitly to recognize two types of inefficiencies, those that arise in the private sector and those that arise from the activity of the public sector. Departures from efficiency in the private sector are defined with reference to the ideal of perfect competition. Departures from efficiency in the public sector are discussed in Chapters VIII and IX. Public policy must be assessed with regard to both types together. Sometimes the cost of correcting departures from efficiency in the private sector is less than the cost of the departure from efficiency itself, sometimes not. The distinction between the two types of inefficiency is essential in deciding when public action is warranted.

Finally, it should be recognized that common property can be appropriated by population growth. Imagine two families, A and B, whose only source of income is the revenue from a mine which they own jointly. If each family owned 50 per cent of the shares, the size of family B would be immaterial to the welfare of the members of family A. An increase in the number of children in family B from two to three reduces the ownership of each person in the next generation of family B from a quarter to a sixth but has no effect on the next generation of family A at all. Population growth in family B dilutes the ownership in family B alone. But suppose instead that the mine were held "in common". Suppose there was an agreement between the families to divide the proceeds of the mine equally among all members of the two families; such an agreement might make sense as insurance if the number of children in each family were seen as an act of God. Now, with such an agreement, each family is adversely affected by an increase in the number of children in the other family. If family A has two children, then an increase in the number of children in family B from two to three decreases the income of each person in the next generation of family A from a quarter of the proceeds of the mine to a fifth. Any population growth dilutes everybody's ownership in this case.

The Malthusian implications of the example are obvious, for much of the world's resources are held in common. The air and the sea are held in common, as each extra person contributes his bit of environmental degradation. National parks, roads, schools and public assets of all kinds are held in common. Even ostensibly private assets are held in common in so far as the tax imposed upon the return to such assets exceeds the cost to the government of protection, provision of roads and other publicly supplied overheads that the assets require. In a liberal society, the right to vote creates a radical equality among all citizens and a degree of common ownership and common responsibility for the nation's resources. Whenever property is held in common, and no matter what form the common property may take, there emerges a gap between the private interest of a family in having children and the public interest in limiting population growth. A family may be influenced in its choice of the number of children by the private cost of bringing up a child, but it is not influenced at all by the effect of total population on the resource base per head in the next generation. Like the fisherman on the lake, the family knows that the effect of its own actions on the welfare of the next generation as a whole is only minutely reflected in the welfare of its own children.[5]

The discrepancy between private and public interest in population growth is especially acute when children are expected to care for their parents in old age. Old people may need children because they cannot convert property in land or business into assets that yield income without the active supervision that the old are no longer able to supply, or because the old are defenceless against predators. In such circumstances, and especially when there are high mortality rates among children, it can be privately advantageous to have a large family, though everybody would be more prosperous in the long run if all families agreed to have fewer children and some other means could be found to save the old from destitution.

There are similar motives within countries, regions or ethnic groups. A small country, threatened by or threatening its neighbours, seeks to enlarge its population to increase the size of its army, despite the fact that the country and its neighbours would all be better off if their populations were contained. Competing religions behave the same. Leaders of ethnic groups within an ethnically diverse nation exhort their followers "to be fruitful and multiply" so as to gain the privileges and the power that majority status conveys. In a world of fixed resources, where the biosphere has a limited capacity to accommodate people, a common, worldwide interest in the control of total population is not always reflected in the incentives upon people, groups or nations.

Property in markets — monopoly
Production and distribution are efficient in the sense of Pareto optimality when the marginal valuation of each good is just equal to its marginal cost, a condition that holds automatically when all consumers and firms are price-takers. Monopoly is not efficient in this sense because the marginal valuation and marginal cost curves, to society, are seen by the monopolist as average revenue and average cost curves. Thus, in maximizing profit, the monopolist chooses output to equate *his* marginal revenue to *his* marginal cost, with the result, as indicated in Figure 32, that the monopolist's output is less than socially optimal.

The emphasis in this discussion is upon the consequences rather than upon the origin of monopoly. Monopoly may arise because, for good reasons or bad, the state has entitled a firm to be the only supplier in a market, or monopoly may arise through cartelization or other developments within the private sector of the economy. Regardless, our concern

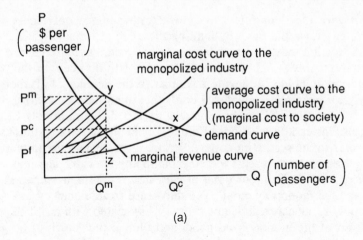

(a)

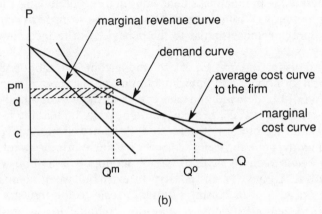

(b)

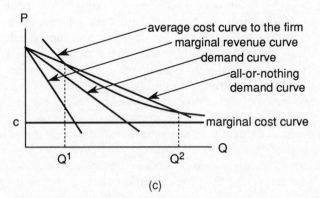

(c)

Figure 32 (a) Contrived monopoly. (b) Profitable natural monopoly. (c) Unprofitable natural monopoly

here is with the departure from efficiency when the only seller in the market can raise the price by limiting the amount for sale.

A distinction may be drawn between secure and insecure monopoly. A secure monopoly is held as a property right with no need on the part of the monopoly-holder to devote resources to the defence of his monopoly against, for example, regulatory boards that might impose controls on his prices or decisions by the bureaucracy to award the monopoly to some-body else instead. Discussions of monopoly in elementary textbooks typi-cally refer to the secure monopoly. We are discussing secure monopoly in this section and will discuss insecure monopoly later on. The importance of the distinction from our point of view lies in the inefficiencies that the two types of monopoly entail. The departure from efficiency in a secure monopoly is the classical deadweight loss associated with insufficient con-sumption of the monopolized good, and there is not much to be gained from analysing the monopolist's behaviour in terms of making and taking, predators and prey. With insecurity of tenure, the struggle to acquire and hold monopoly becomes similar to the behaviour of farmers and bandits in anarchy.

A second distinction may be drawn among contrived monopoly, profit-able natural monopoly and unprofitable natural monopoly, according to the location of the demand and cost curves of the monopolized product. A monopoly is contrived when competition would be feasible in the mo-nopolized industry but is not permitted. A contrived monopoly may be protected by the state, or it may consist of a single firm or cartel that can somehow keep potential rivals at bay. A monopoly is natural when it is socially advantageous for an industry to exist but when competition is infeasible because of increasing returns to scale to the industry and the firm alike. A natural monopoly may be profitable to the monopolist, in which case the granting of a monopoly is sufficient to ensure that the monopolized good will, in fact, be produced. Alternatively, even the granting of a monopoly may be insufficient to induce production of a monopolized good, for an industry may at the same time be socially ad-vantageous yet unprofitable to a monopolist unless additional public as-sistance is supplied. Contrived monopoly, profitable natural monopoly and unprofitable but socially advantageous natural monopoly are illustrated in Figure 32, with price, P, on the vertical axis and quantity, Q, on the horizontal axis. All three diagrams show demand curves, marginal revenue curves, marginal cost curves and average cost curves.

The standard textbook case of contrived monopoly is illustrated in Fig-ure 32a. In interpreting the figure, imagine that total output Q could be produced by many small firms, each just covering its full cost when output is chosen to maximize profit. This situation is consistent with rising aver-age and marginal cost curves to the industry (as shown) when increasing cost is the consequence of upward sloping supply curves of labour and other factors of production to the industry as a whole. If the industry were competitive, the output would be Q^C and the market price would be P^C. Each firm would look upon all prices as invariant with respect to *its* activities, and would produce where *its* marginal cost is just equal to the market price, which, in turn, is equal to the marginal cost to society as a whole. If the industry were monopolized or cartelized, the output would be Q^m, where marginal revenue to the industry is just equal to marginal cost. The price paid by the consumer, P^m, would exceed the marginal revenue to the industry. The price received by factors of production, P^f, would be less than the marginal cost to the industry. The monopoly profit would be $(P^m - P^f)Q^m$, as represented by the shaded area in the figure. The social cost of monopoly is the loss of consumers' and producers' surplus as represented by the triangular area xyz.

Profitable natural monopoly, as illustrated in Figure 32(b), is exemplified by a railroad with a fixed cost in laying the track and a constant marginal cost per passenger or per ton of freight. The average cost curve is downward sloping because each passenger's share of the fixed cost diminishes with the number of passengers. The monopoly is "natural" because the fixed cost of any additional firms would be wasted expenditure. The socially optimal output is Q^0, at which marginal cost equals marginal valuation (price), and the consumers' surplus (the area under the demand curve but above the marginal cost curve) is maximized. The monopolist does not produce at Q^0 because the best price he could get at that output would be the marginal cost, c, and the annualized value of his fixed cost would not be covered. Unregulated, he would choose to produce at Q^m, the quantity for which marginal revenue is equal to marginal cost. The monopoly profit is the shaded area, $P^m abd$, the product of Q^m and the difference between average revenue (price) and average cost. Though the extra fixed cost of a second railroad is a waste of resources, a second railroad might, but need not, be profitable. A second railroad would be profitable only if the original monopoly profit exceeded the (annualized) fixed cost. Otherwise, the monopolist would be quite secure.[6]

Though the monopolist can never break even at the optimal output where price equals marginal cost, he can often turn a profit — a very large profit in some circumstances — by restricting output and raising price. He cannot always do so. There may be goods that are socially advantageous to produce though no firm, not even a secure monopolist, can produce them profitably. At no combination of price and quantity along the demand curve for such goods can the monopolist cover his cost of production, but it is socially desirable to produce those goods, all the same. This case is described in Figure 32(c). Average cost is everywhere above average revenue (the demand curve), signifying that profit is negative regardless of how much is produced. But average cost is still below the all-or-nothing demand curve for values of Q between Q^1 and Q^2, signifying that the consumers' surplus when the socially optimal quantity of Q is produced is still greater than the annualized fixed cost. The all-or-nothing demand curve indicates the price one would pay per unit of Q on an all-or-nothing basis; it answers the question "How much would you pay for Q units if the alternative to buying Q units at that price was to have none at all?'; it takes account of consumers' surplus automatically.

Natural monopoly may be conveyed by network externalities, as exemplified by the telephone system. The defining characteristic of a network externality is that the usefulness of a good depends on the number of people who buy it. A telephone system is best when everybody subscribes; three systems, each serving a third of the population, would definitely be worse than one. The telephone system is a natural monopoly in two respects. It is a natural monopoly because of the large overhead cost of building the telephone line; in this respect it is like the railroad. It is also a natural monopoly because the usefulness of the service to each customer automatically increases with the number of customers. Like other natural monopolies, the telephone company is either nationalized or regulated in many countries on the well founded belief that the telephone company would exact huge monopoly profits if left free to set prices as it pleased.

In the railroad example, the overhead cost that gave rise to the natural monopoly was associated with the firm; a second railroad company would have to build a second railroad. The situation changes substantially when the overhead cost is associated with the industry instead. The difference is that, with large overhead costs to the firm, a monopoly might be expected to accrue automatically to the firm that is clever or lucky enough to enter the industry first, while, with a large overhead cost to the industry, the innovating firm must bear that cost without acquiring any compensating advantage over its late-coming rivals who free-ride over the ground that the innovator has prepared. Monopoly may be required to make entry profitable to the innovator, but that monopoly has to be conferred by the state. The classic example of a monopoly of this kind was the British East India Company, which incurred considerable expense in "protecting" its trade from the French and the Dutch, but had no particular cost advantage over its domestic rivals once its foreign rivals were kept at bay.

Monopolies are conferred by patents. Though there are similarities between inventing and railroad building, there are important differences as well. Control of access to a patented invention is more difficult to enforce and more easily circumvented than control of access to a railroad. There is no analogue in railroad-building to the rule that the patent is conferred upon the one who discovers the new product first, regardless of how close to discovery his rivals may be. There is also a complex interaction between pure research, yielding scientific laws that cannot be patented, and applied research, yielding information about how to make new and patentable products. Nonetheless, the inferences drawn from Figure

32 about the consequences of secure natural monopoly apply equally to secure patents. Too little of the patented product is produced. Consumers are always better off buying a product at the price chosen by the monopoly than they would be if they could not buy the product at all. Even the grant of a patent may not be sufficient to draw forth all socially beneficial inventions.

Monopoly may also be conferred by government as a means of benefiting one group at the expense of the rest of the population. A group may be favoured because it is poor, in which case the grant of a monopoly is seen as a way of redistributing income. A group may be favoured in return for a reward to the grantor of the privilege of monopoly. A group may be favoured as part of the intricate and largely implicit bargain among political parties and interest groups, a matter to be taken up in Chapter IX.

Finally, there is a kind of monopoly power in "brand names", which serve as guarantors of a uniform product but at the same time convey to their owners a degree of flexibility over the pricing of branded goods.

Property as a reward for information
Central to the demonstration that a competitive economy generates optimal production and distribution of goods is the assumption that a producer makes something and is paid by the user for what he makes. The carpenter makes a table that he sells to somebody who wants a table. A doctor makes medical services that he sells to somebody who is sick. Not all activities conform to that pattern. Some activities — mostly, but not entirely, connected with the provision of information — are socially desirable, or are impossible to prevent by the normal application of the law, but conform to a different pattern altogether. An inventor does not make anything; he discovers how to make something. A prospector does not make reserves of ore; he discovers where they are. An advertiser does not make products; he informs people about the existence and qualities of products (though, as we shall see, there is more to advertising than that). A speculator does not make anything; he predicts future prices.

Consider inventing and prospecting. It is clearly in the public interest to induce people to engage in these activities, and the inducement can be provided in one of three ways, all of which are utilized to some extent. The government can hire people as inventors and prospectors. Individuals who engage in these activities privately may be rewarded by the government in accordance with the value of their discoveries. Individuals (or firms) that engage in these activities may be automatically entitled to property which is somehow connected with their discovery, such as mineral rights for successful prospecting and patents for successful invention. Ideally (that is, in a world which differs in some unspecified but desirable way from the world where we live), the second method is the best of the three. An omniscient, honest and costless Royal Commission provides a reward to each inventor and prospector that is commensurate with his marginal contribution to the stock of knowledge. Note that the contribution of the inventor or prospector is not at all the same as the value of what he actually discovers. It might consist in the identification of false trails, areas bare of ore or wrong hypotheses. It might be basic research which contributes to the eventual discovery of useful things but contains no such discovery in itself. It would typically be much less than the full social value of ore discovered or machines invented, for these would be found eventually and the "discoverer's" contribution is to make information available sooner than otherwise. One need only state the sense in which this method of rewarding knowledge-creating activity is ideal to see that it is impractical. It is employed only to the limited extent that outstanding scientists are rewarded with honours, titles of nobility or medals. The first method — direct public financing of knowledge-generating activity — is employed for basic research and geological surveys where the knowledge gained cannot be connected in any immediate and direct way to marketable goods and services.

Our main concern here is with the third type of reward, the granting of a property right that is directly and obviously connected with the success of the activity. A firm invents a machine to perform a certain task. In practice, no outsider can determine how much effort went into the enterprise, what interesting false trails were followed, how close a competitor has come to the invention, or how valuable the machine is to society at large. The patent office need only determine whether the machine has been invented. This is sufficient for the awarding of monopoly rights over the production of the machine. Similarly, no outsider can observe the effort of the prospector, but there is no difficulty in granting the prospector the exclusive mining rights to a limited territory where he claims to have discovered ore, for the rights are valueless if the claim is false. The granting of property rights as prizes for successful invention or prospecting may be the best available way of inducing people to devote labour and resources to these activities, but the correspondence between effort and reward is obviously less immediate and less exact than when a carpenter makes and sells a table. There are departures from efficiency in this form of remuneration.

Remuneration by prizes can be looked upon as occupying a middle ground between perfect competition and anarchy. A prize is for all practical purposes like payment for goods and services when the value of the prize just equals the marginal social product of the actions put forward to win it. A prize creates a microcosm of anarchy when the effort put forward to win the prize yields no social product at all. Invention and prospecting are closer to the pole of perfect competition, though there is reason to believe that the social product of these activities exceeds the value of the prize in many cases. Prizes are also awarded in other circumstances where there is reason to believe that very little of value is generated by the activity put forward to win the prize, but where prize-seeking activity cannot be prevented without interfering with other activity that is socially desirable on balance. Among the activities that are rewarded by prizes in most capitalist economies are inventing, prospecting, litigation and rent-seeking.

Inventing[7]   A patent is a monopoly conferred by the state upon the inventor of a new good or process. In analysing departures from efficiency associated with patents, we restrict our attention to new goods rather than to new processes, but the analyses of goods and processes are very much the same. Suppose that the cost of and the demand for the newly invented good are as indicated in Figure 32(b). Like the railroad in our earlier example, the patent-holding monopolist produces at Q^m, where his monopoly profit (the area $P^m abd$) is maximized, rather than at Q^0, where price equals marginal cost. There is a deadweight loss equal to the area of the triangle aef. Though less well off than he would be if the price of the newly invented good were set equal to marginal cost, the consumer is necessarily better off than he would be if he were unable to buy the new good at all. The consumer's gain is the area eab of the triangle between the demand curve and a line at a height equal to the market price.

A second departure from efficiency is that some worthwhile inventions are not undertaken at all. Having a new good may be worth more than the cost of inventing it, despite the fact that the capitalized value of the patent falls short of the expenditure required to acquire it. This is illustrated in Figure 32(c), where average cost is interpreted as the sum of the cost of production of the invented good and the interest on the cost of the invention.

A third departure from efficiency is the wasteful duplication of inventive activity. From developments in science, or from changes in the economy, it may become evident to many potential inventors at once that a very profitable invention is just around the corner. There ensues a patent race among the would-be inventors. Luck, rather than skill or effort, may determine the winner, and the expected time of the appearance of the invention need not be affected significantly (though it must be affected to some extent) by the number of contestants. In the extreme, one inventor would do, but many enter the contest because the expected reward is many times the cost of participation. Such duplication of inventive activity is wasteful in more or less the same way that excessive fishing is wasteful. One must be careful with this line of argument, because competition for the acquisition of a patent is not always socially undesirable. We shall investigate several cases, beginning with a case in which patent rivalry is clearly undesirable and then modifying the assumptions in ways that lead to different implications.

Suppose (i) it is generally known that a given expenditure on invention yields the information required to produce a new good at a constant marginal cost of c, (ii) that the demand curve for the good to be invented is known in advance, (iii) that the monopoly profit from the patent exceeds the annualized cost of the invention by a factor of four (that the area P^mabd in Figure 32(b) is four times the area bdec), (iv) that each firm competing for the patent must bear the full cost of the invention, (v) that, as long as at least one firm undertakes the required expenditure on invention, the discovery will be made during a particular day, (vi) that production may begin the following day, (vii) that firms undertaking the appropriate expenditure on invention succeed in inventing the new product at randomly chosen times during the discovery day, so that each firm has an equal chance of making the discovery first, (ix) that the patent is awarded to the first firm to invent the product, and (x) that all firms are risk-neutral. It is obvious what happens. Firms enter the patent race as long as expected profit is positive. Since monopoly profit from the patent exceeds the cost of invention by a factor of four, there will be five firms in the race despite the fact that one firm is sufficient to generate the invention. A potential monopoly profit from the patent amounting to four times the cost of the invention is wasted in quintuplication of inventive activity.

Notice that consumers of the new product are unaffected by the excessive inventive activity. They enjoy the same gain from the existence of the new good (and bear the same deadweight loss from the monopoly associated with the patent) regardless of how many firms compete in the patent race.

This extreme and uncompromising description of the waste of resources in duplication of inventive activity serves at once to clarify the phenomenon and to identify the limitations of the analysis. Instead of supposing that expenditure on invention guarantees discovery on a certain day, we might have assumed that each of the n firms undertaking the required expenditure has a probability p of making the discovery. The overall probability of discovery becomes $[1 - (1 - p)^n]$, which is never quite equal to 100 per cent, no matter how many firms enter the race. In that case, the right number of firms in the race, when people as well as firms are risk-neutral, is that for which the annualized cost of invention is just equal to the consumers' surplus from being able to buy the newly invented product (at the price set by the holder of the patent) plus the monopoly profit weighted by the increase in the probability of discovery generated by the "last" firm to enter. The increase in the probability of discovery generated by the nth firm is the difference between the probability that no firm makes the discovery when there are n firms in the race and the probability that no firm makes the discovery when there are $(n - 1)$ firms. The extra probability is $[(1 - p)^{n-1} - (1 - p)^n]$, which is equal to $p(1 - p)^{n-1}$. Thus the socially optimal number of firms is the largest n for which

$$p(1 - p)^n(S + M) > I \tag{6}$$

where M is the monopoly profit, S is the consumers' surplus and I is the

238

annualized cost of the invention (area dbec). If I = \$1 million, S = \$1 million, M = \$4 million and p = 50 per cent, there should be two firms in the patent race. With one firm, the probability of invention is 50 per cent. A second firm raises the probability to 75 per cent. A third firm raises the probability to 87.5 per cent; the extra 12.5 per cent chance of obtaining the invention is not worth the cost of invention (that is, $0.125 \times 5 < 1$).

In the circumstances of this example, the actual (as distinct from the optimal) number of firms induced to enter the patent race by the lure of the monopoly profit that the patent conveys is the largest m for which

$$\left[\frac{1 - (1-p)^m}{m}\right] M > I \tag{7}$$

The term $[1 - (1 - p)^m]/m$ is the probability of any given firm being awarded the patent when there are m firms in the race; it is the ratio of the probability that some firm makes the discovery to the number of competing firms. With the imaginary data we have chosen, three firms choose to enter the patent race, one more than the optimal number. In general, when the probability of discovery is less than 1, one cannot say *a priori* whether there will be too many or too few firms in the race: too many in so far as the average probability of attaining the patent exceeds the increment in the total probability generated by the last firm; too few in so far as the monopoly profit is necessarily less than the sum of monopoly profit plus surplus to consumers. One firm is always sufficient when the probability of discovery is equal to 1.

An increase in the number of firms in the race for a patent may advance the date of the discovery. To model the phenomenon and to show within this context that competition among would-be inventors may still induce too many firms to enter the patent race, suppose that each firm's cost of discovery is \$I per year until the discovery is made, that each firm's probability of discovery is p per year, that the discoverer is awarded a patent, that all firms discount at a rate r, and that there is universal risk neutrality. It follows from the laws of probability that the chance of there being no discovery in the first t years of a patent race among n firms is $(1 - p)^{nt}$, so that the chance of a discovery occurring during the first t years is $[1 - (1 - p)^{nt}]$. Again M and S are the annual monopoly profit to the patent-holder and the annual consumers' surplus from being able to purchase the discovered product at the monopolist's price (the net advantage to consumers of being able to buy the product at that price where the alternative is to be denied the opportunity of buying it at all). The net value of the inventive activity to society as a whole is the difference between the expected present value of the benefits from the discovered product and the expected present value of the costs of discovery. Specifically, when there are n firms in the patent race, the net social value, V(n), of the inventive activity is

$$V(n) = \begin{matrix} \text{net value} \\ \text{of inventive} \\ \text{activity} \end{matrix} = \begin{matrix} \text{expected present} \\ \text{value of the} \\ \text{discovery} \end{matrix} - \begin{matrix} \text{expected present} \\ \text{value of the cost} \\ \text{of the discovery} \end{matrix}$$

$$= \sum_{t=1}^{\infty} \begin{matrix} \text{probability of} \\ \text{having the} \\ \text{invention at time t} \end{matrix} \times \begin{matrix} \text{discount} \\ \text{factor} \end{matrix} \times \begin{matrix} \text{annual value} \\ \text{of the} \\ \text{invention} \end{matrix}$$

$$- \sum_{t=0}^{\infty} \begin{matrix} \text{probability of} \\ \text{not having the} \\ \text{invention at time t} \end{matrix} \times \begin{matrix} \text{discount} \\ \text{factor} \end{matrix} \times \begin{matrix} \text{annual cost of} \\ \text{inventive} \\ \text{activity} \end{matrix}$$

$$= \sum_{t=1}^{\infty} [1 - (1-p)^{nt}] \left(\frac{1}{1+r}\right)^t (M+S) - \sum_{t=0}^{\infty} [(1-p)^{nt}] \left(\frac{1}{1+r}\right)^t (nI) \qquad (8)$$

In constructing the formula, it has been supposed that inventive activity in any year t leads (with a probability p) to a discovery in the year t which permits full production of the invented product to begin in the year t + 1.

As in the earlier example, there is a difference between the value of the inventive activity to society, inclusive of the firms in the patent race and the consumers of the discovered product, and the value of the inventive activity to the firms alone. The latter, defined as $W(n)$, is derived from the former by replacing $M + S$ in equation (8) by M. It follows immediately that $W(n) < V(n)$ for all values of n. The net value of inventive activity to any one of the n firms in the patent race has to be $W(n)/n$.

Inspection of equation (8) should convince the reader that the functions $V(n)$ and $W(n)$ are inverted U-shaped, as indicated in Figure 33 where V and W are drawn as continuous functions of n. Obviously $V(0) = W(0) = 0$ because there can be no benefits or costs if there are no firms in the patent race. At the other extreme, there must be some high values of n (different values for W and for V) for which $V(n)$ and $W(n)$ are once again equal to zero because the term nI in the expression for total cost increases linearly with n while the probabilities are almost unaffected by n once n becomes very large. The functions $V(n)$ and $W(n)$ must be positive in between if the inventive activity is to be worthwhile at all.

The discrepancy between the actual, or equilibrium, number of firms in the patent race and the socially optimal number can now be read off Figure 33. The socially optimal number of firms in the patent race is n^o, the value of n for which $V(n)$ is maximized. The market determines a different number; risk-neutral firms continue to enter the race as long as the net private return of $W(n)/n$ is positive, and an equilibrium number, n^e, is not attained until $W(n) = 0$.

If there were no consumers' surplus to the invention — as would be the case if the invented product were exported and the welfare of foreigners did not enter into the assessment of the benefits and costs of research at

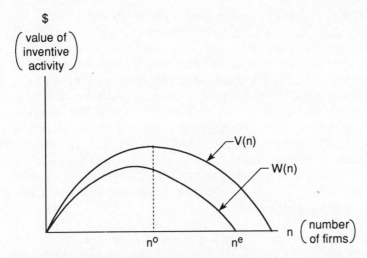

Figure 33 Private and social valuation of inventive activity as a function of the number of firms in a patent race. n^e is the equilibrium number of firms in the patent race, n^o the optimal number of firms in the patent race

home — then the functions $W(n)$ and $V(n)$ would be exactly the same and n^e would be unambiguously larger than n^o. Otherwise, as in the atemporal example above, one cannot be sure because $W(n) < V(n)$ for all values of n. The pattern in Figure 33, in which $n^e > n^o$, is possible but not necessary. It is even possible for the two departures from efficiency in this model of inventive activity — the monopolization made possible by the patent and the common property effect — to just cancel out, so that the equilibrium number of firms in the patent race is optimal.

A departure from efficiency could also arise in the timing of innovative activity. Equation (8) is formulated on the assumption that the firm's cost of inventive activity, I, and probability of discovery remain the same over time. That need not be so. The progress of scientific research may gradually raise p and lower I, so that there is an optimal date to begin inventive activity. It can be shown that a competitive market may begin inventive activity too soon.

An overall assessment of the social consequences of the patenting of inventions must also take account of the contribution to general knowledge of "unsuccessful" inventive activity. It has so far been supposed that the product to be invented is well specified before the research begins and that its economic significance is entirely captured by the demand curve of Figure 32. That need not be so. An increase in the number of firms in a patent race may influence the nature and quality of the invention. No two laboratories follow exactly the same line of research, and it is rarely certain at the outset of research what may be discovered. *Ex post*, when the patents have been awarded, it may be evident that research has been duplicated; *ex ante*, one can never be sure. In the course of seeking to invent, a scientist may discover a law of nature which soon becomes public knowledge. The law itself may be unpatentable and of no monetary value to its discoverer, but it may, nonetheless, facilitate discoveries by other scientists later on. Formally, the value of such discoveries can be included in the measure of surplus, S, in our equations above. The more important the serendipity in invention, the larger is the ratio of S to M, and the more likely that too few firms enter the game and that some socially worthwhile inventions are not attempted at all. Finally, it should be said that, whenever firms have a choice, the patent system creates an incentive to divert research activity away from basic research and toward research with the prospect of a patent in sight.

Prospecting Like the patent, a mineral claim is a property right established as a reward for the discovery of valuable information. In each case, the government certifies the discovery but need not specify its value. In each case, the reward is conditional on discovery, though the social value of the discovery is not necessarily equal to the reward. In each case, a discrepancy between social value and private reward creates a departure from efficiency as an unavoidable by-product of rules which promote activity that is on balance socially desirable.

To clarify the distinction between the market value of discovered minerals in the ground and the social value of the discovery, suppose that geologists know the magnitude but not the location of a country's reserves of a certain mineral. A known quantity of the mineral is somewhere under the ground, but prospecting is still required to locate the mineral so that it can be extracted. Suppose also that the value of identified reserves — the value of the ore above ground less the cost of mining — is (and is expected to remain at) $100 per ton, that the cost of discovery is only $20 a ton if the discovery is made slowly, that the cost rises sharply as prospectors attempt to speed up discovery, and, for convenience, that the rate of interest is zero. Obviously, it is socially optimal to prospect slowly so as to keep the cost of discovery at $20 a ton and acquire a mineral rent of $80 a ton. Competition among prospectors would dissipate the rent. Since the value of the mineral claim is $100 a ton, the rate of prospecting must accelerate to the point where the cost of discovery is $100 a ton as well.

Alternatively, suppose that the search cost over any particular plot of land is invariant at $20 per ton, that the cost has to be borne by each prospecting firm, and that the right to the claim accrues to one of the prospecting firms in a process equivalent to drawing lots. Then five prospecting firms would enter the race when only one firm would do, and, once again, a potential rent of $80 a ton is dissipated. Competition over mineral rights is like the wasteful competition among fishermen in our example of common property above. The loss of rent is qualitatively the same in both cases. The dilemma here is that, when the granting of mineral rights is the only feasible way of inducing people to undertake the risky and expensive business of prospecting, society may have no middle course between offering too large an incentive to prospectors or no incentive at all. The correct reward, which is the shadow price of discovery as distinct from the value of discovered ore, cannot in practice be determined or granted.

A slightly more detailed example may help to clarify the source of the discrepancy between the private and social valuation of mineral discovery.[8] Suppose it is known that a piece of land contains ore with a probability, P, that the value of the ore in the ground would be V if ore is present at all, that the price and value of the ore are expected to remain constant for a long time, that prospecting can determine with certainty whether there is ore and, if so, its exact location, that the cost of prospecting, c(t), decreases over time, i.e. $c' < 0$ and $c'' > 0$, and that the rate of interest is constant at r per cent. Think of the cost of prospecting as incurred instantaneously. On these assumptions, ore will be mined as soon as it is discovered.

The contrast between the socially optimal time for prospecting and the equilibrium time when there is competition among prospectors is reminiscent of the contrast between the equilibrium and the optimal harvesting of fish in equations (4) and (5). The present value of the expected profit from prospecting at time t becomes

$$\pi(t) = [PV - c(t)]e^{-rt} \qquad (9)$$

The socially optimal time for prospecting, t^o, is that for which $\pi(t)$ is maximized. It is identified by the condition

$$r[PV - c(t)] = -c'(t) \qquad (10)$$

which signifies that the cost of postponing the appropriation of the ore by one day is just equal to the benefit from the corresponding reduction in cost.

A monopolist prospector would follow this rule, but prospecting firms in a competitive market would not. Each firm in a competitive market knows that it cannot delay prospecting until the socially optimal moment because some other firm would jump in first. Competition for mineral claims would induce prospecting as soon as the expected profit is positive. Prospecting would take place at t^c for which

$$PV - c(t) = 0 \qquad (11)$$

The competitive moment t^c is necessarily earlier than the socially optimal moment t^o because, by assumption, $c' < 0$.

The relation between market-equilibrium timing and socially optimal timing is illustrated in Figure 34 with time on the horizontal axis and value

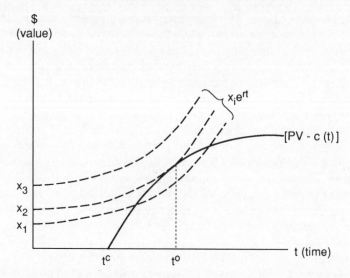

Figure 34 The optimal and the equilibrium time for prospecting. t^o is the optimal time for prospecting, t^c the equilibrium prospecting time in a competitive market

on the vertical axis. The height of unbroken curve is the undiscounted expected profit from prospecting $[PV - c(t)]$ as a function of the date when the prospecting occurs. Its shape is a reflection of the decline over time in the cost of prospecting, $c(t)$. The profit would be negative if prospecting occurred before t^c because cost would exceed the expected value of the discovery. The profit (in current dollars, not present value) increases the longer prospecting is delayed, but the advantage of delay is expected to diminish over time. The broken curves are the loci of points of equal present value; each curve traces out points on the equation $x(t) = x_i e^{-rt}$ for alternative values of x_i, which is a constant represented by the height of the intersection of the curve with the vertical axis.

The meaning of equation (10) above is that the (unbroken) profit curve is tangent to some iso-present value curve at the optimal prospecting time. Profit-maximizing prospectors would not wait that long. They would search the ground for minerals as soon as the expected profit was positive. Someone would enter the game at t^c, and the potential surplus with present value

$$[PV - c(t^o)]e^{-rt^o}$$

would be wasted.

Another possible departure from efficiency in prospecting is analogous to the wasteful duplication of inventive activity. One way or another, the entire community of geologists may simultaneously learn that an area is likely to be rich in ore. With this information, any prospector might be able to discover the whereabouts of the ore in a reasonably short time, and there would be a large potential revenue from prospecting over and above the cost of discovery. Competition among prospectors would dissipate the potential profit in excessive prospecting activity over too short a period of time.

These well known, simple and austere results are useful as an aid to sorting out what is in reality a very complex phenomenon. They must be taken with a grain of salt, for other features of the competitive market for the discovery of ore may, in themselves, imply that there is too little prospecting rather than too much. In particular, unsuccessful prospecting may generate information that is useful to others later on and for which the prospector is not compensated.

Property contested

Litigation There are no lawyers in perfect competition. There are no lawyers because there is no crime. There is no crime because entitlement to property is undisputed and secure, and because *homo economicus* is motivated exclusively by greed. Jealousy, envy, love and all the other motives for crimes not associated with property are quietly assumed away.

To include litigation among the departures from efficiency is not, of course, to deny or belittle the role of the legal profession in the preservation of the liberal society. It is merely to recognize that perfect and costless justice is beyond the capacity of a society of fallible men. Sometimes it is evident what the law requires and how the law will respond to private actions. At other times the law is like a lottery in which one's chance of winning depends on how many tickets one buys. The ideal of the law is to specify rights so perfectly and completely as to eliminate the wasteful competition over entitlement that is the essence of anarchy. The enterprise can never be entirely successful. There remains a region of uncertainty over which wasteful competition may occur. A formal model of litigation is employed in the analysis of anarchy in Chapter III.

Inventing, prospecting and litigation are alike in that all three activities can be looked upon as the seeking of a prize in a contest that is set by the government to provide an incentive for these activities, because the government cannot avoid doing so, or for other reasons. The contest in litigation is different from the contests in invention and prospecting in that the prize is largely unconnected with the social value of the effort to obtain it. To obtain a patent, one must invent. To obtain a mineral claim, one must discover ore. The invention and the discovery are goods in themselves. The prize in litigation is a value that is not created by litigation; it is merely a transfer from one party to another. Litigation is wasteful in itself but necessary as an alternative to other far more wasteful, far less peaceful means of resolving disputes.

Rent-seeking   Rent-seeking is similar to litigation in that it generates no useful by-product, for the prize is a transfer of income created in an act of public policy. The standard example is an import quota. Suppose the government wishes to protect domestic production of sweaters by raising the domestic price. Specifically, let the world price of sweaters be $10, and suppose the domestic price is to be raised, one way or another, to $20. The government could achieve its object with a tariff of $10 per sweater, at which, let it be assumed, 10,000 sweaters would be imported and the revenue from the tariff would be $100,000. A price of $20 could also be maintained by an import quota. An import quota of 10,000 sweaters would do the job because the consumers' price-quantity combination would be the same as if there had been a $10 tariff instead.

The quota itself may be auctioned or it may be assigned without charge to importers. If the quota were auctioned, the equilibrium price of the quota would have to be $10 per sweater and the public revenue from the sale of the quota would be $100,000, just as though the restriction on imports had been effected by a tariff. If the quota were assigned without charge, the difference between the domestic price and the foreign price would accrue as revenue to the privileged importers rather than the government. The $100,000 of public revenue forgone becomes a prize to be competed for by importers and would-be importers, each seeking to persuade the government or its representatives that he is a fit recipient of a share of the quota. Such competition goes by the name of rent-seeking.

Rent-seeking may take many forms. It may consist of lobbying officials responsible for allocating the quota. If the quota is apportioned according to domestic productive capacity, it may consist of excessive acquisition of plant and equipment. It may consist of advertising. If a fixed expenditure on rent-seeking is required for a firm's claim to a share of the quota to be taken seriously, and if the quota is divided up equally among all serious contenders, then the number of contenders will be just sufficient to use up the rent from the quota. If the total value of the quota is V (equal to $100,000 in our example) and the fixed cost of establishing a claim to part of the quota is f, then the number of contenders has to be V/f. The using-up of resources in persuading government to favour one group over another is a departure from efficiency with a distinct family resemblance to the attack and defence model of anarchy in Chapter III.

Though the entire value of a privilege to a group favoured by public policy might be wasted in rent-seeking, there is no reason to suppose that this is universally so. A modest expenditure on rent-seeking may be sufficient to ensure that the privilege is maintained, or the recipient may bear a certain risk of losing his privilege that cannot be reduced significantly by rent-seeking behaviour on his part. Our example, in which the entire profit from entitlement to a quota was wasted in rent-seeking, depended on the assumptions that any firm could compete for the privilege of a quota and that all competitors had an equal chance of winning the prize. Not all profit is wasted if the government is inclined to respect the privilege of the incumbent quota-holder. Similarly, a government may be so determined to favour an industry or region that little or no solicitation by the favoured party is necessary.

On the other hand, what appears at first sight to be a waste of resources in lobbying or rent-seeking may on closer inspection turn out to be bribery. The transfer may be genuine enough, but the ultimate recipient may be the donor rather than the donee. The relation between rent-seeking and bribery may be quite complex. Straightforward bribery may be too risky for all parties concerned, but an environment in which the profits of firms or the incomes of groups of workers depend to a large extent on the favour of the government may create opportunities for politicians and civil servants in the private sector.[9] We return to this matter in Chapter IX.

Monopoly as a prize Except when a monopoly is regulated or in unusual circumstances (as when a firm has the dubious privilege of being the last survivor in a dying industry), the status of monopoly conveys a rent to the monopolist over and above what its resources could be expected to earn elsewhere in the economy. When a monopoly is completely secure, the rent is like a transfer to the monopoly from its customers. When a monopoly is less than completely secure, the rent ceases to be a pure transfer and becomes instead a prize that may, wholly or in part, be wasted. The monopolist devotes resources to preserving his privileges. Other firms devote resources to capturing the monopoly or to destroying it altogether.

Competition for the privilege of monopoly can be of two kinds. Where monopoly is conferred by the government — as with the East India Company — the wasteful competition takes the form of lobbying, by the monopolist to persuade the government to respect its privileges, by its customers to persuade the government to abolish or constrain the monopoly, and by prospective successors to persuade the government that the monopoly power should be in their hands instead. Part of what would otherwise be a pure transfer is converted into a cost, the exact proportion depending on the security of the original monopoly. Alternatively, monopoly may arise out of inter-firm rivalry in the market, in which case competition to maintain, abolish or displace a monopoly takes the form of commercial practices rather than of lobbying. A would-be monopolist may acquire a larger stock of plant and equipment than would be optimal if the monopoly were secure, so as to pre-empt the market and deter potential competitors by assuring them that capacity in the industry would be excessive and profits low in the event that they chose to enter. Monopolists of raw materials may engage in exploration for no other purpose than to bottle up rival sources of supply. A multi-market monopolist may engage in predatory pricing within one market to deter competition in others.

"Predatory pricing" is a well established technical term that is partly, but not entirely, consistent with the use of the term "predatory" in this book. Predatory pricing occurs when a monopolist in several connected markets sets a price below marginal cost in a market where a challenger has appeared. The predatory monopolist is prepared to lose money in the market where he is challenged so long as the challenger is forced to lose money as well. The object of the manoeuvre is to induce the challenger to withdraw and to deter potential challenges elsewhere. A shipping cartel that is challenged on one route immediately engages the challenger in a price war that may be even more unprofitable for the predator than for the prey.

There is considerable dispute among economists on the theoretical question of whether predatory pricing is profitable in the long run, as well as on the empirical question of whether it occurs, or has ever occurred, at all. The dispute seems to turn on the plausibility of the supposition that a monopolist can commit himself today to a course of action that he and the potential challenger both know will be unprofitable tomorrow. Some would argue that predatory pricing is irrational because, if the monopolist is actually challenged, the common interest of the monopolist and the challenger together is to cooperate rather than to fight. Both parties are better off when, for example, the monopolist buys out the assets of the challenger than when the monopolist attempts to bankrupt the challenger by predatory pricing. On the other hand, belief by potential challengers that the monopolist is prepared to engage in predatory pricing, or in other equally unprofitable forms of commercial rivalry, may be sufficient to deter entry, in which case the monopoly profit is preserved for as long as the policy is effective as a deterrent.[10]

As with other forms of prize-seeking behaviour, it is uncertain whether competition for the privilege of holding a monopoly is advantageous or disadvantageous on balance to the economy as a whole. Such competition is advantageous in so far as would-be monopolists neutralize one another, giving rise to a market with lower prices on balance and more of the attributes of perfect competition than would otherwise be the case. Predatory pricing is clearly advantageous to the consumer at the time when predation actually occurs. Predatory pricing is not advantageous in the long run if it leads to the establishment of a monopoly in circumstances where competition might otherwise prevail.

Property in taste: advertising
The incentive to advertise is a consequence of monopoly power, for there would be nothing to gain from advertising by a firm that could sell its

entire output at the going market price. Advertising is expenditure by a firm to shift the demand curve for its product, pushing the curve to the right so that more can be sold at a given price or increasing its elasticity so that price can be raised without too large a drop in sales. It is immaterial to the firm why the shift in the demand curve occurs, except in so far as a knowledge of the psychology of its customers enables the firm to increase the effectiveness of its advertising.

The reason for the shift in the demand curve has a definite bearing on whether advertising is good or bad for society as a whole — on whether advertising belongs in the category of production or in the category of appropriation of what others have produced. Analysis of the effect of advertising on welfare will require a specification of the utility function from which the demand curve, as seen by the monopolist, is derived. Broadly speaking, there can be identified six pure effects of advertising on the consumer, each corresponding to a distinct specification of the consumer's utility function.

(i) Advertising may provide information about the existence or quality of products, as when the exact specifications of a hi-fi set are advertised in a technical magazine.

(ii) Advertising may enhance the quality of goods, not in the sense that the goods themselves are made better by advertising, but in the sense that one feels better when using the goods. On this view of advertising, one really does enjoy one's soft drink more because of the association in one's mind with troupes of dancing girls jumping into ice-cold water.

(iii) Accepting, for the sake of the argument, that advertising does enhance psychic quality, there remains the possibility that, in raising the quality of one good, advertising lowers the quality of close substitutes, so that advertising campaigns by rival firms tend to cancel out. I cannot raise the psychic quality of my product without at the same time lowering the psychic quality of yours. You cannot raise the psychic quality of your product without at the same time lowering the psychic quality of mine. We have here a classic prisoners' dilemma. Each party has an incentive to advertise regardless of what the other does, but both would be better-off with a binding agreement not to advertise at all.

(iv) Advertising may persuade people to act against their real interests. It may induce them to act as though their demand curves were steeper or further to the right than is really the case. It is hard to watch a television advertisement without concluding that viewers are being persuaded to act against their better judgment.

(v) Advertising finances public goods, notably newspapers, radio and television. Newspapers are like natural monopolies in that they have high first-copy costs and negligible marginal cost. Without advertising revenue, newspapers could not show a profit when price is set equal to marginal cost and they might be unable to cover average cost at any price.

Newspapers may be like the railroad, as illustrated in Figure 32(c), that can never turn a profit but is worth having nonetheless because it generates a large consumers' surplus.[11] Newspapers could be financed by the state, but that would create other difficulties. The marriage between advertising and the provision of the daily news may be the best arrangement on balance.

(vi) Advertising may be a signal of quality, subtly conveying to viewers or readers that the advertiser has something substantial to lose if he allows the quality of his product to deteriorate.

These six "pure" effects of advertising — provision of information, augmentation of quality, reduction of quality of goods of rival firms, distortion of taste, financing of public goods, and signal of quality — are described here in some detail one by one, but it should be recognized that advertising is, in practice, a compound of effects that cannot always be disentangled.

These six effects of advertising are examined in a sequence of simple general equilibrium models. In each model, the utility function is specified to reflect a particular effect of advertising, and the amount of advertising that a monopolist advertiser would provide is compared with the socially optimal amount. What is meant by socially optimal in this context is the amount of advertising that I would want the monopolist advertiser to provide if I had an equal chance of occupying the circumstances of each person in the simple economy that is being postulated here. Optimality, in this sense of the term, is identified by the maximization of a straightforward utilitarian social welfare function as discussed in Chapter I.

Begin with advertising as the purveyor of true information. True information might be about the existence or about the quality of a product, but the model is confined to information about existence. Imagine an economy with an unadvertised good that is known to everyone and an advertised good that is not. The number of people who hear about the advertised good is a function of expenditure on advertising. Let x be consumption per head of the advertised good by people who know of its existence, y_1 be consumption per head of the unadvertised good by people who know of the existence of the advertised good, y_2 be consumption per head of the unadvertised good by people who do *not* know of the existence of the advertised good, A be the amount of advertising and $n(A)$ the number of people who hear about the advertised good, where $n' > 0$ and $n'' < 0$.

Assume, for simplicity, that every person has the same productive capacity and that all unit costs of production are constant. Specifically, assume that the cost per unit of the unadvertised good is equal to 1, that the cost per unit of the advertised good is equal to c, that the cost per unit of advertising is also equal to 1 (so that the amount of advertising and the expenditure on advertising are the same) and that, with regard to these prices, each person's productive capacity is I. Hence the production possibility frontier of this economy becomes

$$n(A)[cx + y_1] + (N - n(A)) \, y_2 = NI - A \qquad (12)$$

Assume also that people are identical in their tastes. Each person's utility function is

$$W = u(x) + y \qquad (13)$$

where u is an ordinary concave function ($u' > 0$ and $u'' < 0$) and where $x = 0$ for those who are unaware of the existence of the advertised good.

The unadvertised good is produced by many small firms in competition. The advertised good is produced by a monopolist who chooses a price, P, and an amount of advertising, A, to maximize his profit, π, where

$$\pi = [P(x) - c]x \, n(A) - A \qquad (14)$$

It follows immediately from the form of the utility function, and from the assumption that the price of the unadvertised good is 1, that every consumer who knows about the advertised good chooses a quantity x such that $u_x = P$, where u_x is the marginal utility of x. Advertising determines the number of people who purchase the good.

The profit-maximizing monopolist of the advertised good chooses x and A to maximize the value of π in equation (14). The two first-order conditions are[12]

$$\frac{P - c}{P} = -1/\varepsilon_{xP} \qquad (15)$$

signifying that the mark-up equals the inverse (of the absolute value) of the elasticity of demand, ε_{xP}, and

$$\frac{dn}{dA} = \frac{1}{(P - c)x} = \frac{1}{(u_x - c)x} \qquad (16)$$

where the derivative dn/dA in equation (16) is rate of trade-off *to the monopolist* between advertising expenditure and the number of customers when the amount of advertising is chosen to maximize profit. Define A^m and x^m to be the monopolist's profit-maximizing choice of the amount of advertising and of the quantity per consumer of the advertised good. These can be determined from equations (15) and (16).

The optimal values of x and A can be derived from the maximization of the utilitarian social welfare function

$$S = n(A)[u(x) + y_1] + [N - n(A)]y_2$$

which, on substituting for y_1 and y_2 from equation (12), becomes

$$S = n(A)\left[u(x) + I - \frac{A}{n(A)} - cx \right] + [N - n(A)]I$$

$$= NI + n(A)\left(\frac{u(x)}{x} - c \right)x - A \qquad (17)$$

when the users of the advertised good are assumed to bear the cost of advertising. Maximizing S with respect to the quantity of advertising, we see that

$$\frac{dn}{dA} = \frac{1}{\left(\dfrac{u(x)}{x} - c\right)x} \tag{18}$$

where the derivative dn/dA is the rate of trade-off *to the representative citizen* between the cost of advertising and the increase in his chance of hearing about the advertised product. Define A^S and x^S to be the socially optimal amounts of advertising and of the advertised good.

It follows from a comparison of equations (16) and (18) that, when advertising is genuinely informative, it is in the interest of the monopolist advertiser to advertise too little rather than too much. Equation (16) says that monopolist advertises up to the point where the last dollar of advertising generates just enough new customers that the extra profit, on sales to these customers, is equal to one dollar. Equation (18) is the same except that the social benefit from an extra customer is the sum of the monopoly profit and the consumer's surplus rather than monopoly profit alone. The contrast is illustrated in the demand and supply diagram of Figure 35(a). The socially optimal amount of advertising, A^S, and the monopolists' optimal amount, A^m, can both be read off the "effect of advertising" curve, $n(A)$, in Figure 35(b). It is immediately evident from the figure that $A^S > A^m$ as long as n'' < 0. Unable to capture the full social value of information provided by advertising, the monopolist advertises less than the appropriate amount.

The next pure effect of advertising is the creation of psychic quality. Advertising, on this interpretation, does not teach the customer anything he did not already know, but it associates the product in the mind of the consumer with happiness or success, and thereby makes the product more desirable.[13] The fast car is freedom. The mouthwash is the start of a new life. Since the emphasis now is upon the extent to which a person is affected by advertising, rather than whether he knows about the advertised product at all, it is convenient to drop the assumption that some people learn about the advertised product and others do not, and to assume instead that everybody is affected by advertising to the same extent. Quality creation may be modelled by postulating a utility function of the form

$$W = u(z) + y \tag{19}$$

where utility, W, is a separable function of the amount, y, of the unadvertised good and of the number, z, of quality-corrected units of the advertised good, and where $u' > 0$ and $u'' < 0$. When confronted with prices of 1 per unit of the unadvertised good and P_z per quality-corrected unit of the advertised good, the utility-maximizing consumer chooses a quantity z such that $u_z = P_z$, where u_z is the marginal utility of a quality-corrected unit

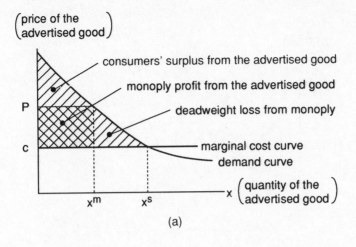

(a)

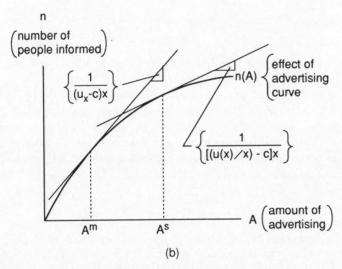

(b)

Figure 35 (a) The market for the advertised good. (b) The technology of advertising. The height of the demand curve is u_x

of the advertised good. The tangible quantity of the advertised good is x. Tangible and quality-corrected quantities are connected by the equation

$$x = q(A)z \qquad (20)$$

The term $q(A)$ in equation (20) may be interpreted as the cost of psychic quality of the advertised good. Think of x units of the tangible good as used to buy z units of the quality-invariant good, where the terms of the

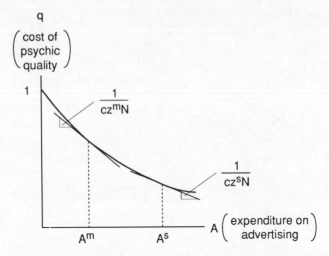

Figure 36 How advertising lowers the cost of psychic quality

purchase depend on the amount of advertising. It is assumed that $q(0) = 1$, $q' < 0$ and $q'' > 0$, as illustrated in Figure 36.

As the provision of psychic quality, advertising can be looked upon in two equivalent ways. Advertising may be seen as shifting the demand curve for the tangible good when the unit cost of the tangible good is invariant. Or advertising may be seen as lowering the unit cost of quality-corrected goods when the demand curve for quality-corrected goods is invariant. The latter procedure is the simpler. The production possibility frontier is

$$Nxc + Ny + A = NI \tag{21}$$

where the meanings of the terms are the same as in equation (12) above. Replacing y in equation (19) with its value from equation (21), and x in the resulting equation with its value from equation (20), we see that the welfare function becomes

$$W = u(z) + I - czq(A) - A/N \tag{22}$$

Once again, the socially optimal values of advertising and of the output of the advertised good are obtained by maximizing the social welfare function. Maximizing W with respect to z and A yields first-order conditions

$$u_z = cq(A) \tag{23}$$

which means that the marginal valuation of the quality-corrected good is just equal to marginal cost, and

$$czq'(A)N = 1 \tag{24}$$

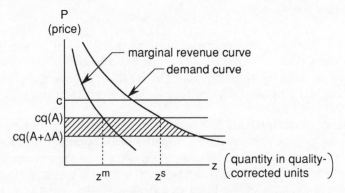

Figure 37 The demand and supply of psychic quality

which means that the marginal reduction in cost brought about by an extra dollar of advertising is just equal to 1. This is illustrated in Figure 37, which is a demand and supply diagram for the quality-corrected good z. Unit cost is shown as independent of z but negatively related to A. The gain in surplus associated with an increase in advertising from A to $A + \Delta A$ is the shaded area in the figure.

Since, by definition, whatever is spent on the tangible good is necessarily spent on the quality-corrected good as well, their costs and values have to be the same. Let P_x and P_z be the prices, as marginal valuations, of the tangible good and the quality-corrected good, and let c_z be the marginal cost of the quality-corrected good. Necessarily, $P_z z = P_x x$ and $c_z z = cx$, which, together with equation (19), imply that

$$P_x = P_z/q(A) = u_z/q(A) \tag{25}$$

$$c_z = c/q(A) \tag{26}$$

and

$$\varepsilon_{xP_x} = \varepsilon_{zP_z} \tag{27}$$

where the symbol ε represents elasticities and ε_{xP_x} is the ordinary elasticity of demand for the tangible good x.

The monopolist, on the other hand, chooses z and A to maximize profit, π, where

$$\pi = (P_x - c)x \, N - A$$

$$= (u_z - c_z)z \, N - A$$

Maximizing with respect to z and A, we obtain the monopolist's first-order conditions,

$$u_z(1 + 1/\varepsilon_{xP_x}) = cq(A) \tag{28}$$

and

$$czq'(A)N = 1 \qquad (29)$$

Equations (28) and (29) together determine the values of z^m and A^m, the monopolist's choices of the quality-corrected quantity of the advertised good and the amount of advertising. The meaning of equation (28) is that the monopolist's optimal expenditure is that for which marginal revenue equals marginal cost.

Comparison of equations (24) and (29) reveals at once how provision of advertising by a monopolist differs from the social optimum. The formulae are the same except for the interpretation of z. Both the monopolist and the ideal planner provide advertising up to the point where the marginal reduction in the cost of the good in quality-corrected units is just equal to the marginal cost of advertising, which is 1. But, since the monopolist produces less ($x^m < x^s$), his cost saving is correspondingly less and his advertising expenditure is less as well. As shown in Figure 36, the monopolist continues to advertise until the marginal reduction in cost, q', is just equal to $1/cz^mN$ while the optimal quantity of advertising is that for which $q' = 1/cz^sN$. The monopolist's advertising, A^m, is less than the optimal amount, A^s, because z^m is less than z^s.

The monopolist under-advertises for essentially the same reason in both the cases we have considered. In both cases, advertising provides a real service to the consumer, provision of information in one case and psychic quality in the other. And in both cases the monopolist who under-provides the good to raise its price has less incentive than the ideal planner to provide the good-augmenting auxiliary service. When advertising is the purveyor of a genuine service to the consumer — the provision of information or quality — it is hardly surprising to discover that the departure from efficiency in this monopolized market is a restriction of output.

The situation changes when firms advertise against one another. Continue to look upon advertising as the purveyor of psychic quality, but suppose there are two advertised goods, produced by rival firms and serving more or less the same need: two makes of cars, soft drinks or soap. Advertising becomes predatory and socially wasteful when the advertising for one good increases the psychic quality of that good at the expense of the psychic quality of the other. Anyone who is prepared to believe that psychic quality is generated by advertising should have no difficulty in believing that quality might be destroyed as well, not only by advertising that knocks the competitor, but by the emphasis upon real or imaginary features that rival products fail to possess.

Formally, one can model competitive advertising by postulating an economy of identical people with utility functions

$$W = u(z_1, z_2) + y \qquad (30)$$

where z_1 and z_2 are quality-corrected amounts of two monopolized goods, each produced by a separate monopolist, and y is the amount of the remaining good which once again is assumed to be produced competitively and which services as the numeraire. The monopolized goods are substitutes, i.e. $\partial^2 u/\partial z_1 \partial z_2 < 0$. Amounts of the two monopolized goods in physical units are x_1 and x_2, which are connected to z_1 and z_2 by the advertising and quality equations,

$$x_1 = q^1(A_1, A_2)z_1 \qquad (31)$$

and

$$x_2 = q^2(A_1, A_2)z_2 \qquad (32)$$

where q^1 and q^2 are indicators of cost per unit of quality and A_1 and A_2 are amounts of advertising. Assume that $\partial q^1/\partial A_1 \equiv q_1^1 < 0$ and $\partial q^2/\partial A_2 \equiv q_2^2 < 0$, signifying that advertising conveys a direct benefit to the advertiser by enhancing the psychic quality of his own product. Also assume that $\partial q^1/\partial A_2 > 0$ and $\partial q^2/\partial A_1 > 0$, signifying that advertising conveys an indirect benefit to the advertiser by lowering the psychic quality of the rival product. The more hyped-up one gets about the virtues of one cola, the less one cares about the other. The reversal of the latter pair of inequalities would imply that advertising expenditures among rival firms are complementary, as would be the case if I cannot advertise my brand of butter without enhancing the psychic quality of other brands as well; this possibility will be ignored here.

The socially optimal quantities of advertising, A_1^s and A_2^s, are determined by maximizing the typical person's utility in equation (30), subject to the constraint of the production possibility frontier

$$c_1 x_1 N + c_2 x_2 N + yN + A_1 + A_2 = NI \qquad (33)$$

or

$$c_1 z_1 q^1(A_1, A_2) + c_2 z_2 q^2(A_1, A_2) + y + A_1/N + A_2/N = I \qquad (34)$$

where c_1 and c_2 are unit costs of tangible goods; these costs are assumed to be constant. Substituting for y in equation (30) and maximizing W with respect to z_1, z_2, A_1 and A_2, we obtain the first-order conditions which, with a little manipulation, become[14]

$$u_1 = c_1 q^1 \qquad (35)$$

$$u_2 = c_2 q^2 \qquad (36)$$

$$A_1^s = -[c_1 x_1 \, \varepsilon_{q^1 A_1} + c_2 x_2 \, \varepsilon_{q^2 A_1}] \, N \qquad (37)$$

and

$$A_2^s = -[c_1 x_1 \, \varepsilon_{q^1 A_2} + c_2 x_2 \, \varepsilon_{q^2 A_2}] \, N \qquad (38)$$

257

where $\varepsilon_{q^1A_1}$ is the elasticity of the cost of quality of the first good with respect to the amount of advertising on that good, that is,

$$\varepsilon_{q^1A_1} \equiv (\partial q^1/\partial A_1)(A_1/q^1)$$

and the other three elasticities are similarly defined. Note that if $c_1x_1 = c_2x_2$ and if the destructive effect of advertising on the quality of the rival good is as strong as the constructive effect upon the quality of the advertised good, i.e., if

$$-\varepsilon_{q^1A_1} = \varepsilon_{q^2A_1} \quad \text{and} \quad -\varepsilon_{q^1A_2} = \varepsilon_{q^2A_1} \tag{39}$$

then the socially-optimal amount of the advertising is necessarily zero; there should be no advertising at all.

Since $\varepsilon_{q^1A_1}$ and $\varepsilon_{q^1A_2}$ are both negative while $\varepsilon_{q^1A_2}$ and $\varepsilon_{q^2A_1}$ are both positive, the equations (37) and (38) can be interpreted to mean that advertising on each good should be carried to the point where the marginal cost saving on production of quality units of that good *less* the marginal cost increase on production of quality units of the other good is just equal to the marginal cost of advertising.

Now consider a monopolist. As the circumstances of the rival monopolists are symmetrical, it is sufficient to restrict the analysis to the monopolist of the first advertised good. For this monopolist, the deterioration of the psychic quality of the second advertised good caused by his own advertising is a *good* rather than a *bad*. It increases the demand for his product. He chooses x_1 and A_1 — or equivalently z_1 and A_1 — to maximize his profit

$$\pi_1 = (P_{x_1} - c_1)x_1N - A_1 = [u_1(z_1,z_2) - c_1q^1(A_1,A_2)]z_1N - A_1 \tag{40}$$

given his conjectures about his rival's behaviour. Such conjectures might be quite elaborate and sophisticated, but it is assumed here that they are not. Instead, the monopolist is assumed to adopt the simple conjecture that his rival's choice of output and advertising, whatever the choice may be, is set independently of his own choice of z_1 and A_1. Even within this restriction, the monopolist's conjecture is not quite pinned down, for the rival might be assumed to hold either x_2 and A_2 or z_2 and A_2 invariant. Assume the former. The monopolist's conjecture about his rival is that the physical and not the psychic quantity is held constant. The distinction is important, because an invariant x_2 allows an increase in advertising on the first good to have a double impact upon its price; the price of the first good increases with advertising because its perceived quality increases and because the quality-corrected (psychic) quantity of a close substitute declines.

Maximizing π_1 in equation (40) with respect to z_1 and A_1, we get first-order conditions

$$u_1(1 + 1/\varepsilon_{x_1P_1}) = c_1q^1 \tag{41}$$

which means that marginal revenue equals marginal cost, and[15]

$$A_1^m = - Nx_1c_1\varepsilon_{q^1A_1} + P_{x_1}x_1\varepsilon_{P_{x1}}x_2\varepsilon_{q^2A_1} \qquad (42)$$

where A_1^m is the monopolist's preferred expenditure on advertising, and where $\varepsilon_{P_{x_i}x_i} \equiv (\partial^2u/\partial z_1\partial z_2)(z_2/(\partial u/\partial z_1))$. The first expression on the right-hand side of equation (42) is the same as the corresponding expression for A_1^s in equation (37), except that x_1 is the monopolists' optimal quantity in one case and the socially optimal quantity in the other. The second expression is entirely different; it is the value of the first good, $P_{x_1}x_1$, scaled up by the percentage change in price caused by the advertising-induced reduction in z_2 for any given value of x_2. By itself, this effect induces the monopolist to advertise more than is socially optimal.

Note particularly that any increase in the absolute value of $\varepsilon_{q_2A_1}$ — the effect of advertising on behalf of the first good upon the perceived quality of the second — has opposite effects on A_1^s and A_1^m. It lowers the socially optimal amount of advertising at the same time as it raises the amount of advertising that the producer of the first good is inclined to undertake.

In the special case where taste is symmetrical between the goods 1 and 2 and where the cost of quality depends upon the difference between A_1 and A_2 $[q^1(A_1,A_2) = h(A_1 - A_2)$ and $q^2(A_1,A_2) = h(A_2 - A_1)]$, the advertising expenditures on the two products must neutralize one another, conveying no net advantage to the producers of either product and leading in the end to a waste of resources in the economy as a whole.

A fourth pure effect of advertising is the creation of what might be called false preferences or false tastes.[16] One acts according to one's true utility function when there is no advertising. Advertising somehow induces one to act as though one's demand curve for the advertised good had shifted upward or toward the right. There is a good deal of reluctance on the part of economists to recognize the existence of such an effect, for it is a deep premise of economics that tastes, as reflected in what people actually buy, are to be respected. Propositions such as that monopoly entails deadweight loss, excise taxes are (in certain conditions) inferior to an income tax, a world with free trade is better than a world with high tariffs — propositions which are the stock-in-trade of economic science — instantly cease to be valid if purchases do not reflect true tastes, for there can be no assurance that the mix of goods chosen at any given prices is utility-maximizing. It appears to be a small step from the assertion that people's purchases fail to reflect their true tastes to the assertion that someone in authority should set matters right and, on the basis of his greater knowledge, should command people to do what they would do willingly and voluntarily if they were aware of their best interests. "You are not maximizing your own true utility function" is treated as an inadmissible argument.

But can one watch a television commercial without concluding that taste is being manipulated? A brand of soap is associated with happy children, a make of car with freedom, a brand of cola with teenagers dancing, a brand of cigarettes (in the good old days) with a cowboy on the range, strong, vigorous and healthy — all without so much as a hint of evidence that one brand of a product is any more likely to achieve these effects than any other. Either the consumer is deluded by advertising, or the advertiser is wasting a great deal of money in the mistaken belief that advertising persuades. There is an apparent impasse between an undeniable fact and an unacceptable implication.

The impasse is only apparent, because the implication is spurious. There is no direct line of inference from the existence of false tastes to excessive interference of government in the lives of citizens. To suppose there is is to fall prey to the Pigovian fallacy, discussed in Chapters I and II, that any departure from efficiency in the private sector of the economy ought to be rectified in the public sector. Recognize that there are departures from efficiency in the public sector as well — departures from efficiency that are likely to be particularly nasty if the government undertakes as amorphous a task as telling citizens where their true interests lie — and economic policy becomes a choice between large departures from efficiency in the private sector and larger departures from efficiency in the public sector. One can admit that advertising sometimes creates false tastes and, at the same time, maintain that the cure is likely to be worse than the disease. To conduct economic policy *as though* all taste were genuine may be a rule of thumb that gives substantially better results than any alternative we know how to apply.

Formally, false taste can be modelled by supposing that the true utility function is $W^t = u(x) + y$ while the advertising-induced utility function is $W^f = v(x,A) + y$, where $v(x,0) = u(x)$ and $v(x,A)$ is an increasing function of A. The consumer acts in the shop as though his utility function were W^f, but he discovers that his function is W^t when he gets the product home. Two extreme cases are illustrated in Figure 38. In both diagrams the original demand curve and the advertising-induced demand curve are downward sloping straight lines. The marginal cost is assumed constant at c, the original demand curve is $D(0)$, and the corresponding marginal revenue curve is $M(0)$. In the absence of advertising, the socially optimal output is x^s, at which price equals marginal cost, and the monopolist chooses the price-quantity combination P^0 and x^0 at which marginal revenue is just equal to marginal cost. The monopoly profit of $(P^0 - c)x^0$ is a pure transfer from consumer to monopolist. The deadweight loss is $1/2(P^0 - c)(x^s - x^0)$ and is represented by the shaded area R_1 in Figure 38(a). The effect of advertising in each case is to raise the demand curve for the advertised product. An amount of advertising A transforms the demand curve from $D(0)$ to $D(A)$. Figures 38(a) and 38(b) differ in the postulated effects of advertising on the shape of the demand curve.

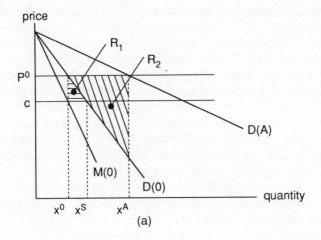

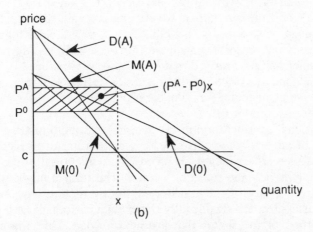

Figure 38 Advertising raises the demand curve for the advertised product: two extreme cases. (a) Rotation of the demand curve around the intersection with the vertical axis. (b) Rotation of the demand curve around the intersection with the cost curve

The assumption in Figure 38(a) is that advertising pivots the demand curve around the vertical axis. On this assumption, the effect of advertising is to increase the quantity demanded but to leave the elasticity of demand unchanged at any given price of the advertised good, so that the monopolist's profit-maximizing price is invariant. With an amount of advertising A, the monopolist's price remains at P^0 but his profit increases from $(P^0 - c)x^0$ to $(P^0 - c)x^A$, a net gain to the monopolist of $(P^0 - c)(x^A - x^0)$. The monopolist would wish to advertise up to the point where $(P^0 - c)(dx/dA) = 1$. One cannot say *a priori* whether $x^A > x^s$ or $x^A < x^s$ at that point.

261

The consumer is harmed because he pays P^0 for each of the extra $x^A - x^0$ units he is induced by advertising to buy, when the average value of these units — as indicated by the height of his true demand curve $D(0)$ — is necessarily less than P^0. The consumer's total loss is the cross-hatched area, R_2, on Figure 38(a), a loss which may or may not exceed the gain to the monopolist. If it turns out that the monopolist's optimal output, x^A, is less than or equal to the socially optimal output (if $x^A \leq x^s$), then the consumer's loss necessarily falls short of the monopolist's gain, signifying that advertising would be beneficial on balance if each consumer were entitled to an equal share of the profit of the monopoly firm. Part of the original deadweight loss would be eliminated. On the other hand, the consumer's loss could exceed the monopolist's gain if, as shown on Figure 38(a), the monopolist's optimal quantity x^A exceeds the socially optimal output by a significant margin.

A curious implication of the assumptions behind Figure 38(a) is that a small amount of advertising can have no effect on the welfare of the consumer. When the amount of advertising is small, the effect on consumption must be small as well, so that x^0 and x^A are close together and the consumer's welfare loss from advertising (the area R_2) is effectively zero. The consumer neither loses nor gains because he is induced to buy a bit more of the good at a price equal to his true marginal valuation. It follows immediately that any net increase in the profit of the advertiser-monopolist is a gain to society as a whole.

An additional consideration in the overall assessment of the social cost or benefit of advertising in this case is that the transfer of income from consumer to advertiser may itself be costly. A fraction β of the transfer, $(P^0 - c)x^A$, may in some sense be wasted. The term β might reflect the redistributive impact of the transfer in the event that stockholders of the advertising firm are significantly richer than customers, or β might be the proportion of the shares that are held abroad. Thus the net social benefit or cost of advertising becomes

$$(P^0 - c)(x^A - x^0)(1 - \beta) - R_2 - A$$

which can be positive or negative. The expression is likely to be positive when A is small and is likely to be negative when A is large.

The other extreme case is illustrated in Figure 38(b). Now the demand curve is assumed to pivot clockwise around the intersection of the demand curve with the marginal cost curve, so that the monopolist's optimal output, x, is independent of the value of A. The symbols in the figure are the same as in Figure 38(a), except that x is the common value of x^0 and x^A, and a distinction has to be drawn between P^0, the profit-maximizing price when there is no advertising, and P^A, the profit-maximizing price when expenditure on advertising is A.

Without advertising, the monopolist chooses a profit-maximizing price-quantity combination of P^0 and x, and his profit is $(P^0 - c)x$. With an amount of advertising A, the monopolist chooses a price-quantity combination of P^A and x, and his profit increases to $(P^A - c)x$. The extra profit generated by advertising is $(P^A - P^0)x$, and the monopolist's optimal amount of advertising is identified by the condition that $x(dP/dA) = 1$. Since quantity, x, is invariant, the effect of advertising in this case is just to transfer income from consumers to the monopolist. There is an unambiguous net social cost to advertising of $A + \beta(P^A - P^0)xN$, the sum of advertising expenditure itself and whatever social cost it is appropriate to attach to the transfer of income.

In the discussion of advertising-induced quality, I referred to advertising as predatory when firms advertise against one another to lure away each other's customers without necessarily affecting the total amount of goods sold or the prices consumers pay. Creation of false taste can be predatory in a different way. It can be the means by which firms extract additional revenue from consumers without providing additional amounts of the advertised good. In this case, the departure from efficiency is the cost of production of the advertising plus whatever weight society attaches to the transfer. Both varieties of taking may occur simultaneously. Advertising for good B may cause an outward shift of the demand curve for good B *and* an inward shift of the demand curve for good C, which is a close substitute for the good B. The advertising for good B by the maker of good B may neutralize the advertising for the good C by the maker of good C, leaving all demand curves where they were before. The net effect would then be that consumers are neither better off nor worse off (except in so far as they are the stockholders of the advertising firms) and that the profits of both firms are reduced by the cost of advertising.

The fifth pure effect of advertising is to finance public goods. Advertisers do not just spend money on advertising. They emit messages that potential customers must somehow be persuaded to receive. The medium itself is not always a source of benefit to consumers. Billboards along roads detract from the view as they catch the eyes of the passing motorist. Television, radio and newspapers, on the other hand, are made available by advertising at a fraction of the total cost of production. To model this effect of advertising, we must combine it with a hypothesis about the impact of advertising on the utility of the advertised good. Assume that advertising creates false taste, that the medium of advertising is television and that television cannot be financed except by advertising. There are now two advertising expenditures, the cost, A_1, of preparing the ad and the cost, A_2, of paying for the television programme with which the ad will appear. Let each person's utility function be

$$W = u(x) + y + m(A_2,A_1) \tag{43}$$

where the function m is the person's benefit from the availability of television. The derivative of m with respect to A_2 is positive, signifying that the welfare of the consumer increases with the amount (the number of hours or the quality) of programming available. The derivative of m with respect to A_1 would be negative if people preferred to see television without ads. The benefit of advertising to the advertiser is that consumers are induced to behave as though their utility for the advertised good were $v(x,A_1,A_2)$ rather than $u(x)$, where the derivatives of v with respect to both A_1 and A_2 would have to be positive over the range of these variables that the advertiser would find profitable to supply. The consumer's demand function for the advertised good becomes $x = D(P,A_1,A_2,I)$, where P is the price of the advertised good and I is the consumer's income. The monopolist advertiser chooses P, A_1 and A_2 to maximize profit which is equal to $(P - c)xN - A_1 - A_2$, and the net social gain from advertising becomes $[m(A_2,A_1) - \beta(P^A - P^0)x]N - A_1 - A_2$ in the special case that is illustrated in Figure 38(b) above. The net social gain is not guaranteed to be positive in this case. The cost of advertising might outweigh the benefit from the provision of the medium, even when advertising is profitable to the advertiser. But the net social gain might very well be positive if, as we have assumed, the television could be financed in no other way.

To assume that television must be financed by advertising or forgone altogether is to rule out private provision without advertising. Private provision without advertising would be difficult because television has some of the properties of a public good; once the television signal is emitted there is little or no extra cost to accommodating an extra viewer and, until recently, there was no feasible technology for charging viewers per programme watched. Even if the viewers could be charged per programme, a fee covering the full cost of producing television programmes would choke off many viewers who would otherwise watch programmes without imposing costs on anybody else. The revenue-maximizing fee might fail to cover the cost of producing television programmes, even in circumstances where the social balance of benefits and costs is favourable. The same applies to advertising in newspapers and magazines and on radio.

Public provision of television is obviously feasible, for it exists in many countries, and it has the advantage that the expenditure on advertising could be avoided. Expenditure A_2 on producing television programmes would be set at the socially optimum level, and advertising expenditure, A_1, would be set at zero. There are several considerations — none of them decisive — on the other side. Programming provided commercially may be more to the taste of the majority of people than programming provided by the state. Advertising may compensate for the deadweight loss in monopoly as explained in the discussion surrounding Figure 38(a). Public provision of television may constitute an impediment to the free flow of information. Television is always a state monopoly in despotic countries, but it has been nationalized in many other countries without becoming subservient to the state and without ceasing to air a wide range of views on important political questions.

The sixth and last of our pure effects of advertising is somewhat like the first in that both pertain to the provision of information.[17] They differ in the kind of information provided. The earlier discussion of advertising as information made no provision for the possibility that the advertiser was not telling the truth. Either the advertiser was naturally truthful or the recipient of the message could always tell truth from falsehood. The advertiser's task was simply to transmit the relevant information about the existence or quality of the advertised good. Now the problem is not so much to transmit the information as to have it believed. The task of advertising is to signal information from advertiser to potential customer by actions which would be unprofitable to the advertiser unless the information were true.

The role of advertising as a signal can be illustrated in the launching of a new product. The manufacturer of a new brand of cookies knows that they are good cookies, good in the sense that a large proportion, π, of those who taste the cookies will like them and will buy them regularly. Potential customers are sceptical. Their subjective probability that they will enjoy the cookies is only ϕ, which is less than π and would not ordinarily be sufficient to justify the trouble of buying a first box or even trying a cookie if it is provided free. How can the cookie-maker convey his knowledge that the potential customer's probability of liking the cookies is really π rather than ϕ? No statement that "these are good cookies" would be believed, for every producer has an incentive to make such statements, even if they are false.

Faced with this problem, the cookie-maker might go to a great deal of visible trouble and expense to offer free cookies for a limited time, in a campaign that would be worthwhile only if the true probability of the customer liking the cookie was closer to π than to ϕ. The customer is induced to reason as follows: "My initial assessment of the probability of liking the cookie must be wrong, because the cookie-maker, who knows more about these cookies than I do, would not spend all that money to offer free cookies if I were right." The situation can be modelled as a simple game between the cookie-maker and the potential customer. The game is played in three stages. First the firm decides whether to offer free cookies. With no offer, the firm gains nothing and the customer gains nothing, as indicated by the symbol (0,0) in Figure 39. If the firm makes the offer, then nature or chance decides whether the customer likes the cookies, with a probability that the firm knows to be π. The third move is made by the customer, who does not know at the time of his move (because he has not yet tasted the cookies) what nature has decreed. He must move in ignorance, as indicated by the large loop around the two square nodes. If the customer does not accept the cookie, then (let it be supposed) it is as though the offer had never been made, and both parties gain or lose nothing. If

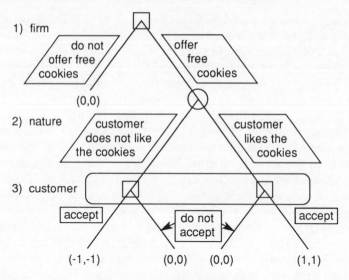

Figure 39 Advertising as a signal

he accepts and likes the cookie, then both parties gain, the firm because it acquires a customer, the customer because he acquires consumer surplus from the addition of a new good to his menu. Let that gain be (1,1). If the customer accepts and doesn't like the cookie, then both parties lose: the firm because it has wasted the cost of the cookie, and the customer because he has tasted a cookie he does not like. Let that loss be (−1,−1).

With these numbers, and on the assumption that the customer knows the pay-off but not the true probability that he will like the cookie, the customer can infer that the advertiser must believe π to be at least 1/2. If π were less than 1/2, the expected return to the firm in making the offer would be negative. A probability of liking the cookie in excess of 1/2 is good enough for the customer as well, for it guarantees him a non-negative expected gain from acceptance. The ploy works (in the sense that the firm's expense in offering free cookies is neither superfluous or wasted) if the customers' original expectation of liking the cookie is less than 1/2.

The essence of advertising as a signal is a demonstration that the producer's claim ought to be believed because the producer has a great deal to lose if the claim turns out to be false. In the example, the claim was that the customer would probably like the cookie. The claim might instead be that a firm will honour the warranty on its product. To establish such a claim, the firm must show that failure to honour the warranty would be unprofitable. Failure to honour the warranty would injure the firm's reputation, reducing the expected benefit of its product to all future customers. This in turn would lead to a reduction in future sales and profit. An essential step in the argument is that the warranted product is generating a great deal of profit for the firm. This can be demonstrated by lavish spending on advertising. Any advertising would do in this context — including a public bonfire of $100 bills — as long as the advertising is seen to be expensive.

That completes the list of the pure effects of advertising: provision of information, conveyance of the psychic quality of the advertised good, destruction of the reputation of competing goods, creation of false taste, finance of public goods and signal of the truth of the advertiser's claims. These effects are not mutually exclusive. A single advertisement can have all six effects at the same time, though some effects may be more important than others. Nor is it evident on balance whether advertising is a departure from efficiency, whether it falls more under the category of making or the category of taking. Certainly there are predatory aspects, especially when rival claims neutralize one another or when the principal effect of advertising is to raise the price of the advertised good rather than to increase the quantity produced. On the other hand, the advertiser becomes a public benefactor when newspapers, magazines, radio and television are provided at low prices to the consumer.

Property in knowledge of the future: speculation
For the purpose of this book, speculation is the use of one's resources to obtain information about how asset prices are likely to change and to use that information profitably in buying assets that are due to appreciate in price. Speculation may or may not be a departure from efficiency, depending on the usefulness to society of the information that is acquired. If the information cannot or will not be used to augment the national income as a whole, then speculation is a subtle variety of predation, for the speculator's gain is matched, dollar for dollar, by a loss to those who sell assets that subsequently rise in price. Sometimes the speculator's information is socially useless, though it is no less valuable to the speculator on that account. But the information acquired by the speculator is not always socially useless. Once disseminated, the information may assist others to invest wisely, more than compensating society for the alternative cost of the labour and resources of the speculator.[18]

An example may clarify matters. Imagine an agricultural economy with two crops, alfalfa and beans, both of which sell on the world market at an invariant price of $1,000 per ton. The production function for alfalfa is

$$Q_a = L_a^{1/2} K_a^{1/2} \tag{44}$$

and the production function for beans is

$$Q_b = B L_b^{1/2} K_b^{1/2} \tag{45}$$

where Q_a and Q_b are outputs in tons, L_a and L_b are numbers of people employed, K_a and K_b are acres of land, the subscripts refer to alfalfa and beans and B is a parameter representing the efficiency of land and labour together in the production of beans. The available land is product-specific.

Beans will not grow on land suitable for alfalfa; alfalfa will not grow on land suitable for beans. Suppose K_a = 98 acres and K_b = 2 acres. Labour, however, is not specialized between crops. There is perfect competition in the market for labour, and workers sort themselves out between crops to equalize the marginal products of labour. There are 100 workers altogether, so that

$$L_a + L_b = 100 \qquad (46)$$

For simplicity, suppose that everything takes place in the course of a single year. The world begins on 1 January, the crop is planted on 1 May, the harvest is gathered on 1 September and the world ends on 31 December. The allocation of labour between alfalfa and beans is irrevocably decided on 1 May, and the biological complication of having no crop until 1 September is ignored. Each person owns an equal share of both types of land, that is, 98/100 acres of alfalfa land and 2/100 acres of bean land. Initially everyone believes that the value of B is 1.

From the symmetry of the problem, it is obvious that the land-labour ratios must be the same for both crops. Think of landowners as hiring workers on 1 May at a wage equal to the expected marginal product of labour, and as pocketing the difference between the value of the crop and the agreed-upon wage once the crop is sold. Competition in the labour and product markets ensures that ninety-eight out of the 100 available workers are employed on alfalfa land, the remaining two workers are employed on bean land, the equilibrium wage is $500 per worker, the expected rent is $500 per acre on both types of land, and, since there is no next year, the price of both types of land is $500 as well.

Now imagine a speculator who owns no land initially and does no agricultural labour. He devotes his time to seeking out information that affects future prices. Suppose he discovers that the true value of B is 2 rather than 1. At the moment of discovery he alone is in possession of the information.

The effect of the discovery on the economy depends very much on when the discovery takes place and on what the speculator can do without revealing his knowledge to others. Clearly, he cannot profit from his information unless there is a capital market. We adopt the simplest and most convenient assumption about the capital market — that one can borrow or lend at a zero rate of interest between any two dates within the year. Suppose, for the moment, that the discovery is made on 1 June after the planting is complete, that the speculator's transactions on the capital market arouse no suspicion among landowners, but that there is no futures market in land. The speculator buys up all the bean land at its market price as of 1 June, and, with the land itself as collateral, borrows the purchase price until after the harvest. He pays $1,000 for the two acres of bean land and, as the owner of the land, inherits a contract to pay $500 to each of the workers employed there. Since his information is correct, the value of the output of beans on that land will turn out to be $4,000 rather than $2,000 as had been expected. With this $4,000 the speculator pays off his $1,000 loan, pays $1,000 to his workers and earns $2,000 for himself.

So far, the essential point of this example is that the speculator has made no contribution to production. His income of $2,000 corresponds a loss of $20 to each of the 100 people from whom he bought the land and to whom the $20 would have accrued as a windfall had the speculator not appeared upon the scene. The unanticipated increase in B from 1 to 2, and the corresponding increase of $2,000 in the national income, would have occurred regardless of his information. His activity as a trader diverts the unanticipated increase in the national income from the rest of the population to himself. On the other hand, if his productivity as a worker were the same as that of everyone else, the diversion of his labour power from agriculture to speculation causes the national income to be $500 less than it would otherwise have been.

Production is affected if the discovery is made in time to shift the allocation of labour between bean land and alfalfa land.[19] Drop the assumption that the speculator's discovery is made on 1 June and suppose instead that the discovery is made on 1 February (three months before planting time), that during the month of February the speculator is able to buy up all the bean land at the original price of $500 per acre, that the speculator's information becomes general knowledge during the month of March, and that this knowledge is taken into account when labour is finally allocated between the two types of land on 1 May. Now competition in the labour market equates the marginal products of labour on both types of land by increasing the number of workers on bean land from 2 to 7.55 and decreasing the number of workers on alfalfa land accordingly from 98 to 92.45. The common marginal product of labour rises from $500 to $515, the rent (and price) of alfalfa land falls from $500 to $485, and the rent (and price) of bean land rises from $500 to $1,943 per acre, allowing the speculator who buys the two acres of bean land at $500 to turn a profit of $2,886.

The national income would be $100,000 if B = 1 as originally expected. It rises from $100,000 to $102,000 if B turns out to equal 2 but the correct value of B is not known until after the crops have been planted. It rises additionally from $102,000 to $102,957 if the true value of B is known in time to adjust the allocation of labour between crops. The initial rise in the national income from $100,000 to $102,000 is captured by the speculator but is in no sense a consequence of his activity; thus far the speculator is a predator. The second rise in the national income from $102,000 to $102,957 would not occur without the information that emerges as a by-product of the speculator's activity. Here the speculator has made a genuine contribution to the welfare of the community. It is a consequence of the numbers we have chosen that the speculator is on balance a predator in the sense that the rest of the population would have been better off without him. His profit is $2,866 and his real contribution is only $957. This result does not hold in general. A slight, and not unreasonable, change in the assumptions could convert the speculator into a net benefactor.

Several considerations so far excluded from our analysis can affect the balance of production and predation in the activity of the speculator. (i) The speculator could increase his income at the expense of the rest of the population if he could participate in the futures market for alfalfa land and for labour. He knows before anybody else that the wage will rise from $500 to $515 and that the price of alfalfa land will fall from $500 to $486. He can benefit from that information by contracting to hire labour at $500 and to sell alfalfa land at $500 at some future date, by which time everyone will have learned the true value of B.

(ii) The potential gain to the speculator is also understated by the emphasis in the example on a once-and-for-all gain in the price of one asset. The position of the non-speculators would be worse if there were many assets that rose and fell in price from time to time and if speculators could predict gains in prices a few minutes, as it were, before they took place. Speculators would then impose a gradual drain of wealth upon the rest of the population. If one randomly chosen asset out of a set of 100 different assets were to rise in price by $99 each day, while all the remaining ninety-nine assets fell by $1 and if the speculator was the first to know which asset that would be, then he could arrange to earn about $99 per day at the expense of the rest of the population.

(iii) The potential gain to the speculator has been exaggerated in our example by an unrealistically strong assumption about the effect of speculative activity on prices. The errant assumption is that the speculator succeeds in buying up all the undervalued assets at the original price that obtained before anybody acquired the new information. Initially, the bean land was owned in equal shares by all the people in the economy. We have assumed that the speculator somehow persuades everybody to part with bean land at $500 per acre without anybody guessing that the speculator knows the land to be underpriced. It is exceedingly difficult to model the speculator's effect upon the prices of the assets he attempts to buy. He earns $2,886 when he buys *all* the bean land at $500 an acre but makes no attempt to take advantage of anticipated changes in the prices of alfalfa land or labour. Suppose, instead, that his attempt to acquire all the bean land led to a gradual rise in price so that his average purchase price over the entire operation was $1,500 rather than just $500. His profit would then be reduced to $886, which is at once less than his real contribution of $957 but greater than his marginal product as a worker of $515.

To discover which assets are undervalued is, as a rule, to discover why they are undervalued, and this information may be useful in the deployment of resources today. To discover that the stock of a firm is undervalued is usually, though not necessarily, to discover that some change might be warranted in the firm's investment policy or that, if the firm is a mining company, the mineral it produces is going to become scarce and ought to be conserved. The prospect of profitable speculation may be the only incentive to acquire certain kinds of socially valuable information.

It is a moot question whether the social value of the informational by-product of speculation is worth the alternative cost of the labour of the speculator and whether other people are made worse off or better off by his activities. He himself can profit from speculation by acquiring information five minutes before it would otherwise be available and, since he cannot usually acquire all the outstanding assets to which his information pertains, he may have an incentive to conceal his reason for believing that some current prices are out of line.

Still more complicated is a market with many speculators and many money managers whose business it is to advise others rather than to speculate for themselves. Collectively these managers must be playing a zero or negative-sum game with their clients' wealth if all investors are advised, for it is impossible for some investors to do better than the market without others doing worse.

Limits upon the domain of prices

Among the assumptions in the proof that a competitive equilibrium is Pareto-optimal are (i) secure property rights and (ii) market-clearing prices for all goods. We have so far been examining the implications of the first of these assumptions. Our enumeration of departures from efficiency has emphasized circumstances where property is not fully appropriated among the actors in the economy and where resources can be employed to appropriate property rather than to produce goods for use or sale. Now we turn to the second assumption. The postulate that there "exists" a set of market clearing prices for all goods is really a network of connected assumptions that have proved enormously fruitful over the years in the application of economics to public affairs, but are nonetheless false in some important respects. The place to begin is the classic description of price formation by Walras.[20]

Let us imagine a market in which only consumers' goods and services are bought and sold, that is to say, exchanged, the sale of any service being affected by the hiring out of a capital good. Once the prices or the ratios of exchange of all these goods and services have been cried at random in terms of one of them selected as the numeraire, each party to the exchange will offer at these prices those goods or services of which he thinks he has relatively too much, and he will demand those articles or services of which he thinks he has relatively too little for his consumption during a certain period of time. The quantities of each thing effectively demanded and offered having been determined in this way, the prices of those things for which the demand exceeds the offer will rise, and prices of those things of which the offer exceeds the demand will fall. New prices having now been cried, each party to the exchange will offer and demand new quantities. And again prices will rise or fall until the demand and the offer of each good and each service are equal. Then the prices will be current equilibrium prices and exchange will effectively take place.

People bring goods to market. Once everybody is assembled, a crier announces a set of arbitrarily chosen prices. Each person, believing he can buy or sell any amounts at these prices, informs the crier of the transactions he wishes to undertake. The crier then adds up all the offers and announces a new set of prices, higher for goods in excess demand, lower for goods in excess supply. People, believing once again that they can buy or sell what they please at these prices, present the crier with a new set of offers, . . . and so on until there are no excess demands or supplies. Only then do transactions actually take place.

This description of price formation rests upon several major assumptions. Firstly, there must exist a set of market-clearing prices, for there would otherwise be no stopping-place in the recontracting process and the crier would carry on establishing new prices, round after round, for ever. As discussed in detail in Chapter I, existence is "proved" in the first theorem of welfare economics, but this in turn requires strong assumptions about the market. Second, it is assumed that all transactions in the economy consist of the purchase of goods and services. Certainly some transactions are properly described in that way. Other transactions are better described as the formation of contracts in which I agree to do thus-and-such, you agree to do thus-and-such, and the profit from our venture is shared according to certain rules. Of course, contracts might be interpreted as an exchange of services among the contracting parties, but there are aspects of the contractual relationship that tend to be overlooked when the emphasis is placed on the production and exchange of goods. In particular, there is a central role for trust, and its opposite, mistrust, in the formation and execution of contracts. Each party is tempted to skimp on his contribution to the common enterprise, and must be on guard against misbehaviour by others. The state can enforce some but not all aspects of contracts. Contracts may be designed in ways that would be inefficient if all parties were guaranteed to fulfil their obligations to the letter, but are, in fact, efficient in an imperfect world where people may fail to discharge their obligations. Third, it is implicit in Walras's account of price formation that people can see what they are buying. There is an important sense in which that is often untrue. When I visit a doctor, I observe that I am buying so many minutes of his time, but I frequently do not know whether the product I hope to obtain — a certain contact with state-of-the-art medical practice — has in fact been purchased. I know that I buy a car, but I do not know whether I have bought the anticipated transport. The general proposition that a competitive equilibrium is Pareto optimal is not true of an economy in which sellers' information about their products is not shared with buyers at the time of sale. Fourth, to assume that everybody in the economy is a price-taker is to assume that nobody bargains, for there can be nothing to bargain about if we can all buy or sell any amount of goods and services at market prices. It is remarkable that, until quite recently, the feature of commercial practice that most characterizes an actual market in a capitalist economy — the haggling and negotiating over prices and terms of contracts — has been abstracted out of sight in the economist's model of how markets work. The abstraction is not innocuous, for bargaining entails a deep indeterminacy that conforms badly to the economist's picture of prices guiding the allocation of goods and services in a competitive economy. Fifth, the story about recontracting over and over again until a set of market-clearing prices is discovered abstracts from the discrepancy between actual prices and market-clearing prices. Prices are set by the actors in the economy on the basis of information that is incomplete, inconsistent from one agent to another, or just plain wrong. There are good reasons for believing that some prices — especially prices of labour time — adjust quite slowly in response to changes in market conditions. Obviously there could be no unemployment of labour if Walras's story were an accurate description of how all prices are formed, because recontracting would continue until everybody had a job or preferred not to work at the going wage. Sixth, it is assumed that everyone obeys the rules. People deliver the goods they have sold and do not steal one another's stocks while waiting for the crier to discover a set of equilibrium prices. This assumption is more nearly true of a market watched over by a policeman than of dealings among traders bound by contracts that are sometimes difficult to interpret or that cannot always be carried out to the letter.

In view of the obvious want of realism in these Walrasian assumptions, one might well ask why they have lasted until quite recently at the core of economic analysis and why they have not been replaced by assumptions that are closer to actual business practice. The answer appears to be that the only alternative would have been silence. These assumptions provided a clear, if not an accurate, picture of the economy and served as a basis for whatever success the economist's model may have had in explaining the world. Propositions about free trade, optimal taxes and tariffs and the regulation of the economy rested, and continue to rest, to a large extent, on the model of perfect competition, modified to take account of monetary policy and the presence of monopoly in some industries. The course of research in economic theory over the last thirty years can be thought of as a gradual chipping away at the Walrasian model of price formation and of its replacement with a more realistic account of transactions in the economy, an account that makes sense of observed phenomena which would have no place in the economy if the Walrasian story were strictly true.

The effect on welfare economics was twofold. On the one hand, it quickly became evident that actual market economies are very far from the ideal of Pareto optimality. Their performance is much less satisfactory than what an omniscient, omnipotent and benevolent despot could supply. In particular, the scope for predatory activity, the waste and the neutralization of effort among competitors are greater than one would suppose if one believed that the Walrasian assumptions were largely true. On the other hand, it became equally evident that there is less to hope for in public policy than had once been believed. As we shall see in Chapter IX, the unobservability of the consequences of actions, the moral hazard, the misuse of positions of trust and the predatory propensities of mankind are, if anything, less constrained in the public sector than in the private sector. People live, and prosper, in the presence of large departures from efficiency that cannot be corrected without imposing greater costs in their place. The remainder of this chapter is a listing of forms of behaviour that arise when the Walrasian postulate of universal price-taking is invalid.

Bargaining

Two parties engage in a venture yielding a profit of V that must somehow be divided between them. To engage in the venture, they must agree upon a pair of incomes — Y_1 for the first party and Y_2 for the second — such that $Y_1 + Y_2 = V$. Furthermore, since participation is voluntary, the income of the first party must exceed his reservation income, $\overline{Y}_1$, defined as the income he would have earned from the resources and labour devoted to the venture if these resources had been deployed elsewhere instead. Similarly, the income of the second party must exceed his reservation income, $\overline{Y}_2$. For the venture to proceed, it is necessary that $Y_1 \geq \overline{Y}_1$ and $Y_2 \geq \overline{Y}_2$. Once these necessary conditions are satisfied, there remains a surplus, $V - \overline{Y}_1 - \overline{Y}_2$, that must somehow be divided up, $Y_1 - \overline{Y}_1$ to the first party and $Y_2 - \overline{Y}_2$ to the second party. The venture cannot proceed without an agreement between the parties on the division of the surplus. The establishment of such an agreement is the bargaining problem.

The bargaining problem is illustrated in Figure 40, with the income of the first party, Y_1, on the vertical axis and the income of the second party Y_2, on the horizontal axis. The downward sloping line VV, at 45° to both axes, is the locus of all possible allocations between the parties of the profit from the venture. Not all points on this line are in accordance with the minimal requirements of the bargain. Points to the left of B_1 are unacceptable because the second party is not provided with the minimum income required to induce him to participate. Points to the right of B_2 are unacceptable to the first party. The mutually acceptable points are those between B_1 and B_2, where B_1 is the best among these points for the first party and B_2 is best for the second.

Bargaining problems can arise in many ways. The two parties may be

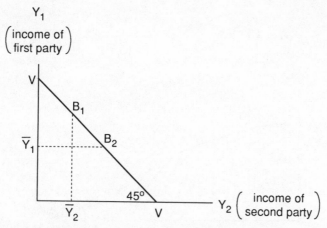

Figure 40   The bargaining problem. V is the total income from the venture, $\overline{Y}_1$ the reservation income of the first party, $\overline{Y}_2$ the reservation income of the second party

locked in a business venture as we have supposed. The parties might be a firm and a union in a company town. The parties might be a duopoly of firms that would benefit from collusion if they could agree on a division of the spoils. The parties might be the buyer and the seller of a house. Nor is the problem limited to relations between a pair of agents. There may be any number of parties in the venture. A bargaining problem arises whenever total income within the venture exceeds the sum of what participants could earn apart from the venture.

Two aspects of the problem need emphasis. The first is that the problem cannot arise in a Walrasian framework where everybody is a price-taker. The existence of a venture yielding rents to the participants collectively is inconsistent with universal price-taking behaviour, for there is no market-determined price of participation. The second is that the problem is insoluble. We shall proceed immediately to discuss a number of "solutions" to the bargaining problem, but each of these solutions is to a slightly different problem or is based on principles other than the maximization of utility by selfish actors. No procedure yields a unique point on the segment $B_1 B_2$ as the outcome of optimizing behaviour by both parties in these circumstances. There is no analogue to the derivation of a unique competitive equilibrium as the outcome of utility maximization by all consumers and profit maximization by all firms. The bargaining problem represents a fundamental indeterminacy at the core of actual markets.

A class of solutions to the bargaining problem is based on the concept of fairness.[21] The two parties in the problem described in Figure 40 might agree to split the difference so that

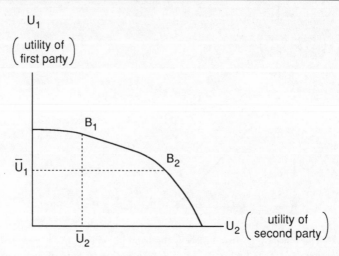

Figure 41 Bargaining over utilities. $\overline{U}_1$ is the reservation utility of the first party, $\overline{U}_2$ the reservation utility of the second party

$$Y_1 = \overline{Y}_1 + S/2 \quad \text{and} \quad Y_2 = \overline{Y}_2 + S/2 \tag{47}$$

where S is the surplus, $(V - \overline{Y}_1 - \overline{Y}_2)$. There is no denying that people do have a sense of fairness, and that splitting the difference is considered a reasonable way to behave. To say, as we have in the preceding paragraph, that there is no solution to the bargaining problem is to say concepts of fairness are inconsistent with ordinary selfish utility maximization and that a person should not be considered as irrational if he chooses to be stubborn rather than fair. Furthermore, the rule in equation (47) is one of many possible methods of splitting a difference, and there is no obvious reason why that method is superior to its competitors.

It is useful at this point to shift the analysis from incomes to utilities. Let $U_1(Y_1,0)$ be the utility of the first party when his income is Y_1 outside the venture, and let $U_1(Y_1,v)$ be his utility when his income is Y_1 within the venture. A pair of functions, $U_2(Y_2,0)$ and $U_2(Y_2,v)$, may be similarly defined. Think of the utility functions as unique up to a linear transformation, as is the case when utility is defined to reflect one's comportment toward risk.[22] The venture itself may now be looked upon as generating a utility possibility frontier rather than a fixed income, V. The utility possibility frontier of the venture is illustrated in Figure 41, which is a generalization of Figure 40. The distribution of utilities must lie on the segment of the frontier between B_1 and B_2 if both parties are to be better off within the venture than they would otherwise be.

One would like to generalize equation (47) by splitting the difference in utilities rather than in incomes but to do so in a way that is independent of the representations of the utility functions of the two parties. The Nash bargaining solution[23] is such a generalization. Choose incomes Y_1 and Y_2 to maximize the product

$$[U_1(Y_1,v) - \overline{U}_1] \cdot [U_2(Y_2,v) - \overline{U}_2]$$

where $Y_1 + Y_2 = V$ and where $\overline{U}_1$ and $\overline{U}_2$ are reservation utilities such that $\overline{U}_1 = U_1(\overline{Y}_1,0)$ and $\overline{U}_2 = U_2(\overline{Y}_2,0)$. Clearly this solution makes both parties better off than they would be outside the venture if the venture is viable at all, and the allocation of utilities between the contending parties is efficient in the sense that the utilities themselves lie on, rather than below, the utility possibility frontier of Figure 41.

Whether the Nash bargaining solution is really fair is a question that cannot be resolved by objective analysis. Each reader must resolve the question for himself by an appeal to his own sense of right. Whether the solution corresponds to what bargainers actually do is an empirical matter. The existence of wars, strikes and negotiations that break down from time to time is proof enough that there is more to bargaining than can be represented by the Nash bargaining solution.

Another concept of "fairness" would reward each participant in a venture in accordance with his contribution.[24] This concept has little meaning in a venture with only two parties because it allows each party to claim the entire surplus on the grounds that no surplus would be obtainable without his participation. The concept becomes meaningful when there are three or more participants and when the venture can be conducted (less profitably) without the full contingent of participants. Consider a venture with three participants, called 1, 2 and 3. Profit, V, depends on who is engaged in the venture. In particular, suppose $V(1) = 0$, $V(2) = 1$, $V(3) = 2$, $V(2,3) = 3$, $V(1,3) = 4$, $V(1,2) = 5$ and $V(1,2,3) = 16$ where, for instance, $V(2,3)$ is defined as the profit from the venture if parties 2 and 3 participate but party 1 does not. The meaning of "contribution" is not immediately evident in this context, but an unambiguous meaning can be assigned for any given order in which people join the venture. Suppose party 2 enters first, followed by party 3 and then party 1. In that sequence, the contribution of party 1 would be $V(1,2,3) - V(2,3) = 13$, the contribution of party 3 would be $V(2,3) - V(2) = 2$, and the contribution of party 2 would be $V(2) = 1$. With three participants, there are six possible orders in which they can enter the venture. An allocation among the participants according to the principle of fairness-as-contribution might award each person the average of his contributions over all six possible orders of entry. These awards are called Shapley values.[25] The awards to the three parties in this example would be 5.5, 5.5 and 5.

A third solution to the bargaining problem is based upon a set of assumptions about what the parties can say to one another, the order of speech, and what happens if the parties fail to agree.[26] Consider first a simple variant of this bargaining solution. Two parties engage in a venture with a total income of V. The bargaining problem is to divide V into Y_1, accruing to party 1, and Y_2, accruing to party 2. Suppose that participation in the venture does not diminish outside income, so that both reservation incomes (within the venture) are equal to zero. The bargaining begins with an offer by party 1 to party 2. Party 1 says, "I offer you an income of Y_2, and I will keep the difference between V and Y_2 for myself." Party 1 is allowed to choose the value of Y_2 in this sentence, but otherwise the sentence must be exactly as written. Then party 2 is allowed to say either "Yes" or "No" — nothing else at all. If he says "Yes", the venture proceeds, party 1 gets $V - Y_2$ and party 2 gets Y_2. If he says "No", the venture does not proceed and both parties get nothing.

What does party 1 say, and how does party 2 respond? Party 1 has the upper hand, for he can offer party 2 an income of next to nothing, ε, and party 2 has no choice but to accept. If allowed to speak, party 2 might protest. He might try to commit himself to accept no less than some $\hat{Y}_2$ which is substantially larger than ε. He cannot do so because, by assumption, he is limited to answering a single question with a yes or a no. Party 1 gets the entire surplus. A similar line of reasoning shows that party 2 would get the entire surplus if he were entitled to make the one and only offer and if party 1 had to respond with a yes or a no.

An interesting extension of this procedure yields a division of the surplus between the two parties rather than an assignment of the entire surplus to one party or the other. Again two parties face one another across the bargaining table, they are required to speak in turn and they are limited in what they can say. But now the rules are different in two respects: the bargaining takes place in a sequence of rounds and the surplus shrinks from one round to the next. The simplest way to think about shrinkage of surplus is to suppose that each party is taxed a fixed percentage of his income for each round of bargaining until the agreement finally takes place. Let V, the value of the venture, be unchanging from one round to the next, and let Z_1 and Z_2 be the amounts accruing to parties 1 and 2 regardless of when the deal is struck, so that $V = Z_1 + Z_2$. But the parties do not get to keep Z_1 and Z_2 unless the deal is struck on the very first round. When the deal is struck on the nth round of bargaining, the parties get to keep $Y_1(n)$ and $Y_2(n)$ such that

$$Y_1(n) = Z_1/(1 + r_1)^{(n-1)} \quad \text{and} \quad Y_2(n) = Z_2/(1 + r_2)^{(n-1)} \qquad (48)$$

where r_1 and r_2 are fixed positive numbers that might be thought of as tax rates but could equally well be interpreted as interest rates. In the latter interpretation, bargaining is a time-consuming process, $Y_1(n)$ and $Y_2(n)$ are present values of incomes accruing n periods in the future, and r_1 and r_2 are indicators of the parties' impatience to reach a deal. The bargaining

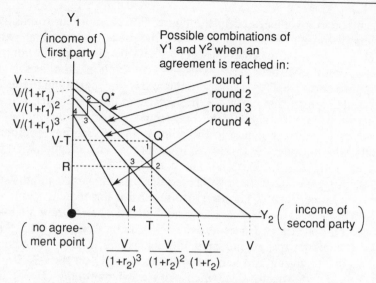

Figure 42 Bargaining as a sequence of offers.

might be supposed to proceed for ever unless an agreement is reached, or it might terminate after N rounds, in which case the venture itself is terminated, so that $Y_1 = Y_2 = 0$. At each round in the sequence, one party proposes a deal and the other has the choice of acceptance or rejection. If the deal is accepted, the bargaining terminates. Otherwise, the parties switch roles in the next round. The outcome of this process is determinate. It depends on the permissible number of rounds in the bargaining game, on the values of r_1 and r_2 and on which party gets to propose a deal in the first round.

Let party 1 begin. He says, "I offer you Z_2 and will keep $V - Z_2$ for myself." Party 2 then says "Yes" or "No". If yes, then $Y_2 = Z_2$, $Y_1 = V - Z_2$ and the bargaining is over. If no, then the second round begins. In this round, party 2 says, "I offer you Z_1 and will keep $V - Z_1$ for myself." Party 1 responds with a yes or a no. If yes, then $Y_1 = Z_1/(1 + r_1)$, $Y_2 = Z_2/(1 + r_2)$ and the bargaining is over. If no, then the third round begins, in which it is again the turn of party 1 to propose a division of V. The parties exchange roles, round after round, until either a bargain is struck or all benefit from the venture is eliminated.

The options of the bargainers and the "solution" to the bargaining problem are illustrated in Figure 42, which is an extension of Figure 40 above. Suppose, for convenience, that a maximum of four rounds of bargaining is permitted. Although the total income from the venture remains constant at V, the locus of feasible combinations of incomes Y_1 and Y_2 shifts inward at each round, as illustrated in the figure. For example, in round 2, the maximal income to party 1 is $v/(1 + r_1)$, the maximal income to party 2 is $v/(1 + r_2)$, and all feasible pairs, Y_1 and Y_2, lie on a straight line from $v/(1 + r_1)$ on the vertical axis to $v/(1 + r_2)$ on the horizontal axis.

Suppose party 1 makes the offer in the first round, party 2 in the second, party 1 in the third, and party 2 in the fourth and last. The logical outcome of this procedure is that, on the first round, party 1 offers party 2 an income of Y_2, corresponding to the point Q in the diagram, and party 2 accepts. The reasoning is as follows. Imagine that no agreement had been reached on the first three rounds and party 2 is making the final offer on the fourth round. Since there will be no fifth round, party 1 might as well accept anything party 2 chooses to offer. Knowing that, party 2 offers virtually nothing. He offers ε (a very small number) and keeps $V/(1 + r_2)^3$ — ε for himself. Party 1 accepts. The result is that party 2 gets to keep $V/(1 + r_2)^3$ and party 1 gets to keep nothing, as indicated by the point 4 at the end of the zigzag line beginning at the point Q on the VV frontier. Now consider the third stage, when party 1 is making the offer. Party 1 knows that party 2 can get a net income for himself of $V/(1 + r_2)^3$ if the bargaining proceeds to the fourth stage; this income becomes, in effect, the reservation income of party 2. Party 2 accepts no less at the third stage but need not be offered more. So party 1 would choose the point 3 on the zigzag line beginning at Q, yielding an income of $V/(1 + r_2)^3$ to party 2 and a net income of R for himself. The same line of reasoning leads party 2 to offer party 1 a net income of R at the second stage, and it leads party 1 to offer party 2 an income of T at the first stage, leaving party 1 with an income of $V - T$ for himself as represented by the point Q. Alternatively, had party 2 made the first offer — giving participant 1 the advantage of the final offer — then the outcome of the bargaining would have been Y_1 and Y_2, corresponding to the point Q*.

Several propositions are plausible, if not obvious, from inspection of Figure 42, and can be proved rigorously. First, with a fixed number of rounds, it is advantageous to be able to make the last offer. Second, if the number of rounds of bargaining is unlimited, the points Q and Q* come together into a unique bargaining solution. Third, the ratio of Y_1 to Y_2 in the unique bargaining solution is an increasing function of the ratio of r_1 to r_2. The meaning of this last proposition is that the less impatient party with the lower discount rate gets the best of the bargain.

One aspect of this bargaining procedure ought to be particularly noted. When people bargain over a surplus, as illustrated in Figure 40, there is a distinct advantage to the person who can commit himself first. If one of the parties can say "I'll abandon the venture unless I get the entire surplus, except for some small amount ε," and if he can create conditions where he has to exercise his threat, then that party has won, for the other party has no choice but to agree.[27] The rule which allows party 1 to make the first offer and gives party 2 no option other than to agree or to scuttle the entire venture is equivalent to an institution that gives party 1 (or party 2 if he gets to make the offer) the means to commit himself and thereby provides him with the entire surplus. A complex bargaining procedure with several stages of offers and counter-offers is like a division of the commitment between the parties. Each is induced by the order of speech to commit himself up to a point but no further. This division of commitment is what generates the unique division of the surplus. It is to a large extent the absence of a division of commitment that differentiates actual bargaining from bargaining under a multi-stage priority rule. Without a prior division of commitment there can be no unique outcome that the theorist can predict in advance, in the sense that he can predict price and output from conditions of supply and demand.

With only one stage of bargaining, the priority model is almost equivalent to assigning a property right in the venture to the party who is allowed to make the first offer. This situation might arise naturally when, for example, a person holds the patent to a new good that can be produced only with the assistance of a partner with a certain set of skills, and when there are many potential partners with these skills and with the same reservation wage. Then the patent-holder can command the entire surplus if he hires well. We shall presently be considering a number of variations on this theme. Features of the priority models of bargaining can sometimes be created artificially, as when a realtor goes back and forth with offers from buyer to seller. Though delay can be more costly for one party than for another, there are, as a rule, no natural stages of bargaining, no restrictions on speech, no hard-and-fast barriers against one party committing himself never to accept less than a certain amount, and there is no universal empirical regularity that the bargain is always struck at the first instant of negotiation, as the theory would lead one to predict. The great merit of the theory is that it does generate an agreement which is the consequence of rational maximizing behaviour by both parties. Its great fault is that it is not really a theory of bargaining. The haggling, the threats, the commitment, the delays and the general disorder in real bargaining are all abstracted away, leaving in their place an orderly process which is quite unlike what happens when actual deals are struck.

Information about goods

Implicit in Walras's account of price formation and in the proof of the existence and optimality of a competitive equilibrium is the assumption that people recognize goods and know their quality. This assumption may be invalid in two distinct ways with quite different economic consequences. There may be a pure and universally recognized risk in which everyone knows that mutually exclusive events A and B occur with probabilities p and $(1 - p)$. A light bulb may last for a shorter or longer period of time.

A farmer's effort may result in a larger or a smaller crop, depending on the weather. A house may or may not burn down in the course of the year. A venture may or may not succeed, depending on the whims of the market. The presence of pure risk does not invalidate the proof of the existence and optimality of a competitive equilibrium, for the usual assumptions are easily extended to cover this phenomenon. A second kind of ignorance can play havoc with the market. Ignorance may be one-sided in the sense that one party to a transaction knows whether event A or event B will occur but the other party does not. One-sided ignorance occurs when, for example, the seller knows whether he has a high-quality item but the buyer does not know and has no way of finding out. Such asymmetric information converts price into a rough indicator of quality and may destroy the mechanism by which prices equilibrate markets.

Some pure risks can be eliminated by pooling. If the probability of a house burning down is 1 per cent per decade, if risks to different houses are uncorrelated, and if the administration cost of insurance is negligible, then the risk of fire can be transformed by insurance into the equivalent of a 1 per cent addition to the rate of depreciation of the housing stock. Every year the house owners pay 1 per cent of the value of their houses into a common fund to finance the acquisition of new houses for the people whose houses have burned down that year.

Pure risk cannot always be pooled away. A critical assumption in the housing example is that the risks to different houses are uncorrelated. Risk cannot be pooled away if, for example, the only circumstance in which my house might burn down is a great conflagration of all the houses in my community. The best I can do to protect myself in that case is to accumulate a fund for the purchase of a new house. Nor can society arrange to pool the good years and the bad years over the business cycle, for in that case there would be no business cycle. All that can be done is to share the burden of depression so that it does not fall disproportionately on any segment of the population.

Regardless of whether pure risk can be pooled away, it entails no necessary departure from efficiency. As discussed in connection with the second theorem of welfare economics in Chapter I, the proposition that a competitive equilibrium is Pareto optimal is equivalent to the proposition that an omniscient, omnipotent and benevolent dictator can do no better for the people than the people can do for themselves with the appropriate initial distribution of wealth. The proposition can be extended to cover pure risk, as long as the dictator has no greater predictive power with regard to uncertain events than the people themselves. The dictator must have no special ability to predict the weather, the occurrences of natural disasters, or whose house is destined to burn down. The proof of the existence and optimality of a competitive equilibrium extends to an uncertain world whenever uncertainty can be reduced to a lottery in which one state of nature is chosen at random from a set of states of nature with universally recognized attributes and probabilities of occurrence. In principle, a price can be established for each good in each state of nature, and this enlarged set of prices clears the market under more or less the same set of assumptions under which ordinary prices can be said to clear the market in a riskless world.[28]

That is not true of a market where traders are unequally informed. A competitive equilibrium is not Pareto optimal and may not exist at all in a market where, for instance, sellers are fully informed about the quality of goods offered for sale while buyers are altogether uninformed but are at the same time aware that they are at a disadvantage. The standard example of the disintegration of markets and the corresponding inefficiency of the competitive economy in the presence of one-sided ignorance is the market for second-hand cars.[29] Suppose the quality of second-hand cars can vary from 0 to 1, where a car of quality 1 is as good as new and a car of quality 0 is worthless. The distribution of qualities among cars in the second-hand market is assumed to be rectangular, so that the probability of a randomly chosen car being of a quality less than or equal to q is precisely q. It follows immediately from these assumptions that the average quality of all cars in the entire market is 1/2 and, more generally, that the average quality of all "cars of quality less than q" is q/2. If nobody in the market — not the seller, not the buyer — could determine the quality of a car, if everyone agreed that price should vary directly with quality, if everyone was risk-neutral, and if the going price of new cars were $10,000, then *all* second-hand cars would sell at $5,000. All second-hand cars must sell at the same price because, by assumption, nobody can distinguish a high-quality car from a low-quality car until the sale is complete. Buyers will discover the true value of their cars eventually, but the market would not be upset on that account.

The market works quite differently if the seller knows the quality of the car but the buyer does not. Modelling this case requires some care in the specification of the preferences of the buyers and sellers. Suppose the buyers have an infinitely elastic demand for cars as measured in quality-corrected units; they are prepared to pay $10,000 for a new car, and to pay $10,000 × q for a car when its expected quality is q. To be a willing seller in this market one must own a car *and*, if its quality is q, one must be prepared to sell that car at some reservation price less than $10,000 × q. Suppose, once again, that the distribution of second-hand cars owned by the would-be sellers is rectangular, with a maximum quality of 1 and an average quality of 1/2. In such a market, the price of second-hand cars can no longer be $5,000 per car, for at that price some "sellers" of high quality cars would withhold their cars from the market, lowering the average quality of cars for sale, and thereby lowering the price which the buyers are prepared to pay for the second-hand cars that they are offered.

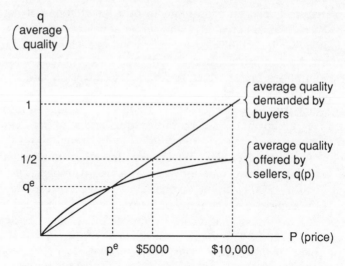

Figure 43 The market for cars as an example of one-sided ignorance

Progressive withdrawal of high-quality cars from this market may, but need not, eliminate the market altogether.

The fate of the market depends on the sellers' reservation prices of cars in quality-corrected units. If these prices are close to $10,000 (that is, if a seller's reservation price, p, for a car of quality, q, is not much below $10,000 × q) then the market will be destroyed. Otherwise, some, but not necessarily all, of the cars for sale will be sold. Suppose each seller has a reservation price which depends on the quality of his car and on how badly he wants to dispose of it. Some sellers are prepared to accept almost any price; others insist on a price commensurate with quality. Suppose the behaviour of sellers as a group can be represented by a function

$$q = q(p) \qquad (48)$$

where q is the average quality of cars offered for sale and p is the price of cars in the second-hand market, and where $q' > 0$. Everybody in the market, buyer and seller alike, is aware of this function. It is known how average quality varies with price, even though buyers are ignorant of the quality of any particular car offered for sale. The assumed shape of the function q is illustrated in Figure 43. Average quality has to be 1/2 when p = $10,000 because all owners of second-hand cars are happy to sell their cars when the price of a second-hand car is equal to the price of a new car. The function begins at the origin of the graph because nobody is prepared to give his car away. The function would be linear if the only cars offered for sale at a price p were those of quality less than or equal to p/10,000, as would be the case if each seller demanded a price per unit of quality equivalent to the price per unit of quality in a new car. The curve is drawn concave on the assumption that many sellers in the second-hand market are prepared to accept a considerably lower price per unit of quality to dispose of their cars. Buyers, on the other hand, are unwilling to pay more than $10,000 per unit of quality. Their reservation price per unit of average quality is shown on the upward-sloping straight line from the origin to the point (1, 10,000).

The equilibrium, if there is one, occurs where the two curves cross, the point (q^e, p^e) in Figure 43. Clearly, our assumptions imply that average quality must be less than 1/2 and the market price of second-hand cars must be less than $5,000. Whether there is equilibrium at all in this market depends on the proportion of sellers who are so anxious to dispose of their cars that they are prepared to accept a low price per unit of quality. If that proportion is quite small, the sellers' curve never rises above the buyers' curve and no second-hand market can be sustained.

The welfare loss from one-sided ignorance is the loss to those would-be sellers who are forced to keep their cars because they have no means of persuading buyers of the cars' true quality. There is no welfare loss associated with the cars that are sold, because any discrepancy between price and quality is a pure transfer between buyer and seller. Consider the seller i who has a car of quality q^i and a reservation price of p^i. The reservation price p^i must be less than $10,000 q^i$ for this person to be a seller at all. Now suppose the market price is p^e. The would-be seller i fails to dispose of his car if $p^i > p^e$. Thus a disappointed seller is characterized by the relation $p^e < p^i < 10,000 q^i$, and the social cost associated with his disappointment is $10,000 q^i - p^i$, the difference between what a buyer would be prepared to pay for the car if its quality could be certified, $10,000 q^i$, and the seller's valuation of the car, p^i. Suppose, for example, that the market price of used cars is $4,000, and consider a person who owns a car of quality 0.8 that he would be prepared to sell for as little as $5,000. The welfare loss from the thwarted transaction is $3,000, because the car would be worth $8,000 to the demanders if its true quality were known.

A similar phenomenon may occur in the labour market, and may be part of the explanation for the wage stickiness that is sometimes alleged to be a contributory cause of business cycles.[30] Consider a bifurcated labour market in which some workers are employed by firms and others are self-employed. Suppose the distribution of quality of labour is rectangular and that quality, q, varies from 0 to 1. The marginal product of labour in the self-employed sector of the economy is w per unit of quality, so that a worker of quality q can earn an income of wq. Firms that cannot identify the quality of workers have to offer *all* workers a wage of w to ensure that high-quality workers are not systematically turned away. The equilibrium wage per unit of quality becomes 2w, which is twice the average income

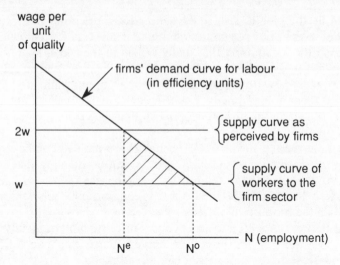

Figure 44 One-sided ignorance in the market for labour

per unit of quality in the self-employed sector. The equilibrium in the labour market is illustrated in Figure 44.

The true supply curve of labour, which would be revealed to the firm if the quality of each worker were identified, is the horizontal line at a height w. The apparent supply curve of labour to a firm that has to pay all workers a wage of w, equivalent to a wage of 2w per unit of quality, is the horizontal line at a height 2w. The market equilibrium number of workers hired by firms is N^e, which is less than the number N^o that would be hired if one-sided ignorance were eliminated. In these circumstances, all workers in the self-employed sector would rather work for firms (except for workers whose quality is exactly 1).

It is characteristic of such markets — as distinct from ordinary markets with complete or symmetrical information — that no worker from the self-employed sector can get a job in the firm sector by offering to accept a wage which is less than the going wage w. On receiving an offer to work at a wage $w - \Delta w$, the employer must reason as follows: if this man is prepared to work for a wage $w - \Delta w$, then the quality of his labour cannot exceed $(w - \Delta w)/w$, for, otherwise, he would be better off self-employed. Hence his expected quality is $(w - \Delta w)/2w$ and his average quality per dollar of wage is $1/2w$, which is precisely what the firm is paying to those it already hires at a wage w. The offer would therefore be refused. Stickiness in wages is alleged to arise from the firm's inability to distinguish between a general willingness of all workers to accept a low wage in bad economic conditions and a low-quality worker who offers the firm a dubious bargain.

There is a similar explanation of credit rationing. Firms denied credit may offer to pay the bank a higher rate of interest than the bank is receiving from its customers. A bank must refuse such an offer because the firm's willingness to pay a high rate of interest on a loan may be a sign that the firm is a poor credit risk.

The market for insurance may be destroyed in a process called adverse selection if customers have better information than the insurance company about the risks they bear.[31] Consider fire insurance. It could happen that (i) every home-owner would benefit from fire insurance and the insurance company would earn a profit if the premium on each house could be set to reflect the risk of fire to that house or if nobody knew whether the risk to his house was greater or less than the average, but (ii) no market can be sustained because home-owners know their risks while the company knows no more than the average riskiness in the community as a whole. If the company offered insurance at a premium representing the average risk, it would lose those potential customers whose risk is very low, too low to justify the paying of a premium based on the average risk in the community as a whole. The company would then have to raise its rates to account for the fact that the houses of its customers are a bit more likely to burn down than the average in the community as a whole. More customers are lost and the rates go up again. If people are quite risk-averse, the process might stop before the market is wiped out altogether, but there is no guarantee that any part of the market will be preserved. Adverse selection is like a Gresham's law of insurance: bad risks chase out good. The good risks, like owners of good used cars, are the losers, for they remain uninsured.

Departures from efficiency associated with one-sided ignorance give rise to incentives within the public sector and within the private sector to provide the missing information. An instance of public provision of information is the grading of wheat and other commodities for export. Without public certification of quality, the importer would be in the position of car-buyer in our example. There would have to be a large enough gap between the quality-adjusted values of wheat in the importing country and in the exporting country to make it worthwhile for the importer to pay the going price in the exporting country for the best wheat when the actual quality received is only average. The effect would be to reduce exports or destroy the market altogether. Public certification ensures that the price of each grade of wheat is the same (except for transport costs) in both countries.

Within the private sector, each seller of a high-quality product has an incentive to devote resources to proving that the quality of his product is really high. In the equilibrium of our automobile example, the owner of a car of quality 0.8 could sell it for $8,000 rather than just $4,000 if he could find a way of demonstrating the truth to a buyer. He would pay up to $4,000 to a professional certifier in whose honesty everyone could rely. In the labour market this certification may be supplied by education. The student need not actually learn anything at university. The university does the job of identifying capable young men and women, as long as study is made difficult enough that less capable men and women are unlikely to earn their degree or are discouraged from entering university at all. This may be an expensive way to differentiate among members of the labour force, but worth the price if there is no cheaper method of certification.[32]

Malfeasance

Another implicit assumption in Walras's model of price formation and in the proof of the Pareto optimality of the competitive equilibrium is that buyers get what they pay for. Goods and services, once purchased, are actually delivered. When I pay for three bags of sugar, I expect to receive three bags and not two. This assumption is reasonable enough for the spot purchase of goods. The assumption is not always reasonable for contracts. Parties to a contract may observe one another's performance imperfectly or may be unable to compel one another to discharge obligations to the letter. Enforcement of contracts becomes especially difficult when the parties' obligations cannot be specified completely (because the success of an undertaking depends on responses to unforeseen developments in the market) or when parties' obligations are not simultaneous (so that the party who fulfils his obligation today has no assurance that his partners will fulfil theirs tomorrow). Contracts that would be mutually advantageous if they could be perfectly and costlessly enforced may cease to be advantageous if the parties to the contract may cheat or shirk. Without actually breaking the law, actors in the economy may deal with one another in ways that are similar in some respects to the behaviour of farmers and bandits in conditions of anarchy.[33]

The employment contract will serve as an example. A firm hires workers who may or may not behave honestly. Malfeasance, in this instance, is the stealing of materials from the firm. A worker who steals (without getting caught) acquires a certain benefit for himself and imposes a certain cost on his employer. The cost must exceed the benefit, for otherwise there would be room for a deal in which the employee accepts a cut in his wage on the understanding that the "stealing" of materials from the firm is permissible. The firm monitors workers to detect malfeasant behaviour. The monitoring is only partially effective, but the larger the firm's expenditure on monitoring the greater is the probability that stealing will be detected. The worker caught stealing is punished. Workers are assumed to vary in their ability to steal without being detected.

Punishment may take many forms. (i) It may consist of the usual penalties administered by the state, fines or imprisonment for specific forms of misconduct. Our example of malfeasance is theft of material, a common crime punishable by the state. Other types of malfeasance are not punishable in that way. Shirking is not an indictable offence, though it can be no less costly to the employer than the theft of material. Managers or people in positions of trust can sometimes siphon income into their own pockets without actually breaking the law.

(ii) Termination of employment is a form of punishment when it is costly to find a new job or when workers once fired are stigmatized by the market. Suppose the market favours workers who have never been fired over workers who have been fired; the going wage for the former is w and the going wage for the latter is w – s. In that case, the punishment in being fired is a loss of s per year for the rest of the worker's life.

(iii) The employee might post a bond at the time of his employment, a sum of money that is returned with interest when the employee leaves the firm, except in the event of detected malfeasance.[34] This is an ideal solution from the point of view of the employer, for the punishment, which is a cost to the malfeasant worker, is a benefit rather than a cost to the firm. There are two drawbacks to this form of punishment. The first is that it blocks the hiring of workers who do not have the assets to cover the bond. A worker who shirks does not care whether the cost of his shirking is borne by the firm that employs him or by the lender who advances him the money to pay for the bond. Consequently, a bond is no deterrent to malfeasance unless it is financed out of the worker's own assets or the lender can punish the worker in ways that are not open to the firm. The other drawback to bonding is that it presents a temptation to malfeasance on the part of the employer. Just as the law cannot identify and punish shirking on the part of the worker, so too the law is unable to prove the firm wrong if the firm claims that the worker has shirked. The worker may not trust the firm to decide whether and in what circumstances to forfeit a large bond.

(iv) When bonding the worker is infeasible and when termination of employment would not otherwise be an adequate deterrent, the employer might, in his own interest, agree to pay a wage in excess of what an equally skilled worker could earn elsewhere, so as to increase the cost to the employee of being fired. Loss of a "trust" wage might supply the required extra deterrence. One would expect to observe an "economy of high wages" in any occupation where the cost of malfeasance to the employer is significant and where monitoring is expensive.

(v) Piecework is not punishment, but it plays the same role as punishment in this context. The worker has no incentive to shirk if his income depends upon his productivity. The difficulty with this mode of deterring malfeasance is that it is often impossible to identify each worker's contribution to a group performing an assigned task or to the firm as a whole. What is the contribution of one worker on an assembly line or of the vice-president in charge of finance? It may in practice be advantageous to pay workers according to some rough-and-ready measure of their output, but it is not always so. Payment according to contribution may not always be advantageous to the employer or to the employee. A worker's contribution may vary greatly from year to year, so that a worker paid according to his contribution to output may be compelled to bear a risk that could more easily be borne by the employer, whose total income may be larger and who can spread risk over many employees. The design of methods of compensation is often a complex trade-off between incentives and risk-bearing. The standard argument in favour of sharecropping and profit-sharing between owner and workers is that sharecropping and profit-sharing represent good compromises between fixed wages, which would be the best allocation of risk between the parties, and fixed rents to owners of land or capital, which would provide the appropriate incentive to labour in a world where malfeasance is endemic.

(vi) An old age pension administered by the employer may be like a bond for good behaviour or like a trust wage. It is like a bond for good behaviour if the worker is paid less in the firm when he is young than he could earn in jobs without pensions, so that the present value of the worker's lifetime earnings in the firm (including entitlement to the old age pension) is not augmented by the arrangement. It is like a trust wage if the worker's lifetime earnings in the firm exceed what he could have earned elsewhere. The deterrent effect of the pension increases over time; this may be satisfactory to the firm if the amount of harm that the worker can do to the firm through malfeasance and the profitability of malfeasance to the worker increase as the worker acquires seniority and responsibility within the firm. An old age pension administered by the firm shares the principal drawback of bonding as an incentive upon the worker, that it exposes the worker to a risk of malfeasance on the part of the firm, for it constitutes no deterrent to malfeasance by the worker unless the firm reserves the right to deny the pension if the worker misbehaves.

(vii) Punishment may also consist of denial of promotion within the firm.[35]

The profit-maximizing firm selects a mix of "punishments" to minimize its cost per unit of penalty to the malfeasant worker. Of course, opportunities to punish are not the same from firm to firm or from time to time. One firm can get away with demanding a bond from its workers, in which case the cost of punishment might be zero or even negative. Another firm can rely on the stigma of dismissal. Another firm must offer above-market wages if the firing of a worker is to be a sufficient deterrent to malfeasance.

Let P be the dollar equivalent of the cost to a worker of being punished for malfeasance, Q be the cost (per worker) to the employer of imposing punishment, c be the cost of malfeasance to the employer, b be the benefit of malfeasance to the worker (where $b < c$), m be the employer's monitoring cost per worker, π be the probability that malfeasance is detected, and r be an indicator of the worker's ability to escape detection. As there is no single "right" way to measure r within the terms of this problem, we may as well assume for convenience that r is scaled between 0 and 1, and that the proportion of workers for whom $r < \bar{r}$ is precisely $\bar{r}$. The advantage of this normalization is that r now plays a dual role as the measure of ability to escape detection *and* the proportion of workers whose ability to escape detection is at least r. The probability of a worker being caught in the event that he steals is $\pi(m,r)$, where, of course, $\partial\pi/\partial m > 0$ and $\partial\pi/\partial r < 0$, signifying that the probability increases with the firm's monitoring effort and decreases with the worker's intrinsic ability to escape detection. Assume also that the cost of malfeasance to the employer, c, must be borne regardless of whether malfeasance is detected. Punishment in this example is deterrence, not restitution. A worker caught stealing must forgo the loot, b, and bear a cost of punishment P. Think of the loot as being destroyed in the event that malfeasance is detected; perhaps the recovered loot is no longer of use to the firm but is retrieved regardless, as a deterrent.

The "cost of punishment" requires some explanation. Punishment must be costly in equilibrium to the punished and to the punisher alike. That punishment must be costly to the punished is implicit in the very meaning of the term, for otherwise punishment is no deterrent. That punishment must be costly to the punisher is also required, for there would otherwise be nothing to stop the punisher from increasing P without limit until all malfeasance is deterred. The fact that punishment is never infinite and not all malfeasance is deterred must signify that punishment is costly to the punisher at the margin. Thus it is assumed that $Q = Q(P)$ where $Q' > 0$ and $Q'' > 0$, where P is the dollar value of the harm to the person punished of whatever punishment is imposed and Q is the corresponding average cost to the punisher.

Equilibrium in the "market" for malfeasance is a balance between the behaviour of the worker who steals when it is advantageous to do so and the employer who chooses profit-maximizing levels of monitoring and punishment. In this example, the worker is the "robber" and the firm is the "cop". In reality, the parties might easily exchange roles, and the general paradigm applies to a wide variety of transactions.

An amoral and risk-neutral worker chooses to steal from his employer when the expected gain, $b(1 - \pi(m,r))$, exceeds the expected cost of punishment, $P\pi(m,r)$. Thus a worker whose ability to escape detection is r steals whenever $b(1 - \pi(m,r)) > P\pi(m,r)$, that is, when

$$\pi(m,r) \leq b/(b + P) \tag{49}$$

In these circumstances there must be a critical value, $\bar{r}$, such that a person steals if his r exceeds $\bar{r}$ and is honest otherwise. The value of $\bar{r}$ is identified from equation (49) by transforming the inequality into an equality. Specifically,

$$\bar{r} = \bar{r}(m,P) \tag{50}$$

where $\partial\bar{r}/\partial m > 0$ and $\partial\bar{r}/\partial P > 0$.

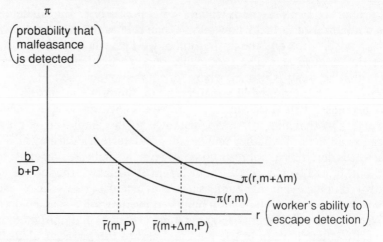

Figure 45 Monitoring and malfeasance (for a constant P). $\bar{r}(m,P)$ is the proportion of workers who are 'honest' when the monitoring cost is m

The worker's behaviour is illustrated in Figure 45, with his ability to escape detection, r, on the horizontal axis and the probability of detection, π, on the vertical axis. The curves show π as a function of r for alternative values of m. Since r is at once a measure of the worker's ability to escape detection and, in the light of equation (50), of the proportion of workers who remain honest at any given m and P, the proportion of workers who remain honest is indicated by the intersection of the curve $\pi(m,r)$ with a horizontal line at a distance $b/(b + P)$ above the axis. For a given punishment, P, an increase in monitoring cost from m to $m + \Delta m$ shifts the curve $\pi(m,r)$ to the right and increases the proportion of workers who refrain from stealing from $\bar{r}(m,P)$ to $\bar{r}(m+\Delta m,P)$.

For a fixed monitoring cost, m, the firm's choice of punishment is illustrated in Figure 46. On the horizontal axis is the severity of punishment, P, as perceived by the worker. On the vertical axis is the cost to the firm per worker of malfeasance and of its efforts to deter malfeasance. As long as punishment deters crime at the margin, an increase in the severity of punishment leads to an increase in the proportion of workers who remain honest and, therefore, to a decrease in the cost of malfeasance itself as indicated by the downward sloping curve. In principle, the deterrent effect of an increase in the severity of punishment might be so great, and the incidence of crime so dramatically reduced, that the total cost of punishment declines with the severity of punishment. That cannot be so at the firm's optimal values of P and m, for, if it were so, the chosen value of P would be too small and the firm would have every incentive to increase P. At any equilibrium where not all malfeasance is deterred, the cost of

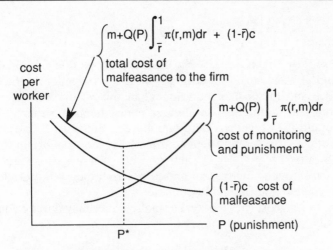

Figure 46 Punishment and malfeasance (for a constant m)

punishment per worker must increase with severity, as shown by the up-ward sloping curve in Figure 46. The total cost of malfeasance — inclusive of the direct cost, the cost of monitoring and the cost of punishment — must be U-shaped. The optimal punishment occurs at the trough of the U-shaped curve.

Given the behaviour of workers, the firm chooses m and P to minimize the total cost of malfeasance, inclusive of monitoring, m, administering punishment, $Q(P)\int_{\bar{r}}^{1}\pi(r,m)dr$, and bearing the cost of the remaining, un-deterred malfeasance $(1-\bar{r})c$. The firm's problem is to choose values of m and P that minimize the expression

$$m + Q(P)\int_{\bar{r}}^{1}\pi(r,m)dr + (1-\bar{r})c$$

where $\bar{r}$ depends upon m and P in accordance with equation (50) above. The first-order conditions to this problem are easily computed and easily interpreted. The first-order condition with respect to monitoring cost, m, is

$$1 + Q(P)\int_{\bar{r}}^{1}\pi_m(r,m)\,dr = [Q(P)\pi(\bar{r},m) + c]\frac{\partial\bar{r}}{\partial m} \qquad (51)$$

To increase m by 1 is to incur a direct cost of 1 plus an additional cost of punishment due to the fact that a larger proportion of malfeasant workers are detected. On the other side of the equation is the saving in the cost of malfeasance to the firm and in the cost of punishment of those workers who are induced by the increase in m to become honest. The first-order condition with respect to the severity of punishment, P, is

$$\frac{\partial Q}{\partial P}\left[\int_{\bar{r}}^{1}\pi(r,m)\,dr\right] = \left[Q(P)\pi(\bar{r},m) + c\right]\frac{\partial \bar{r}}{\partial P} \tag{52}$$

To increase P by 1 is to increase the cost of every worker punished by an amount $\partial Q/\partial P$. The corresponding benefit is the reduction in the cost of malfeasance and the cost of punishment of those workers who are deterred from malfeasance by the greater punishment. In principle, equations (51) and (52) together yield equilibrium values of P and m, from which all other variables may be determined. Let the equilibrium values of the variables be P*, m*, $\bar{r}$*, Q* and π* when workers, from their point of view, are optimally malfeasant and firms, from their point of view, are optimally vigilant and optimally punitive.

The total social cost (per worker) of malfeasance may now be compiled. It is the sum of the loss to the firm,

$$m^* + Q(P^*)\int_{\bar{r}}^{1}\pi(r,m^*)\,dr + (1 - \bar{r}^*)c$$

plus the cost of punishment to malfeasant workers who are detected

$$P^*\int_{\bar{r}}^{1}\pi(r,m^*)\,dr$$

minus the gain to workers who steal successfully

$$b\int_{\bar{r}}^{1}(1 - \pi(r,m^*))\,dr$$

These costs can be rearranged more or less in accordance with three of the four categories in the classification of the social cost of theft as introduced in the discussion of banditry in Chapter III. The costs become: (i) the cost of punishment to the malfeasant worker

$$\equiv P^*\int_{\bar{r}}^{1}\pi(r,m^*)\,dr$$

(ii) the cost to the employer in protecting himself

$$\equiv m^* + Q(P^*)\int_{\bar{r}}^{1}\pi(r,m^*)\,dr$$

(iii) the destruction of property

$$\equiv c(1 - \bar{r}^*) - b\int_{\bar{r}}^{1}(1 - \pi(r,m^*))\,dr$$

on the assumption that all malfeasance is harmful to the firm but only undetected malfeasance is beneficial to the workers. The fourth category, deadweight loss, is not formally incorporated into the model of malfeasance. A deadweight loss would emerge when consumption is diverted from goods produced in industries where malfeasance is especially prevalent to goods produced in industries where malfeasance is less prevalent.

Whenever a principal employs an agent there is an incentive on the part of the agent to work less and to serve the principal with less diligence than would be agreed upon by the principal and agent together if both parties could be sure that the agreement would be honoured completely. Malfeasance is endemic in any economy: the employee shirks, steals from his employer or fails to watch out for ways to improve productivity. The employer skimps on expenditure on accident prevention or to reduce the incidence of industrial disease. The company as the agent of the stock-holders takes risks that are inconsistent with the terms on which bonds are issued because the entire potential gain accrues to the stockholder, while large losses would be borne in part by bondholders. The manager of a firm finds ways of diverting income from stockholders to himself or resists a take-over bid to preserve his job. A person whose house is insured against fire has a less than optimal incentive to engage in expenditure on fire prevention. Holders of cost-plus contracts may not exercise due diligence in buying material at the lowest price. Stockbrokers may find reasons to change their clients' portfolios frequently. Lawyers on *per diem* may spin a case out.

Each of these cases is analogous to our example of the worker who might steal from his employer. The principal typically devotes resources to monitoring his agent and to some equivalent of punishment when malfeasance is detected. The agent on the other hand is quite willing to trade off a large loss of income to his principal against a small gain of income to himself if he can do so in circumstance where the risk of detection is small and the punishment is not too serious. Thus, for example, an elected official who does not steal small sums of money for fear of imprisonment might happily act in a way that is equivalent to transferring large amounts of money from taxpayers to firms engaged in business with the government if there is a prospect of his being hired by such firms when his term of office is done.

The analysis of information, adverse selection and the principal–agent problem, all major preoccupations of the economics profession over the last twenty-five years, has led to a radical transformation in the way the competitive economy is perceived. Perfect competition — with prices determined in accordance with Walras's process and with price-taking behaviour by all consumers and firms — is the perfect absence of competition as the term is understood on the street. To compete as the term is commonly understood is to argue, perhaps to cheat, to bargain, to make deals, and to beat one's competitor. You cannot do any of those things as a price-taker. Perhaps it is a question of distance. Given a body of data on house prices and characteristics (including location) of the houses that are sold, and knowing that some of the good and bad points of particular houses are not captured in the data on characteristics, one might infer that buyers and sellers were all price-takers. Within limits, that would be true. But if one watches the activities of buyer, seller and realtor from the day a house is put on the market to the day the new owner moves in, one must conclude that there is a range of indeterminacy over which vigorous negotiation takes place. The transaction cost — inclusive of the labour time of the seller, prospective buyer, realtor and lawyer — amounts to about 10 per cent of the price. There is a core of anarchy at the centre of what is on the whole an efficient and orderly process.

Contract and purchase

A contract is "an agreement between two or more parties to do something". A purchase is "the transfer of a good or service from one person to another in return for money". Contract is the broader term, on these definitions, for "the transfer of a good or service" is a special case of "an agreement between two or more parties". All purchases are contracts, but not all contracts are purchases. A contract to buy a house is a purchase. A contract to acquire a spouse is not. Nor is a contract between firms to embark on a joint venture or a contract among consulting engineers to form a partnership. The distinction matters because the prototype of a transaction in Walras's description of price formation and in his discussion of the perfectly competitive economy is the purchase rather than the contract, and because certain aspects of contracts other than simple purchases have important implications for the efficiency of a market economy.

Though the enforcement of private contracts is one of the functions of the state, there are types of contracts that cannot or will not be enforced. The state will not enforce a contract to sell oneself into slavery or to commit an illegal act. The state cannot enforce a contract unless its provisions are precise enough for the state to determine whether a violation has occurred. The state cannot enforce a contract that requires, for example, exceptional diligence by a worker; the most it can do is to refrain from actions that prevent the dismissal of a worker who in the opinion of the firm does not display that quality. This consideration is a matter of degree, for no contract can be absolutely unambiguous, regardless of the circumstances. A contract is always incomplete, for it is impossible to account in the written document for every contingency that might affect the obligations of the parties. Perhaps a signatory literally cannot meet his obligations under the contract, or cannot do so without bearing costs that are significantly greater than anybody thought possible at the time the contract was signed. Union and management may disagree as to whether a company is justified in penalizing a worker under the terms of the labour contract. Partners in a law firm may come into conflict over the direction of the firm. A professor may claim to be wrongfully dismissed from his university.

The essential incompleteness of contracts has several implications. It implies that a contract must always be understood against the background of the laws and customs of the society in which it is signed. It implies that parties to a contract can never be certain that they will not end up in litigation over the interpretation of the contract. It implies that, in practice, most contracts are always being renegotiated at the edges to account for changes in circumstances. Contracts involve the parties in bargaining, not only when the deal embodied in the contract is arranged, but later on, as the contract must be continually reinterpreted.[36]

The prospect of malfeasance and the desire to minimize the cost of bargaining in contractual arrangements may affect the nature of the contracts themselves. Contracts which would be best if each party's actions under the contracts could be costlessly observed, so that the law would enforce compliance to the letter, might be inappropriate in an environment where this is not so. We have already mentioned sharecropping. The "best" contract between landowner and farm worker would be a fixed wage, so that the farm worker, who can ill afford to bear the financial risk associated with uncertainty in the weather or with the variability of farm prices, need not be obliged to do so. That is not the best contract when the effort of the worker cannot be observed, because it does not provide sufficient incentive to diligence on his part. Similarly, the "best" contract between inventors and the rest of society would be to reward the inventor with a lump sum payment if the patent office could determine both the originality of the invention and its value to society. The invention could then become part of the common stock of knowledge and the use of the new product would not be restricted by royalties. That is not the best contract in practice because the patent office cannot determine the true value of an invention and because a requirement upon the patent office to estimate the true value of inventions would in all probability entail costly negotiation and considerable malfeasance. The inclusion of a partially firm-financed old age pension as part of the compensation of the worker is poor risk management, because subsequent bankruptcy of the firm would entail the loss of one's pension along with one's job. It may nonetheless be the optimal labour contract once problems of malfeasance and negotiation are taken into account.

Some implications of the discrepancy between Walras's description of price formation and actual behaviour in the market

Unemployment of labour
There is no involuntary unemployment of labour in an economy when everyone is a price-taker because, by definition, each worker can supply as little or as much labour as he pleases at the going wage. If more people want to work than there are jobs available at the going wage, then Walras's crier announces another, lower wage and everybody recontracts, over and over again until all prices and wages are right. Unemployment must be explained as the consequence of features of real markets that are abstracted out of Walras's account.

One explanation is that some prices move slowly. Walras envisioned a process of infinitely rapid recontracting in which no trade takes place until a set of prices has been discovered at which all markets clear. In reality, trade takes place at "false" prices — prices that are obviously not clearing the market — because consumers are unwilling to wait for goods and sellers are unwilling to hold stocks until such time as markets clear. Some prices do move quickly. There is no excess demand or supply for shares on the stock exchange or for minerals traded on the London or Chicago markets. Walras's assumptions might be true of these items. The price of labour on the other hand varies considerably less than the price of shares or minerals, from day to day or from year to year, and the quantity purchased varies instead. There is no crash on the labour market but there can be an excess supply.

Wage stickiness can be explained in part by the presence of long-term contracts between unions and firms. Even without unions, there may be an understanding between workers and firms that wages will not change rapidly from day to day. By not changing wages frequently the firm provides the worker with a kind of income assurance, and the owner bears the major part of the risk due to fluctuations in price or in demand for output. In return, the worker may accept a lower wage in the long run. Wages may also be relatively stable because workers already in the firm are less than perfect substitutes for workers outside the firm. Employers may be afraid to cut wages for fear of losing workers who have built up skills that are particular to or especially useful to the firm. This concern is reinforced by the possibility of adverse selection. A firm dare not replace a significant part of its labour force with outsiders willing to work at a lower wage, for fear that people willing to accept a low wage are not capable of earning a high wage in trades where skill can be immediately recognized.[37]

Interactions among markets may contribute to wage stickiness. Suppose the equilibrium wage in all industries falls from 10 to 5 owing to a sharp contraction in the money supply that is expected to reduce all prices and wages accordingly. The appropriate wage in any particular industry may, nevertheless, remain well above 5 until such time as all wages have fallen. No employer can get away with offering 5 while other employers are still offering 10 because workers — particularly the best workers — may still have a chance of finding work elsewhere at 10 and because a money wage of 5 would constitute a low real wage in the initial disequilibrium before all prices and wages have fallen. One would expect wages to edge down gradually and unemployment to rise during the transition.[38]

Another possible source of involuntary unemployment of labour is the dependence of the efficiency of labour upon the real wage. Possible reasons for this dependence will be discussed presently. For the moment, suppose that the input of labour per worker in efficiency units, e, increases with the real wage, w, though at a decreasing rate. Specifically, suppose

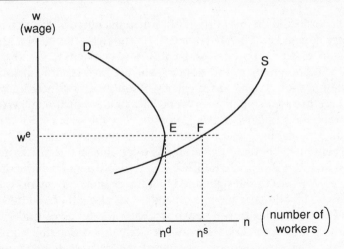

Figure 47 Involuntary unemployment of labour when efficiency is affected by the wage rate

that $e = e(w)$, that $e' \geq 0$ and that $e'' \leq 0$. To focus upon the implications of this assumption, suppose also that labour is the only factor of production, so that the production function becomes

$$Q = f(e(w)n) \tag{53}$$

where n is the number of workers, Q is total output, $f' > 0$ and $f'' \leq 0$.

A distinction needs to be drawn between the wage *per se*, w, and the wage *per efficiency unit of labour*, $w/e(w)$. An increase in the former does not necessarily lead to an increase in the latter, and it is only the latter that is of interest to the firm in its hiring decisions. The significance of this distinction is that there may be a certain wage, w^e, called the "efficiency wage", which is the *minimum* a firm would be prepared to pay (even if workers were prepared to accept less) because the wage per efficiency unit of labour, $w/e(w)$, is minimized at w^e. The firm would never voluntarily pay its workers less than w^e per worker because the lower wage per hour is a higher wage in efficiency units of labour.[39]

The market is illustrated in Figure 47, with wage per hour on the vertical axis and the number of workers on the horizontal axis. There is a normal upward sloping supply curve of labour, indicating that n^s workers would be prepared to work for the firm if the offered wage were w^e. The demand curve is backward-bending. The meaning of the upward sloping portion of the demand curve below the efficiency wage is this: if a firm were compelled to offer a wage w that was less than w^e and if the firm could choose the number of workers to hire at that wage, it would hire fewer workers at the wage, w, than it would hire at the efficiency wage, w^e, because the wage in efficiency units would actually exceed the efficiency wage. A firm would never locate on this portion of its demand curve voluntarily, and its voluntary demand curve may be said to terminate at the point E. In these circumstances the firm offers a wage of w^e and demands n^d workers at that wage, and there remain $n^s - n^d$ workers who are involuntarily unemployed.

To the question of why the efficiency of labour might increase with the wage there are two standard answers. The first is nutritional. Without a certain minimal standard of living, workers lack the strength to work well. This is an explanation of chronic rather than cyclical unemployment, though a cycle could be generated by variations over time in a country's terms of trade. As the terms of trade improve, the derived demand curve of labour in Figure 47 moves to the right and involuntary unemployment is reduced accordingly. Involuntary unemployment ceases altogether and the equilibrium real wage begins to rise above w^e when the terms of trade get high enough that the point E overtakes the point F, so that the equilibrium occurs at a downward sloping portion of the derived demand curve for labour. This tragic explanation of involuntary unemployment is only relevant to very poor countries.

The other explanation of the backward-bending derived demand curve for labour pertains to the "economy of high wages" as discussed above in connection with malfeasance. The function $e(w)$ becomes $e(w - \overline{w})$ where w is the wage paid to employed workers within the firm, and $\overline{w}$ is the worker's reservation wage at which he is indifferent between continuing in the job and being fired. Imagine a situation where a certain fraction of the employed workers leave the work force each year owing to illness or retirement and where these workers are replaced at random from the pool of unemployed, so that the expected duration of unemployment and the corresponding $\overline{w}$ depend upon the number of unemployed. The key assumption in this interpretation of involuntary unemployment is that $e(w - \overline{w})$ represents the worker's willingness to work diligently as a function of his fear of being fired for malfeasance. In this case there can never be full employment because employers must, in their own interest, raise wages as soon as the rate of unemployment falls below a critical level. This phenomenon is not confined to poor countries. It can take place anywhere if the conditions are right.

The second explanation of the dependence of efficiency upon the wage is not illogical, but it is open to a number of objections concerning the relevance of the assumptions to actual labour markets. It too is an explanation of chronic rather than cyclical unemployment. There should always be involuntary unemployment of this type if it occurs at all, for there is no reason to suppose that the propensity to malfeasance varies over the business cycle. It is a better explanation of involuntary unemployment among would-be accountants, company presidents and drivers of Brinks trucks whose conditions of work entail particularly large opportunities for malfeasance than of involuntary unemployment among the general run of workers who are reasonably well supervised on the job. One may at the same time be involuntarily unemployed in the sense of wanting (and being able to perform well in) a high-paying job in a position of trust, and employed in the sense that one holds another job at a lower rate of pay. That interpretation of involuntary unemployment is not what is usually meant by the term. The explanation also requires that the taking away of a high-paying job is the cheapest punishment a firm can inflict upon a malfeasant worker. If being fired carried a stigma, so that a person once fired would command a lower wage than one who had never been fired, then trust wages would be unnecessary and firms would not need to be concerned that their workers would cheat them if there were full employment. In an economy with many different skills and with jobs that vary considerably in their opportunities for malfeasance, one would expect to see a good deal of variation in wages for similarly skilled people, but this alone need not imply that involuntary unemployment of labour. The "efficiency wage" explanation is coherent, but not necessarily correct.

Existence of the firm
Strictly speaking, there is no place for the firm in perfect competition. If each person acts as a price-taker in apportioning his income among goods and if the owner of every factor of production, including labour, is a price-taker in the determination of where and with which other factors of production his human and non-human capital is employed, then the mix of factors of production we now call a firm would come together automatically, each factor attaching itself to the bundle of other factors for which the value of its marginal product (and therefore its remuneration) is maximized. The price mechanism itself would induce what would otherwise be profit-maximizing behaviour by the firm. The auctioneer calls out the price of an automobile and the prices of all inputs — steel, rubber, machines, land and so on — to be assembled at the appropriate times and places. The factors of production arrive, perform their tasks at the agreed-upon prices, and the automobile is produced.

The auctioneer is a very busy man. He must call a price for each task and must continue adjusting all prices until, for example, the worker who stands at a certain location in the assembly line, tightening a particular bolt, is paid a wage high enough that the job is the worker's best alternative but low enough that nobody else is prepared to do the job for less. The auctioneer is also very knowledgeable. To call prices for each task, he must know what those tasks are, right down to the very last detail. He must know every production process intimately and master every organization chart before he can begin to call out prices for the tasks to be assigned, including responsibility for dealing with unforeseen contingencies.

The auctioneer's task is easier in one respect than the task of the manager of a firm. The assumptions in the model of perfect competition leave no place for malfeasance. The person who contracts to perform a certain task can be guaranteed to do so, regardless of monitoring or punishment for misbehaviour. Walras's process attaches prices to all goods and services in an environment where everyone agrees about the nature of each good and service and where nobody need doubt whether a good or service that he has bought will actually be delivered. The firm is made superfluous in perfect competition by endowing the auctioneer with knowledge which is in fact scattered throughout society and by abstracting from predatory behaviour that no auctioneer, no matter how knowledgeable, could control. Firms exist in an environment where neither of these conditions obtains.

A distinction should be drawn between the "existence" of competitive equilibrium prices and the process by which they emerge. "Existence" as the term is understood in the study of general equilibrium is a shadowy and mathematical form of being. All it means is that God could tell us the prices that would clear all markets. It carries no warranty that these "existing" prices and the actual market prices are one and the same. Walras's process is an imaginary experiment that carries a suggestion of how actual prices might be drawn toward the market-clearing ideal. The process, suggestive as it is, is highly artificial. If the full process is required to make actual prices clear the market completely, then obviously the actual prices are at best an approximation to the ideal.

Under these circumstances, society has two principal methods of allocating resources. It can rely on a price mechanism which can, at best, yield prices that approximate the market clearing ideal, or it can rely on a system of command that by-passes the price mechanism in the economy as a whole or in selected parts of the economy. The firm is a system of command in a part of the economy where the required coordination among factors of production is too intricate and the cost of bargaining over the allocation of tasks and the sharing of rewards would be too great to be entrusted to the price mechanism alone. Firms are, in the famous phrase of D.H. Robertson, "islands of conscious power in the ocean of unconscious cooperation".[40]

"The distinguishing mark of the firm is the suppression of the price mechanism" by a contract in which the worker "agrees to obey the directions of an entrepreneur *within certain limits*".[41] In an uncertain environment where owners of cooperating factors of production may not agree what to produce, which factors belong together, what each worker is to do in the common enterprise, or how to identify and punish those who do not pull their weight, it is efficient for one agent (who may be a person or a group of people) to be entrusted with the task of administering the firm.

Certain traits and characteristics of the firm are mandated by its role as partial replacement for the price mechanism in areas where the price mechanism cannot be expected to perform well.

(i) The firm requires an agent to decide what to produce, how to organize production, how much to invest, how much to advertise, who is to be hired, who is to be fired, how much money to borrow, when to make use of the bond market, how much effort to devote to research, and so on. This agent must inevitably stand at the peak of a chain of command encompassing all the workers in the firm.

(ii) The agent who bears the final responsibility for running the firm must at the same time be the residual income claimant. As a rule, one does not accept to be directed by a boss unless one's remuneration is fixed by contract. If factor incomes are fixed by contract and if the income of the firm as a whole is uncertain, then there must be an unpredictable residual that someone must bear. If each worker is to be paid a fixed wage for doing as he is told, then someone must be prepared to accept the difference between the revenue and the cost of the firm. The residual income claimant cannot divest himself of ultimate control, for, in that case, the controller would have every incentive to enhance his own income and to allow residual income to become small or negative. The key word in the preceding sentence is "ultimate". The residual income claimant may hire a team of managers to conduct the day-to-day business of the firm, but the residual income claimant must reserve the authority to remove managers if profit is not maximized.[42]

(iii) As owner of the firm, the residual income claimant must bear final responsibility for monitoring factors of production. The responsibility for monitoring devolves upon the residual income claimant because nobody else has the same incentive to attend to the job. Shirking is, necessarily, at the expense of the residual income claimant. He alone bears the cost of shirking and has the proper financial incentive to put a stop to it.[43]

(iv) Within the firm, there is an affinity among the functions of generalship (deciding what to do), residual income-bearing and ownership of capital. No one is willing to bear the residual income without the ultimate authority to organize and direct the firms. No one is tolerated as residual income bearer unless he owns a significant part of the capital of the firm, though capital in this context may consist of a patent, special skill or knowledge of the market. One cannot bear the residual income unless one has something to lose in the event that the residual income is negative. An owner without capital imposes an unacceptable risk on bond-holders or other lenders. If the firm is prosperous, the owner earns a significant portion of the profit. If the firm is unprosperous, the bond-holders and lenders would be compelled by the bankruptcy laws to take the entire loss.

(v) The firm is a domain of command in an otherwise impersonal world of prices. To be sure, obedience is limited to agreed-upon working hours and to an agreed-upon range of tasks, but within these prescribed limits the boss tells the worker what to do and the worker does it. Domination and subservience, even to this limited extent, affect the way parties begin to feel about one another. The worker begins to feel timid in the presence of, and perhaps even inferior to, his boss who knows and directs the entire enterprise in which the worker plays a routine and minor part. At the same time, the worker begins to resent the boss who orders him about and who can fire him, if not at will, than for prescribed misbehaviour. The boss, on the other hand, cannot help feeling a certain sense of superiority to the workers he commands. Perhaps he begins to see himself as their father, the one who knows what is best for them, who catches them when they try to shirk their duties and who sets them on the right path. This inevitable antagonism between the boss and worker is exacerbated by the unavoidable lack of precision in the specification of the limits to the command-obedience relation, as exemplified by the secretary's "duty" to provide coffee which was once thought of as part of the job and is now usually excluded as humiliating. The boss, of course, wants these limits as broad as possible, and the worker wants them as narrow as possible.

If the firm is the home of obedience and command, then the market is the home of freedom, of being one's own boss. There is an independence in producing directly for a market of customers who cannot tell you what to do and whose only hold over you is the option not to buy what you produce. The market is also the great source of independence for the worker within a firm. A worker who is dissatisfied with his present employment can seek alternative employment in a competitive market where he can command the going value of the marginal product of his labour. That is why the sting of command cannot be removed by placing firms in the public domain, where, so it is said, the worker can work for himself as citizen rather than for a boss. What stings is the need to obey, regardless of who is ultimately at the peak of the hierarchy of which one is a part. Nationalization of all industry serves to close the only route of escape for one who finds his present position intolerable and to remove the major impediment to arrogance on the part of the boss — the ability of the worker to quit one job and find another.

None of these considerations matters in the ideal economy for which a competitive equilibrium is proved to be Pareto optimal. There is no subordination because everybody follows prices. There is no monitoring because there is no malfeasance. There is no residual income because the future is parcelled out into states of the world, so that each good in each state has its contingent price. There is no task of coordination because the auctioneer has the organization of industry and the specification of each task worked out before he starts calling prices. There is for all practical purposes no firm.

Voting within the private sector of the economy
The solution to one problem of coordination immediately gives rise to another. We have so far spoken of entrepreneurship as though the entrepreneur were one person who directs the firm, is the sole residual income

claimant and owns the equity capital all by himself. That may be true of small firms, but not of large ones. Large firms may have many owners because there is a mismatch between the distribution of wealth among citizens and the distribution of assets among firms, and because many wealth-holders, who are risk-averse or who do not wish to take the responsibility of running firms, prefer partial ownership of large firms to full ownership of firms that are commensurate with their wealth. The device that makes this possible is voting by majority rule among shareholders.

Voting by shareholders of a corporation has a good deal in common with voting for candidates in an election or for bills in the legislature, but there are two important differences. The first is the composition of the electorate. One person has one vote in a political election. One share has one vote in the corporation, with no limits on how many shares a person may own. The second is the subordination of the corporation to the state. There is in principle no higher authority than the legislature, but the corporation is bound by laws and regulations. Thus, while the diseases of voting discussed in connection with the liberal society have their counterparts in the government of the corporation, the virulence of and remedies for these diseases are not the same.

Conflict of interest among shareholders is constrained by their common interest in maximizing the profit of the corporation, but is not eliminated altogether. Conflict of interest may arise through genuine differences of opinion as to how profitability is to be attained. Some investors, believing the firm to have excellent prospects, want low dividends and large borrowing to finance investment. Other investors are less sanguine and would prefer large dividends now. Some investors want the firm to take large risks with the possibility of high returns. Other investors are more modest in their objectives for the firm. Some investors are enthusiastic about the ability of the firm's current management. Others are not. Where such differences exist, it matters who manages the firm and which stockholders' views are represented in the conduct of management.

When the interests of shareholders are alike, a take-over of the firm may be no more than the replacement of a less efficient by a more efficient management or the exploitation of synergies among firms. Suppose the incumbent management can earn $10 per share, while a new management can earn as much as $20. Discounting at 10 per cent, the share price cannot exceed $100 if the incumbent management cannot be dislodged, as might be the case if the incumbent management is that of the founder of the firm who has grown lazy or less enterprising with the passage of time, or who cannot cope with the large enterprise that his firm has become. All stockholders gain as the share price rises toward $200 in response to information that the incumbent management is not firmly entrenched and might be displaced in a proxy fight or take-over bid.

Conflict over control is not necessarily so benign, for control may be the source of advantages that are not shared equally among all stockholders. One cannot watch the manoeuvres of the predator and target in a take-over controversy, or observe the resulting rise in the price of the shares of the targeted firm, or observe the differences between the prices of voting and non-voting shares, without concluding that something of great value is acquired when the control of the firm passes from one party to another.

The greatest advantage in the control of the firm is the exploitation of other stockholders and, perhaps, of bond-holders as well. He who controls the firm would like to confine its profit to his shares or to his pocket while denying dividends to other stockholders. The ploy would, of course, be manifestly illegal. A major objective of the law of corporation finance is to put all shares on an equal footing. The return to the shares of a minor-ity shareholder should be no less than the return to the shares of the majority shareholder or of a coalition of shareholders who together hold a majority of the shares. The regulation of security markets is intended to ensure that this is so, or is as nearly so as can be arranged.

There are, nonetheless, several reasons for believing that control might be of value *per se*, apart from any effect it may have in raising the stock price. (i) Control is a source of jobs. Typically, a corporate raider has an organization of people who become and remain loyal when there is a prospect of high-paying and responsible jobs in acquired companies. Or the control of the firm may be a source of high incomes and valuable work experience for one's family or friends. (ii) Control may be turned into wealth by judicious transfer pricing. A person who controls two firms, one with a substantial proportion of shares owned by others and a second that he owns outright, can augment his wealth by transferring income from the first firm to the second. Assets can be exchanged advantageously. Particu-larly attractive investments can be reserved for the wholly-owned firm. Favourable contracts can be negotiated. The best managers can be fun-nelled into the wholly-owned firm without regard for the minority share-holders of the other.[44] (iii) Control may be sought out of a sheer love of activity. It can be fun to control an empire, even when one earns less money than if somebody else were in control. (iv) Control may be advan-tageous in dealings with the government. The larger one's empire, the more of other people's money can be assigned as contributions to political parties, the more influence one has over jobs and prosperity in various constituencies, and the greater is one's scope for offering remunerative employment to ex-civil servants and ex-politicians who have been sympa-thetic. Such influence can be employed to enhance the wealth of the stockholders of a firm one controls or it can be used to enhance one's own wealth through, for example, favourable treatment of a wholly-owned firm.

Some of these ploys are illegal. Perhaps all might be illegal in an ideal regulatory regime. In practice, the perquisites of control cannot be elim-inated altogether. Control of the firm carries the right to appoint the lawyers and the accountants, who can be expected to serve the interests of their employer up to the very limit of the law. Only in rare cases can minority shareholders be dispossessed altogether. The ordinary fallibility of the law virtually guarantees that minority shareholders are exploited to some extent and that control is valuable for its own sake.

Ownership of 51 per cent of the shares of a firm is always sufficient for control, but is not always necessary. Control might be maintained with substantially less than 51 per cent of the shares if management is reasonably efficient and the controlling party is not too greedy. In practice, it may be prohibitively expensive for a raider to dispossess the holder of a substantial minority of the stock because a large block of shares cannot be acquired by purchase without generating a substantial rise in price (which might render the acquisition unprofitable) and because management with full access to the list of stockholders and a position of trust built up over the years can often expect to win against a raider in a proxy fight.

Permanent and unchallengeable control can be maintained with no share ownership at all through intercorporate shareholding. The simplest scheme is for each of two equal-sized companies with the same board of directors to own 51 per cent of the other's shares. The intercorporate dividends are not taxable. The 49 per cent minority in each company, who may or may not be the same people, have no chance of electing directors to either company. The companies may have separate businesses, or they may in effect be two halves of the same business. This scheme, in the blatant form described here, would be illegal in most countries, but it is a pure and extreme case of a practice which is quite common, the use of interlocking firms to maintain control of a large amount of other people's capital with a small amount of capital of one's own. There is of course some question as to why minority shareholders would allow themselves to be manoeuvred into the situation described here.[45]

A similar outcome can be obtained by dividing the ownership of the firm into voting and non-voting shares, a practice that is legal in Canada but illegal in many states of the United States. In principle, there is no lower limit to the ratio of the number of voting shares to the number on non-voting shares, so that one could maintain control of a firm with virtually no entitlement to dividends at all. In practice, it would not pay the originator of a firm to try to maintain control with little or no entitlement to dividends because the prospective holders of non-voting shares would be unwilling to enter into an arrangement where the firm was controlled by someone with little personal interest in its dividends. Non-voting shares are most often issued when the founder of the firm wishes to preserve control in his own hands or in the hands of his children.

It is difficult to say whether or to what extent competition for control of a firm represents a departure from efficiency. There is no doubt that a take-over bid is costly in legal fees, in the use of the time of the managements of the acquiring firm and the target firm, and in providing a potential target with incentives for actions that may at the same time reduce the risk of take-over and lower the profitability of the firm. No omniscient, omnipotent and benevolent despot would allow resources to be used in such activity. On the other hand, take-overs, like law enforcement, may be necessary in an imperfect society, for the threat of a take-over can be a major goad to efficiency in an environment where management might otherwise ignore the interests of stockholders altogether. The market for ownership is a segment of the economy in which malfeasance is endemic, the assumptions of the model of perfect competition are especially at variance with observed behaviour, and all known institutional arrangements are inefficient to some extent.

A second domain of voting within the private sector of the economy is the trade union. Workers cannot bargain collectively without a common programme, and they cannot form a common programme without a method of resolving disputes among themselves. Majority rule voting is a prerequisite to the unionization of workers.

Voting in a trade union is different in certain respects from voting in a corporation and from voting in society at large. A trade union is like Parliament in that each participant has one, and only one, vote. There is no analogue to the acquisition by one person of control of a firm through the purchase of 51 per cent of the shares. Membership of a union also differs from ownership of a firm in the privileges that membership conveys. Ideally, all shareholders are paid the same dividend per share. The "dividend" from belonging to a union is holding a job. This dividend is not enjoyed equally by all union members, for some union members are employed and others are temporarily or permanently laid off. The union may be confronted with a trade-off between wages and unemployment; the higher the wage, the greater the rate of unemployment among union members. With a prior agreement that workers are to be laid off in accordance with seniority, the choice of a wage rate becomes a single-peaked issue on which the first preference of the median voter on the seniority scale can be expected to prevail.[46]

Seniority, however, is not the only source of conflict among the members of a trade union. Majority coalitions among trade unionists might be established to advance the interests of a particular ethnic group, language, race, class or region. A dominant group may preserve the good jobs for itself and arrange for those outside the group to bear the brunt of unemployment. Yet another difference between voting by the members of a union and voting by the shareholders of a firm is that the union faces an especially complex boundary problem. It is not always clear who has the right to join a union and to vote in union elections. Some unions are open to anyone; others are closed.

Notes

1 There is an almost perfect analogy between the fishing example in the text and the classic problem, which was a source of controversy between Pigou and Knight, of the wide bumpy road and the narrow smooth road. Both roads go from A to B. The wide road can accommodate any amount of traffic, and each car on that road can make the journey in a given time, t^0. The time, t, required for the journey on the narrow smooth road varies with the amount of traffic, n, that is, $t = t(n)$ where $t' > 0$ and $t'' > 0$ because this road becomes congested. With free access to both roads, people allocate themselves between roads so that average travel time is the same on both roads, that is, $t(n) = t^0$. The optimal use of the narrow road is that which minimizes total travel time on both roads. The optimal n is that which minimizes the expression $nt(n) + (N - n)t^0$, where N is the total number of travellers from A to B; this value of n is identified by the condition that $t'(n) = t^0$. On the road problem, see Frank Knight, "Fallacies in the Interpretation of Social Cost", *Quarterly Journal of Economics*, 1924. The classic on common property is Scott Gordon, "The Economic Theory of a Common Property Resource: the Fishery", *Journal of Political Economy*, 1954, 124–42.

2 Though equation (5) can be derived in a multi-period or continuous-time framework, a simpler and more instructive procedure is to suppose that the lake lasts for only two fishing seasons and then disappears altogether. Let the production function in both seasons be

$$C = C(N,S)$$

where C is the catch in any season, S is the stock of fish in the lake at the start of the fishing season and N is the number of fishermen that season. Let P and W be the price of fish and the wage of labour, and designate the years by the superscripts 1 and 2. The stock of fish at the beginning of the first season is given as $\overline{S}$. The stock of fish at the beginning of the second season, S^2, depends on the size of the catch in the first season, specifically,

$$S^2 = (\overline{S} - C^1)(1 + g)$$

where $\overline{S} - C^1$ is the stock of fish that remains in the lake at the end of the first season and g is the rate of growth of the fish stock during the winter.

Over both seasons together, the present value of the total net benefit from fishing in the lake is

$$\pi = [P^1C(N^1,\overline{S}) - W^1N^1] + \frac{1}{1+r} [P^2C(N^2,(\overline{S} - C^1)(1 + g)) - W^2N^2] \qquad (54)$$

Maximizing π with respect to N^1 yields the first order condition

$$[P^1C^1_N - W^1] - \frac{1}{1+r} [P^2 C^2_s C^1_N (1 + g)] = 0 \qquad (55)$$

where C^1_N means

$$\frac{\partial}{\partial N^1} C(N^1,\overline{S})$$

and C_s^2 means

$$\frac{\partial}{\partial S^2} C(N^2, S^2)$$

Dropping the superscript 1, equation (55) may be rewritten as

$$P\partial C(N,S)/\partial N = W + q \qquad (56)$$

where, by definition

$$q \equiv \frac{1}{1+r} [P^2 C_s^2 C_N^1 (1+g)] \qquad (57)$$

Equation (56) is precisely equation (5) in the text. The variable q may be interpreted as the shadow price of the future consequences of the addition of one fisherman today — the present value of the loss of catch next year through the reduction in stock next year resulting from the extra catch today.

As long as prices and wages are independent of the choice of the number of fishermen each year, the maximization of the present value of benefit, π, is the appropriate criterion from the point of view of the profit-maximizing owner of the lake and from the point of view of society as a whole. However, the interest of an owner diverges from the interest of society as a whole when ownership is insecure. With a probability ϕ that the lake will be expropriated in the interval between seasons, the present value of the lake to its owner becomes

$$\pi^0 = [P^1 C(N^1, \overline{S}) - W^1 N^1] + \frac{(1-\phi)}{1+r} [P^2 C(N^2, (\overline{S} - C^1)(1+g)) - W^2 N^2] \qquad (58)$$

and the first-order condition for the owner's optimal choice of N^1 becomes

$$P\partial C(N,S)/\partial N - W = (1 - \phi)q \qquad (59)$$

which differs from the condition for the socially optimal choice in equation (5) by the inclusion of the term $(1 - \phi)$ on the right-hand side. Inspection of Figure 30 shows that N^1 increases steadily with ϕ. The owner of the lake has less and less incentive to show restraint in his exploitation of the lake today, as he has less and less chance of reaping the benefit of that restraint tomorrow.

3   Externalities can be classified according to the number of people affected, with direct person-to-person externalities at one end of the scale and common property at the other. The examples mentioned in the text are about externalities that affect common property. Meade's famous story of the apples and the bees and Coase's story of cows wandering among the farmer's crops are about direct person-to-person externalities. See J. Meade, "External Economies and Diseconomies in a Competitive Situation", *Economic Journal*, 1952, and R. Coase, "The Problem of Social Cost", *Journal of Law and Economics*, 1960. The significance of the distinction between these two types of externalities is that direct person-to-person externalities can often be eliminated by the assignment of the appropriate property rights, either to the perpetrator of the externality or to the victim. Consider the farmer and herder example. If the farmer has the property right, then the herder must keep his cattle off the farmer's field unless the parties can strike a bargain in which the farmer is compensated for the damage to his crops. If the herder has the

property right, then the farmer may not interfere with cattle grazing in his field unless the parties can strike a bargain in which the herder is compensated for the loss of revenue from his herd. In either case, the outcome of the bargain is Pareto optimal, though the distribution of benefits between the parties is not the same. There can be no such bargaining when the externality takes the form of a deterioration of common property, for it is in the nature of common property that nobody can be found to pay the perpetrator of the externality to desist. W. Baumol, "On Taxation and the Control of Externalities", *American Economic Review*, 1972, 307–22. When individual property rights cannot be established in the first place, they cannot be bargained away.

4 Public property in the context of immigration is discussed in D. Usher, "Public Property and the Effects of Migration upon Other Residents of the Migrants' Countries of Origin and Destination", *Journal of Political Economy*, 1977, 151–68.

5 The adverse effect of population growth upon income per head could be counterbalanced by economies to scale. In the example of the two families in the text, it was assumed that the total income from common property is unaffected by the size of the population, so that population growth lowers income per head. The force of the example would remain undiminished if total output increased with population (because the work force increases too) as long as output per person declines as a consequence of the diminishing marginal product of labour. However, population growth need not lead to a reduction in output per head if the rate of technical change were an increasing function of the absolute size of the work force or of the absolute size of the corps of scientists and engineers. For an argument that this is actually the case, see Julian Simon, *The Ultimate Resource*, Princeton University Press, 1981.

I remain unpersuaded. Certainly the national income has more than kept pace with population in many countries, but the causal connection may be from income to population, not the other way round, as the scale argument would require. A more plausible story is that exogenous technical change (where exogenous in this context means no more than that the rate of technical change is more or less unaffected by the rate of population growth) leads to an increase in the national income which, in turn, makes possible a high rate of population growth. I believe that income per head would be larger in most countries today — especially the poor countries — if there were fewer people to contend with. There would be more capital per person. There would be more land, more forests and more minerals per person. Land and resources may have once been so abundant that their marginal products were virtually zero, but that has not been so for many, many years.

6 The story would not be changed significantly if it were assumed that marginal cost declines with output.

7 In writing this section, I have benefited greatly from conversations with my colleague John Hartwick, who has made a deep study of resources and invention, and with three former students at Queen's, Jeroen Swinkles, Irene Henriques and Perry Sadorsky. Anything which may appear both original and correct in this section is probably due to one of them. On prizes and rivalry in research and prospecting, see R.R. Nelson, "Uncertainty, Learning and the Economics of Parallel Research and Development Efforts", *Review of Economics and Statistics*, 1961, 351–64; P. Tandon, "Rivalry and the Excessive Allocation of Resources to Research", *Bell Journal of Economics*, 1983, 152-65; J. Hartwick, "Efficient Prizes in

Prototype Development Contests", *Economic Letters*, 1982, 375–79; J. Brander and B. Spencer, "Strategic Commitment with R & D: the Symmetric Case", *Bell Journal of Economics*, 1983, 225–35; and J. Swinkels, "Efficiency of Innovative Activity", B.A. thesis in Economics, Queen's University, 1985; Irene M. Henriques, "Four Essays on Research and Development and Spillovers", Ph.D. thesis, Queen's University, 1990; Perry A. Sadorsky, "Three Essays on the Exploration for Non-Renewable Resources", Ph.D. thesis, Queen's University, 1990.

8 The example in the text is a modification of the model developed by Y. Barzel in "Optimal Timing of Innovations", *Review of Economics and Statistics*, 1968, 348–55.

9 The concept of rent-seeking was introduced by Gordon Tullock in "The Welfare Costs of Tariffs, Monopolies and Theft", *Western Economic Journal*, 1967, 224–32. The name "rent-seeking" first appeared in Ann Krueger, "The Political Economy of a Rent-seeking Society", *American Economic Review*, 1974, 29–303. Somehow the name stuck. This is a pity, for, in my opinion, the term "rent-seeking" is one of the least expressive terms in the entire lexicon of economics. First, the term employs an arcane usage of the word "rent". Rent in common speech means the return to property, the income of the landlord. Rent in the context of rent-seeking means a return to any factor in excess of its alternative cost. Second, one may seek rents, in the latter sense of the term, in ways that have nothing to do with rent-seeking as the expression is commonly employed. One seeks rent in one's choice of occupation; one hopes to find a job that is just right in the sense of being distinctly preferable to the next best alternative. One seeks rent when one enters an especially profitable business venture. Firms always seek rent, in ordinary commercial transactions and in their dealings with government; there is nothing in the term "rent-seeking" to suggest the wasteful competition for public favour that the term has recently come to mean. A number of important papers on rent-seeking, including the two cited above, are included in James Buchanan, *et al.*, *Toward a Theory of the Rent-seeking Society*, Texas A & M University Press, 1980.

10 Steven McGee is the leading proponent of the view that predatory pricing is an illusion. See his "Predatory Price Cutting: the Standard Oil (N.J.) Case", *Journal of Law and Economics*, 1958, 137–69, as well as "Predatory Pricing Revisited", *Journal of Law and Economics*, 1980, 289–330. Specialists in industrial organization have talked about predatory pricing for many years. The recent revival of interest in the subject is an offshoot of game theory which has proved useful in specifying the conditions under which predatory pricing might be profitable. In "The Chain Store Paradox" (*Theory and Decision*, 1978, 127–59), Reinhard Selten showed that predatory behaviour cannot be part of an equilibrium between an incumbent monopolist and a *finite group* of potential challengers, where, one by one, the potential challengers have to choose to take on the monopolist in some sub-market or to desist from doing so. The case against an equilibrium with predatory pricing is an argument by induction. At the last challenge, it would clearly be in the interest of the monopolist to cooperate rather than to fight. That being the case, the second-to-last challenger would have no fear of entering the market because the monopolist, who will cooperate at the last round, has every incentive to cooperate at the second-to-last round as well. And so on, until cooperative behaviour — as distinct from predatory pricing — becomes the monopolist's equilibrium response at every stage. Selten refers to this as a paradox because, notwithstanding his counter-example, he believes that predatory pricing would be practised and would be profitable to the predator in this situation. For myself, I do not find the example entirely convincing. The example shows the impossibility of a "sub-game perfect" equilibrium in which nobody can commit himself to actions that will be disadvantageous at the time when they are to be undertaken; I think such commitments are sometimes possible. The example is of a finite chain of challenges; I do not see that it applies to cases where no "last" challenge can be identified. It has been argued by David M. Kreps and Robert Wilson ("Reputation and Imperfect Information", *Journal of Economic Theory*, 1982, 253–79) and by Paul Milgrom and John Roberts ("Predation Reputation and Entry Deterrence", *Journal of Economic Theory*, 1982, 280–312) that Selten's result can be broken by abandoning *either* the assumption that challengers have full information about the costs of the incumbent monopolist *or* the assumption that the monopolist must behave "rationally". In either case, predatory pricing by the monopolist today provides the monopolist with a reputation for predatory behaviour that may be sufficient to deter challenges tomorrow. The entire debate is reviewed in Louis Philips, *The Economics of Imperfect Information*, Cambridge University Press, 1988, chapter 7.

11   Harold Hotelling, "The General Welfare in Relation to Problems of Taxation and Utility Rates", *Econometrica*, 1938, 242–69.

12   Differentiating π in equation (14) by x and A, we see that

$$\pi_x = (P'x + P - c)n = 0$$

and that

$$\pi_A = (P(x) - c)x \, dn/dA - 1 = 0$$

from which equations (15) and (16) follow immediately. Equation (15) is a modification of a formula first derived by R. Dorfman and P. Steiner in "Optimal Advertising and Optimal Quality", *American Economic Review*, 1954.

13   The *locus classicus* of this argument is G. Stigler and G. Becker, "De Gustibus non est Disputandum", *American Economic Review*, March 1977. In this article, psychic quality is treated as a stock rather than as a flow. Welfare is $u(z) + y$, as is assumed here, but z is made to depend on cumulative advertising rather than on current advertising. Specifically $z = Sx$ where

$$S = g \left(\sum_{t=0}^{\infty} \frac{A_t}{(1+r)^t} \right)$$

where A_t is advertising undertaken t years ago and where r is the rate of deterioration of past advertising. My treatment of psychic quality follows L. Nichols, "Advertising and Economic Welfare", *American Economic Review*, March 1985. Note that the capitalization of advertising is no protection against false taste, as discussed below.

14   Replacing y in equation (30) with its value in equation (33), the social welfare function of the typical person becomes

$$W = u(z_1, z_2) + I - c_1 z_1 q^1(A_1, A_2) - c_2 z_2 q^2(A_1, A_2) - A_1/N - A_2/N$$

The first-order conditions are:

$$W_{z_1} = u_1 - c_1 q^2 = 0$$

$$W_{z_2} = u_2 - c_2 q^2 = 0$$

$$W_{A_1} = -c_1 z_1 q_1^1 - c_2 z_2 q_1^2 - 1/N = 0$$

$$W_{A_2} = -c_1 q_1 q_2^1 - c_2 z_2 q_2^2 - 1/N = 0$$

where q_1^1 means $\partial q^1/\partial A_1$ and so on. The equations for W_{A_1} and W_{A_2} imply that

$$c_1 x_1(q_1^1/q^1) + c_2 x_2(q_1^2/q^2) = -1/N$$

and

$$c_1 x_1(q_2^1/q^1) + c_2 x_2(q_2^2/q^2) = -/N$$

from which equations (37) and (38) in the text follow immediately.

15 Differentiating equation (40) with respect to z_1 and A_1 and observing that $z_2 = x_2 q^2 (A_1, A_2)$ and $\partial z_2/\partial A_1 = x_2 q_1^2$, we obtain the first-order conditions

$$\partial \pi_1/\partial z_1 = u_1 - c_1 q^1 + z_1 u_{11}$$

$$= u_1(1 + z_1 u_{11}/u_1) - c_1 q^1$$

$$= u_1(1 + 1/\varepsilon_{x_1, P_1}) - c_1 q^1 = 0$$

which is equation (41) in the text, and

$$\partial \pi_1/\partial A_1 = z_1(u_{12}\partial z_2/\partial A_1 - c_1 q_1^1)N - 1$$

$$= z_1(u_{12}x_2 q_1^2 - c_1 q_1^1)N - 1$$

$$= -x_1 c_1(q_1^1/q^1)N + z_1(u_{12}z_2/u_1)(q_1^2/q^2)N - 1 = 0$$

which, when multiplied by A_1^m, becomes equation (42) in the text.

16 See A. Dixit and V. Norman, "Advertising and Welfare", *Bell Journal of Economics*, spring 1978. Figure 38 in the text is a modification of a figure in that article.

17 On advertising as a signal see R. Schmalensee, "A Model of Advertising and Product Quality", *Journal of Political Economy*, 1978, 485, and P. Milgrom and J. Roberts, "Price and Advertising Signals of Product Quality", *Journal of Political Economy*, August 1986.

18 This interpretation of speculation is based on the work of Jack Hirschleifer. See his "The Private and Social Value of Information and the Reward for Inventive Activity", *American Economic Review*, 1971 561–74, and "Speculation and Equilibrium: Information, Risk and Markets", *Quarterly Journal of Economics*, 1975, 519–42. In Hirschleifer's model, the role of information is to identify errors in the market's assessment of the odds of different occurrences. For simplicity I adopt the less realistic assumption that the speculator can discover the truth.

19 From the production functions, it follows immediately that the marginal products of labour on alfalfa land and bean land are respectively

$$\frac{1}{2}\left(\frac{K_a}{L_a}\right)^{1/2}$$

and

Table 8   *Shapley values of fair allocation*

Order of entry	Contribution of first party	Contribution of second party	Contribution of third party
[1,2,3]	0	5	11
[1,3,2]	0	12	4
[2,1,3]	4	1	11
[2,3,1]	13	1	2
[3,1,2]	3	12	1
[3,2,1]	13	2	1
Average contribution	5.5	5.5	5

$$\frac{1}{2} B \left(\frac{K_b}{L - L_a} \right)^{1/2}$$

where $K_a = 98$, $K_b = 2$ and $L = 100$. Equating these marginal products, we see that

$$L_a = L \frac{[49/B^2]}{[1 + (49/B^2)]}$$

so that $L_a = 98$ and $L_b = 2$ when $B = 1$, and $L_a = 92.45$ and $L_b = 7.55$ when $B = 2$. Thus, when $B = 2$ and when labour is appropriately distributed between alfalfa land and bean land, the value of alfalfa production is \$95,185, the value of bean production is \$7,772 and the total national income becomes \$102,957. The marginal product of alfalfa land is \$486 per acre, the marginal product of bean land is \$1,943 per acre and the marginal product of labour is \$415 per worker.

20   Léon Walras, *Elements of Pure Economics*, translated by William Jaffe, Allen & Unwin, 1954, 41–2. The first edition of this work appeared in 1874.

21   For an excellent short discussion of fair allocation, see Anatol Rapoport, *N-Person Game Theory*, University of Michigan Press, 1970. For a summary of research on fair or cooperative solutions to the bargaining problem, see chapters 6 and 7 of M. Shubik, *Game Theory in the Social Sciences*, M.I.T. Press, 1983.

22   A utility function reflecting the subject's comportment toward risk may be constructed as follows. Choose any two numbers N and M such that $N \geq M$. Then choose a very low income, $\underline{Y}$, and a very high income, Y. Let $U(\underline{Y}) \equiv M$ and $U(\overline{Y}) \equiv N$. For any income, Y, between $\underline{Y}$ and $\overline{Y}$, let $U(Y) = M + \pi(N - M)$, where π is determined as follows: π is a probability such that the person to whom the function applies is indifferent between (i) a certainty of an income Y and (ii) a probability π of having an income $\overline{Y}$ and a probability $(1 - \pi)$ of having an income $\underline{Y}$. Any linear transformation of the utility function $U(Y)$ is equivalent to a different choice of M and N. It can be shown that the utility functions corresponding to all arbitrary choices of M, N, $\underline{Y}$ and $\overline{Y}$ are linear transformations of one another as long as the person to whom the utility functions belong is consistent in his behaviour. See H. Raiffa, *Decision Analysis*, Random House, 1968.

23   J.F. Nash Jr, "The Bargaining Problem", *Econometrica*, 1950, 155–62.

24 Fairness as contribution is discussed in Rapoport's *N-Person Game Theory*.

25 The Shapley values are constructed as shown in Table 8.

26 See J. Sutton, "Non-cooperative Bargaining Theory: an Introduction", *Review of Economic Studies*, 1986, 709–24.

27 On this phenomenon, see T. Schelling, "An Essay on Bargaining" in *The Strategy of Conflict*, Harvard University Press, 1960. The second party agrees in these conditions as long as he is not concerned about a loss of reputation for toughness, which may affect his ability to deal with other negotiations in the future.

28 See K. Arrow and F. Hahn, *General Competitive Analysis*, Holden-Day, 1971, chapter 5, section 6, and J. Hirschleifer, "Investment Decisions under Uncertainty: Choice Theoretic Approaches" and "Investment Decisions under Uncertainty: Applications of the State Preference Approach", *Quarterly Journal of Economics*, 1965, 1966.

29 The source of this example is G. Akerlof, "The Market for Lemons: Qualitative Uncertainty and the Market Mechanism", *Quarterly Journal of Economics*, 1970, 488–500.

30 J.E. Stiglitz, "The Causes and Consequences of the Dependence of Quality on Price", *Journal of Economic Literature*, 1987, 1–48.

31 M. Rothschild and J. Stiglitz, "Equilibrium in Competitive Insurance Markets: an Essay on the Economics of Imperfect Information", *Quarterly Journal of Economics*, 1976, 629–50.

32 M. Spence, "Job Market Signaling", *Quarterly Journal of Economics*, 1973, 355–74.

33 There is a vast literature on malfeasance in the private sector. The subject is often referred to as "the principal-agent problem". See, for example, G. Becker and G. Stigler, "Law Enforcement, Malfeasance and the Compensation of Enforcers", *Journal of Legal Studies*, 1974, 1–18; S. Ross, "The Economic Theory of Agency: the Principal's Problem", *American Economic Review*, 1973, 134–9; M. Jensen and W. Meckling, "The Theory of the Firm's Managerial Behaviour: Agency Costs and Ownership Structure", *Journal of Financial Economics*, 1976, 305–60. The example in the text is a modification of an example in Becker and Stigler.

34 C. Eaton and W. White, "Agent Compensation and the Limits of Bonding", *Economic Inquiry*, 1982, 330–43.

35 E. Lazear and S. Rosen, "Rank-order Tournaments as Optimum Labour Contracts", *Journal of Political Economy*, 1981, 841–64.

36 The inevitable incompleteness of contracts, and the consequences of that incompleteness in actual markets, have been studied in detail in O.E. Williamson, *The Economic Institutions of Capitalism*, Collier-Macmillan, 1985. On the subject of contracts, I have benefited considerably from conversations with my colleague John Baldwin.

37 For an excellent collection of readings on the role of one-sided information and malfeasance as explanations of wage stickiness and of involuntary unemployment, see G. Akerlof and J. Yellen, eds., *Efficiency Wage Models of the Labour Market*, Cambridge University Press, 1986.

38 This consideration has been alleged to lie at the core of Keynesian economics. See Axel Leijonhufvud, *Keynesian Economics and the Economics of Keynes*, Oxford University Press, 1968.

39 Suppose all workers are equally skilled and are willing to accept employment at a wage $\bar{w}$. Firms cannot obtain workers at a wage less than $\bar{w}$, though, of course, firms could pay more if they wished to do so. When the price of the product is P, the firm's profit as a function of the number of workers, n, becomes

$$\pi = Pf(e(w)n) - wn$$

where w is the wage actually paid rather than the minimum workers are prepared to accept. Transforming labour input and wage into efficiency units, the profit function becomes

$$\pi = Pf(m) - vm$$

where $m \equiv e(w)n$ and $v \equiv w/e(w)$. The firm chooses m such that $Pf' = v$. It chooses the lowest possible value of v, which is not the same as choosing the lowest value of w that workers are prepared to accept. The two are only the same when

$$\frac{dv}{dw} = \frac{e(w) - we'(w)}{e(w)^2} > 0$$

a condition which is reversed whenever the elasticity of the efficiency wage with respect to the actual wage $[e'w/e]$ is greater than 1. This elasticity is likely to be low when wages are high, but it may exceed 1 when wages are low.

40 D.H. Robertson, *Control of Industry*, p. 85.

41 Ronald Coase, "The Nature of the Firm" in G. Stigler and K. Boulding, *AEA Readings in Price Theory* (reprint of an article from *Economica*, 1937). The sentence in the text is a compound of quotations from pp. 334 and 337.

42 The role of the residual income claimant has been stressed by Frank Knight in *Risk, Uncertainty and Profit*, 1921. The quotation below is from p. 271 of the reprint by the London School of Economics (No. 16 in the series of Reprints of Scarce Tracts in Economic and Political Science).

The essence of enterprise is the specialization of the function of responsible direction of economic life, the neglected feature of which is the inseparability of these two elements, responsibility and control. Under the enterprise system, a special social class, the business men, direct economic activity; they are in the strict sense the producers, while the great mass of the population merely furnish them with productive services, placing their persons and their property at the disposal of this class; the entrepreneurs also guarantee to those who furnish productive services a fixed remuneration. Accurately to define these functions and trace them through the social structure will be a long task, for the specialization is never complete; but at the end of it we shall find that in a free society the two are essentially inseparable. Any degree of effective exercise of judgment, or making decisions, is in a free society coupled with a corresponding degree of uncertainty-bearing, of taking the responsibility of those decisions.

With the specialization of function goes also differentiation of reward. The produce of society is similarly divided into two kinds of income, and two only, contractual income, which is essentially rent, as economic theory has described incomes, and residual income or profit.

43 This aspect of ownership has been stressed particularly in A.A. Alchain and H. Demsetz, "Production, Information Cost, and Economic Organization", *American Economic Review*, 1972, 777–95. On reading the different explanations for the existence of the firm, one is reminded of the old tale of the blind men and the elephant.

44 A recent law case illustrates this beautifully. The Canadian Tire Corporation is a franchiser of hardware and automotive stores. Each dealer uses the Canadian Tire name and buys products from the company but is otherwise privately owned and, within the rules of the franchise, independent. To keep a tight control on his business, the founder of Canadian Tire financed the firm with a large proportion of non-voting shares and a small proportion of voting shares, which he held himself. On the death of the founder, his children offered to sell their voting shares to an association of the dealers. The dealers offered to pay the family $160 per share for their voting shares at a time when non-voting shares were selling for $20. The holders of non-voting shares claimed that the proposed sale was illegal because of a provision in the contract between the corporation and the holders of the non-voting shares that the non-voting shares would acquire voting rights in the event of a transfer of control of the firm. Holders of the non-voting shares claimed that the dealers might not buy the corporation unless they were prepared to buy all the shares at the same price. The legal question was complex and irrelevant to our concerns. The point is that holders of non-voting shares believed that their shares would not be worth much if the dealers controlled the company. *Globe and Mail*, 11 December, 1986, section B, 1–2.

45 Two firms control the South African diamond cartel, the Anglo-American Corporation and De Beers. Anglo-American controls 33 per cent of the shares of De Beers, 7 per cent directly and another 26 per cent through the Anglo-American Investment Trust, which is 52 per cent owned by the Anglo-American Corporation. De Beers, on the other hand, owns 38 per cent of the Anglo-American Corporation. Thus 17 per cent private ownership of the two corporations would be sufficient for absolute and unchallengeable control once the boards of directors of the two corporations were in the right hands. A smaller percentage would probably be sufficient in practice. The percentages are from *The Economist*, 1 July 1989, p. 60.

46 See G.M. Grossman, "Union Wages, Temporary Layoffs, and Seniority", *American Economic Review*, 1983, 277–90.

Chapter VIII

The public sector in a liberal society

What should governments do? What should governments desist from doing? Consideration of these questions will occupy the rest of the book. Though simply stated, the questions themselves are somewhat ambiguous. Four aspects of these questions should be identified before we proceed to the questions themselves.

(i) The questions are posed with reference to some notion of the common good; otherwise the questions make no sense at all.

(ii) The answers must depend in part on the technical and behavioural constraints in society.

(iii) The answers must depend on the extent to which governments can be expected to recognize the common good as a criterion for their actions.

(iv) The effects of public policy are not confined to the welfare of the citizen within an invariant set of institutions; public policy can affect the institutions themselves and may do so in ways that are not intended by the policy-makers.

Questions about what governments should do or desist from doing are posed in the context of a conversation among citizens, a conversation that cannot proceed unless each citizen is prepared to recognize that public policy must balance his interests against the interests of his neighbours. We cannot usefully talk to one another about public policy unless each person is prepared to recognize a standard over and above his own personal gain. Furthermore, the weighting of the interests of all citizens in the determination of public policy, and the recognition of a common good as implied in that weighting, are for all practical purposes equivalent to the specification of a social welfare function.

One may be uncomfortable with the notion of the social welfare function, but there is no escape from it. Any statement to the effect that such-and-such an organization of society is better than the alternatives is logically equivalent to a statement about levels of social welfare. Without a postulated social welfare function or some equivalent construction lurking in the background, one cannot evaluate public policy at all. The social welfare function may be nothing more than a specification of one's sense of the common good, a criterion over and above crude self-interest and without which talk about what government ought to do or about how society ought to be organized is foolishness and hypocrisy. To employ a social welfare function in this sense of the term is not to deny that each person may have his own unique sense of the common good. Nor is it to postulate the existence of a God-given function that the public sector must seek to maximize. Nor is it to suppose that the public sector seeks to maximize the value of the social welfare function without regard to political pressures or to the self-interests of officials, politicians and soldiers. The social welfare function is requirement and prerequisite for discourse about the economy, for, in strict logic, one cannot claim that the government is not acting properly without a concept or notion of what the proper actions of government would be.

Over and above the specification of the common good, a determination of appropriate public policy requires a specification of the constraints to public action. There is a lesson to be learned from the standard method of analysis of economics, in which optimal decisions, public or private, are derived as the maximization of an objective function subject to constraints. In the discipline of public finance, upon which this chapter draws to a very great extent, the appropriate form of taxation is made to depend upon the behaviour of self-interested taxpayers in reorganizing their affairs to limit the size of the tax bill; the best tax in the absence of diversionary measures by the taxpayer is not necessarily the best tax when these are taken into account. The choice among alternative ways of redistributing income to the poor is not independent of the manoeuvres of potential recipients to make themselves eligible. A publicly administered old age pension was unthinkable in the Middle Ages when the administrative machinery was unavailable and could not be constructed. It is desired by the great majority of citizens in many countries today, and it may become inappropriate tomorrow for as yet unanticipated reasons.

At a minimum, the study of despotism in Chapter IV served to emphasize that governments are at least partly self-serving and that the common assumption in much of the literature of public finance that governments choose their actions to maximize the value of a social welfare function may be dangerously misleading.[1] It is one thing to discuss public policy with reference to a notion of the common good; it is quite another to suppose that the government knows no other criterion. The social welfare function is a devious construction which can lead the unwary to forget that people differ in their assessments of the common good, that the best policy for a benevolent, omniscient and omnipotent government (such as is often postulated in the economic analysis of the public sector) is not necessarily the appropriate policy for the partly responsible, partly self-seeking governments of fallible men which are the best we can hope for in this imperfect world, that optimal welfare-maximizing policy is in practice unattainable and that crude self-interest is not confined to the private sector. One may recognize an ideal for the evaluation of public policy without at the same time supposing that actual governments are likely to be guided by that ideal exclusively in their actions from day to day. In discussing public policy, it is essential to avoid what was referred to in Chapter I as the displacement fallacy: the displacement of the social welfare function from the conscience of the citizen judging policy to the criterion of the government of the day.

The displacement fallacy is at the core of a dichotomy in traditional welfare economics between public sector altruism and private sector greed. Within the market, agents are assumed to deploy their resources selfishly, the consumer in choosing goods to maximize the value of a utility function that takes no account of the circumstances of his neighbours, and the property owner in maximizing the return from his resources or his firm regardless of the consequences of his actions upon workers, the environment or the nation as a whole. But let the agents enter the public sector, and they are assumed to behave quite differently. No longer do they engage in the single-minded pursuit of their own income and pleasure. They become public-spirited; they serve the common interest exclusively; they maximize a social welfare function which is, if not the will of God, then a manifestation of the conscience of mankind.

This view is, in my opinion, not altogether wrong. There is a degree of altruism in most people, an altruism more likely to show itself in public affairs than in private business dealings. Man really is a social animal to some extent. But the dichotomy between public sector altruism and private sector greed is the wrong starting point for the study of the scope of the public sector in the liberal society or for the analysis of departures from efficiency in the public sector. The liberal society is defined by the conjunction of private property in the economy and voting by majority rule in the legislature. The starting-point for our study of the liberal society is the assumption that people are no less selfish as voters than as participants in the market. While not denying that there is a degree of decency, honour and public-spiritedness in most men, I claim that it would be contrary to the purpose of our investigation and imprudent in the extreme to assess the role of government on the premise that no other sentiments need be considered.

From the discussion of the liberal society in Chapter V and the discussion of transitions in Chapter VI we bring the propositions that the institutions of the liberal society are fragile and that the viability of the liberal society may depend in part on what the government chooses to do. Though the analysis is far less precise and satisfactory in its implications than I would like it to be, it does inculcate a sense of caution, an appreciation of the fact that public policy may have consequences well beyond the usual range of considerations in economic analysis, and, perhaps, a reluctance to employ the public sector unless the measurable advantages of doing so are overwhelming.

The division of labour between this chapter and the next is that this chapter concentrates upon the tasks of government and on the cost of using the public sector, while the next chapter deals with the role of self-interest within the public sector and to some extent with the effect of public policy on the institutions of the liberal society. Of course, these matters can never be disentangled altogether, but it is expedient to discuss them sequentially. Following well worn grooves in public finance, the list of tasks includes the protection of property, the provision of public goods, correction for market failure and the redistribution of income. Items on the list are discussed under the tentative assumption that the government is reasonably efficient and more or less devoted to the welfare of the citizen. Among the costs are the classical deadweight in taxation as taxpayers divert effort from high-productivity, highly taxed activities to low-productivity, less highly taxed activities, and the corresponding inefficiencies on the expenditure side of the budget. There is some discussion of the inevitable conflict between the rights of people as voters and the rights of people as property-holders, with special reference to the principle of eminent domain and to cost-benefit analysis. The chapter concludes with a discussion of giving and taking by the public sector.

The tasks of the public sector

The enforcement of property rights

Whatever else it may do, the government must enforce the rules for the allocation of the national income among citizens, in accordance with the returns to one's property or on some other principle altogether. The government must take steps to avoid a condition of anarchy where a significant portion of the resources of the society are devoted to the squabble over the apportionment of goods among people rather than to the production of goods. The first and fundamental task of government is to provide the police, the judges and the prisons without which civilization is impossible. Romantics may wish that these instruments of coercion were unnecessary, but, faced with a choice of occupying the place of a randomly chosen person in a society with public protection of property or in a society without public protection of property, it is doubtful that even romantics would opt for the latter.

Enforcement of property rights can be represented as the suppression of banditry in a development of the model of despotism in Chapter IV. A valuable feature of the model in the present context is that the enforcement of property rights need not be complete. Banditry is suppressed to

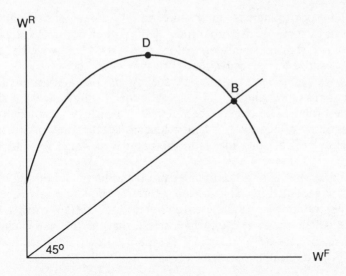

Figure 48   The welfare of rulers and farmers in a despotic society (D) and in a society with a benevolent government (B)

a great extent — and farmers are typically better off on that account than they would be in a state of anarchy — but banditry is not eliminated altogether. What needs to be modified in the model of despotism is the potentially large disparity between the income of rulers and that of ordinary citizens.

Specifically, let the three social classes be farmers, bandits and policemen instead of farmers, bandits and rulers as in the original model of despotism. Think of the policemen, not just as ordinary cops, but as law enforcement officers of all kinds, including judges, legislators and prison officials. Then make the assumption, consistent with the general premise in this chapter, that the governors rule in the interest of the governed. The parameters of the model — the tax rate, the number of policemen and their wages — are chosen to maximize the welfare of farmers (rather than that of rulers as in the model of despotism) with the proviso that policemen are not worse off than farmers. The contrast between benevolent government and despotism is illustrated in Figure 48, with policemen's welfare (W^R) on the vertical axis and farmers' welfare (W^F) on the horizontal axis. The figure shows the locus of feasible combinations of W^R and W^F, where W^R is maximal for every value of W^F. With a given number of policemen in a world without banditry or tax-induced disincentives to labour, the curve connecting W^R and W^F would have to be a downward sloping straight line, for taxation of farmers is just a dollar-for-dollar transfer of income from farmers to policemen. Otherwise total output shrinks as policemen seek to increase their share, and the curve connecting W^R and W^F acquires some of the properties of the Laffer curve. As drawn, the curve is hive-shaped, signifying that there is a limit below which farmers' incomes cannot be reduced without dragging down the incomes of policemen as well. One way or another, society chooses among the feasible combinations of W^R and W^F. In a despotic society, the policemen are self-interested rulers who choose the point D at which W^R is maximized regardless of the value of W^F. A benevolent society that does not favour one social class over another moves to the point B at which W^R and W^F are equal.

The curve in Figure 48 can be derived from the model of despotism in Table 2 as modified in Table 4. Reinterpret the tables so that R refers to policemen rather than rulers. Leave equations (1) to (20) exactly as they are, but delete equation (21), which stated that the tax rate is chosen to maximize the income of rulers, W^R, come what may. Replace it with an equation of the form

$$W^R = \alpha W^F \qquad \text{(21' with reference to Table 4)}$$

where α is a constant which may be thought of as the slope of a line through the origin in Figure 48. The curve in the figure becomes the locus of combinations of W^F and W^R corresponding to all possible a. Benevolent government is that for which $\alpha = 1$; equation (21') is then representable by a line at 45° from the origin.

Part of the task of protecting property rights is to specify crimes and prescribe punishments. The choice of the severity of punishment could be ignored in our discussion of anarchy and despotism in Chapters III and IV because it was assumed that all crime is punishable by execution, an assumption which was hardly realistic but which did serve to simplify an already complex model designed to cast light on other aspects of society. In a liberal society the choice of punishments for the different crimes is an intricate trade-off between the effect of severity of punishment as a deterrent to crime[2] and a mix of considerations which, together, may be thought of as the cost of severity. A crime may be deterred by a high probability of conviction coupled with a small penalty or by a low probability of conviction coupled with a high penalty. Thus an increase in the severity of penalties can generally be expected either to decrease the incidence of crime when the probability of detection is constant or to permit a decrease in the probability — and the cost — of detection with no corresponding increase in the incidence of crime. Among the constraints upon the severity of punishment are the risk of an innocent person being convicted by mistake,[3] the incentive on the part of the criminal to commit large, profitable crimes instead of small, less profitable crimes unless the punishment for the latter is less severe,[4] the incentive on the part of the criminal to commit additional crimes in the attempt to avoid detection,[5] the fact that it may be socially desirable to commit certain crimes in extreme circumstances,[6] the mores of the community as manifested in the unwillingness of policemen to make arrests and the unwillingness of juries to convict the guilty when the punishment is seen as excessive,[7] and the danger, when small crimes entail a small probability of a large penalty, of placing a great deal of discretionary power in the hands of the police.

The specification of property rights

Ideally, each person's rights, including ordinary property rights, rights conferred by patents, rights acquired through private contracts, rights of beneficiaries of government programmes and civil rights of all kinds, should be so well defined that it is obvious to everyone when they are violated. The role of government with regard to rights could then be limited to enforcement. In an imperfect and ever-changing world, that can never be the case. Try as it may to define rights exactly, the government inevitably finds itself obliged to clarify ambiguities in the structure of rights, to modify existing rights and to invent new rights from time to time. The well specified property rights in the proof of the Pareto optimality of the competitive equilibrium are ideal in the double sense that they constitute a limit that is approached by actual property rights in actual markets to a greater or lesser extent, and that they constitute a goal of public policy in legislation and administration. The public sector is often compelled to act whenever that goal is not fully attained.

The rights of property are not rights of people over things; they are rights of people over other people regarding the usage of things. As such, the rights of property are inevitably limited in scope. The boundaries of property rights must change from time to time, giving rise to conflicts among interested parties that only the government can resolve. One cannot help suspecting that somewhere in the origins of most of the large fortunes is to be found an indispensable public decision that conveyed property rights where none was thought to exist or that favoured one party over another. Consider these cases:

(i) Zoning laws are always subject to interpretation and revision by the city council. The value of my property depends to a greater or lesser extent on what I am allowed to do with it and what my neighbour is allowed to do with his. The skill of the developer is, in large measure, his ability to persuade the city council that his proposal is good for the city. Substantial resources are devoted to that endeavour.

(ii) Patent law distinguishes between inventions that can be patented and scientific discoveries that cannot. This distinction is never so precise that it is obvious to everyone when a new invention has been made. Prior to a U.S. Supreme Court decision on the subject, it was uncertain whether new micro-organisms developed by genetic engineering would be covered by patents. The Court's decision to allow the patenting of micro-organisms created property rights where none existed before, enhanced the fortunes of those in a favourable position to occupy the new rights, and more than justified a considerable expenditure on litigation. The computer chip gave rise to litigation of a different kind. The courts had to decide between an early but incompletely designed model of the computer chip and a slightly later but better designed version. A decision of the lower court was reversed on appeal, signifying, if nothing else, that it was not obvious who had the right to the patent.[8]

(iii) Redistribution of income typically conveys ambiguous property rights. My entitlement to an old age pension is no less my property than my entitlement to my house. Both are mine because the laws decree that they are mine and protect me from arbitrary seizure of these goods by the government of the day. Both convey rights that are subject to redefinition from time to time. But there is a difference between these rights, in degree if not in kind. Though property taxation and zoning laws may vary, I have reasonable assurance that the rights of house ownership will be approximately the same tomorrow as they are today. The amount of the old age pension, on the other hand, may be high or low as a consequence of a series of political decisions from now until the time of my retirement. In establishing a large publicly supplied old age pension a country creates property rights with consequences that will be determined for each person only as the outcome of a complex political bargain between the old and the young at the time when he is retired. There is a similar difficulty with unemployment insurance, national health insurance and other redistributive activities, a difficulty which is not in itself sufficient to warrant the abandonment of these measures, but which should be weighed in the balance along with other considerations in the evaluation of proposals for reform.[9]

(iv) Protection of property, broadly defined, includes the enforcement of rights acquired by patents on inventions, by copyright on literary or artistic production and by contract. When two or more parties sign a contract of a kind that the state is willing to enforce, they necessarily impose on the state an obligation to enforce compliance with the terms of the contract in the event that one party fails to discharge his obligations. In connection with this obligation, the government must decide which contracts ought to be enforced. No government is prepared to enforce a contract in which a person sells himself into slavery or is obliged to commit an illegal act. Choosing which contracts to enforce is a weighing of the benefits to the contracting parties, the costs or benefits to third parties of the actions mandated by the contract and the cost to the state of enforcing the contract. Presumably, the contract must be advantageous to the contracting parties, for why else, barring irrationality, would it be signed? A contract need not be advantageous to third parties, and the cost of enforcement cannot always be passed on to the contracting parties themselves. Consider Charles Dickens's England, where, for the sake of the argument, the

maintenance of commerce is assumed to require the threat of imprisonment for failure to pay one's debts. The debtors' prison is a cost to the
state of the enforcement of contracts without which England would have
been a very much less prosperous place. The benefits of the institution
may well have exceeded the cost. Nowadays the balance of costs and
benefits is seen differently, and a contract to pay a debt which one cannot
pay without literally starving oneself and one's family is simply unenforceable.

Public enforcement of private contracts is nowhere more contentious
than in the governance of corporations. Shares of stock in a corporation
differ from ordinary property because the shareholder, as owner, is not
personally liable for the debts of the corporation. In creating a fictitious
person, the state must decide what he is empowered to do. The state must
establish a body of law about the control of the corporation, the obligations of the controlling interest toward minority shareholders, whether
a distinction can be drawn between voting and non-voting shares, the
frequency of stockholders' meetings, proxy voting, poison pills, provision
of information to the public, treatment of workers, bankruptcy, charitable
donations, contributions to political parties, access to labour unions, liability for accidents and so on. The legislature bears the ultimate responsibility
for the legal framework of the corporation, but part of that responsibility
may be delegated to the stock exchange or to the courts. Similarly, labour
unions operate within a framework of rules about such matters as when a
union is certified as the bargaining agent of a group of workers, how union
leaders are chosen, how actively a union may pursue a conflict with employers, and so on.

(v) Contracts cannot be written to provide for every relevant contingency. What rights has A over B when, through no fault of his own, B fails
to meet his obligation under a contract to A? When does A have the right
to refuse to pay B because the service rendered by B is inadequate? Much
of the businessman's time is occupied negotiating about such matters and
a great deal of expensive litigation occurs when negotiation breaks down.[10]
The intrinsic incompleteness of contracts is nowhere more troublesome
than in the private administration of natural monopolies. The right to
operate a telephone service is granted to a private firm because private
provision is expected to be more efficient and cheaper than the direct
operation of the service by the state. On the other hand, a private monopoly of the telephone service can be expected to use its monopoly power
to raise the price of telephone calls above the cost of production. The
telephone company is therefore regulated to control prices without depriving the company of a normal rate of profit on its investment. This
inevitably gives rise to a two-sided risk of malfeasance. The telephone
company has every incentive to pretend that its costs are larger than they
really are and to devote resources to influencing the regulatory agency to

be sympathetic to the company's concerns. The jurisdiction that regulates the company has every incentive to keep the cost of the service low, even if that is tantamount to the gradual expropriation of the assets and the accumulated investment of the company. There is no perfect resolution of this dilemma. The property right of the telephone company is necessarily ambiguous and subject to negotiation at the edges.[11]

(vi) The boundary between the rights of workers and the rights of firms is ill defined. Firms, especially large and impersonal firms, are constrained in their right to hire and fire workers. As a rule, a firm cannot refuse to hire a person for no other reason than the colour of his skin. Workers, once hired, have some tenure in their jobs, varying from full and official tenure for academics and civil servants to the obligation on the part of the firm to compensate certain classes of workers if they are let go, to the rule in many circumstances that workers whose performance on the job is satisfactory cannot be dismissed because they are disliked by their employers. Such general rules can never be unambiguous in their application. They require litigation and they change from time to time in response to changes in the mores of the community.

(vii) The law itself is necessarily ambiguous. Virtually every Supreme Court case attests to the fact that there may be no logical connection between the letter of the law and the resolution of the conflict at hand. The recent conflict between Texaco and Pennzoil turned on whether a contract had actually come into effect. There is every indication that both parties sincerely believed themselves to be in the right, and that the Court's decision, which in effect awarded a substantial portion of one company to the owners of another, came as a complete surprise to the losing party. One might expect that after centuries of litigation there would be little room for dispute as to whether a contract exists, but it was not so.[12]

(viii) The tax structure is itself an aspect of property. Ownership of agricultural land is ultimately the entitlement to a stream of income from the rent of that land, and the value of the rent depends critically on whether the crops are subsidized or taxed. It is probably fair to say that at least half the value of agricultural land in America and Western Europe is capitalized subsidy and that farmers' incomes are largely dependent upon decisions in the public sector. The same is true to a greater or lesser degree of every industry and occupation.

It is in this context that one should place the concept of horizontal equity. Tax systems might be used — and have on occasion been used — to overturn property rights completely. Property is not property unless it governs the allocation of the national income, at least to some extent. The connection between property and income is severed when a government is prepared to establish *ad hominem* taxation, or to impose a special tax on a particular social class up to the limit of what would otherwise be its full income. In practice, taxation always bears more heavily on some people than on others, if only because people differ in their ability to escape from tax into leisure or do-it-yourself production. The ideal of horizontal equity is that the tax system should be designed to minimize discrimination among taxpayers so that each person pays his "fair" share of the cost of public sector expenditure.[13]

(ix) Government bears the responsibility for a large corpus of rules that create, limit and modify the right to practise certain occupations. The usual rationale for these rules — such as the restriction of the right to practise medicine to those who have graduated from approved medical schools and have passed the qualifying exams of the College of Physicians — is that users of the services of practitioners would not otherwise know who is skilled and who is not. Opinions differ as to how far that argument goes. Licensing is necessarily the denial of the right to enter an occupation to people who would like to do so, and it is not infrequently an instrument of monopolization. The risk of monopolization — of restricting entry to a trade or profession to raise the incomes of practitioners — is particularly great when governments delegate the setting of standards to an organization representing the members of the profession. Professional organizations with the authority to screen out unsuitable applicants have the means to do so but the incentive to exclude many suitable applicants as well.

Rule-making necessarily involves the government in jurisdictional disputes. Practitioners of every licensed trade have an interest in extending the range of its functions, for the degree of monopoly power depends on the proportion between the number of people allowed into a trade and the range of tasks that practitioners of the trade are entitled to perform. The carpenters' union and the plumbers' union conflict over the right to build wooden supports for pipes. Doctors try to abolish or circumscribe the right of midwives to deliver babies. Lawyers try to guard the right to transfer residential property from seller to buyer. My favourite jurisdictional dispute is between doctors and podiatrists over the definition of a foot.

Though no government could divest itself altogether of its rule-making obligations, every government has a good deal of leeway in deciding where to impose rules and where not. Anti-trust laws may be strict, moderate or non-existent. The list of licensed occupations may be long or short. The circumstances under which the courts are prepared to intervene in disputes between firms and labour unions may be many or few. Optimal regulation may depend to a large extent on the honesty of government, as discussed below.

Provision of public goods
As a technical term within the science of economics, "public goods" are goods that enter a person's utility function in a special way. The *total* supply of a public good enters simultaneously into *every* person's utility. By contrast, the total supply of a "private good" is divided up among people,

and each person's portion enters his utility function exclusively. In an economy with n persons and two goods (one public and the other private), the utility function of any person i can be written as $U^i(x_i,G)$, where x_i is *his* consumption of the private good, G is *total* availability of the public good. Total availability of the private good, X, is the sum of the amounts allocated to each person i, that is, $X = \left[\sum_{i=1}^{n} x_i\right]$.

A television signal is a public good in this sense, for my benefit in having a channel available is at nobody else's expense. If I eat one less loaf of bread, that loaf is available to be eaten by somebody else. If I choose not to watch television, the amount of television available to the rest of the community is not at all increased. Uncongested roads are pure public goods, or would be except for the effect of additional traffic on the cost of maintenance. Education is a hybrid of public and private goods. It is a private good in so far as the education of a child enhances his own earning power and enjoyment of life. It is a public good in so far as an educated citizenry is in everyone's interest, for an educated citizenry may be a requirement for economic growth and for the preservation of the values and mores of a liberal society. Within the confines of the farmers, bandits and rulers model, each person's education is a public good if, by enhancing his productivity as a farmer, it makes farming relatively more attractive than banditry and thereby reduces the equilibrium number of bandits, causing the national income to be very much larger than can be accounted for by the increase in productivity alone. (With reference to Figure 8, education may raise the "income of the worker" curve so that the equilibrium moves to the left.)

Pure research yielding information about the laws of nature rather than immediately patentable products is a public good because one person's acquisition of information does not thereby reduce the stock of information available for others to acquire. In fact, knowledge is the most public of all goods, for its benefits are worldwide, and not limited, like those of defence, to any one country. Some aspects of the environment, such as the percentage of greenhouse gases in the atmosphere, can also be thought of as worldwide (positive or negative) public goods.

There is a discrepancy in the provision of public goods between private profitability and social gain. For ordinary private goods, the competitive economy can be trusted to provide the right amounts of each, right in the sense of Pareto optimality that no change in the composition of output could make everybody better off. For public goods, this is not so. Socially advantageous public goods would be under-provided if their production were left to the private sector of a competitive economy, and they might not be provided at all. The reason is that each person is inclined to "buy" public goods up to the point where *his* marginal valuation is just equal to marginal cost, while the right amount of public goods is that for which the *sum of everybody's* marginal valuation is just equal to the marginal cost, a condition reflecting the place of public goods in the utility function.[14] Specifically, the right amount of public goods is that for which

$$\sum_{i=1}^{n} MB_i = MC \tag{1}$$

where n is the number of people in the economy, MB_i is the benefit that person i derives from an extra unit of the public good and MC is the marginal cost of the public good. Equation (1) — known as the Samuelson rule — will be modified and reinterpreted later on in this chapter.

Though the term "public goods" is too entrenched in the lexicon of economics ever to be removed, it is a loaded and, in some respects, misleading term. One and the same term is employed to denote a technical characteristic that a good may or may not possess and to convey a prescription for the role of the public sector. Use of the phrase "public goods" would seem to suggest that these, and only these, goods ought to be provided in the public sector, as though the proper role of government could be determined by the meanings of words rather than by the needs of citizens. Though, in fact, most public goods are, and ought to be, produced by or for the government, some public goods are produced in the private sector, and governments may have good reason to produce or to supply some "private" goods. Public goods, such as roads and bridges, are provided directly by government. So too is basic research. The incentive to undertake applied research is promoted by the granting of a monopoly on inventions. The provision of television, though regulated, can be left within the private sector because television is a vehicle for advertising as well as a source of entertainment. In this instance, a private good for which consumers can be made to pay is piggy-backed on to the "public" good to make private provision profitable.

Obviously a responsibility of government, the provision of security is not quite a public good as the term is ordinarily defined. Consider once again the model of despotism as converted in this chapter into a model of a benevolent government engaged in the suppression of banditry. The natural measure of security is the number of policemen, n^R. For security to be a public good in the strict technical sense of the term, the utility, u^i, function of each person i would have to be of the form $u^i(x_i, n^R)$ where x_i is the consumption of person i of the private good or goods and n^R is total provision of security. The utility function in the model is not like that at all. The utilities of farmers, bandits and rulers (as set out in equations (14) and (15) of Table 2 and in equation (18) of Table 4) are functions of ordinary income, Y, and of personal mortality rates, V, which together can be thought of as components of a vector of private goods x_i. Provision of security, n^R, affects welfare indirectly through the intermediary of the variables Y and V, but there is no direct or additional effect on welfare once the equilibrium values of Y and V have been determined. While it is true that everybody gains more or less equally from the activity of the police, it is still inappropriate to include security together with other ordinary goods and services in the utility function. Such a procedure would be double-counting, because security is a precondition for the acquisition of other goods and services. The value of security is the value of private goods one would not otherwise possess. For security to be a public good, there would have to be a trade-off in production between private goods and security, so that society could have more private goods at the margin if fewer resources were devoted to security. It is the essence of security that the right amount is that for which total provision of private goods is maximized. Nor would it be correct to say that security is a "public" factor of production, for security cannot be combined in a production function together with, for example, labour and machines to yield a certain amount of output.[15]

Rectification of departures from efficiency in the private sector
As discussed in the last chapter, the production of private goods may spin off public goods or bads. A factory upstream pollutes drinking water downstream. Production of electricity causes smog in cities and acid rain that destroys forests miles away. Fertilization of crops releases chemicals into the ecosystem, destroying whole species of animals. Innocent-seeming spray guns for deodorants emit gases that slowly destroy the ozone layer of the atmosphere and subject people to a risk of cancer. Use of fossil fuels for heating, cooking or industrial production, and the conversion of forests into farm land or pasture land, increase the percentage of carbon dioxide in the atmosphere, causing a gradual warming of the earth.

The progress of science and technology over the last few hundred years has provided the Western world with a standard of living and a personal longevity far beyond the wildest dreams of our ancestors. This has been achieved, not just for the few, but for the many. Prosperity has already been extended to much of Asia and to a lesser degree throughout the world. At the same time, the progress of science and technology has made possible a dangerously high rate of world population growth, and yielded substances which, if misused, can literally destroy the basis of life on this planet, as a by-product of war or of ordinary money-making activity. This prospect naturally conveys new regulatory responsibilities to the public sector. Noxious by-products of consumer goods and industrial processes may be regulated by taxation, by subsidization of pollution abatement equipment, by outright prohibition of offending activities or by mandatory use of environmentally friendly technology. Choice of methods is a topic beyond the scope of this book.[16]

Markets can be inefficient in other ways as well. Monopoly pervades the economy, from the corner grocery store with influence upon local prices to large firms with influence upon prices in major sectors of the economy. Efforts by workers and by firms to prevent accidents on the job are likely to be inadequate. Externalities crop up everywhere because everybody is affected to some extent by the activity of his neighbours. Advertising is often harmful on balance. Much of the activity of the businessman is predatory. Vast resources are wasted in bargaining. Speculation can be socially advantageous, but is often no more than the taking by the well informed from the rest of the community. Speculation is advantageous if socially useful information is uncovered in the attempt to foretell which asset prices are due to rise, but there is no guarantee that the value of such information will be commensurate with the resources devoted to speculation. The main product of speculation may be millionaires. There is no corner of the private sector that an omniscient, omnipotent and benevolent dictator could not improve to some extent. Little in the private sector is left untainted in our discussion of departures from efficiency in Chapter VII.

But, as will be discussed in the latter half of this chapter and in Chapter IX, the appropriate course of action in response to departures from efficiency in the private sector must take account of the costs of using the public sector and of the fact that actual governments are not the omnipotent, omniscient and benevolent despots of traditional welfare economics. Where departures from efficiency are large and lethal, the government must act. In other cases, it need not do so. One of the minor themes of this book is our objection to the Pigovian fallacy that *all* departures from efficiency in the private sector ought to be corrected; many departures from efficiency ought not to be corrected because the required public activity would generate greater inefficiencies in their place.

The redistribution of income
There is an unavoidable tension within a liberal society between people's essential equality as voters and their essential inequality as holders of property (where property is defined broadly to include valuable skills as well as land and capital). The source of the tension is that there is no universally accepted line of division between the domains of property and voting. This is in part a conflict between rich and poor. The rich naturally wish to extend the range of things that money can buy, while the poor naturally want citizenship to entail a broad spectrum of rights. The battle is fought over medical care, the old age pension, the progressivity of taxation, access to the media at election time, availability of legal services and so on. For example, public provision of medical care may be more or less inclusive. There may be a small fixed fee for each consultation as a means of discouraging excessive and unnecessary usage of medical service. Dentistry or psychiatry may be covered. Decisions on each of these points

automatically pit the rich against the poor in conflict over the specification of property rights. Each party wishes to expand the domain of its comparative advantage, voting for the poor and property for the rich.

The conflict between the rights of property-holders and the rights of voters is not just a conflict between rich and poor. Ultimately — formal constitutional provisions notwithstanding — a determined and long-lived majority of the voters can do as it pleases with the property of the minority, even if that entails the complete dispossession of one part of the population for the benefit of another. As already discussed in some detail in Chapter V, there are two main reasons why the majority may have an interest in showing restraint. The first is that a society where the rights of property are very severely restricted is likely to be inefficient in the sense of having a lower national income than would otherwise be the case; a majority coalition seeks the optimal trade-off between the size of the pie and the share that is assigned to its members. The second is that a society where a majority is prepared to dispossess a minority completely is unlikely to remain a liberal society. The preservation of a system of voting by majority rule requires that the losers accept the outcome of the vote peacefully and that the faction in power today does not employ the state's monopoly of the means of violence to maintain itself in office indefinitely. That requirement will not be satisfied if a change in government entails the total dispossession of a significant proportion of the population. The only protection for the minority is a system of rights — including property rights — that the party in power is prepared to respect. Property rights can be modified, but not dispensed with altogether if the liberal society is to be preserved. Implicitly or explicitly, voters can often be expected to understand these considerations and to adapt their behaviour accordingly. The conflict between the rights of citizens as voters and the rights of citizens as property-holders does not vanish on that account, but it may, with luck, be contained within manageable bounds.[17]

In this context, a distinction may be drawn between two types of public transfers of income from one group of citizens to another. A transfer may be a systematic narrowing of the income distribution, making the poor richer and rich poorer without altering the ordering of people on the side of rich and poor. This type of transfer is exemplified by an increase in the progressivity of the income tax. Alternatively, a transfer may be from a favoured group to a disfavoured group, regardless of who is rich and who is poor. Rent control and subsidization of farmers are redistributions of this kind.

A good deal of confusion is engendered by the common use of the word "redistribution" to cover both types of transfers. The usage conveys an aura of generosity to policies that are essentially discriminatory. Elsewhere I have suggested that the word "redistribution" be restricted to the narrowing of the gap between rich and poor, and that a new word — I suggested "reassignment" — be employed to denote transfers of income between favoured and unfavoured groups. There is, however, an ambiguity in this terminology. Redistribution and reassignment are not like boxes in which public policies may be unambiguously placed. They are more like the poles of a continuum. Some policies are almost pure redistribution in the sense that the distribution of income is narrowed and hardly anybody changes place on the scale of rich and poor. Other policies have relatively major effects on particular sub-groups of the population and relatively minor effects on the variance of income distribution as a whole. I think that the advantages of the distinction between reassignment and redistribution outweigh the cost of the ambiguity, and I shall, from now on, employ the word "redistribution" in the restricted sense of the term.[18]

There are two main reasons for including redistribution among the minimal functions of government in a liberal society. The first is that some degree of redistribution is desired by the great majority of citizens, regardless of whether they are likely to be net payers to or net receivers from the redistributive system. A listing of the motives for redistribution is the main subject of this section. The second reason is that redistribution of income is self-limiting. None of the motives for redistribution would warrant its extension to the point of full *ex post* equality of income. If A is better off than B before a redistribution of income (as distinct from a reassignment), then A is better off after the redistribution as well, so that a large part of the incentives to work, save and innovate that are the great virtue of property and markets are preserved. The chaos intrinsic to the exploitation problem does not extend to the ordinary redistribution of income.

Motives for the redistribution of income may be characterized under the headings of taking and giving. The former refers to the use of the vote by the poor to modify the privileges of the rich. The latter refers to the willingness of the rich to share some of their good fortune with the poor. These are discussed in turn, with the giving motive subdivided under the heading of insurance, altruism, the prevention of crime and the preservation of the liberal society.

Taking Imagine a society where each person's utility is a function of his consumption, C, and his hours of work, L (i.e. $u = u(C,L)$ such that $u_C > 0$ and $u_L < 0$), where everyone is alike in his tastes, where labour is the only factor of production, and where people differ in skills, so that the gross income, y_i, of person i is given by

$$y_i = s_i L_i \tag{2}$$

The variable L_i is the hours of labour supplied by person i, and s_i is a parameter signifying his level of skill.

Suppose that redistribution in this society is effected by a lump sum transfer of T to each person, financed by a proportional income tax at a rate t, so that each person's consumption, C_i, becomes

$$C_i = (1 - t)y_i + T \tag{3}$$

For convenience, it is assumed that government has no role in the economy other than to redistribute income. Budget balance is represented by the constraint

$$t\bar{y} = T \tag{4}$$

where $\bar{y}$ is average income; the left-hand side of the equation is average revenue, and the right-hand side is average expenditure per person.

The self-limiting property of redistribution as taking by poor voters is a consequence of the fact that total income — the pool available for consumption — is not invariant. The reason is that redistribution typically reduces the incentive to work. Once the government has chosen the redistributive parameters, T and t, each person i chooses his labour supply, L_i, to maximize his utility, $u(C_i,L_i)$ subject to his post-tax, post-transfer budget constraint

$$C_i = (1 - t)s_iL_i + T \tag{5}$$

giving rise to supply of labour functions

$$L_i = L_i(s_i,t,T) \tag{6}$$

with the property that L_i decreases with the size of the transfer (i.e. $\partial L_i/\partial T < 0$). Now, plugging the supply of labour functions of equation (6) into the budget constraint of equation (4), one immediately obtains a function connecting the size of transfer, T, with the rate of taxation required to finance it

$$T = h(t) \tag{7}$$

This function is illustrated in Figure 49 with transfer per person on the vertical axis and the tax rate on the horizontal axis. The function is drawn as an inverted U, signifying that the size of the transfer increases with the rate of tax as long as the tax rate is not too large, but that the possible transfer per head actually falls when the tax rate exceeds some limit. To see this, it is sufficient to observe that nobody would work at all if the tax rate were as high as 100 per cent, in which case there would be no income and no transfer either. This function, which is essentially a Laffer curve, represents the redistributive options among which society may choose. A policy of redistribution is a choice of a pair, T and t, from among the set of all feasible pairs represented by the function h.

As an intermediate step in the analysis of how a society with majority rule voting goes about choosing the degree of redistribution, suppose that the choice were assigned to person i, who might be anybody on the scale

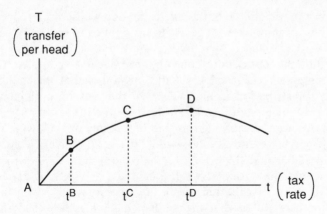

Figure 49   Transfer payments and tax rates

of rich and poor. It is easily shown[19] that his first choice is indicated by the condition

$$s_i L_i = T' \tag{8}$$

The direct loss of income per unit increase in the rate of tax, $s_i L_i$, is just equal to the indirect gain from the increase in the transfer made possible by the increase in the tax. The utility of person i is as large as it can be when equation (8) holds.

Three simple propositions follow immediately from equation (8). The first is that if anybody's labour supply is reduced by the transfer to zero, his preferred rate of tax is t^D in Figure 49, at which $T' = 0$ and the transfer is as large as it can be. The second is that a person whose income is above average wants no transfer; his preferred tax rate is 0, as indicated by the point A or Figure 49. (Strictly speaking, equation (8) cannot hold for such a person because his income, $s_i L_i$, is greater than T' for every possible value of t. Thus $t = 0$ is a boundary condition of the maximization problem.) The third proposition is that, for someone whose preferred rate of tax lies between these limits, the desired amount of redistribution is a decreasing function of pre-tax income, which, under our assumptions, can for all practical purposes be represented by the skill parameter s_i. If person B is more skilled than person C, and if their preferred tax rates are t^B and t^C, then $t^B < t^C$ as shown on the figure.

Since, as indicated by equation (7), the degree of redistribution can be represented by the parameter t and since each person has a unique preferred value of t as indicated by equation (8), the choice of a degree of redistribution, on the assumptions made so far, is a single-peaked issue with a unique electoral equilibrium which is the first best t of the median voter. (Line up all voters according to the size of their preferred values of

t. The voter in the middle of the line is the one whose preferences prevail because he can combine with voters to his right or to his left to defeat any value of t other than his own first best in a pairwise vote.)

An additional consideration must be introduced to complete the story. Nothing assumed so far rules out the possibility that the median voter wants no redistribution at all. We know that voters' optimal tax rates all lie in the range from 0 to t^D in Figure 49 and that, among all voters, optimal rates are a decreasing function of income, or skill, with a concentration at $t = 0$ for those voters with greater than average incomes. It remains possible that $t = 0$ for over half the voters, so that the median voter is within this group. To rule out that possibility, it need only be assumed that the distribution of pre-tax income at any given tax rate is skewed to the right so that the median income is less than the mean. Among five voters, a distribution that conforms to this assumption is (3,4, 5,7,11) with a mean of 6 and a median of 5, while a distribution that fails to conform is (1,3,5,5,6) with a mean of 4 and a median of 5. The assumption is innocuous because, in reality, distributions of income are always skewed to the right, with many somewhat poor people and a few very rich. The fact that incomes can be high without limit but can rarely be negative almost guarantees the appropriate skewness of the distribution. Thus it can reasonably be expected that the electoral equilibrium will be a point like B or C on Figure 49 rather than a point like A. An equilibrium at D is possible, too, but seems unlikely. A majority of voters are not likely to be induced by the combination of welfare and a progressive income tax to stop work altogether.

Compare this story with exploitation by voting as described in Chapter V. Now there is a unique electoral equilibrium; then there was none. Now each person preserves his rank in the ordering of rich and poor; then a person could fall from the top to the bottom of the income distribution, or rise from the bottom to the top, depending on essentially unpredictable incidents in the process of coalition formation. The redistribution of income, as distinct from reassignment, is an orderly self-limiting process which reduces the perogatives of property to some extent but presents no threat to the institution of property itself.

But this welcome feature of the redistribution of income requires a stronger constraint than the preservation of the ordering of people in passing from the pre-tax, pre-transfer distribution to the post-tax, post-transfer distribution. It was assumed in connection with equation (3) that a lump sum transfer to each person is financed by a proportional tax. The assumption transformed redistribution into a clean, single-peaked issue with a unique electoral equilibrium. Without that assumption, and with nothing more than the preservation of one's ordering on the side of rich and poor, the vote is no longer confined to a single variable, t, and voting on redistribution is no longer, strictly speaking, single-peaked. For instance, the ordering of voters on the scale of rich and poor need not be altered by a change in the tax schedule that leaves a little more net income for the very rich and the very poor and a little less for a minority of voters in the middle. This may not matter a great deal if voters are not too sensitive in their behaviour to small changes in net income. In practice, redistribution of income may be almost single-peaked, and that may be sufficient.

The essential orderliness of the determination of the degree of redistribution in the circumstances we have been examining is of the greatest significance in the context of this book, where "taking" is cast in the role of the enemy, not only of efficiency, but of democracy as well. Anarchy wastes resources as effort is diverted from making goods to taking what others have made. Despotism is the extreme limit of taking by the ruling class. Foremost among the diseases of the liberal society is the development of an unwillingness of people to live with the outcome of government by majority rule as groups vie with one another for inclusion in a majority coalition when the power of the state is employed to take income and other advantages from those who are left out. Yet here we have a case where taking appears to be restrained. Redistribution as taking is still the enemy of efficiency to some extent, but the degree of inefficiency may be quite bearable, and redistribution as taking appears not to be the enemy of democracy at all.

Insurance The "insurance" motive for redistribution is to protect oneself from the ups and down of the market. No matter how well off one is today, one can never be quite certain that one will continue to be well off tomorrow. The market is inherently dangerous. Skills become obsolete, firms fail, investments turn sour, and bonds may lose their value through inflation. In an uncertain world it may be to everyone's advantage to have a degree of pooling of risk through redistributive taxation or through public provision of welfare, especially for the old, who have little chance to become prosperous if they are not prosperous already.

The insurance motive is best introduced in a society where each child born today has a fixed probability, π, of becoming prosperous, coupled with a probability $(1 - \pi)$ of becoming unprosperous. The assumption — which will be relaxed presently — is not just that prosperity depends on luck, but that it depends on nothing else and that one cannot improve one's chance of becoming prosperous by effort and hard work. Think of prosperity as something attained altogether or not at all, rather than as something attainable to a greater or lesser degree. One's income if one is prosperous is y^P. One's income if one is unprosperous is y^U, where, of course, $y^P > y^U$. Life in this society is a gamble with a probability π of winning y^P and a probability $(1 - \pi)$ of winning y^U. Suppose, finally, that people are identically risk-averse, specifically that, when confronted with risk, each person acts so as to maximize his expected utility, W.

$$W = \pi u(C^P) + (1 - \pi)u(C^U) \qquad (9)$$

where C^P is one's consumption if one is prosperous, C^U is one's consumption if one is unprosperous and u is an ordinary utility function with diminishing marginal utility of income (i.e. $u' > 0$ and $u'' < 0$). Utility depends on consumption but not, as was assumed in the discussion of taking, on labour supply.

Redistribution is the transfer of T dollars to each unprosperous person, whose consumption rises from y^U to $y^U + T$. The transfer is financed by a tax on each prosperous person, whose consumption must fall from y^P to $y^P - T(1 - \pi)/\pi$ if the government's budget is to be balanced. Let $W(T)$ be each person's expected utility at birth when there is to be a transfer of T dollars to each unprosperous person. Expected utility becomes

$$W(T) = \pi u(y^P - T(1 - \pi)/\pi) + (1 - \pi)u(y^U+T) \qquad (10)$$

Now imagine the infants in this society as deciding collectively on the size of the transfer. There is, at that age, no conflict of interest among them, for their chances of becoming prosperous are the same. They unanimously agree upon whatever transfer, T, serves to maximize their welfare $W(T)$. The optimal transfer is identified by the first-order condition $W'(T) = 0$, which can be satisfied only when all risk is pooled away, that is, when $T = \pi(y^P - y^U)$ so that

$$C^P \equiv y^P - T(1 - \pi)/\pi = y^U + T \equiv C^U \qquad (11)$$

Everybody is as well off as he can be in this model when the transfer from rich to poor is large enough that everybody's consumption turns out to be the same regardless of his income.[20]

This is really two propositions; one weak, one strong. The weak proposition, which is all I really wish to cull from the example, is that some pooling of the risks of the market can be universally advantageous. The strong proposition, that *all* risk of the market should be pooled away, is a direct consequence of the assumption that one cannot improve one's chances of becoming prosperous by hard work. The assumption will be relaxed below when we come to assess the costs of public sector activity, and the strong proposition will no longer be valid.

Recognition of the parallel between public redistribution and private insurance — both reducing the variance of income at the expense of some reduction of average income — raises the question of why public redistribution is required at all. In so far as public redistribution is a form of insurance, it would seem to be duplicating facilities already available in the market, possibly at considerably lower cost. What, it may be asked, differentiates the provision of insurance from the provision of food, clothing and automobiles to justify public provision in the form of redistribution of income? Why the compulsion in public provision of insurance? Why cannot people decide for themselves whether to insure or not?

There would seem to be two answers to these questions. The first has to do with the general availability of information. We can insure our houses against fire because neither we nor the insurance company know whose house will burn down. We cannot privately insure ourselves against our failure to prosper because too much is known about us — by the insurance company and by ourselves — when we reach the age of twenty or twenty-five at which we can be expected to have the legal and personal maturity to take out such insurance. I cannot insure privately against the contingency that my parents are too poor to provide me with a good education or that I have a low I.Q., or that I am handicapped, or that I am sickly, for these events will have occurred by the time I apply for insurance. I can, however, take out such insurance for my children and grandchildren through the intermediary of the public sector.

The other reason is adverse selection. Private insurance against poverty would be accepted by those who believe they are likely to become poor, and rejected by those who believe that they are unlikely to become poor. The refusal of those who are unlikely to become poor to take out insurance, coupled with disincentive effects upon those who do, would either render the provision of such insurance unprofitable or cause the terms of the insurance to be so unfavourable to the insured that most of the potential benefit would be lost. Some risks, such as the risk of fire or the risk of automobile accidents, can be effectively insured in the private sector. Other risks, notably the risk of poverty, cannot.

Altruism Though redistribution as insurance involves giving *ex post* from rich to poor, it involves no giving *ex ante* when the programme is introduced, for nobody knows whether he will gain or lose from the programme. Altruism is unambiguously giving; the prosperous may be genuinely concerned about the welfare of the unprosperous, and quite willing to share their good fortune to some extent.[21]

To model altruism as a motive for the redistribution of income, suppose, once again, that some people are prosperous and others are unprosperous, but now suppose that prosperity is a consequence of property or skill, rather than a random event, and that there is no longer any doubt as to who is, or is about to become, rich. Society consists of n^P prosperous people, each with a pre-tax, pre-transfer income of y^P, and n^U unprosperous people, each with a pre-tax, pre-transfer income of y^P. By definition, $y^U < y^P$. Altruism can be represented by the inclusion of the income of others as an argument in one's own utility function. Specifically, let the utility function be

$$U = u(C^P;C^U) \text{ when one is prosperous} \qquad (12a)$$

where $\partial u/\partial C^P > 0$ and $\partial u/\partial C^U > 0$, and

$$U = u(C^U) \text{ when one is not prosperous} \qquad (12b)$$

where $\partial u / \partial C^U > 0$, where $u(C^P;C^U) > u(C^U)$ as long as $C^P > C^U$, but where $u(C^P;C^U) = u(C^U)$ in the limiting case for which $C^P = C^U$. The consumption variables C^P and C^U — as distinct from y^P and y^U — are the post-tax, post-transfer incomes of the prosperous and the unprosperous. The functions $u(C^P;C^U)$ and $u(C^U)$ must be interpreted carefully. The argument C^P in the first function and the argument C^U in the second are to be understood as one's own private consumption rather than as average consumption of one's social class. By contrast, the argument C^U in the function $u(C^P;C^U)$ is to be understood as the average consumption of the unprosperous. The meaning of equation (12) is not that the prosperous have a monopoly on concern for others. It is, instead, that concern for others is concentrated upon those who are less fortunate than oneself. I will sacrifice nothing, on this assumption, to augment the income of one who is already better off than I, but I will sacrifice something to augment the average incomes of those who are worse off than I.

In these circumstances, the cost to each prosperous person of a universal subsidy of T to each unprosperous person is Tn^U/n^P, and the optimal subsidy — from the point of view of the prosperous — is that which maximizes the utility of the prosperous, $U(y^P - Tn^U/n^P; y^U + T)$. The optimal subsidy might be zero, is not so large as to equalize the post-tax and post-transfer incomes of the rich and poor, and is likely to be between these limits.

Again the question arises as to why the transfer cannot be undertaken privately without the intermediary of the state. If each prosperous person is prepared to vote for a transfer of T to each unprosperous person at a cost to himself of Tn^U/n^P, why would he not be prepared to donate Tn^U/n^P privately, in which case the transfer to each unprosperous person would be T just the same? The answer to this question depends critically on the nature of altruism and the form of the utility function. If what mattered to the giver were the size of the gift, if the utility function of the prosperous were of the form $u(C^P;T)$, then private charity would indeed be sufficient. But if what matters is the average income of a class of unprosperous people, then public redistribution and private charity are not equivalent in the assessment of the giver.

The reason is that public redistribution involves compulsion upon all prosperous people to do their share. Suppose I am a prosperous person who wishes to provide an extra dollar of income to *every* unprosperous person. The cost to me of providing the extra dollar by an additional public transfer is only n^U/n^P dollars. The cost of providing the extra dollar by a private act of charity on my part would be a full n^U dollars. The difference of $n^U(1 - 1/n^P)$ dollars comes out of the pockets of other prosperous people. Were I as concerned about the incomes of other prosperous people as I am about the incomes of the unprosperous, then there would be no net advantage in a public transfer as far as I am concerned.

There is a net advantage because the incomes of other prosperous people do not enter as arguments into my utility function, while the incomes of the unprosperous do. In short, provision of income to the unprosperous may be like a public good among the prosperous. Each prosperous person gains slightly, but equally, from every donation. Public provision of transfers prevents each prosperous person from free-riding on the contributions of the rest. All prosperous people gain from compulsory transfers to the unprosperous.

Altruism as a motive for redistribution may not be focused on income exclusively. There is a sense in most people that the sick should be cared for and that people should not be allowed to die of illnesses that can be cured at a modest cost. Equally, there is a sense that all children should be reasonably well educated, regardless of whether their parents can afford the cost of education. Insurance and altruism are connected as motives for redistribution. If people in certain unfortunate circumstances are to be helped out in any case, they might as well have been provided with insurance so that they can help themselves.

Deterrence of crime   Recall the model of despotism in which rulers dared not tax farmers too heavily for fear that impoverished farmers would turn to banditry. In setting the tax rate, rulers had to draw a balance between the benefit of the extra revenue from a rise in the tax rate and the cost of the resulting increase in the incidence of banditry. A similar phenomenon is to be found in a liberal society. If, in the absence of redistribution, it is advantageous for the destitute to turn to crime, it may be advantageous for the wealthy to redistribute income to some extent.

Consider once again the "benevolent" variant of the model of despotism that was used in the discussion of the protection of property rights. Once again, rulers become policemen, but, to explain redistribution as a deterrent to crime, it is now assumed that there are two classes of farmers, the rich and the poor. Thus the model contains four groups of people: prosperous farmers from among whom policemen are hired, unprosperous farmers some of whom turn to banditry, policemen and bandits. Normally, one would suppose there to be a continuum among farmers from poorest to richest, but for convenience it is assumed here that there are two distinct groups with pre-tax, pre-transfer incomes of y^P and y^U, as in the preceding models of redistribution. To focus on giving as a motive for redistribution, assume that prosperous farmers constitute a clear majority in this society and that public decisions are made in their interest exclusively.

Think of the life of the bandit as so disagreeable that banditry would be avoided if a modest income were obtainable in another occupation. Since the expected utility of all bandits is the same, and since the utility of prosperous farmers is greater than the utility of unprosperous farmers, it must be the case *either* that all bandits are drawn from the ranks of the unprosperous farmers *or* that *all* potentially unprosperous farmers and *some* potentially prosperous farmers turn to banditry. In the former case, the equilibrium is such that bandits are as well off as unprosperous farmers. In the latter case, the equilibrium is such that there are no practising unprosperous farmers and bandits are as well off as prosperous farmers. Assume the former case. Also, assume for convenience that bandits steal only from prosperous farmers and leave the unprosperous farmers alone.

The story can be told without developing the full analytics of the model. Let S be the cost of banditry to each prosperous farmer, and suppose that S is a function of the number of bandits, n^B, i.e. $S = S(n^B)$ where $S' > 0$. To a prosperous farmer, the cost of banditry is the sum of the value of what is stolen, the expense and inconvenience of defending himself against bandits, and his share of total government expenditure in hunting and punishing bandits. The post-tax, post-transfer income of each prosperous farmer becomes

$$y^P - S(n^B) - T(n^U - n^B)/n^P$$

where T is the transfer to each unprosperous farmer, n^P is again the number of prosperous farmers and n^U is the number of unprosperous farmers as the number would be in the absence of banditry. Of the n^U possible unprosperous farmers, $n^U - n^B$ is the number of those who remain in farming and are recipients of the transfer. Suppose, finally, that the number of bandits is a decreasing function of the net income, $y^U + T$, of unprosperous farmers

$$n^B = f(y^U + T), \qquad f' < 0 \tag{13}$$

Prosperous farmers choose a transfer, T, to maximize their net incomes, or, equivalently, to minimize the sum of the costs of banditry and of the transfer

$$S(n^B) + T[n^U - n^B]/n^P$$

In principle the optimal transfer might be zero, but it might also be positive. If positive, the optimal transfer is identified by the first-order condition

$$n^P f' S' = f'T + [n^U - n^B] \tag{14}$$

The left-hand side of this equation is the reduction in the cost of banditry to all prosperous farmers resulting from a one-dollar increase in the transfer. The right-hand side is the sum of the total cost of the extra transfer to those unprosperous farmers who were already honest, $[n^U - n^B]$, and the cost of the transfer to ex-bandits who are induced to become honest, $f'T$.

Preservation of the liberal society Redistribution of income may help to keep the dictator away. If a great gap is allowed to emerge between the incomes of the overprivileged rich and the underprivileged poor, the people at the bottom of the heap may come to believe that their best chance of advancement lies in sweeping away the entire paraphernalia of the liberal society, property, voting and all. A majority of voters who are of this opinion could terminate the liberal society in one last vote or in a curtailment of the "rights" of property so severe as to destroy the economic foundation of the institution of majority rule voting. A substantial minority of voters who are of this opinion would constitute a ready-made faction and support in Parliament for any anti-democratic party that might come along. A wide gap between the incomes of the rich and the poor would pose a danger to the liberal society. Redistribution of income might head off this danger.

The logic of this argument for redistribution can be illustrated in a simple example. A country contains ten people, nine poor and one rich. Each poor person earns $20,000 and the rich person earns $220,000, so that the total national income is $400,000. As the poor constitute an overwhelming majority of the population, they could easily vote away the liberal society or stage a revolution to overturn the distribution of income. Whether they would wish to do so depends on what they expect from the post-revolutionary society. Suppose (i) that the revolution will lead, by one route or another, to the establishment of a despotic society with a small predatory ruling class and many disfranchised and oppressed subjects, (ii) that nobody can predict in advance of the transition to the despotic society whether he will turn out to be a ruler or a subject, and (iii) that every person sees the option of taking his chances on the new despotic society as the equivalent of living in a liberal society with an income of $30,000. Now consider a redistribution of income which raises each poor person's income by $12,000, from $20,000 to $32,000. The usual disincentives associated with the redistribution of income cause the total national income to fall from $400,000 to $350,000, so that the income of the one rich person is reduced from $220,000 to $62,000. On these assumptions, everybody is in favour of the redistribution of income, the poor because their incomes are increased and the rich as the only alternative to the establishment of a despotic society. When undertaken judiciously, redistribution can serve as a defence of the liberal society because a larger proportion of the population in a liberal society is prepared to try its luck with a new form of political and economic organization — as long as status in the liberal society is not preserved in the new society — when the post-tax, post-transfer distribution of income is wide than when it is narrow.

The political argument for the redistribution of income bears a family resemblance to the taking argument and the deterrence-of-crime argument as discussed above, as well as to some of the constraints upon the ruling class in a despotic society. Just as rulers must moderate their exploitation of subjects for fear of rebellion, so the rich in a liberal society must, in their own interest, acquiesce in the moderation of the privileges of wealth.

That completes our list of motives for the redistribution of income through the intermediary of the public sector: taking, insurance, altruism, deterrence of crime, and the preservation of the liberal society. Generally, some or all of these motives are combined as the justification for any particular redistribution programme. All five would seem to be operative in the old age pension. It is in part taking, for the old constitute a formidable and single-minded group of voters. It is in part insurance, for nobody can be absolutely sure that he will not be poor when he becomes old. It is in part altruism, for most of those who are themselves prosperous would sacrifice something to avoid destitution among the old. It is in part deterrence of crime, for people facing destitution as they grow old might turn to crime. It is in part political, for people facing destitution as they grow old might support political parties with illiberal aims. All five motives may also be operative in the provision of welfare, though the deterrence-of-crime motive is probably of greater importance for this programme than for the old age pension. Unemployment insurance is genuine insurance to some extent, but the other motives, especially taking and the deterrence of crime, are probably important as well. I would imagine that the insurance motive is also dominant in the public provision of medical care, though altruism — the unwillingness to allow the poor or improvident to die or to suffer illness for want of medical attention — must be important as well.

Counter-cyclical policy
Every capitalist society is characterized by alternating periods of prosperity and depression, and governments must choose what, if anything, to do about it. Counter-cyclical policy might be restricted to maintaining a constant rate of growth of the money supply, as Milton Friedman has proposed. It might include active manipulation of the deficit by varying tax rates and total public spending over the course of the business cycle. It might include bail-outs of unsuccessful firms in bad times. Counter-cyclical policy is mentioned here to complete a list of the necessary functions of government. The evaluation of alternative policies is beyond the scope of this book.

The cost of using the public sector

The cost of using the public sector can be classified under four headings: minimal resource cost, perverse incentives in the private sector, weakening of property rights and predatory behaviour within the public sector. Suppose a country is considering the introduction of socialized medicine. The minimal resource cost includes the necessary expenditure on doctors, nurses and hospitals, together with overhead costs borne by the Ministry of Health in administering the system and by the Ministry of Justice in detecting and punishing fraud associated with the public provision of medical care. Costs associated with perverse incentives in the private sector include the marginal deadweight loss due to increases in tax rates required to finance the public medical service, the marginal cost of tax evasion and the effect of public provision on people's willingness to care for themselves. The weakening of property rights occurs not only because money can no longer purchase health care but because every extension of the role of government is an extension of the range of ambiguity over the scope and limits of property rights. For instance, the return on investment in acquiring medical skills becomes dependent on public decisions as to how well medical practitioners are to be paid. The final cost, associated with predatory behaviour within the public sector, is a mixture of considerations including differences, if any, between the public and private sectors in the incentive to work hard, the possibility that bureaucrats will distort public decisions in their own interest, the possibility that services will be provided disproportionally on regional, linguistic, economic, religious or racial lines, and the cost of voters' manoeuvrings to turn the medical services to the advantage of their own group. The emphasis in this chapter is primarily on perverse incentives in the private sector and to a lesser extent on the weakening of property rights. Predatory government is the subject of the next chapter.

The minimal cost of resources employed

The "minimal resource cost of the public sector" may be interpreted broadly or narrowly. On the narrow interpretation, it is the cost of manning and supplying the army, providing education and medical care (if these are in the public sector), building roads, collecting taxes, and so on, as the cost would be if the public sector were a perfectly coordinated and well oiled machine, headed by a planner who decides what is to be done and staffed by public servants who allocate tasks among themselves and purchase what needs to be purchased to fulfil the plan as inexpensively as possible. Minimal cost in this sense is the cost to an omniscient, benevolent and omnipotent despot, where omnipotence is, of course, restricted to the despot's authority over the functionaries of the government and does not extend to the private sector.

On the broader interpretation, minimal cost takes account of the actual characteristics of bureaucracy. A useful distinction can be drawn between bureaucratic malfeasance as discussed under the heading of predatory government in the next chapter and the ordinary difficulties that arise when honest but fallible men undertake tasks collectively in a public hierarchy. Like any large bureaucracy, the government is inevitably confronted with the dual problem of passing information up and passing orders down the steps of the hierarchy. Collectively, officials know a very great deal more than any particular official, from the Prime Minister to the lowest clerk, can hope to assimilate. The law-makers' intentions are distorted to some extent in the Ministers' regulations; the regulations, in turn, are distorted by the officials who apply them. Inevitably, bureaucracy is a great sprawling beast whose brain has some influence over the actions of the limbs, but not full control.[22]

In this respect, public bureaucracy and private bureaucracy within the corporation are alike, but there are features of public bureaucracy which render it especially rigid, unwieldy and costly to operate. The difference between public and private bureaucracy is not just a matter of size, though governments tend to be larger than even the largest corporation and are somewhat less flexible on that account. The difference lies in the criteria of the organizations.

No matter how large they may be, corporations are geared to the maximization of profit, which plays a dual role as the unique well defined objective and as the measure of the extent to which the objective has been achieved. While it is not always immediately evident how each activity of the corporation contributes to profit or whether actual profit is as large as can reasonably be expected in the circumstances of the corporation, it is at least evident whether a corporation is doing well in comparison with its competitors, and it is often possible to say of a manager whether he is contributing sufficiently to the overall profitability of the corporation. When a corporation ceases to produce goods that are worth more to the consumer than other goods that could have been made with the same input of resources, that corporation becomes unprofitable and will ultimately be eliminated if it cannot be reformed. In principle, every action of the corporation can be judged with reference to a single, all-encompassing criterion. Managers and employees can be allowed a degree of discretion and independence because actions that are detrimental to the corporation can be spotted in the profit figures.

By contrast, governments have a multiplicity of criteria. Many objectives compete for the government's attention. In principle, the multiplicity of criteria can be subsumed into a social welfare function, so that the maximization of social welfare becomes the public analogue to the maximization of profit on the part of the corporation. But the maximization of social welfare is at best a vague and ill specified criterion. As discussed in Chapter I, the social welfare function is no more than the precise expression of the citizen's conception of the common good, and there is no basis for presuming that each citizen's conception is the same. Nor is the maximization of the social welfare function the only consideration; public action is inevitably a response to conflicting demands and influences in society.

The absence of a single clear criterion for the public sector has several consequences for the cost of public sector activity. First, it requires that the public sector be a good deal more rule-bound than would be warranted in large firms in the private sector. With a clear criterion of success, people up and down the hierarchy can be allowed a degree of discretion, in the expectation that they will be rewarded if their actions turn out well and that they will be penalized otherwise. Without a clear criterion of success, discretion within the ranks of the hierarchy is a recipe for chaos. It is in the very nature of a public bureaucracy that officials must be circumspect, judicious and not especially entrepreneurial. Typically, public officials are more secure in their jobs than their counterparts in the private sector, and this security, like tenure in the university, may in some instances be a refuge for laziness and inefficiency. One expects the Post Office to be a bit hidebound in its ways. One expects an activity administered within the public sector to be more like the Post Office than like Federal Express. This is a consequence of the environment of bureaucracy.

Bureaucratic management means, under democracy, management in strict accordance with the law and the budget. It is not for the personnel of the administration and the judges to inquire what should be done for public welfare and how public funds should be spent. This is the task of the Sovereign, the people and their representatives.[23]

The environment of bureaucracy may engender an attitude on the part of the official in which his particular job and his particular objective takes on greater importance than might be warranted in the light of a broader view of the role of government. The doctor, under socialized medicine, cares about healing the sick but places little value on the time of the patient or the cost to the state of the treatment he prescribes. The policeman cares too much about solving the crime and too little about the rights of citizens he encounters in his investigation. The professor is programmed to believe that no amount of money spent on education is enough. The regulator is too punctilious in the administration of "his" regulations. The fire inspector is concerned about fire, the health inspector about health, the city planner about the appearance of the city, and the tax authority about taxation. The cost of public services, the citizen's time and trouble in conforming with the regulations and aspects of life that do not fall neatly into any regulatory category receive too little weight in public decision-making.

In the absence of a simple substitute for profitability as a criterion for the public sector, the public administration of any domain of the economy involves costs over and above the rock-bottom resource cost of doing whatever the public sector chooses to do. Such costs should be taken into account in deciding upon the scope of the public sector. In particular, the full cost of public administration should be weighed along with other costs of public activity, to be discussed below, in the decision whether to take corrective action over departures from efficiency in the private sector, or to desist, in the belief that, on balance, the benefits of corrective action are not worth the cost. Public action is costly, even in the best of times when bureaucratic behaviour has not yet crossed the line between inefficiency and corruption.[24]

Perverse incentives in the private sector

Costs associated with perverse incentives within the private sector include deadweight loss in taxation, concealment of taxable income, intimidation cost, transfer-seeking and commodity effects. The general principle running through all these topics is that, whenever the government takes, it creates an incentive for each person to rearrange his affairs so as to pass the burden of the taking on to somebody else; and, whenever the government gives, it creates an incentive for each person to rearrange his affairs so as to get as large a share as he can. Such manoeuvrings are privately advantageous but socially disadvantageous, and their social cost has to be set against the benefits of what the public sector provides.

A decision is to be made about, for instance, the provision of guns to the army. The manufacturer is prepared to supply any number of guns at a fixed price per gun. The government, as the disinterested servant of its citizens, chooses a number of guns in accordance with citizens' preferences for protection as well as for the ordinary goods and services that must be forgone when guns are bought instead. People's desire for protection may be represented as a community demand curve showing how marginal valuation[25] of protection declines with the number of guns bought. What rule should the government follow in deciding how many guns to buy? If there were no perverse incentives to taxation or public expenditure — if minimal resource cost were the only consideration — then the appropriate rule would be for the government to buy just enough guns that the sum of all citizens' valuations of the protection afforded by an additional gun is equal to the price of guns, as signified by equation (1) above. But if each dollar of public expenditure entails, for instance, an additional dollar of costs associated with perverse incentives in the private sector, then the government should purchase guns — or anything else — only up to the point where the benefit of an extra dollar of expenditure on guns is at least two dollars, one dollar of resource cost and one dollar of other costs. To recognize these other costs where they have not been recognized before is, of course, to reduce public expenditure. Fewer projects and programmes can pass a two-for-one test than a one-for-one test. One of the central problems in public finance is to determine how large the benefit–cost ratio must be for public expenditure to be justified.

Deadweight loss in taxation[26] Deadweight loss is best analysed in stages, beginning with a simple example and proceeding to the analysis of the entire tax system. Consider a carpenter whose house requires plumbing and a plumber whose house requires carpentry. Both parties can do both jobs, but each is naturally better at his own trade. The carpenter could do the job of plumbing in ten hours, but the plumber can do it in six hours. Similarly, the plumber could do the job of carpentry in ten hours, but the carpenter can do it in six hours. The two jobs may be allocated on a do-it-yourself basis, by barter or by purchase. Obviously the efficient procedures are purchase and barter, for these procedures require a total of twelve hours of work for the two jobs together instead of the twenty hours that would be required if each party did his own repairs. We rule out barter by supposing that the parties are unaware of one another's requirements. That leaves a choice between purchase and do-it-yourself. Suppose the wages of carpenters and plumbers are both $20 per hour, so that the cost of each job is $120. Suppose also that the rate of income tax is 50 per cent. The tax has no effect on the time required to complete both jobs on a do-it-yourself basis. But, with a 50 per cent tax, each party would need to work twelve hours to earn the $240 that is required to pay for the carpentry or the plumbing out of after-tax earnings. It would, therefore, be in each party's interest to do the job himself in ten hours, despite the fact that he could hire somebody else to do it in six hours. The effect of the tax in this instance is to induce each party to waste four hours of labour, with a social value of $80. In total, eight hours or $160 worth of output or leisure is lost, and not one penny of tax is collected on the transaction. This $160 is just as much a cost of the public service financed by the tax as is another $160 that is actually paid for goods purchased by the government. This $160 is a part of the *deadweight loss*, or, as it is sometimes called, *excess burden*, of the tax system. The full cost of any public activity includes deadweight loss as well as the overhead cost and resource cost of that activity. This example is of a portion of the tax base that vanishes altogether in response to taxation. In the example to follow, the tax base shrinks in response to taxation, but does not vanish.

Imagine a society in which the only public expenditure is on guns for the army and the only source of public revenue is the taxation of water from a public well. There is no scarcity of water, anybody can use as much water as he pleases without depriving anybody else and the price of water to the user is just the tax per gallon that he must pay. Initially, the government finances a certain purchase of guns with a certain rate of tax. This example is about the full cost to society of the purchase of one extra gun. To purchase that gun, the government must increase tax revenue slightly by increasing the rate of tax. The taxpayer's response to the increase in the price he must pay for water is to use less. The unused water is wasted in the sense that it has no alternative use and makes no direct contribution to the production of the gun. Thus the full social cost of the extra gun is

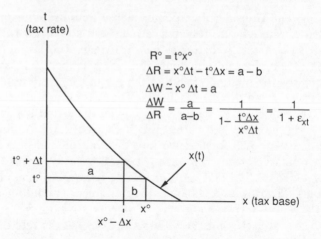

$R° = t°x°$

$\Delta R = x°\Delta t - t°\Delta x = a - b$

$\Delta W \stackrel{\sim}{=} x° \, \Delta t = a$

$\dfrac{\Delta W}{\Delta R} = \dfrac{a}{a-b} = \dfrac{1}{1 - \dfrac{t°\Delta x}{x°\Delta t}} = \dfrac{1}{1 + \varepsilon_{xt}}$

Figure 50   Marginal revenue and marginal deadweight loss

the loss of other goods that could have been made with the resources diverted to the production of the gun, together with the loss of the water that is not used because the increase in the tax has made the water slightly more expensive. The waste, or deadweight loss, is exactly analogous to the wastage of labour in the preceding example.

The magnitude of the waste as a proportion of the extra tax revenue is illustrated with the aid of the demand curve, $x(t)$, in Figure 50, where the quantity of water, x, is shown on the horizontal axis and the tax, t (which is the price of water to the consumer), is shown on the vertical axis. There is no need to represent the supply curve. Since water is abundant, one may think of the supply curve as lying along the horizontal axis. Initially, the tax is t^0, the quantity of water demanded is x^0 and the revenue from taxation is t^0x^0. Let Δt be the increase in the tax that is required for the purchase of the extra gun; the tax has to be increased from t^0 to $t^0 + \Delta t$. The demand for water shrinks accordingly by an amount Δx, where, for convenience, Δx is defined positively so that $\Delta x = x(t^0) - x(t^0 + \Delta t)$. The waste, or deadweight loss, is the value of the water that is not used because the tax has been increased. It is approximately $t^0 \Delta x$ which is represented in the figure by the area b. Note that the little triangular area at the top of the column b is being ignored; the area is approximately $\frac{1}{2}\Delta t \Delta x$ which, as the product of two small changes, is itself very small. The ratio of this triangular area to the area of the rectangle b approaches zero as Δt approaches zero.

The increase in tax revenue, called ΔR, is the difference between the new revenue and the old revenue. Specifically,

$$\Delta R = (t^0 + \Delta t)(x^0 - \Delta x) - t^0 x^0 = x^0 \Delta t - t^0 \Delta x - \Delta t \Delta x$$

$$\cong x^0 \Delta t - t^0 \Delta x = \text{area a (in Figure 50)} - \text{area b} \qquad (15)$$

when $\Delta t \Delta x$ is ignored. The full social cost, called ΔW, of the extra tax is the sum of the resource cost (equal to the extra revenue) and the waste.

$$\Delta W = [\text{area a} - \text{area b}] + \text{area b} = \text{area a} = x^0 \Delta t \qquad (16)$$

The social cost, ΔW, is seen by the consumer as the increase in the cost of the water that he buys. Despite the loss to the tax collector, the contraction of the tax base from x^0 to $x^0 - \Delta x$ is neither a gain nor a loss to the consumer because it is a shift in purchasing power between goods, water, and other things that are of virtually equal value at the margin. It follows immediately that the marginal cost of taxation to the taxpayer is greater than the marginal revenue from the tax.

$$\Delta W = x^0 \Delta t > x^0 \Delta t - t^0 \Delta x = \Delta R \qquad (17)$$

The appropriate quantity of guns depends upon the marginal social cost of taxation as well as upon the cost and benefits of the guns themselves. The rule for identifying the appropriate quantity of guns is to equate $\Delta W / \Delta R$ to the citizens' marginal valuation of guns expressed as a multiple of their marginal cost. If ΔW and ΔR were equal, as would be the case if the demand curve for water were vertical, then there would be no cost to taxation over and above the resource cost of making the extra gun, and guns costing a dollar from the manufacturer should be purchased up to the point where the sum of all citizens' marginal valuations of a gun is just equal to \$1. Otherwise, if $\Delta W / \Delta R$ were greater than 1, fewer guns should be purchased because their full cost per dollar of expenditure is greater than \$1. The higher the marginal social cost of taxation, the smaller is the appropriate purchase of guns as long as the citizens' demand curve for guns is downward-sloping.

The value of $\Delta W / \Delta R$ can be determined from the shape of the demand curve for water. From equations (16) and (17), it follows at once that the marginal social cost per dollar of tax revenue becomes

$$\frac{\Delta W}{\Delta R} = \frac{\text{area a}}{\text{area a} - \text{area b}} = \frac{x^0 \, \Delta t}{x^0 \, \Delta t - t^0 \, \Delta x} = \frac{1}{1 - \dfrac{t^0 \, \Delta x}{x^0 \, \Delta x}} = \frac{1}{1 + \varepsilon_{xt}} \qquad (18)$$

where ε_{xt} is the elasticity of demand for water from the taxed well. Thus $\Delta W / \Delta R$ has to be greater than 1 as long as ε_{xt} is negative and the government is not so foolish or misinformed as to raise the tax rate beyond the level at which a higher rate yields no extra revenue; the significance of the latter qualification will be discussed below. If the elasticity of demand for water from the well were -0.5, the value of $\Delta W/\Delta R$ would be 2, signifying that the government should buy guns up to the point where the public's marginal valuation of guns is twice the price from the manufacturer.

The principles in the guns and water example can be generalized to a more realistic economy with many kinds of taxes and many kinds of public expenditure. Depending on the context, the quantity of water, x, becomes the base for any given tax or for the tax system as a whole, the tax on water, t, becomes the rate of the given tax or an average rate for the tax system as a whole, and the demand curve in Figure 50 shows the sensitivity of the tax base to the corresponding tax rate. The transition from the guns and water example to a real economy entails complications and qualifications that will be discussed presently, after some of the implications of equation (18) have been examined. Though measurement of deadweight loss in any real economy is considerably more complex than the simple example might suggest, the tax-induced diversion of purchasing power from more taxed to less taxed activities remains as an unavoidable social cost of public expenditure over and above the cost of the resources that the government employs, and the full marginal cost of public revenue, as represented by $\Delta W/\Delta R$, may be very much greater than 1.

The estimate of 2 for $\Delta W/\Delta R$ in the guns and water example is critically dependent on the assumed elasticity of demand for water, but the number itself is not preposterous and not altogether out of line with the empirical evidence.[27] The value of $\Delta W/\Delta R$ for any actual economy can only be estimated with the aid of some strong simplifying assumptions. A variety of assumptions have been employed and, not surprisingly, the estimates have varied considerably. The number 2 lies within the range of these estimates. If 2 were the correct number, it would signify that all public goods and public programmes are really twice as expensive as they appear to be. Ignoring ordinary overhead costs, the payment by the government of $1 for military equipment, in the transfer of income to the poor or to subsidize investment, would have an effect upon the taxpayer that is equivalent to a lump sum (and therefore non-distortionary) tax of $2. Arguments for public expenditure to defend ourselves, to provide infrastructure, to correct for market failure, or to provide transfers for worthy groups of people seem less compelling when the cost to the taxpayer is $2 for each dollar of expenditure than when the cost is only one. To be sure, many activities of government are fully worth the price. If the protection of the ozone layer of the atmosphere requires large public expenditure, then that expenditure must be borne, regardless of whether a dollar of revenue costs the taxpayer one dollar or two.

The guns and water example teaches a second lesson that was not immediately evident in the plumber and carpenter example. As a general rule, deadweight loss per dollar of public expenditure tends to increase together with total tax revenue, so that a project worth doing when the public sector is small may no longer be worth doing when the public sector is large. Suppose a road improvement yields a present value of benefits amounting to one and a half times its cost, where cost is interpreted, as accountants would understand the term, to include the amount of public revenue required to undertake the project regardless of the consequences for the economy of the steps that must be taken to acquire that revenue. Such a project might be worthwhile if and only if total public expenditure is, for instance, less than 35 per cent of the national income. The connections among t, R and $\Delta W/\Delta R$ can be seen at once from Figure 50. When the tax rate is low, the area b has to be small relative to the area a, and the value of $\Delta W/\Delta R$, which is equal to (area a)/(area a – area b), cannot be much greater than 1. In fact, $\Delta W/\Delta R$ approaches 1 as t approaches zero. As t is increased, the area b increases relative to the area a, and $\Delta W/\Delta R$ increases too. Eventually, as t is increased more and more, $\Delta W/\Delta R$ must exceed 1.5, which is the cut-off point beyond which the project is no longer socially advantageous. The more society chooses to do through the intermediary of the government, the more stringent the test for any new public activity must be.

If the demand curve were a downward-sloping straight line, the rise in $\Delta W/\Delta R$ would be continuous up to infinity. As long as the demand curve touches both axes — indicating that there is a finite tax base as t approaches zero and that there is some value of t so high that the tax base vanishes altogether — there must be some tax at which total revenue is maximized. At that tax, $\Delta W/\Delta R$ has risen to infinity, signifying that any increase in the tax generates extra deadweight loss but no extra revenue.

This consideration is the explanation of the seemingly odd implication of equation (18) that the marginal cost of public revenue turns negative when the absolute value of the elasticity of the tax base to the tax rate, ε_{xt}, is greater than 1. The process by which $\Delta W/\Delta R$ first grows without limit and then turns negative is best illustrated by converting Figure 50 to a Laffer curve. Figure 51 is derived from Figure 50 by changing the units on the axes. The vertical axis shows tax revenue xt (which was an area in Figure 50), the horizontal axis shows the tax rate t, and the Laffer curve shows how tax revenue varies with the tax rate. The curve is an inverted U with a maximal tax revenue at a tax rate of t*. By definition, the change in revenue resulting from a small increase in t is

$$\frac{dR}{dt} = x + t\frac{dx}{dt} = x(1 + \varepsilon_{xt}) \tag{19}$$

where ε_{xt} is the elasticity of tax base to tax rate. The elasticity of the Laffer curve is

$$\frac{t}{R}\frac{dR}{dt} = 1 + \varepsilon_{xt} \tag{20}$$

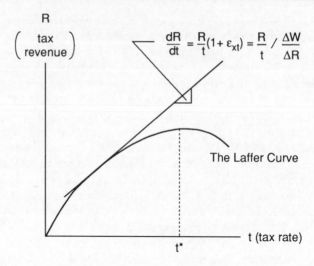

Figure 51 Tax rates and tax revenues

which is the inverse of the marginal social cost of tax revenue, $\Delta W/\Delta R$. The marginal social cost of tax revenue is positive and growing on the good (left) side of the Laffer curve. It rises to infinity at the top of the curve, signifying that a further increase in the rate of tax has costs but no benefits. It is negative on the wrong side of the Laffer curve, signifying that a reduction in the rate of tax would have benefits but no costs.

The generalization of equation (18) — that $\Delta W/\Delta R = 1/(1 + \varepsilon_{xt})$ — from the guns and water example to a more realistic depiction of the economy is a large topic that cannot be treated here in detail, but some aspects of the topic can be usefully and briefly discussed. Production of the taxed good presents no problem at all, though the elasticity of tax base to tax rate, ε_{xt}, is no longer equal to the elasticity of demand. It now depends on both the elasticity of demand for the taxed good and its elasticity of supply. Specifically

$$\varepsilon_{xt} = \frac{-t\varepsilon^S\varepsilon^D}{P^D\varepsilon^S + P^S\varepsilon^D} \tag{21}$$

where P^D, P^S and t are gross-of-tax price, net-of-tax price and tax per unit so that $P^D - P^S = t$, and where ε^D and ε^S are the *absolute values* of the elasticities of demand and supply. It follows immediately from equation (21) that there is no marginal deadweight loss from taxation and that $\Delta W/\Delta R = 0$ if either $\varepsilon^S = 0$ or $\varepsilon^D = 0$. On the other hand, it is easy enough to pick plausible values of ε^S, ε^D and t for which the ratio $\Delta W/\Delta R$ is very large. For example, the set $\varepsilon^S = 1/2$, $\varepsilon^D = 1/2$, and $t = P^S$ (which is equivalent to a sales tax of 50 per cent of the retail price) yields a value of $\Delta W/\Delta R$ of 1.2, the set of $\varepsilon^S = 1$, $\varepsilon^D = 1$ and $t = P^S$ yields a value of $\Delta W/\Delta R$ of 1.5, and the set $\varepsilon^S = 10$, $\varepsilon^D = 2$ and $t = P^S$ yields a value of $\Delta W/\Delta R$ of 11, signifying that the full social cost of taxation would be eleven times the tax revenue!

Externalities in the taxed good require a more substantial modification to equation (18), but present no major conceptual problems. When an increase in a tax leads to a reduction in the demand for the taxed good, the value of that reduction, $t^0\Delta x$, is seen as a loss of tax revenue to the community as a whole. There may be an additional loss or gain if the presence of the taxed good conveys costs or benefits over and above the benefit of the good to the immediate purchaser. Consider a tax on gasoline. Suppose the cost of production of gasoline is 50 cents per gallon, the tax is 50 cents, and the retail price is therefore equal to $1 per gallon. The externality associated with gasoline is that the fumes from the exhaust of automobiles pollute the atmosphere. The harm done by pollution, to all consumers together, is valued at 25 cents per gallon of gasoline. Consumers respond to taxation by adjusting their purchases so that the benefit from a gallon of gasoline is just equal to the benefit of a dollar's worth of other, untaxed goods. They do so despite the fact that gasoline costs only 50 cents to produce and despite the fact that each gallon of gasoline does 25 cents worth of harm to other people. Now consider a slight increase, Δt, in the rate of the tax, leading to a reduction in gasoline consumption of Δx. The net social loss from the reduction in gasoline consumption is no longer equal to $50\Delta x$ cents, which is the value of the area b in Figure 50. The net social loss is only $25\Delta x$ cents, which is the difference between the tax loss of $50\Delta x$ cents and the externality gain of $25\Delta x$ cents. The measure of $\Delta W/\Delta R$ in equation (18) would be a substantial over-estimate in this case. By the same token, the measure of $\Delta W/\Delta R$ in equation (18) would be an under-estimate if the taxed good were the bearer of a positive externality or if the untaxed good were the bearer of a negative externality, as would be the case if taxed work is conducive to good conduct and clean living while untaxed leisure is conducive to dissipation and crime.

Equation (18) should also be modified for the direct impact, if any, of the provision of the publicly-supplied good upon the demand for the taxed good. If the provision of guns made one thirsty or in need of a bath, the combined effect of taxation and the provision of guns upon the demand for water would be different from what one would infer from the demand curve, $x(t)$, alone. This connection seems a bit far-fetched in the guns and water example, but other examples may be more compelling. If the public expenditure is for a city park and if the effect of the park is to induce people to substitute in the use of their time from taxed labour to untaxed leisure, then the resulting loss of tax revenue has to be counted as part of the cost of the park. On the other hand, if the public expenditure is for a marina and if the effect of the marina is to induce people to work more and take less leisure in order to purchase expensive and highly taxed

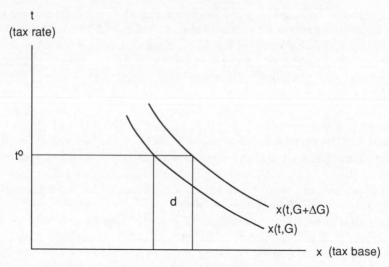

Figure 52   Deadweight loss from the provision of public goods

yachts, then the resulting increase in tax revenue is a hidden benefit of the marina.

The situation is illustrated in Figure 52, which is a modification of Figure 50. The axes are the same, and the demand curve x(t,G) in Figure 52 should be thought of as identical to the demand curve x(t) in Figure 50. The term G refers to the quantity of whatever the government purchases with its tax revenue. The shift of the demand curve when that quantity increases from G to G + ΔG is the effect of the publicly supplied goods on the taxpayer's purchases of taxed goods. As the figure is drawn, the shift is to the right. Consequently, the area d which is equal to $t^0(\partial x/\partial G)\Delta G$ is a hidden gain from public expenditure. Note, however, that one cannot say *a priori* whether the shift in the demand curve x(t,G) is to the right or to the left. As drawn, the curve covers the example of the marina. The example of the park would correspond to a leftward shift in the curve.[28]

Interactions among taxes constitute the main impediment to the generalization of the guns and water example to more complex tax systems. The crucial assumption in the derivation of equation (18) was that an increase in taxation diverts purchasing power from taxed to untaxed goods. For equation (18) to be strictly valid, the tax-induced shift in purchasing power must be from the taxed good to another good that is not taxed at all. This requirement is met in the guns and water example where, by assumption, all goods other than water are untaxed. Equation (18) ceases to be valid when there are many taxed goods and when an increase in the tax on one good diverts the taxpayer's expenditure to another equally-taxed good, so that the decrease in revenue from the tax on the one good is balanced by an equal increase in revenue from the tax on the other.[29] In that case, the value of t°Δx, as represented by the area b in Figure 50, can no longer be interpreted as a deduction from total tax revenue. If there were no escape from the tax collector, if absolutely every activity one might engage in were subject to the same rate of tax and if no tax could be evaded, then the economy-wide counterpart of the demand curve for water in Figure 50 would be vertical. The area b would vanish, $\Delta W/\Delta R$ would be equal to 1 and no deadweight loss need be considered in calculating costs and benefits of public expenditure.

But the mere multiplicity of taxes does not invalidate the lessons of the guns and water example. The analysis carries over, almost unchanged, to an economy where all goods are taxed if some goods are taxed at a high rate and other goods are taxed at a lower rate. In that case, the calculation of $\Delta W/\Delta R$ remains as it was, except that the tax, t, has to be understood as the excess of one rate over the other. With many goods and many kinds of taxes, a mix of rates may be chosen to minimize total deadweight loss by equalizing the ratios of appropriately-measured marginal welfare cost to marginal revenue for each tax in the system. When such tax rates are chosen, a unique value of $\Delta W/\Delta R$ may, in principle, be identified for the economy as a whole. Otherwise, an estimate of the economy-wide $\Delta W/\Delta R$ based on a simple model of the economy can be useful and instructive if not entirely accurate. Regardless of the impediments to accurate measurement, the economy-side counterpart of the demand curve for water remains downward sloping, the tax base shrinks as tax rates are increased and the Laffer curve retains its characteristic shape because the tax collector can be escaped to some extent. Among the taxpayer's ways of escape are the shift of activity from the production of taxed goods to untaxed leisure, barter or do-it-yourself activities, the shift of purchasing power from more-taxed future consumption to less-taxed current consumption and the shift of effort from the production of goods to legal tax avoidance and illegal tax evasion.

The disparity between rates of taxation on present and future consumption is a direct consequence of the double taxation of saving in the income tax. If the price of apples is and will remain at 50 cents each and if the rate of interest, interpreted as a reflection of the marginal rate of substitution in production between present and future goods, is 5 per cent a year, then the social cost, P^S, of providing one apple thirty years hence is 11.16 cents; $P^S = 50e^{-0.05 \times 30} = 11.16$. When the rate of the income tax is 50 per cent, a person who wishes to put aside enough money today to buy himself an apple thirty years hence has to invest considerably more than 11.16 cents. Ignoring transaction cost, a firm that can earn 5 per cent on its capital is prepared to pay that rate on its loans, and the saver can expect to earn 5 per cent on his money. But the annual interest on one's saving is counted as part of one's income and subject to income tax at a rate of

50 per cent. Thus, a return of 5 per cent before tax translates into a return of only 2.5 per cent after tax, at which the present value of 50 cents in thirty years is 23.62 cents; $P^D = 50e^{-0.025\times30} = 23.62$. This is the sum one must put aside today to buy an apple then. With an interest rate of 5 per cent and an income tax rate of 50 per cent, the effect of the double taxation of saving on the price today of apples delivered thirty years hence is to create a gap between the demand price of 23.62 cents and the supply price of only 11.16 cents, as though "future apples" were being taxed at a rate of 47 per cent of the retail price. When the income tax rate is low, the implicit excise tax on future consumption is low as well and the resulting deadweight loss is small. Raise the rate of the income tax and there is created an incentive for the taxpayer to shift from more-taxed future consumption to less taxed present consumption — from investment to present consumption — generating a deadweight loss and reducing the tax base, exactly as in the guns and water example.

Concealment of taxable income[30]   The contraction of the tax base in response to an increase in the tax rate has so far been attributed to a tax-induced shift of purchasing power from more valuable taxed goods to less valuable untaxed goods. A similar, and additional, contraction, with a similar impact on the ratio of marginal cost to taxpayers per unit of tax revenue, occurs when an increase in the tax rate induces taxpayers to devote extra resources to tax avoidance. The general principle is that people devote resources to legal or illegal tax avoidance up to the point where the marginal cost of tax avoidance is just equal to the tax saved. Hence, when a tax is increased from t to $t + \Delta t$, it pays the taxpayer to devote a bit of extra resources to tax avoidance because the return to tax avoidance is greater by Δt than it was before. The magnitude of this effect depends upon the cost of concealment of the tax base. Let this be $C(v)$ where v is the amount of the taxable base that is concealed from the tax collector or sheltered from taxation in some other way. The optimal v from the point of view of the taxpayer is defined by the condition $dC/dv = t$. As shown in Appendix VIII.2, the measure of $\Delta W/\Delta R$ in equation (18) remains valid in this case but the elasticity of tax base to tax rate increases, to account for the effect of concealment. Specifically

$$\varepsilon_{xt} \equiv -\left\{\varepsilon^D \frac{y}{x} + \varepsilon^C \frac{v}{x}\right\} \tag{22}$$

in the special case where the elasticity of supply of the taxed goods is infinite. In this formula, y is total consumption of the taxed good, x is the amount on which tax is paid, v is the amount concealed (so that $y = x + v$), ε^D is the absolute value of the elasticity of demand for the taxed good, and ε^C is the elasticity of the cost of concealment with respect to the amount of the potential base that is concealed. The marginal cost to the taxpayer associated with an increase in public revenue may be high *either* because ε^C is high *or* because ε^D is high. Anything that causes the tax base to contract as the tax rate increases drives up the marginal social cost of public revenue.

Legal tax avoidance and illegal tax evasion have been placed on exactly the same footing in equation (22) because they are, in essential respects, the same from the point of view of the amoral taxpayer. Each entails the non-payment of tax at some cost — the use of resources to discover ways of making income tax-exempt in one case, and the use of resources to hide income, together with the risk of punishment, in the other. Each course of action proceeds up to the point where its marginal cost per dollar of tax saved is just equal to 1. Each drives up the marginal cost of public funds by causing the tax base to shrink as the tax rate increases. The two are not the same from the point of view of the general public or the government because they involve different types and amounts of intimidation cost.

Intimidation cost   Virtually any task that the public sector is called upon to perform involves the establishment of rules. Rules require enforcement. Enforcement entails costs which must be counted as part of the total cost of public programmes. Among these costs are the citizens' time and money devoted to evading the rules without getting caught, the cost to the government of identifying infractions of the rules, and the cost to the government (and ultimately to the taxpayer) of punishing people identified as rule-breakers. These last two items may together be identified as intimidation cost, the cost borne by the government in enforcing compliance with the rules. Any increase in public expenditure requires a corresponding increase in tax rates; the increase in tax rates induces taxpayers to devote extra resources to tax evasion; the increase in tax evasion induces the government to devote more resources to detection and punishment; the extra intimidation cost is part of the full cost of the original public expenditure.

Marginal deadweight loss, marginal concealment cost and marginal intimidation cost *may* be strictly additive, though there are circumstances where this is not quite so. These costs are strictly additive when tax evasion is costly but foolproof, as would be the case if evasion consisted of working underground where productivity is low but the tax collector cannot find you. Suppose that 1,000 cameras are sold when the tax is $50 per camera, and that, of these, 200 are sold on the black market, where the tax is not paid. Suppose also that an increase in the tax to $51 per camera leads to a reduction in total sales to 995 cameras, of which 205 are now sold on the black market, so that tax is paid on only 790 instead of 800 cameras. Finally, suppose that the rise in the tax leads to an increase in enforcement costs from $3,000 to $3,100, to ensure that sales on the black market are not larger than has been assumed. These numbers must be the joint outcome of complex optimizations by tax evaders and tax collectors, the nature of which does not concern us here.

The marginal cost to the taxpayer of the increase in the tax, ΔW, is \$800 — the product of the original tax base of 800 cameras and the increase in the tax. The marginal revenue is only \$290; it is the new revenue of \$40,290 ($= 790 \times 51$) less the original revenue of \$40,000 ($= 800 \times 50$). In addition, there is an extra cost to the government of \$100 in monitoring tax collection, so that the net gain in revenue, ΔR, is reduced to \$190. Thus the marginal social cost per dollar of net revenue, when all the hidden costs we have considered so far are taken into account, is

$$\frac{\Delta W}{\Delta R} = \frac{800}{190} = 4.21$$

If a new item of public expenditure has to be financed by an extra tax on cameras, or if, as would be socially optimal, the value of $\Delta W/\Delta R$ is the same — and turns out to equal 4.21 — for all sources of tax revenue, then that expenditure is worthwhile only if the benefits are just over 4.2 times the resource cost of the new item of public expenditure.

Concealment cost, borne by the tax evader, and intimidation cost, borne by the government, remain additive when punishment is by imprisonment. They cease to be additive when punishment consists of a fine, for in that case the private *cost* of paying the fine is matched by a public *benefit* from the receipt of the revenue from the fine. To the tax evader, the source of evasion cost is irrelevant; it may be the reduction in productivity in working underground, the expected fine or the uncertainty when evasion may or may not be detected. He evades up to the point where marginal cost equals the tax saved, regardless of how the cost is composed. To the government — that is, to the citizen in his capacity as beneficiary of publicly supplied goods — the fine is a benefit that must be set against other forms of intimidation cost, so that only the net cost matters. The \$3,000 of intimidation cost in our example must be thought of as the difference between expenditure on police, prisons, revenue agents and so on and the revenue from fines.

How transfers magnify deadweight loss[31]   We have so far been reasoning as though all citizens are exactly alike, each having an equal share of all costs and all benefits of public activity. The analysis carries over to the transfer of income from rich to poor, through the progressive income tax or the provision of welfare, but costs and benefits must be reassessed. The critical statistic in this analysis is the ratio of the full cost to the payers of the transfer to the full benefit to the recipients, where full costs and benefits are defined to allow for hidden costs of taxation. Call this ratio Q. The full cost of a transfer is the reduction, B^P, in the welfare of all net payers, who, by assumption, are prosperous. The full benefit from a transfer is the increase, B^U, in the welfare of all net recipients, who, by assumption, are unprosperous. By definition, Q equals B^P/B^U. With no deadweight loss in taxation, the values of B^P and B^U must be the same, so that $Q = 1$. Otherwise the value of Q is necessarily greater than 1, signifying that the transfer itself is costly. A value of Q of, for instance, 4 signifies that it is necessary to impose costs on net payers that are the equivalent of a lump sum tax of \$4 in order to convey benefits to net recipients that are the equivalent of a lump sum subsidy of \$1.

Three general types of transfers can be identified. In the first, only the ultimate payers are taxed and only the ultimate receivers are allowed to share in the transfer. This is exemplified by welfare payments to the very poor where the payments are financed by an income tax with a high enough personal exemption that the very poor pay no tax. In the second type of transfer, both payers and receivers are taxed at the same rate but only the net recipients are eligible for benefits. This is exemplified by subsidies to farmers or for investment in selected industries. In the third type of transfer, which is our main concern in this section, both groups are gross recipients as well as taxpayers, but taxes are proportional to income while transfers are constant per head so that the poor become net recipients and the rich net payers. The old age pension is a transfer of this kind. In equations (23), (24) and (26) below, the value of Q is shown as a function of $\Delta W/\Delta R$ and other variables in the economy; these equations are derived in Appendix VIII.3.

In the first type of transfer where the net beneficiary pays no tax and the net benefactor receives no transfer, the value of Q is simply the marginal cost of public revenue.

$$Q^1 = \Delta W/\Delta R \qquad (23)$$

where $\Delta W/\Delta R$ is defined in equation (18). The assumption behind this formula is that the benefactor incurs a deadweight loss when his tax is increased, but the beneficiary receives his income as a lump sum. In the second type of transfer, where the revenue to finance the transfer is acquired by a general tax on beneficiary and benefactor alike, the deadweight loss is borne by both parties and the value of Q is larger.

$$Q^2 = \left(\frac{\Delta W}{\Delta R} \frac{1}{1 - [(\Delta W/\Delta R) - 1] \, (n^U y^U / n^P y^P)} \right) \qquad (24)$$

where n^U and y^U are the number and income per head of net recipients, and where n^P and y^P are the number and income per head of net payers. The value of Q^2 is necessarily equal to 1 when $\Delta W/\Delta R$ is equal to 1, and it is normally greater than $\Delta W/\Delta R$ when $\Delta W/\Delta R$ is greater than 1. However, Q^2 can turn negative — signifying that even net recipients are harmed on balance by redistribution — if $\Delta W/\Delta R$ is large and if the total pre-transfer income of the net recipients is large relative to the total pre-transfer income of the net payers, that is, if

$$[(n^U y^U)/(n^P y^P)] > 1/[(\Delta W/\Delta R) - 1)] \tag{25}$$

The meaning of this inequality is that the transfer is on balance costly to net recipients, as well as to net payers, when the recipient's net income from the transfer is outweighed by the recipient's share of the resulting deadweight loss.

In the third type of transfer, where everybody pays tax in proportion to income and everybody receives the same transfer per head, the value of Q becomes

$$Q^3 = \frac{n^P((\Delta W/\Delta R)y^P - \bar{y})}{n^U(\bar{y} - (\Delta W/\Delta R)y^U)} \tag{26}$$

where $\bar{y}$ is average income per head in the population as a whole. In this case, the transfer can be beneficial to the net recipients only if $\Delta W/\Delta R < \bar{y}/y^U$, that is, if the marginal cost of public funds is less than the ratio of average income per head, $\bar{y}$, in the population as a whole to the income per head of the net recipients of the transfer, y^U. Otherwise the net recipients' share of the transfer is less than its share of the burden of taxation, and the transfer is of no net benefit to anybody at all.

It may be useful to compare the costs of the three forms of transfer within the same numerical example. Suppose $\Delta W/\Delta R = 1.5$, $n^U = n^P$, $y^U = 1$, $y^P = 3$ and, accordingly, $\bar{y} = 2$. Then

$$Q^1 = 1.5$$

$$Q^2 = 1.5/[\,1 - (0.5)(1/3)] = 1.8$$

$$Q^3 = [(1.5)(3) - 2]/[2 - (1.5)] = 5 \tag{27}$$

Even a low marginal cost of public funds yields a high marginal cost of transfers when a great deal of money has to flow through the public sector to effect a small net transfer between one group and another.

The "obvious" moral to be drawn from the comparison of the costs of these three forms of transfers is that the first is the cheapest and therefore the best. The moral is that transfer programmes should be targeted as closely as possible to the group or groups that are the intended beneficiaries; programmes designed to better the condition of the poor should be means-tested rather than universal. There is some force to this argument, but it is not decisive. On the other side is the moral argument that means-tested programmes should be avoided because they are humiliating to the recipients, and the economic argument that restricted transfers may give rise to private behaviour that is similar in kind and no less costly than the private response to taxation which is the source of ordinary deadweight loss.

Waste of resources in benefit-seeking The central proposition to emerge from our examination of tax evasion and tax avoidance is that private

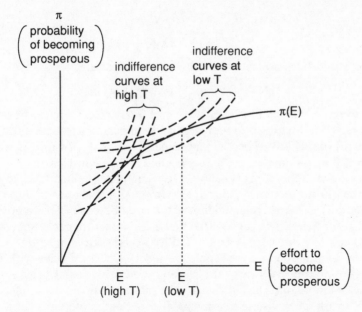

Figure 53 Effort determined by the transfer to the unprosperous

manoeuvres to avoid tax place a wedge between the marginal cost of tax to the taxpayer and the marginal revenue acquired by the government. There is a comparable proposition about the expenditure side of the budget. A similar, and additional, wedge is created by private manoeuvres in response to public provision of goods, transfers or privileges. Suppose once again that society consists of two classes of people, the prosperous and the unprosperous. But nobody is born into a social class. Every person has the same prospects at birth, represented by a probability of becoming prosperous, π, which is a function of his effort, E, where effort may be thought of as working long hours, saving, diligence or anything at all to improve one's chance of becoming prosperous. An effort function, $\pi(E)$, with an assumed diminishing marginal effectiveness of effort (that is, $\pi' > 0$ and $\pi'' < 0$), is illustrated in Figure 53, with π on the vertical axis and E on the horizontal axis.

Each person's utility depends upon his consumption, C, which is a 'good', and his effort, E, which is a "bad". The utility function is $u(C,E)$, with diminishing marginal utility of consumption and increasing marginal disutility of effort. Each prosperous person earns a gross income of y^P and each unprosperous person earns a gross income of y^U, where $y^U < y^P$. In the absence of transfers, consumption and gross income would be the same. In the presence of a transfer of T to each unprosperous person financed by a universal proportional income tax at a rate t, the consumption of the unprosperous, C^U, and of the prosperous, C^P, is:

$$C^U = (1 - t) \, y^U + T \tag{28}$$

$$C^P = (1 - t) \, y^P \tag{29}$$

where T and t are connected by the budget constraint

$$(1 - \pi)T = t \, ((1 - \pi)y^U + \pi y^P) \tag{30}$$

From the original utility function connecting C and E there can be derived an expected utility function representing each person's welfare as dependent on his probability of becoming prosperous, π, and his effort, E, with y^P, y^U and T as parameters.[32] The associated indifference curves are commensurate with the effort function, $\pi(E)$, and may be illustrated, together with the effort function, in Figure 53. However, the shapes of these indifference curves are not independent of the size of the transfer. In principle, the transfer T could be set so large that a person no longer cared whether he was initially prosperous or not. Utility would then depend on E alone, and the indifference curves would be a set of vertical lines with utility increasing to the left. Lower the transfer, and pre-transfer prosperity becomes desirable once again, causing the indifference curves connecting π and E to tilt clockwise. The smaller T, the greater the value of a given increase in one's probability of becoming prosperous, and the flatter the indifference curves must be.

Two sets of indifference curves — a relatively flat set corresponding to a low value of T and a relatively steep set corresponding to a high value T — are combined with the effort function $\pi(E)$ in Figure 53 to illustrate how the optimal E is chosen and how this varies with the size of the transfer. At any given T, a person chooses E to place himself on the highest possible indifference curve consistent with the effort function. It is immediately evident from the figure that a person supplies a high level of effort when the transfer is small and a low level of effort when the transfer is large.[33]

This is a classic "moral hazard" problem. If people could form binding contracts for effort and redistribution of income, they would choose full insurance (a value of T high enough that $C^P = C^U$) and a value of E high enough to maximize utility in that case. When such contracts are not enforceable, the value of T must be very much lower, to provide people with an incentive for effort. Any selective transfer creates an incentive for all potential recipients to make themselves eligible for the transfer by creating, or by not avoiding, the conditions in which the transfer is supplied. Actions to make oneself eligible for a transfer may bring about a reduction in the national income as a whole.

This general principle has many manifestations. Unemployment insurance reduces the incentive of those with jobs to keep them, of those currently unemployed to look for jobs, and of all workers to acquire assets to tide them over periods of unemployment.[34] Provision of welfare reduces one's incentive to avoid becoming poor. Provision of special benefits to unmarried mothers is often claimed to be a major cause of the recent increase in illegitimacy among the poor. Medicare reduces one's incentive to keep well and avoid accidents. Bail-outs of firms that would otherwise fail reduce the firms' incentive to avoid actions that might lead to failure. Deposit insurance diminishes the bank's incentive to be prudent in its investments. As with the deadweight loss in taxation, these private incentives generated by public activity have to be counted as part of the cost of this activity, a cost which is worth bearing when the benefit is substantial, but not otherwise.

Commodity effects   A second and complementary principle about the effect of public expenditure on private incentives is that small in-kind transfers have no effect on the market as a whole. Suppose it is determined that lettuce is particularly good for you, and there is a public decision to induce people to consume more lettuce by providing each person with one free (that is, tax-financed) head of lettuce per month. The policy would have some effect if many people were accustomed to eating less than one head of lettuce per month. It would have no effect at all if everybody normally ate, for example, three heads of lettuce per month. Given one lettuce free, people would merely reduce their normal purchase and would consume the same amount as before. To influence lettuce consumption, the government would need to provide more than people normally consume or to subsidize *all* lettuce consumption.

The general principles in this example are illustrated in Figure 54. The government wishes to promote the consumption of a certain good. Demand and supply curves for that good are shown on each of the three sections of the figure, with price, P, on the vertical axis and quantity per head, Q, on the horizontal axis. The supply curve is flat at a price P^S. The market equilibrium quantity in the absence of public provision is Q^0. Suppose the government believes it can force an increase in the consumption of the good by providing each person with an in-kind transfer of Q^T per head, where $Q^T < Q^0$. It is immediately evident from figure 54(a) that the government is mistaken. As long as the demand and supply curves remain invariant, a public provision of Q^T can have no effect upon the total consumption of the good, for neither the marginal valuation nor the marginal cost of the good is affected at all. Public provision reduces private provision accordingly. The demand and supply curves would remain invariant if every person's tax bill were increased by an amount $\$P^S Q^T$ to cover the cost of the transfer and if there were no marginal deadweight loss to taxation. Otherwise, total consumption might vary a bit, but a decrease would be as likely as an increase. A *decrease* in total consumption might be expected when there is a high marginal deadweight loss to taxation and a high income elasticity of demand for the transferred good!

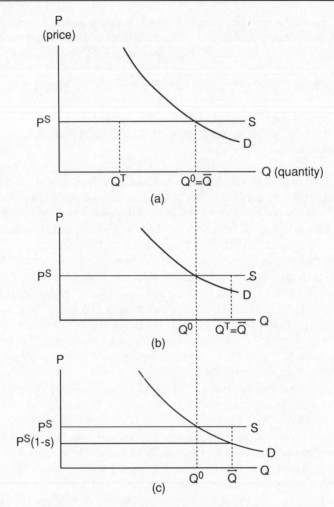

Figure 54 Public provision and private consumption. Q^0 is the quantity consumed with no public provision, Q^T the amount of public provision, and $\overline{Q}$ the quantity consumed with some public provision or subsidy

Two ways for the government to influence total consumption are illustrated in Figures 54(b) and (c). The first, illustrated in Figure 54(b), is to provide more of the good than people would be prepared to buy for themselves at the going price. Here $Q^T > Q^0$. The effect of public provision in this case is to drive out all private provision. The public provision of Q^T has effected a net increase in consumption of $Q^T - Q^0$. Public policy is beneficial in such a case if the social gain, however measured, from the extra provision of the good, $Q^T - Q^0$, exceeds the marginal excess burden of the tax required to finance the purchase of total consumption, Q^T.

The same extra provision, $Q^T - Q^0$, can be obtained at lower cost to the treasury by subsidization as illustrated in Figure 54(c). A subsidy of a portion s of the cost price reduces the market price from P^S to $P^S(1 - s)$ and increases the quantity demanded from Q^0 to $\overline{Q}$. In this case, an increase in consumption of $\overline{Q} - Q^0$ has been bought with an expenditure of $sP^0\overline{Q}$ per person rather than an expenditure of $P^0\overline{Q}$. The saving is not just a reduction in the transfer from all taxpayers to consumers of the subsidized good; it is a saving of real resources that would otherwise be wasted in tax evasion or tax avoidance.

The general principle that you cannot affect a market by a partial subsidization has many applications. The improvement of the housing of the poor brought about by public housing is nowhere near commensurate with the amount of housing provided under the programme and might in certain circumstances be altogether illusory. Public housing could actually worsen the accommodation of the poor if, for example, each poor family would have occupied 1,000 square feet in the absence of public housing and is offered 900 square feet at a low rent under the public housing programme. Of course, even in this extreme case where public housing fails to improve accommodation, it must succeed as a vehicle for transferring purchasing power to the poor if the public housing is occupied at all. What is more likely, however, is that public housing offers better accommodation to most beneficiaries than they would otherwise obtain, so that the situation is more like that depicted in Figure 54(b) than like that depicted in Figure 54(a).

The principle is also exemplified, with some complications, by the old age pension.[35] Consider a bachelor whose sole motive for saving is to provide for his old age, who retires at the age of sixty-five and who, in the absence of a publicly funded old age pension, would have accumulated $200,000 of capital at that time. If the public pension provides a stream of income with a present value at his sixty-fifth birthday of $100,000, it would be rational for that person to accumulate $100,000 less over the course of his working years, especially if he is taxed during those years to finance the old age pensions of others. When the public pension is funded, the reduction of $100,000 in cumulative private saving is matched by an increase of $100,000 in cumulative public saving and there is no net effect upon total investment or capital formation, though the title to the capital has changed. However, when the public pension is unfunded and pay-as-you-go, there is no public saving to match the decline in private saving, and there must be a reduction in net capital formation. What appears to the recipient of the old age pension as a substitution of public saving for private saving may constitute a reduction in saving for the economy as a whole, depending on how the public pension is financed.

It is essential to the argument that the recipient of the old age pension be a bachelor. The polar opposite case is that of a family whose capital today has been accumulated over many generations and whose investment decisions take account of the interests of many generations to come. For such a family, a pay-as-you-go old age pension can have no effect whatsoever on consumption and saving today because anticipated benefits from the old age pension and anticipated taxes to finance those benefits just cancel out, leaving the present value of post-tax and post-transfer income as it would be without the old age pension and without the taxes to finance it. A family's allocation of consumption over time is no more affected by the taxes and transfers associated with the old age pension than a person's allocation of consumption over the months of a year is affected by the fact that the income tax is collected all at once in April. In both cases, lending and borrowing are timed to preserve the optimal stream of consumption within the given resource constraint.

Even for the bachelor, there are important qualifications to the argument that the pension leads to a reduction in private saving, dollar for dollar. The income of the old is certainly augmented by the old age pension if the amount of the pension exceeds what the person would have provided for himself in its absence. The case where the pension has no effect on the consumption of the old is covered by Figure 54(a), where Q is reinterpreted as the annual consumption of the retired and P is the rate of substitution in use between consumption in one's working years and consumption in retirement. The case where the pension does affect the consumption of the old is covered by Figure 54(b). A country's decision to establish an old age pension is in part a manifestation of the political influence of the old, but it is also in part a judgment that there are enough people whose savings in the absence of a pension would be less than the pension — the circumstances described in Figure 54(b) — to justify the social cost of the circulation of income through the tax and transfer system of the government.

Predatory government   The catalogue of the tasks and costs of government in this chapter was prepared under the working assumption that governments are reasonably disinterested in their choice and administration of policies. Since predatory government is the subject of the next chapter, it need only be said at this point that, the less disinterested a government, the greater the full cost of any public sector activity, and the smaller the appropriate scope of the public sector is likely to be. For example, the case for a publicly financed old age pension is very different in a society where the civil service can easily determine who is eligible and who is not and where there are high standards of conduct in the civil service — so that bureaucrats dispensing cheques to the old will not demand compensation from legitimate recipients or recognize fraudulent claims — than in a society where these conditions do not obtain.

The conduct of government

There is an unavoidable tension between the two principles of entitlement in a liberal society, between the claims of people as voters and the claims of people as holders of property. At one extreme, the rights of voters — the power conferred by majority rule voting — could be extended to the point where a majority in Parliament can take anything from anybody, where no property is secure, and where a man's fortune depends primarily on his political standing. At the opposite extreme, the rights of property could be extended to the point where even the clean redistribution of income is blocked because it constitutes a public taking from one group for the benefit of another. In practice the first extreme is avoided — in so far as it is avoided — because voters understand that total disregard for property rights would mean destruction of the liberal society, and the second extreme is avoided because it could only be established in a dictatorship of judges or soldiers prepared to ignore the wishes of the great majority of the population over a long period of time.

Liberal society is characterized by a domain within which voting is predominant, a domain within which property is predominant and a grey area in between where the methods of allocation conflict. As equal voters, people choose their leaders, the scope of government expenditure, the tax system and the extent of redistribution of income. As holders of unequal amounts of property, people choose how society's capital is to be deployed, what is produced, and for whom. Within the grey area between the domains of property and voting are the rules of eminent domain, public sector giving and cost-benefit analysis. These will be discussed in turn.

Eminent domain
The state wishes to build a road, hospital, school or courthouse on land that is privately owned. The normal rules of conduct for the public sector allow the state to appropriate the land, regardless of whether the owner wishes to part with it, but require the state to compensate the owner according to the fair market value of the land. The Fifth Amendment to the constitution of the United States includes the provision "nor shall private property be taken for public use without just compensation".

The meaning of this provision of the American constitution, and of comparable rules in other countries, is straightforward enough when physical property is taken away from its owner for public use, but there are many instances where people's wealth is diminished by public action and no compensation is paid. For example, the rights of property are materially affected by the public provision of medical care. With private provision, the purchase of medical care or medical insurance is one of the uses of the income from property. With public provision, one's discretionary income is reduced by the increase in taxation made necessary to finance medical services, and access to medical care becomes a citizen's right regardless of whether he is rich or poor. In a society with any degree of progressivity in taxation, the passage from private to public financing of medical care is a taking of property from the rich and the healthy for the benefit of the poor and the unhealthy. The rights of voters, who elect a government that establishes and preserves a system of public medical care, takes precedence over the rights of property-holders.

In the public appropriation of land and buildings, the taking of property is compensated. In the establisment of new programmes in the public sector, the taking of property is not normally compensated. Indeed, compensation for net losers would be inconsistent with the redistributive motive in many public programmes. However, the presence of a redistributive motive cannot be the entire explanation of why taking is compensated in some circumstances but not in others, for compensation would not be denied in the taking of land and buildings when the owner of the expropriated property is especially rich. What exactly is the difference between these cases that justifies such different treatment with regard to compensation?

Some would argue that there is no difference. On this view, if an act of the state reduces the value of one's property, then one ought to be compensated, the only exceptions being where the action would be permissible to a private person, or where each person's benefit from the public action can be expected to outweigh the cost of the reduction in the value of his property.[36] An example of the first exception is the loss to local firms when the wages they must pay to their workers are driven up because a large government project is established in the locality. An example of the second is taxation to finance public buildings; the tax is taken, but those from whom the tax is taken are compensated by the object of public expenditure.

Others would argue that there is an important distinction to be drawn between changes in universally applicable rules (even if some people gain and others lose thereby) and victimization of identifiable people for the public good.[37] The political consequences may be entirely different. A government with the authority to take land for public purposes without compensating its original owner can use that authority to punish or intimidate opponents of the party in power. The granting of such authority would constitute a substantial raising of the stakes of competition for office among political parties in an election. If my party wins the election, you will be expropriated. If your party wins the election, I will be expropriated. Authority to appropriate land without compensation moves politics that much closer to the exploitation paradigm of Chapter V and threatens the institution of majority rule voting. Public provision of medical care carries no such baggage, though it does provide governments with the means to discriminate among voters to some extent.

Drawing the line between taking that is compensated and changes in the rules for which no compensation is warranted has been the source of much confusion and great ingenuity of argument among the judges who must ultimately decide what to do. Should the owners of Grand Central Station be compensated when the City of New York forbids the construction of a skyscraper on top of the building because the building is an historical landmark? The U.S. Supreme Court decided not, despite the fact that the skyscraper would in all probability have been permitted if the original builders of the station had taken less pride in the city and put up an equally functional but less attractive structure. Should the owner of a brickworks in a residential district be compensated when ordered to discontinue business because the brickworks is a nuisance to occupants of houses near by? Would it matter if the brickworks had been in operation long before the district became residential? Is the owner of a gold mine entitled to compensation when the government orders the mine to be shut down to free miners for employment in other mines during a war? Is the owner of cedar trees entitled to compensation when the state cuts the trees down because they harbour a fungus that is dangerous to apple trees near by? Is the owner of marsh land entitled to compensation when a law is passed forbidding him to drain the marsh and convert the land for residential construction because it has come to be believed that the destruction of marsh land has adverse environmental consequences? In each of these cases there would seem to be sufficient justification for the actions of the government in appropriating property or changing property rights in ways that benefit some people at the expense of others. The question is how to distinguish between a compensatable taking by the state and a state-induced harm that is part of the normal and uncompensatable risk of doing business. In dealing with particular cases, the courts have been required to answer this question as best they can. Apparently the answers have, in practice, involved a complex trade-off among several considerations — security of property, constraint on discrimination by the state, cost of adjudication, cost of rent-seeking and comparative efficiency (effect on total national income) of alternative forms of economic organization.[38]

Giving and taking
There is a widespread view about the proper conduct of government according to which government may *give* but not *take*. The state is often looked upon as analogous to a person who may dispose of his property as he sees fit but may not appropriate the property of another. In the words of a distinguished Canadian jurist, the state is

capable of making gifts or contracts like any other person, to whomsoever it chooses to benefit . . . and may attach conditions to the gift, failure to observe which will cause its discontinuance. These simple but significant powers exist in our constitutional law though no mention of them can be found in [the written constitution].[39]

Regional and industrial policies in Canada and in many other countries attest to the existence of such powers no matter what the constitutions may say.

Tolerance of giving contrasts sharply with the general intolerance of taking as embodied in the principle of eminent domain and in the principle of "horizontal equity". As discussed above, the principle of horizontal equity is that equals should be taxed equally, that no person should be taxed more than his neighbour unless the difference can be justified by a difference in pre-tax incomes. Both principles are essential to the defence of the liberal society, for widespread respect for the rules of the liberal society would be difficult to maintain if governments could take property without compensation or if taxes varied greatly according to one's occupation, place of residence, religion or influence with the government of the day. The two principles merge in the extreme. The ultimate violation of the principle of horizontal equity is *ad hominem* taxation which is for all practical purposes the taking of property by means of the tax system and the empowerment of the government of the day to impoverish its opponents.

Tolerance of giving is reflected on the expenditure side of the public accounts. Regions may not be taxed differently, but most federal countries are quite prepared to employ elaborate systems of intergovernmental grants that may be broadly progressive in their overall impact but that contain large elements of political and administrative discretion. Firm-specific investment grants are tolerated, but not the penalization of firms that fail to invest as the government thinks they should. Canada maintains a vast array of programmes of subsidies to create jobs, to help deserving industries, notably farming and fishing, to promote desirable investment, to improve public services in certain parts of the country, to assist firms that might otherwise fail or to bail out investors in unprofitable institutions. This is considered quite within the proper scope of government. By contrast, special taxes to divest labour from certain parts of the country, to harm undeserving industries, to discourage undesirable investment, to reduce public services in certain parts of the country, to reduce excess profits or excess returns to investment would be generally considered beyond the range of what is appropriate for governments to do.

The flaw in the analogy between governments and people that justifies public sector giving but not public sector taking should be immediately evident. If I give you a book, then you have a book which you would not otherwise possess, and I have deprived myself of the book or the cost of the book. If the government gives you a book, it has not deprived itself of anything, for there is no public sector self to be deprived. If the government gives you a book, it has simultaneously taken the book from me in my capacity as taxpayer. Every government giving is at the same time a taking; every government taking is at the same time a giving to those whose tax burdens are thereby reduced. Politicians naturally employ a rhetoric of giving, and are only too pleased to accept the praise and thanks of the recipients, but, as an accounting identity, there can be no net giving at all.

It is difficult to understand the discrepancy in attitudes toward giving and taking, though several partial and not entirely convincing explanations may be proposed. Perhaps the analogy between persons and governments is persuasive despite the fact that it breaks down under close examination. Perhaps a certain leeway for giving is required as a source of rewards for participants in party politics; volunteers serving as foot soldiers in the ranks of political parties — an army without which democracy might not be viable at all — may have to be induced by the spoils of office, which are better provided, or better concealed, as expenditures rather than as tax exemptions.

Perhaps risk aversion is important. Suppose a person had to choose between two fair gambles, the first with a small probability of a large gain balanced by a much larger probability of a small loss, and the second with the small probability of a large loss balanced by the much larger probability of a small gain. (For example, the first gamble might involve a 1 per cent chance of a gain of $10,000, balanced by a 99 per cent chance of a loss of $101, and the second might involve a 1 per cent chance of a loss of $10,000, balanced by a 99 per cent chance of a gain of $101.) Normally, a risk-averse person would choose the former gamble as long as the expected return on the two gambles was the same. The effect on the general population of infrequent public sector giving is like a gamble with a small probability of a large win and the near certainty of a small loss. This may be preferable to selective taking, which is like the other, less attractive gamble. Of course, the validity of this argument depends on the frequency of public sector giving.

These arguments may have some force when public sector giving is an infrequent event affecting a small part of the population. They break down completely when giving becomes so pervasive that the numbers of net gainers (those for whom the value of gifts exceeds the cost of taxes to finance other people's gifts) and net losers is more or less the same. Tolerence of public sector giving may be corruptive to the liberal society.

Costs and benefits

Conflict between the rights of people as equal voters and as unequal owners of property extends to the rules governing the scope and application of cost–benefit analysis. Consider medical care once again. In establishing public provision of medical care, the legislature does not simply arrange for the provision to each person of a certain amount of a homogeneous stuff called medicine. It sets up an entire medical service, and thereby empowers the Ministry of Health or its delegates to make thousands of complex decisions which necessarily benefit some people at the expense of others. One way or another, the Ministry of Health or its delegates must decide how many doctors to hire, how well doctors in each sub-speciality are to be paid, what aspects of each doctor's medical practice he may determine for himself and what aspects must conform to Ministerial directives (whether, for example, doctors may set up in practice where they choose or are to be assigned to places in accordance with the Ministry's judgment of where they are needed), where hospitals are to be built, which medical procedures are to be denied patients because the procedures are too expensive, how scarce hospital beds are to be allocated among patents, what drugs are to be made available, and so on.

The ideal for the public administration of medical care is that each of these decisions should be so bound by impersonal rules that there is no room for political influence in determining who is entitled to what. Consider the opposite extreme. If the Ministry of Health under the guidance of the Cabinet can give or withhold medical services at will, then one's standing with the party in power may become, quite literally, a matter of life and death. Cronies of politicians in office and of high officials can expect the best of medical care immediately. Mortality rates among their opponents turn out to be higher than among their supporters. If you want a modern hospital and well trained specialists in your constituency, then you had better have voted for the party in office.

Medical care is just one example of a general principle. Roads, schools, military installations (a bad if it consists, for example, of a firing range for large cannon) or public enterprises have to be allocated among constituencies. In the absence of principles as to how this is to be done, it is difficult if not impossible to prevent the government in office from employing its authority over the allocation of public expenditure to discriminate against its political opponents, bribing each constituency with money appropriated from other constituencies, raising the stakes of office, magnifying the exploitation problem and, in the extreme, rendering the liberal society inviable in the long run. Hence the political role of cost–benefit analysis.

Cost–benefit analysis is the attempt to subordinate public sector decision-making to a general rule that everybody, or almost everybody, is inclined to accept because the rule itself is fair, because the outcome is efficient or, simply, because the rule is seen as the only alternative to political allocation. Any such rule is for all practical purposes the application of a rudimentary social welfare function by the government to some domain of the economy. The standard rule in cost–benefit analysis is (i) within a limited budget, to choose projects and set the characteristics of each project to maximize the sum of benefits "to whomsoever they may accrue" and (ii) in choosing the size of the budget for each department of government, to maximize the difference between total benefit and total cost, inclusive, of course, of deadweight loss and other costs of private manoeuvres to evade taxation. The corresponding measure of social welfare is just the national income, broadly defined, at current prices. Among the virtues of this rule are that dollars of benefits to all consumers are equally weighted, that nobody is deliberately favoured over anybody else, that decisions of government can be monitored by an outside observer and that there appears to be no other procedure which is more advantageous to the representative consumer in the long run.

Cost–benefit analysis is inevitably a socialist, or collectivist, corner in an otherwise capitalist economy. Modified to some extent, the rules of cost–benefit analysis would be appropriate for an entirely socialized economy, but they are confined in the liberal society to particular domains of activity that have been assigned by the legislature to the public sector. Maximization of a social welfare function is the right criterion for officials in the Ministry of Health, *within its proper domain of authority*, just as winning wars is the right criterion for the Ministry of Defence, *within a different set of socially imposed constraints*. The constraints are essential. The choosing between the interests of one man and another is acceptable only within limited and well specified domains of public activity, and would become intolerable and corrosive to a liberal society if the limits were not respected.

The efficiency criterion for cost–benefit analysis is not so well defined that the evaluation of policies or programmes can be entirely mechanical. This is in part because a complete and accurate evaluation of a project or programme requires information that is not readily available to the government. Suppose the Ministry of Health is attempting to determine the optimal number and allocation to localities of paediatricians. The Ministry can at best form a rough estimate of the demand curve for the services of paediatricians in each locality. It may, of course, ask people what they would be prepared to pay for the services of an extra paediatrician, if those services were not provided free by the national health service, but it cannot expect such questions to be answered accurately. People cannot easily determine what they would do or pay in hypothetical situations, and, more important, they have an incentive *not* to tell the truth because they know that their chance of getting the extra paediatrician — or any other public service — is improved when a high value is claimed for the service.[40]

Quantification of benefits raises a different set of problems. A principal benefit of medical expenditure is the lengthening of life. On certain conditions,[41] this benefit can be quantified in accordance with the citizen's evaluation of his own life as reflected in the amount he would be willing to pay to avoid, for instance, a one-in-a-thousand risk of losing his life today. As a general rule, that may be satisfactory for evaluating the benefits of expenditures for the prevention of diseases or accidents that may strike more or less randomly across the age distribution of the population. Rough indirect evidence can be acquired indicating what the appropriate valuation should be. It is another matter to place values on age-specific improvements in mortality rates, as one must, implicitly, in decisions concerning pre-natal care or the provision of coronary by-pass surgery. The value that an elderly man places on the — let us say — extra year of life that a coronary by-pass can be expected to provide may be quite different from what a young adult would choose if he were setting the rules that would apply in his own care, and in the care of his children, during the rest of his life. With private provision of medical care, such decisions are determined in the market for medical services and in the market for insurance, leaving government with the option of not involving itself in the matter. Public medical care requires public allocative decisions which are essentially "tragic choices" over matters where society is reluctant to make collective choices at all.[42]

A similar problem arises in comparing benefits to rich people with benefits to poor people. Consider a society with equal numbers of rich and poor where the value of the life of the rich is $6 million (this means that a rich person would be prepared to pay up to $6,000 to avoid a one-in-a-thousand chance of losing his own life, not that his life is worth $6 million in some abstract sense) the value of life of the poor is $2 million and there is a social consensus that the government is prepared to pay up to $4 million to save a randomly chosen life, in medical care, prevention of traffic accidents and so on. Now consider the treatment of ulcers, which, let it be supposed, is entirely a disease of the rich; rich people sometimes get ulcers, poor people never do. The question is whether, to save a randomly chosen life (randomly chosen among the rich) by expenditure on research into and the treatment of ulcers, the Ministry of Health should be prepared to spend up to $6 million, which is the value that beneficiaries put on the public activity, or only $4 million, which is what the government is prepared to spend on other, more widespread, diseases. If public valuations are to reflect private valuations come what may, then $6 million is the appropriate figure. If public valuations are abstracted from all considerations of wealth, then $4 million is the appropriate figure.

The problem is not confined to medical expenditure or to expenditure on projects that save lives. Any public service (such as road repair in wealthy and poor parts of the city) with differential impacts on rich and poor people can be assigned benefits in accordance with one of two procedures, neither of which is right, or wrong, beyond dispute. Benefits can be assigned according to the actual valuation of the expected users, in which case the upkeep of roads will be superior in wealthy parts of the city. Or benefits can be assigned according to the average valuation of the type of services in the country as a whole. In favour of the former procedure is that it alone is Pareto optimal. It reflects what potential victims of disease or users of public services would be prepared to spend for themselves. In favour of the latter is the conviction that, once medical care is placed in the public domain, it should be administered to all citizens independently of how their valuations are affected by their wealth. Once placed within the public domain, provision of medical care becomes a right of citizenship which, like the right to vote, is not to be commensurate with money. My own preference is for the latter procedure because I think it appropriate to place public services in the domain of voting, where all people are equal, rather than in the domain of property, where all dollars are equal.

A different argument points in the opposite direction. Instead of simply assuming that the government seeks to maximize the monetary value of all benefits for any given level of public expenditure, we might have stepped back to the more fundamental "veil of ignorance" test. The right pattern of expenditure for the Ministry of Health would then be whatever generates the society I would most like to enter if I had an equal chance of occupying the status of every person there. Though it is not entirely clear what rules this test implies, a case can be made that the test justifies the use of welfare weights to reflect the diminishing marginal utility of income. Cost–benefit analysis would in effect be conducted in utils rather than in dollars, where the util value of a dollar's worth of benefits is greater for the poor than for the rich. A dollar of benefit accruing to the rich would be weighted less than a dollar of benefit accruing to the poor.

There is, however, something anomalous in this utilitarian approach to cost–benefit analysis. An omniscient, omnipotent and benevolent despot might well act as a utilitarian in planning the entire economy, and he would have no hesitation in arbitrarily transferring income from A to B if he believed that B could make better use of the money. There would be no rich and no poor, except in so far as people differed in their needs or capacity for enjoyment. By contrast, an economy based on private property allows considerable disparities of income and, in so far as people's tastes are more or less the same, considerable disparities among people in their marginal utilities of income. The anomaly in the use of welfare weights in cost–benefit analysis arises from the discrepancy between practices in the public and private sectors. There is something odd about, for instance, giving poor patients priority of access to heart transplants because rich patients, by virtue of the fact that they are rich, have priority of access to the nation's supply of yachts.

Conceptual difficulties are also to be found on the cost side. It is by no means obvious what to do when the cost of medical care varies markedly in different parts of the country. Given the enormous cost of getting doctors to people or people to doctors in the Canadian Arctic, there is some question whether any northern medical service could be justified on a strict comparison of dollars of benefit and dollars of cost. Yet northern citizens are clearly entitled to some degree of medical care. A balancing of rights and costs is required, though it is unclear exactly how the balance should be drawn.

Evaluation of inputs to public services becomes problematic when the government exerts an influence over their price. Public provision of medical care implies public influence upon the remuneration of doctors. The government is not entirely unconstrained in this matter. In Canada, where public medical care is administered by the provinces, the government of each province must recognize that doctors would be induced to emigrate to another province or to the United States if remuneration were low, and that the average quality of doctors in the province would eventually reflect the average wage. But there is, at least in the short run, a good deal of leeway for each provincial government in setting doctors' wages, for doctors, once established in a place, are reluctant to move. This has the dual effect of creating a large and rather influential group within society whose wages are determined as the consequence of public decisions rather than by the market, and of generating a certain ambiguity as to the appropriate cost of medical services.

Partly as a consequence of these difficulties in specifying benefits and costs, and partly because voters and politicians will inevitably become engaged when large projects are involved, the decision to place any segment of the economy within the public sector must inevitably extend the range of political allocation of income in the economy, pushing society that much closer to the pure exploitation paradigm as described in Chapter V. This is not a decisive argument against the public provision of any particular good or service, because the liberal society can tolerate a degree of political allocation. No society based on private property and majority rule voting would ever be observed if that were not so. An increase in the extent of political allocation of income is nonetheless a cost of the public provision of goods and services, a cost that should be considered along with ordinary resource cost, deadweight loss in taxation, administrative overhead and intimidation cost in deciding whether any particular public project or programme should be undertaken.

Appendix VIII.1 Derivation of marginal social cost of public revenue for an excise tax on a commodity with an upward-sloping supply curve

There are only two goods in the economy, one taxed and the other not. Let x be the quantity produced and consumed per head of the taxed good, let $P^D(x)$ be its marginal valuation in terms of the untaxed good and let $P^S(x)$ be its marginal cost in terms of the untaxed good; $P^S(x)$ is the extra amount of the untaxed good that could be produced with the resources that are released when one less unit of the taxed good is produced. In the absence of tax, the demand and supply prices would be the same. With a tax of t^0 per unit, the market equilibrium output of the taxed good is x^0 such that

$$P^D(x^0) - P^S(x^0) = t^0 \tag{31}$$

The market for the taxed good is illustrated in Figure 55, with price on the vertical axis and quantity on the horizontal axis. As shown on the figure, a tax of

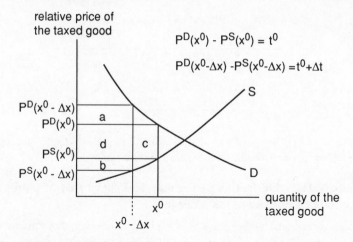

Figure 55 Marginal revenue (a + b – c) and marginal deadweight loss (c) resulting from an increase in the tax rate from t^0 to $t^0 + \Delta t$

t^0 yields a revenue of $[P^D(x^0) - P^S(x^0)]x^0$ which is represented by the area d + c. When the tax is increased from t to $t^0 + \Delta t$, the output falls from x^0 to $x^0 - \Delta x$, the demand price rises to $P^D(x^0 - \Delta x)$, the supply prices falls to $P^S(x^0 - \Delta x)$, and tax revenue becomes $[P^D(x^0 - \Delta x) - P^S(x^0 - \Delta x)](x^0 - \Delta x)$, which is represented by the area a + b + d. The change in tax revenue, ΔR, is equal to a + b – c. The effect on the welfare of the consumer, called ΔW, is the sum of two parts, (i) the increase in tax paid, a + b – c, which, with stable demand and supply curves, must correspond to a loss of potential consumption of the untaxed good, and (ii) the loss of consumers' and producers' surplus associated with the tax-induced reduction in the consumption of the taxed good. The consumer's marginal reallocation of purchasing power from the taxed to the untaxed good is socially disadvantageous because the marginal valuation of the taxed good in terms of the untaxed good, $P^D(x^0)$, exceeds its marginal cost $P^S(x^0)$. This second effect, measured by the area of the box c on the diagram, is the marginal deadweight loss associated with the marginal increase in tax; it is similar to the tax-induced waste of eight hours of labour in the carpenter and plumber example.

Pulling all this together, we see that the ratio of the full marginal cost to consumers to marginal revenue generated by a small increase in tax is

$$\Delta W/\Delta R = [\Delta \text{ tax paid} + \Delta \text{ deadweight loss}] \, / \, [\Delta \text{ tax paid}]$$

$$= \frac{(a+b-c)+c}{a+b-c} = \frac{a+b}{a+b-c} \tag{32}$$

where the values of a, b and c can be read off Figure 55. Specifically, $a = x^0 \Delta P^D$, $b = x^0 \Delta P^S$ and $c = (P^D - P^S)\Delta x$. It follows that

$$\frac{\Delta W}{\Delta R} = \frac{x^0 \Delta P^D + x^0 \Delta P^S}{x^0 \Delta P^D + x^0 \Delta P^S - (P^D - P^S)\Delta x} = \frac{1}{1 - \dfrac{t^0 \Delta x}{x^0 \Delta t}} = \frac{1}{1 + \varepsilon_{xt}} \tag{33}$$

because $(\Delta P^D + \Delta P^S) = \Delta t$ and $P^D - P^S = t^0$. But

$$\frac{t^0 \Delta x}{x^0 \Delta t} = \frac{t^0}{x^0 \dfrac{\Delta P^D}{\Delta x} + x^0 \dfrac{\Delta P^S}{\Delta x}} = \frac{t^0}{P^D \left(\dfrac{x^0 \Delta P^D}{P^D \Delta x}\right) + P^S \left(\dfrac{x^0 \Delta P^S}{P^S \Delta x}\right)}$$

$$= \frac{t^0}{(P^D/\varepsilon^D) + (P^S/\varepsilon^S)} = \frac{t \varepsilon^D \varepsilon^S}{P^D \varepsilon^S + P^S \varepsilon^D} \tag{34}$$

where ε^S and ε^D are the absolute values of the elasticities of supply and demand. Equation (34) is reproduced as equation (5) in the text.

Appendix VIII.2   Derivation of the marginal social cost of public revenue in the presence of tax evasion

In the discussion surrounding Figure 50 in the text, deadweight loss was introduced by the example of taxation of water from a well. Reconsider that example with the additional assumption that, though no labour is required to draw water from the well, it is nonetheless costly to conceal the drawing of water from the watchful tax collector. Let the cost of concealment be $C(v)$ where v is the amount of water on which the tax is not paid. The taxpayer's optimal v is defined by the condition that $C' = t$, where C' is the marginal cost of tax evasion and t is the amount of tax saved. The formula in equation (18) for identifying the marginal cost of public revenue remains valid in the presence of tax evasion as long as the variable x is reinterpreted as the amount of water on which tax is actually paid rather than as the amount of water consumed. Define y to be the amount of water consumed. Necessarily

$$y = x + v \tag{35}$$

The relation between marginal revenue from the tax, ΔR, and marginal social cost, ΔW, is illustrated in Figure 56, which is a development of Figure 50. The demand for water is the same in both figures. The new feature in Figure 56 is the marginal cost of concealment, which is shown as increasing with the amount of water concealed. The derivation of the marginal social cost of tax revenue is now almost the same as in the earlier case. As may be read off the figure, a rise in the tax per unit of water from t^0 to $t^0 + \Delta t$ leads to a decrease in consumption from y^0 to $y^0 - \Delta y$ and an increase in evasion from v^0 to $v^0 + \Delta v$. Note that Δy and Δv are defined so that positive values signify a reduction in the tax base. Note also that $\Delta x = \Delta y + \Delta v$. Revenue changes from $x^0 t^0$ to $(x^0 - \Delta x)(t^0 + \Delta t)$. Ignoring products of first differences, the change in revenue becomes

$$\Delta R = x^0 \Delta t - t^0 \Delta x \tag{36}$$

which is the area $a - b - c$. The change in welfare is

$$\Delta W = x^0 \Delta t \tag{37}$$

which is the area a. Marginal social cost per unit of revenue becomes

$$\frac{\Delta W}{\Delta R} = \frac{1}{1 - \dfrac{t^0 \Delta x}{x^0 \Delta t}} = \frac{1}{1 + \varepsilon_{xt}} \tag{38}$$

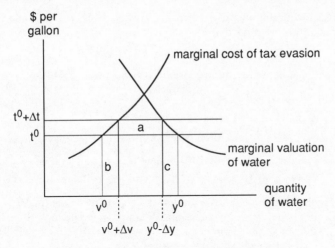

Figure 56 Tax evasion and deadweight loss

which is precisely equation (18) in the text. In an economy without tax evasion, ε_{xt} was just the elasticity of demand for water. Now it depends on both the elasticity of demand, ε^D, and the elasticity of the cost of tax evasion, ε^C.

$$-\varepsilon_{xt} = \frac{t^0 \Delta x}{x^0 \Delta t} = \frac{t^0(\Delta y + \Delta v)}{x^0 \Delta t}$$

$$= \left(\frac{t^0 \Delta y}{y^0 \Delta t}\right)\frac{y^0}{x^0} + \left(\frac{t^0 \Delta v}{v^0 \Delta t}\right)\frac{v^0}{x^0}$$

$$= \varepsilon^D(y^0/x^0) + \varepsilon^C(v^0/x^0) \tag{39}$$

where $\varepsilon^D \equiv |t^0 \Delta y / y^0 \Delta t|$ and $\varepsilon^C \equiv |t^0 \Delta v / v^0 \Delta t|$. This is equation (22) in the text.

Appendix VIII.3 Derivation of Q_1, Q_2 and Q_3 in equations (9), (10) and (12)

The key assumption in the derivation of the expressions for Q_1, Q_2 and Q_3 is that the elasticity of the tax base to the tax rate is the same for both groups. It follows that the ratio of the marginal burden of tax to the marginal tax collected is also the same for both groups. Define S to be the common value. Specifically

$$\Delta W^U / \Delta R^U = \Delta W^P / \Delta R^P \equiv S \tag{40}$$

where ΔW^U and ΔW^P are the marginal costs of taxation of the two groups, and ΔR^U and ΔR^P are the corresponding marginal tax revenues.

Define T^U to be the transfer per head to the net recipients. Define T^P to be the transfer per head to the net payers; T^P could be zero and must be small enough that transfers received remain less than the group's share of the taxes to finance the transfers. Let ΔT^U be an increase in payment per head to the net recipients and let ΔT^P be an increase (which could be negative) in payment per head to the net payers. The accounting identity between marginal public revenue and marginal public expenditure requires that

$$n^U \Delta T^U + n^P \Delta T^P = n^U \Delta R^U + n^P \Delta R^P \tag{41}$$

The net marginal benefit to all unprosperous people is

$$B^U \equiv (\Delta T^U - \Delta W^U) n^U \tag{42}$$

The net marginal cost to all prosperous people is

$$B^P \equiv (\Delta W^P - \Delta T^P) n^P \tag{43}$$

The ratio of total net cost to total net benefit is

$$Q = B^P/B^U = [n^P(\Delta W^P - \Delta T^P)]/[n^U(\Delta T^U - \Delta W^U)] \tag{44}$$

Note that in the absence of deadweight loss in taxation the values of ΔW^U and ΔR^U would have to be the same, the values of ΔW^P and ΔR^P would have to be the same as well, and it would follow immediately from equation (41) that $Q = 1$. Otherwise — when $S > 1$ — the value of Q may be quite high.

The first type of transfer is defined by the property that the net receiver pays no tax and the net payer receives no transfer, specifically that $\Delta R^U = \Delta T^P = 0$ so that ΔW^U is also equal to zero and Q becomes

$$Q^1 = n^P(\Delta W^P)/n^U \Delta T^U = S \tag{45}$$

because $\Delta W^P = S \Delta R^P$ and $n^P \Delta R^P = n^U \Delta T^U$. That is equation (12) in the text.

The second type of transfer is defined by the property that the net payer receives no transfer (i.e. $\Delta T^P = 0$) but both groups are taxed. Assume that each group's tax is proportional to its income so that $\Delta R^P/\Delta R^U = y^P/y^U$. The value of Q becomes

$$Q^2 = [n^P \Delta W^P]/[n^U(\Delta T^U - \Delta W^U)]$$

$$= [n^P \Delta R^P S]/[n^U(\Delta T^U - S \Delta R^U)] \text{ by equation (40)}$$

$$= [n^P \Delta R^P S]/\left[n^U \left\{ \frac{n^U \Delta R^U + n^P \Delta R^P}{n^U} \right\} - S \Delta R^U \right] \text{ by equation (41)}$$

$$= Sn^P y^P/\{n^U y^U + n^P y^P - Sn^U y^U\} \text{ because } \Delta R^P/\Delta R^U = y^P/y^U$$

$$= S/[1 - (S - 1)(n^U y^U)/(n^P y^P)] \tag{46}$$

which is equation (13) in the text.

In the third the transfer is universal in the double sense that everybody pays the same *rate* of tax and everybody receives the same *amount* of transfer. The marginal tax payments are constrained so that $\Delta R^P/\Delta R^U = y^P/y^U$ and the transfer per head becomes $\Delta T^U = \Delta T^P = (n^P \Delta R^P + n^U \Delta R^U)/(n^P + n^U)$. Consequently, the value of Q is

$$Q^3 = n^P(\Delta W^P - \Delta T^P)/n^U(\Delta T^U - \Delta W^U)$$

$$= \frac{n^P[S \Delta R^P - (n^P \Delta R^P + n^U \Delta R^U)/(n^P + n^U)]}{n^U[((n^P \Delta R^P + n^U \Delta R^U)/(n^P + n^U)) - S \Delta R^U]}$$

$$= \frac{n^P[Sy^P - (n^P y^P + n^U y^U)/(n^P + n^U)]}{n^U[((n^P y^P + n^U y^U)/(n^P + n^U)) - Sy^U]}$$

$$= [n^P(Sy^P - \bar{y})]/[n^U(\bar{y} - Sy^U)] \tag{47}$$

where, by definition, $\bar{y} = (n^p y^p + n^u y^u)/(n^p + n^u)$. Equation (47) is equation (26) in the text.

Notes

1 See, for instance, G. Brennan and J.M. Buchanan, *The Power to Tax: Analytical Foundations of Fiscal Constitutions*, Cambridge University Press, 1980, in which (i) a sharp distinction is drawn between the interests of citizens and the interests of government, and (ii) public policy is formulated in a context where citizens can constrain the government to some extent but not altogether. The model is discussed in Chapter IX below.

2 The doctrine of utilitarianism was employed by Bentham as a criterion for the designation of crimes and the choice of punishments. See Jeremy Bentham, *An Introduction to the Principles of Moral and Legislation* (originally published in 1789) ed. J.H. Burns and H.L. Hart, Methuen, 1970 — a surprisingly modern treatment of what is now called the discipline of law and economics. Equally surprising is that the economic approach to the law was largely ignored for over a hundred years after the publication of Bentham's book. The modern revival begins with the appearance of Gary S. Becker, "Crime and Punishment: an Economic Approach", *Journal of Political Economy*, 1968, 169–217.

3 Bentham recognized the risk of wrongful conviction as a major constraint upon the severity of punishment, *op. cit.*, chapter XVII, section 14.

4 "You might as well be hanged for a sheep as for a lamb." It follows that those who would rather that the thief steal the lamb should arrange a lesser penalty for lamb-stealing than for sheep-stealing.

5 An old conundrum in the economics of crime and punishment is the argument that hanging is the proper punishment for parking violations because, with such severe punishment, there would be no parking violations and no hangings on that account. A standard answer is that if one did happen to park illegally one would surely bring a machine gun along to deal with witnesses or policemen passing by.

6 This consideration is recognized by Becker and analysed in detail by A.M. Polinsky and S. Shavell, "The Optimal Use of Fines and Imprisonment", *Journal of Public Economics*, 1984, 89–99.

7 Michael Ignatieff, *A Just Measure of Pain: the Penitentiary in the Industrial Revolution*, Penguin Books, 1989, 19.

8 The semiconductor was invented more or less simultaneously by Jack Kilby, working for Texas Instruments, and Robert Noyse, working for Fairchild Semiconductor Corporation. Kilby was the first to apply for a patent. Noyse applied a few months later with a better description of the product. The patent was first granted to Kilby. Fairchild's lawyers contested the decision. The lower court upheld Kilby's claim, but that decision was reversed by a higher court, which granted the patent to Noyse. Apparently, the higher court's decision turned on the question of whether the words "laid down on" could be taken to mean the same as "adherent to". The story is told in T.R. Reid, *The Chip*, Simon & Schuster, 1984.

9 On the comparison between property as entitlement to transfers from the government and ordinary property as ownership of the means of production, see Charles Reich, "The New Property", *Yale Law Review*, 1964, 733–87.

10 See Oliver Williamson, *The Economic Institutions of Capitalism: Firms, Markets and Relational Contracting*, Free Press, 1985.

11 On the double moral hazard in the regulation of natural monopoly, see John Baldwin, *Regulatory Failure and Renewal: the Evolution of the Natural Monopoly Contract*, Economic Council of Canada, 1989.

12 *New York Times*, 19 December 1985, p. 29.

13 Though he does not employ the term, the classic plea for horizontal equity in taxation is by Henry Simons in *Personal Income Taxation* (University of Chicago Press, 1938). In *The Theory of Public Finance* (McGraw-Hill, 1959, 160–82), Richard Musgrave distinguishes horizontal and vertical equity, the former being the equal treatment of equals in taxation and the latter being the equalization of net incomes by the progressivity of the tax system. The distinction automatically raises the question of how to define "equals". The standard answer has been that people are equal for tax purpose if their incomes, broadly defined, are the same. There is, however, an ongoing debate as to whether the proper tax base is income, as Simons defined the term, or consumption.

14 The classic derivation of this formula is P.A. Samuelson, "The Pure Theory of Public Expenditures", *Review of Economics and Statistics*, 1954, 387–9. With reference to the utility functions $U^i(x_i, G)$, and with private goods as the numeraire, the marginal benefit of public goods to person i is $(\partial U^i / \partial G)/(\partial U^i/\partial x_i)$, and the marginal cost is the technical rate of trade-off in production between X and G at the margin.

15 This argument is developed at length in D. Usher, "Police, Punishment and Public Goods", *Public Finance*, 1986, 96–115. For general equilibrium analysis of crime and punishment, see P.A. Neher, "The Pure Theory of Muggery", *American Economic Review*, 1978, 437–45, and William Furlong, "A General Equilibrium Model of Crime Commission and Prevention", *Journal of Public Economics*, 1987, 87–103.

16 For an introduction to this topic, see E.S. Mills and P.E. Graves, *The Economics of Environmental Quality*, Norton, 1986.

17 It is tempting to suppose that one can resolve the conflict between the rights of people as property-holders and the rights of people as voters by reference to the social contract. All social institutions are seen as the outcome of a pact among citizens; my rights today are nothing other than my original rights as modified by permissible legislation (legislation consistent with the original social contract) and private contracts among citizens. Legislation not consistent with the original contract is unconstitutional and should be struck down as invalid by the courts. I believe that a contractarian resolution to the conflict between property and voting is fundamentally illusory because there is no real agreement among citizens as to the terms of the contract. Those who wish to see the enhancement of the rights of property see the social contract as a contract to preserve property, and they see political institutions as the outcome of a subsidiary agreement among property-holders. Those who wish to see the rights of voters enhanced at the expense of the rights of property-holders see the original contract as a contract to maintain certain political institutions, and they see property rights as an instrument which society may use, modify or abolish altogether as it sees fit. There may be compelling prudential reasons for preserving or enhancing property rights, but the original contract, on this view, contains no injunction to do so. I cannot see how conflict between those who wish to extend the rights of people as equal voters and those who wish to extend the rights of people as holders of unequal amounts of property can be resolved, or even clarified, by reference to a real or imagined contract.

These two interpretations of "the" social contract would seem to have their roots in the distinction between the contract of society and the contract of government; some contractarians assume that the only contract is a contract of society, others assume that the only contract is a contract of government, and still others allow for two distinct contracts. On this matter, see W.J. Gough, *The Social Contract*, Oxford University Press, 1957. For the modern usage of contractarian theory, see James M. Buchanan, *The Limits of Liberty*, University of Chicago Press, 1975, and H.S. Gordon, "The New Contractarians", *Journal of Political Economy*, 1976.

18 I discuss the distinction between redistribution and reassignment at greater length in *The Economic Prerequisite to Democracy*, Blackwell, 1980, chapter 3.

19 Person i chooses to maximize his utility $u(C_i L_i)$ subject to his budget constraint

$$C_i = (1 - t)s_i L_i + T(t)$$

The Lagrangian of this problem is

$$\pounds = u(C_i, L_i) - \lambda[C_i - (1 - t)s_i L_i - T(t)]$$

From the envelope theorem, it follows that

$$du/dt = \pounds_t = \lambda[s_i L_i + T']$$

His optimal t is that for which $du/dt = 0$, from which equation (8) follows at once.

20 This model of taking is really a simple model of optimal taxation where optimality is the first best of the median voter, who, in this case, happens to be unprosperous. For a more general model see A. Atkinson, "How Progressive should the Income Tax be?" in E. Phelps, ed., *Economic Justice*, Penguin Books, 1973.

21 For a more thorough analysis of altruism, see H. Hochman and J. Rogers, "Pareto Optimal Redistribution", *American Economic Review*, 1969, 542–57.

22 On communication in organizations where all participants have a common objective, see J. Marschak, "Elements for a Theory of Teams", in *Economic Information, Decisions and Prediction*, Dordrecht, 1979. See also J. Marschak and R. Radner, The *Economic Theory of Teams*, Yale University Press, 1972.

23 L. von Mises, *Bureaucracy*, Yale University Press, 1944, 45. Mises goes on to say that:

The objectives of public administration cannot be measured in money terms and cannot be checked by accountancy methods. Take a nation-wide police system like the F.B.I. There is no yardstick available that could establish whether the expenses incurred by one of its regional or local branches were not excessive. The expenditures of a police station are not reimbursed by its successful management and do not vary in proportion to the success attained. If the head of the whole bureau were to leave his subordinate station chiefs a free hand with regard to money expenditure, the result would be a large increase in costs as every one of them would be zealous to improve the service of his branch as much as possible. It would become impossible for the top executive to keep the expenditures within the appropriations allocated by the representatives of the people or within any limits whatever. It is not because of punctiliousness that the administrative regulations fix how much can be spent by each local office for cleaning the premises, for furniture repairs, and for lighting and heating. Within a business concern such things can be left without hesitation to the discretion of the responsible local manager. He will not spend more than necessary because it is, as it were, his money; if he wastes the concern's money, he jeopardizes the branch's profit and thereby indirectly hurts his own interests. But it is another matter with the local chief of a government agency. In spending more money he can, very often at least, improve the result of his conduct of affairs. Thrift must be imposed on him by regimentation.

24 Bureaucratic delay is not necessarily the outcome of corrupt practices on the part of officials. It may stem from an excessive concern to do one's job right, to have all the forms completed in proper sequence as required by the laws. While it is true that bureaucratic delay is fertile ground for corruption, there is no absolutely necessary connection. On the economic analysis of bureaucracy, see P.M. Jackson, *The Political Economy of Bureaucracy*, Philip Allan, 1982, and A. Breton and R. Wintrobe, *The Logic of Bureaucratic Conduct*, Cambridge University Press, 1982.

25 By the community's marginal valuation I mean the sum of the valuations of all citizens, on the assumption that guns are a pure public good.

26 The concept of deadweight loss in taxation is central to modern public finance. See, for example, Robin Boadway and David Wildasin, *Public Sector Economics*, Little Brown, 1984.

27 There is a wide variation among estimates of marginal cost of public funds because such estimates are very sensitive to assumptions about the magnitudes of the underlying elasticities of demand and supply. In the earliest empirical paper on the subject, Campbell (Harry Campbell, "Deadweight Loss and Commodity Taxation in Canada", *Canadian Journal of Economics*, 1975, 441–77) estimates marginal social costs of taxation to be about $1.25 per dollar of public expenditure. Browning (Edgar Browning, "The Marginal Cost of Public Funds", *Journal of Political Economy*, 1976, 283–98) estimates the comparable figure for the United States to be between $1.09 and $1.16. The papers differ in that Campbell estimates the loss from the reorientation of consumption brought about by excise taxation, while Browning is concerned with the labour–leisure choice as affected by the income tax. Stuart (Charles Stuart, "Welfare Cost per Dollar of Additional Revenue in the United States", *American Economic Review*, 1985, 352–62) derives a series of estimates varying, according to the assumptions about elasticities of labour supply and other aspects of the economy, between $1.07 and $2.33.

28 Equation (18) abstracts from the effect of the provision of the public expenditure on the taxpayer's purchase of the taxed good. The cost benefit rule when this is taken into account becomes

$$\sum_{i=1}^{n} MRS_i = \left[\frac{1}{1 + \varepsilon_{xt}} \right] \left[MRT - t \sum_{i=1}^{n} \frac{\partial x_i}{\partial G} \right]$$

In this equation, i refers to one of the n people in the community, MRS_i is his marginal valuation of the public good, MRT is the marginal cost of the public good, and the derivatives $\partial x_i / \partial G$ are the effects on consumption of the taxed goods x_i of a small increase in the supply of the public good. On this matter, see A.B. Atkinson and N. Stern, "Pigou, Taxation and Public Goods", *Review of Economic*

Studies, 1974, 119–28, and David Wildasin, "On Public Good Provision with Distortionary Taxation", *Economic Inquiry*, April 1984. The effect of the provision of public goods upon the demand for taxed private goods is captured in the term

$$t \sum_{i=1}^{n} \frac{\partial x_i}{\partial G}$$

29 On the neutralization of deadweight loss when all goods are taxed at equal rates, see Milton Friedman, "The 'Welfare' Effects of an Income Tax and an Excise Tax", *Journal of Political Economy*, (1952), 25–33. When leisure cannot be taxed, it is advantageous for the community to levy high taxes on goods that are especially complementary to leisure. See W.J. Corlett and D.C. Hague, "Complementarity and the Excess Burden of Taxation", *Review of Economic Studies*, (1953–4), 21–30. In principle, one can compute a set of "optimal" excise taxes for any given amount of tax revenue, where optimality refers to the minimization of aggregate deadweight loss in the economy as a whole. On the theory of optimal taxation, see Anthony B. Atkinson and Joseph E. Stiglitz, *Lectures on Public Economics* (1980). For an attempt to compute optimal taxes, see E. Ahmad and N. Stern, "The Theory of Reform and Indian Indirect Taxes", *Journal of Public Economics* (1984), 259–98. When a set of excise taxes is chosen arbitrarily or at random, there may be negative deadweight losses associated with especially low tax rates on some commodities. Increases in the rates of taxes on these commodities could reduce the overall deadweight loss by diverting purchasing power to other commodities with higher tax rates. This possibility is closed automatically when the tax structure is designed to make the community as well off as it can be within the existing technical and behavioural constraints.

30 A burgeoning literature on the social cost of tax evasion is surveyed by F.A. Cowell in *Cheating the Government*, M.I.T. Press, 1990.

31 For empirical work on the cost of transfers, see Edgar K. Browning and William R. Johnson, "The Trade-off between Equality and Efficiency", *Journal of Political Economy*, 1984, 175–203, and Charles L. Ballard, "The Marginal Efficiency Cost of Redistribution", *American Economic Review*, 1988, 1019–33. Both papers present ratios of losses to the top four quintiles of the American population to gains to the bottom quintiles. Their estimates depend critically upon assumed elasticities of the tax base to the tax rate. Browning and Johnson's "preferred" estimate is 3.49. Ballard's preferred estimate is between 1.5 and 2.5.

32 A person's expected utility, W, is

$$W = \pi u(C^P, E) + (1 - \pi)u(C^U, E)$$

which is a function of π, E, C^P and C^U in the first instance. However, equations (28), (29) and (30) allow C^P and C^U to be expressed as functions of Y^P, Y^U and T, which permits W to be expressed as a function of π and E with Y^P, Y^U and T as parameters.

33 For given t and T, expected utility can be written as

$$W = \pi(E)u((1 - t)Y^P, E) + (1 - \pi(E))u((1 - t)Y^U + T, E)$$

Effort, E, is chosen to maximize W, so that

$$\pi'(u^P - u^U) + \pi u_E^P + (1 - \pi)u_E^U = 0$$

where u^P and u^U are the values of utility if one is prosperous and if one is unprosperous. Since $\pi' > 0$ and the difference $(u^P - u^U)$ gets smaller as T increases, the expression $\pi u_E^P + (1 - \pi)u_E^U$ must get smaller too. This can happen only when E is reduced; diminishing marginal disutility of labour implies that E and the absolute value of u_E must increase or decrease together.

34 On the effect of unemployment insurance upon the incidence of unemployment see Dale T. Mortensen, "Unemployment Insurance and Job Search Decisions", *Industrial and Labour Relations Review*, 1977, 505–17, and Robert H. Topel, "On Layoffs and Unemployment Insurance", *American Review*, 1983, 541–59. The effect of provision of welfare for unmarried mothers upon the incidence of illegitimacy is discussed in Charles Murray, *Losing Ground: American Social Policy, 1950–80*, Basic Books, 1984, and Victor R. Fuchs, *How We Live*, Harvard University Press, 1983, chapter 4.

35 Two seminal articles on the effects of public indebtedness and saving are Martin Feldstein, "Social Security, Induced Retirement, and Aggregate Capital Accumulation", *Journal of Political Economy*, 1974, 905–26, and Robert Barro, "Are Government Bonds Net Wealth?", *Journal of Political Economy*, 1974, 1095–17. Both papers apply equally well to public indebtedness financed by bonds and to public indebtedness in the form of promises to pay old age pensions. Feldstein argues that public indebtedness substitutes for private capital formation when one's motivation for saving is to provide for one's old age. Barro argues that public indebtedness has no effect upon private capital formation when people expect to make bequests for their children.

36 A leading proponent of this point of view is Richard A. Epstein in *Takings: Private Property and the Power of Eminent Domain*, Harvard University Press, 1985. A great economic and political edifice is built upon one phrase in the Fifth Amendment of the U.S. constitution, "nor shall private property be taken for public use, without just compensation". Epstein argues that the plain meaning of these words is that much of the social legislation in the United States is unconstitutional. The book is an elegant construction which, at a minimum, forces the reader to decide what he means by property rights and what he believes the proper limits to property should be. For myself, I object more to Epstein's premises than to his logic. First, there is reason to doubt whether the word "taking" meant the same to the Founding Fathers as it does to Epstein. Apparently, a taking was exemplified by the billeting of soldiers in private houses, while price control, which to Epstein is the epitome of a taking without compensation, was not thought of as taking in 1789. On this matter, see Frank I. Michelman, "Property, Utility and Fairness: Comments on the Ethical Foundations of 'Just Compensation Law'", *Harvard Law Review*, 1968, 1165–258. If one is bound by the constitution at all, it must surely be in accordance with the meanings of words at the time when the constitution was adopted. Our obligations to one another cannot change for no other reason than that the usage of words has changed.

Second, if Epstein were right as to the meaning of taking, if the "true" meaning had been recognized over the entire 200 years since the establishment of the U.S. constitution and if the Supreme Court had held to the true meaning, then the Fifth Amendment would surely by now have been amended, for the great majority of the American people seemed to want a set of policies that Epstein claims to be unconstitutional. An interpretation that has been relied upon for centuries becomes the correct interpretation no matter what the Founding Fathers intended. Nobody is about to render important laws unconstitutional because of discoveries about the Founding Fathers' usage of key terms in the constitutional document.

Third, and perhaps most important, the Epstein programme of law reform requires an activism on the part of the judiciary that might in the end be corrosive to democratic government. Judges would have to take it upon themselves to invalidate much of the social legislation of the United States. This, in turn, would carry the twin dangers of a major increase in the political influence and partisanship in the appointment of judges and of a loss in respect for the judicial process in the nation at large. The judiciary is respected in its supervision of the laws when it confines itself to cases of manifest discrimination, to interpretations when the law itself is ambiguous, or to judgments in circumstances where most people want to do what is right but cannot make up their minds where right lies. As discussed in Chapter VI, a judiciary prepared to block social legislation which is not manifestly discriminatory and which is favoured by the great majority of voters is in danger of losing the respect that is required for its necessary, but minimal, role in society.

37 See, especially, Joseph L. Sax, "Takings and the Police Power", *Yale Law Journal*, 1964, 36–76, "Takings, Private Property and Public Rights", *Yale Law Journal*, 1971, 149–86, and "Some Thoughts on the Decline of Private Property", *Washington Law Review*, 1983, 481–96.

38 All the cases in this paragraph are examined by Epstein or in the literature cited in note 37. It is interesting that Ronald Coase denies the very existence of the problem. In "The Problem of Social Cost", *Journal of Law and Economics*, 1961, 1–44, p. 14, he cites a judicial opinion that a party to a dispute had a certain right by the "doctrine of lost grant". This doctrine states "that if a legal right is proved to have existed and been exercised for a number of years the law ought to presume that it had a legal origin". Coase goes on to argue, "The reasoning employed by the courts in determining legal rights will often seem strange to an economist because many of the factors on which the decision turns are, to an economist, irrelevant. Because of this, situations which are, from an economic point of view, identical will be treated quite differently by the courts. The economic problem in all cases of harmful effects is how to maximize the value of production . . . . In deciding this question, the 'doctrine of lost grant' is about as relevant as the colour of the judge's eyes." A case could perhaps be made for Coase's position if judges were gods, all-knowing and impervious to special pleading or sympathy with one or another party to a dispute. Surely, a degree of respect for prior rights reduces the precariousness of legal proceedings and economizes on transaction cost to some extent.

39 F.R. Scott, cited in James Mallory, *The Structure of Canadian Government*, revised edition, Gage, 1984, 408.

40 A number of schemes for eliciting truthful responses from potential recipients of public largess are discussed in R. Boadway and D. Wildasin, *Public Sector Economics*, Little Brown, 1984, chapter 6.

41 The conditions and the exceptions are discussed in D. Usher, "The Value of Life for Decision Making in the Public Sector", *Social Philosophy and Policy*, spring 1985, 168–91.

42   The phrase is from the title of a book by Guido Calabresi and Philip Babbit, *Tragic Choices*, Norton, 1978.

Chapter IX

Predatory government

Just as market failure can be looked upon as a vestige of anarchy within the private sector of the economy, so predatory government can be looked upon as a vestige of despotism within the public sector. I have so far presented two opposite pictures of the public sector: the selfless and disinterested servant of the common good as described in traditional welfare economics and the ruling class in the despotic society where the only constraint upon the exploitation of the ordinary citizen is his capacity to rebel, or to turn to banditry, if pushed too far. It is the purpose of this chapter to say something about governments at neither extreme, to describe predatory aspects of government within the confines of the liberal society and, where possible, to draw implications about the role of government in a society with a less than completely predatory government.

Predatory activity within the public sector of a liberal society may consist (i) of appropriation of income and privileges by a ruling class of politicians, soldiers, civil servants and police, (ii) of capture of the instruments of government by groups in the private sector that exercise a disproportionate influence upon the state, and (iii) of exploitation or subjugation of the rest of society by any majority of voters. Predation by a ruling class is similar in some respects to despotism, but more constrained. Predation by capture and predation by voting are alike in that both involve the domination of the state by a group or coalition of groups in the private sector. They differ in the means by which government is dominated. Predation by capture involves lobbying, financial contributions to political parties, bribery, terrorism or commonality of interest between personnel of the government and representatives of the dominant groups in the private sector. Predation by voting involves the formation of a majority coalition to elect a government pledged to favour its supporters. These forms of predation will be discussed, one by one.

Predation by a ruling class

Liberal society differs from despotism in the constraints upon the ruling class. In a despotic society, rulers are constrained in their exploitation of subjects by the fear of rebellion or by the effect of oppression upon the productivity of the economy. In a liberal society, rulers are constrained by the prospect that they will be turned out in the next election. Ideally, the constraint of the ballot box would be sufficient to ensure that public decisions are responsive to the will of the electorate and that the rewards of office are held down to what the personnel of the government could earn in the private sector. In practice, a liberal society is never quite as it should be, and public officials can be expected to act in their own interest, at the expense of the electorate, to a greater or lesser extent.

Liberal society differs less from despotism in the instruments of government than in how these instruments are employed. In both societies, the army stands ready to suppress domestic rebellion and to intimidate would-be foreign aggressors. In both societies, the police are prepared to use violence against citizens who break the rules. In both societies, the government sets limits on public discussion through censorship or other means of influencing the press. Sometimes the instruments of government can be employed by political leaders to enhance the perquisites of office and to maintain their tenure indefinitely. Sometimes they can be employed by the army to overthrow the elected leaders or to place limits on what political leaders — duly elected or otherwise — can do. The instruments of government may be used for the subversion rather than for the preservation of the liberal society.

When liberal society works as it should, the predatory tendencies of government are constrained by a conditional obedience to authority. Soldiers obey their officers, juniors obey their superiors in the civil service, and the leaders of the army and the civil service obey the head of state only in so far as the commands conform to the laws, customs and traditions of society. The instruments of government are not too powerful to be contained within a liberal society as long as a President about to be impeached cannot command the secret service to arrest members of Congress and judges of the Supreme Court; and as long as the general, who is obeyed instantly on the field of battle, would lose his authority over his troops if he commanded them to assassinate the Prime Minister and the Members of Parliament. A liberal society can be compatible with the extensive hierarchy that modern government requires only if that hierarchy automatically breaks down when commands exceed the limits prescribed by the laws and customs of society.[1]

To draw a distinction between acceptable and unacceptable commands is not necessarily to claim that there is a clear and distinct line of division between the two or to deny the existence of a middle ground between completely predatory government in a despotic society and the completely public-serving government in an ideal liberal society. The purpose of this chapter is to explore the middle ground. Though the prospect of the loss of office at the next election and the conditional obedience in the hierarchy of government do serve as a defence against the gross excesses of a despotic society, it is too much to expect that the formidable powers of government will never be used to enrich the personnel of the public sector at the expense of the rest of society or to provide officials with income and privileges in excess of what they could expect if they had employed their talents in the private sector instead.

The constrained Leviathan

A good starting place for the analysis of predatory government within the confines of a liberal society is the model of the constitution-constrained Leviathan as developed by Brennan and Buchanan in *The Power to Tax*.[2] Imagine an undifferentiated ruling class that seeks to maximize its own income, regardless of the welfare of its subjects, but is constrained by a constitution that everybody, ruler and subject alike, is bound to respect. From a purely analytical point of view, the Brennan and Buchanan model differs from the model of despotism in Chapter IV, not in the objective function of the ruler, but in the replacement of the constraint imposed by banditry with a constraint upon the mix of taxes that the constitution allows. The term "Leviathan", taken over from Hobbes, is a useful shorthand for the undifferentiated revenue-maximizing state.

At the core of the model is a dichotomy between a ruler, who chooses the tax rates, and subjects, who choose the tax base on which the rates are imposed. The model can be thought of as a two-stage game in which the first move is by subjects choosing the tax base, the second move is by the ruler choosing tax rates, and each party's reward depends on both parties' moves. To make the formal analysis plausible, think of the subjects as attending a constitutional convention to choose a tax base. Subjects know that the ruler will respect the constitutionally sanctioned base but will at the same time be entirely free to impose whatever rates he pleases on the base that is supplied. Ruler and subject must both be seen as benefiting from public goods, for, if the ruler spent the entire tax revenue on his own pleasures, there would be no point in giving him any tax base at all. Subjects are prepared to supply the ruler with some tax base because they know that he, as well as they, is a beneficiary of the army, the police and a variety of services that can be produced only within the public sector. Better to have part of the public revenue siphoned off for the ruler's personal pleasures than to have no public revenue — and no public goods — at all. The subjects' problem in choosing the tax base is to provide the ruler with revenue to run the state while denying him the means to impoverish his subjects with unnecessarily burdensome taxation. The subjects may, for instance, allow excise taxes on gasoline, tobacco, salt and cheese, as well as tariffs on some or all imports, but not an income tax or a poll tax.

Though the ruler is legally free to set tax rates as high as he pleases within the prescribed base, he is in fact constrained by the taxpayers' response to the rates that he sets. If the rate of tax on any commodity is set too high, the taxpayer may contract his purchases of the commodity so drastically that the tax revenue is actually less than if the rate had been lower. There is in effect a Laffer curve for the Leviathan as well as for other forms of government. The subjects' problem at the constitutional convention is to choose the tax base at which their utility is maximized, with due regard for the behaviour of the ruler, who is unconcerned about the welfare of his subjects but who does need some public goods and who recognizes that a rise in any tax rate leads to a contraction in the corresponding tax base.

The model is to some degree reminiscent of the relations between Parliament and the King in early seventeenth-century England.[3] Parliament could levy or refuse to levy taxes, but it would be an infringement upon the majesty and perogative of the King for Parliament to demand a full account of how the money is spent. As in the model, the King could choose the allocation of state funds among competing uses, his own pleasures, rewards to his favourites and protection of the kingdom. But the powers of Parliament were both greater and less than the powers of the citizen in the constitutional convention of the Brennan and Buchanan model, greater because Parliament chose the amount of tax and not just the tax base, less because Parliament could be dissolved at the pleasure of the King.

The immediate purpose of the model is to construct a canon of principles for the subject in choosing a tax base. The ultimate purpose is two fold: to supply an interesting alternative to the model of the selfless and social welfare-maximizing government that is the staple of traditional welfare economics, and to rationalize the tax limitation referenda that were prevalent in the United States at the time *The Power to Tax* was written. The principles themselves are of considerable interest, for they represent a complete overturning of ordinary public finance as designed for a welfare-maximizing government. In particular, it is shown that a narrow tax base is almost always preferable, from the point of view of the subject, to a broad tax base, and that, for a given dollar value of the base, it makes almost no difference which taxes are allowed.[4] However, our concern here is not with the principles *per se*, but with the main assumptions of the model as a basis for understanding predatory government within a predominantly liberal society. A critique of the model will serve as the framework for examining predation by the personnel of the government. The critique is focused on two key assumptions in the Brennan and Buchanan model, that government is an undifferentiated revenue-maximizing entity and that it is constrained by the subjects' control of the tax base.

On abandoning the assumption that government is the selfless maximizer of the social welfare, the natural place to go is to the opposite extreme, namely, that government maximizes its own revenue without regard for the well-being of the ordinary citizen. As a working hypothesis, the maximization of revenue by governments bears a family resemblance to the maximization of profit by firms, or, more generally, to the maximization of income as a criterion of economic behaviour. The analogy between governments and firms is what makes the hypothesis plausible. To maximize revenue is, in certain circumstances, to maximize the incomes of the personnel of the government, whose behaviour in the workplace is deemed to be no different from the behaviour of other actors in the economy.

The analogy between public revenue and private income in the model of the revenue-maximizing Leviathan is, nonetheless, weak in two important respects. First, there is no differentiation between total revenue and revenue per public official. Even an increase in the salary component of public expenditure can fail to be beneficial to the individual bureaucrat or politician if the increase is used to hire more public officials rather than to increase the wages of those already employed. Other things being equal, an increase in the average salary of public officials must be reflected as an increase in total public expenditure, but the converse is not true. Expansion in the scope of the public sector[5] could be accompanied by a decrease in average salaries if the addition of a new responsibility of government — such as the provision of day care — coincided with a period of austerity, as would be the case if Parliament were reluctant to provide the extra funds to finance the new purchases of goods and services.

Second, and of greater importance, the analogy fails to take account of conflicts of interest within the personnel of the public sector. Strictly speaking, the model sees bureaucrats, soldiers, judges, policemen and politicians of all political parties as in cahoots for the purpose of squeezing as much income as can be squeezed from the general public. One cannot help suspecting that the assumption is not altogether wrong. Certainly, the rhetoric of tax revolts suggests that many people believe the assumption to be at least partially right. It cannot be entirely right within the confines of a liberal society. Politicians hoping to be re-elected have an acquired interest in lowering tax rates and in keeping down the incomes and privileges of other personnel of the government. Soldiers have a special interest in the incomes of soldiers, officials have a special interest in the incomes of officials, and judges have a special interest in the incomes of judges, but each group becomes the enemy of the rest in competition for shares of a given revenue pie. A public sector with many divergent interests is less of a threat to the subjects than the undifferentiated Leviathan as postulated in the model.

Realistic or not, the revenue maximization hypothesis becomes interesting when coupled with an assumption about the constraints upon the ability of the government to acquire revenue. In standard microeconomics, the entrepreneur maximizes profit but he does not grab the entire national income. He is constrained by conditions of production and by the terms under which he can acquire factor supplies. A theory of the revenue-maximizing government requires comparable constraints within the public sector. The theory is virtually indistinguishable from the theory of government as the maximizer of social welfare in the special case where the constraint is the control exercised by the public through the intermediary of elections and representative government. The theory takes on content when the usual political constraint is seen as weak and ineffectual, and another quite different constraint is put in its place.

The great virtue, in my opinion, of Brennan and Buchanan's constitutionally constrained Leviathan is as a contrast to and foil for the benevolent government in traditional welfare economics. Neither view of government is particularly realistic on balance, yet each may be adopted unthinkingly if no alternative is discussed. Deny it as we may, the working assumption in traditional welfare economics is that government has internalized the social welfare function and has adopted the subjects' interest as its own. This assumption prevails by default when no other motive is recognized in the determination of public policy. As I argued in the introductory chapter of this book, a social welfare function can be justified as a representation of the reader's sense of the common good. It *will* be looked upon as the objective of government unless some explicit alternative is put forward. Theories are defeated by theories, never by facts alone. It is in this context that the story of the constitution-constrained Leviathan is useful, for the story is a half-truth presented to an audience that is already in possession of the other half.[6]

All the same, the sharp dichotomy in the model between the tax base chosen by the citizen and the tax rate chosen by the government is surely an exaggeration. It is hard to imagine that control of the government by the voters is at once so weak as to have no influence whatever upon the choice of tax rates and so strong as to be an absolute barrier to the types of taxes that are prescribed in the constitution. A government with enough independence from its subjects to set tax rates at will would surely be free to choose the tax base as well. In defence of Brennan and Buchanan's division of the power to tax between ruler and subject, it might be argued that the exaggeration contains a grain of truth because the subject has more control over the tax base than over the tax rates. Should that be so, there might be room for a general model incorporating traditional welfare economics and the tax base-constrained Leviathan as special cases.

There is a similar but more fundamental dichotomy in *The Power to Tax* between constitutions and elections. Governments are rigidly constrained by constitutions. They are not constrained by elections at all. The absence of an electoral constraint is not a conclusion of the model in the usual sense that elections are formally incorporated into the model and found to have no effect on the behaviour of governments. There is no formal dismissal of the view of the man on the street that the predatory inclinations of bureaucrats, politicians and soldiers are to some extent held in check by the incumbent politician's fear of being tossed out of office in the next election if the actions of the government are unpopular or if tax rates rise beyond what citizens are prepared to pay. The common view that elections matter is not tested and found wanting. It is ignored.

The procedure is an instance of a common, almost universal, practice in the social sciences of darkening the stage as the spotlight is directed to a particular actor in the play. The scope of a model is deliberately restricted to clarify the phenomenon one wishes to understand. Brennan and Buchanan focus upon the constitutional constraint. They must, and do, believe that the electoral constraint is in some respects weak or inadequate, for otherwise the study of the constitutional constraint would cease to be interesting. Their procedure is to abstract from the electoral constraint altogether and to assume that the constitutional restriction on the tax base is an unevadable constraint upon the Leviathan.

Brennan and Buchanan participate in what might be called "the myth of the self-enforcing constitution". The constitution is seen as representing an absolute barrier to the predatory inclinations of officials, soldiers, judges and politicians. In the absence of constitutional restraints, the personnel of the government can exploit their subjects as they please; a constitutional prohibition is a line that can never, never be crossed.

The myth is at least partly correct. Constitutions do constrain governments to some extent. Again and again we see governments quietly and humbly deferring to the rulings of the Supreme Court. At the same time, it must be recognized that the Supreme Court is itself an agency of the government and is in the long run manipulable through the government's authority to appoint judges who can be expected to interpret the constitution in acceptable ways. In practice, the meaning of the constitution is never self-evident. A government intent on increasing the role of the state appoints judges who are likely to turn a blind eye when, for instance, a component of the allowable tax base is interpreted more broadly than the framers of the constitution had intended. The gasoline tax may, for example, be assessed in proportion to the income of the taxpayer. And, of course, a government intent on reducing the size of the state would appoint judges whose interpretations would lean in the opposite direction.

The harm in the myth of the self-enforcing constitution is not so much that it is wrong as that it leads one to be unreasonably and dangerously sanguine about the efficacy of courts and constitutions as constraints upon the behaviour of government. Courts interpreting constitutions are respected, even venerated, when their influence is restricted to a few fundamental matters where widely held moral convictions appear to conflict, where the great majority of the citizens want "right" to be done but are not entirely sure what constitutes the right in a given situation (for instance, in rules pertaining to racial discrimination) or where laws extend into territory that should be covered by constitutional amendment. But respect for and independence of the courts can be maintained only if the courts are not over-used. Courts can be and are subverted by despotic governments. Equally, a constitution that required the courts to void economic legislation supported by a majority of voters could generate a political reaction that would in the end destroy the authority of the courts altogether. A constitutional prohibition on all but a few, narrowly specified types of taxation would lead the government of the day to appoint judges prepared to decree that the tax system which the government wanted to adopt was "really" consistent with the prohibition. The stakes in having a sympathetic judiciary would rise, political disposition would become increasingly important relative to probity or competence in judicial appointments, and the rights of citizens would be less adequately protected, without achieving the economic effects that the prohibition on certain types of taxation was intended to procure.[7]

Notwithstanding these reservations about the model of the constrained Leviathan as a basis for the study of predatory government, the model is useful as a first step away from the extremes of traditional welfare economics and of despotic government and towards a middle ground occupied by an imperfect liberal society. In particular, the model raises two large questions: what are the rewards of office in a liberal society? And what are the constraints upon the personnel of the public sector in seeking these rewards? I shall discuss these questions in turn.

Rewards of office
Rewards of office may be of several kinds. First among them is income, including current salary, expected future salary for as long as one remains in the public service, and the options available in the event that one wishes to transfer from the public to the private sector at some point in one's career. Expected future salary depends upon one's prospects of promotion. Options in the private sector depend on experience, contacts and obligations acquired within the public service. The pecuniary motive is in no way unique to the public sector. Nor is it intrinsically anti-social, for, in the public sector as in the private sector, there is an elaborate structure of incentives — comprising punishment for gross misbehaviour, dismissal, salary increases and promotion — to enlist selfish motives for the purposes of the organization.

The enlistment mechanism is probably effective to some extent, but never completely so. There is reason to suppose that the agency problem

— the difficulty, as discussed in Chapter VII, in all contractual relations of binding agents together so that each does as he has contracted to do when it is in his personal interest to do otherwise — is of greater importance in the public sector than in the private sector. It is at least arguable that the prospect of a political party losing office in the next election is less of a constraint upon the actions of politicians, soldiers and civil servants than is the prospect of bankruptcy upon the actions of entrepreneurs, investors and workers in the private sector. Allowing that incentives in the public sector do work as they should to some extent, it must be recognized that these incentives are inevitably less than completely effective in tying the private pecuniary interest of public officials to the common good.

The re-employment of ex-public officials in the private sector is a grey area between legitimate use of one's skills and outright corruption. A considerable part of the lifetime income of senior bureaucrats is the remuneration from employment in the private sector on retirement. Senior military men take positions with defence contractors. Ex-politicians become lobbyists on the strength of their contacts with former colleagues still in office. Public officials who have learned the ins and outs of bureaucracy are hired by firms that can make use of their special experience. Boards of directors of large corporations include personages who were once prominent in government and may become so again. It is perfectly reasonable that people who leave the public service should have the opportunity to make a living elsewhere and to use acquired skills where they yield the largest social product. A civil service from which one could not resign, or be fired, without risk of destitution would have a dangerously strong hold over its employees, who would then be inclined to follow orders, regardless of whether they were legal, and who would be unlikely to protest about wrongdoing. On the other hand, the offer of a job on retirement may be tantamount to bribery. A firm with a reputation for employing ex-officials of the department of government to which it applies for licences, entitlement to import and "sensible" interpretations of regulations may get a more sympathetic hearing from the bureaucracy than a firm with a policy of never employing ex-officials at all, or of offering them insultingly low wages.

Unlike bribery, which can sometimes be detected and punished, the reciprocation of favours leaves no evidence that could be brought out in a court of law. Nobody, not even the parties to the transaction, knows whether the hiring of an ex-official by a firm that does a great deal of business with the government, or that must appeal frequently to the government for interpretations of its regulations, is a straightforward employment of someone whose skills are useful to the firm or a bribe. Public control of contacts between firms and ex-bureaucrats can be exercised only by rules of thumb such as that nobody, on resigning from the civil service, can work for or give advice to a firm that has had dealings with his department until at least two years after his resignation, or that no ex-civil servant may lobby the department where he once worked.

Further along the road to bribery, though quite legal or quietly permitted in some countries, is what might be called political speculation. A politician or senior bureaucrat who is at the same time a businessman can ensure favourable treatment for a firm he happens to own. Thus a firm is worth more in his hands than in the hands of someone outside the ruling group.[8] His speculations invariably prosper as he buys firms, provides them with valuable contracts, and resells them at their new higher value or includes them as part of his own commercial organization. Sometimes political speculation is undertaken directly by the person in office. Sometimes title is held by a member of the family. Sometimes the politician or general works through a surrogate, preferably a person from a politically unpopular group such as the Chinese in Indonesia, whose position would be quite untenable but for his political support, just as the Great Khan employed Marco Polo in his enterprises.[9]

Finally, among the pecuniary rewards is the income from bribery, the taking of money for performing services to the general public that should be performed free or for favouring one person over another in the disposition of favours. This will be discussed below under the heading of constraints upon the personnel of the government.

Over and above the pecuniary rewards of office are the rewards of the job itself, the authority to command, the sheer interest of the job, and the knowledge that one is exerting an influence upon the world, that one's actions matter, for good or evil, to a great many people. Indeed, there are those who argue that it is only by participation in the life of the community that one becomes fully human. Man, it is said, is a social animal. To the ancient Greeks, the proper activity of a free man was to take part in the deliberation about and the governing of his state, to engage in *action* as distinct from mere *labour* or *work*.[10] That is hardly a tenable position today unless the sphere of action is enlarged to include the leadership in large corporations and the activity of the scientist, who has surely no less influence upon the human condition than the politician or businessman. There is nonetheless an attraction to high office, to influence upon the development of one's society, to the attainment of a kind of immortality in one's society or, more crudely, in the inclusion of one's name in the history books. Of course, men enter politics with pecuniary motives, but it would be wrong to suppose that there are no other motives.[11]

Non-pecuniary motives are not necessarily altruistic. The politician or soldier who leads his people into war may be sacrificing his countrymen for his own glory rather than for their benefit, and he may take considerable satisfaction in the sacrifice, regardless of the outcome. It is rare for a politician to step down because he believes somebody else can do a better job than he. Sincerely held attachment to policies or programmes may have as much to do with their efficacy in carrying the politician to office as with their efficacy in promoting the common good. Desire for influence is a mixed motive which is sometimes beneficial and sometimes harmful to the population as a whole. As with pecuniary motives, this motive can be directed one way or another, depending on how society is organized.

Constraints upon the personnel of the government
Four constraints are discussed — rebellion by subjects, private sector incentives, elections and the law. Of these, the first two are mentioned briefly and the last two are covered at some length.

Predatory government is constrained in its exploitation of its subjects by the threat of rebellion when their standard of living and the general circumstances of their lives are seen as very much worse than might be expected after a change in government. Recall the model of the despotic hierarchy in Chapter IV. For a given probability of success, a rebellion at any level of the hierarchy, from top to bottom, becomes increasingly likely the greater the disparity between present income and income as it would become after a successful rebellion. Rulers, in their own interest, must see to it that their subjects do not become so desperate that a rebellion appears, on balance, as an attractive alternative to passive obedience.

While this constraint is genuine and is ignored by rulers at their peril, it is cold comfort to subjects whose incomes may be far below what could be expected from a more subject-oriented government. Recall also that the no-rebellion constraint in the model of despotism depends on the probability of success of rebellion and the severity of retribution should the rebellion fail, as well as on the increase in incomes that successful rebels can expect. A ruler may concentrate on the first two deterrents. A small, wealthy, cohesive and determined ruling class may subjugate a large population without too much risk of a successful uprising against its authority. Stalin died in his bed, as did most of the emperors of China.

Harsh treatment of subjects can also destroy the subject's incentive to work and to accumulate, thereby reducing the potential tax revenue that a ruler can expect from his domain. This is Hobbes's argument, already quoted in Chapter IV, that "the greatest pressure of Sovereign Governors, proceeded not from any delight, or profit, they can expect in the damage, or weakening of their own subjects, in whose vigor, consisteth their own strength and glory". This is the essence of the model of rulers, bandits and farmers in Chapter IV; rulers have to treat farmers with some consideration lest farmers turn to banditry, simultaneously reducing tax revenue and increasing the expenses and dangers that the rulers must bear. The best outcome for the Leviathan may be compatible with a less than total impoverishment of the subjects.

As constraints on the personnel of the government, the prospect of rebellion by subjects and the effect of repression on the incentive to work, save and innovate are essentially the same in the liberal society as in a society that is entirely despotic. But a liberal society has two other constraints on the ruling class, constraints that are considerably more binding and can be expected to provide the subject with a happier, more prosperous and freer life than could be had in a despotic society. The liberal society provides the subject with the opportunity to replace government in *elections*; and, though this has not been emphasized so far, the *law*, applying as it does to ruler and subject alike, represents an independent constraint on the amount of exploitation possible. Ideally, these institutions would abolish exploitation altogether, by tying rulers' actions to the social welfare function and ensuring that the personnel of the government earn no more than their talents could command in the private sector. To some extent they do. Our discussions of these constraints will emphasize the reasons they do so imperfectly.

Voting and elections are discussed in the latter half of this chapter with special emphasis on the exploitation by the majority of the minority, and largely without reference to the personnel of the public sector. Here the emphasis is on "throwing the rascals out" if they fail to behave in the interest of the electorate as a whole. With frequent elections, and with a well informed electorate, the government might be induced to behave well and to demand no more for its services than the going wage in the private sector for its personnel. With elections every few years, there remains some scope for public sector predation.

Imagine a political party coming to power with a five-year term of office before it must submit itself to the electorate once again. Presumably politicians seek office because the rewards of office exceed what they could obtain in the private sector. Suppose for the moment that the politician's only reward is monetary and suppose that his income in the private sector would be $100 per day. If he accepts no more than $100 in the public sector, the entire advantage of attaining office is lost, and he might as well not have sought office at all. On the other hand, he knows that if he takes too much he will be turned out of office at the next election. His problem is to take just enough that the voter is prepared to re-elect him.[12] One might suppose that the rational politician would simply take what he can during his term of office, because the benefit from re-election is not worth the cost of the restraint that would be required to persuade voters that he was worthy of re-election. This may sometimes be a rational strategy. It need not be if law or custom places an upper limit on what one may safely take. The voter, on the other hand, is prepared to re-elect the incumbent as long as his income does not exceed $100 by too great a margin, for the voter knows that a rival politician whom he might elect instead would also appropriate a premium over the private sector wage. It is difficult to say what the minimal premium would be, but it is evident that some premium would emerge. There would be an equilibrium rent for the party in power, below which it could remain in power indefinitely. The problem is, of course, greatly compounded by the fact that the party in power has a platform of policies that are of special interest to some segment of the voters, who dare not abandon "their" party unless it becomes very greedy indeed.

This analysis is based on the assumption that the election is strictly "fair" in the sense that the party in power has no influence on the outcome except in so far as its policies and its predatory behaviour affect its popularity among the electorate as a whole. The assumption is never strictly true. The party in power can employ its influence to buy or bully the constituencies one by one.

Elections may be partially or totally fraudulent. Improper practices vary all the way from stuffing ballots in a few critical elections, through the employment of hoodlums to intimidate voters and electoral officials in constituencies known to favour opposition parties, to outright falsification of election results. It is unclear who is fooled or what is gained from totally fraudulent elections, but such elections do sometimes take place. The authority of the incumbent government over the means of communication may be employed to advertise liberally for candidates of the party in power and to restrict access to the media by candidates of the opposition party. Censorship may limit the scope of criticism of the party in power. The personnel of the opposition parties may be constrained in a variety of ways to reduce access to voters and to discourage competent people from participating in politics. Candidates and party workers may be banned from certain parts of the country or may be physically harassed. Where the means of production are owned by the state, remunerative employment or access to education for their children may be denied to people who oppose the ruling party.

Governments may maintain themselves in office indefinitely by buying votes. This may be accomplished directly for cash or for drink, as was the practice in eighteenth-century England and remains the practice in many countries to this day. A more common practice is to buy constituencies with public works. The location of the new hospital or the new industrial plant is made to depend on satisfactory behaviour by the voters in the districts where the facilities are to be built.[13] The road paved up to the ballot box is the paradigm of these techniques. Vote-buying may be a reward or a punishment. It is a reward when public services are directed to constituencies that voted for the party in office. It is a punishment when recalcitrant constituencies are taxed to finance these services or are systematically by-passed in the allocation of funds and advantages at the disposal of the government in office.

Vote-buying with public works creates a prisoner's dilemma among constituencies. Voters in all constituencies might be better-off if the incumbent party were defeated in the election, but everybody votes for that party nonetheless because it is in his interest to do so. We have here an instance of Tullock's law that personal interest takes precedence over class interest when the two conflict. Suppose, for simplicity, that all voters in a constituency are alike and that the typical voter's utility depends in the first instance on amounts of goods consumed. Utility may nonetheless depend on the outcome of the election, for each person's consumption depends on the disposition of the party in power toward his constituency — favourable if his constituency votes for the party in power, unfavourable otherwise. Thus the typical voter's utility function can be represented indirectly as $U(e,v)$, where e is the outcome of the election and v is his constituency's vote. With only one opposition party, the variables e and v can be confined to the values 0 and 1; $e = 1$ means that the incumbent party is elected, $e = 0$ means that the opposition party is elected, $v = 1$ means that the constituency elects a Member of Parliament from the incumbent party, and $v = 0$ means that the constituency elects a Member of Parliament from the opposition party.

This specification of the circumstances of the voter reveals a certain ambiguity in the statement that a voter favours one party over another. Suppose, for instance, that he is said to favour the opposition. The statement may mean that

$$U(0,0) > U(1,1) \tag{1}$$

which signifies that he is better off with a win for the opposition than with a win for the incumbent party, provided that he personally voted for the winning party and can enjoy his share of the spoils of office. Alternatively, the statement may mean that

$$U(0,0) > U(1,0) \tag{2}$$

$$U(0,1) > U(1,1) \tag{3}$$

which signifies an unconditional preference for the opposition regardless of one's own vote.

An additional consideration has to be introduced. A person's interest in voting for the incumbent or for the opposition depends on his assessment of the incumbent's probability of winning the election and on how that probability is affected by his constituency's vote. Let $p(v)$ be the probability that the incumbent wins, where $p(1)$ is that probability when one's constituency elects a Member of Parliament from the incumbent party and $p(0)$ is that probability when one's constituency elects a Member of Parliament from the opposition. Obviously $p(1)$ must be greater than or equal to $p(0)$ but the difference between the two must be small, for there is not much chance of either party winning by a majority of just one constituency. Whether the constituency votes for the incumbent party or for the opposition depends on the expected utility of the typical voter in each case. The expected utility is

$$E(1) \equiv p(1)\, U(1,1) + (1 - p(1))\, U(0,1) \tag{4}$$

if the constituency elects a Member of Parliament from the incumbent party, and it is

$$E(0) \equiv p(0)\, U(1,0) + (1 - p(0))\, U(0,0) \tag{5}$$

if the constituency elects a Member of Parliament from the opposition. A constituency that favours the opposition in the sense of equations (2) and (3) will attain a greater expected utility by voting for the opposition if its vote has a significant effect on the outcome of the election as a whole (i.e. if $p(1)$ is significantly greater than $p(0)$) and if the incumbent party is disinclined or unable to punish voters who opposed it (i.e. if $U(1,1)$ is not significantly greater than $U(1,0)$). But these conditions may not obtain. A vindictive incumbent may cause $U(1,1)$ to be considerably larger than $U(1,0)$ so that

$$E(1) > E(0) \tag{6}$$

despite the fact that the opposition party is preferred. The incumbent party wins by rewarding constituencies that vote appropriately and by punishing constituencies that do not.

Suppose, for example, that $p(1) = 0.8$ and $p(0) = 0.75$, signifying that the outcome of the election is uncertain, that the incumbent party is thought to have a 75 per cent chance of winning even if one's constituency votes for the opposition, and that one's constituency's vote for the incumbent party raises the incumbent's probability of winning from 75 per cent to 80 per cent. Suppose also that $U(0,0) = 100$, $U(0,1) = 90$, $U(1,1) = 50$ and $U(1,0) = 10$. The best outcome for one's constituency is for the opposition to win and to be supported by one's constituency. Close behind is for the opposition to win without one's constituency's support; presumably the opposition party is not vindictive. Next is a win for the incumbent party supported by the constituency. Last by a wide margin is a win for the incumbent party unsupported by the constituency. The large gap between $U(1,1)$ and $U(1,0)$ signifies that the incumbent party rewards its supporters and punishes its opponents. With these numbers, the value of $E(1)$ is 58 and the value of $E(0)$ is 32.5. The constituency votes for the incumbent party despite the fact that it would very much prefer the opposition to win the election. If all constituencies are alike and if utilities and probabilities are as specified here (in particular, if each constituency is so unconfident about the willingness of other constituencies to vote against the incumbent party that $p(0)$ is as high as 75 per cent), then the incumbent party wins unanimously. The vindictiveness of the incumbent party facilitates its win at the ballot box, provided only that its presence as the incumbent, aided perhaps by well chosen advertising campaign, creates a belief in the minds of voters that a win is quite likely.

As a means of cajoling voters to support the incumbent party, vote-buying and election fraud are mutually reinforcing techniques. What we are calling vote-buying is necessarily a system of rewards *and* punishments because dollars spent on one constituency must necessarily be raised by taxation of other constituencies. Since the gain to some constituencies is necessarily balanced by the loss to others, vote-buying can be expected to deliver elections only when votes are cast in fear rather than in gratitude. Every constituency may fear the displeasure of the incumbent party, but the gratitude of constituencies that have been favoured must be balanced against remembrance in other constituencies of past harm. In this context, it is essential for voters to believe that the incumbent party has a significant chance of being re-elected, for there would otherwise be nothing to fear in voting for the opposition. A general understanding that the party in office is prepared to use its control over the election machinery to doctor election results if necessary, or even a well founded suspicion that it may do so, serves to increase the voter's subjective probability that the incumbent party will be re-elected and to raise $E(1)$ in equation (4) above $E(0)$ in equation (5), so that it becomes advantageous to vote for the incumbent even though one would prefer the opposition to win. A government prepared to doctor elections and buy votes may be required to do very little of either.

The force of the example is weakened somewhat by the fact that constituencies are collections of people, some of whom vote for the opposition and some for the incumbent. It is more difficult for the party in power to punish a constituency for electing a Member of Parliament from the opposition party when a significant proportion of the voters behave loyally than when the vote was almost unanimous. Of greater importance is the fact that each voter, knowing that his influence within the constituency is negligible and that nobody will ever discover how he, personally, voted, may choose to vote his conscience rather than his pocket book, or may simply refuse to allow himself to be bullied.

A final constraint on predation by the personnel of the public sector is the law. I spoke at the outset of this chapter of the provisional obedience to authority which is essential for the maintenance of a liberal society. Soldiers obey their general in war, but the bonds of military authority must dissolve if the general commands his soldiers to usurp the authority of the civilian heads of state. The President is obeyed by the army, but not if he commands the execution of his political rivals. The law specifies the limits of obedience, and the point at which authority becomes void. In considering this matter, we are to some extent back in the world of the constrained Leviathan, with one major difference. The constrained Leviathan was a single entity or personality supposed to be representative of the government as a whole in its dealing with ordinary people. Now, instead, we are dealing with particular people or groups within the public sector whose interests may diverge both from the general population of subjects and from the rest of the personnel of the public sector. If citizens make laws, as Brennan and Buchanan might have supposed, and if laws are universally obeyed within the public sector, then predatory government is all but abolished and we are transported once again to the domain of traditional welfare economics. But laws are not completely and universally obeyed, not in the private sector and not in the public sector either.

A useful distinction can be drawn between exploitation of the citizenry by the entire personnel of the government acting cohesively, as in the Brennan and Buchanan model — a taking by the entire governing class in command of the law — and the taking by some members of the governing classes in violation of the law. The word "corruption" is usually restricted to the latter. Corruption has special properties that distinguish it from taking by a ruling class as a whole, though, of course, there are activities with attributes of both.

The economics of corruption
Broadly speaking, corruption may be defined as the selling of authority. It is the selling by officials or politicians of favours to one man in the private sector at the expense of another or of the general public. Corruption may consist of kickbacks on government contracts, bribes to the police to over-look infractions of the law, the selling of offices, the selling of credentials, winking at falsification of tax returns or demanding payment for licences to which the applicants are entitled. Corruption may be more or less con-spiratorial, ranging all the way from uncoordinated acts of impropriety by officials, through organized malfeasance by entire police departments or branches of government, to government-wide predatory activity that is in the limit indistinguishable from despotism.[14]

It is sometimes argued that corruption involves no social cost because corruption is a mere transfer of income from the private sector to public officials. This argument is generally false in my opinion. Corruption is like theft or banditry, which, as discussed at length in Chapter III, involves a considerable waste of resources as income is transferred to the predator from the prey. Though corruption takes place within the public sector, it has more in common with anarchy than with despotism, which may be a relatively clean and wasteless transfer of income. The waste in corruption stems from the tenuousness of the connection between private gain to the corrupt official and the loss to others from his actions.

Consider an amoral official whose decision to engage in a corrupt act, or to desist from doing so, is, like that of any potential criminal, a balanc-ing of expected gains and losses. His decision is a weighting of *his* benefit if the corrupt act is undetected, the punishment if the act is detected and the probability of detection. The social cost of the corrupt act may be very much greater than the expected benefit to the amoral official, but that is none of his concern. Social cost does not enter into his calculation except in so far as the punishment and the probability of detection are made commensurate with social cost. In particular, if the amoral official is sure that a corrupt act will be undetected, he will commit the act regardless of how small the value of his personal benefit, or of how large the social cost, as long as he has no more lucrative alternatives.

A privilege inappropriately granted to firm A yields a benefit of $10 to that firm and a cost of $2,000 to the general public. Firm A offers the official a bribe of $5. Obviously, the official rejects the bribe if there is a significant probability of detection and if the punishment is severe. He also rejects the bribe if those who are harmed in the transaction can come up with a larger competing bribe, as they could well afford to do, for they would willingly pay, say, $15 to avoid a $2,000 loss. Neither of these conditions need obtain. Firm A may be in a position to offer an undetectable bribe, while those harmed by the official's decision may be too dispersed to arrange for the provision of a competing bribe or they may be unable to make the bribe undetectable, as the subscription to finance a bribe might come to the notice of the police. The undetectable bribe might take the form of an unspoken offer of employment at an unspecified time when the official retires from the public service.

The social cost of bribery may take many forms: the loss of potential benefit when a contract is granted to the less efficient firm, the reduction in use of a licensed service when the cost is driven up by bribes paid by practitioners, the harm to consumers of services when licences are granted to unqualified practitioners, and the waste of resources in rent-seeking when opportunities for rent-seeking behaviour are deliberately created for the benefit of the dispensers of rent. This last point needs some elaboration.

The discussion of rent-seeking in Chapter VII emphasized competition among firms for favours in the gift of the government. Rent-seeking was looked upon as participation in a lottery where resources employed to procure a ticket are typically, though not necessarily, wasted. A contract yielding $1 million of profit is awarded at random to a "suitable" firm, where suitability refers to the acquisition of a machine that costs $100,000 and has no use apart from the contract. If only one firm buys the machine, that firm is sure to win the contract and to pocket the $1 million over and above the cost of the machine. Clearly, this windfall gain is competed away. As long as firms are risk-neutral, each of eleven firms purchases a suitable machine though only one randomly chosen firm is awarded the contract. Of the total of $1,100,000 spent by the eleven firms on the contract-specific machinery, all but $100,000 is wasted. What, at first, appears as a transfer from the government to one privileged or lucky firm turns out to be a social waste in circumstances where *ex ante* profits are normal. Complete dissipation of rent occurs when there is no limit to the number of firms that are able to seek rents and when all firms seeking rents are alike. Otherwise, if the number of potential rent-seekers is limited, or if it is quite costly for a firm to augment its initial chance of the prize, the prize is only partly wasted. It should also be noted that what goes by the name of rent-seeking may not be wasteful of all, for, as discussed in Chapter VII, the steps required by a firm to position itself as a possible recipient of rent may be socially advantageous.

Positioning, however, is not the only form of rent-seeking. Rent-seeking may also consist of lobbying, in which case the cost of rent-seeking is the businessman's time in negotiating with officials, his expenditure on professional lobbyists, or his expenditure on advertising to persuade voters of the desirability of his enterprise and to convince politicians that voters are persuaded. What goes by the name of rent-seeking may also be bribery in the form of direct payment to influential officials or in the form of a more or less explicit promise of favours. From the point of view of the rent-seeker, it is irrelevant whether the steps he must take to get a chance of the prize consist of positioning, as in the example of the purchase of a machine, lobbying or bribery. His only concern is to draw the best balance between the size of the prize, his total expenditure to increase his chance of getting it, and his probability of success. The nature of rent-seeking is of great concern to the corrupt official.[15]

As long as there is some component of bribery in rent-seeking, it may be advantageous for corrupt officials or politicians to create circumstances where rent is to be dispensed. Suppose — for good reasons or bad — an industry is to be protected, and the government must choose whether to protect the industry by tariffs or by quotas distributed free of charge to certain privileged firms. Tariffs are preferable in most circumstances because they generate public revenue, while "free" quotas do not. A totally predatory government would levy a tariff and use the proceeds to augment officials' wages. A corrupt government, which cannot use tariff revenue to augment officials' wages directly but is quite willing to increase officials' income if that can be accomplished secretly, might prefer quotas. The quotas would not be auctioned off. They would be awarded to privileged firms on the understanding that the recipients of quotas were beholden to the officials from whom the quotas were obtained. If the revenue from the tariff would have been $2,000, if an equivalent quota would be worth $2,000 to the fortunate recipient, if the potential profit to the recipient of the quota is certain to be dissipated in wasteful rent-seeking, but if the dispenser of the subsidy can expect to skim off $5 of benefit with no risk of detection, then the decision to protect domestic industry by a quota rather than by a tariff generates a riskless gain to officials of $5 and a loss to the general public of $2,000 of potential tax revenue. The decision is advantageous to officials when no alternative form of corruption is more profitable.

More generally, when agents in the private sector compete for publicly created rent, the value of the rent can be divided into four components: (i) windfalls to rent-seekers, (ii) rewards to officials dispensing rents, (iii) waste, and (iv) benefits to the public that are incidental to the rent-seeking activity.

An example will show how the components fit together. An industrial process discovered in a government research laboratory is to be licensed to a firm in the private sector. The licence could be auctioned off, in which case the revenue from the auction would accrue to the country as a whole. An alternative is to donate the right to employ the newly discovered process to a "worthy" firm, in which case the revenue from the patent becomes the objective of rent-seeking activity.

The variables in the problem are these: R is the rent to be allocated to one firm in the contest, N the number of firms that are *potentially* eligible for the contest, F the cost to each potentially eligible firm of entering the contest, n the number of firms that choose to enter the contest, B_i the bribe of firm i (where $i = 1, \ldots, n$), P_i the probability that firm i will win the contest, α the fraction of F that is socially useful, β the fraction of bribes wasted by the bribe-taker in covering his tracks, and γ a weighting in the equation for P_i. The apportionment of rent among the four components depends critically on how each firm's probability of success is affected by its behaviour in the contest. To keep the analysis simple, suppose that all entrants are alike in their circumstances and their behaviour, and that each firm's probability of success is a weighted average of two factors, the number of firms in the contest and the ratio of that firm's bribe to the total of all bribes by all contestants. Specifically, when n firms enter the contest and each firm j offers a bribe B_j, the probability, P_i, that the winner of the contest is firm i becomes

$$P_i = \gamma/n + (1 - \gamma) B_i / \sum_{j=1}^{n} B_j \qquad (7)$$

where the parameter γ is a weighting of the importance of bribery and is confined to the range [0,1]. If $\gamma = 1$, then bribery is useless and the winner is chosen by lot among the n firms entering the contest. If $\gamma = 0$, then bribery alone determines the winner.

Having entered the contest at a cost of F, a risk-neutral firm i chooses its bribe B_i to maximize its *expected net rent*, which is equal to $RP_i - B_i - F$. Since, by assumption, all firms are identical, the common value of the optimal rent-maximizing bribe when there are n contestants is[16]

$$B(n) = (1 - \gamma)R (n - 1)/n^2 \qquad (8)$$

With no restrictions on the number of firms that may enter the contest, and with identical contestants, competition among potential entrants would drive all expected net rents to zero. Allowing for indivisibilities, the equilibrium value of n would be determined by the inequalities

$$RP(n) - B(n) - F > 0 > RP(n + 1) - B(n + 1) - F \qquad (9)$$

where $P(n)$ is the common value of P_i when there are n firms in the race. Equation (9) means that net rent is still positive (though probably very small) when there are n firms in the race, but that each firm's net rent would turn negative if one more firm were to enter. Note that $P(n)$ is necessarily equal to $1/n$ when all firms are alike.

Suppose, on the contrary, that the number of eligible entrants, N, is less than the number of firms required to dissipate the rent entirely, so that $RP(N) - B(N) - F > 0$ and $RP(N + 1) - B(N + 1) - F > 0$ as well.

In these circumstances the four components of rent are as follows:

windfall to rent-seekers	$R - NB(N) - FN$
net bribes to officials	$(1 - \beta) N B(N)$
waste	$(1 - \alpha)NF + \beta NB(N)$
public benefit	αNF

Obviously one cannot say much *a priori* about the relative sizes of these components, but a simple numerical example is sufficient to show that public benefit may be a very small part, and waste may be a very large part, of the total rent. Suppose that the rent, R, is $1 million, that the number of firms, N, in a position to compete for the rent is five, that the fixed cost of applying for the rent, F, which in this example may be thought of as the cost of training workers to use the new technology, is $100,000 per contestant, and that the parameters α, β and γ are all equal to $1/2$. With these values, the optimal bribe $B(5)$ according to equation (8) is $80,000 per firm, the total windfall gain to the successful rent-seeking firm is $820,000, the unremunerated expenditure by the four remaining rent-seeking firms $720,000, the net gain to rent-seeking firms as a whole is $100,000, the net income to bribe-taking dispensers of rents is $200,000, the benefit to the public is $250,000 and the pure waste is $450,000. With these values, the public exchanges a potential benefit of $1 million for a net benefit from firms' training of workers of $250,000. In the process, dispensers of rent pick up $200,000 that, by assumption, would not have been available if the technology had been auctioned off among the interested firms.

Different figures could have produced radically different results. There would have been no bribery had it been assumed that $\gamma = 1$, signifying that each eligible firm has an equal chance of the prize. Public benefit would have been very much greater had it been assumed that $\alpha = 1$, signifying that all firms' positioning expenditure is socially advantageous. In fact, values of α in excess of 1 are not impossible; the standard argument for the patenting of inventions boils down to the assumption that $\gamma = 1$ and $\alpha \geq 1$ when F consists of inventive activity. Equally, however, net bribes could be very small and waste could be a very large proportion of the rent if β is close to 1 and α is close to 0, as is often assumed in discussions of

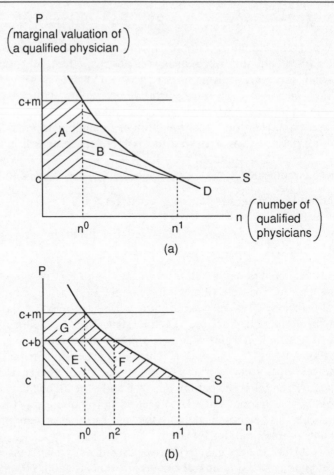

Figure 57 The benefits of licensing under alternative assumptions

rent-seeking behaviour in international trade. Any net gain to public officials — no matter how small — is sufficient to induce officials to institute
a rent-seeking contest, regardless of the net loss to the public — no matter
how large — if the officials have no better alternative.

This principle may be illustrated by a second example from a different
quarter of the bureaucracy, the licensing of physicians. To simplify the
example, we abstract from the sequence of entrance and exit of physicians
from the labour force, and suppose that the entire national supply of
physicians enters the labour force all at once. The market for physicians
is illustrated in the demand and supply curves for physicians in Figure 57.
The horizontal axis shows the number of physicians. The vertical axis
shows the "price" of physicians, P, interpreted as the present value of their
services (or their earnings) over their working lives. The height of the

demand curve is the patients' marginal valuation, as a present value, of the lifetime services of a physician. The supply curve is assumed to be flat. Its height, c, is at once the alternative cost of becoming a physician — inclusive of training cost and earnings in the physician's next best option — and the minimal present value of lifetime remuneration that a physician is prepared to accept. The demand and supply curves in both parts of Figure 57 are assumed to be identical.

The role of the government in this example is to determine whether a person who claims to be a physician is really qualified; it is to protect the public from charlatans posing as physicians. Think of the demand curve in Figure 57 as pertaining to qualified physicians, and suppose that the government can take advantage of economies of scale in identifying professional qualifications. Assume the following:

(i)   Nobody employs a physician unless he is known to be qualified.
(ii) Individual patients can determine whether physicians are qualified at a cost, to all patients together, of m per physician, so that the supply curve of *qualified* physicians as seen by patients who must certify qualifications for themselves is horizontal at a height $c + m$ above the horizontal axis.
(iii) A lump sum payment by the government of L is sufficient to identify all qualified physicians at no marginal cost.
(iv^0) (An assumption to be replaced presently.) The licensing procedure is conducted honestly, without bribery and at no marginal cost to the qualified physician or to the general public.

The costs and benefits of public licensing are now easily compared. Without public licensing, the cost to the public per physician is $c + m$, and the number of physicians demanded is n^0, as shown in Figure 57(a). Introduce public licensing, and the cost per physician falls from $c + m$ to c, providing a gain to users of physicians' services equal to the shaded area $A + B$. The area A is the saving on the n^0 doctors already employed and the area B is the gain in the form of consumers' surplus from employing $n^1 - n^0$ more physicians at a cost of c per doctor. The net benefit of licensing is therefore equal to $A + B - L(\Delta W/\Delta R)$, where the third term in the expression is the lump sum cost, L, of public licensing, scaled up by the marginal social cost per dollar of tax revenue, $\Delta W/\Delta R$, as defined in Chapter VIII. Public licensing is advantageous if this net benefit is positive. Assume it to be so.

The effect of corruption by public officials depends critically on their opportunities and constraints. Two among many possibilities will be examined. Suppose, first, that the corrupt official dare not license unqualified physicians for fear that his actions will be discovered, but that he can demand as large a bribe from qualified physicians as the market will bear and can keep all revenue from bribery. Assumption (iv^0) is now replaced by (iv^1)   The corrupt official can demand a bribe per qualified physician up to but not in excess of m, which is the cost to the patient of certifying the doctor's qualifications for himself.

Depending on the shape of the demand curve, the optimal bribe from the point of view of the official could be less than or equal to m. Suppose it is just m. Suppose also that income from bribery can be looked upon as a mere transfer from one party to another, where the transfer itself involves no social cost — where all dollars are counted as equal, in the well known phrase from cost–benefit analysis, "to whomsoever they may accrue". With a bribe of m, the number of physicians employed is no greater when physicians are licensed than when they are not, for, in each case, the marginal cost to the patient is c + m. Without licensing, the m represents the patients' cost of discovering which doctors are qualified. With licensing, the m is part of the fee that the doctor requires to cover the alternative cost of his time, his training cost and his bribe. The surplus, B, that would accrue if licensing were conducted honestly is now lost, and the net gain from public licensing of doctors is reduced from A + B − L(ΔW/ΔR) to A − L(ΔW/ΔR). The resource cost, A, to the patient is now converted into a transfer to the corrupt official, but it is still saved because it shows up as somebody's income. (It may even show up as a tax reduction if officials are paid less than what they could earn in the private sector because they are expected to acquire extra income from bribes. In that case, the net benefit from licensing is (A − L)(ΔW/ΔR) rather than A − L(ΔW/ΔR). Bribery would be socially advantageous if (A − L) (ΔW/ΔR) were greater than A + B − L(ΔW/ΔR).)

All this depends on the assumption (iv^1) that the entire bribe is a pure transfer rather than a social cost. That may not be so. Part of the potential gross transfer, A, may be wasted in the following ways. (i) Though corrupt officials as a class have an incentive to avoid licensing unqualified physicians, the average quality of physicians may be lower when officials are corrupt than when they were honest. (ii) There may be some cost, to physicians or to the officials themselves, in delivering the bribe. For example, to avoid detection, the bribe might have to be paid through the intermediary of lawyers who would demand a cut. Transaction cost in bribe-taking must reduce the net income of the bribe-taker to something less than the bribe, m, per physician. (iii) Bribe-takers may bear a risk of punishment, in the form of a fine or imprisonment. The net gain to the bribe-taker becomes the bribe less the expected cost of punishment. (iv) The government may bear a cost of hunting and punishing bribe-takers. This cost is converted into a benefit whenever punishment takes the form of a fine. The net cost to the government becomes the cost of detection of corrupt practices *plus* the cost of imprisonment *minus* the revenue from fines. (The situation is analogous to the government's efforts to stop tax evasion, as discussed above.) All four items are genuine costs of public licensing of physicians, in that they would all be avoided if the government left the licensing of physicians to the market.

In this environment, where bribe-taking might be detected and punished, the optimal bribe, b, is likely to be less than the cost of private certification, m. The situation would then be as portrayed in Figure 57(b), where the demand and supply curves are the same as in Figure 57(a), the number of physicians licensed is n^2 (which is less than n^1 but greater than n^0), and the sum of the three areas G, E and F is the same as the sum of the two areas A and B in Figure 57(a). Assumption (iv^1) is now replaced by

(iv^2) The optimal bribe, b, from the point of view of the officials is less than m, and a fraction, f, of the physician's expenditure on bribes, E, is wasted.

The net benefit from the licensing of physicians becomes

$$G + (1 - f)E - L(\Delta W/\Delta R)$$

where G is the surplus that remains to consumers from the licensing of physicians and $(1 - f)E$ is the amount of the bribe that accrues as net income to the bribe-taker. The net cost of bribery is

$$A + B - G - (1 - f)E$$

which is the difference between $(A + B - L(\Delta W/\Delta R))$, the net benefit from licensing in the absence of bribery, and $(G + (1 - f)E - L(\Delta W/\Delta R))$, which is the net benefit of licensing in the presence of bribery. It could easily turn out that

$$A + B - L(\Delta W/\Delta R) > 0 > G + (1 - f)E - L(\Delta W/\Delta R) \qquad (10)$$

signifying that licensing physicians is socially advantageous when officials are honest but not otherwise. The net benefit to the bribe-takers, $(1 - f)E$, may be very small by comparison with the social cost of bribery, $A + B - G - (1 - f)E$, for the bribe-taker is concerned with the former exclusively.

Together, these examples of corrupt practice — the rent-seeking contest and the licensing of physicians — suggest some general principles about the role of corruption in the economy. The most important is that corruption is not just a transfer between civilians and officials. It is a waste of resources, the magnitude of which can be very much larger than the net gain to the corrupt official. The waste encompasses all the costs of anarchy. Think of the bribe-taker as the bandit and of the rest of society as the farmer in the original model of anarchy in Chapter III. The analogue of the wasted labour of the bandit is the bribe-taker's cost in accepting bribes without drawing punishment upon himself. The analogue of the wasted labour of the farmer is the time and effort of society as a whole in hunting

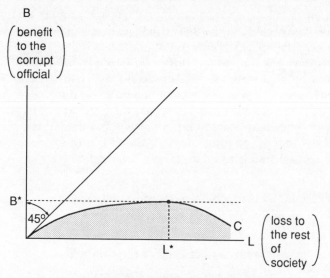

Figure 58 The social cost of corruption

and punishing bribe-takers, and of rent-seekers in positioning themselves
to become eligible for a chance of the prize. There is a deadweight loss as
resources are diverted from corruption-laden activities (the area B in Figure 57). There is destruction of product, as the public sector's tasks are ill
performed in a corrupt environment. Like the bandit, the corrupt official
cares for none of these impositions. He engages in corrupt practice if and
only if it is personally advantageous to do so. In both the examples we
have considered, the ratio of social loss to private gain could be made as
large as one pleases by a not wildly improbable choice of parameters.

This point can be emphasized with the aid of the simple diagram in
Figure 58, which is really a transposition and relabelling of figure 3(c) in
the appendix to Chapter I. Consider a corrupt official who has to choose
among alternative courses of action, each represented by a point on the
figure, with a certain expected benefit to himself and a certain expected
loss to the rest of society. The vertical axis shows the benefit, B, to the
corrupt official. The horizontal axis shows the loss, L, to the rest of society.
The curve C demarcates the boundary of the cluster of points in the figure;
it signifies the largest available B for each and every possible value of L.
All pure transfers are represented by points on a line at 45° through the
origin. From among his options on the curve C, the corrupt official chooses
the point (B*,L*) at which B is largest. At that point the ratio of L* to B*
could be very large. In general, the curve C is well below the 45° line.

A system of corruption deterrence, imposed perhaps by a higher level
of government, can be thought of as the attempt to push the peak of the
curve C to the left. The benefit, B, of corruption must be seen as a utility-

like measure that takes account of the cost of being punished if corrupt activities are detected as well as of the income acquired if they are not. The ideal in corruption deterrence is to rotate the entire curve C below the horizontal axis so that the best point for society as a whole, the origin, is the best point for the potentially corrupt official as well.

It is sometimes argued that corruption is conducive to overall efficiency in the public sector as a means of cutting through red tape that would, but for corruption, bind industry in senseless regulations. That may be true, but the red tape itself should be seen as part of the corrupt environment. Regulations may sometimes be adopted for the express purpose of creating a market in which they may be circumvented. It would be foolish to argue that corruption is never socially advantageous, but the moral of the story of corruption as a sword for cutting red tape is that the red tape should be eliminated.[17]

Two propositions follow immediately. First, an efficient despotism, such as is postulated in the Brennan and Buchanan model, would not be corrupt in the sense of the term employed here. Corruption is like a tax imposed by an official for his own benefit rather than to augment the revenue of the government as a whole. If a corrupt act were consistent with the maximization of total public revenue in a fully despotic society, it would be made legitimate and therefore no longer corrupt. If not, the act would be forbidden, and revenue would be maximized in some other way. Corruption is inexpedient for the Leviathan because it is wasteful. The despot can avoid the waste by taxing his subjects directly. The despot licenses physicians honestly and then acquires revenue through an appropriate mix of income and sales taxes. The despot would rather auction off a new technology than give it away in a rent-seeking contest. Corruption is a feature of inefficient governments that may or may not be despotic.

Second, the appropriate role of the government in society is smaller when government is corrupt than when it is honest. Should physicians he licensed? The answer may be "yes" if the licensing procedure is honest, but "no" otherwise. Do citizens benefit from public provision of medical care? The answer may be "yes" if the public medical service is run honestly, but "no" otherwise. Should a state-owned industry be privatized? The answer may be "no" if public ownership affects the conduct of the industry so as to generate large external benefits at the expense of long-term profitability and if the industry can be administered honestly, but the answer may be "yes" if public ownership represents a diversion of profit to the pockets of officials and their political masters. The political moral of this analysis of corruption is that the proper scope of the public sector depends very much on the probity of the government. Countries that are sure of the integrity of their governments might risk a considerable degree of regulation of the economy and an elaborate system of redistribution of income; countries not sure of the integrity of their governments might be better off with strict and unqualified *laissez-faire*.

Predation by capture

The "executive of the modern state is but a committee for managing the common affairs of the whole bourgeoisie".[18] This famous quotation from Karl Marx is the most extreme statement I know of what is commonly called the capture thesis: that, regardless of formal rules or constitutional pronouncements, government is run for the benefit of a group or groups in the private sector that "captures" the personnel of government for its own ends. A critique of Marx's statement will serve as a general introduction to the subject. The statement is not altogether wrong. I suppose that if one had to choose a group within the private sector which, man for man, exerts the greatest influence upon the government, that group would have to be the owners and administrators of large amounts of capital. Members of this group have the funds to contribute to the campaigns of political parties, the wherewithal to provide lucrative jobs for ex-politicians and bureaucrats, and a day-to-day influence upon the economy that justifies consultation on a wide range of issues. Such advantages must convey privilege.

Responsibility for the view of capitalists as a ruling class rests to some extent on the economists, especially the classical economists from whom Marx drew many of his ideas. Though the classical economists held no such view, they prepared the ground by ignoring the personnel of the government in their analysis of the distribution of income. David Ricardo defined economics as the science that explains the division of the national income among the owners of three, and only three, factors of production: land, labour and capital. In his formal analysis of society, Marx employed the classical economists' model of the autonomous private sector. With only workers, landowners and capitalists to choose from, it is not unreasonable to suppose that capitalists dominate.

In evaluating this extreme version of capture, it is useful to begin by differentiating between capture and influence. It would be foolish to deny that the rich exert a disproportionate influence upon politicians, the judiciary and the civil service. A rich man who can afford to hire the best and most influential lawyer and who is of the same social class as the judge can expect a lighter sentence for any given crime than would be meted out to a poor man without these advantages. Owners of large businesses are likely to have greater influence upon regulations than ordinary people who are also affected by regulatory decisions. If the capture thesis implied no more than that, there would be few to disagree, and the role of the capture thesis would be as a reminder of aspects of society that might otherwise be overlooked. The capture thesis becomes interesting when its claims are comprehensive, when regulators are the puppets of the regulated and officials are the lackeys and running-dogs of the bourgeoisie. Essential to this extreme and challenging variant of capture is that the entire electoral process be a dumb show with no real impact upon the behaviour of government or the lives of ordinary people. Whichever party is elected, its leaders are bribed or bullied to serve the bourgeoisie, and the hopes of the electorate that their interests will be represented in public decision-making are bound to be disappointed. (Propositions of this sort are the stock-in-trade of would-be political leaders who claim that they alone have the strength of character to resist the blandishments of the rich.) Also required for this extreme form of the capture thesis is that public officials — politicians, civil servants and soldiers — who are better organized than the rich, and who might perfectly well employ their monopoly of the means of violence to exploit the rich and the poor together, must somehow decline to do so.

Marx's view of the bourgeoisie as dominating the state has this in common with Brennan and Buchanan's model of the Leviathan state: both model a class as though it were a person. Brennan and Buchanan model the government as an entity with a well defined interest and a unified will. Marx sees the bourgeoisie in the same light. Brennan and Buchanan can at least justify their abstraction by an appeal to the fact that governments are organized as hierarchies. Marx has no such justification. It is difficult to imagine a mechanism by which the entire business community can act in concert. Businesses have competing interests as well as common interests, and the lure of profit can induce individual firms to act against the interest of the business community as a whole. Whatever else it may do, the business community does not have the unity of purpose to deny goods to the government when the government has, or prints, the cash to buy them.[19]

If it comes down to a choice between the personnel of the government and the bourgeoisie as candidates for the ruling class, the advantage would seem to lie on balance with the former. The picture of government as the servant of capital would seem to take no account of the government's monopoly of the means of violence. The power to specify and restrict the laws of property, or to expropriate property altogether, may be more than sufficient to intimidate the capitalist class. Soldiers and politicians are more likely to become rich than businessmen are to become powerful, as, for instance, when the soldiers of the army of William the Conqueror became the legitimate landowners of England. An alliance, of course, is possible. Soldiers and politicians empower privileged businessmen to acquire large incomes that are only partly expropriated.

More generally, there may be a great many capturers within a liberal society.[20] Regulatory boards may gradually come under the influence of those whom they are empowered to regulate. Businessmen in one industry may persuade government to impose tariffs on competing products, to the detriment of businessmen in other industries and of the general public. Wealthy contributors to political parties may expect a sympathetic hearing from legislators in disputes with officialdom or with ordinary citizens over the interpretation of the law. Each of a great number of citizens or groups may capture a corner of government, and there may be no single dominant group that can be said to have captured the government as a whole.

Finally, whether there be one capturer or many, the analysis of capture must come to terms with the existence of voting as a means of choosing the personnel of the government. Is the choice of government through voting a defence against capture, a means of capture, a sham or perhaps a combination of all three? It can be said in Marx's defence that when he and Engels published *The Communist Manifesto,* from which the quotation above is taken, the franchise was everywhere restricted to property-holders. Universal franchise was one of their principal "demands". Even today, some economists argue that elections have no influence upon the distribution of income.[21] By contrast, the model of exploitation by voting, as presented in Chapter V and to be discussed again in this chapter, allows for capture by coalitions of voters in circumstances where there is *no* political analogue to the equilibrium in a competitive market.

These considerations, while sufficient, in my opinion, to exorcise the spectre of full capture of the state by the bourgeoisie, raise a number of questions that occupy the remainder of this chapter. (i) What would an uncaptured government be like? One cannot speak coherently of capture, by one group or many, without some idea, however vague, of what an uncaptured government would do. (ii) What exactly is captured and by whom? (iii) How is capture done? By bribery, by contributions to political parties, by voting? (iv) How does the state, or the potential victims of capture, defend against danger?

The first of these questions is at the same time easy and difficult to answer. The easy answer is that an uncaptured government is one that serves the common good. As discussed in Chapter I, the notion of the common good is indispensable to discourse about public policy. You cannot persuade me that such-and-such a policy is good for the country as a whole without a prior agreement among us that there is such a good and a general, though perhaps vague, understanding as to what that good entails. Identification of capture rests on a similar basis in common understanding.

To put the point formally, an uncaptured government is one that acts, or desists from acting, so as to maximize the value of a social welfare function with due regard to all the technical and social constraints upon its actions. In choosing among options, it may seek to create or maintain the society that "I" would most like to enter if I had an equal chance of occupying the circumstances of each and every person in that society. Despite one's unease about the concept of a social welfare function, there is no escape from the need to invoke the concept — or some logically equivalent notion under a different name — in constructing an ideal of governmental behaviour. Presumably an ideal government would respect property rights in the belief that a society without property rights would not long remain either prosperous or democratic.

Characterization of an uncaptured government becomes problematic when it is recognized that people differ in their notions of the common good, when the deficiencies of government are taken into account (so that one's ideal of a government of fallible and self-interested people is quite different from what one would want of a government guaranteed to have internalized the social welfare function), and in view of the fundamental indeterminacy of majority rule voting. Even those who revere voting as the best method in this imperfect world of subjecting government to the interests of the governed must recognize that the outcome of any particular vote is likely to reflect the interests of some voters at the expense of others, and is not what one would choose if one had an equal chance of occupying each and every place in society.

Thus, turning to the second question, it must be recognized that the identification of the fruits of capture is also to some degree a matter of opinion. A decision of government seen by a beneficiary as sound policy in the public interest may be seen by others as nothing more than the booty brought home when one has succeeded in diverting all or part of the government to one's own interest at the expense of society as a whole. Furthermore, it is not possible to categorize any type of economic policy as absolutely and invariably inappropriate, regardless of circumstances. The list in Chapter VII of private sector departures from efficiency is long and diverse enough to provide *some* justification for almost anything a government might choose to do. The most that can be said is that certain types of policy are usually adopted to benefit some group at the expense of the rest of society. The author's own judgment is necessarily engaged in the construction of a list of the objects of capture.

The first and perhaps most valuable prize to be captured is *discrimination*, the reservation of a significant privilege for a particular segment of the population that is usually, but not necessarily, defined by religion, language, possessions or race. The greatest such privilege, and the instrument for acquiring other privileges as well, is the right to vote. Before the turn of the century, the right to vote was denied in most countries to people without property or a substantial income. It is arguable that such restrictions were necessary to keep the vote from those who would in all probability have made use of it to destroy the system of private property upon which democracy, then as now, depended; universal franchise may be self-destructive in the absence of a fair degree of prosperity.[22] All the same, the enfranchised can be expected to serve the interests of their group at the expense of the rest of society. In eighteenth-century England a Parliament of landowners saw fit to impose the death penalty for poaching and for the unauthorized gathering of wood from private forests.[23] One suspects that such laws could not have been passed by a Parliament more representative of all ranks of society. A Parliament of whites in South Africa imposes economic and residential discrimination on blacks. A white electorate in the southern United States saw fit to impose separate and much inferior schooling upon the black community as well as outright prohibition from the better jobs and from residence in certain neighbourhoods.

Discrimination can arise without restrictions on the right to vote. A racial, religious or differently constituted group may be favoured because it represents a majority of the voters or because it is particularly influential for some other reason. In Malaysia, for example, places in the army and the civil service are closed to the large Chinese minority, and the right to open a new business is made conditional on substantial participation of Malays.[24] In the Province of Ontario the right to state funding for parochial schools is granted to Catholics but denied to practitioners of all other religions. Unpopular minorities may be restricted by quota in the number of places in university that they are allowed to occupy. The *numerus clausus* was once a fact of life in North America, and in a curious way is becoming so again, though its application to gender is probably transitory and harmless in the long run.

Whenever public officials are drawn predominantly from one segment of society, there is a danger that other segments of society will be disadvantaged in their dealings with the government. The process may be quite subtle and need not be reflected in laws or regulations. There is a good deal of evidence that blacks in the United States and Indians in Canada are more severely punished that other citizens for any given crime.[25] At a time when Canada imposed the death penalty for murder, a sentence of death could be commuted by the Federal Cabinet to a term in prison. Commutation was considerably less likely to be granted for Indians than for others.[26]

It is a mark of good government that the power of public officials to discriminate among citizens — granting a privilege here, denying a privilege there — be limited to the greatest possible extent. Such discrimination cannot be eliminated altogether. In the best of circumstances, politicians, officials and, of course, judges have to exercise discretion as to who is the most worthy recipient of a government contract, where a particular investment is to be located or the appropriate severity of punishment for a particular crime. The benefit of the doubt is likely to go to the party that captures the sympathy of the official who is empowered to decide among competing claims.

A favoured group or faction may also be rewarded by *price control* or *price supports*. In some circumstances, these may be beneficial to the community as a whole, but they are often employed for no other purpose than to benefit more influential traders at the expense of less influential traders. Advocates of rent control, for example, point to poor widows and orphans pushed on to the street by unconscionably high rents. The actual beneficiaries are likely to be the sitting tenants, who are more numerous than landlords but not necessarily poor. The resulting disincentive to the upkeep of rental accommodation is harmful to everybody, landlord and tenant alike. The incentive to convert rental accommodation to condominiums and the disincentive to new construction of rental accommodation are harmful to precisely those groups that rent control is allegedly designed to protect. In general, control of the price of any good creates a scarcity of that good and requires a rule for allocating the available supply. With rent control, the rule is that scarce rent-controlled accommodation accrues, in the first instance, to the sitting tenants and, over time, to new tenants who buy their way into a rent-controlled accommodation with key money or are lucky enough to find a vacant place. With ordinary price control (such as is often imposed in wartime), the available supply is allocated by rationing. With agricultural price supports, there is an excess supply rather than an excess demand. The excess supply may be bought up by the state or it may be controlled artificially by quotas on agricultural output. When price control takes the form of fixed exchange rates, scarce foreign exchange is often allocated according to the political influence of rival claimants.

Quantity restrictions are similar in their effects upon the economy. Quotas on agricultural production, such as are mandated by the Canadian system of marketing boards, raise the incomes of quota-holders by raising food prices to consumers. To an even greater extent than with rent control, the benefits are entirely restricted to the original recipients of quotas when the system is first introduced. The reason is that the quotas can be sold. On the day the Egg Marketing Board acquired its authority to restrict output, a total quota for all egg producers was set to ensure that their gain from the rise in price outweighed their loss from the fall in production, and the quota was somehow distributed among the egg producers in business at that time. Thereafter, anybody leaving the industry could sell his quota, anybody wishing to enter had to buy one, and the price of a quota would find a level at which the new egg producer would earn the going rate of return on his investment in the purchase of a farm and a quota together.

Quantitative restrictions on international trade convey benefits to domestic producers at the expense of domestic consumers while, at the same time, reducing the national income somewhat because domestic prices fail to reflect world scarcities. Industries with negative value-added at world prices can sometimes thrive in a protected environment Domestic labour and resources in such industries would be altogether wasted, but the returns to these factors of production might be substantial regardless. Automobile assembly conforms to this pattern in many countries. The effects of quantitative restrictions upon the domestic economy depend in part on who gets the quota and whether it is a gift or a sale. If the quota is put to auction each year, then its effect upon the economy is like that of a tariff with a variable rate, high when imports would otherwise be quite large, low when imports would otherwise be smaller. If the quota is allocated among foreign suppliers, it is as though the revenue from the tariff were donated abroad like foreign aid. If the quota is allocated among domestic importers, it is as though the revenue from the tariff were given away to privileged groups at home.

Broadly speaking, *trade taxes* — tariffs and export taxes — can have three main effects upon the economy: a financial effect as a source of public revenue, a strategic effect on world prices of goods for which a country has some monopoly power, and a distributive effect as protected industries gain at the expense of the rest of the economy.[27] The financial effect has at times been very important. A strong case can be made for tariffs when tax evasion is rampant but the tariff is less evadable than other forms of taxation. The combined deadweight loss and cost of collection have at many periods of history been lower, at moderate rates, for the tariff than for alternative sources of public revenue. This remains the case in many countries today. The strategic effect of the tariff is the exercise of a country's monopoly power over its trading partners.

But tariffs have often been imposed where other taxes could be collected at relatively low cost and where a country has no significant monopoly power in world markets. Then tariffs, or export subsidies, are employed for their distributive effects and despite the fact that they make the country as a whole worse off than if public revenue were acquired by other forms of taxation. A tariff raises the domestic price of the imported goods, augmenting incomes of domestic producers at the expense of domestic consumers. An export tax lowers the domestic price of the exported good, benefiting home consumers of the exported product at the expense of the exporters. At the time of the second oil crisis, Canada established a National Energy Policy that taxed the export of petroleum and subsidized its import, driving the Canadian domestic price below the world price and thereby transferring purchasing power from western Canada (which exports petroleum to eastern Canada and the United States) to eastern Canada (which imports petroleum from western Canada and from overseas).[28] Thailand is a major exporter and consumer of rice. For many years, Thailand imposed an export tax on rice amounting at times to half the world price, lowering the domestic price substantially, raising the real incomes of rice consumers in the city and reducing the real incomes of rice producers on the farms.[29] Motivation for both these institutions was mixed and complex, but one suspects that their distributive implications were on balance desired by the framers' economic policy.

Groups, firms or people can also be favoured by *subsidies*. I have in the preceding chapter called attention to the curious asymmetry between public attitudes toward "giving" and "taking" by the public sector. People are more willing to tolerate *ad hominem* subsidies than *ad hominem* taxes, despite the fact that a gift to one person is a tax on others, and vice versa. A special tax on investment by one identifiable firm is considered a major violation of the principles of good government, but a special subsidy on the investment of its rival is generally accepted with equanimity.

Public subsidization of investment may be general or firm-specific. Subsidies are general when, for example, all investment is made eligible for a tax credit. Subsidies are firm-specific when they are awarded to designated investments in designated firms and are denied to other firms. Firm-specific may be provided *ad hoc* by the bureaucracy or the Cabinet. They may also be provided in programmes designed to favour investments in specific areas of the country, industries, types of firms (such as firms owned by native people), or projects that are especially innovative and different from the normal run of business activity. Sometimes a project is only considered for a subsidy if it would not be commercially viable otherwise.

Firm-specific subsidization of investment is often alleged to "create jobs", a claim that attributes the total employment associated with the subsidized project to the subsidy itself.[30] Politicians running for office or civil servants justifying their activities will proudly point to the many jobs "they" have created with the subsidies to investment that they grant. Such claims may be justified. Though the social value of investment is usually reflected in private profitability, there are instances where this is not so and where subsidization is on balance advantageous. Investments to create new products may generate social benefits that cannot be captured in the return to the entrepreneur. Even the grant of a patent may be insufficient to enable the innovator to cover the cost of investment, though the consumer surplus from the new product may be more than sufficient to justify the cost of the inventive activity. Similarly, an investment in a depressed region may be privately unprofitable without a subsidy but socially advantageous if the investment provides work to those who would otherwise be on welfare because they have no other source of employment.

While it is true that firm-specific subsidization of investment may be socially advantageous in certain cases, it is highly unlikely that a programme of firm-specific subsidization or that *ad hoc* subsidization by politicians or bureaucrats will be socially advantageous on balance. A distinction must be drawn here between the benefit of the subsidy and the benefit of the subsidized investment. Obviously the investment itself must be beneficial on balance for the subsidization to be justified. That is a necessary but not a sufficient condition for the subsidy to be socially advantageous. An additional, but absolutely necessary, requirement for the subsidy to be beneficial is that the investment would not be profitable otherwise. The reason why firm-specific subsidization is unlikely to be beneficial in practice is that it is difficult, bordering on impossible, for public officials to determine with an acceptable degree of certainty whether these two conditions obtain in a particular case.

Knowing that subsidies are available, there is an incentive for firms to claim that projects are unique when they are not or that projects would not be commercially viable without subsidization. Such claims are difficult to verify, and even more difficult to refute by the public officials whose task it is to determine whether they are valid. Projects can be substitutable in many subtle ways. The introduction of a subsidized project in a region may drive up the wage of labour, and thereby drive out an established firm that would have remained viable otherwise. Or the introduction of the subsidized project might forestall the development of another as yet un-recognized project that would not require a subsidy at all. The subsidized project might use up local savings that would otherwise have been chan-nelled by the banks to other investment in the region. Firm-specific subsidization of investment might possibly increase the total investment in the favoured categories, but there is no assurance that this will occur, and there is a virtual certainty that the increment to investment, if any, will be well short of the total value of subsidized investment. The jobs "created" may in reality be transferred from other projects or firms. Subsidized firms might bump unsubsidized firms, just as public provision bumps an equal amount of private provision in the circumstances of Figure 54 in Chapter VIII.

These difficulties with firm-specific investment subsidies are compounded by a problem of information. Public officials administering a programme of firm-specific investment subsidies must either rely on judgment and intuition in deciding whether a project is appropriate for subsidization, or fall back on simple general rules — such as to subsidize all investment within a region — that lead inevitably to the support of many projects that would go forward regardless. Furthermore, the same want of a precise criterion that makes the initial evaluation problematical removes all pos-sibility of a proper *ex post* audit. It can, of course, be determined whether the subsidized investment actually takes place and whether the new project employs as many workers as was claimed in the initial application. What cannot be determined *ex post* is whether the subsidy was really necessary, whether the subsidized firm bumped some existing firm from the market or forestalled another investment that would have appeared if the subsidy had not been granted. The usual measure of "success" in this context — that the subsidized project is thriving — might equally well be treated as a measure of failure.

Absence of a solid criterion for evaluating firm-specific investment sub-sidies creates an opening for dishonesty in government. A perfectly ad-ministered subsidy programme would convey no net advantage to the re-cipients, for the subsidies would be no larger than necessary to induce firms to engage in some socially advantageous but privately unprofitable

428

behaviour. But an imperfect programme, such as any actual programme must be, necessarily conveys large windfall gains to many if not all the recipients, who, as owners of firms, are normally rich and who might be expected to reward their benefactors. Public subsidization of investment may in the end be little more than the appointment of rich men.

Redundancy of a portion of the firm-specific investment subsidies raises the distinct possibility that a large programme of subsidies may inhibit more investment than it promotes. The mechanism by which this perverse outcome may occur is as follows. Suppose that each dollar of subsidy-induced investment requires x dollars of subsidy, that the increase in tax rates required to generate the x dollars of extra revenue to finance the subsidy entails a reduction in domestic saving of y dollars per dollar of extra tax revenue, and that — with due allowance for the foreign response to the increase in domestic tax rates and the decrease in domestic saving — the overall tax-generated reduction in domestic investment is z dollars per dollar reduction in saving. The net change in investment becomes 1 − xyz. This expression could be positive, signifying that subsidization does generate net investment, but that need not be so.

The value of x is almost certainly greater than 1. (The value of x might be less than 1 in a perfectly administered programme because only part of the cost of the investment would be covered by the subsidy, but that is most unlikely in practice because many subsidized projects would have gone forward regardless and because some subsidized projects bump established firms or other unsubsidized projects.) The value of y is greater than the marginal propensity to consume out of post-tax income because of the double taxation of saving under the income tax; the increase in the tax rate accentuates the bias against saving under the income tax and reduces saving accordingly. The value of z would be equal to 1 if foreign investment were unresponsive to domestic saving, but z is probably less than 1 otherwise. One cannot say *a priori* whether the primary effect of the subsidization of projects that would not be viable in the absence of subsidies is outweighed by the secondary effect of the churning of money through the tax system. The balance could go either way.

That completes our brief list of the rewards of capture, a list intended to jog the memory of the reader as to the range of gifts that government may provide to sufficiently grateful or sufficiently influential supporters. We need not dwell on the details, as they are adequately covered elsewhere in the literature of economics. It remains to mention the means by which gifts are obtained. These may be classified as coalition formation in voting and direct influence of private agents over public officials. Voting is the subject of the next and final section of the book. Direct influence includes bribery, hiring lobbyists with access to public officials, contributions to political parties, the employment of ex-civil servants *pour encourager les autres*, and political advertising in favour of one's policies or of cooperative politicians. Direct influence over public officials may be effected by punishments as well as by rewards. Customs officials, policemen or judges may be intimidated by threats of violence from well organized criminals in a position to carry out such threats if their demands are ignored. Intimidation of public officials usually requires an organization of criminals, such as the Mafia, or it may be effected by groups such as the Shining Path which span the boundary between politics and crime.[31] One would like to think of the state as secure enough in its monopoly of the means of violence to be impervious to capture by intimidation, but it is not always so.

Predation by voting

Democratic government has often been opposed on the grounds that it is destined to self-destruct. The basis of this classic anti-democratic argument is a paradigm of voting according to which a majority of voters — constituted along the lines of language, geography, religion or any badge whatever that serves to differentiate between majority and minority groups — acquires command of the powers of government and employs those powers to exploit the minority. The excluded minority can expect to be impoverished or, at best, left with no more income than is necessary to stay alive and working. Recognizing the fate of the minority in a system of majority rule voting, the citizen would be unwilling to abide by the rules of the electoral game, especially as there is no guarantee that one's fellow citizens will continue to respect the rules when the rules decree that their day in office is at an end. The personnel and supporters of the party in office might be unwilling to risk their privileges, their fortunes and perhaps their very lives to the vagaries of the ballot box. Better to fight while you have the means to do so than to hand over the government's monopoly of violence to your political opponents.

I believe that this consideration has played an important role in many instances where democratic government has broken down. The interesting question from the point of view of this book is not why democratic government sometimes breaks down but why it ever fails to do so. In practice, majorities do not dispossess minorities altogether and there is far greater willingness on the part of most people to accept the outcome of the vote than the exploitation paradigm and the anti-democratic argument would lead one to expect. Why might this be so? What are the constraints upon the majority coalition? How much reliance can be placed upon these constraints to preserve the liberal society indefinitely? Or is the liberal society an unstable hiatus between two less desirable but more stable forms of society?

The problem has been frequently posed as a conflict between rich and poor. The *locus classicus* of this formulation is the Putney debates of 1647 within Cromwell's army about the extent of the franchise when Parliament was to become supreme after the beheading of the King. A group of radical reformers, called Levellers, advocated a universal, or nearly universal, franchise. Cromwell's side argued for property qualifications, without which "we shall plainly go to take away all property and interest that any man hath either in land by inheritance, or in estate by possession, or anything else".[32] The vote, so the argument goes, provides the poor with the means to expropriate the rich. While it is probably true that, dollar for dollar, the gain to the poor from expropriation is less than the loss to the rich, massive expropriation might still be beneficial on balance to the expropriators.

Predation by voting is not limited to transactions between rich and poor. Any majority coalition would seem to be empowered to expropriate or take advantage of people who are not included in the coalition. There may be a "majority of minorities"; a coalition of small groups, each with its own special interest, may succeed in dominating the legislature. Religion, language, race, geography and occupation are useful in cementing a majority coaltion, but they are not necessary. In principle, members of a predatory majority need have nothing at all in common other than an intention to exploit.

How does a liberal society preserve itself against such potentially destructive forces? A liberal society requires that the party in power should be prepared to surrender its authority over the civil service, the army and the police when the electorate decrees that it shall do so. Supporters of the party in office must acquiesce in the transfer of power to the opposition and be prepared to live by the laws and administrative decisions of its successor. Somehow the party in office and in command of a majority of the legislature must be prepared to exercise a substantial degree of restraint in dealings with its would-be successors; and it must be reasonably confident that its successors will, in their turn, exercise restraint when they come to office. Such restraint does not seem to be inherent in the rules of a liberal society as described so far.

A partial response to the anti-democratic argument has already been proposed in Chapter V. It was argued there that respect for property rights constitutes a defence against exploitation of the minority at the hands of the majority. Hence the combination of property and voting as the two defining features of the liberal society. Without well established property rights, there is really no alternative to the political allocation of the entire national income among citizens and no principle to which the minority not represented by the party in office can appeal to defend itself against political predation. Property is absolutely necessary for the preservation of the institution of voting by majority rule, but it may not be sufficient. In the remainder of this chapter a number of social, political and economic considerations will be discussed that, together with property rights, may serve as defences of the liberal society.

It is useful to begin with a reconsideration of the simple voting model that was introduced in Chapter V, a model with no electoral equilibrium at all when voters are unable to form stable coalitions and with a multiplicity of exploitative equilibria in the presence of plausible coalition-forming behaviour. Imagine a society with a population of n and a fixed national income of nY, where Y is the income per head. Suppose n is an odd number. Define a platform to be a set of incomes $\{y_1 \ldots y_n\}$ where y_i is the income of the person i and where

$$\sum_{i=1}^{n} y_i = nY \tag{11}$$

There are no property rights in this society, and the total national income is to be allocated among people by majority rule voting. An electoral equilibrium, if there were one, would be a platform of incomes that defeats all other platforms in a pairwise vote.

There can be no political equilibrium in this society because *any* platform can be defeated by an infinity of other platforms with higher incomes for some $(n + 1)/2$ people and lower incomes for the rest. Consider the platform

$$P = \{y_1 \ldots y_{(n+1)/2}, y_{(n+3)/2} \ldots y_n\} \tag{12}$$

This platform can be defeated by another platform in which some majority of the voters — suppose the majority consists of the first $(n + 1)/2$ voters — receives an additional income of ε, and the incomes of all other voters are reduced by $\varepsilon(n + 1)/(n - 1)$ to preserve the national income unchanged. The new platform is

$$P' = \{y'_1 \ldots y'_{(n+1)/2}, y'_{(n+3)/2} \ldots y'_n\} \tag{13}$$

where $y'_i = y_i + \varepsilon$ for $i \leq (n + 1)/2$ and $y'_i = y_i - \varepsilon(n + 1)/(n - 1)$ for $i > (n + 1)/2$. The new platform, P', defeats the original platform, P, because P' is preferred by a majority of the voters. It follows immediately that every platform is indirectly preferred to every other platform in the sense that between any pair of platforms, P_a and P_b, there is a chain of platforms $P_1 \ldots P_m$ such that P_a is preferred to P_1, P_1 is preferred to P_2, and so on, until finally P_m is preferred to P_b. This is true as long as there are at least three voters. Clearly, there is no political equilibrium. Nor is there any basis for predicting which of the many potential $(n + 1)/2$-member sub-groups of the population will coalesce into an effective majority coalition. The composition of the majority coalition is an accident of the history of organization that would seem to defy formal analysis.

The argument extends immediately from completely selfish individuals to completely selfish groups. Suppose that the national income is fixed, that the total population is composed of m distinct groups, that the incomes of people within any group have to be the same, and that the policy of each group is to maximize the average income of its members. By definition

$$nY = \sum_{i=1}^{m} n_i y_i \tag{14}$$

where n_i is the number of people in the ith group and y_i is the average income in that group. In this context, a platform is a set $\{y_1 \ldots y_m\}$. Once again, there is no predicting the composition of the majority coalition.

Nor, other than zero, is there any lower limit to the incomes of people who are excluded from the majority coalition. Nothing within the example obliges the majority to provide the minority with any income at all. A bare majority might coalesce around a platform in which each member of the coalition receives an income of $2nY/(n + 1)$ and nobody in the excluded minority receives anything. Total and complete exploitation of the minority is, in a sense, the natural outcome of self-interested voting in that it is consistent with the usual assumption in economic analysis that people are unlimitedly greedy; the implications of modifying that assumption will be examined below. Equality of income among the members of the majority coalition is also reasonable when it is recognized that any member of the majority coalition whose income exceeds the incomes of others in the coalition is at risk of being evicted from the coalition and replaced by someone chosen from among the excluded minority.

"Majority" must be understood in this context as the majority in the legislature rather than as the majority of the voters. No such distinction would be necessary in a plebiscite, where a proposition is either accepted or rejected. In actual politics, the preferences of voters are filtered through a complex electoral mechanism with an independent influence upon the final outcome. In the usual first-past-the-post method of electing legislators to represent constituencies, a policy favoured by a majority of the voters may be defeated because those in favour of that policy are split between two parties seeking office, while the vote of those who oppose the policy are concentrated on a third party that wins more votes than either of the other two. Suppose, for example, that 40 per cent of the voters favour policy x, and 60 per cent of the voters oppose it. An election fought exclusively on whether or not to adopt policy x may be won by the party in favour of x if the opposition is split equally between two parties that, perhaps because of personal jealousy among politicians, cannot join forces in the election. A policy supported by a minority of voters may also win if the voters are distributed asymmetrically among the constituencies. With the same percentages, for and against policy x, that policy would command the support of a majority of 70 per cent of the constituencies if the 40 per cent of the population in favour were spread evenly over 70 per cent of the constituencies so that they constituted a majority of four-sevenths in each, while the 60 per cent of the population opposed to the policy constituted

100 per cent of the voters in the remaining 30 per cent of the constituencies and three-sevenths of the voters in the 70 per cent of the constituencies where the proponents of the policy were in the majority.[33]

The exploitation problem is really two connected difficulties. The first is that voting about incomes is *capricious* in the sense that there is no telling who the members of the majority coalition will turn out to be. Any sufficiently large collection of people or groups will do. The second is that voting about incomes is *precarious* in that the losers in the process — those who find themselves among the excluded minority — appear in danger of being wiped out completely, of being left with nothing, of losing all that they might otherwise possess. Thus in asking how actual liberal societies may differ from the stark and unattractive picture of voting I have presented so far, one might divide the question in two: is there, or under what circumstances might there be, an electoral equilibrium in voting about policies or incomes in a liberal society; and what, if anything constrains the majority from expropriating the minority completely? These, to the best of my knowledge, are not questions to which clear and universal answers can be provided. The best I can do is to identify conditions under which some approximation to an electoral equilibrium might be found, and to put forward reasons why majorities might be sufficiently restrained in their dealings with minorities to avert the breakdown of the liberal society that would surely follow if voting were as precarious as it appears to be in our exposition of the exploitation paradigm.

The remainder of the chapter is an attempt to break this simple example of exploitation by a majority of voters. It is an attempt to moderate the dismal implications for the stability of the liberal society by showing that the assumptions of the exploitation paradigm are unreflective of the actual conditions when people vote. The attempt is not entirely successful. The force of the example can be lessened to some extent, but exploitation by a majority of voters remains a danger nonetheless. The value of the analysis is in sharpening the diagnosis of the diseases of the liberal society and in suggesting how the patient can best be protected by an appropriate choice of public policy. Considerations that have so far been abstracted from or overlooked will be discussed one by one.

Insensitivity to the platforms of political parties
The anti-democratic argument has been developed within an exceedingly spare model of voting and elections. There are no political parties, and people are assumed to be exquisitely sensitive to their own incomes when they cast their votes for one platform or another. These assumptions will now be relaxed. By itself, the introduction of political parties does not change the story significantly. The introduction of a degree of voter insensitivity to offers of income in the platforms of rival political parties may in some circumstances create the electoral equilibrium that is missing so far,

but the circumstances where this is so are much more restricted than is usually recognized in the literature on voting theory. Consider an economy with these characteristics:

(α) The national income is to be allocated among three equal-sized groups of voters, where everyone within a group is treated identically but income per head may differ among the groups. The groups are A, B and C, their incomes per head are y_A, y_B and y_C, and the national income *per head* in the country as a whole is Y. Since all three groups are the same size, it follows as an accounting identity that

$$y_A + y_B + y_C = 3Y \tag{15}$$

The assumption that everybody's income is the same within each group is for analytical convenience and may be relaxed without lessening the force of the example.

(β) There are two political parties, R and D. The parties seek office but not income.[34] On attaining office, a party is empowered to choose the incomes of citizens y_A, y_B and y_C. Parties can commit themselves at election time to a choice of incomes. They do so by announcing platforms $\{y_A^R, y_B^R, y_C^R\}$ and $\{y_A^D, y_B^D, y_C^D\}$ where, for instance, y_A^R is the income that party R promises to supply to group A in the event that party R wins the election. All platforms must be consistent with the national income accounting identity in equation (15).

(υ) Define v_A^R as the percentage of people in group A who vote for party R, and define v_A^D, v_B^R, v_B^D, v_C^R and v_C^D accordingly. By definition, all these numbers are positive or zero and

$$v_A^R + v_A^D = v_B^R + v_B^D = v_C^R + v_C^D = 100 \tag{16}$$

Votes are determined in response to the offers of income in the platforms of the political parties. The overall percentage of votes for party R is

$$V^R = (v_A^R + v_B^R + v_C^R)/3 \tag{17a}$$

and the overall percentage of votes for party D is

$$V^D = (v_A^D + v_B^D + v_C^D)/3 \tag{17b}$$

where, by definition, $V^R + V^D = 100$. The winner in the election is the party with more than 50 per cent of the votes. It is convenient to suppose that, in the event of a tie, the winner is determined by the flip of a coin.

(δ^0) (To be modified presently) Each person votes for the party that offers him the largest income.

Together these four blocks of assumptions reproduce the exploitation paradigm in the context of party politics. The electoral equilibrium, if there were one, would be a pair of platforms such that neither party could gain votes by altering its platform, given the platform of the other. The symmetry of the assumptions guarantees that such an electoral equilibrium would have to be a tie in which V^R and V^D were both 50 per cent. Clearly there can be no electoral equilibrium in the model, for, starting from that equilibrium, it would be possible for either party to gain votes and win the election by offering $2 less to each person in one group and $1 more to each person in both the other groups.

Voters who can be expected to understand the essential instability of this process might behave differently than is assumed in (δ^0). They might be prepared to stick with a political party that offers to share the entire national income equally among its supporters, with nothing left over for anybody else. Such behaviour leads to a "nasty" equilibrium where, for instance, party R wins with a platform $\{0,3Y/2,3Y/2\}$ which provides all the available income to groups B and C and nothing to group A. To get such an equilibrium, it must be assumed that party R is the first to offer a sufficiently attractive platform to the two groups in the majority coalition and that members of groups B and C are "loyal" to party R because they know that any switch of allegiance to party D will set off a train of events that could lead eventually to their exclusion from a new majority coalition. Obviously, this nasty equilibrium is bad news for the liberal society. Nobody can be expected to adhere to the conventions of majority rule voting if total impoverishment of minorities is to be expected.[35]

A far more acceptable equilibrium can emerge if it is assumed that voters are somewhat insensitive to the platforms of the political parties. Assumption (δ^0) above carries the implication that, for instance, v_A^R can take only three extreme values: $v_A^R = 100$ when $y_A^R > y_A^D$; $v_A^R = 50$ when $y_A^R = y_A^D$; and $v_A^R = 0$ when $y_A^R < y_A^D$. A hundred per cent of the people in group A vote for party R when party R offers the higher income, the vote is split evenly when both parties offer the same income, and nobody votes for party R when party D offers the higher income. As an alternative, it might be reasonable to introduce a degree of continuity in voting behaviour. Perhaps party platforms are misperceived. Perhaps voters have a degree of party loyalty; the most loyal supporters require a big disparity in offers of income to induce them to change their vote, while others are induced to switch parties on the basis of a small difference in offers of income. Perhaps voters within groups differ in their assessment of the abilities of the party leaders.

With identical groups of voters and identical vote-maximizing political parties, it can be shown that a degree of insensitivity of voters to offers of income in the platforms of the rival political parties may lead to the emergence of an electoral equilibrium in which everybody's income is the same, an equilibrium in which each party offers a platform $\{Y,Y,Y\}$ and the winner of the election is determined by the toss of a coin. To get that equilibrium, it must be assumed that each group's percentage of votes for any political party varies gradually with the offer of income to the group in the party's platform, and that voters' sensitivity to offers varies, in a manner to be discussed, with the offers themselves. Suppose for the sake of the argument that there is an electoral equilibrium platform, that party D adheres rigidly to the electoral equilibrium platform, but that party R offers $1 more to everybody in groups B and C, and $2 less to everybody in group A. This is a winning strategy when all voters are assumed to be extremely sensitive to small differences in income. It need not be a winning strategy when each group's vote for party R varies continuously with the income offered to that group by the party platform. It is not a winning strategy when, for example, the responses of any group to changes in the offer of income by party R are as follows: provision of *one* extra dollar induces *one* extra member of the group to vote for party R; withdrawal of *one* dollar leads to the withdrawal of *one* vote; withdrawal of *two* dollars leads to the withdrawal of *three* votes; withdrawal of *three* dollars leads to the withdrawal of *six* votes; and so on. On this assumption, party R no longer gains the vote of the entire groups A and B by offering $1 more than its rival. It gains only one vote from each of the two beneficiaries of its manoeuvre and it loses three votes from the injured party. Party R loses one vote on balance, which is enough to swing the election to party D. The relation between votes and offers in this example is a particular case of a more general condition for the existence for electoral equilibrium; any concave relation would have done as well.

If each group's vote for any party can be expressed as a concave function of the income offered to that group in the party's platform and as a convex function of the income offered in the platform of the rival party, then there exists an electoral equilibrium pair of platforms from which neither party has an incentive to deviate. This proposition is known as the "probabilistic voting theorem". In so far as the theorem is true and is a reasonable representation of the circumstances of democratic politics, it is the sought-for escape from the exploitation paradigm and the anti-democratic argument. I shall argue here that the theorem is true, that it is not irrelevant to democratic politics, but that its assumptions are much stronger and much less representative of the circumstances of elections than is commonly believed. The theorem is proved formally elsewhere.[36] To make the theorem plausible and to focus on the limits to its applicability, it is convenient to employ a specific example. Replace assumption (δ^0) above with the following assumption about the voters' responses to the offers of the political parties.

(δ^1) The groups' percentages of votes for party R are dependent on the offers of incomes of both political parties as indicated by the votes-to-offers functions:

$$v_A^R = X \text{ where } X = 50 + S_A[(U_A(y_A^R) - U_A(y_A^D)] \qquad (18a)$$
$$\text{as long as } 0 < X < 100, \text{ and otherwise } v_A^R = 0$$
$$\text{when } X < 0 \text{ and } v_A^R = 100 \text{ when } X > 100$$

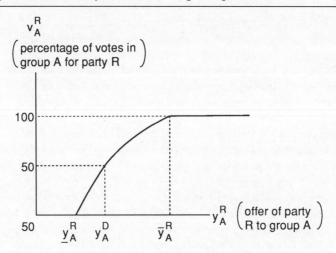

Figure 59 The response of voters to offers in the platform of a political party

$$v_B^R = X \text{ where } X = 50 + S_B[(U_B(y_B^R) - U_B(y_B^D)] \qquad (18b)$$
$$\text{as long as } 0 < X < 100, \text{ and otherwise } v_B^R = 0$$
$$\text{when } X < 0 \text{ and } v_B^R = 100 \text{ when } X > 100$$

$$v_C^R = X \text{ where } X = 50 + S_C[(U_C(y_C^R) - U_C(y_C^D)] \qquad (18c)$$
$$\text{as long as } 0 < X < 100, \text{ and otherwise } v_C^R = 0$$
$$\text{when } X < 0 \text{ and } v_C^R = 100 \text{ when if } X > 100$$

The U_A, U_B and U_C are ordinary utility of income functions with an assumed diminishing marginal utility of income, i.e. $U_A' > 0$ and $U_A'' < 0$, etc. Diminishing marginal utility of income will prove critical in establishing the electoral equilibrium, for this property of the utility function conveys the required concavity of the votes-to-offers functions in equation (18). The terms S_A, S_B and S_C are sensitivity parameters; they show, for instance, the extent to which group A increases its vote for party R in response to an increase in the gap between the utilities of group A in the offers of the two political parties. Each function is defined to ensure concavity between vote shares of 0 per cent and 100 per cent and to allow for the possibility that nobody in a group is prepared to vote for a political party which is seen as exploiting that group for the benefit of other groups in the population.

The meaning of equation (18a), for example, is that equal numbers of people in group A vote for each party if the offers, y_A^R and y_A^D, are the same, and that, otherwise, the percentage voting for party R increases with y_A^R and decreases with y_A^D, as indicated in Figure 59. The vertical axis shows the percentage of people in group A who vote for party R. The horizontal axis shows the income offered by party R to a person in group A. The curve shows how these are related for a given offer to group A by party

D. The curve is nicely concave as long as not everybody in group A votes for the same party, but there is assumed to be a minimal income $\underline{y}_A^R$ below which nobody in group A votes for party R.

For this example, the proof of the "probabilistic voting theorem" is now straightforward. If there is an electoral equilibrium, it is represented by a pair of platforms, $\{y_A^R, y_B^R, y_C^R\}$ and $\{y_A^D, y_B^D, y_C^D\}$, each maximizing a party's total vote, V^R and V^D, subject to the income constraint and with due regard to the platform chosen by the other political party.[37] By symmetry, since there is assumed to be no intrinsic difference between the parties, their electoral equilibrium platforms have to be the same. The equilibria are identified by the first-order conditions

$$S_A U_A' (y_A^*) = S_B U_A' (y_B^*) = S_C U_C' (y_C^*) \tag{19}$$

where y_A^*, y_B^* and y_C^* are the incomes in the common equilibrium platform, U_A' is the marginal utility of income for people in group A, and so on.

It follows immediately that a person's income in the electoral equilibrium is an increasing function of his sensitivity to offers; the greater S_A, for instance, the smaller is U_A' in equilibrium, and the larger y_A^* must be. Suppose $Y = 1,000$ and all utility functions are logarithmic. By symmetry, if S_A, S_B and S_C are the same, then $y_A^* = y_B^* = y_C^* = 1,000$. But, if $S_A = S_B = 100$ while $S_C = 200$, then equation (19) requires that $1/y_A^* = 1/y_B^* = 2/y_B^*$, so that $y_A^* = y_B^* = 750$ while $y_C^* = 1,500$.

Does that dispose altogether of the anti-democratic argument? Some authors have argued that it does.[38] In support of this view, they point to the existence of the electoral equilibrium and to the fact that the equilibrium is not too bad. Nobody is denied income altogether, and there is full equality of income in some circumstances.

Against this claim, and in support of the proposition that the anti-democratic argument cannot be dispensed with so easily, it may be argued that even the existence of an electoral equilibrium is not sufficient to remove the possibility of exploitation by voting. In fact, as will be shown presently, the possibility of exploitation by voting is not eliminated in the example where the electoral equilibrium has just been derived. A distinction has to be drawn in this context between *local* and *global* equilibrium. A local electoral equilibrium is one from which small deviations in the platform of any party must lose that party votes. That is what is identified by the first-order condition in equation (19) above. A global equilibrium is one from which any deviation whatever loses votes for the deviating party. That is what is required to exorcise the spectre of exploitation by voting. That, in turn, requires that the votes-to-offers functions of equation (18) be globally and not just locally concave. Note that the votes-to-offers function in Figure 59 is locally concave in the vicinity of y_A^D, which is the offer to group A in the electoral equilibrium. As drawn, the function is not globally concave because there is a kink at $\underline{y}_A^R$. The function would be globally concave only if it were so flat that it intersected to the left with the vertical rather than with the horizontal axis.

To appreciate the significance, strength and want of realism of the concavity assumption in the probabilistic voting theorem, consider once again the basic idea of the theorem. What makes the theorem go is that, starting from the electoral equilibrium, each additional withdrawal of a dollar from the offer by a political party to any group of voters induces that group to withdraw a progressively larger and larger percentage of its votes; a \$1 reduction in y_A^R leads to a 1 per cent reduction in v_A^R, an additional \$1 reduction leads to an additional 2 per cent reduction in v_A^R (so that v_A^R becomes 3 per cent less than it was at the electoral equilibrium), and so on. If that is what is going on, there can come a time when the income of group A has been so reduced that v_A^R falls to 0, signifying that nobody in group A votes for party R at all. The case illustrated in Figure 59 is where v_A^R is reduced to 0 once the income per head of people in group A is reduced to y_A^R.

The possibility of exploitation by voting arises because, once group A has withdrawn all its votes from party R, it has lost the capacity to inflict further punishment on party R if party R chooses to reduce its income still further. Now a new strategy is open to party R. It can pick up extra votes from people in groups B and C without losing votes from people in group A, by increasing its offers to groups B and C and reducing its offer to group A accordingly, exactly as in the circumstances of assumption (δ^0) above.

Consider once again the rivalry between party R and party D when the votes-to-offers function are as specified in equation (18), the national income per head is 1,000 and the three sensitivity parameters, S_A, S_B and S_C, are the same. By symmetry, the electoral equilibrium must be $y_A^* = y_B^* = y_C^* = 1,000$. When both parties choose that platform, then each has a 50 per cent chance of winning the election and a small deviation by either party from the electoral equilibrium is guaranteed to lose that party the election. But the possibility of gaining votes by exploiting one of the three groups has not been eliminated! It is easily shown that when the common value of the sensitivity parameters is 100 and when party D adheres rigidly to the platform {1,000, 1,000, 1,000}, the party R — which has nothing to gain from a small deviation from the electoral equilibrium platform — can nonetheless win the election by tendering a platform {0, 1,500, 1,500}.

The options for party R are shown in Figure 60 with its percentage of votes, V^R, on the vertical axis and the assumedly common offer of income to people in groups B and C on the horizontal axis. By definition, the offer of income to group A is what is left over from the offers to groups B and C. For instance, if \$1,200 is offered to everybody in groups B and C, then, since average income is \$1,000, the offer to people in group A must be

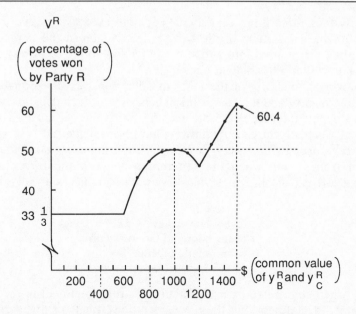

Figure 60 The percentage of votes won by party R as dependent on the degree of exploitation of group A. The platform of party D is {$1,000, $1,000, $1,000}, which is the (local) electoral equilibrium

$600. The electoral equilibrium platform is {1,000, 1,000, 1,000}. The curve shows that party R wins half the votes if it adheres to that platform and that it loses votes (as it must if equilibrium means anything at all) by deviating, as long as the deviation is not too large. But once the common offer to groups B and C rises to about $1,200, the party R has lost all the votes of group A and can only gain from increasing the offers to groups B and C still further. The platform {800, 1,100, 1,100} reduces the total vote of party R from 50 per cent to 49.3 per cent, but the loss is eventually made up as the offer to group A is reduced, and the vote for party R rises to 60.4 per cent once group A has been wiped out altogether with a platform of {0, 1,500, 1,500}.

Everything depends on the size of the sensitivity parameters. If they are quite small, the votes-to-offers function in Figure 59 is rather flat, the right-hand side of the function intersects with the vertical axis, the required concavity obtains over the whole range of possible offers and any deviation whatsoever by party R from the electoral equilibrium platform must cause party R to lose the election. But if the sensitivity parameters are quite large, then the votes-to-votes functions are steep, the function intersects with the horizontal axis as indicated on the figure, and the possibility of exploitation by voting of minorities by majorities appears once again. In the limit, as the sensitivity parameters get very large, the vote of group A for party R is either 0 per cent or 100 per cent, except over a very small range in which the offers of the two parties are almost the same. Then assumption (δ^1) merges into assumption (δ^0) and voting conforms to the original exploitation paradigm once again.[39]

Is universal concavity of the votes-to-offers function a reasonable assumption to make about actual political behaviour? Much depends on why voters do not automatically vote for the party that offers the largest income in its platform. Several answers have been suggested. Voters may misperceive small differences in offers. People may be more likely to abstain from voting when the differences between the offers of the political parties is small. People may have prior identification with political parties;

> . . . every boy and every gal
> That's born into the world alive
> Is either a little Liberal
> Or else a little Conservative!

except when confronted by substantially different treatment in the party platforms. I can accept that these considerations, singly or together, may account for a certain local concavity in the votes-to-offers function as shown in Figure 59, but I find it hard to believe that they are important enough in practice to neutralize the anti-democratic argument.

A second, and quite different, objection to the probabilistic voting theorem is that it proves too much. The entire distribution of income is determined as the outcome of rivalry between political parties seeking votes, with nothing left over to be accounted for by the distribution of property, skill, inheritance or any of the other considerations that are commonly believed to explain why some people are rich and other people are poor. Strictly speaking, the theorem implies that a person is rich not because he is highly skilled, not because he is the owner of large amounts of property, not because he has been lucky in his market transactions, not for any of the reasons that economists commonly invoke to explain the distribution of income. He is rich because, and only because, he is highly sensitive to the offers of the rival political parties. As the theory has been constructed, there is no place for a *status quo* in the economy that political parties and voters have come to respect.

This consideration raises two questions: whether the political explanation of the distribution of income in the strict version of the probabilistic voting theorem can somehow be combined in a larger theory with the usual economic explanations, and whether the theory can be brought down to earth as an explanation of the actual behaviour of political parties. In practice, both difficulties are dealt with simultaneously by a switch in the arguments of the votes-to-offers function from incomes to transfers or to other transfer-like variables. The probabilistic voting theorem might be used to explain the magnitudes of the old age pension, the terms of unemployment insurance, or the pattern of tariffs.[40]

Though the substitution of policies for incomes may serve to connect the theorem to the reality of public policy in some contexts, the procedure has several difficulties of its own. There is no explanation within the theory of why political parties choose the types of policies that they do. For instance, a political explanation of tariffs requires a prior assumption that political parties are prepared to redistribute incomes through the medium of tariffs but not by direct taxes or subsidies on the sectors of the economy that are affected by the tariffs. There must be a *status quo* in which redistribution by means of tariffs is permitted but redistribution by other means is not. Furthermore, though it remains possible for members of a group to compare the platforms of political parties, it is no longer possible to classify platforms as favourable or unfavourable to a group in any absolute sense. When the entire national income was allocated in the platforms of the political parties it was possible to say that group A was favoured over group B if members of group A were assigned higher incomes than members of group B. That is not so when platforms assign tariffs, for a high tariff on goods produced by group A may be looked upon as part of the *status quo*. The tariff may have been in force for so long that its effects have been completely capitalized into land prices and the present "beneficiaries" of the tariff are earning no more than the ordinary rate of return on their investments. In that case, the tariff itself is no longer a transfer to group A, and its removal would be seen as a transfer from group A to the rest of society. Finally, when policies rather than incomes are the arguments in the votes-to-offers function, one can no longer appeal to a common utility of income function in comparing the reactions of different groups to changes in public policies. A high tariff may represent a small percentage change in the incomes of those affected by the tariff, while a low tariff may represent a large percentage change in the incomes of the beneficiaries.

Nevertheless, it may be in the context of transfers that the true political significance of the probabilistic voting theorem is to be found. If there is a *status quo* of civil rights, property rights and acquired entitlement to public programmes, if voters are more responsive to losses than to gains in the offers of rival political parties, and if large reallocations of welfare are eschewed in the belief that you cannot redivide the pie without reducing the size of the pie or placing democratic government in jeopardy, then the *status quo* may represent a political equilibrium. It would represent an equilibrium in the sense that no political party could command the votes of a majority of the electorate with a platform representing any significant deviation from the *status quo*. This cannot be the whole story. Allowance must be made for changes in economic and social conditions and for swings of public opinion that affect the political equilibrium from time to time.

The significance of this line of reasoning is that the probabilistic voting theorem is not on its own sufficient to break the exploitation paradigm. Only in the context of a widespread respect for established rights can it serve to explain how a political equilibrium can arise and why a political party may be reluctant to rely too heavily in its platform on measures that benefit a majority of voters at the expense of the rest.

Altruism

A second major abstraction in the original statement of the exploitation paradigm was that voters are strictly selfish and unlimitedly greedy. That is surely false. One's utility may depend primarily on one's own income, but it is unreasonable to suppose that people are completely insensitive to the incomes of others, especially when the others are very poor. As we shall see, a degree of altruism does not dispose of the exploitation paradigm altogether, but it does constrain the majority to some extent, and it does place a lower limit on the amount one stands to lose through exclusion from the majority coalition. Suppose, once again, that society consists of n people, each of whose income is to be determined in voting by majority rule, that n is an odd number, and that the national income is invariant.

Altruism is introduced by allowing each person's utility to depend on his own income and on the incomes of every other person in his society. A convenient specification of a utility function of a person j who may, but need not, be altruistic is

$$U^j = \sum_{i=1}^n P_i^j \ln y_i \tag{20}$$

where P_i^j is the degree of concern of person j for person i (the intensity of preference of person j for the income of person i), y_i is the income of person i, and

$$\sum_{i=1}^n P_i^j = 1 \tag{21}$$

for all j. If person j is entirely selfish then $P_i^j = 1$ and $P_j^j = 0$ for all $i \neq j$. Assume instead that $P_j^j < 1$ for all i and j, that everybody in this society is equally altruistic and that each person's altruism is directed equally to every other person. Together, these assumptions imply a common degree of selfishness, P, such that

$$P_1^1 = P_2^2 \ldots = P_n^n \equiv P < 1 \tag{22}$$

and

$$P_i^j = (1 - P)/(n - 1) \tag{23}$$

for all $i \neq j$. The term $(1 - P)/(n - 1)$ can be thought of as each person's degree of concern for every other person.

To abstract from rivalry over the allocation of income within the majority coalition, let it be assumed that an agreement is somehow reached within the majority coalition to provide the same income for each of its members and to provide another, smaller income to each person in the excluded minority. A bare majority of $(n + 1)/2$ people forms a winning coalition in the legislature and chooses a pair of incomes, y_A for each person in the coalition and y_B for each person among the excluded minority, subject to the national income constraint

$$\frac{n+1}{2} y_A + \frac{n-1}{2} y_B = nY \tag{24}$$

where Y is national income per head, which is assumed to be invariant.

Consider a typical member of the majority coalition. His income is y_A, and he belongs to a society consisting of $(n-1)/2$ *other* members of the majority coalition whose incomes are also y_A, and $(n-1)/2$ people in the excluded minority whose incomes are y_B. From equation (20), it follows that *his* utility, U, becomes

$$U = P \ln y_A + \left[\frac{1-P}{n-1}\right]\frac{(n-1)}{2}\ln y_A + \left[\frac{1-P}{n-1}\right]\frac{(n-1)}{2}\ln y_B$$

$$= P \ln y_A + (1-P)\frac{\ln y_A + \ln y_B}{2} \tag{25}$$

His degrees of selfishness, P, and altruism, $(1 - P)$, serve as weights in his utility function, covering his own income and a logarithmic average income in the rest of society.

Think of this person as choosing y_A and y_B to maximize his utility, U. He could reserve the entire national income for members of group A, but he does not do so if he is at all altruistic. He chooses a pair of incomes, y_A and y_B, by maximizing his utility, V, in equation (25) with respect to the national income constraint in equation (24). His preference is indicated by the first-order condition

$$\frac{y_A}{y_B} = \left[\frac{P + (1-P)/2}{(1-P)/2}\right]\left(\frac{n-1}{n+1}\right) \tag{26}$$

which has a simple economic interpretation. If a person is so selfish that $P = 1$, then $y_B = 0$ and all the national income accrues to members of group A, as in the original exploitation paradigm. At the other extreme, if a person is so completely altruistic that no less weight is placed on another's income than on his own, then $P = 1/n$ and his preferred values of y_A and y_B are equal. Alternative degrees of selfishness and altruism are illustrated in Figure 61, with y_A (the income of members of the majority coalition) on the vertical axis, y_B (the income of those excluded from the majority

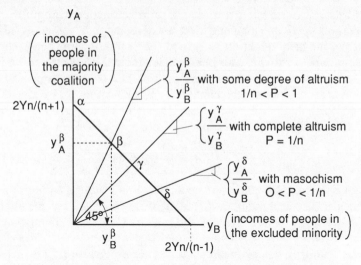

Figure 61 Predatory voting in the presence of altruism

coalition) on the horizontal axis, and with alternative ratios of y^A to y^B represented by the slopes of the four diagonal lines through the origin, corresponding to pure selfishness (the vertical line), some altruism (the line with slope greater than 45°), complete altruism (the line with slope equal to 45 per cent) and masochism (the line with slope less than 45 per cent). The resulting pairs of incomes, y_A and y_B, are represented by the points α, β, γ, and δ.

The significance of altruism — or of any feature of society that lowers a person's intensity of preference for his own income to something less than 1 — is that each person's stake in the outcome of the electoral process is considerably reduced. When everybody's intensity of preference for his own income is equal to 1, the cost of not being a part of the majority coalition is a fall in one's income from $2Yn/(n + 1)$ to nothing. When everybody's intensity of preference for his own income corresponds to the line through β, the cost of not being a part of the majority coalition is a fall in one's income from y_A^β to y_B^β. The greater the degree of concern of one voter for another, the smaller the gap between y_A^β and y_B^β and the greater the likelihood — when a host of other considerations are taken into account — that the losers at the game of voting by majority rule are content to abide by the customs of society and to desist from becoming the enemies of the state.

Production constraints
Another key provision in the original statement of the exploitation paradigm is that the national income is fixed. That is a convenient assumption

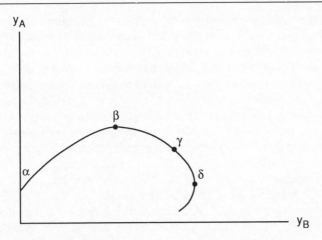

Figure 62   The income possibility curve when redistribution is costly. γ is the *status quo*

for demonstrating the presence or absence of an electoral equilibrium and for showing the role of altruism as a constraint upon exploitation, but it obscures the fact that exploitation by voting is also constrained on the production side of the economy. The size of the pie is not independent of how the pie is shared.

The basic proposition is illustrated in Figure 62, which is a variant of Figure 61 above. Interpretations of the axes are the same; the vertical axis shows income per head, y_A, of the members of the majority coalition and the horizontal axis shows the income per head, y_B, among the excluded minority. The figures differ in two important respects. The first is that γ need no longer be a reflection of altruism. Now it represents the *status quo* distribution of income, which is primarily a reflection of the historically given distribution of property and skills. The second difference is in the shape of curve αβγδ, signifying the options for redistribution between the majority and the minority. When the national income is invariant the curve must be a straight line, as was indicated in Figure 61. When the national income is not invariant — when the pie shrinks as it is redistributed — the curve becomes as indicated in Figure 62. The curve in Figure 62 signifies that a majority of voters can still benefit from laws or regulations which, one way or another, transfer income from the minority to the majority, but each extra dollar taken from the minority yields a progressively smaller gain to the majority and there comes a time — well before the minority is dispossessed altogether — when there is nothing to be gained by the majority from additional exploitation of the minority. The best that the majority can do for itself is to move the economy to the point β at which the direct gain from additional redistribution is offset, dollar for dollar, by the indirect loss from the resulting shrinkage in the national income. At

447

the point α where the minority is expropriated altogether, the majority is worse off than it would be at the point β; the doubling back of the curve $\alpha\beta\gamma\delta$ provides the minority group with a certain natural protection. The point δ represents the mix of incomes that would be chosen if the minority controlled the government and effected *its* optimal redistribution.

Contraction of the national income in response to policies that transfer income from one group to another has been discussed already in Chapter VIII with reference to the disincentives in programmes of redistribution of income from rich to poor: unemployment insurance, welfare, socialized medicine, progressive income taxation and so on. But relative income (prior to redistribution) may not be the basis on which the majority coalition is formed and, even if it were, the majority coalition might be of the rich or of some group in the middle of the income distribution rather than of the poor. People in the upper half of the income distribution might establish a majority coalition with a programme of regressive taxation, little or no public provision of services, low welfare payments and minimal public contribution to the destitute. Even such a programme might encounter a production constraint, associated in this case with increases in crime and in the cost of the criminal justice system. A majority coalition may be formed along industrial lines. Workers and owners of firms in certain industries may coalesce around a programme of tariff protection for the products of the industries within the coalition. The contraction of the pie in this case is the welfare loss associated with tariffs. This loss may be a considerable deterrent to the majority coalition because the coalition must, by definition, contain a great many industries and the practitioners of each industry weigh the benefits of their own protection against the cost of protection to other industries in the coalition. One can think of the coalition as establishing a common rate of protection for all the industries within the coalition. Since welfare loss from protection tends to increase with the square of the rate of protection,[41] there has to be an optimal rate of protection — optimal for the members of the majority coalition rather than for the nation as a whole — beyond which coalition members stand to lose more as consumers of the products of their coalition partners than they stand to gain as producers from the extra protection the industries on which their own livelihoods depend. There is an optimal degree of protection beyond which additional protection would confer no additional benefit to the firms and workers in the industries within the coalition.

The pie may shrink for political as well as economic reasons. Expropriation of the minority by the majority may take many forms. Those excluded from the majority coalition may be taxed disproportionately, expropriated, disfranchised, exiled, enslaved or killed. The response of the minority might be proportional to the provocation. When exclusion from the majority coalition represents a substantial loss of income and privilege, one would expect to see high expenditures by all parties to influence the outcome of the vote. One would expect to see a great deal of political agitation — from strikes to public demonstrations, to civil disobedience, to outright terrorism — designed to persuade the party in power that oppression of the minority will be ultimately unprofitable, and a resulting rise in public expenditure to preserve order. All these moves are costly, to members of the majority coalition as well as to those who are excluded.

Cost, in this context, goes well beyond the reduction in amounts of goods and services available for ordinary consumption. Cost must be thought of as inclusive of the risk of falling victim to crime and of the loss of civil rights, in addition to amounts of goods and services consumed. Extreme forms of expropriation of minorities are especially damaging to the non-material, intangible aspects of welfare. Members of the majority coalition may be prosperous in the sense of enjoying large amounts of goods and services, but they may be less well off in some broader sense than if they had been moderate in their treatment of the minority. Disfranchisement or exile of the minority is particularly dangerous because members of the original majority risk consignment to a minority in the new reduced electorate.[42] These extremes of expropriation are not usually in the interest of the would-be expropriators, but there have been circumstances — as when majority and minority are defined on racial lines and when there is a great deal of hostility between the races — where these extremes have been observed.

Connections among groups

Similar to altruism but distinct enough to be worth discussing on its own is the realization by each member of the majority coalition that he may in time cross over to the minority. One who is now poor (and who as a member of a majority coalition of the poor favours high minimum wages, substantial welfare payments and a steep rate of progressivity of the income tax) may be reluctant to harm the rich too much because he may become well off, or his children may become well off, or he may have prosperous relatives about whom he is concerned. The steelmaker who is a member of the majority coalition from which the farmer is excluded may nonetheless be somewhat concerned about the farmer's welfare and reluctant to support policies that harm the farmer a great deal because the steelmaker may in time become a farmer, or his children may become farmers, or he may have relatives and friends who are farmers.

Ignoring differences in incomes among members of the majority coalition and among people in the excluded minority, this consideration may be formalized as follows. Let $y_A(s)$ be the average income of the members of the majority coalition and $y_B(s)$ be the average income of people in the excluded minority, where both incomes are expressed as functions of the share, s, of total national income accruing to the members of the majority coalition. Clearly there must be some range of s within which

$$\frac{d}{ds} (y_A(s)) > 0 \quad \text{and} \quad \frac{d}{ds} (y_B(s)) < 0 \tag{27}$$

for otherwise there would be no conflict of interest between the groups. Also, let u(y) be the common utility of income function, and let π be the probability that a person who is now a member of the majority coalition remains within the coalition, and is not transferred to the minority, when the policy by which majority exploits minority comes into effect. On these assumptions, members of the majority coalition choose s to maximize expected utility,

$$\pi u (y^A (s)) + (1 - \pi) u (y^B((s)) \tag{28}$$

The value of s for which $y^A(s)$ is maximized may be well short of 1 because total national income may fall significantly as s rises. But now we see that this "killing the goose" argument is supplemented by another consideration. It is reinforced substantially by an "uncertainty" argument. The majority coalition may choose an s well short of that for which $y^A(s)$ is maximized because the typical member of the coalition is uncertain as to how long he will remain a member. The greater the reduction of total national income in response to policy designed to augment the share of the members of the majority coalition, the greater the chance that people now in the majority will find themselves among the minority when those policies take effect (or the greater the bond of sympathy between majority and minority) and the greater the degree of risk aversion as represented by the concavity of the utility function, the less predatory is the majority likely to be and the better is the lot of the excluded minority.

Speaking of democracy, Aristotle[43] said that "a state cannot be constituted from any chance body of persons . . . Most of the states that have admitted members of another stock, either at the time of their foundation or later, have been troubled by sedition". One can accept the force of Aristotle's logic without at the same time subscribing entirely to his conclusion. The major premise in the argument would seem to be that people of different stock have a high intensity of preference for policies affecting their own groups and a considerably greater degree of sympathy and identification with others in their group than with citizens belonging to other groups. A state composed of many stocks is less likely to coalesce around a common policy than a state that is initially more unified. A corollary to this proposition is that, the more diverse a society, the stronger must be the system of entitlements and the more circumscribed the government if the liberal society is to be sustained.

Laws, policies and incomes
The exploitation paradigm has been discussed so far in the context of the allocation of the national income among voters, but Acts of Parliament are

about laws rather than about incomes, and policy as formulated by the executive branch of government does not simply consist of taking from one person and giving to another. Much of politics is not directly allocative, though it may have an allocative component. Punishment of crimes, conduct of foreign affairs, education, national defence and the choice of leaders are matters about which conflict of interest among citizens may be unimportant by comparison with their common interest in choosing the best policy for society as a whole. Can we then say that the dangers to the liberal society as exemplified in the exploitation paradigm are confined to direct allocation of income by the state, or do these dangers seep out into legislation and policy of all kinds? Are ordinary legislation and policy-making a mere cover for conflicts over the allocation of the national income among people, or are they fundamentally different types of public decisions? I cannot supply simple and straightforward answers to these questions. The best I can do is to show by example when policy and legislation acquire characteristics of the exploitation paradigm and when not.

The prospects for the emergence of an electoral equilibrium in voting about platforms of issues, rather than about incomes directly, is the subject of this section and the next. The present section is a discussion of an example with a unique, stable electoral equilibrium. The next section is a discussion of several examples without such equilibria and where voting about platforms of issues inherits the instability and the potentiality for exploitation that we observed in voting about the allocation of the national income.

That there *may be* a voting equilibrium when there is more than one issue to be resolved and when there is a diversity of preference among voters, is established as follows: The important assumptions are numbered for convenience. Suppose (i) there are only two objects of public expenditure, the army and the navy, and (ii) there is a firm consensus about the size of each voter's tax share, regardless of the total amount of public expenditure. Each voter's utility function can be written as

$$U^i = U^i (E_A, E_N, c^i) \tag{29}$$

where i refers to the voter, U^i is his utility, c^i is his consumption of ordinary goods and services, E_A is the public expenditure on the army and E_N is the public expenditure on the navy. When a voter's pre-tax income is y^i, his consumption c^i becomes

$$c^i = y^i - t^i(E_A + E_N) \tag{30}$$

where t^i is his predetermined tax share. Substituting for c^i in equation (29), the utility function becomes

$$U^i = V^i(E_A, E_N) \tag{31}$$

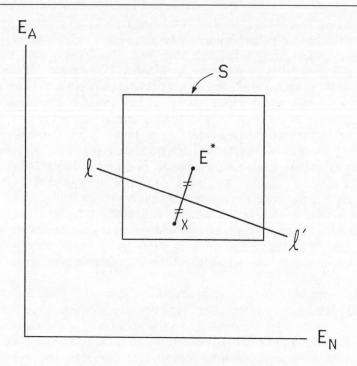

Figure 63   An electoral equilibrium

As long as his original utility function in equation (29) has the usual shape (in the space comprising E_A, E_N and c^i), a voter i has a first preference, E_A^i and E_N^i, and the indifference curves of his derived utility function in equation (31) are successively larger loops around the point representing his first preference.

Introduce two more assumptions: (iii) every voter's indifference curves are perfect circles around his first preference point, so that any two points in the E_A – E_N space are ranked by person i according to their distance from his first preference point, and (iv) there are a great many voters whose first preferences are spread out *with uniform density* on a square, S, in the E_A – E_N space as illustrated in Figure 63, with E_A on the vertical axis and E_N on the horizontal axis. Each voter's indifference curves are concentric circles around his first preference point, wherever within S that happens to be.

On these assumptions, there is an unassailable electoral equilibrium, $E^* \equiv (E_A^*, E_N^*)$, in the middle of the square. To prove this statement, it must be shown that the combination of public expenditures represented by the point E^* is preferred by some majority to any other combination. Choose some other combination as represented in the figure by the point

x. Draw a line from x to E*. Draw another line, indicated by (l,l′), perpendicular to the line from x to E* and cutting it in half. As long as the point x is within the square or close to it, the line (l,l′) must divide the square into two parts, with E* in one part and x in the other. By construction, every point in the part of the square containing E* is closer to E* than to x, while every point in the part containing x is closer to x than to E*. Furthermore, since E* is in the middle of the square, the part of the square that contains E* must be greater in area than the part that contains x. Each point in the square translates into an equal number of votes because, by assumptions (iii) and (iv), the indifference curves are circles and the density of first preferences is everywhere the same. Thus, the combination of expenditures represented by the point E* must win in a pairwise vote over every other combination. The point E* is a genuine electoral equilibrium.

In assessing the significance of this example, note that the dimensionality of the problem is not, in itself, critical. An electoral equilibrium would emerge with any number of public expenditures — the army, the navy, the air force and so on — as long as all of the other assumptions are maintained. Nor does the space in which the first preferences are contained have to be a perfect square; any symmetric shape, such as a circle, would have done as well, though a triangle would not. A good deal of sophisticated theorizing has been devoted to discovering how far the assumptions can be relaxed without destroying the electoral equilibrium and whether, or in what circumstances, a requirement for a super-majority, such as 65%, would protect a *status quo*.[44]

The crucial assumptions in this example are about the shapes and locations of the indifference curves over alternative public expenditures. To appreciate the significance of these assumptions, it is helpful to contrast the voting milieu in Figure 7 with the voting milieu in Figure 2 of Chapter V, where the object of public choice is to allocate a fixed national income among all voters. Here, regardless of the number of voters, only two dimensions, or as many dimensions as there are objects of public expenditure, need to be considered. There, since each voter was concerned about his own income exclusively, the number of dimensions had to be as large as the number of voters. Here, it is not unreasonable to suppose that the first bests of voters tend to cluster together in a way that, without too much distortion, can be represented by a dense, compact and symmetric set. There, the first bests of the different voters were as far apart as they could be, each as high as technically possible on its own unique axis. Here, the indifference curves are loops. There, they are planes, each reflecting one's own income exclusively, regardless of the incomes of the rest of the community. Here, it is not unreasonable to imagine that there might be an electoral equilibrium. There, no such equilibrium exists.

The contrast between this example and the earlier discussion of voting about the allocation of income serves to highlight the importance of assumption (ii) above, that there already exists a consensus about the appropriate value of each person's tax share, for the unconstrained choice of tax shares is for all practical purposes a choice of incomes. Thus, as there is no electoral equilibrium in the allocation of incomes, there can be no electoral equilibrium in the allocation of tax shares either, unless, as discussed in Chapter VIII, the allocation of tax shares is severely constrained or unless voters are assumed to set aside their immediate self-interest for the common good. Our example of electoral equilibrium rests on a prior public decision that could not itself have been the outcome of an electoral equilibrium, and must have been reached in some other way. Rules about tax shares are an aspect of property, and may be thought of as having evolved through the same half-understood process by which property itself evolved.

The moral of this example is that, for all practical purposes, there may be an electoral equilibrium — or a sufficiently small range of indeterminancy that the legislature can easily cope with the remaining diversity of interest — when public expenditure cannot be allocated directly among citizens. "Unallocatable" public expenditure is an imperfect vehicle for exploitation by voting, and poses less of a threat to democratic institutions than the direct determination of the incomes of citizens. But the threat is not eliminated altogether. To assume, as we did, that indifference curves are circles around first preferences that lie uniformly within a square is, in effect, to rule out strong intensities of preferences among voters for one issue over another. It will now be shown how the essentials of the exploitation paradigm can reemerge in voting about platforms of issues when this assumption is relaxed.

A majority of minorities
Suppose there are several issues to be resolved. If each voter is concerned about one and only one issue, then there would seem to be a very close analogy with the exploitation paradigm in which each voter is concerned about his own income exclusively, and one would expect the consequences for voting by majority rule to be more or less the same. This section is a discussion of examples in which voters' preferences over issues are biased toward one issue, though the bias need not be so pronounced that all other issues are ignored. Now, there may or may not be an electoral equilibrium among platforms of issues depending on how close the constellation of preferences lies to the extreme of the exploitation paradigm. These examples have strong implications about the significance of political extremism for the stability of the liberal society.[45]

Define a "majority of minorities" as a majority coalition composed of groups of voters, none of which constitutes a majority in itself, each of which has a favourite policy on some issue of the day, and each of which is so concerned about *its* issue that it is prepared to adhere to the policies of its coalition partners on other issues as long as the right policy on its issue is adopted. The original exploitation problem conformed more or less to that pattern because each member of the majority coalition was exclusively concerned with his own income.

A majority of minorities may form over the juxtaposition of two or more single-peaked issues. Imagine a society with only two issues to be resolved, two bills to be passed or rejected by the legislature. Passage of the first bill is indicated by x, and its rejection is indicated by $\bar{x}$. Passage of the second bill is indicated by y, and its rejection is indicated by $\bar{y}$. To make the example concrete, think of x as a bill to introduce the death penalty, of $\bar{x}$ as the maintenance of a criminal justice system with no death penalty, of y as a bill to prohibit abortion, and of $\bar{y}$ as a legal system where abortion is not a crime. For simplicity, intermediate options are ignored. Society consists of three people, one whom favours x but not y, a second who favours y but not x, and a third who favours neither. Both issues are trivially single-peaked. In a plebiscite between x and $\bar{x}$, the winner is $\bar{x}$ by a two-to-one majority. In a plebiscite between y and $\bar{y}$ the winner is $\bar{y}$ by a two-to-one majority. Can it then be inferred that the platform $(\bar{x},\bar{y})$ is preferred by a majority of voters to any other platform? Not necessarily.

The four possible platforms are: (x,y) which means that both bills pass, $(\bar{x},\bar{y})$ which means that neither does; $(x,\bar{y})$ which means that the first bill passes but not the second; and $(\bar{x},y)$ which means that the second bill passes but not the first. The preferences of the three voters — indicated by the symbols D_1, D_2 and D_3 — are complete orderings of these four joint outcomes. For example, the preference of voter 3 might be

$$D_3: (\bar{x},\bar{y}), (x,\bar{y}), (\bar{x},y), (x,y)$$

which means that the third person is opposed to both bills but would prefer the first to the second if one of the two must be passed.

Whether the "plebiscites equilibrium" $(\bar{x},\bar{y})$ is a true electoral equilibrium, in the sense that it is preferred by some majority of voters to every other platform, depends not merely on voters' preferences for x against $\bar{x}$ and for y against $\bar{y}$ but on the complete ordering of the four possible platforms. In some circumstances the platform $(\bar{x},\bar{y})$ is invincible. In others it can be defeated by a majority of minorities. Let the preference orderings of the three voters be

$$D_1: (x,\bar{y}), (x,y), (\bar{x},\bar{y}), (\bar{x},y)$$
$$D_2: (\bar{x},y), (x,y), (\bar{x},\bar{y}), (x,\bar{y})$$
$$D_3: (\bar{x},\bar{y}), (x,\bar{y}), (\bar{x},y), (x,y)$$

These orderings are consistent with the assumptions in the preceding paragraphs about each person's preferences for x against $\bar{x}$ and for y against ȳ, but new information is added. The ordering D_1 signifies that person 1 cares more about the choice between x and x̄ than about the choice between y and ȳ, while the ordering D_2 shows that person 2 has the opposite intensity of preference. These are precisely the conditions in which a majority of minorities may emerge.

The plebiscites equilibrium (x̄,ȳ) is the outcome of a pair of independent votes — x against x̄, and y against ȳ — but a political party with (x,y) as its platform can nonetheless win an election by a two-to-one margin against a political party with a platform (x̄,ȳ). Alternatively, when voters themselves are the legislature, the outcome (x,y) may emerge through vote trading.[46] A deal is struck between voter 1 and voter 2. Voter 1, whose true preference is for ȳ rather than y, commits himself to vote for y nonetheless, on the understanding that voter 2, whose true preference is for x̄ rather than x, commits himself to vote for x. The net effect of the trade is that both bills are passed. Though the outcome (x,y) is neither voter's first preference, it is better for both than if they had voted sincerely. Each party gets what he wants most in the trade and gives up what he considers secondary. The excluded minority is, of course, harmed by the trade; the third person in our example gets his least favoured outcome, (x,y), rather than his most favoured, (x̄,ȳ), which would have been the outcome if everybody had voted sincerely. The legislature adopts the death penalty and the prohibition of abortion despite the fact that neither policy is, by itself, favoured by a majority of voters.

To see the importance of compatible intensities of preference[47] within the majority of minorities, consider another structure of preferences, which is also consistent with a two-to-one majority for x̄ in a plebiscite with x and with a two-to-one majority for ȳ in a plebiscite with y, and which is constructed from the original table by reversing the order of preference of (x,y) and (x̄,ȳ) for persons 1 and 2:

$$D_1: (x,\bar{y}), (\bar{x},\bar{y}), (x,y), (\bar{x},y)$$

$$D_2: (\bar{x},y), (\bar{x},\bar{y}), (x,y), (x,\bar{y})$$

$$D_3: (\bar{x},\bar{y}), (x,\bar{y}), (\bar{y},x), (x,y)$$

Now persons 1 and 2 can be said to have low intensities of preference for x and y respectively, and vote-trading is no longer possible because no deal makes both participants better off. The only feasible deal is the one we have already considered: to vote for the platform (x,y). But that is worse than (x̄,ȳ) for persons 1 and 2, and (x̄,ȳ) is already the first best for person 3.

The moral of this story is that a majority of minorities can form only among extremists, among people or groups that are intensely concerned with one particular issue and are prepared to form coalitions with anybody to get their way on that issue alone. Political theorists often argue that democracy requires a fair degree of consensus among voters. Consensus

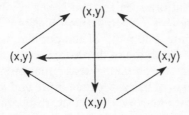

Figure 64   Absence of an electoral equilibrium. An arrow from one platform to another signifies that the former defeats the latter in a pairwise vote

can be interpreted as a low enough intensity of preference for one's immediate self-interest — one's town, or one's occupation, or one's language group — that an effective majority of minorities is unable to form. Advocates of the death penalty and the prohibition of abortion can both get their way if they care about nothing else, but the route to coalition is closed if they detest one another's programmes.

Successful vote-trading is always associated with the absence of an electoral equilibrium.[46] Whenever vote-trading changes the outcome in the legislature from what it would be if everyone voted sincerely on every bill, there is introduced an intransitivity in the voting procedure. Go back to the original structure of preferences. The outcome of sincere voting is $(\bar{x},\bar{y})$. We have shown that a majority nonetheless prefers the platform (x,y) to the platform $(\bar{x},\bar{y})$. But that is not the end of the story. The platform (x,y) does not win in a pairwise vote with any other platform. It is defeated by the platform $(x,\bar{y})$ and by the platform $(\bar{x},y)$, while these in turn are both defeated in voting by the platform $(\bar{x},\bar{y})$. There is a complete cycle. Persons 1 and 2 prefer (x,y) to $(\bar{x},\bar{y})$, persons 1 and 3 prefer $(\bar{x},y)$ to (x,y), and persons 2 and 3 prefer platform $(\bar{x},\bar{y})$ to $(\bar{x},y)$. The full constellation of outcomes of pairwise votes between platforms can be determined immediately from the structure of preferences, D_1, D_2 and D_3. These outcomes are shown on the directed graph in Figure 64.

High intensity of preference provides "natural" minorities with a chance to prevail as part of a majority coalition, but this chance is procured at the cost of intransitivity in the voting procedure and a corresponding instability in the state. When bills are considered one at a time and when legislators vote sincerely, there may be a unique outcome. Combine bills into platforms or allow for vote-trading, and the outcome depends upon the exigencies of voting, the skill of politicians and the accidents of who combines with whom to form a majority coalition.

A variation on this theme is worth examining briefly. Suppose two issues are to be resolved, the expenditure on the army and whether to impose the death penalty. Expenditure on the army can be high, H, medium, M, or low, L. The death penalty may be imposed, x, or not imposed, $\bar{x}$. For each of the six possible platforms on the two issues combined, Table 9 shows the assumed proportion of the population which prefers that platform over all others. For example, one-ninth of the population wants high military expenditure and the imposition of the death penalty as the punishment for murder. The numbers are chosen so that equal proportions of the population favour each level of military expenditure and a two-to-one majority is opposed to the death penalty. Obviously, if the issues are resolved one at a time and if everybody votes sincerely, the median voter theorem guarantees that there will be a medium-sized army and the two-to-one majority guarantees that there will be no death penalty.

Table 9   Distribution of first preferences

Platforms:	(H,x)	(H,x̄)	(M,x)	(M,x̄)	(L,x)	(L,x̄)
Proportions of voters:	1/9	2/9	1/9	2/9	1/9	2/9

The outcome may or may not be impervious to political manipulation. Despite the opposition to the death penalty by two out of three voters, the death penalty might be adopted as part of the platform of a successful political party or in vote-trading among legislators. Whether this actually happens depends on the entire structure of preferences of all voters, and not just upon the proportions of first preferences among the six platforms. The proponents of the death penalty can prevail if their intensity of preference regarding the death penalty is high, while the corresponding intensity of preference of the opponents of the death penalty is low. Table 10 shows a structure of preferences that is consistent with Table 9 but amenable to political manipulation. The table is constructed on the assumption that preferences are identical within each of the six groups. Each group's preference is shown along a row with platforms ordered, left to right, from the most to the least preferred, except where equal signs indicate a tie. From Table 10 one can determine the outcome of every pairwise vote between platforms, and these are shown on the directed graph in Figure

Table 10   Distribution of complete orderings of preference

Group	Proportion of voters	Orders of preference					
(i)	1/9	(H,x)	(M,x)	(L,x)	(H,x̄)	(M,x̄)	(L,x̄)
(ii)	2/9	(H,x̄)	(H,x)	(Mx̄)	(M,x)	(L,x̄)	(L,x)
(iii)	1/9	(M,x)	(H,x) =	(L,x)	(M,x̄)	(H,x̄) =	(L,x̄)
(iv)	2/9	(M,x̄)	(M,x)	(L,x̄) =	(H,x̄)	(L,x) =	(H,x)
(v)	1/9	(L,x)	(M,x)	(H,x)	(L,x̄)	(M,x̄)	(H,x̄)
(vi)	2/9	(L,x̄)	(L,x)	(M,x̄)	(M,x)	(H,x̄)	(H,x)

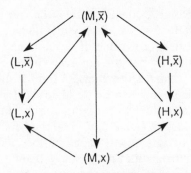

Figure 65   The outcomes of all votes between pairs of platforms. An arrow from one platform to another signifies that the former defeats the latter in a pairwise vote

65. An arrow from one platform to another signifies that the former defeats the latter in a pairwise vote. Missing arrows signify a tie.

Obviously, $(M,\bar{x}) \to (M,x)$, $(L,\bar{x}) \to (L,x)$ and $(H,\bar{x}) \to (H,x)$ because more people prefer $\bar{x}$ to x than prefer x to $\bar{x}$. The interesting connections are $(L,x) \to (M,\bar{x})$ and $(H,x) \to (M,\bar{x})$. The plebiscites equilibrium is $(M,\bar{x})$; this is the winning combination when votes on military expenditure and the death penalty are conducted separately and there is no vote-trading among groups. That platform is now defeated by two extreme platforms, (H,x) and (L,x), each of which captures five-ninths of the total vote, representing a coalition of *all* those who favour the death penalty and some of those who do not but are attracted to the platform by its extreme position on military expenditure. Each of these winning coalitions is a majority of minorities.

The plebiscites equilibrium is not a full electoral equilibrium in the circumstances described in Table 10 because those who favour the death penalty order platforms primarily according to whether the death penalty is to be imposed and only secondarily according to the amount of military expenditure, while those who oppose the death penalty behave in the opposite way. A different set of orderings could have produced a different result. The plebiscites equilibrium would have been a genuine electoral equilibrium that wins in a pairwise vote against any other platform if intensities of preference were the same among those who favour the death penalty as among those who oppose it.

Finally, note that vote-trading may or may not be efficient in the sense of maximizing the national income. To take an extreme example, imagine a society of five people (A, B, C, D and E) where all public revenue is financed by a poll tax (everybody has to pay one-fifth of the total public expenditure, whatever that may be) and the legislature has to decide whether to build each of five roads (also designated by A, B, C, D and E). All roads are of benefit to all voters, but each road benefits one voter more than the rest. Road A conveys $100 of benefit to person A and $25 of benefit to each of B, C, D and E. Road B conveys $100 of benefits to person B and $25 of benefit to each of A, C, D and E, and so on. Each road costs $150, so that no person, not even the chief beneficiary, would be prepared to build a road all by himself, though the sum of the benefit to all voters ($200) is larger than the total cost ($150). If the five people voted on each road separately, no road would be built, because the tax cost of each road to each person is $30 while the benefit to four of the five people is only $25. An agreement among all five people to build all five roads supplies each person with $200 worth of benefits at a tax cost of only $150. The agreement makes everybody better off.

However, against a proposal to build all five roads, a coalition of any three voters — say A, B and C — may form in support of a programme of building only those roads that are especially beneficial to the coalition members. As members of the majority coalition, persons A, B and C would each save $60 in tax and lose $50 worth of road use, for a net gain of $10. As the excluded minority, persons D and E would each save $60 in tax and lose $125 worth of road use, for a net loss of $65. In blocking the two roads that are especially beneficial to the excluded minority, the coalition trades $30 of net benefits to itself against $130 of net loss to others, wiping out $100 of benefits to society as a whole. With majority rule voting, the coalition prevails regardless.

Government v. voters
Exploitation by voting is also constrained by the intrinsic unreliability of political parties. I have so far been reasoning as though political parties could commit themselves irrevocably to a platform benefiting a segment of the population at the expense of the rest. Contemporary liberal societies are not usually like that. In a parliamentary system, citizens vote for Members of Parliament who are attached to political parties that are only weakly committed to particular policies. There are times — times of danger for democratic government — when society is so sharply polarized that members of the majority coalition are immediately identifiable and are represented by a single political party which is irreversibly committed to the interests of its supporters. Then the only constraint upon the majority is the potential loss of income as those who are left out of the majority coalition respond by emigration, crime or rebellion. Normally, majority and minority are not so clearly differentiated and the threat to the minority is not so grave. Normally, there is no organization of the majority coalition outside the political parties, while the political parties, in turn, have an interest in ambiguity, in being all things to all men, and may easily shift policies while in office to appeal to some new majority in the next election. Minorities have less to fear from majorities when the composition of the majority coalition is ill defined and when political parties are to

some degree untrustworthy than when, as has been assumed, a winning political party can commit itself irrevocably to the service of a majority coalition in the electorate.

Equally important is the voters' fear — shared by the members of the majority coalition and by the rest of the population — of the power of the government itself. The governing classes — the executive, the legislators, the bureaucracy and the army — have a permanent interest in the enlargement of the perquisites of office, the salaries of public officials, and the influence of government upon the economy. There is a tension between the majority of voters who elect the legislature and executive — and who need not re-elect them if public policy does not conform to the will of the majority — and the governing classes that are inevitably tempted to employ the instruments of government for their own ends. Public officials can be held accountable to the electorate and can be induced to relinquish office when defeated in elections as long as the number of officials that have to be replaced is not too large and the loss of office is not too great a burden. Numbers matter because those about to be removed from office in an election are unlikely to resist, or to employ the instruments of government to remain in office, when the number of defeated politicians and bureaucrats to be replaced is small by comparison with the great majority of citizens who want the rules to be obeyed. The burden matters because defeated politicians and dismissed bureaucrats are less likely to accept the verdict of the election peacefully when they face punishment at the hands of their successors, or catastrophic loss of income, than when the cost of departure is small because, for example, ex-politicians can expect lucrative positions in the private sector.

Taking from minorities — notably by progressivity in the income tax or by tariffs — can sometimes be effected with no increase in the scope or powers of government, but thoroughgoing exploitation requires a substantial role for the public sector. It is difficult to exclude the minority from leading positions in the economy or from the ownership of property without at the same time empowering the government to involve itself more extensively in the economy and in the lives of ordinary citizens than many members of the majority coalition would be prepared to tolerate. In a society of blue people and green people, the blues cannot be confined to menial jobs unless there is a substantial internal security force to ensure that no blue person works in any other capacity and to suppress rebellion among discontented blues. But, once established, the security force may oppress the greens as well. A government devoted to assisting the greens in exploiting the blues is likely to be corrupt because the greenish majority cannot turn against its party in the next election without at the same time abandoning the source of its privileges. These considerations may provoke the greens who are in the majority to think twice about restricting the economic opportunities of the blues. A predator of a predator makes life easier for

461

the prey. Frequently, though not invariably, the majority cannot seriously disadvantage the minority without at the same time enlarging the powers of a ruling class that can be expected to prey on majority and minority alike.

Political institutions and parliamentary procedure

A predatory majority is constrained to some extent by the machinery of government. In the original exposition of the exploitation paradigm, there was assumed to be a direct conduit from the interests of the majority coalition, through the platform of the winning political party, to legislation once that party takes office. The assumption was useful in conveying the essence of a difficulty with majority rule voting. It nonetheless abstracts from much of the detail of political life, from the rules and institutions, the separation of powers, and the checks and balances among branches of government that are specifically designed to protect an otherwise exposed minority. The classic division of government into executive, legislature and judiciary, each with its own jealously guarded realm of authority, protects the citizen from the government as a ruling class and from his fellow citizens in their capacity as a majority coalition. An independent judiciary is a better guardian of the rights of the minority than a judiciary that functions at the pleasure of other branches of government. A potentially predatory majority in one House of the legislature can be blocked and neutralized by a different but equally predatory majority in the other House. A degree of independence between the executive and the legislature is an impediment to the squelching by government of the unpopular individual or the outnumbered group. The division of powers stands at the same time as a defence against predation by a ruling class. Predation by rulers can never be eliminated altogether. Officials, politicians and soldiers will inevitably acquire privileges at the expense of the population. There is, however, more scope for whistle-blowing by officials and for civil disobedience in response to laws that are unjust in themselves or unjustly administered when the laws are made, administered and enforced by separate branches of government, each jealous of its range of authority, than when all government is a single hierarchy that may promulgate laws and punish infractions as it sees fit.[49]

Government in a liberal society is, in a sense, explicitly designed to be ineffectual. It is intended to respond slowly and imperfectly to the demands of the majority of voters, as a check on predation by voting and in the hope that most of society's business will be conducted within the private sector of the economy. The division of powers is clearest in the United States, where the sphere of authority of each branch of government is specified in the constitution. Similar constraints are instilled in parliamentary government by the formal authority of Parliament over the Cabinet, the division of Parliament into an Upper and a Lower House, and some degree of independence for the judiciary.

The majority is also constrained by the ceremony of democracy. In Canada the passage of a law requires three readings of a bill in the House of Commons, with extensive debate at the second reading. The bill must then be ratified by the Senate, which cannot stop a bill permanently but can send it back to the House of Commons, with or without amendments, for reconsideration. Only then is the bill proclaimed as law by the Governor General. Passage of a bill is an intricate political dance in which both government and opposition must follow steps prescribed by custom but not necessarily written down as constitution or as law. Canada is in no way unusual in this regard. Comparable ceremony is to be found in every democratic country. There are strong pressures on government and opposition to follow the steps exactly. Citizen voters cherish the ceremony and would normally be inclined to punish a political party for breach of ceremony by withholding votes in the next election or, in extreme cases, by civil disobedience. Respect for the ceremony by citizen voters is traditional, but it has a solid basis in rational self-interest, for democratic government might not last if the ceremony were abandoned altogether.

An important aspect of the ceremony of democracy is the "right" of the opposition party to refuse to play its prescribed role in the passage of legislation. The option of refusing to follow the regular procedures provides the opposition with a means of expressing the extreme concern of the classes of voters it represents. Refusal enables the minority to say to the majority that a proposed law is intolerable and that government by majority rule is not working as it should if such laws are to be passed. The party in power must then reconsider its policies in the light of the extreme displeasure of the opposition. The filibuster in the U.S. Congress is such a breach of ceremony. So too is the denial of a quorum by a determined opposition, or the refusal of the opposition to enter the House of Commons when its presence, if not its votes, is required for the passage of legislation.[50] A party which disrupts the ceremony of democracy regularly or for reasons that voters see as less than fundamental is unlikely to have much support at the polls. Breach of the ceremony by a minority party might provoke the majority party to pare down the ceremony to ensure the passage of a bill and might, perhaps, lead to a situation where there is some dispute whether a bill has passed or not. But the tactic frequently succeeds, at least in the short run. The party in power may amend the offending bill, or withdraw it altogether, or allow it to die the natural death of bills not passed into law before Parliament is prorogued, or accept an election on the issue in question.

These constraints upon the acquisitiveness of the majority faction apply, not only to the current majority, but to any future majority from which members of today's majority may be excluded. Thus does the majority acquire a double reason for restraint: the arguments for moderation apply to the majority today, and, since they apply with equal force to a new majority tomorrow, provide the members of today's majority with some basis for confidence that their moderation will be reciprocated. Each party comes to believe that the other would not be too greedy in its exercise of office and would be inclined to show restraint.

These constraints are powerful but not decisive. Insensitivity to offers of rival political parties, altruism, the dependence of the size of the pie on how it is shared, uncertainty about one's future role in society, common interest in policies, the unreliability of political parties, the division of powers, the ceremony of democracy and the fear of the ruling class are all to some extent curbs upon predation by voting and may, singly or in combination, be necessary conditions for the preservation of a liberal society. They are not sufficient. Despite these constraints, it remains possible for a determined majority — or for a minority which somehow succeeds in acquiring a majority of the seats in the legislature — to enforce its will on the minority in any matter whatsoever. If the entire national income were really up for grabs, a majority coalition would one way or another congeal around some nucleus; race, religion, language, wealth and region would all do equally well. Even the realization that democratic government may be at stake is an insufficient deterrent. Fear of exclusion from a majority coalition drives each voter to the shelter of that very coalition, seeking entry before the membership is closed, though everyone knows that he would be better off if nobody acted in that way. Only with assurance of "fair" treatment at the hands of a government that one does not support is one willing to play by the rules of democracy. Such assurance requires a standard of fairness, and that, in turn, requires the allocation among voters of the national income and other advantages to be, at least in part, determined by considerations outside and prior to the sphere of political activity. Thus we return to a consideration that was central to the analysis of the liberal society in Chapter V: the mutual dependence between property and voting.

Property and civil rights

To speak of "predation by voting" is to suppose the existence of a standard, *status quo* or system of equity[51] against which predation may be identified. If, out of a total income of 100, I honestly believe myself to be entitled to 80 and you to be entitled to only 20, while you, on the other hand, believe that you are entitled 80 and I am entitled to only 20, then there can be no agreement between us about the meaning of predatory behaviour. You see me as a predator if I succeed in taking 80. I see myself as taking no more than is my due. The constraints on predation by voting that we have been discussing become all but meaningless without a common understanding as to when predation occurs. Why shouldn't the party of the blues expropriate the property of the greens and remove the greens from lucrative and powerful positions in the industrial hierarchy? What right had the greens to be rich and to hold high office when there were equally deserving blues with neither wealth nor office? The only possible answer to these questions is with reference to a non-political standard which both blues and greens have come to respect because the standard is worthy *per se* or because of a general recognition that the abandonment of the standard is, in effect, the abandonment of the liberal society. Government by majority rule voting is not viable without a general willingness on the part of the losers in an election to accept the result peacefully and on the part of the party in power, and its supporters, to risk loss of control of government when the time comes to call an election. That willingness will be forthcoming only if the stakes in the election are not too high. The preservation of democracy requires rules of allocation among citizens that the electorate cannot or will not easily overturn.

The required standard is supplied — if supplied at all — by the outcome of the market with an historically given distribution of human and physical capital. Let it be admitted that there is no real justification for the given distribution of property, that the government must defend and, to some extent, define property rights, that there is some predation by rulers, by capture and by voting within the public sector, that the government has a substantial role to play in providing public goods, correcting market failure and redistributing income between rich and poor, and that everything touched by the government must benefit some citizens at the expense of others. Despite all that, it remains true that the market is at least partially autonomous. The market does supply a rough standard against which predation by voting can be identified. The market is not one standard among many, from which the legislature may choose. It is the only non-political mechanism for producing goods and services and for allocating income to citizens. There is simply no other, and the reader who doubts this statement need only ask himself what that other might be.

One might suppose that full equality of income would serve as an alternative standard of allocation, but that is illusory. Incentives to work, save and innovate would be destroyed. The market would sooner or later be replaced by a less attractive method of compelling each person to pull his weight. People at the top of the industrial and governmental hierarchies would one way or another employ their authority to acquire income and privilege. Alternatively, one might suppose that people's contribution to the national product would serve as an alternative standard of allocation, but that too is illusory. One's contribution is in part a consequence of one's status in the industrial hierarchy. Contribution is not measurable by any universally acceptable standard. The assessment of each person's contribution would have to be entrusted, along with the administration of the economy, to a cadre of economic planners who would be ultimately responsible to the government. Government can displace the market, but it cannot do so without at the same time acquiring greater powers over the lives and fortunes of citizens than is consistent with the maintenance of democratic institutions.

Property rights provide the legislature with a way of *not* voting on precisely those issues that would be so divisive as to destroy the consensual basis of the voting. Without property rights, all incomes would have to be determined within the legislature. Without property rights that the legislature is prepared to respect, a man's entire fortune would come to depend on his success in manoeuvring himself into a majority coalition and negotiating a good deal with his fellow members, or upon his capacity to rebel if the legislature failed to take account of his interests. Without property rights, the appeal to violence would become irresistible. The outcome of the market may be modified, extreme poverty may be alleviated and the distribution of income may be narrowed by various social programmes. Property and markets remain as an indispensable requirement for a government with majority rule voting.

Markets, voting and the powers of government

In the models of anarchy and despotism, the distribution of income among social classes was determined in an equilibrium where violence or the threat of violence had an essential role to play. Each party took what he dared. An increase in one's capacity to harm one's neighbour could be expected to increase one's share of the pie. By contrast, the distribution of income in the liberal society seemed to depend exclusively on the prior distribution of property and the exigencies of voting, with no *explicit* reference to violence at all. This asymmetry in the treatment of violence raises questions about the liberal society. Where did violence go? Has violence been abolished? Or are rules of property and voting a cover for a distribution of income that is really determined by violence and the threat of violence, so that the liberal society is much more like despotism than one might at first suppose? What is the role of violence in the liberal society?

These questions might be dismissed with the simple observation that violence is not really absent at all. The liberal society can be described without reference to violence, but violence is there all the same as a sanction for obedience to the rules. Actual liberal societies — societies where most of the means of production are privately owned and where voting is essential in choosing leaders and legislation — must confer a monopoly of large-scale violence upon the state to deter crime and insurrection. The army, the police, the civil service and the politicians in office must be empowered to enforce the laws, protect property rights and uphold electoral procedures. A distinction can, nonetheless, be drawn between the liberal society with no place for violence once the rules are obeyed and the alternative societies, anarchy and despotism, where violence is an inextricable part of ordinary transactions.

The important question about violence in the liberal society is not whether it is present but how it can be constrained. The question is why the custodians of the means of violence allow themselves to be bound by the rules of property and voting, why they are prepared to uphold the laws rather than to secure advantages for themselves or to reconstitute themselves as a despotic ruling class. Organized in hierarchies, they have a greater capacity to act cohesively than other groups or coalitions in society. By virtue of their occupations, they may have the most to lose when a ruling party is turned out of office in an election. The constraint would seem to be a combination of fear and respect.

To say that violence becomes the sanction for obedience to the laws is to say that men in office cannot do just as they please. Deference to authority becomes conditional. Obedience is withdrawn from officials who overstep the bounds of their authority. More generally, a concerted attempt to overturn the laws, dispense with property rights, disregard voting or abolish the liberal society altogether would be resisted by a large enough segment of the population that the attempt would be unlikely to succeed. Thus the personnel of the government are induced by the ever-present threat of withdrawal of obedience to deploy their monopoly of violence in accordance with and in defence of the laws. Ideally, the laws guard the guardians. A self-enforcing expectational equilibrium keeps the liberal society on track and creates the appearance that there is no appeal to violence at all. Each person is prepared to obey the rules and to do his part in punishing rule-breakers in the belief that others would punish him if he did not.

That cannot be the whole story, for, in an open society, an expectational equilibrium requires that expectations be well-founded. The liberal society cannot be preserved by fear of retribution based upon the illusion of widespread support. The support must be genuine. The threat of punishment may be adequate to secure most people's compliance with ordinary laws, but not to deter concerted actions by well-organized groups within government or the private sector. There is too much communication and coordination among would-be usurpers who may cease to fear retribution because they expect to establish a despotic society in which they become the ruling class. Opposition may be silenced because a *putsch* may be as dangerous to oppose as to support. There must be a reasonable basis for the expectation that most people, within the governmental classes and within the general population, will defend the liberal society. There must be a widely held and well-founded conviction that the liberal society is worthy of support. In the last resort, the rules of the liberal society are respected and obeyed because each person sees himself as better off within the liberal society than he could expect to become in any plausible alternative, or, to be more specific, because allegiance to the liberal society is sufficiently widespread that no attempt to displace it is likely to succeed. A person must have more to gain from the continuance of the liberal society than from the advancement of his group or class in the event that the liberal society is displaced. A person must, as it were, be able to say to himself that, all things considered, the liberal society is his best bet for a decent and prosperous life for himself, his children and his grandchildren.

Respect for the liberal society is a necessary, but by no means sufficient, condition. I suspect that throughout most of recorded history the advantages of office were so great and the consequences of loss of office so devastating, if not lethal, that the liberal society could not have been established or, if established, could not have been preserved. There would be little chance for the establishment or preservation of voting with universal suffrage as a means of decision-making in the public sector in a largely illiterate society with a widely dispersed population and little or no communication among ordinary citizens. The most the common man could hope for would be a stable and somewhat benevolent despotism without too much strife from dissension within the ruling class.

Nor can majority-rule voting be maintained in a modern industrial society in the absence of strong property rights. In a society without property rights, the government's control over the means of violence would be augmented by control over the means of production and communication. Authority to fill all the top jobs and set all the salaries in all the hierarchies in the economy – industry, services, newspapers, television and transport — would be added to the authority over the hierarchies in the civil service and the army that is already required to perform the normal tasks of government in a liberal society, as set out in Chapter VIII. The exercise of such authority would not be entirely innocent. Predatory government is especially difficult to constrain in this context because, as discussed in Chapter I, there is no universally recognized social welfare function by which decisions of government that are not public-serving could be unambiguously identified, and because the range of matters that would have to be settled by voting would extend well beyond the domain — exemplified by the army and navy example in the preceding section — within which an electoral equilibrium might be expected.

The privileges of office would be magnified, as would the capacity of the party in office today to victimize its opponents. Office would become the sole object of ambition and the means to all other ends. Loss of office would be a fall from the top to the bottom of society, without the financial security that the private sector provides and with little prospect of returning to office again. Politicians, bureaucrats and soldiers who understand the virtues of the liberal society, who are prepared to undergo some sacrifice to preserve it and who would ordinarily accept loss of office in an election when the alternative is a step toward despotism, albeit a despotism where they form the upper class, may cling to power regardless when voting is not backed by property and the means of production are owned and administered by the state. To a far greater extent than at present, political parties would become the catalysts of interest groups defined by race, language, region or any other badge for distinguishing the privileged from the unprivileged. In the absence of strong property rights, the party in office would be irresistibly tempted to subvert the electoral process when loss of office seemed likely because, for instance, a rival party had succeeded in mobilizing a majority coalition among the unprivileged members of society. With the magnification of the privileges of office, the office-holders' temptation to dispense with elections would be reinforced by a well founded fear that their successors, on making the same comparison between office and loss of office, would refuse to step down in their turn. One might cease to see the choice as between the continuance or discontinuance of the liberal society. One might come to see the choice as between two despotisms, my despotism and that of my opponents.

It is uncertain how large and influential the government can become without destroying the economic foundation of majority rule voting. Full public ownership of the means of production is clearly incompatible with democratic government. A substantial public sector and a considerable influence of government upon the economy must be tolerable, for otherwise no liberal society – no society with an economy based on private property and a politics based on voting – could ever have been established. Somewhere between full public ownership of the means of production and extreme *laissez-faire* is a line that the liberal society cannot cross or a grey area within which politics becomes increasingly factious and unwieldy as the public sector expands, until eventually the liberal society dissolves into despotism.

Throughout most of this century, and in virtually every country in the world, there has been a marked upward trend in the government's share of the gross national product and involvement in the economy. The trend was especially disturbing because the expansion of government was only partly voluntary. The expansion of government was to a great extent a consequence of fundamental changes in technology and society, not a simple political decision which could be simply reversed. As society became more complex, an ever larger share of the national income seemed to be required for the rock-bottom minimal functions of government in protecting property and providing public goods, inclusive of research, public health and, to a degree, education. Environmental externalities became progressively more dangerous and geographically extensive, so that production in one country affected the health and safety of people throughout the world. Improvements in communication have magnified economies of scale, causing markets to look less and less like the model of perfect competition in which the nice theorems of welfare economics can be said to hold unambiguously. Economies of scale in the control of firms have accentuated many of the worst departures from efficiency in speculative activity. Oligopoly has become more prevalent, regulation more extensive and the perquisites of office correspondly greater. As a gradual working out of the implications of universal franchise, or as a consequence of innovations in accounting and computing, the government has acquired responsibility for the redistribution of a substantial share of the national income through the old age pension, unemployment insurance, welfare and so on. Markets, luck or life itself inevitably churn up gross inequalities of income. The losers in this process, those who fear becoming losers and the altruistic invoke the fundamental equality of people as voters to moderate inequality to some extent.

Solid economic reasons for the involvement of government in the economy do not change the fact that the expansion of government can threaten democratic institutions. I began the study of the interaction between markets and voting in the mid-1970s when the role of government was still expanding throughout the Western world and Communism still seemed to be a going concern. It seemed then that many countries were absent-mindedly chipping away at the foundations of the liberal society, and manoeuvring themselves into circumstances where democratic government would in time cease to be viable. In the 1980s the expansion of government appeared to be slowing down in most Western countries and markets were being re-established in what was the Communist world. There was also a great ideological shift away from government intervention in the economy and toward a much greater reliance on markets. Perhaps the governments of most Western countries had expanded up to or beyond the point where the great majority of voters wanted their governments to be. Certainly the contrast in economic development between East Europe and East Asia has taught the world a lesson it will not quickly forget. On the other hand, the proliferation of environmental externalities, the magnification of economies of scale, the natural development of technology and the intensification of nationalism and religious fanaticism will in all probability impose new tasks on government or threaten the liberal society in as yet unexpected ways. Government's role in the economy may expand once again unless old tasks can be sloughed off as new ones are acquired.

The emphasis in this book has been upon analysis rather than prescription, the book itself has covered much of the conventional ground of welfare economics and public finance, and there has been considerable agreement with commonly held views in these fields. But the paraphernalia of bandits, rulers, anarchy, despotism and predation — in extending the scope of economic analysis beyond the property-respecting, welfare-maximizing societies which are its traditional domain — served to emphasize a few general propositions about public policy, propositions which, although hardly surprising or original, do not flow naturally from traditional welfare economics. The central proposition is an extension of the political argument for private property: that the legislature and the bureaucracy should be as little involved as possible in the determination of who is to be rich and who is to be poor, for political allocation of income is an invitation to predatory government. Thus, in all public policy, universally applicable rules are preferable to narrowly focused projects or programmes. On this principle, the redistribution of income should be nation-wide, not tailored to this or that region, occupation or social class which happens to capture the sympathy of the legislature at the moment or is able to mobilize support among the electorate. Similarly, encouragement of investment through the tax system is preferable to industrial policy in which a department of government is empowered to designate regions, industries or even firms as recipients of public largess. There is a comparable political argument against tariffs, price control and subsidies of all kinds, an argument that need not be decisive in any particular case but should weigh in the balance along with standard economic considerations. One can recognize the usual reasons for government involvement in the economy — protection of property, correction of market failure, redistribution of income and provision of public goods — and still maintain that these reasons are not necessarily decisive. The benefit of involvement may be outweighed by the economic cost of the usual inefficiencies of public action and the political cost of the enlargement of the public sector. As public expenditure entails public influence on the allocation of income among citizens, the full social cost per dollar of expenditure on projects or programmes must necessarily increase together with the size of the public sector, not just (as discussed in chapter VIII) because of the increase in the marginal deadweight loss from taxation, but because political institutions become increasingly unwieldy. The larger the public sector, the more carefully must each new project or programme be scrutinized, and the more stringent should the test for new items of public expenditure become.

The liberal society is valuable for its own sake and as the political and economic basis of freedom, prosperity, civil rights and the rule of law, but the liberal society is not eternal. It can be destroyed piecemeal and by mistake as government programmes are introduced, one after another, without regard to the totality of their effects.

Notes

1 Part of the tragedy of the Soviet Union since the revolution of 1917 is that the hierarchy of the Communist Party did not break down when it should have done. Robert Conquest, *The Great Terror: Stalin's Purge of the Thirties*, Macmillan, 1973.

2 G. Brennan and J.M. Buchanan, *The Power to Tax: Analytical Foundations of a Fiscal Constitution*, Cambridge University Press, 1980.

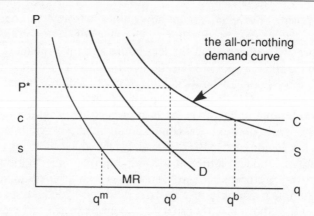

Figure 66 The 'market' for a bureaucratically supplied good

3 "A fundamental characteristic of parliament" (in early seventeenth-century England) was "its dependence on the will of the king, who called it into being and dissolved it as he saw fit. Kings summoned parliament for money . . . and not because they were constitutionally bound to submit themselves to criticism". Derek Hirst, *Authority and Conflict: England 1603–1658*, Harvard University Press, 1986, 36. How Parliament's authority to withhold money was to some degree transformed into influence over policy is chronicled in C. Russell, *Parliaments and English Politics, 1621–1629*, Oxford University Press, 1979.

4 These propositions are developed in Brennan and Buchanan, *The Power to Tax*, chapters 3 and 4.

5 It is a matter of some debate whether public officials have a class interest in the expansion of government. On the one hand, each bureaucrat can be expected to want to expand his empire within the bureaucracy. On the other hand, bureaucrats may share with every other occupational group the incentive to limit their numbers so as to raise the equilibrium wage for their services. On these matters, see Gordon Tullock's "Dynamic Hypothesis on Bureaucracy", *Public Choice*, 1974, 127–31, as well as P.N. Courant, E.M. Gramlich and D.L. Rubinfeld, "Public Employee Market Power and the Level of Government Spending", *American Economic Review*, 1979, 806–17.

6 The constitutionally imposed tax base is not the only possible alternative to the welfare-maximizing despot of traditional welfare economics. In fact, the Brennan and Buchanan model, though in my opinion the most interesting in its class, is a latecomer among the models of the constrained revenue-maximizing or output-maximizing bureaucrat. In *Bureaucracy and Representative Government* (Aldine Press, 1971) W.A. Niskanen postulated a bureaucracy that is only loosely controlled by voters and politicians. The spirit, if not the detail, of Niskanen's model is captured by imagining a bureaucracy which supplies a not altogether indispensable good and which is constrained in its expenditure by the rule that citizens must not be worse off than they would be if the bureaucracy were abolished, taxation reduced accordingly and none of the good supplied by anybody else.

The "market" for the bureaucratically supplied good is illustrated on the demand and supply diagram in Figure 66. Three types of demand curve are shown, the

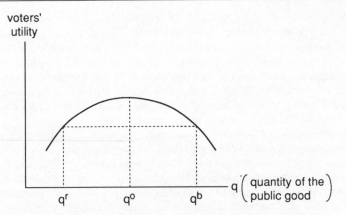

voters'
utility

q^r q^o q^b q $\left(\begin{array}{l}\text{quantity of the}\\\text{public good}\end{array}\right)$

Figure 67   Voters' utility and the supply of a public good

ordinary demand curve, D, the marginal revenue curve, MR, and the all-or-nothing demand curve indicating what citizens would be prepared to pay per unit if the alternative were to be denied the good altogether. Note that the ordinary demand curve is marginal to the all-or-nothing demand curve. The supply curve, S, is assumed to be horizontal; its height, s, is the minimal cost per unit on the assumptions that bureaucrats who produce the good are paid no more than they would earn in the private sector and that there are no bureaucratic perquisites of office. Parallel to and above the supply curve is a cost curve, C (at height c), for a constant level of bureaucratic perquisites per unit of output. If the good were produced in the private sector, an ordinary monopoly would produce q^m units and a competitive industry would produce q^o units, which is optimal.

If the bureaucracy could produce as much or as little of the good as it pleased, subject only to the constraint of the all-or-nothing demand curve, it would produce the optimal quantity q^o at a tax-price of P* per unit and would pocket the excess over minimal average cost, q^o(P* − s). If the bureaucracy were additionally constrained not to exceed a cost per unit of c, it would produce q^b units, which exceeds optimal output, and the value of its perquisites would be q^b(c − s). Output under competition is just right.

A different constraint is employed by T. Romer and H. Rosenthal, in "Bureaucrats versus Voters: on the Political Economy of Resource Allocation by Direct Democracy", *Quarterly Journal of Economics*, 1979, 563–87. In their model, bureaucrats set agendas to cheat voters into accepting a greater public output than the voters would really prefer. Reduced to its simplest terms, the model is this: suppose that all voters are alike and that their common utility as a function of the quantity of a public good supplied (q) is an inverted U as shown in Figure 67. Voters' utility must, of course, be dependent both on the quantity of the public good and on their net income after payment of the tax to finance the purchase of the public good. The voters' first best outcome is q^o. The bureaucrat is assumed to want as much expenditure as he can induce the voter to finance. The amount of the public good is to be determined in a referendum.

The crux of the Romer and Rosenthal model is that the referendum confronts the voter with a choice between a reservation quantity, q^r, of the public good which would usually be the *status quo* prior to the referendum and another higher quantity which the bureaucrat is empowered to choose. Though the bureaucrat knows that voters want q^o, he does not propose it in the referendum. Instead, he proposes quantity q^b, which is larger than q^o and is just preferable in the eyes of the voters to the reservation quantity, q^r. Voters' utility of q^b is just marginally larger than their utility of q^r, though utilities of both are substantially lower than the utility of the optimal quantity, q^o. In a choice between q^r and q^b, the voter opts for the latter which is what the bureaucrat wants him to do.

Like all the models of constrained government, the Romer and Rosenthal model is open to the objection that voters who elect the politicians who appoint bureaucrats will not allow themselves to be led by the nose in this way. The model is also open to the objection that the reservation quantity q^r cannot be made low at any given time without output being *less* than what voters prefer at some previous time. Alternation over time between q^r and q^b may mean that output is optimal on an average. Such alternation may be an entirely innocent consequence of the fact that voting takes place infrequently because it is expensive.

7 On the dubious constitutional basis and the political dangers of judicial activism, see Lino A. Graglia, "Judicial Activism: Even on the Right, it's Wrong", *Public Interest*, spring, 1989.

8 Anastasio Somoza said of himself, "I go abroad seeking investors to come into this country. Getting foreign investment is a big part of my job. Often that isn't easy. So to convince potential investors that Nicaragua is sound and has a future, I offer to take a piece of the action myself. I put my money where my mouth is." Quoted in Bernard Diederich, *Somoza and the Legacy of U.S. Involvement in Central America*, Dutton, 1981, 143. By the time of his overthrow, Somoza had accumulated a fortune that he estimated at about $100 million and that others have estimated at about half a billion dollars. He owned the dealership of Mercedes Benz. "The police and traffic cops used Mercedes, as did most politicians and the National Guard Brass. Even the city's garbage trucks were Mercedes Benz." (Diederich, pp. 132 and 327.)

9 The rights of the Chinese are severely restricted in Indonesia and the Chinese community bore the brunt of the anti-communist massacre of 1966 in which half a million people lost their lives. Nonetheless, a small group of Chinese, called *cukong*, have become the richest people in Indonesia in a symbiotic relation with the soldiers who rule the country. The *cukong* are given monopolies of certain industries on the understanding that their military benefactors are suitably rewarded. See Hamish McDonald, *Suharto's Indonesia*, Fontana Books, 1980, 53, 118–22.

10 In *The Human Condition* (University of Chicago Press, 1958), Hannah Arendt revives the ancient distinction among labour, work and action as a basis for analysing developments in society today.

11 On the pecuniary motives for seeking office, I know of no better account than L.B. Namier's chapter entitled "Why Men enter Parliament" in *The Structure of Politics at the Accession of George*, second edition, St Martin's Press, 1957.

12 This matter is discussed by Dennis C. Mueller in *Public Choice* II, Cambridge University Press, 1989, especially chapter 11.

13 A political party called the Union Nationale governed the Province of Quebec from 1936 to 1939 and again from 1944 to 1960 under the undisputed leadership of Maurice Duplessis. The Union Nationale held no monopoly on electoral bribery in Canada, but was something of a champion at this sport. Two classic quotations from Mr Duplessis: to the electors of one riding, "I warned you in 1948 not to vote for the Liberal candidate. You did not listen to me. Unfortunately your riding has not obtained the subsidies, grants that would have made you happy. I hope that you will have learned a lesson and that you will vote against the Liberal candidate this time." To the electors of another riding: "If you want to help build the bridge, then all you have to do is to vote for the Union Nationale candidate" because if he "asks for help he will get it. If, on the other hand you vote for the Liberal candidate, then the government will respect your opinions." The source of these quotations is Herbert Quinn, *The Union Nationale*, University of Toronto Press, 1963, 137. They are cited (and the former translated) in Jeffrey Simpson, *Spoils of Power: the Politics of Patronage*, Collins, 1988.

The Union Nationale resorted to fraud and bullying as well as to bribery. Thugs smashed up committee rooms of Liberal candidates and intimidated supporters (Quinn, 145). Tampering with the enumeration and counting of votes was made possible by electoral laws that assigned the supervision of elections to government officials exclusively, without representation from the opposition. The rules were such that votes could be sold (Quinn, 149). Many newspapers were brought into line by lucrative printing contracts and the threat of their withdrawal. All this, as Simpson shows, is in the grand Canadian tradition.

The interesting question about electoral bribery is not why it frequently works, but why it so often fails to work. The Union Nationale lost the election of 1960 to the Liberals, won the next election, and lost again in 1970. Perhaps the explanation lies in the secret ballot, which makes vengeance against individual voters infeasible and creates a free-rider problem among voters, each of whom knows that he bears a small cost in voting his conscience. Perhaps there was a general realization among political activists in the Union Nationale that excessive repression would be disadvantageous for everybody in the province.

14 On the economics of corruption, see Susan Rose-Akerman, *Corruption: a Study in Political Economy*, Academic Press, 1978. For a nice collection of examples, see Arnold J. Heidenheimer, ed., *Political Corruption: Readings in Comparative Analysis*, Holt Rinehart & Winston, 1970. See also F.T. Lui, "A Dynamic Model of Corruption Deterrence", *Journal of Public Economics*, 1986, 215–36.

15 Socially advantageous rent-seeking is discussed by Robert J. Michaels, in "The Design of Rent-seeking Competitions", *Public Choice*, 1988, 17–29. On the connection between rent-seeking and corruption, see Elie Appelbaum and Eliakim Katz, "Seeking Rents by Setting Rents: the Political Economy of Rent-Seeking", *Economic Journal*, 1987, 685–99.

16

$$\frac{\partial}{\partial B_i}(RP_i - B_i - F) = \frac{\partial}{\partial B_i}\left(\frac{R\gamma}{n} + \frac{(1-\gamma)B_i R}{\sum_{j=1}^{n} B_j} - B_i - F \right)$$

$$= \left[(1 - \gamma) \left(\sum_{j=1}^{n} B_j - B_i \right) R / \left(\sum_{j=1}^{n} B_j \right)^2 \right] - 1$$

Setting this derivative equal to zero and noting that $B_i = B_j \equiv B$ for all i and j, we see that $(1 - \gamma) R(n - 1)/n^2 = B$, which is equation (8) in the text.

17 On how red tape can tie a country in knots, see Hernando de Soto, *The Other Path: the Invisible Revolution in the Third World*, Harper & Row, 1989.

18 Karl Marx and Friedrich Engels, *Manifesto of the Communist Party* (1848), ed. Samuel H. Beer, Crofts Classics, 1955, 12.

19 The free-rider problem in political activity for the benefit of one's social class is examined extensively in Mancur Olsen, *The Logic of Collective Action*, Harvard University Press, 1965.

20 The leading exponent of the theory of capture in this context is George S. Stigler, whose principal essays on the subject are collected in *The Citizen and the State*, University of Chicago Press, 1975. A classic capture is the application of the United States Reclamation Act to farming in California. To assist small farmers, the Act provided for water to be sold at subsidized prices to farms of less than 160 acres. Though the Act itself remains unamended, political pressure led to the provision of subsidized water to corporate farms of tens or hundreds of thousands of acres. See Marc Reisner, *Cadillac Desert*, Viking, 1986, 349. This book is a gold mine of capture stories.

21 Gary Becker says of his model of the equilibrium of political influence that he "presented a theory of rational political behaviour, yet [has] hardly mentioned voting. This neglect is not accidental because I believe that voter preferences are frequently not an *independent* force in political behaviour. These "preferences" can be manipulated and created through the information provided by interested pressure groups, who raise their political influence partly by changing the revealed "preferences" of enough voters and politicians." (Gary S. Becker, "A Theory of Competition among Pressure Groups for Political Influence", *Quarterly Journal of Economics*, 1983, 371–400, p. 392. Becker speaks of his theory as a formalization of a well established view in political science represented particularly by Arthur F. Bentley (*The Process of Government*, University of Chicago Press, 1908), David B. Truman (*The Governmental Process*, Knopf, 1971) and Robert A. Dahl (*Polyarchy: Participation and Opposition*, Yale University Press, 1971).

Becker postulated an equilibrium of influence that is formally similar to the equilibrium among rent-seekers as discussed above, except that probabilities of being awarded a prize are replaced by transfers which are negative or positive, large or small, depending on the amounts of an ill specified political expenditure by the competing groups. The model makes no allowance for coalitions among groups. Nor is there an explanation of why "government" responds to political expenditure as it is assumed to do.

22 This was a common view among the classical economists. Their reasons for distrusting universal franchise, and their general preference for property qualifications, are examined in W.D. Grampp, "The Politics of the Classical Economists", *Quarterly Journal of Economics*, 1948, 714–47. The main articles in the famous debate on universal franchise between James Mill, who favoured it, and T.B.

Macaulay, who was opposed, are reprinted in J. Lively and J. Rees, *Utilitarian Logic and Politics*, Oxford University Press, 1978.

23 By the "Black Act" of 1723, it became a capital offence to appear "armed with swords, fire-arms or other offensive weapons, and having his or their faces blacked" in any forest or park "wherein any deer have been or shall be usually kept", or to hunt, wound or steal deer, hares, rabbits or fish off private land, or to cut down trees "planted in any avenue, or growing in any garden, orchard or plantation". (E.P. Thompson, *Whigs and Hunters*, Pantheon Books, 1975.)

24 In the wake of a major race riot in 1969 in which tens of thousands (the number is in dispute) of Chinese died at the hands of the Malays, the government of Malaysia established a New Economic Policy designed to increase the role of the Malays in business, which had been largely dominated by the local Chinese and by foreigners. Among the provisions of the New Economic Policy were that major businesses must hire at least 30 per cent Malays at all levels from top management to workers, that major businesses must be at least 30 per cent owned by Malays as a condition of doing business in the country, that places in university should be reserved for Malays. The New Economic Policy was silent on the overwhelming predominance of Malays in the civil service, the army and the police. See R.S. Milne and Diane K. Mauzy, *Politics and Government in Malaysia*, University of British Columbia Press, 1978, chapter 10.

25 Samuel R. Gross and Robert Mauro, *Death and Discrimination: Racial Disparities in Capital Sentencing*, Northeastern University Press, 1989.

26 Kennith Avio, "The Quality of Mercy: Exercise of Royal Perogative in Canada", *Canadian Public Policy*, 1987, 366–79.

27 On arguments for tariffs, see W.M. Corden, *Trade Policy and Economic Welfare*, Clarendon Press, 1974.

28 Canadian energy policy in the 1980s was a mixture of import subsidization, export taxation, subsidization of exploration and preference for Canadian-owned firms. See C. Green, *Industrial Organization and Policy*, second edition, 1985, 362.

29 See D. Usher, "The Thai Rice Trade" in T. Silcock, *Thailand: Social and Economic Studies in Development*, Australian National University Press, 1967.

30 Canada has developed an elaborate system of subsidization of investment. For programmes of the federal government, see *ABC: Assistance to Business in Canada 1981–82*, Ministry of State for Economic Development, Government of Canada, 1984.

31 Richard Bird of the University of Toronto once told me about a customs officer in Columbia who was propositioned as follows. You will let pass uninspected a shipment through your border crossing at such-and-such a time. If you do, when you get home, you will find under your door an envelope containing a good deal of money. If you do not, when you get home, you will find your wife and children gone. Is that bribery? What can one reasonably expect the poor customs officer to do?

32 The Putney debates are reproduced in A.P.S. Woodhouse, *Puritanism and Liberty; Being the Army Debates, 1647–49*, second edition, University of Chicago Press. The quotation is from p. 55.

33 See James Buchanan and Gordon Tullock, *The Calculus of Consent*, University of Michigan Press, 1962, chapter 16.

34 Political parties do not seek to maximize votes. They seek to win elections, which may or may not amount to the same thing. To say that political parties maximize votes is in some respects like saying that hockey teams maximize their scores. In a sense they do, but a team is, as a rule, not less satisfied with a win of four goals to three than with a loss of eight goals to nine. Similarly, a party that seeks to maximize votes would presumably maximize expected votes as well, in which case, in a two-party race, it would prefer a 30 per cent chance of winning 80 per cent of the votes together with a 70 per cent chance of winning 49 per cent of the votes to a certainty of winning 51 per cent of the votes. This implication of the hypothesis is clearly false. Furthermore, as William Riker pointed out many years ago, vote-maximization is at variance with the "size principle". A rationally administered political party may prefer to win by a margin that is safely above the 50 per cent mark but not overwhelming. The reason is that a party with the support of an overwhelming majority of the electorate is prone to fission, as a bare majority of its supporters comes to realize that they could do better for themselves in a new party with a smaller base of support and no need to placate superfluous adherents. A party with too large a base in the electorate is intrinsically undisciplined and unstable. On the size principle, see William Riker, *A Theory of Political Coalition*, Yale University Press, 1962. The vote-maximization hypothesis is usually attributed to Anthony Downs. See his *An Economic Theory of Democracy*, Harper & Row, 1957.

35 There are six possible nasty equilibria: groups A and B voting for party R, groups A and B voting for party D, groups A and C voting for party R, and so on. These are known in game theory as bargaining sets. See Martin Shubik, *A Game-theoretical Approach to Political Economy,* M.I.T. Press, 1987, 342.

36 For a good introduction to and bibliography of the probabilistic voting theorem, see Dennis C. Mueller, *Public Choice II*, Cambridge University Press, 1989, chapter 11. The theorem is called probabilistic because there is an isomorphism between the proportion of each group that votes for a given political party and the probability that each member of the group does so.

37 The Lagrangian of the problem is

$$\pounds = V^R - \lambda \left[y_A^R + y_B^R + y_C^R - 3Y \right]$$
$$= 50 + S_A \left[U_A (Y_A^R) - U_A (Y_A^D) \right] + S_B \left[U_B (Y_B^D) - U_B (y_B^D) \right]$$
$$+ S_C \left[U_C (Y_C^R) - U_C (Y_C^D) \right] - \lambda \left[y_A^R + y_B^R + y_C^R - 3Y \right]$$

Differentiating with respect to y_A^R, y_B^R and y_C^R, the first order conditions become:

$$\pounds y_A^R = S_A U_A' (y_A^R) - \lambda = 0$$
$$\pounds y_B^R = S_B U_A' (y_B^R) - \lambda = 0$$
$$\pounds y_C^R = S_C U_C' (y_C^R) - \lambda = 0$$

from which follows equation (19) in the text. If all three utility functions, U_A, U_B and U_C, are the same and all sensitivity parameters, S_A, S_B and S_C, are the same as well, then, by symmetry, the equilibrium platform has to be {Y, Y, Y}. Note, particularly, that V^R is minimized rather than maximized unless the second-order conditions are right. Maximization requires that U_A'', U_B'' and U_C'' are all negative; V^R must be a concave function of y_A^R, y_B^R and y_C^R.

38 For a proof that the outcome of probabilistic voting may maximize social welfare in some circumstances, see John O. Ledyard, "The Pure Theory of Large Two-candidate Elections", *Public Choice*, 1984, 7–41. See also Randall L. Calvert, *Models of Imperfect Information in Politics*, Harwood Academic Publications, 1986.

39 It is not necessary for this result that every last member of group A withdraw his vote for party R when the offer to group A falls below y_A^R; one diehard supporter of party R is not sufficient to restore the global equilibrium. The assurance of global equilibrium is lost if the votes-to-offers function ceases to be concave — a much weaker condition.

40 For an appeal to the probabilistic voting theorem in this context, see S.P. Magee, W.A. Brock and L. Young, *Black Hole Tariffs and Endogenous Policy Theory*, Cambridge University Press, 1989, especially chapter 3.

41 A standard result in international trade. See Arnold C. Harberger, *Taxation and Welfare*, Little Brown, 1974, chapter 2.

42 In 1647, at the end of the Great Civil War, the Parliament of England remained divided between the "Presbyterians", who still hoped to reach an accommodation with Charles I, and the "Independents", who had come to believe that accommodation was undesirable or impossible. The Independents and their allies in the army dared not dissolve Parliament and call a new election, for they had no assurance of popular support. The outcome was Pride's Purge, in which over a hundred members of Parliament were forcibly removed and as many more withdrew in protest: "the highest and most detestable Force and Breach of Privilege and Freedom ever offered to any Parliament of England". The event is described in Robert Ashton, *The English Civil War*, Norton, 1978. The contemporary quotation is from p. 343.

A similar event occurred in the French Revolution. By 1793 the National Convention was divided into three factions: the Jacobins, the Girondins and a middle group called the Marsh. The Jacobins were the principal support in the Convention for the Committee of Public Safety, which, spurred on by the radicals in Paris, pursued a policy of military expansion abroad and economic regimentation at home. Tension between Jacobins and the Girondists rose to the point where each had reason to fear a *coup d'état* by the other. The people of Paris surrounded the Convention and forced the arrest of enough of the delegates of the Girondins that the Committee of Public Safety was for a time unchallenged. (Leo Gershoy, *The French Revolution and Napoleon*, Meredith, 1964, chapter X.)

The general election in Hungary in November 1945 produced a Parliament with a 60 per cent majority for the Smallholders' Party, 17 per cent for the Social Democrats, 17 per cent for the Communists and 5 per cent for the National Peasants' Party. A year later the Communists had entire control of the government, owing to the presence of the Russian army and to the Russian insistence that the political police be entirely under the jurisdiction of the Communists. The technique for acquiring control was to eliminate the opposition bit by bit — in the words of Matyas Rákosi, who engineered the transition, "sliced off like salami". First the right wing of the Smallholders Party was removed, without protest from the Social Democrats or even the remaining members of the Smallholders' Party. Right-wing Social Democrats were next. Then a conspiracy was "discovered" among the remaining members of the Smallholders Party. A number of Deputies who were not actually purged had the good sense to flee the country. (Paul Ignotus,

Hungary, Ernest Benn, 1972, p. 200. I am indebted for this reference to Lucien Karshmar, Professor of History at Queen's.)

In all three cases, a minority prevailed over a majority by purging the legislature. Of course, external force had to be applied to induce the purged delegates to depart: the English Army in 1647, the Paris mob in 1792 and the Russian army, acting through the political police, in 1945. In each case, conflicts within the legislature were irreconcilable except by force, and government by majority rule voting was, at least temporarily, doomed. Except in extreme circumstances, members of a majority faction within the legislature would not acquiesce in the forceable removal of their opponents because they know where such actions lead.

43 Aristotle, *The Politics of Aristotle*, Ernest Barker (ed.), Oxford University Press, 1958, 210. On consensus and democracy, see Elias Berg, *Democracy and the Majority Principle*, Scandinavian University Books, 1956.

44 The example is taken from Gordon Tullock, "The General Irrelevance of the General Impossibility Theorem", *Quarterly Journal of Economics*, 1967, 256–270. Tullock had little to say about the precise conditions for the existence of an electoral equilibrium, but the matter has been discussed at great length in subsequent literature. See, particularly, P.B. Simpson, "On Defining Areas of Voter Choice: Professor Tullock on Stable Voting", *Quarterly Journal of Economics*, 1969, 478–90, O.A. Davis, M.H. DeGroot and M.J. Hinich, "Social Preference Orderings and Majority Rule", *Econometrica*, 1972, 147–57, and A. Caplin and B. Nalebuff, "On 64% Majority Rule", *Econometrica*, 1988, 787–814. Nothing in this literature holds out much hope for an electoral equilibrium in the unconstrained choice of tax shares or in direct allocation of income among citizens.

45 The classic discussion of the majority of minorities is in Robert Dahl, *A Preface to Democratic Theory*, University of Chicago Press, 1956.

46 For a fuller discussion of vote-trading, see William H. Riker, *Liberalism against Populism: a Confrontation between the Theory of Democracy and the Theory of Social Choice*, W.H. Freeman, 1982, especially chapters 6–8.

47 Intensity of preference may be interpreted as a weighting of objectives in a utility function. In equation (20), an altruistic person, j, places a certain weight P_i^j in his utility function on the income of person i. Person j has a high intensity of preference for the welfare of person 3 as compared with the welfare of person 2 if $P_3^j > P_2^j$. Intensity of preference is in some respects like a relative price. Where two issues are to be resolved in the legislature, the intensity of preference of person j for issue x as against issue y can be represented as the ratio of P_x^j to P_y^j when the utility function of person j with regard to these issues is assumed to take special form:

$$V^j = P_x^j\, \delta_x^j + P_y^j\, \delta_y^j$$

where $\delta_x^j = 1$ if the legislature's choice between x and $\bar{x}$ corresponds to the preferences of person j, $\delta_x^j = 0$ otherwise, $\delta_y^j = 1$ if the legislature's choice between y and $\bar{y}$ corresponds to the preferences of person j, and $\delta_y^j = 0$ otherwise.

48 The electoral equilibrium, if there is one, is what the legislature would choose in the absence of vote-trading and if the issues were resolved individually, one by one. Otherwise there is a "top cycle" of outcomes, each of which is defeated by some other outcome in the cycle. On the top cycle, see Joseph B. Kadane,

"On the Division of the Question", *Public Choice*, 13, 1972, 47–54. See also Thomas Schwartz, "Collective Choice: Separation of Issues and Vote Trading", *American Political Science Review*, 1977, 999–1010.

49 On the role of checks and balances in preserving democratic government, see *The Federalist Papers*, especially in Nos. 47, 48, 49 and 51 by James Madison (first published in 1787–88). There is a family resemblance between the old concept of checks and balances and the recently developed concept of "structure-induced equilibrium". It is claimed that the organization and procedure of Congress are designed to generate a unique outcome in circumstances where there might otherwise be an intransitivity among alternatives. For a good exposition, see Kenneth Shepsle and Barry Weingast, "Structure-induced Equilibrium and Legislative Choice", *Public Choice*, 1981, 503–19. For an argument, with which I am inclined to agree, that political structures are not strong enough to withstand a majority bent on exploitation of the minority see William Riker, "Implications from the Disequilibrium of Majority Rule for the Study of Institutions", *American Political Science Review*, 1980, 432–46, and his *The Art of Political Manipulation*, Yale University Press, 1986.

50 In the Parliament of Canada in 1982 the Conservative Party, then in opposition, opposed a bill on energy policy, on the ground that the bill was dangerously and unconstitutionally comprehensive. When called to vote on the bill, the Conservatives refused to enter Parliament, thereby blocking all voting and legislation. The bells calling Members of Parliament to vote rang continuously for two weeks, until a compromise was reached. The Liberals, then in power, agreed to divide up the bill, and the Conservatives returned to the House. The story is told in C.E.S. Franks, *The Parliament of Canada*, University of Toronto Press, 1987, 133.

51 See Dan Usher, *The Economic Prerequisite to Democracy*, Blackwell, 1981.

Index